Domino® 5 Web Programming with XML, Java™, and JavaScript™

Randall A. Tamura

que®

A Division of Macmillan USA
201 West 103rd Street
Indianapolis, Indiana 46290

DOMINO® 5 WEB PROGRAMMING WITH XML, JAVA, AND JAVASCRIPT™

Copyright © 2000 by Que® Corporation

International Standard Book Number: 0-7897-2275-5

Library of Congress Catalog Card Number: 99-068219

Printed in the United States of America

First Printing: August, 2000

02 01 00   4   3   2   1

TRADEMARKS

WARNING AND DISCLAIMER

Associate Publisher
Tracy Dunkelberger

Acquisitions Editor
Michelle Newcomb

Development Editor
Laura Bulcher

Managing Editor
Thomas Hayes

Project Editor
Tonya Simpson

Copy Editor
Cynthia Fields

Indexer
Johnna VanHoose

Proofreader
Megan Wade

Technical Editors
Leigh Weber
Karen Hobert
Cameron Martin
Victor Mascari
Tim Patterson
Gene Stuckey
Andrew Walt

Database Conversion Specialist
Steve Kern

Team Coordinator
Cindy Teeters

Media Developer
Michael Hunter

Interior Designer
Ruth Lewis

Cover Designer
Maureen McCarty

Copywriter
Eric Borgert

Production
Mark Walchle

CONTENTS AT A GLANCE

CONTENTS

About the Author

Randall A. Tamura is Vice President of Engineering for PeopleLink, an Internet company that provides outsourcing of community services for Web sites. He is the author of four books on Notes and Domino, including the best-selling *Special Edition Using Lotus Notes and Domino R5*.

Tamura has more than 25 years of experience in the computer field, and has been working with Notes and Domino since release 3. Before joining PeopleLink, he was the president of Graphware Corporation, which provided Notes and Domino consulting services. Before founding Graphware, Tamura was the general manager of IBM's Engineering Systems Development organization in the Los Angeles area.

DEDICATION

I dedicate this book to my family. My wife, Mari, and my son, Eric, are the center of my universe. I'm proud of Eric for accomplishing the rank of Eagle Scout in the last few months. My parents, Bud and Fumi, are and have always been supportive of me.

ACKNOWLEDGMENTS

I would like to thank the many people who helped make this book possible. Michelle Newcomb, my acquisitions editor, helped get this book through the Macmillan maze. Laura Bulcher, the development editor, carefully went through all the chapters. Thanks to Karen Hobert, Victor Mascari, Tim Patterson, Leigh Weber, Cameron Martin, Gene Stuckey, and Andrew Walt for their help. Leigh did the technical edit for most of the book, and he, as well as the other tech editors, made many valuable suggestions to improve the book. Project editor Tonya Simpson helped keep this project on track, and copy editor Cynthia Fields smoothed out the jagged edges of my English.

I also would like to thank many of the people at Lotus and Iris who helped by providing me with much of the information I needed for this book. Chris Reckling of Lotus and Ned Batchelder of Iris both provided invaluable information about the new XML support beginning in release 5.0.3 of Domino. For this I am very grateful. John Stack and Jim Frederick provided the actual beta code for 5.0.3 so that I could actually test and develop many of the examples in the book. A conversation with Mark Judd at Lotusphere convinced me to include a chapter on XSL in the XML section.

Finally, as always, I would like to thank you, the reader, for investing the money to purchase this book, and also the time to read it. I hope this book is a valuable tool for you to use in building great Web sites.

TELL US WHAT YOU THINK!

As the reader of this book, *you* are our most important critic and commentator. We value your opinion and want to know what we're doing right, what we could do better, what areas you'd like to see us publish in, and any other words of wisdom you're willing to pass our way.

As an Associate Publisher for Que, I welcome your comments. You can fax, email, or write me directly to let me know what you did or didn't like about this book—as well as what we can do to make our books stronger.

Please note that I cannot help you with technical problems related to the topic of this book, and that due to the high volume of mail I receive, I might not be able to reply to every message.

When you write, please be sure to include this book's title and author as well as your name and phone or fax number. I will carefully review your comments and share them with the author and editors who worked on the book.

Fax: 317-581-4666

Email: quetechnical@macmillanusa.com

Mail: Associate Publisher
             Que
             201 West 103rd Street
             Indianapolis, IN 46290 USA

INTRODUCTION

You're probably reading this introduction in the bookstore as you ponder whether to make the investment of buying this book. Let me take a few paragraphs to tell you what this book is about and why I think you should make that investment. In short, I'm excited about XML, Java, and JavaScript and their integration with Lotus Domino. They are key technologies now and will be strategically important in the future.

I've been writing books about Lotus Notes and Domino for several years. Over the time period since the launches of release 4 and release 5 of Notes and Domino, major changes have occurred in information technology, most notably the exponential rise in the importance of the Internet. With that change, Lotus has grown and enhanced their Notes and Domino products to accommodate the needs of the industry and the Internet. We're on the edge of the next transition with the advent of XML.

Microsoft, Lotus, IBM, and many other companies in the industry are moving toward XML as a model for data storage and exchange. Microsoft's Internet Explorer Web browser, for example, already has XML support in release 5. Notes and Domino have some support in 5.0.2 with more in 5.0.3 and even more to come in the future. IBM developed a parser called XML for Java (XML4J) that has been donated as the basis for the Apache XML project's parser and that is now integrated into Domino as of release 5.0.3. XML is the basis for everything from Web phones (WAP/WML) to streaming media integration (SMIL) to electronic data interchange formats.

A few years ago, Java was a fledgling technology, just starting to gain acceptance in the industry, but no longer. Java is now a mature technology and many companies have already deployed mission-critical applications on the Java platform. It is one of the major options for server-side Web programming. Many tools are now available for Java, and it would be rare to find a vendor that does not have Java support of some kind.

JavaScript has been available in one form or another for several years. For client-side Web browser programming, there really are no other practical choices for a browser-independent scripting language. JavaScript provides the client-side programming glue to piece together your HTML, Java applets, graphics, and other dynamic effects.

So, each of the technologies—XML, Java, and JavaScript—alone is important to making state-of-the-art Web applications. By combining these tools with the power of the Domino server, you have a solid basis for your Web development for years to come.

This book brings together these important Web technologies as well as several others to give you an explanation of how they work and how they integrate with Domino, and examples of how you can use them to build your Web applications. In this book, I show you how to perform client-side validation of a credit card number in JavaScript. You'll see an example of the XML-based WML (Wireless Markup Language), which is the language used to program WAP (Wireless Access Protocol) phones. Also, I show you how you can use JDBC to access relational database systems from your Java programs and how to integrate them with both XML and Domino.

These are just a few of the examples contained in this book, along with a complete reference of the Java Domino Object classes, which will be a great resource. But wait, there's more. You'll also get, for no additional charge, the complete text of this book on the CD-ROM in Notes database format. This will enable you to perform a full text search for any topic found within this book. So, even though the paper index in the back of this book is great, you might be able to find something with a full text search by combining keywords not specifically found in the paper index.

So, tuck this book under your arm and take it over to the cash register at the bookstore and check it out. If you bought this book using the Web from an e-tailer, good for you; thank you for investing in this book without even being able to browse this introduction before you filled your electronic cart. I hope you find this book was worth it. If so, write a good review of this book on your favorite online bookstore's Web site.

WHO SHOULD READ THIS BOOK

Of course, I'm tempted to say that everyone should read this book. Unfortunately, I don't think my parents, brothers, or even my wife would find this book too useful or interesting. So, sadly, there are some people for whom this book would not be appropriate. Surely, however, you are not one of them.

This book will be useful and interesting to people who work for companies that either now have a Web site or are contemplating having a Web site. If you are currently using Domino or are thinking about using it then you are even more likely to find some important information. If you want to find out about using XML with Domino, this is the only book that I know of at the time of this printing that covers the topic. This book can save you some time searching elsewhere.

This book is for developers. One of my other books, *Special Edition Using Lotus Notes and Domino R5*, contains information about Domino system administration, but this book does not. In this book, I've included practical information for developers, such as how to debug with the Domino Java AgentRunner. I've included programming tricks and techniques with JavaScript and information on how to traverse the parse tree of the XML Document Object Model, which appears to be sparsely covered (if at all) in the Lotus documentation.

So, if you're still contemplating buying this book, take it now to the checkout stand.

How This Book Is Organized

This book is organized into five parts. Part I, "The Domino Designer and Domino Programming," covers the important aspects of user interface programming with the Domino Designer. It covers the traditional Notes and Domino design elements such as forms, views, folders, navigators, outlines, and framesets. Part II, "Programming the Client with HTML and JavaScript," covers HTML, JavaScript, and how they integrate with Domino. This part also explains JavaScript techniques such as how to validate a credit card number in JavaScript.

Part III, "Using Java with Notes and Domino," covers the difference between Java agents, applets, and applications. It explains how to create Java agents within the Domino Designer as well as with third-party programs such as Symantec's Visual Café and IBM's Visual Age for Java. Java applets, which run in a Web browser, can now use the Domino Object classes to access Domino databases on the server through CORBA and IIOP. This part shows you how to build regular applets as well as an applet that can access Domino.

Part IV, "The Domino Objects for Java," is a complete reference of all the classes, properties, and methods for the Domino Object classes. Part V, "Enterprise Integration Using XML, Java, and Domino," covers the basics of XML, how to use XSL (Extensible Stylesheet Language), and how to serve XML from Domino. It also shows you how you can use Domino's new `parseXML` method to parse an XML document, how to access relational databases with JDBC, and how to use Java Server Pages (JSPs) with Websphere and Domino integration.

Conventions Used in This Book

This book uses the following conventions:

- Menu names are separated from menu options by a comma. For example, "File, Open" means "Select the File menu and choose the Open option."
- New terms appear in *italic*.
- Words that you type appear in regular text in `monospace`.
- Placeholders (words that stand for what you actually type) in regular text appear in *`italic monospace`*.

- All code appears in monospace.
- Placeholders in code appear in *italic monospace*.
- When a line of code is too long to fit on only one line of this book, it is broken at a convenient place and continued to the next line. The continuation of the line is preceded by a code continuation character (➡). When you see a line of code that has this character, it means that you should type the code as one long line without breaking it.
- An ellipsis (…) indicates that the remaining or intervening code required to complete a statement or code structure is omitted for the sake of brevity.

THE DOMINO DESIGNER AND DOMINO PROGRAMMING

DOMINO ARCHITECTURE AND WEB APPLICATIONS

In this chapter

Lotus Notes and Domino have always had a client/server architecture. Originally, this architecture was based on proprietary technology, but now it has evolved to a standards-based communications infrastructure. With the list of standards including TCP/IP, LDAP for directory access, IIOP and CORBA for distributed objects, HTML, Java, and JavaScript, among many others, Lotus Notes and Domino provide a powerful platform for Internet, intranet, or extranet development.

In this chapter I'll introduce you to some of the technologies you can use to program Lotus Notes and Domino for the Web. These same technologies can also be used within your company to develop applications that can be accessed via Web browsers or Notes clients. The capability to use either or both types of clients makes Domino a good choice for your client/server computing platform. In later chapters I'll go into much more detail about these technologies. The purpose of this chapter is to give you an overview of all the programmability options before we focus on Java and JavaScript in the rest of the book.

CLIENT/SERVER COMPUTING

Fundamentally, the objective in client/server computing is to distribute the computing workload so that you can accommodate more users and obtain more throughput. In the computing literature there has been a discussion about the relative merits of thin clients and fat clients. Essentially, a *thin client* performs very little processing and relies on the server for most computing tasks. *Fat clients*, on the other hand, offload computing tasks from the server, usually allowing more clients to be attached to a single server.

THE NOTES CLIENT WITH THE DOMINO SERVER

The Notes client provides end users with tremendous functionality. Some might call this a fat client, but I don't think that Notes is necessarily overweight. Essentially, Notes is a desktop database manager and communication package. It provides support for applications such as email, calendaring, and contact management. In addition, because of the replication features, you can store, manage, and execute complete applications in the Notes client on the desktop.

All this power, however, comes at a price of disk storage and complexity. When a company installs Notes clients, it typically requires an administrator to administrate the users, passwords, and installation of software. Thus, in the past it has been unusual to find the Notes client being used by an individual at home unless it is to access a corporate network remotely.

The trend with Notes and Domino, however, is to make the Notes client usable as a Web browser and capable of being used with servers other than Domino. Domino also is moving toward a model where it can support Web browser clients as well as Notes clients. For example, Domino can execute agents on the server on behalf of any client, including Web browser clients.

THE WEB BROWSER AND WEB SERVER

Web servers and Web browsers have traditionally fallen into the thin client model because Web browsers have had limited functionality. It has been relatively difficult to develop complex applications for Web browsers because they haven't been capable. Web browsers, however, are becoming more and more powerful because of several factors.

JavaScript, developed by Netscape as a language to add user interactivity to the browser, is becoming more prevalent as well as more powerful. JavaScript is usually used to implement mouse rollovers, field input validation, and other simple client-side functionality.

Java applets are also being used to add intelligent functions on a Web browser client. Java can be used to develop complete user interfaces, simple controls, database access, and more. The Java language can also be used on the server. In this capacity, programs known as servlets, Java Server Pages (JSPs), or Enterprise JavaBeans (EJB) can be developed to provide additional server-side functions.

The main constraint to large, Java-based applications in a Web browser is communication bandwidth. On the Internet, most users still connect with modems, which are too slow to download large (say 1MB) Java applets. As bandwidth improves via cable modems, ISDN, DSL lines, and so forth, more and larger applications for the Internet will be possible. In corporate environments, bandwidth is usually sufficient to handle large Java applets. Thus, Java applets might be more useful today in corporate intranets than on the Web because of the bandwidth constraints.

MOVING FROM LOCAL AREA NETWORKS TO INTERNET STANDARDS

Several layers of communications protocols are used in a networked environment. The lower layers of the protocol deal with hardware and the management of the movement of the data. Moving packets of data from a source computer through the network to the destination is the responsibility of these protocols.

Higher-layer protocols are used by applications to communicate between say, a client application and a server application. Often, to the user, both of these components are just pieces of a single application. The Notes client and Domino server, for example, can use special protocols to transfer database information from one to the other.

When the client and server parts of an application are relatively tightly coupled, the protocols used don't really matter too much as long as the client and server can communicate. However, as we move more and more toward the use of Internet protocols, even within corporations, standards become much more important.

Using standard protocols allows the client and server programs to become less dependent on one another and allows users to select software pieces more independently. Web servers and browsers are the most successful example of this phenomenon. Many different kinds of Web servers are available, running on many different kinds of hardware platforms. You can use one of several Web browsers to access these Web servers. The magic that makes this possible is the Hypertext Transfer Protocol (HTTP) and the associated data format, Hypertext Markup Language (HTML). By standardizing the content and meaning of data flowing via HTTP, we can see the benefits of a diversity of Web servers and browsers.

You can see the Domino and Web architecture in Figure 1.1. I'll be discussing the various components of this figure throughout this chapter.

Figure 1.1
The Domino/Web architecture.

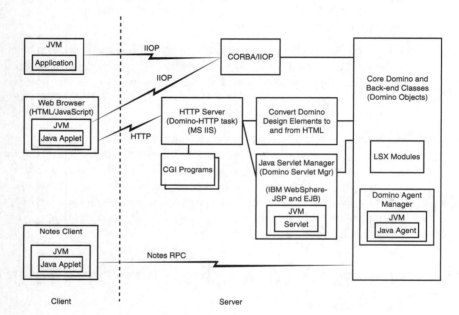

In Figure 1.1, the client technologies are on the left side of the diagram and the server technologies are on the right side. The figure is simplified to illustrate where you can use various programming languages and communication protocols. In Figure 1.1 notice that the Web server can be either Domino (HTTP task) or Microsoft Internet Information Server (IIS), but not both. Also, the Domino servlet manager or WebSphere (but not both) may be used as the Java Servlet Manager.

Here are the abbreviations used in Figure 1.1:

- CGI (Common Gateway Interface)—A standardized interface for external programs to work with Web servers. Programs can be written in C, C++, Perl, or other languages.

- CORBA (Common Object Request Broker Architecture)—This is an architecture (not a product) that allows distributed components written in different programming languages to communicate. A user of a component can make remote calls over a communication network using IIOP. This function is similar to a remote procedure call (RPC).

- EJB (Enterprise JavaBeans)—These are server-based components that enable you to access databases in an object-oriented manner.

- HTTP (Hypertext Transfer Protocol)—The protocol used by most Web servers and browsers.

- IIOP (Internet Inter-ORB Protocol)—An object-oriented protocol for allowing distributed objects to communicate. This is the protocol used to communicate between ORBs.

- JSP (Java Server Pages)—A standard for incorporating Java-based logic with Web pages.

- JVM (Java Virtual Machine)—The environment that interprets and executes Java instructions.

- LSX (Lotus Software Extensions [Formerly LotusScript Extensions])—Allows software components to be written that integrate with both LotusScript and Java within the Notes/Domino environment.

- ORB (Object Request Broker)—A program that allows clients and servers to communicate. Through the use of an ORB, the client does not need to know the details of the location of the server.

- RPC (Remote Procedure Call)—Generically, this technology allows a subroutine to be called over a network. The Notes client and server implement a specific version of this called Notes RPC.

CLIENT-SIDE TECHNOLOGIES

The discussion so far has been fairly abstract, so let's look at some specific technologies in the Notes client and Web browsers and see how they compare. In essence, Lotus is using the Web technologies I've discussed—JavaScript and Java—to implement capabilities that have traditionally been available in the Notes client.

Notice in Figure 1.1 that there are actually three different types of clients shown on the left. The first is a standalone Java application program, the second is a Web browser with an embedded applet, and the third type of client is the Notes client. Although all three client types are shown, you will typically be using only one of these clients at a time. These different types of clients can eventually access the Domino backend through several different communications mechanisms. Three protocols used are the Notes RPC, HTTP, and IIOP. I'll discuss these in more detail shortly.

Let's first take a look at the programmability features of the Notes client. Then we will cover the client technologies that have traditionally been available in Web browsers. All the Web technologies are now also available within the Notes client as well.

DOMINO DESIGN ELEMENTS

Domino design elements such as forms, views, and navigators have long been a staple of the user interface for the Notes client. Each of these design elements provides a programming capability. You can provide programming code to handle actions that occur within a particular object.

For example, if the user pushes a button, you can program the Click event to take some action. Each of the different types of objects, such as forms and views, has its own set of events that you can program. The programs you supply for these actions are sometimes called scripts, and hence this is the reason Lotus chose LotusScript as the name for its version of Basic. You can usually supply the event-object scripting in formula language, LotusScript, JavaScript, or with simple actions.

FORMULA LANGUAGE

Formula language is a variant of the language that was originally available in Lotus 1-2-3. It was adapted and enhanced for use in Lotus Notes. With its long history of allowing customers to move their applications from release to release, the formula language is still supported in Release 5 of Notes.

Formulas, in fact, still play an important role in many contexts within Notes. They are used, for example, in default values, view selection, input translation, and for several other purposes. Basically, a formula is an expression that is evaluated and results in a value. The use of the resultant value depends on the formula context.

The formula language consists of a large number of functions, each beginning with an @. Sometimes this language is called @formula language and the functions are called @functions. Here is an example of an @formula:

```
@if(@IsNewDoc;"New Document"; DocTitle)
```

This is an example of a formula you might find as a window title. It will check the status of the document and if it is new, the title will be New Document. If the document has previously been created, it will extract the value of a field called DocTitle and use that for the window title.

SIMPLE ACTIONS

Simple actions are pre-programmed actions that are commonly required in Domino databases. There are simple actions for replacing a value in a field of a document, copying documents, sending email messages, running agents, and even sending an automated reply to an email message. These simple actions can be set up and executed without too much programming knowledge.

LOTUSSCRIPT

LotusScript is the Lotus version of the Basic language. The language is similar to Microsoft Visual Basic but there are differences. For one, LotusScript is available on all the Notes/Domino platforms, meaning Windows, Macintosh, AIX, HP/UX, Solaris, UNIX, AS/400, RS/6000, S/390, and Linux. Microsoft Visual Basic only runs on the proprietary Microsoft Windows operating system platforms.

LotusScript can be used in several different contexts in the Notes client, including the scripting of object events as well as client-side agents. LotusScript is also available in some other Lotus products such as its spreadsheet product, 1-2-3.

Although it is available within Notes, LotusScript cannot be used to create standalone applications. This is different from Java, which can be used to create standalone applications as well as for use within the Notes, Web browser, or server environments.

DOMINO OBJECTS

There is a set of classes that you can use to access data within Domino databases. These classes are sometimes called the Domino back-end classes to distinguish them from the front-end classes that deal with the Notes client user interface.

The *nom du jour* for the back-end set of classes is Domino Objects. Prior to that, they were called the *Domino Object Model* (DOM). The problem with the name Domino Object Model (DOM) is that it conflicts with a JavaScript concept called the *Document Object Model* (DOM), which provides a similar concept but completely different set of classes for JavaScript.

Regardless of their current naming, these classes allow a programmer to find and open particular Domino databases, manipulate the data within a database, traverse documents within views, and examine individual fields within a particular document.

Although abbreviated out of Figure 1.1, the Domino Objects can be used in either the Notes client or on the Domino server. Notes and Domino handle any communication between the client and server automatically. In Figure 1.1 you'll notice the remote procedure call (RPC) interface is used between the client and the server.

Although LotusScript can access the front-end classes, they are not available within Java, so I will not cover the front-end classes much in this book. These classes are not available in Java because the front-end classes are wrappers around much of the code found in the Notes client itself. To separate the Notes client code from the database functionality, Lotus separated the front-end classes from the back-end classes. If you use the front-end classes with LotusScript in addition to the back-end classes, be careful because there are two separate paths into the database and you might find subtle inconsistencies.

LOTUS SOFTWARE EXTENSION (LSX) MODULES

Lotus has cleverly renamed LSX modules without having to change the acronym. LSX modules were originally named LotusScript Extensions. Originally, these add-on, user-supplied modules were extensions to LotusScript. With version 2 of the LSX toolkit, Lotus has introduced the Java adapter, which now allows LSX modules to work with Java as well as LotusScript.

You usually will create an LSX module in C++ with the LSX toolkit. LSX modules expose an object-oriented interface to LotusScript or Java programs. You can develop your own classes and methods, and they will be accessible in LotusScript or Java. Typical applications for LSX extensions are for database access, rich text applications, and any other type of custom data or communication application.

Although it is not shown in Figure 1.1, you can also use LSX modules with the Notes client if it is appropriate. For example, an LSX module can be used to process rich text. This type of service can be provided on the Notes client.

WEB BROWSERS AND HTML

When people think of a user interface or client for the Internet, most would think of a Web browser. Browsers are primarily programs that format and display Hypertext Markup Language (HTML) code. Although many Web browsers are available, the two most prominent are Netscape Navigator and Microsoft Internet Explorer. With R5 of Notes, all the Web technologies described in this section can be used within the Notes client as well as Web browsers.

HYPERTEXT MARKUP LANGUAGE (HTML)

Hypertext Markup Language (HTML) is the *lingua franca* of the Internet. It is based on Standard Generalized Markup Language (SGML) but has been tailored and updated for the World Wide Web. HTML 4.0 has been approved by the World Wide Web Consortium (W3C) as a standard and is in wide use.

The language itself consists of tags surrounded by angle brackets. Here is a very simple HTML document:

```
<HTML>
<HEAD>
<TITLE>A Sample</TITLE>
</HEAD>
<BODY>
<H1>Hello, HTML</H1>
</BODY>
</HTML>
```

In the example, note that the tags may be nested, and each tag specifies a component of the document's structure. HTML elements usually have a start and end tag. The end tag uses the same word as the start tag, but the end tag contains a forward slash. In the example, the pair of tags <TITLE></TITLE> is nested within the <HEAD> element. This document structure is parsed and stored within the browser. At that time it is also available for access via JavaScript.

JAVASCRIPT

JavaScript was invented by Netscape to provide interactivity in the browser. As you probably already know, JavaScript is not Java and it isn't a lightweight or simplified version of Java. In fact, it originally was called LiveScript, and its name was changed to JavaScript to provide a marketing benefit to the language.

JavaScript is an interpreted language, and because Netscape and Microsoft developed separate implementations (the Microsoft version is actually called JScript), there are language differences between the differing implementations. In addition, each version of the browser has brought differences in the associated JavaScript language. JavaScript was first introduced in Netscape Navigator 2. Since that time, both Netscape and Microsoft have improved their products. There is now a large core subset of the language that can be used with both Netscape and Microsoft browsers.

One of the main features of JavaScript is the capability to access and/or create HTML documents. The JavaScript programs actually reside on a Web page and can be used to read or update values found within the document's structure. In fact, JavaScript can be used to dynamically create the entire contents of a Web page.

JavaScript programs are always sent from the server to the client in human-readable text. Contrast this with Java programs, which are typically downloaded in binary.

JavaScript accesses the objects of a page via a set of objects called the Document Object Model (DOM). Don't confuse this with the Domino Object Model, which is another name for the back-end classes of Domino. Key objects in the JavaScript DOM are the *window*, *document*, and *form*. Again, don't confuse these terms with Domino objects that use the same names. In JavaScript these objects typically appear in lowercase, and when associated with JavaScript, the context will help you differentiate from the Domino objects with similar names. Part II, "Programming the Client with HTML and JavaScript," covers this in more detail.

JAVA APPLETS

Java was introduced in May, 1995 at the Sun World conference. The development team at Sun had used the code name *Live Oak*, but the name *Oak* was already trademarked and was not available, so Sun chose the name Java instead. In only the few short years since that time, the language has become extremely popular.

The Java language closely resembles C++, but without some of the error-prone features of C++. Java, for example, does not have pointer variables, but it does use a memory garbage collection scheme, so memory management in Java is easier and less prone to leakage than in C++.

The Java language can be used for several different purposes. One purpose is for applets. Another purpose is for complete applications. You can write standalone Java applications that can run on a variety of platforms and are not dependent upon Notes, Domino, or Web browsers. Finally, you can use Java to implement server-side functions as well as client-side functions. One main use for Java, however, is for applets in Web browsers.

In Figure 1.1, you can see several occurrences of the *Java Virtual Machine* (JVM), which is the environment that runs the Java programs. It is important to note that each JVM runs independently of the other JVMs that might also be running on the same computer. In particular, you must be careful of the version number of each JVM. The two prominent major versions are 1.1.x and 2.x (previously called 1.2). Differing versions of the JVM might be running on the same computer at the same time (because they have differing capabilities), so be careful that you are running the version you expect.

Applets are written in Java and are downloaded (in binary) from the Web server to the browser. Applets can provide simple functionality such as animation or they can provide application-level logic. Domino can download several built-in applets for functions such as managing views, action buttons, and rich text editing.

Security for Java applets is stronger than for Java applications. Downloaded applets, for example, cannot communicate with servers other than the server from which they are downloaded. They also cannot invoke programs and manipulate files on your hard disk. This is good, because a malicious Java applet could be downloaded and create havoc on your machine without these security constraints. Java applications do not have these restrictions. You can write a Java application that can communicate with any server, access files from the hard disk, and invoke other programs. The Web browser is typically the program providing the secure environment, not the Java language itself.

Applets that conform to an additional set of specific guidelines are called *JavaBeans*. The JavaBeans guidelines allow developers to create components that can be easily used with graphical Java development environments. Many commercial JavaBeans are available for purchase or downloading from the Internet. By using JavaBeans you can more quickly and easily create your application by leveraging the use of components that have already been designed and tested. JavaBeans are conceptually similar to Microsoft ActiveX components.

CORBA

CORBA, which stands for *Common Object Request Broker Architecture*, is an architecture specification for implementing distributed objects. A distributed object is one where some logic is located on the client and some is on the server. By using CORBA, a Java program running in a Web browser client (or Java application) can invoke methods that use the Domino objects.

The key is that the programmer can develop the application in an object-oriented style, and program as if the object resides on the client. In reality, CORBA will make all communication transparent so that the programmer does not need to write explicit communication code. This greatly eases the implementation task and allows faster development of the application. Domino takes this one step further by handling most of the details of CORBA itself on behalf of the programmer.

SERVER-SIDE TECHNOLOGIES

On the server side of client/server computing there are also many technologies at work. You can use these technologies to program the actions of the server in response to client requests. We'll first look at the Domino technologies and then some of the technologies traditionally associated with Web servers.

DESIGN ELEMENTS, FORMULA LANGUAGE, AND SIMPLE ACTIONS

Notes and Domino have long provided functions to support a remote client transparently to the programmer. As a developer you could develop applications using forms, views, and other design elements and really not worry too much whether these design elements are located on the client or server. Notes and Domino take care of the distribution of function.

For example, after you develop a Domino database, if you locate it on a server, it will work with Notes clients cooperatively. If you copy or replicate that database to a Notes client, the same database can operate independently of the Domino server.

You have many tools that you can use to program a Domino database. The formula language has long been a part of the Notes development interface and was previously described in the section titled "Formula Language." You can use formulas to select documents for a view, define one field based on the values of other fields, and for many other purposes. In R5, features were added to the formula language to support Internet addressing, hard/soft document deletion, and National language support, among several other features.

When you use the design elements or formula language on the server but with a Web browser as the client, the Domino server must translate the actions into HTML. The Domino server does this automatically. Because of this translation, however, some of the user interface elements appear differently in a Web browser than they do in the Notes client.

If the JavaScript option is enabled, the Domino server can generate JavaScript to be sent to the browser as well as the HTML. This allows the Domino server to offload some of the processing to the Web browser client.

Notice in Figure 1.1 a box that performs the function of converting Domino design elements to and from HTML. The original internal code name for this component was Domino. Eventually, Lotus renamed the entire server after the code name for the HTML conversion module (and got legal clearance from a certain pizza company).

DOMINO AGENTS

Agents are small programs that can be triggered by various events either in the Notes client (but not running on Web browsers) or on the server. Triggers can occur when mail arrives, at specific time intervals, when documents are added to a database, and so forth. The agent itself can be written in formula language, LotusScript, Java, or by using simple actions, which were described in the section titled "Client-Side Technologies."

Agents can be run on a Domino server in response to a URL request from a client. When used in this way, agents can execute any of the database and computing functions they would normally perform, and they produce an HTML page as output. The HTML page is then sent to the client as the response to the URL request.

These HTML-producing agents are similar to servlets. There are a few differences between agents and servlets. First, agents can be programmed in formula language, simple actions, or in LotusScript as well as Java. Servlets can be programmed only in Java. Second, agents are stored within the context of a Domino database, so they have Domino security protection and can be replicated. Servlets are typically stored in the file system of the Web server.

DOMINO WEB SERVER API (DSAPI)

DSAPI stands for *Domino Web Server Application Programming Interface*. This interface is specific to the Domino Web server and enables you to add custom authentication (for example, looking up users in your own corporate directory), or for logging, filtering, or translating uniform resource locator (URL) addresses. The DSAPI is normally programmed in the C programming language, although with work, you might be able to use other languages as well. The DSAPI interface is similar to the Microsoft ISAPI interface for the Microsoft Internet Information Server (IIS).

To implement a DSAPI filter, you implement at least two entry points in your C program: `FilterInit` and `HttpFilterProc`. `FilterInit` enables you to initialize your filter program and specify what types of events you would like to monitor. Events include authentication and processing of URL addresses, among several others. Your `HttpFilterProc` entry point is called when the events occur. You will be passed information about the type of event, and you can either handle the event or tell Domino to use its own default handling.

WEB (HTTP) SERVERS

The Domino server performs many functions. One function is to read the Domino databases and collaborate with Notes clients. Another is to read these same databases and convert them to HTML for Web browsers. Finally, Domino is a Web server because it can serve the HTML pages to Web browsers. In this capacity it has capabilities that it shares with all Web servers.

The different functions of Domino do not all have to be used together. For example, you can configure Domino to read Domino databases and convert them to HTML, but then use another Web server, such as Microsoft IIS, to serve the HTML to the clients. In Figure 1.1 you'll notice that the HTTP server can either be the Domino HTTP server or Microsoft IIS.

Strictly speaking, a Web server just needs to supply HTML to Web browser clients. Practically, however, most Web servers provide many other functions, including some features for programmability on the server. I'll describe some of these Web server capabilities in the next few sections.

COMMON GATEWAY INTERFACE (CGI)

The granddaddy of server-side technologies is the *Common Gateway Interface* (CGI). This interface was defined so that developers could add functionality to a Web server without needing to modify the server itself. CGI programs are typically written in C, C++, or a language called Perl and are accessed via a URL address.

Each time a client invokes a CGI program, a new process is spawned on the server, the request is satisfied, and the result is returned to the client. There is a great overhead in creating and destroying these server processes, so for simple tasks they can degrade performance.

CGI programs would be suitable if you have an existing legacy application and want to convert it for use with the Web. If the amount of computing is relatively large compared to the number of times it will be invoked, you might want to consider CGI programs. Many companies these days, however, are looking seriously at implementing server-side functionality using servlets.

SERVLETS

Servlets are Java programs that run on the server. They have a performance advantage over CGI programs because they can be loaded and stay running on the server for multiple clients or client requests. Servlets, like CGI programs, will typically receive parameters via the URL address like so:

```
http://www.acme.com/servlet/dbquery?firstname=fred&lastname=flintstone
```

Servlets can parse the URL parameters and generally will create a dynamic HTML page for return to the client. The client then displays the page.

A servlet manager loads, unloads, and generally manages the servlets. Domino has a built-in servlet manager that works in conjunction with the HTTP server task.

Domino can also use third-party servlet managers. In particular, it can work with the IBM WebSphere server (refer to Figure 1.1). When used in this mode, Domino allows WebSphere to manage the servlets. This configuration is beneficial because the WebSphere server has many more functions than the built-in Domino servlet manager. For example, WebSphere supports Java Server Pages (JSPs), Enterprise JavaBeans (EJBs), XML, ease of administration functions, and many other features. WebSphere is very complementary with Domino because when used together there is not that much overlap in function, but their use together leverages the strength of both servers.

JAVA SERVER PAGES (JSPs)

Java Server Pages (JSPs) are not explicitly supported in Domino, but can be used when Domino is used in conjunction with the IBM WebSphere server. You can think of JSPs as just-in-time Java. This means you can use snippets of Java code directly within the HTML of the Web page, and the Java code will be dynamically compiled and executed by the server. This is the Java analog to Microsoft Active Server Pages (ASPs).

One of the main goals of the use of JSPs is that they allow the separation of the form of a Web page from its content. The layout and graphical appearance of a Web page is separated from the back-end data management required to fill in the blanks on the page. In Listing 1.1 you can see an example of a Java Server Page.

LISTING 1.1   AN EXAMPLE OF A JAVA SERVER PAGE

```
<HTML>
<HEAD>
<TITLE>JSP Test</TITLE>
```

continues

LISTING 1.1   CONTINUED

```
</HEAD>
<BODY>
<H1>
<% if (null == request.getParameter("with")) {
out.println("JSP Rocks");
    }
else {
out.println("JSP rocks with " + request.getParameter("with"));
    }
%>
</H1>
</BODY>
</HTML>
```

A user could invoke this sample with the following URL:

```
http://server/JSPTest.jsp
```

The output would be a page with the text JSP Rocks. If it is invoked with the following URL, the output would be a page with the text JSP rocks with style and grace:

```
http://server/JSPTest.jsp?with=style+and+grace
```

Notice that you must use plus signs (+) instead of blanks in URLs. Plus signs are automatically converted into blanks (see Figure 1.2).

Figure 1.2
Using IBM WebSphere with Domino for Java Server Pages.

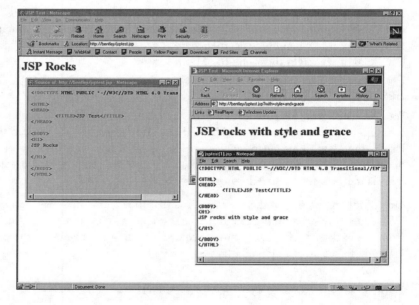

In Figure 1.2 notice that the resulting HTML no longer contains any Java and is strictly HTML code that the browser can handle.

The Java code that is supplied within the JSP is compiled at the time the page is invoked. This means that the page can be developed without the use of a Java compiler and all the associated tools. When the page is invoked, the code is automatically compiled, converted into a servlet, loaded, and managed by the WebSphere server.

In a more realistic example, the Java code included in the Web page would make calls to Java code that was developed by a back-end Java programmer. The Web page designer can concentrate on the logic of the Web page, but another person can program the access of data from the database. This is really pretty cool.

CORBA AND ENTERPRISE JAVABEANS (EJBS)

The CORBA technology on the server allows clients to use distributed objects and remote method invocation. In the specific case of Domino, CORBA is used to allow Java applets to access Domino databases on the server. The use of CORBA with Domino is largely transparent to the programmer.

When used natively, CORBA requires you to describe your remote interfaces with the *Interface Definition Language* (IDL). The IDL specification is then compiled and produces programs that run on both the client and server that implement the communication. The IDL statements and the corresponding programs for the Domino objects have been developed by Lotus, and as a user of these objects you do not need to worry about the IDL definitions.

You can use CORBA with Java yourself, however, to build distributed object-oriented programs. This task is not for the faint of heart, however, because you'll need to understand a lot about this technology, including IDL statements, object request brokers (ORBs), stubs, and skeletons. Some Java programming environments may ease this task for you. Although CORBA allows the use of distributed objects, it does not support transaction-processing functions. This is a higher level of function and is provided by the Enterprise JavaBeans specification.

Enterprise JavaBeans (EJB) is another technology that you can use if you combine IBM WebSphere with Domino. Just as JavaBeans is a component specification, EJB is a component model for server-side functionality. You should be aware, however, that Enterprise JavaBeans are not really JavaBeans. The component models for these two specifications are completely different, and other than their similarity in names, they have nothing to do with one another.

EJB enables you to use and develop standardized components for transaction-oriented applications. You can manage attributes such as security, persistence, and resource management using Enterprise JavaBeans. The specification enables you to develop components that fit within a larger, standardized framework. In essence, you can develop the business logic that will run on the server, and EJB will supply a lot of the plumbing required.

There are two types of Enterprise JavaBeans: entity beans and session beans. Entity beans are used to model objects that must be persistent and are usually stored in a database system.

Session beans are not persistent and usually deal with processes that manipulate the data. For example, in an e-commerce application, you might use entity beans to represents items for sale and you might use session beans to represent a shopping cart used during the purchasing process.

PROGRAMMING LANGUAGE AVAILABILITY

We've gone quickly through some of the key technologies and languages available for Web development. Although by no means exhaustive, this introduction has shown you many of the primary tools you'll use for the Web. Because there are so many different technologies and so many different options for choosing a programming language or tool, I've summarized in Table 1.1 a list of key object situations and the primary programming language choices. In the next section I'll discuss how you can choose among the available languages.

TABLE 1.1   AVAILABILITY OF PROGRAMMING LANGUAGES

Object Situation	LotusScript	JavaScript	Java	Formula Language	Simple Actions	C/C++	HTML
Object scripting (for example, buttons)	X	X		X	X		
Domino Objects	X		X				
Notes client agent	X		X	X	X		
Applet/ JavaBean			X				
LSX Module	X-Use		X-Use		X-Create		
Web browser		X	X				X-Intr
Notes client browser	X	X	X	X	X		X-Intr
Domino server		X-Gen				X-Add-in	X-Gen
Domino server agent	X		X	X	X		X-Gen
Domino server servlet			X				X-Gen
Java Server Pages (JSP)			X				X-Gen
CGI Programs					X	X-Gen	
Standalone application		X			X		

Legend:

- X-Use—Programmer can use the object within the language specified
- X-Create—Programmer can create this object using the language
- X-Intr—The object specified can interpret the given language
- X-Gen—The object generates the given language for a client
- X-Add-in—A Domino server add-in program can be written in C/C++

CHOOSING A LANGUAGE OR TOOL

With all these choices, which language or tool should you use and why? This is a good question. The answer is, it depends primarily on what you're trying to do and your background and experience.

As I mentioned previously, you are restricted to using certain languages for the various features in Notes and Domino. For example, to make an applet, you must use Java. To write scripts for objects, you can use several other languages but not Java. When you are creating an LSX module, you will typically use C/C++ but not LotusScript or Java. So in many cases the initial selection of language is done for you by the context.

In programming scripts for objects, though, you can still use LotusScript or JavaScript. If you're familiar with BASIC, go with LotusScript. If you're familiar with either JavaScript or JScript, use the JavaScript support in Notes. This book, in fact, will teach you how to do just that. The world is moving more and more toward Internet standards. As JavaScript becomes more popular in general, more programmers and programs will be available in JavaScript.

When programming agents, you can use LotusScript or Java (or formula language or simple actions), but you cannot use JavaScript. In this case again, use the tool most comfortable for you. If the situation is simple enough, use a simple action. For example, to replace a single value within a document, you could use a simple action. Usually, there are several ways to accomplish your goal, and you can pick any of the options. If you're really ambitious, you can learn them all and pick the tool that seems just right for the occasion.

CHOOSING WHERE YOUR PROGRAM EXECUTES

In essence, you really have only two generic choices for where your program executes: the client or the server. In general, code that you write for the client should typically be small and fast and limited in function. For example, field validation is an example of a good application for client-side code. Accessing a large Domino database or a SQL database is an application that is better suited for the server-side execution.

As client computers become more powerful, you might consider providing more functionality on the client in a Web browser. With CORBA support as well as some of the new functionality of XML, it might be feasible to offload functions to the client. However, you should be very careful in doing this today and make sure that you benchmark performance before you deploy a large application that has a lot of code in the client. As mentioned previously, bandwidth may be a greater concern than the actual processing capability of the client.

In local area networks where communication bandwidth is relatively plentiful, downloading a megabyte of code to the client would not be a big problem. When designing applications for use with the Internet, however, keep in mind that most users will be using 56K modems, which would drastically change the user experience.

I'll show you in later chapters how you can use server-side programming to create dynamic Web content. In other words, rather than a page of HTML that is generated by a Webmaster, the HTML page is completely generated by the server based on data in a database. This is a key capability that is used in e-commerce. Imagine a catalog with thousands or millions of entries. It would be impossible for a Webmaster to generate Web pages for these items. This is clearly a job for server-side code.

A WORD ABOUT XML

Extensible Markup Language, or XML, is one of the newer standards for the Internet. Although it is similar to HTML, XML is not a specialized version of HTML nor is it a superset of HTML. In fact, the purpose of XML is quite different from HTML. The purpose of HTML is to provide a language for displaying Web pages and allowing user interaction with these pages.

The purpose of XML, on the other hand, is to provide a language that can describe any kind of business data. Whereas the primary purpose of HTML is for data display, the purpose of XML is to logically organize, store, and communicate the information.

XML can be used for a variety of different applications. To be meaningful, a file that is in XML format must also be associated with a document type definition (DTD) file. A DTD supplies the allowable syntactic format for a given XML document type. For example, you can define several different XML document types for a single application. In an e-commerce application for selling CDs, for example, you might define an Artist XML document type, a CD XML document type, a Customer XML document type, and a CreditCard XML document type. Each of these different document types would define the data that is required. Here is an example of what the Artist XML document might look like:

```
<ARTIST>
<NAME>David Benoit</NAME>
<GENRE>Jazz</GENRE>
<INSTRUMENT>Piano</INSTRUMENT>
</ARTIST>
```

Alternatively, with a different DTD specification, you could require the XML to look like this:

```
<ARTIST NAME="David Benoit"/>
<GENRE>Jazz</GENRE>
<INSTRUMENT>Piano</INSTRUMENT>
</ARTIST>
```

The choice between these two formats or a multitude of other formats is up to the DTD designer. To some extent the choices are a matter of style, but different choices may allow for different semantic meanings for the data.

Lotus has used XML for internal communication between its Java applets and the Domino server since release 5.0. The use of XML in Domino will continue to increase, so it is important to understand this technology.

SUMMARY

In this chapter I have covered the important programmability features of Notes and Domino. Lotus has traditionally provided a client/server model of programming but now is moving to supporting this model via Internet protocol standards. Whereas previously you had to use the Notes client with the Domino server, now both components are becoming more useful as separate pieces.

There are many choices for programming languages and tools on both the client and the server. Your choice of language will depend on your application as well as your background and experience. Many times there is more than one method for implementing a solution. On the client, for example, you can now use JavaScript as well as LotusScript to script objects. JavaBeans, which are specialized Java components, provide you with component technology that can be used to implement user interface elements.

You can use servlets as well as agents on your Domino server. With the IBM WebSphere Application Server, you can also include Java server pages or Enterprise JavaBeans.

This chapter has given you only an overview of these features. In the rest of this book I will elaborate on these features and show you how you can use them in your own applications.

CHAPTER REVIEW

Here are some questions for you to consider:

1. Suppose you are developing the following e-commerce application with Domino for use on the Internet. It is a Web site devoted to selling supplies for sailboats. Items include sails, lines, navigation equipment, motors, oars, and so forth.

   a. Which Domino technologies would you use in the design of your Web site?

   b. Suppose you already had a relational database system that included your parts and inventory. Would that change your design?

   c. How could you use Domino's strengths to incorporate customer support into your Web site?

2. What are the relative merits of using LotusScript or JavaScript for providing client-side programming?

3. Are Enterprise JavaBeans just specialized versions of regular JavaBeans? Can you describe situations in which you should use each of these technologies?

4. What are the relative merits of using Domino agents or servlets for server-side programming? How does each of these compare with CGI programs?

5. What is the biggest benefit of the CORBA support in Domino? Would you consider using Domino CORBA support for an Internet application? Why or why not?

6. What are some of the benefits of using IBM WebSphere in conjunction with Domino?

CHAPTER 2

DOMINO DESIGNER AND THE INTEGRATED DEVELOPMENT ENVIRONMENT (IDE)

In this chapter

If you are familiar with a previous release of Notes and Domino, you will immediately see that the Domino Designer IDE has been updated significantly. The main objective of the newly designed environment is that it can be used by two distinct user groups: designers familiar with the original Notes designer interface and designers familiar with existing third-party Web development tools.

The new designer interface makes it easy to develop Web pages using native HTML or by using traditional Notes and Domino design elements. People familiar with tools such as NetObjects Fusion or Microsoft FrontPage should be able to learn quickly and begin to develop pages using the Domino Designer.

This chapter is meant to be an overview of the Domino Designer. It will provide you with an introduction to the various parts of the Designer and how to use them. I'll cover the various different types of design elements you can use. Later chapters in this part cover each of the major design element types in more detail.

STARTING THE DOMINO DESIGNER

In previous releases of Notes, the Domino Designer was part of the client user interface. Starting with release 5, the Domino Designer is a separate executable program. You can start the Designer directly from your operating system. For example, in Windows, you can select the program from your Start button or by clicking an icon if you have placed one on your desktop.

You can also start the Designer by clicking the Domino Designer icon in the regular Notes client. The Domino Designer icon is one of the new navigation icons located in the bookmarks section of the regular Notes client (see Figure 2.1).

Figure 2.1
The Domino Designer icon appears in the regular Notes client.

Note that the icon will not appear if you do not have the Domino Designer client installed. After you launch the Designer client, you will notice that it appears in a window that is separate from the Notes client. You can have both windows open at once, and if you also have the administration client installed, it is even possible to have all three client windows opened at once.

Another way to open the Designer is to open a database in the regular Notes client, and then select View, Design from the menus. At this point, the Designer client will be launched if it is not already running. If you have previously developed Notes and Domino applications, this method is already familiar to you. It seems a little strange at first when a menu option launches a completely separate application, but this enables you to immediately start working with the new designer. You launch it in a way that is very familiar, and you can later start to launch it as a separate application if you choose.

THE DOMINO DESIGNER WINDOW

After the Designer client is launched, you see the welcome screen for the Designer. From this window, you can either create a new database or you can open an existing database. If you create a new database, you can base the new database on a database template, which will incorporate the template's design elements into the new database. Figure 2.2 shows an example of a newly created database that is based on the discussion template. By using a template rather than a blank database, you can modify an existing set of design elements quickly to suit your needs.

PART

1

CH

2

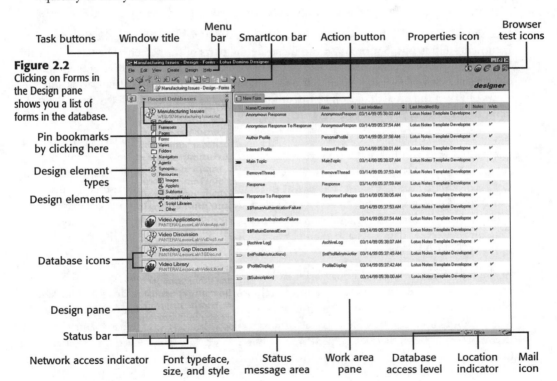

Figure 2.2
Clicking on Forms in the Design pane shows you a list of forms in the database.

THE PARTS OF THE DOMINO DESIGNER WINDOW

Notice that you can have several databases open at once in the Designer. Domino Designer keeps track of the most recently used databases and makes them easily available to you. In Figure 2.2, you can see the various parts of the Domino designer window. This window is similar in many respects to the Notes client, but there are some subtle differences.

The top line contains the window title, just as in the Notes client. As you change your context by clicking on the various design elements in the Design pane, you see the window title change. For example, it can include the name of the database and the design element type you are viewing.

The menu bar appears just below the window title. The menu bar is context-sensitive, so as you change from one design element type to another, the menus will change. Most of the elements will contain the following menu items: File, Edit, View, Create, Design, and Help. To the right of the menu bar, you see icons that are useful for testing your database. These icons are different from the ones that appear in the regular Notes client. In the regular Notes client, this area contains the Universal Navigation icons. In the Domino Designer, this area contains the Properties icon followed by icons for previewing your design. You will normally see at least the Properties, Notes Preview, and Domino Preview icons. Following these three, you may optionally see the Microsoft Internet Explorer Preview icon and/or the Netscape Navigator Preview icon. Both the IE and Navigator icons appear in Figure 2.2.

In Figure 2.2, you see the SmartIcon bar below the menu bar. By default, the SmartIcon bar is turned off, but I have turned it on to illustrate the parts of the screen. The left side of this bar contains the universal SmartIcons, and the right side is context-sensitive and contains SmartIcons useful for design tasks. For example, there are icons for creating forms and views. To turn the SmartIcons on or off and to modify the icons on the left side of the bar, you can select File, Preferences, SmartIcon Settings from the menu.

Below the SmartIcon bar are the task buttons. These buttons enable you to switch from one open window to another. Each time you open a new design element, a new task button appears. You can easily switch from one element to another by clicking its task button. You can even design within several databases at the same time. This is a very useful feature because it is now much easier to review and copy design elements from one database to another. You just open the design element of the first database, copy it to the Clipboard, click on the second database, and then paste. To close a window, click on the X that appears to the right of the name.

At the far left is a column of bookmarks. In Figure 2.2, there is only one icon in the bookmarks column. The Design pane is immediately to the right of the bookmarks. The regular Notes client does not contain a Design pane. When the Design pane is open, it displays the most recently used databases and all the different types of design elements within each one. If you prefer to leave the Design pane open while you work, you can click on the small icon in the upper-left corner of the Design pane. In release 5.0, this icon is rectangular; beginning in release 5.0.1 it is triangular. A pull-down menu will appear. Enable the Pin Bookmarks On Screen option, which will leave the Design pane open. With this option enabled, when you close and reopen the Design pane, it stays open. If you disable this option, after each use of the Design pane, it automatically closes again. In release 5.0.1, there is also a pin icon in the upper-right corner of the design pane below the X. You can enable and disable the Pin Bookmarks option by clicking this icon.

The large main area on the right of the screen is called the Work pane. The contents of this pane change as your context changes. It can contain a list of design elements, or it can contain the work area for a particular element that you are editing.

THE STATUS BAR

The status bar is located at the bottom of your screen. It appears in all contexts, gives you useful information about various aspects of your Notes session, and also allows you to change certain settings (refer to Figure 2.2).

The status bar is divided into eight sections. Here are descriptions of these sections:

- Network access indicator—The network access indicator shows a lightning bolt when Notes is accessing the network. If you are using a mobile connection, a modem with flashing lights appears.

- Font typeface indicator—The Font Typeface shows the current font typeface when you are editing a document. If you click this indicator, you can change the current typeface by selecting one of the fonts that appears in the pop-up list.

- Font size indicator—The font size indicator works like the font typeface indicator. You can view the current size and change it by clicking it and selecting from the list.

- Font style indicator—The style indicator shows you the current style, if there is one, and allows you to change the style by clicking the indicator. This indicator, as with the font typeface and size indicators, appears only when you are editing a document or certain design elements such as a form, subform, and the Help Using and Help About elements.

- Status message area—The fifth section is the status message area. Notes displays status messages here, and you can find a recent history of messages by clicking this indicator.

- Database access level icon—This icon visibly shows your access level for the currently selected database. If you click this icon, you will get more detailed access-level information.

- Location indicator—The location indicator shows you the name of the current location document. If you click this indicator, you will see a complete list of all your locations, and you can select a new location from the list or edit your current location document.

- Mail icon—The mail icon displays an inbox when you have new mail. Otherwise, this icon shows an envelope. If you click this icon, you can send and receive mail, open your mail database, and create a new email message.

THE DESIGN ELEMENTS

The Design pane of Figure 2.2 shows you the types of design elements that are available to you. Many of these design elements might be familiar to you from previous releases of Notes and Domino. There are also some new design elements, such as outlines, framesets, pages, images, and applets. The purpose of these new design elements is to make it easier for you to develop applications for your intranet or your Internet Web site.

When you click on a design element type in the Design pane on the left, the Work pane on the right shows you a view containing the actual elements of that type stored in your database. For example, in Figure 2.2, Forms has been chosen on the left, and on the right is the list of forms in the database. Notice that the format of the right pane is similar to a regular Notes view. In this case, you can see the name of the design element with an optional comment, an optional alias, and information about the time of last modification, with the name of the user who last modified the element.

If you double-click on the name of an actual design element in the Work pane on the right, the selected design element is placed in edit mode. Here is the list of design elements you can use:

- Outlines—Outlines are a new design element in release 5. Outlines are essentially high-level navigation tools. In Web site design terminology, an outline is similar to a site map or the navigational elements that frequently appear at the left of a Web page. In Notes/Domino terminology, you can think of an outline as a way to program the traditional Navigation pane. This is the pane that normally lists all the views of a database.

- Framesets—Frames are the Web terminology for panes in Notes. Although in previous releases of Notes the end user could manipulate the panes to a small degree, the database designer could not easily create panes or frames to control the user experience. Framesets are layouts that are used to control the display of multiple frames to the user.

- Pages—Pages are very familiar to Web designers. Pages contain the main information to be displayed to the end user. Of course, pages can be very complex if they include sophisticated HTML or JavaScript or invoke Java applets. If you have a Domino background, pages are similar to a Domino form. The main difference is that pages cannot contain Domino fields. They can contain HTML INPUT fields.

- Forms—Forms are a part of the traditional Notes/Domino system. A form is a visual template through which you view a document. This template typically contains static information as well as field definitions. Information from a document is extracted and displayed in the field locations on the form and then rendered to the display.

- Views—Views enable you to see a tabular summary of information from many documents at once. With a formula, you can select the documents you want to see in the view. The view columns typically extract information from the documents in the database.

- Folders—Folders are similar to views. They present data in a tabular format. The major difference is that in a view the documents are selected by a formula, whereas in a folder the documents can be any arbitrary collection. Folders are typically used by an end user to organize documents in a database.

- Navigators—Navigators were introduced in release 4 of Notes and Domino to provide users with a graphical method for navigating through a database. If the Designer includes a navigator with various links to a database, the user can just click on an area of the navigator. The major function of a navigator can now also be accomplished with an outline or page design element.

- Agents—Agents are small programs that are associated with a database and can be run automatically or under user control. They can be written in LotusScript, Java, or formula language, and they can be run on either the Domino server or the Notes client.

Below the Agents design element, you can see the word *Synopsis*. This is not actually a design element. By clicking on this word, you can obtain a synopsis, or summary, of all the design elements used within your database, so it is actually a command rather than a design element. It is located within the list of design element types so that it is readily accessible, no matter what editing task you are performing.

PART

I

CH

2

The following design elements can be found within the Resources *twistie* with the other design elements. A twistie is a small triangle, typically to the left of the name of a collapsible section. If you click the twistie next to the word Resources, an additional group of resource items will appear. These resources represent items that can be shared within the database.

- Images—Image resources are a new feature of release 5 that enable you to store images once and reuse them throughout your database. You give each image a name and can then reference the image from other design elements, such as pages, forms, and subforms. Domino supports industry standard formats, such as GIF, BMP, and JPEG.

- Applets—Java applets are small programs written in Java that execute within the browser environment, including the Notes client. The shared applets feature of the Domino Designer enables you to save a Java applet in a central location in the database, give the applet a name, and then reuse it throughout the database. In release 5, with Java and CORBA support, there are now mechanisms to enable Java applets in Web browsers to access the Domino Object Model on the server.

- Subforms—Subforms are similar to forms in almost all major respects. The difference is that a subform may be reused by incorporating it on several different forms. A subform may not be used by itself. Typical uses for subforms include headers and other information that you would like to reuse for consistency across multiple forms. You can also conditionally include different subforms within a form, depending on context.

- Shared fields—Shared fields are field definitions with attributes such as data type, programming, security, and formulas that can be shared across multiple Domino forms. By using shared fields, you can implement consistency in formula programming across several forms or subforms.

- Script libraries—You can use script libraries to share common LotusScript or Java code. Code that is stored within a script library can be used throughout a database.

- Shared actions (within the Other section)—Actions are small programs that are typically used in forms and views. Actions can be invoked by the user by clicking an action button or from the menus. Either or both of these options are enabled by the Designer.

- Other—The Other section also includes the database icon, the Using Database and About Database documents, and the Database Script, which is invoked when the database is opened.

I'll now provide a summary of the various design elements of Domino Designer release 5. Each of these elements is covered in more detail in later chapters, but this chapter gives you an overview of the various elements.

OUTLINES

If you double-click on the name of a design element in the Work pane on the right, you enter edit mode on the element (see Figure 2.3).

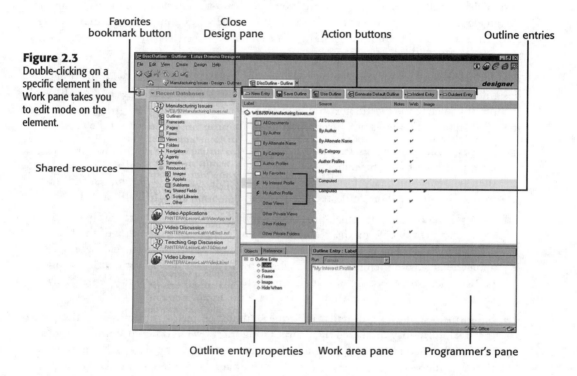

Figure 2.3
Double-clicking on a specific element in the Work pane takes you to edit mode on the element.

Figure 2.3 shows the design environment for outlines. The screen layout in the Work area pane of each of the different design elements (such as outlines, framesets, pages, forms, and so forth) is different, but the outline layout is fairly typical.

To the right of the Design pane, the window layout is a three-pane view. The work area for outlines is in the top pane. The bottom-right pane is called the Programmer's pane and includes two parts. On the left is typically an area where you can see your object list and reference material. In the right of the Programmer's pane, you can usually enter information that affects the design element.

The action buttons, just below the task buttons, show you the actions you can take with the current design element type. For outlines, you can create new entries, save the outline, use (embed) an outline on a page, generate a default outline, and control indentation of the outline entries. In Figure 2.3, you can see there are several outline entries. They begin with the following: All Documents, By Author, By Alternate Name, and By Category.

For each outline entry, you can determine whether the entry applies to the Notes client, a Web client, or both by looking at the check marks to the right of each outline entry. You can also supply a small image to replace the little icon that appears next to the outline entry label.

In the InfoList pane in the left half of the Programmer's pane, you can see the important properties and methods of the object. For example, in Figure 2.3, you can see all the properties of an outline entry. In this case, there are five properties of an outline entry: Label, Source, Frame, Image, and Hide When.

To modify a property for an entry, first select the entry in the upper pane, and then select the property on the left in the Programmer's pane. In the Programmer's pane on the right, you can enter a definition for the property.

I cover outlines in more detail in Chapter 6, "Using Outlines, Framesets, and Navigators."

FRAMESETS

Framesets are a new feature of release 5 of Notes and Domino. Figure 2.4 shows the frameset designer. I have hidden the Design pane in this case because when you are designing frames, it is usually easier to work if you have as much screen real estate as possible.

Figure 2.4
You can design the layout of your frames with the frameset designer.

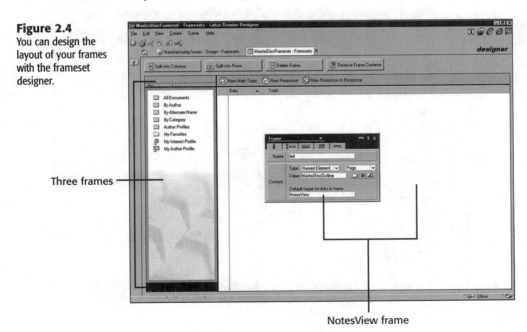

Three frames

NotesView frame

Notice that with the frameset designer, you can add and delete frames, move frame borders, and change the contents of each frame. In Figure 2.4, there are actually four frames defined, three on the left and one on the right. The middle frame on the left is highlighted. You can see in the properties box that the content of this middle frame on the left is a page called MasterDiscOutline. This page contains an outline control, and when the user selects one of the items from the outline on the page, the default target is the right frame. The right frame is called NotesView, and the target is specified at the bottom of the properties box.

I cover framesets in more detail in Chapter 6.

PAGES

Pages are design elements that were introduced in Domino Designer release 5 (see Figure 2.5). If you are familiar with other Web design tools, pages are easy to understand. If you are coming from a Notes/Domino background, pages are like a simplified form. First, like a form, you can use certain design elements. For example, you can insert horizontal rules, sections, hotspots, tables, pictures, navigators, and several other elements. However, you cannot add fields to a page. A page can be useful as a container for an embedded view. Remember, however, that you do not create documents via pages, and pages will not appear in any view. Also, any content that you place on a page will not be full text–indexed or searched because it is a design element, not a document. You can refer to a page by name in a URL.

Figure 2.5
You can define rich text and hotspots on pages.

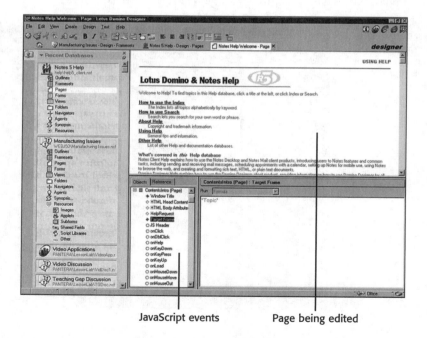

JavaScript events   Page being edited

Figure 2.5 shows you a page from a Help file. Normally, you want to use standard documents and forms, but with the page capability, you can perform special processing on a single page if you need it. Remember that pages are not full text–indexed. In this case, the Help database uses a page for the welcome page, which typically is not needed in a search. When you define a page, you can use the Domino Designer rich text editor to edit the page in a WYSIWYG manner. You can change fonts and make text bold. In addition, you can also edit the page as if it were HTML text. By opening the page properties box and checking the Treat Page Contents As HTML box, you can add HTML markup directly to the page. As you can see from Figure 2.5, Domino also supports JavaScript, and you can define JavaScript processing with the Designer.

> **Tip**
>
> Be careful when using both fonts and colors. When your page is displayed on the Web by a user's Web browser, you have no control over the level of software, the fonts installed on the user's machine, or the capabilities of the user's display adapter. You should try not to use fancy fonts or extreme colors. One trick you can use to allow the display of an arbitrary font is to render the font into a bitmap. Then you can display the bitmap image. By implementing fonts this way, the user does not have to have any particular fonts loaded. If you do use bitmaps for the Web, make sure that you carefully watch their size because large bitmaps can cause long download times for users connected by modem.

I cover pages and how to use them in more detail in Chapter 3, "Developing Pages with the Domino Designer."

FORMS AND SUBFORMS

Forms are like visual templates that can be used to display documents. Documents in Notes and Domino are the fundamental data structure. Nearly all data in Notes and Domino is stored in a document within a database. Even design elements are stored in special documents within the database.

A document stores information by name in items. Each item can hold one or more values, but usually each item stores a single value. The values can be text, date/time, or numeric. Each item within a document has a name, so you can retrieve the value by name.

In Figure 2.6, you can see a Domino form being edited in the middle of the screen. In the form, you can see that there are several fields, each with a box surrounding the field name. This form displays documents by associating field names in the form with item names in the document. Whenever there is an item in the document with the same name as the field, the value of the item is displayed.

While you are editing the form, you can see static information and the various fields that have been defined for the form. For example, in Figure 2.6, you see the static text Subject: and Category:. Note that there is also a field called Subject. You can tell the difference because field names are those with a box surrounding them, such as DateComposed, WebCategories, and NewCats. The icon to the right of the name signifies the type of the data field. For example, the little 16 within a calendar means that it is a date field, so DateComposed will display a date. WebCategories has a little down arrow, which indicates that it is a drop-down list. NewCats as well as the Subject field both have a *T*, which indicates that they are text fields. A rich text field, such as the one called Body, is symbolized by an italic *T*. As you work with the Designer, you will learn the symbols, which are very useful. In the Designer windows in Figure 2.6, you'll notice that an extra pane appears on the right side of the form. This pane is called the Action pane and contains a list of the actions that have been defined. Actions can be displayed either as action buttons or in the Action menu, or both. When you highlight an action in the Action pane, it is selected in the object window of the Design pane at the bottom of the screen. You can supply a program that will execute when a user activates an action.

Figure 2.6
Forms use fields to display information from documents.

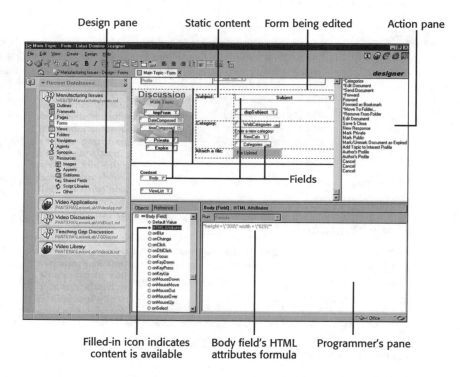

The left side of the Programmer's pane at the bottom displays the objects available within the form. There is a global object, the form object, field objects, embedded objects, and actions within the form. Each object typically has methods and properties. You can see in Figure 2.6 that the Body field has extra HTML attributes defined. These attributes are displayed in the right half of the Programmer's pane and will be used with an HTML client.

Tip

One great new feature the Programmer's pane offers is the capability to see whether a property or method contains a definition. In previous versions of Notes and Domino, you had to pull down a list box and then open an element to find out whether anything was defined. Usually, nothing was defined and it caused wasted effort. Now, the icon for a property is filled in when there is a definition. You can see at a glance the properties and methods that have a definition, and you can go directly to them to find out what they do.

You edit subforms just as you edit forms. The major difference between forms and subforms is that subforms may be referenced from several different forms in the database. The subforms design element type is found within the resources area in the Design pane. I cover both forms and subforms in more detail in Chapter 4, "Creating and Using Forms and Subforms."

VIEWS AND FOLDERS

Views are used to display summary information from documents (see Figure 2.7). Just as a form displays a single document to the user, a view displays information from a set of documents. Typically, each row of a view is information extracted from a single document, so if 20 rows are displayed, they represent 20 different documents.

Reference information is available on this tab   Action pane

Figure 2.7
You can control many aspects about the design of your views.

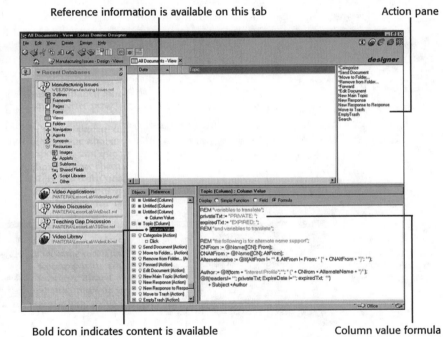

Bold icon indicates content is available   Column value formula

In Figure 2.7, you can see the Designer panes for editing views. The main Work pane shows the view itself, and just to the right you can see the Action pane. The Action pane shows the view actions available and is similar to the form Action pane. The Programmer pane at the bottom shows the objects on the left and the definitions on the right. In Figure 2.7, you can see that the value to be displayed in the Topic column is calculated using a formula. You can use simple functions, document fields, or formulas to display information in views.

In Figure 2.7, in the left side of the Programmer's pane, you can see that there is a second tab next to the Objects tab. This tab is for reference information. If you click the Reference tab, you can find the names of all the fields stored in the database, along with reference information for @formulas and @commands. I cover views and folders in more detail in Chapter 5, "Designing Views and Folders."

NAVIGATORS

Navigators were introduced in release 4 of Notes and Domino. In some ways, they were a precursor to the current Page concept. You can add graphic elements to navigators, provide links to multiple different locations, and use them to provide an attractive user interface. There are several reasons why you might want to use navigators.

First, you might already have navigators within your database, so they are provided in release 5 for compatibility with release 4.x. Second, navigators provide an opportunity to use a simple set of graphic editing tools, which a page element does not provide. If you want to create graphic elements with associated hotspot links, navigators are a good choice. Third, you may now embed a navigator within a page, so you can get the best of both worlds.

I cover navigators in more detail in Chapter 6.

AGENTS

An *agent* is a program that is contained in a Domino database (see Figure 2.8). It can be written in LotusScript, Java, or formula language, or it can be a simple action entered from a dialog box. An agent can be triggered to run in several ways, for example when certain events occur, at specific time intervals, or manually by a user.

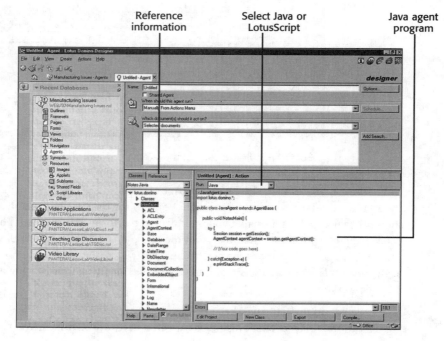

Reference information   Select Java or LotusScript   Java agent program

Figure 2.8
Agents can be written in Java (shown here), LotusScript, formula language, or in simple actions.

In Figure 2.8, you can see the Domino Designer panes for agents. At the top half of the work area pane you see the name of the agent and whether the agent is shared or private. You also specify the triggering mechanism for this agent, which can be a time interval or an event, such as a new document being created within the database.

When the agent is run, it can access a set of applicable documents. For example, if the agent is triggered when a new document is pasted, the pasted document is available. If the agent is run on a schedule, such as hourly, the documents can either be the new and modified documents or the complete set of all documents in the database. You can even add more complex search criteria, if needed by your agent.

The Programmer's pane below includes two parts. In the right part, you can write your agents in Java, as shown, or in LotusScript, formula language, or simple actions. Reference information can appear on the left. In this section for Java, you find information for both the Domino Objects as well as the core Java classes (such as `java.awt`, `java.lang`, and so forth). If you explore the reference material and you find a method you want to use, you can double-click on it and it will be transferred into the Design pane programming area. I cover Java Agent programming in more detail in Chapter 12, "Java Agents, Applets, and Applications"; Chapter 13, "Creating Java Agents with the Domino Designer IDE"; and Chapter 14, "Using the Domino Designer and Third-Party IDEs with Java."

RESOURCES

There are five major types of resources within the Resources twistie and five additional types of resources contained in the Other category. The five major types are images, applets, subforms, shared fields, and script libraries. Of these five types, images and applets are new shared resources in release 5 of Domino. I've already discussed subforms, so in the next few sections I cover images, applets, shared fields, and script libraries. Storing information in shared resources allows you to replicate these resources with the database. If the resources were stored in the file system, as they are for most Web servers, the resources could not easily be replicated.

IMAGES

Image resources enable you to import an image that will be used in several places on your Web site and store them only once in your database. You can give your resources a name, as shown in Figure 2.9, and then reference the image name from other parts of your database.

Image resources are valuable for storing logos, headers, or other graphics that you want to display on several pages throughout your site. In addition, you store multiple images within one image resource. This saves additional overhead if you have a group of related images.

Figure 2.9
Image libraries save space by enabling you to store and name a single copy of an image resource.

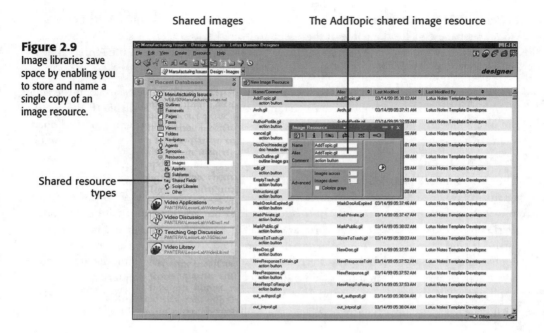

Shared images   The AddTopic shared image resource

Shared resource types

APPLETS

Applets are Java programs that are downloaded from a server and executed within a Web browser. Here are the typical steps in applet development and execution:

1. The applet is developed in the Java language within a Java development environment, such as IBM Visual Age for Java, Borland JBuilder, NetObjects Bean Builder, Symantec Visual Café, or Microsoft Visual J++.

Note

If you use Microsoft Visual J++, you might have some difficulties, depending on the version you use. Before a court decree, Microsoft was using some nonstandard calling conventions for Java. Microsoft has recently released a version of Visual J++ that complies with Sun Microsystems' Java Native Interface (JNI) definition. If you use Visual J++, be sure to carefully test your Java applets for compatibility.

2. The applet is compiled in the development environment to create a set of class files. Class files are similar to compiler object code. They are binary files that define machine operations. The class files, however, are machine-independent. They are read and operate within a virtual machine called the Java Virtual Machine, or JVM. All the major Web browsers as well as the Notes client and the Domino server include a JVM. The JVM is the component that enforces applet security by disallowing the Java program from accessing system resources, such as the file system.

3. Class files can optionally be grouped in an archive file that can be of type ZIP, JAR, or CAB. These formats store a collection of files in a compressed format.

4. The archive files are stored in a directory or within a Domino database in a location where the Web server can find them.

5. A Web page is developed that references the applet via special HTML tags. The tags specify the applet name and any parameters required by the applet.

6. When a user is viewing the Web page that references the Java applet, the applet class files are sent from the server to the Web client and are loaded into the Web browser's JVM for execution.

7. The applet runs either continuously or to completion within the JVM.

Notice the difference between agents and applets. Domino agents may be written in any of several languages, including Java, LotusScript, formula language, or simple actions. Applets may be written only in Java. Agents can be triggered on a scheduled basis or when documents arrive in a database. Agents can run on either the Notes client or the server but cannot run in a non-Notes Web browser. Applets are triggered via HTML tags and run only on the client. Applets can run in either a Web browser or the Notes client, but not on the server.

You can develop agents in Java within the Domino Designer, but the Designer does not contain facilities for developing applets. You must use another third-party tool to develop applets. After they have been created, you can import the Java applet class files into your database. I cover applets in more detail in Chapter 15, "Developing Java Applets for Use with Domino."

Shared Fields

A Domino field is defined in the context of a form. Pages cannot contain fields. Fields are used for data input and display. They may contain formatting information as well as programming information. Fields can have formulas that can perform input validation and translation, for example.

Normally, each form contains the definition of the fields it contains. However, you might have an application in which certain fields are displayed on several separate forms within an application. Some common examples might be a name, document creation date, or other user information.

Shared fields enable you to define common programming attributes of a field and then share the definitions across multiple forms. For example, suppose you have a field that has complex input validation requirements. You can program the validation formula once, share the field, and then any time the field is used, the validation formula will always be the same.

Script Libraries

Script libraries enable you to store subroutines that are used throughout your database. You can create either LotusScript or Java libraries, but you cannot mix LotusScript and Java types within the library. You may, however, have two or more separate script libraries, so you can have one or more of each type. You give each script library a separate name. Note that (as of release 5.0.1) you cannot use the script library feature to store JavaScript programs, only LotusScript and Java.

After you create a script library, you can add subroutines to the library and then reference them from other locations in your database. Sharing your LotusScript or Java code in a shared library is a good technique to promote reuse.

SUMMARY

In this chapter, I showed you how to invoke the Domino Designer. This program is now separate from the Notes client. You can either invoke the executable module directly from your desktop or from within the Notes client.

After you start the Designer, many different types of design elements are available for your use. Some of the new elements in release 5 include outlines, framesets, and pages. You can use these elements to create a Web site without even using the original Domino design elements. Of course, through the use of the traditional Domino forms and views, you have additional powerful tools at your disposal.

Release 5 enables you to use many different types of shared resources within a database. This cuts down on the amount of storage needed to house a Web site. In addition, by storing all the design elements within a database rather than in the operating system file structure, the elements are more easily managed.

In following chapters, I show you more detail on how to use the design elements to create applications that can be Web-enabled.

In this chapter, I gave you information about how to use the IDE. In addition, I gave you an introduction to some of the major Domino design elements.

CHAPTER REVIEW

1. To write a Web application that displays in a Web browser and requests a name and address from the user, would it be more appropriate to use a Domino form or a page? Why?

2. Suppose I wanted to create a Domino database to store an inventory of parts and display this inventory as a list of items to the user. What Domino design element should I use?

3. What are some differences between a Domino agent and an applet?

4. Can I use the shared library feature to store JavaScript programs?

5. What are some of the benefits of using shared resources for your images, applets, and so on?

6. Besides the help system, where could you find reference information about the Domino objects or Java classes in Domino Designer?

7. Can you use the Domino Designer to develop Java applets? What are some other tools available from various vendors for developing Java applets, applications, and agents?

DEVELOPING PAGES WITH THE DOMINO DESIGNER

In this chapter

In previous releases of Notes and Domino, the major user interface element was the form. A Domino form enables you to place static text and graphic elements together with fields as a template for display. The form is combined with different document data items, and it is displayed to the end user.

Release 5 of Notes and Domino introduces a new Web development paradigm, the page. Well, it is not really new. This paradigm is exactly the one used by other Web page development tools and is now available for use within the Domino Designer. Now Domino provides the best of previous releases of Domino with the best of the other Web development tools, and you can mix and match their capabilities.

USING THE PAGE EDITOR

And now, here's something completely different. If you are already familiar with Notes and Domino design but relatively new to Web design, let me show you how different page development can be from previous releases. To illustrate, first I'll create a new, blank database called Page Design.

You can follow along by starting the Domino Designer from your desktop. To create a new database, you can press the Create New Database icon on the Designer welcome page, or you can select File, Database, New, from the menu. Give the new database the name Page Design for the title and filename. You can leave the server Local and the template name -Blank-. I've created my database in my WEBJ50 directory, but you can use Domino's root directory or another directory that you create.

CREATING YOUR FIRST PAGE

After the database has been created, click the Pages design element in the design pane within the database. Your screen should resemble Figure 3.1.

Follow these steps to create a new page:

1. Open the database you want to use for your page.
2. Select the Pages icon in the Design pane.
3. Click the New Page action button. Your new page will appear.

Here is where things get interesting. To follow along with this example, perform the following steps:

1. Open a properties box by clicking the Properties icon in the upper-right area of your screen or by selecting Text, Text Properties. Use the default font (Default Sans Serif) and change the size to 24 points and the style to Bold.
2. Enter Some Text on the first line of the page.

3. Skip one line, and then from the menus select Text, Pass-Thru HTML. Notice that the font size will change to 10 points and the style changes automatically to Plain.

4. Type the following on the page:

```
<h1>This is a Header 1</h1>
```

Figure 3.1
The Domino Designer with the Pages design element selected.

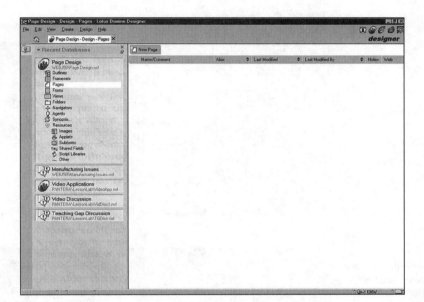

This line uses Hypertext Markup Language (HTML) tags. HTML tags normally have a beginning tag and a matching end tag. In this case, <h1> begins the header text and </h1> ends it. When you read HTML, a tag preceded by a slash means that it is the closing tag of a pair. Notice that the HTML text has a gray background so that you can differentiate HTML from text entered directly on your page. At this point, your screen should look like Figure 3.2.

This is a good point to test your Web page. The icons in the upper-right part of your screen can be used to invoke a Web browser. If you have Internet Explorer or Netscape Navigator installed (or both), you will see their respective icons. To preview your test page, do the following:

1. Click one of the browser icons to test your Web page. If you prefer, you can also select Design, Preview in Web Browser. At this point, you see a listing of Web browser choices. Choose the Web browser you want to use.

2. You will be prompted for a name for your page. You can name your page anything. I chose PageTest.

3. Click OK, and your Web browser should appear. The browser selected by Domino Designer will be the browser you have chosen. In Figure 3.3 I've moved the Domino Designer to the left and placed the browser on the right so you can see both the Designer version and the browser version side by side.

PART

I

CH

3

Figure 3.2
You can enter some text directly on your page along with some HTML.

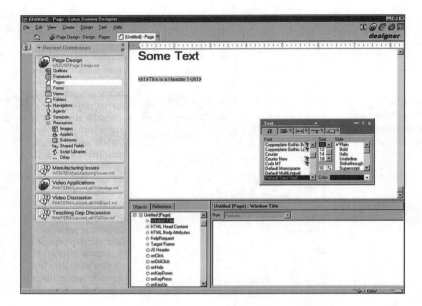

Figure 3.3
You can preview your page with Internet Explorer (shown) or Netscape Navigator.

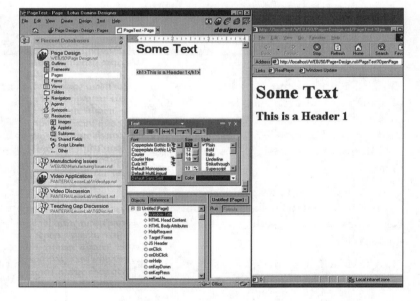

Here are several points to notice about your first Web page:

- The font for Some Text doesn't seem right, and the size is large but slightly different than the source.

- The size for This is a Header 1 is larger than the input, and the font is also different. Also, the beginning and ending tags are gone.

- Notice that the uniform resource locator (URL) address in the browser window includes localhost, the database name, the page name, and the command to open the page.

I wanted to show you immediately the importance and convenience of testing your Web page designs with the browser buttons in the upper-right corner of your screen. Here are some explanations of why your Web page looks different than you might think it should:

- The first line does not appear in the browser as it does in the Designer because fonts in the Designer are not necessarily available to the browser when your page is displayed. Because of this, standard Web fonts have been defined. Because we used the default font (Default Sans Serif), no font information was sent to the Web browser, and the text displays in the default font for the browser, which is Times Roman. Sizes are also standardized and, by default, are not available with fine granularity, so the browser uses an approximation to the size.
- A size is associated by default with the h1 tag, and it is used for the text. Other heading tags—h2, h3, and so forth—are defined and use different styles. The font is also associated with the h1 tag, and the default browser font is used again for the h1 tag.

PART
I
CH
3

I should note here that with HTML you can control many different aspects of the presentation. I cover HTML in more detail in Chapter 7, "Using Hypertext Markup Language (HTML) for Page Design."

As an alternative to using the Pass-Thru HTML text property, you can enclose text within square brackets ([ ]), and it will be treated as Pass-Thru HTML. This makes it very easy and convenient to mix HTML source directly in your page without resorting to menu items all the time. Here is how our example would look if we used the bracket syntax:

```
[<h1>This is a Header 1</h1>]
```

PAGE PROPERTIES

The Page Info tab of the Page properties box appears in Figure 3.4.

Background ⌐   ⌐ Launch
Page Info ⌐   ⌐ Security

Figure 3.4
You can treat an entire page as HTML.

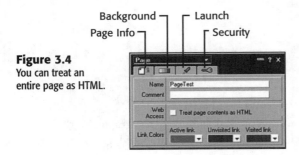

Notice that you can treat an entire page as HTML. To do so, just check the box titled Treat Page Contents as HTML. If you check this box, you don't have to include the square brackets because your entire page will be treated as HTML automatically. This is an extremely useful setting if you are new to Domino but are already familiar with HTML, or if you want to use a separate HTML editing tool and just import your HTML.

I have shown you three different ways to specify HTML in your page:

- Create text on the page, and then highlight the text and give it the Pass-Thru HTML attribute. You do this on the Text menu. You can mix and match HTML and non-HTML with this method.

- Place square brackets ([ ]) around any text on the page that you want to be considered HTML. You do not have to use the menus. You can mix and match HTML and non-HTML with this method.

- Go to the Page properties box and check the box labeled Treat Page Contents as HTML. This will treat the entire page contents as HTML. This makes it easier to import text directly from another HTML authoring tool. Remember that when you turn on the HTML setting, the text in the page will use HTML formatting rules (such as its handling of spaces) as opposed to Domino's formatting rules.

In the Page properties dialog box you can also set the colors for the Active Link, Unvisited Link, and Visited Link. Normally, you should just leave these set at the default values.

PASTING AND IMPORTING GRAPHIC BACKGROUNDS

You can specify a specific color or a graphic image as a background for your page. To change the graphic background, do the following:

1. Open the Page properties box for the page.

2. Click the Background tab (see Figure 3.5). You can select a background color by opening the drop-down box.

Figure 3.5
You can set the background color and image with the Page properties box.

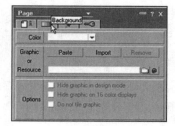

3. Use one of the following methods to obtain a graphic background:
   - You can use another graphics editing program and copy the graphic to the Clipboard. After you have copied the graphic to the Clipboard, go to the Page properties dialog box and click the Paste button.

- If you want to import an image for your background from a file, click the Import button. You will be prompted and can locate your file. The graphic import file types supported are BMP, GIF, JPEG, PCX, or TIFF 5.0.

- If you have saved your graphic image as an image resource, type the name or click the folder icon on the Image Resource line. You can specify a formula by clicking the @ symbol. The formula must result in the name of an image resource.

4. (Optional) You can specify that you want to hide the image during design or for 16-color displays. Turning off the image during design makes it easier to edit your page. On 16-color displays, sometimes 256-color (or higher) photos or graphics look more like modern art than an attractive background. This can be distracting to users, so you can turn off the background.

5. (Optional) You can specify that you want to turn off tiling of the graphic background. Normally, by default, graphic backgrounds are tiled.

ENHANCING YOUR PAGE

There are a multitude of features in the Domino Designer for creating user interface elements. These elements include tables, pictures, and sections, among many others. Let's look at some of the features you can use within the page editor to enhance your pages.

CREATING TABLES

Although you can use the Domino designer to create your page with a WYSIWYG (What You See Is What You Get) editor, Domino will eventually convert your page to HTML before sending it to the Web browser. One of the limitations (features) of HTML is that text lines will automatically wrap as the browser does formatting for you. So, if you carefully line up your input text into columns, the browser will cheerfully ignore the columns you set up. What can you do to format your text so that you get the artistic look you want from your page?

You can use tables. In fact, using tables is an important technique because tables can be used as formatting tools in addition to their traditional purpose as a means to display text and numbers. HTML 4 has additional formatting capabilities and styles to accomplish positioning, but many users are not yet using the latest browsers, so learning how to use tables is still valuable.

With release 5 of Domino Designer, you can create several different styles of tables, including a tabbed interface, a timed interface, and a table that will display different rows depending on the contents of a field (in a form). To format different elements of a page, however, all you need is the basic type of table. I'll show you the other types later.

To create a basic table, do the following:

1. Place the cursor on the page (or form) where you want your table to appear.
2. Select Create, Table. You will see a dialog box, as in Figure 3.6. We are interested in creating a basic table, which uses the first icon button. You can leave the default number of rows and columns or enter the number of rows and columns you want to use for your table. Your table can fit the window width or be a fixed-width table. The default is for your table to have a fixed width.

Figure 3.6
When creating a table, you can enter its size, its width type, and the type of table.

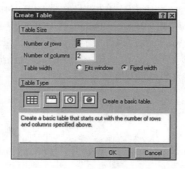

3. Click OK to create your table.

By default, tables are created with borders displayed and will extend to the full width of your page.

ADDING ROWS AND COLUMNS

After you have created your table, you might want to add rows or columns. There are several ways to add rows and columns, depending on where and how many you want to add. Click your mouse cursor inside the table, and then click the Table menu (see Figure 3.7).

Figure 3.7
There are several ways to add and delete rows and columns of your table.

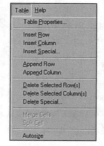

If you want to add rows to the end of your table, you can select the Append Row option. The row will be added to the bottom of your table. To add a column to your table, select the Append Column menu option. The column will be appended on the right side of your table.

To insert a row or column at the beginning or middle of your table, select the Insert Row or Insert Column menu option. The row or column will be inserted before the selected row or column. You can also add a new row by tabbing out of the last cell of a table in design mode. A new row is automatically added for you.

Use the Insert Special menu option when you want to insert or append more than one row or column. The Insert Row/Column dialog box will appear (see Figure 3.8).

Figure 3.8
Use Insert Special to insert more than one row or column to your table.

Enter the number of rows or columns you want to add, and then select Insert to insert before the currently selected row or column. Use Append to append the desired items to the end of the table.

DELETING ROWS AND COLUMNS

Deleting rows and columns operates similarly to inserting. Follow these steps to delete rows or columns:

1. Select a cell—either the topmost cell in a set of rows or the leftmost cell in a set of columns—that you want to delete.

2. Drag the mouse to select cells in the rest of the rows or columns. If you are deleting rows, you must have at least one cell selected in each row you are about to delete. If you are deleting columns, make sure to select at least one cell in each column to be deleted.

3. After you select the cells, select Table, Delete Selected Row(s) to delete rows, and Table, Delete Selected Columns to delete columns.

Note

Delete Special can be used as a shortcut to delete a contiguous set of rows or columns. First, select the topmost or leftmost cell (as in step 1 in the previous instructions). Then, select Delete Special. You will be prompted for the number of rows or columns to delete.

TABLE PROPERTIES

You can view the table properties by clicking the Properties icon, by issuing Edit, Properties, or by pressing Alt+Enter on the keyboard. You can also click inside any cell of a table, and then select Table, Table Properties. When the properties box appears, if Table is not listed on the top line of the dialog box, you can click the drop-down box and select Table (see Figure 3.9).

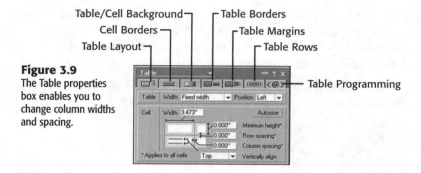

Figure 3.9
The Table properties box enables you to change column widths and spacing.

Table Programming

The Table Layout tab (the first tab) of the properties box enables you to change the type of width to use (Fixed, Fit to Window, or Fit with Margins), the position of the table (Left, Right, or Center), and the fixed spacing between columns and rows. Note that the amount you enter into the columns and rows fields applies to all columns and rows. Also, the sizes you enter apply to each side of the cell. For example, if you enter a column space of 0.5", you will get 0.5 inch on both the left and right side of the column. This means that you will get a full inch between columns. Note that column spacing, row spacing, and minimum height are not supported in Web applications. Some of these values can affect the width of a cell, however, which is supported on a column-by-column basis.

CHANGING TABLE BORDERS AND MARGINS

Figure 3.10 shows the Cell Borders tab. This tab affects cell borders, not the border for the entire table. The Border tab controls the border for the entire table.

Figure 3.10
The Cell Borders tab enables you to change the cell border style, color, and thickness.

You can specify the style of the cell borders as Solid, Ridge, or Groove. Clicking the Color drop-down enables you to select a color for the borders. If you click the Set All To 0 button, you will get no borders because the thickness of all borders will be zero. If you set all the borders to 1, you will get the default thickness. Note that the style options Ridge and Groove, as well as individual cell coloring, are not supported for Web browsers. You can set the border color for a table, but all cells will be the same color.

Setting all borders to zero, along with setting the widths of columns, enables you to specify text formatting on your page. By using tables, you can place elements relatively easily. You can specify spacing between separate items for viewing just by changing the table column widths. This is especially useful if your target audience will be Web browsers.

If you are familiar with layout regions in Notes, you should be aware that they cannot be rendered to Web browsers. Typically, in previous releases of Notes and Domino, you might have used a layout region for precise positioning. You should become familiar with tables as another means to accomplish formatting because you can use tables with zero thickness to manipulate positions, and this will work fine with either browsers or Notes clients. You can open a discussion database in Domino Designer and look at the Main Topic form to see these zero thickness tables at work to position text within a form.

The Table Borders tab is used to change settings that affect the whole table rather than specific cells. You can see the Table Borders tab in Figure 3.11.

Figure 3.11
The Table Borders tab enables you to change the table border style, color, thickness, and spacing.

In the Table Borders tab, you can set the style of the table border to None or one of eight predefined styles, such as Solid, Double, or Dotted. This is the line style used for the border surrounding the table. The cells each have their own border, but you can have an extra border around the entire table. You can set the thickness of the table border as well as its color. You can change the spacing between the table and its border. This spacing is called the Inside spacing. The Outside setting is the space outside the table border that separates the table from its surroundings. (The Outside setting was originally called Outer Space in one of the early beta versions of Notes. I guess they figured that option was out of this world.) To set thickness, inside spacing, and outside spacing, first select the one you want using the drop-down box, and then adjust the Top, Bottom, Left, and Right numbers (refer to Figure 3.11). Each of the three parameters can have four different numbers. You can use the spinner controls to the right of the dialog box to increment or decrement all four values at once. Finally, you can add a shadow effect by checking the Drop Shadow check box. If a shadow is enabled, you can control its width.

The Table Margins tab appears immediately to the right of the Table Border tab and can be used to specify the left and right margins for the table. You can specify each margin as either an offset measurement or a percentage of the window. The table margins affect the table as a whole, not the individual cells.

IMPLEMENTING NEWSPAPER-STYLE COLUMNS

With release 5, you can format columns within your table in newspaper style, with text flowing from one column of a table to the next column (see Figure 3.12).

Figure 3.12
The Table Margins tab enables you to create newspaper-style flowing from one column to another.

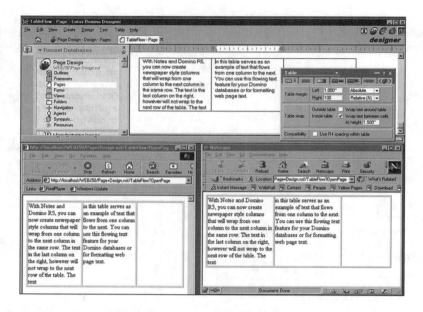

In Figure 3.12, you can see the table within the Domino Designer as well as within Web browsers. The figure shows you formatting in the Domino Designer, Netscape Navigator, and Microsoft Internet Explorer. The newspaper-style flowing is obtained by checking the Inside Table Wrap Between Cells. When you enable this feature, you must specify the column height in the At Height input field.

Text will flow between cells within the same row. Text will not wrap from the last cell on the right to the next table row. If you enter more text in the right column than the column height setting, the table row height will just expand to accommodate the larger height.

SETTING TABLE/CELL BACKGROUNDS

In release 5, there are many new options for setting background colors and/or images in tables. The Table/Cell Background tab is the third tab in the Table properties box (see Figure 3.13).

Tables for the Web must be a solid color. However, because you might be developing applications that will be used by Notes clients as well as Web browsers, I'll describe the options for completeness.

You can set a table color style in the properties box. This will give colors to the entire table at once. Two colors are involved; one called Color, and the other called Body. You can change these colors with the drop-down boxes in the dialog box. By default, two shades of gray are used with the Body color: dark gray and the highlight color light gray. In the Table Style drop-down list, you can select from one of the following styles:

- None—No automatic row or column header highlighting.
- Solid—The table is all one color. This is the only option supported for Web browsers.

- Alternating rows—Alternate rows are different colors. By default, two shades of gray are used.

- Alternating columns—Alternate columns are different colors. By default, two shades of gray are used.

- Left and Top—The top row and the left column are highlighted. I have changed the colors so that the header color is dark and the body color is light gray. This is a table that an accountant or spreadsheet guru would love (refer to Figure 3.13).

- Left—The left column is highlighted with the color you specify.

- Right and Top—The top row and the right column are highlighted. This is a bit unusual. Perhaps left-handed accountants might like this one or you could use it to highlight row totals on the right.

- Right—The right column is highlighted with your color.

- Top—The top row is highlighted.

Figure 3.13
The Table/Cell Background tab enables you to set cell backgrounds, headers, and gradients.

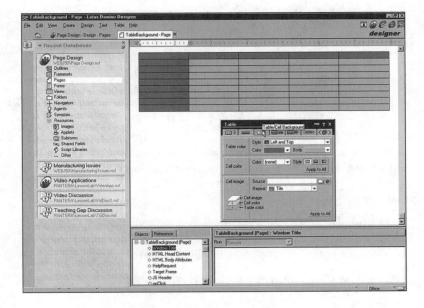

You can override any of the default styles by highlighting one or more cells, and then clicking the cell color drop-down icon to select a color. A color palette will appear. If you select a color, it overlays the default color of the style. To make the style color show through again, you can click the (none) button, which is the second icon (of four) and appears in the top row at the top-right of the color palette.

You can make gradients (gradual color shifts) within a cell by using three selections: The Color field will be the starting color, the To field color will be the ending color, and the direction can be set to either Top to Bottom or Left to Right. You specify the direction by clicking one of the Style buttons. Gradients will display only if you are using a Notes client. Internet Explorer and Netscape Navigator will both display a solid background color.

The final option on the Table/Cell Background tab is to set the Cell image. With this option, you can include an image within a table cell. You can use this feature to format an attractive page (see Figure 3.14).

Figure 3.14
You can include a background image within a table cell.

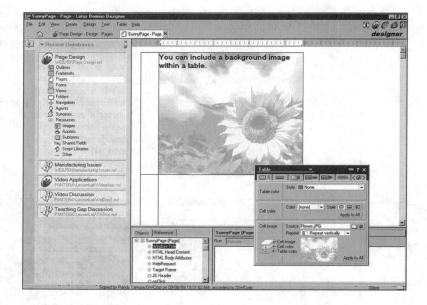

You can include an image by name by using a formula or from your image library. Images from your image library are resources and will replicate along with your database. Unfortunately, cell images are not supported on the Web.

MERGING AND SPLITTING CELLS

In Figure 3.15, I used another table technique known as *cell merging*. In this case, I merged all the cells in the top row to become a single cell. After that, I used a gradient that stretches across the entire width of the title, and I centered the text within the long cell.

Follow these steps to merge several cells into one cell:

1. Select the cells within the table that you want to merge.

2. Select Table, Merge Cells. This option is valid in the menu only if you have more than one table cell selected. You can select cells in row-wise direction or column-wise direction. You can also select cells that have already been merged previously.

3. Your cells are now merged. Note that when merging cells that already contain text, Domino places the text of the cells into the leftmost (or topmost) cell separated by newline characters.

Figure 3.15
You can merge cells to get a continuous gradient and centered text.

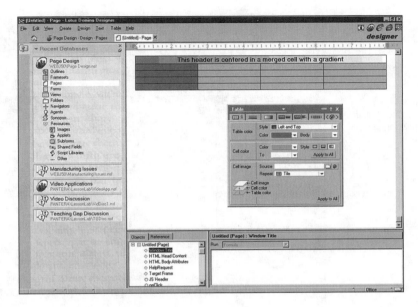

Follow these steps to split cells that have been previously merged:

1. Select a cell that was previously merged within the table.

2. Select Table, Split Cell. This option is valid in the menu only if you have selected a cell that was previously merged. Your cells are now split back into their original, elementary state before being merged. If you merged cells more than once, the previous state is not kept. Your cells will split back into their original, single state. If there is text in the merged cell, it will be placed into the leftmost (or topmost) cell upon the split.

ADVANCED FUN WITH TABLES

There are several special effects that you can create with tables. They all revolve around a concept called the collapsible table, which you can create either initially or on the Advanced tab of the Table properties box. The one factor that these tables have in common is that only a single row of the table is shown at a time. Various methods are used to determine which row to show. There are three types of special tables:

- Tabbed tables—Each row of the table will correspond to one tab of the tabbed table. Only the row containing the selected tab will appear.

- Timed tables—Each row of the table will appear for a specified amount of time. The default is two seconds. You can use these tables to display animation.

- Programmatic control—In addition to the table, you must supply a field. The name of the field is the same as the table name with a $ prefix. The contents of the field determines which row to display. You can programmatically update the field, which can then be used to select the row.

You can create a table of any of these three types or the standard table type initially and later convert it to any of the other types. You control the type of table on the Table Rows tab of the Table properties box. This is the sixth tab in the properties box. Look at the example in Figure 3.16.

Figure 3.16
A tabbed table with five rows and four columns.

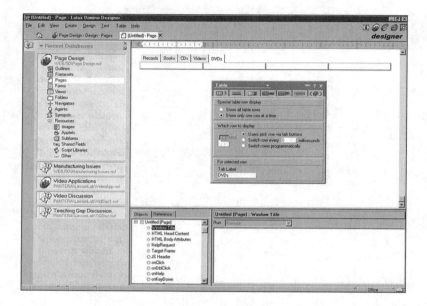

I created a tabbed table with five rows and four columns. You can create a tabbed table on the Create Table dialog box by clicking on the Tabbed Table icon (the second icon) in the Table Type section, entering the number of rows and columns, and then clicking OK.

After you create the table, you can add information to each table row. In Figure 3.16, you see that I have added tab labels for each row. To add a tab label, first select the tab on the page, and then enter a tab label in the bottom of the Table Rows tab of the properties box. Because there are five rows in this example, there are five tabs. You must select the tab and enter the name separately for each tab. One common use might be to use only a single column with several rows. In this way, you could create a tabbed interface similar to a dialog box.

Another option for tables is to use the timed table option. This will show each row for a fixed amount of time. The default is two seconds, but you can adjust this time. In Figure 3.16, you see that you can set the second radio button option in the middle of the properties box. The timed display can be used to create an animated appearance to the user. Timed tables are not supported on the Web.

To use this option, create a table with several rows and one column. Each row should contain a graphic file—from your image library, for example. Set the timer for the amount of time you want to show each graphic. You can specify a transition effect such as left-to-right, dissolve, or explode, among several others. You can also specify that you want to cycle through the graphics continually or when clicked by the user.

Tip

New with release 5 of Domino, you can include nested tables, or tables within tables. This is particularly useful with tabbed tables—you can include a tabbed table within a tabbed table. This technique is used in the Domino Public Directory database.

The final type of single-row table gives you programmatic control over the table to be displayed to the user. Normally, this table type should be used with a form because fields are not allowed in a page. I describe fields and forms and the programmatic control of tables in Chapter 4, "Creating and Using Forms and Subforms."

EMBEDDING PICTURES

Earlier in this chapter, I showed you how to change the background color and set an image as your page background. In this section, I cover the embedding of smaller graphic elements, such as buttons, on your page. There are several methods for using graphic elements on your page, depending on how you want to use them.

IMPORTING GRAPHIC FILES

One way you can use a graphic image is to embed it directly on your page. To embed a graphic picture on your page, perform the following steps:

1. Create or open the page you want to use for your graphic.

2. Move your cursor to the location where you want to place your picture and select Create, Picture. You will see a dialog box similar to Figure 3.17.

3. Notice that you can choose among a variety of graphics file formats. The most common Web formats are GIF and JPEG formats. BMP is a native Windows format. Several other graphics formats are popular as well. Select the format you want to use. Note that if you choose a format other than BMP, JPEG, or GIF, Domino must do a conversion on the graphic file. If possible, you might want to consider converting your graphics to JPEG or GIF yourself (so you can control the conversion aspects such as color, dithering, and so on), and you might also want to consider using shared image resources (described in the next section).

4. After you select your format, the files of that type will appear in the dialog box. In this case, you can see a PushMe.JPG file.

5. You can double-click on the file you want to import, or you can single-click on the file you want to import, and then click the Import button. Your graphic will then appear on your page.

Figure 3.17
The Import dialog box appears after you issue the Create Picture menu command to import graphics.

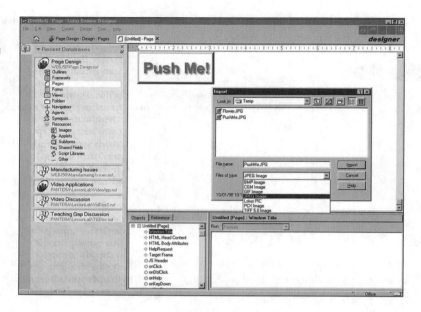

USING IMAGE RESOURCES

An important new feature of release 5 is the capability to store graphic images in an image resource library. You can then reference the images from other locations in your database. In previous releases of Domino, shared images were not as important because the forms and subforms and their contents are already shared resources. With the advent of pages, however, it is important to have shared images; otherwise, the identical images will be duplicated on each page and will take up unnecessary space.

Follow these steps to save a new image in your image resource library:

1. Open the Resources twistie and select Images in the Design pane.

2. Click the New Image Resource action button. An Open dialog box will appear.

3. Select the type of image you want to store in your image resource library. Note that only GIF, JPEG, and BMP type images are supported. This is more restrictive than the types available for direct import to a page.

4. Double-click on the file you want to put into your library. You can also single-click on the file and click Open. The image will be stored in your image resource library.

5. (Optional) You can add an alias to the image resource by opening the properties box for the image and entering an alias into the box. If you refer to this image via an alias, you will be free to change the image later without changing any programs that refer to the image in the library. You can also enter a comment that will appear when you view the list of image resources (see Figure 3.18).

Figure 3.18
The Image Resource properties dialog box.

After you have stored the image resource in your library, you can use it on your page. Follow these steps to use the image resource on your page:

1. Create or open the page you want to use for your graphic.

2. Move your cursor to the location where you want to place your picture and select Create, Image Resource. You will be prompted for an image name and an image type, and you will see a list of the available images (see Figure 3.19).

Figure 3.19
The Insert Image Resource selection dialog box.

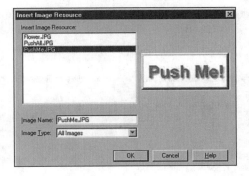

3. If you click on an image name, you will see a preview of the image on the right side of the dialog box. After you have found the image you want to include, select its name and click OK.

4. Your image will be displayed on your page.

USING AN IMAGE RESOURCE SET

You might have noticed in Figure 3.18 there are fields for specifying the number of images across and down within a single image resource. There are two types of image resource sets (also sometimes called image wells), horizontal and vertical. Horizontal resource sets can be used to specify rollover images for a single graphic. Vertical image resource sets are used to specify different sized icons for use in the bookmark bar.

By specifying four images horizontally, you can control the image used by the Notes client for these situations:

■ Normal image

■ Mouse Rollover image (while mouse is over the image)

- Selected image (while the image has the focus)
- Clicked image (when image is clicked)

You must store all four images in a single graphic (for example, GIF or JPEG) file. You combine the images using some other graphic editing program. Separate each image from the others by a single pixel-wide line. Even if you are not using one of the states, you must supply a graphics image. You can, of course, use the same image in more than one of the four positions, which can give the appearance that the image is not changing.

> **Note**
>
> The image rollover feature of image resources is supported only in the Notes client. It will not work with Web browsers. To implement rollovers in Web browsers you should use JavaScript. I'll show you how to do this in Chapter 11, "JavaScript Techniques with Domino."

Vertical image resource sets are used for icons used in the bookmark bar. The standard bookmark icons are located in the bookmark.nsf database. Each bookmark icon has three sizes: small, medium, and large. The small icons are 16×16, medium is 24×24, and large is 32×32 pixels. All three of these different sized icons are stored in the same image resource (see Figure 3.20).

Figure 3.20
The Image Resource properties box with three icons vertically.

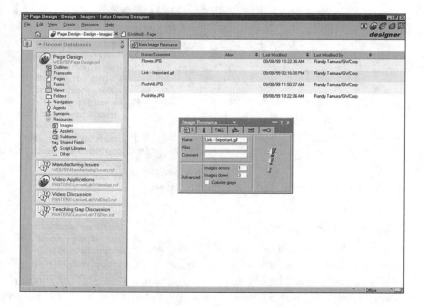

To create one of these image resource sets, use a graphic editor and create an image that is 98 pixels high and 32 pixels wide. Each of the three icons has a single pixel line separating them. The top icon is the large one, the middle is the medium-sized one, and the bottom is the small icon. Each icon should be positioned in the upper-left corner of the graphic image (see Figure 3.21).

Figure 3.21
Map of vertical image resource used for bookmark bar.

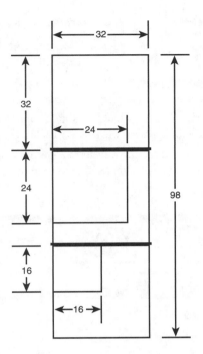

As a user, you can change the size of icon used in the bookmark bar by issuing File, Preferences, User Preferences. You can change the Bookmark icon size in the User Preferences dialog box.

ORGANIZING DATA WITH RULES, SECTIONS, AND PAGE BREAKS

To make your page look better and provide more organization, you can use horizontal rules and sections. A horizontal rule is just a line that goes across the page. With the rule properties, however, you can modify the width and height of the rule. The width can be expressed as a percentage, or you can specify an exact measurement, such as inches.

For Notes clients, rules can also include color gradients, which start in one color and gradually change to another color. The gradients change colors from top to bottom. Gradient rules are not supported on the Web. To create a horizontal rule, move your cursor to the location on the page or form where you want your rule to appear. Then, select Create, Horizontal Rule. After your rule has been created, you can change its properties via the properties box. You can see an example of a rule with a gradient in Figure 3.22.

Creating sections is easy and fun. Here is what you do to create a section:

1. Move the cursor to where you want to create your section. Type all the text that you want included in the section.

2. After the text has been entered on the page, select the text you want to make into the section with the keyboard or the mouse.

3. Select Create, Section to create your section. The first line of the text that you selected will become the section title and will display if the section is closed.

4. (Optional) After the section has been created, you can change the title with the Section properties box. You can also change the rules that are used to automatically expand and collapse the section (see Figure 3.22).

Figure 3.22
The Section proper-
ties box can be used
to control the
expand/collapse
rules.

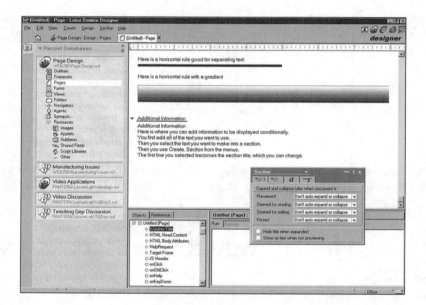

You can control printer page breaks by inserting a page break. To insert a page break, first move the cursor to the location where you want your page to break, and then choose Create, Page Break. Note that the page break will not affect formatting for display in either the Notes client or Web browsers. It is strictly an aid to formatting your printed output.

SUMMARY

In this chapter, I showed you how to create pages and we explored the major design elements for the user interface. Pages can contain graphics, tables, hotspots, text, and several other objects. In addition, you can create HTML for a page with another editor and import the HTML into Domino Designer.

I showed you how to use tables and gave you examples of the various kinds of formatting you can do with tables. You can also position graphics and text through the use of tables for a Web browser. Tables can be used to format newspaper-style text and spreadsheet-like data and can be embellished with graphics.

With special tables that show only a single row, you can implement a tabbed interface for your users. This will allow you to provide many more choices to the users, but without overwhelming them. These single-row tables can also be used with a timer to implement a crude animation.

In this chapter you learned how to import graphics directly onto a page as well as into an image library. By using an image set with multiple images, you can implement mouse rollovers in the Notes client.

Finally, rules allow you to improve your user interface by separating areas of your page. They can cover the entire width of the window or can be a fixed length. Sections also allow you to provide additional information to a user that can be optionally expanded. I'll cover additional topics on tables and sections in the next chapter.

PART

I

CH

3

CHAPTER REVIEW

1. Create a page that contains a graphic, such as a corporate logo, in the upper-right corner. It should be exactly five inches from the left margin. Make sure the graphic is also positioned properly when viewed both by the Notes client and a Web browser.

2. Create a page that contains a tabbed dialog interface. There should be three tabs, and each tab should contain a different graphic image. When the user selects a different tab, the associated image will display.

3. What are three different ways that you can code HTML directly on a page?

4. What different graphic formats are supported when you import a graphic picture from the file system directly onto a page? What graphic formats are supported for image resources?

5. There are two types of image resource sets: horizontal and vertical. What can you do with a horizontal set and what can you do with a vertical set? How many images should there be in each type?

6. Create a page that contains a tabbed dialog interface with two tabs. Create a nested table within each tab. The nested table on the first tab should have five rows and two columns. The second tab should have a nested table with three rows and six columns. Color each nested table with a different set of background colors.

7. Create a page that contains a section. Inside the section create a table with four rows and three columns. In addition to the table, there should be text both before and after the table. You should be able to show and hide the section, including the table. Set the properties so that the table is always initially collapsed when it is opened for reading.

CHAPTER 4

CREATING AND USING FORMS AND SUBFORMS

In this chapter

DESIGNING FORMS

In the last chapter, I covered most of the basics of page creation and use, so let's move on to forms. Forms have always been a fundamental part of Notes and Domino, so if you're familiar with previous releases, you probably already know a lot about forms. If you have not used previous releases of Notes or Domino, you get an introduction to how forms and documents work in the next sections.

FORMS AND DOCUMENTS

In Domino, the *document* is the fundamental unit of storage for information. Documents contain named items to store information. The item has a data type, such as numeric or text, and if the item contains multiple values, they are all the same type. A typical item within a document might contain, for example, a name, address, or phone number. Sometimes these document items are also called fields.

You might have hundreds or thousands (or more) of documents in a database. The documents do not all have to have the same item names. For example, one document might contain the items Name and Address, and another document might contain TotalAmount and DueDate.

Not all the data contained within documents is necessarily visible to a user. Documents contain data, but they are typically used with user interface elements, such as forms and views. Forms and views are the means to present information stored within documents to the user. Views present summary information from many documents, and forms enable you to see detailed information from one document.

A *form* is like a visual template. By this, I mean that the form in Domino is much like a blank paper form. Think for a moment about the form you fill out in the dentist's office with your name, address, and medical history. This form indicates the information desired and leaves several blank areas for you to fill in.

With Domino forms, the blank areas are called fields. Each field within a form has a field name so you can reference it and obtain the information you need. A form contains both static information and field information. It is a visual object, much like the page design element that I showed you in the previous chapter.

Suppose Domino is showing an empty form to a user. When the user fills the empty fields of the form, the information is stored in a document. Domino separates the user interface (form) from the field data stored within the document. This way, you can view the same fields with different forms, and you can change the look and feel of your application without changing the underlying data stored in the document fields.

What happens if the names in the document don't match the names in the form? Actually, this happens quite often and is normal. If the document contains items that have names that do not appear on the form, the values are not displayed to the user. If the form contains field names that don't appear in the document, when the user enters a value, it automatically creates a corresponding item value in the document.

When serving forms and documents to a Web browser, Domino works a little differently. Because Web browsers support HTML (Hypertext Markup Language), Domino forms and documents must first be converted to HTML. This conversion happens on the server before sending the information to the Web client.

To recap, forms are used for visual display to a user, and documents are used to store data within the database. The correspondence of names in forms and documents enables Domino to display fields filled in with the values from a document. For display to a Web browser, Domino first merges the form definition with the document values and then converts the result to HTML, which is then sent to the browser.

HOW DO FORMS AND DOCUMENTS COMPARE TO PAGES?

We have now talked about pages, forms, and documents. How are these all used and how do they compare? In Table 4.1, an *X* indicates that the feature is available. There might be minor exceptions, but I've tried to show you the major differences so you can contrast the database elements.

TABLE 4.1   COMPARISON OF PAGES, FORMS, AND DOCUMENTS

	Pages	Forms	Documents
Visual User Interface	X	X	
Can be viewed in a Web browser	X	X	
Stores field data values			X
Can contain Domino field definitions		X	
Can contain HTML formatting and INPUT items (HTML-type fields)	X	X	
Is a design element	X	X	
Full text searched			X
Data can be shown in views			X
Single element can be used with multiple documents		X	

CREATING A NEW FORM

To create a new form in your database, follow these steps:

1. In the Domino Designer, open the database where you want your form to appear. If you are following along, create a new, blank database called Form Design. I have created this database in my WEBJ50 directory, but you can put it in any convenient directory.

2. Click on Forms in the Design Pane.

3. Click the New Form action button. Your new form will appear.

The Form editor is similar to the Page editor. You have a large area at the top to lay out your form and the Programmer's pane on the bottom to manipulate details of the elements within the form.

COPYING FORMS FROM ANOTHER DATABASE

With Domino Designer it is especially easy to copy an existing form from another database. It is usually much easier to start with a form that is already created and modify it rather than to start with a blank form. Follow these steps to copy one or more forms from another database:

1. In the Domino Designer, open both the source and destination databases.

2. In the source database, click on the word Forms in the Design pane. This will bring up a list of the forms in the Work pane.

3. To copy a single form, click on the form in the Work pane on the right. To select a set of contiguous forms, use the Shift key and click on the start and end forms. To select non-contiguous forms, use the Ctrl key and click on each form to be copied.

4. After you have selected the forms you want to copy, press Ctrl+C on the keyboard or select Edit, Copy from the menus. Your forms will be copied to the clipboard.

5. Switch to the destination database and click on the word Forms in the Design pane. Press Ctrl+V on the keyboard or select Edit, Paste from the menus. Your forms will be copied from the clipboard to your destination database.

FORM PROPERTIES

After you have created your new form or have copied it from another source, you can adjust its properties. In Figure 4.1 you see the Form Info tab of the Form properties box.

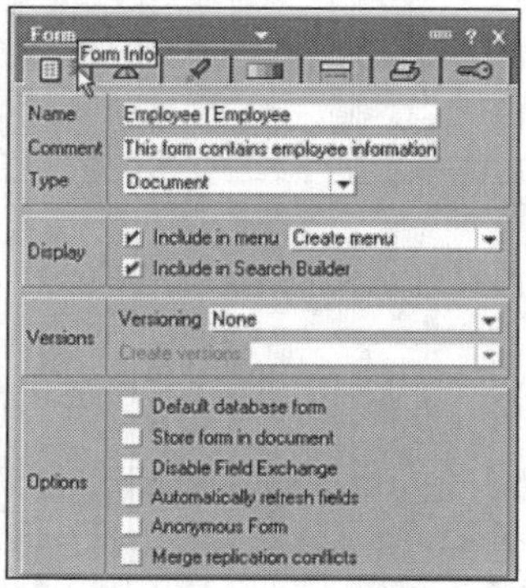

Figure 4.1
You can change the name, alias, and form options in the Form properties box.

THE FORM NAME

In the Form Info tab you specify the most important properties of the form. In the Name field, you specify both the name and alias of the form. Separate the name and alias by a vertical bar. The alias is important because it enables you to assign a name that can be used during programming for the form. In essence, the name and alias are like an external and internal name for the form.

You might want to change the text that appears to users when you update the form. By assigning an alias and using it within your programming, you do not need to change any of your programming code. Thus, you should normally always assign an alias to a form, even if it is the same name as the external name for the form.

The comment field displays in the listing of the forms, so it is a convenient place to describe the contents of the form. The document type can be Document (the default), Response, or Response to Response. These different document types affect the way the document behaves when displayed in a view. The details of the different types are described in Chapter 5, "Designing Views and Folders."

THE FORM MENU DISPLAY OPTIONS

In the Display section you can choose to include the form in the Create menu or the Create-Other dialog, or to inhibit display within the menus. You can disable the menu display if you want to use the form for administrative or other purposes that normal users of the database do not require. You might have some forms that you would like to make available to normal users of the database, but which are not frequently used. Thus, you would like to remove them from the main menu selection so that the Create menu does not get too cluttered. In this case, choose the Create-Other dialog option. The form can still be used for creation, but it will not be displayed in the main list of forms.

You can choose to include or exclude the form from use within the Search builder.

USING THE FORM VERSIONING OPTIONS

When a user edits an existing document and then saves it, two generic actions can occur:

- The document can be saved overlaying and replacing the existing document.
- The document can be saved in addition to any previous existing document without replacing the old version.

If Versioning is set to None, the first option is used: Any saved document overlays and replaces the previous version of the document. If you want to save previous versions of the document, you can use the versioning feature. Be careful when designing Web applications, however; versioning is not supported on the Web.

When using versioning, you have three choices. Note that when you use any of these versioning options, you will not get any save conflicts or replication conflicts. A save conflict occurs when two or more users on the same server simultaneously edit and save the same document. A replication conflict occurs during replication when two or more users on different servers edit and save copies of the same document. Both save conflicts and replication conflicts are indicated by a black diamond next to the offending document in a view. When you use versioning, you avoid these document conflicts because any changes are saved as new, separate documents and the previous documents are retained in the database.

If you create a view that supports a response hierarchy, the main and response documents will appear as follows:

- New versions become responses—In this case, the existing document remains the main document and new documents are shown underneath the original.
- Prior versions become responses—By using this option, the newest version of the document becomes the main document. All prior versions are shown as subordinate.
- New versions become siblings—With this option, the original document and all new documents are main documents.

After you have selected the type of versioning to use, you can also select when new versions are made. The default is Automatic-File, Save. This default will cause a new version to be created every time the document is saved. The other choice is Manual, File, New Version, which allows the user to control when a new version is created. In this case, the user must select File, Save as New Version to save a new version of the document.

OTHER FORM OPTIONS

A list of checkbox options is below the version settings. Here is the meaning of these options:

- Default Database Form—This option selects this form to be the default for the database. A database is not required to have a default form, but if it exists, there can be no more than one default form.
- Store Form in Document—This option enables you to store the form with the document instead of separately. You would use this option if the form is to be emailed to a user or database where the form might otherwise not be available. You normally do not want to enable this option because it can use a large amount of extra storage. Note that if a document is saved with a form, it can be rendered on the Web. However, saving a new document with its form is not supported on the Web.
- Disable Field Exchange—This option disables Notes/FX data exchange using OLE with other applications. Field Exchange is not supported on the Web.
- Automatically Refresh Fields—By using this setting, you can have the Notes client automatically recalculate and refresh computed fields as the user enters information. Domino does not support automatically refreshing fields for Web browser clients. You can provide some support for this capability by writing your own programs in JavaScript for Web browsers.

- Anonymous Form—Notes and Domino normally keep track of the identities of the creator of a document and users who subsequently edit it. This information is kept in a field called $UpdatedBy. For some applications, you might want to keep the identities of document editors unknown. One example might be an employee survey for which you would like to guarantee anonymity. If you enable the Anonymous Form option, then the $UpdatedBy field will not be created and a field called $Anonymous with a value of 1 (true) will be created instead. Anonymous forms are not supported in Web browsers.

- Merge Replication Conflicts—If this option is enabled, Domino examines document changes on a field-by-field basis. If two users on different servers modify different fields of the same document, the changes are merged and a replication conflict document is not created. If, however, the two documents contain modifications to the same field, a replication conflict is still generated. Be careful when enabling this option because you can get some unexpected results. For example, suppose a document containing customer information is located on two different servers. A user on one server modifies the Name field, and a user on the other server modifies the Address field. Domino will merge these two changes, but are you sure this is the result you really want? The new name associated with the new address might not be correct at all. The creation of a replication conflict document would otherwise highlight this situation and enable you to correct it manually, whereas the Merge Replication Conflicts option would silently allow the changes without notification.

PART

I

CH

4

FORM DEFAULTS

The form defaults enable you to specify what happens when certain events occur in the lifetime of a document created with the specified form. These events are when the document is first created, when it is opened for editing, when it is closed, and when it is accessed from the Web. In Figure 4.2 you can see the Defaults tab of the Form properties dialog box.

Figure 4.2
The Defaults tab enables you to specify actions during the lifetime of a document.

DOCUMENT CREATION

The On Create section enables you to specify what happens when a document is first created. This option involves inheritance from an existing document. You use this option to save the user from typing information that already exists in another document. You have two choices:

- Formulas Inherit Values from Selected Document—The selected document might be contained in a view or it might be an existing document that is displayed. Check this option to allow the newly created document to obtain values from the selected document. Normally, you should name fields that inherit values with the same field name in both the source and destination forms. The value specification in each field in the receiving form should contain the field name to be inherited. When using this option to create a new document from the Web, you must use the following syntax:

  `http://server/db.nsf/receiveform?OpenForm&ParentUNID=hexvalue`

- Inherit Entire Selected Document into Rich Text Field—The primary use of this option is in a mail database. When you reply to an email message, you might want to include the original message when sending a reply. After you select this option you can choose the field where you would like the document embedded; you have three choices for the operation:

  - Link—Only a link and not the full text of the document is stored. This option is not supported on the Web.

  - Collapsible rich text—The source document is included in a collapsible section so that it does not clutter the main document. This option is not supported on the Web.

  - Rich text—The source document is directly included into the destination document in the specified rich text field. This option is supported on the Web if the database property Use JavaScript When Generating Pages is enabled and the document resides in the same database.

DOCUMENT OPENING AND CLOSING

When opening an existing document you can automatically enable Edit Mode. By selecting this option, you make it easier for users to quickly edit a document. If the document is used frequently or primarily in read-only mode, you should leave this option disabled.

The Show Context Pane option enables you to show the context pane when documents associated with this form are displayed. You can choose either a Doclink or Parent for the context pane information. The Show Context Pane option is not supported on the Web. You can achieve similar results by using framesets for Web applications.

The Present Mail Send Dialog option can be enabled when a document is closed. This enables you to easily enable a particular document as an email message.

WEB ACCESS TO DOCUMENTS

In Chapter 3, "Developing Pages with the Domino Designer," I discussed the Treat Document Contents as HTML option. This option is also available for forms. It is very convenient if you are importing HTML from another source, if you are familiar with HTML, or if you want to combine HTML with Domino features.

Generate HTML for All Fields is a very useful option. You use this option to have Domino generate `<INPUT TYPE=HIDDEN>` HTML fields for Domino hidden fields. If you do not enable this option, hidden fields will not generate any HTML and therefore might not operate correctly.

Hidden fields are particularly useful when combining Domino features with JavaScript. In particular, hidden fields are accessible to JavaScript, so they enable you to write code on Domino that can set field information and transmit it to a Web browser client. The information can then be obtained and used by a JavaScript program in a Web browser, modified and sent back to Domino, all without appearing visible to the end user. I'll show you more details about the use of this option when I describe HTML and JavaScript in Part II, "Programming the Client with HTML and JavaScript."

WORKING WITH FIELDS

Fields can be placed on forms but not pages. They represent the blank areas of a paper form. In the United States, we fill out forms to pay our taxes to the Internal Revenue Service (IRS). If you are outside the U.S., you probably pay taxes to your own government. (If not, let me know where you live.) On those forms for taxes, the blank boxes where you enter your numbers are fields. The good news is that working with fields in Domino is much less painful than filling in the fields on tax forms.

ADDING FIELDS TO A FORM

To create a new field on your form, do the following:

1. Open the form on which you want to add the field.

2. Select Create, Field. Your new field will be created with the name Untitled (see Figure 4.3).

Figure 4.3
You can change the name and type of fields in the Properties box.

Each field on the form must have a unique name, so if you enter a name that already exists, the Domino Designer will automatically append a numeric suffix. For example, the second unnamed field will be Untitled2.

One of your first tasks should be to change the field name. A set of fields called Untitled, Untitled2, and Untitled3 would be pretty boring, not to mention rather hard to debug. An important part of application design is to have naming conventions for the various design elements.

NAMING CONVENTIONS

When you create field names, you have great flexibility. You can call your fields just about anything you want, and they won't complain to you. You can call one field Input, another Output, and a third one TextField. The main characteristic of all three of these names is that they are terrible field names. They are valid and Domino won't complain, but they represent poor programming practice.

Officially, field names must begin with a letter, or $, or _. Following the initial letter, names may use letters, numbers, $, and _. Names in Notes/Domino are not case-sensitive; however, both Java and JavaScript use case-sensitive naming, so try to use a consistent capitalization scheme and stick with it. Names cannot contain spaces and may be up to 32 bytes. For single-byte character languages, this is the same as 32 characters. For multibyte languages, you can use only half as many characters.

Your field names should be meaningful in their context. For example, the field names LastName, FirstName, and PhoneNumber are much better names because you can almost immediately tell just from their variable names how these fields will be used. The field PhoneNumber is a little ambiguous, however. Is that field a numeric field or a character field? Well, the answer is it might be either. Normally, phone numbers are stored as text strings, but with the field name PhoneNumber it becomes a little more ambiguous. What can we do?

Another convention that is becoming widespread is to add a prefix to the variable name and to use capitalization to help make the name easier to read. The prefix represents the data type of the variable, and the rest of the variable name follows. Here are some sample prefixes:

c or txt	Text (character) field
n	Numeric field
rt	Rich text
dt	Date/time

Using these prefixes, the field names would become txtLastName, txtFirstName, and txtPhoneNumber. Some people use c for character. This is shorter, so if you prefer, it could be cLastName, cFirstName, and cPhoneNumber. Notice that by using cPhoneNumber and nPhoneNumber, you can immediately see which field is a character field and which field is a numeric field.

As you can see by the examples, you typically use a lowercase letter for the data type with an initial capital letter for the variable name. You also can use internal capitalization of words. Although capitalization is not significant to Notes or Domino, it is to both Java and JavaScript.

If you will be using JavaScript, remember that Domino will store and serve field names just as you type them into the Domino Designer, including capitalization. Thus, even though capitalization is not important to Domino, it is to JavaScript and you must be careful of the capitalization you use with field names. Because Java will access the fields via the back-end classes rather than as part of the language, capitalization of field names does not affect Java.

It does not really matter which conventions you use, but you should definitely find a naming convention for your entire organization, and then standardize on this convention. By using one style of naming variables, you will promote easier maintenance for your entire group. It will become much easier for one person to read another person's code.

Naming conventions are also a simple, easy way to improve your productivity because you will spend less time trying to remember the data types of each of your variables. You really appreciate these conventions the most when you must maintain code someone else has written.

FIELD DATA TYPES

I've alluded to the fact that several different types of data can be stored in documents. The basic data types include text, rich text, date/time, and number values, but most data is stored as text. Several kinds of user interface elements (called field types) can be used to display and obtain information from users. In Figure 4.4, you see the various types of fields that can be used on a form. An icon on the right side of the field shows its type.

Figure 4.4
There are many different types of fields you can use on a form.

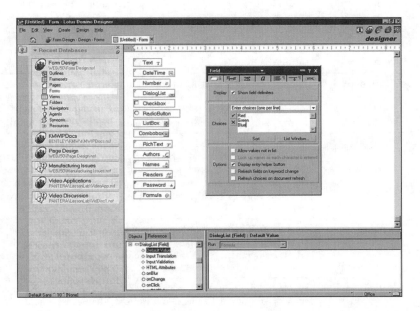

Several field types can be used to display lists of information. User interface types for lists include Dialog list, Checkbox, Radio button, Listbox, and Combobox. These field types typically store text information. In Figure 4.4 you can see the control tab for a dialog list where you can enter the list of items that the user can choose or you can specify a formula to be used to populate the list. Table 4.2 describes the various field types.

TABLE 4.2   FIELD DATA TYPES

Data Type	Description
Text	A text field can hold letters, numbers, and special characters. A designer can assign formatting attributes, such as bold or italic, to regular text fields, but after they are set, the end user cannot change the formatting.
Date/Time	Date/time fields store date and/or time information. They can be displayed in a variety of formats, including date-only or time-only.
Number	Use number fields to store numeric information that will be used in calculations. Numbers can be displayed in a variety of formats, including decimal, percent, scientific, and currency.
Dialog list	A dialog list field displays a list of choices. In the Notes client, a dialog list can optionally have a helper button so the user can choose one of a set of predefined values. The helper button is not supported on the Web. You can specify the choices by formula or by typing them directly, or you can allow the user to add a choice not in the list.
Checkbox	You use a checkbox when you have a set of options and you want to allow the user to select zero, one, or more of the available options.
Radio Button	Radio buttons are used with a set of selections where only one choice is allowed from the set.
ListBox	A listbox shows a scrollable list of choices. The list can contain predefined values or values specified by a formula, or you can allow the user to add a value that is not in the list.
Combobox	A combobox is similar to a listbox but takes up less screen space. It is shown as a single line with a drop-down button. The user can click on the button to reveal a list of choices. As with the other list options, you can predefine values, enter a formula, or allow the user to add values that are not in the list.
Rich Text	Rich text fields enable the user to add formatting information such as bold and italic. These fields can also hold extra information, such as attachments, hotspots, doclinks, and tables. Rich text fields cannot be displayed in views. In Web browsers, full support for rich text fields is provided via the rich text applet. If you use regular HTML, multiple-line, plain-text support is available for rich text fields.
Authors	Authors fields basically affect users with Author-level ACL access. If a document contains an authors field and the user's name is stored in it, the user is allowed to edit the document, even if he or she did not originally create it. This type of field cannot be used to override the ACL.
Names	Names fields are used to store names when you don't need to associate rights such as Authors or Readers. You can use a names type field when you want to display the Notes name in a particular format.

Data Type	Description
Readers	The readers field is used to control reading rights to users who otherwise would be able to read a document. If a readers field exists and contains usernames, only users found within the field can read the document. Even if a user has Manager ACL privilege, if that user is not listed in the readers field for the document, he or she cannot read it. This field refines ACL privileges.
Password	A password field is used to show asterisks on the screen for data entry.
Formula	A formula field is used to store the text value of a selection formula. This type of field is used within the Headlines subscription database.

EDITABLE AND COMPUTED FIELDS

In addition to the data type of the field, each field has an attribute of being editable or computed. Here are the types and what they mean:

Data Entry	Description
Editable	In editable fields, the user can enter data directly into the field. This is the most common type of field.
Computed	The value of a computed field is determined by a formula. A user cannot enter data into the field; it is for output only. A computed field is reevaluated whenever the form is created, refreshed, or saved. The computed value is saved in the document.
Computed When Composed	A computed when composed field is also specified by a formula. The formula is evaluated at the time the document is created, but it is never reevaluated. The value is saved in the document.
Computed for Display	The value of a computed for display field is evaluated at the time the document is created or opened. It is reevaluated whenever the document is saved or refreshed. Although the value is reevaluated when the document is saved, the value of a computed for display field is not stored in the document. Another implication of this is that computed for display fields may not be used in views because there is no value stored in the document.

OTHER FIELD ATTRIBUTES

When you create fields, you can specify many other attributes with the Field properties box. You can specify several attributes dealing with the display of the field:

- Allow Multiple Values—This enables the field to accept multiple values. The values are stored internally as a list. This checkbox is particularly valuable with any of the list and name type fields.

- Compute After Validation—This checkbox applies only to computed fields. This is useful when a field is dependent upon other fields. If checked, the field will be computed only after the validation occurs on other fields. Note that this option is not supported for Web browsers.

PART

I

CH

4

- Style: Notes Style/Native OS Style—Notes style is the standard style for controls. Certain controls, such as the date/time controls, are supported only in the Notes client when the Native OS Style box is checked. Native OS style controls are not supported by Web browsers.

- Show Field Delimiters—This normally enabled option causes the brackets that surround editable fields to appear. If you disable this option, make sure you provide prompts for the user because there will be no visible marking within the window to tell the user there is a field that accepts user input.

In addition to the basic properties just mentioned, the properties box enables you to change the following attributes for fields:

- Date/Time Formatting (in Control)—Several options enable you to specify the style of date formats. You can, for example, specify that you always want four-digit years, four-digit years for 21st century only, or to show year only when it is not this year. You can specify the order of day of week, day, month, and year. When you show times, you can show hours, minutes, and seconds, and perform time zone adjustments. You can also require the user to enter four-digit years.

- Date/Time Formatting (in Layout Region)—Within a layout region, a date/time field has a calendar control that enables a user to pick dates visually. This is not available in a regular form date control.

- Number Format (in Control)—This enables you to specify numbers as decimal, percent, scientific, or currency. You can control the number of decimal digits displayed, use parentheses when negative, and use punctuation at thousands.

- Help Description (in Advanced)—This enables you to specify a help text message for the field. The Help Description is not supported for Web browsers.

- Multi-Value Options (in Advanced)—This enables you to specify the separators that can be used by a user when entering multiple values. The choices are space, comma, semicolon, new line, and blank line. This section also enables you to choose the separator used for display between multiple values in a multivalue field.

- Security Options (in Advanced)—This enables you to sign the field, enable encryption, or require at least Editor access to use a field. The Enable Encryption and Sign If Mailed or Saved options are not supported in Web browsers.

- Font (in Font)—This enables you to specify a typeface, point size, and style for the field.

- Alignment (in Paragraph Alignment)—This enables you to specify whether the field will be left-aligned, right-aligned, centered, or justified. It also enables you to specify first-line indentation style, list styling (numbered, bulleted, and so forth), and paragraph spacing (single, one-and-a-half, double). Paragraph type can also be specified for right-to-left languages.

- Hide Paragraph (in Paragraph Hide When)—This enables you to control hiding the paragraph from Notes clients or Web browsers. You also can control hiding when the document is previewed and opened for reading or editing. You can specify a formula that controls the hiding.

- HTML (in Field Extra HTML)—This enables you to add an ID, Class, Style, Title, or other extra HTML attributes. Some particularly useful attributes are SIZE and MAXLENGTH. When Domino converts the field to HTML, it converts it to an HTML <INPUT> field. The HTML SIZE parameter on an <INPUT> field specifies the width onscreen. The MAXLENGTH parameter specifies how many characters can be input into the field. You may also specify HTML attributes in the field's pseudo-event called HTML Attributes. You can find out more about HTML in Chapter 7, "Using Hypertext Markup Language (HTML) for Page Design."

FIELD FORMULAS: DEFAULT VALUE, INPUT TRANSLATION, AND INPUT VALIDATION

Domino fields can have three special formulas associated with them called the Default Value, Input Translation, and Input Validation formulas. All three formulas are optional. The Default Value formula provides an initial default value for the field. This enables the user to leave a field blank, and the Designer can specify the initial value.

The Input Translation and Input Validation formulas are run whenever a document is refreshed or saved. The Translation formula enables you to do processing that will put the data in a canonical format. In other words, you can capitalize words, you can trim leading and trailing blanks, and you can replace user input with codes you look up.

After input translation is performed, the Input Validation formula is run. This formula evaluates to Success or Failure. If successful, the field passes validation. If it fails, the user is prompted with an error message you provide and must edit the field to correct the problem.

SINGLE-USE AND SHARED FIELDS

The most common type of field is called a single-use field, whose definition is included with the form on which it is created. Sometimes, however, you might want to define a field that will be used on several forms. In this case, you can create a shared field, which is a shared resource. Remember that here we are talking about the field definition itself, not any data that is stored within any documents. You do not need to use a shared field to share data within documents.

Shared field definitions enable you to define attributes of the field, such as its formula definitions. For example, suppose you want to create a field to be used for part numbers. You want to perform an input translation and/or validation on the part numbers, so you specify formulas associated with the field. By making this field a shared field, you can use the part number entry field throughout your database, and the formulas will be shared.

You can easily create a shared field by creating a regular, single-use field and then converting it to a shared field. To convert a single-use field into a shared field, select the field, and then select Design, Share This Field.

To convert a shared field back into a single-use field, select the field, and then use Edit, Cut followed by Edit, Paste.

After you have created a shared field, you can use it on a form by doing the following:

1. Open the form you want to use for your shared field.

2. Move the cursor to the location where you want your shared field to appear.

3. Select Create, Insert Shared Field. A dialog box will open displaying the names of the available shared fields.

4. Select the desired shared field and click OK. Your shared field will be inserted into the form.

CREATING FORM ACTIONS

Actions are programs that can be implemented using predefined simple actions; or you can write your own custom actions in LotusScript, JavaScript, or formula language. Simple actions include modifying a field, copying a document to a database or folder, running an agent, or sending a mail message.

Actions can be invoked by clicking an action button in a form or view. They can also be displayed in the Action menu. The Action Bar, if displayed, appears just above the document or view window. Because the action buttons do not appear inside the window, they are independent of any scrolling of the document window itself.

You can associate actions with individual forms or views, or you can create shared actions. Shared actions are useful whenever you need to provide functions that might be common across several forms or views. Shared actions are found in the Design pane under Resources, Other, Shared Actions.

Six predefined actions appear with an asterisk in the Action pane. If these actions appear on a form, the action will apply to the currently viewed document. If the action appears on a view, the user can select one or more documents and apply the action to the selected documents. The predefined actions do not work on the Web; however, you can use shared actions with a formula and @commands instead. The following are the predefined actions:

- Categorize—This opens a dialog box that enables a user to add and remove categories from a document being viewed or listed in a view. To use this feature, the form must have a keyword field named Categories.

- Edit Document—This enables editing of a document currently being viewed or listed in a view. This does not enable a user to override the ACL; it just provides a convenient method to put the document into edit mode.

- Send Document—This sends the document to a user or mail-in database. The form must contain a `SendTo` field, and the value within the field supplies the destination.

- Forward—This forwards the document in an email message.

- Move To Folder—This moves the selected document(s) to a folder.

- Remove from Folder—This removes the selected document(s) from a folder.

In addition to the built-in actions, you can define your own actions. Programmer-defined actions can appear in the Action Bar and/or the Action menu. In Figure 4.5, I have defined the Lights, Camera action. You can specify the action to take with a formula, simple action, LotusScript, or JavaScript program. The example uses LotusScript, and when the action button is clicked, a message box will appear. In Figure 4.5, I have specified a custom graphic to be used instead of one of the standard Domino graphics. You can see the result of the custom graphic in the upper-right corner of the screen. You can also specify a graphic button to appear in the action button by selecting one of the Notes graphics in the Action properties box.

Figure 4.5
When you can define your own actions, you can see them in the Action pane.

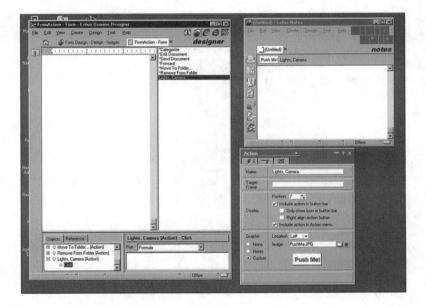

The complete list of action graphics that can be used appears in Figure 4.6. Release 5 has added 24 new graphics that can be used for a total of 156 choices. The first one is used to indicate that no graphic should be displayed, so there are actually 155 displayable graphics.

Figure 4.6
You can choose from
156 different Notes
graphics for actions.

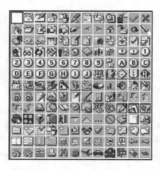

PROGRAMMATIC CONTROL OF TABLES

In Chapter 3, I introduced tables but did not cover the programmatic control of tables
because you must use fields for this feature. Because you cannot use fields on pages, I
deferred discussion of the topic until now.

Let's now examine how you can control the display table information. Figure 4.7 shows the
Table dialog box. Notice that the option Switch Rows Programmatically has been checked.
You can optionally show the tabs when you use the programmatic selection method.

Figure 4.7
You can programmat-
ically show rows of a
table.

At the bottom of the dialog box, I can give the tab a label. This label is used for display
only and not for the selection of the row. In Figure 4.8, you can see the dialog box for the
HTML header.

In the Table Programming tab, you give the table its name, and you also give a name to
each row. You can pick the row to display either by its name or by its 0-origin numeric row
index. In this example, I named the table MediaTypes. The name of the row shown is
Records, which is the first row.

Figure 4.8
Name the table and its rows within the Table Programming tab.

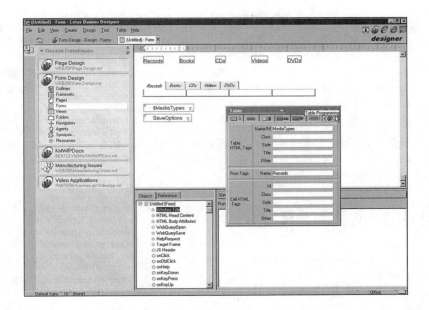

PART

I

CH

4

Note

The row names are case sensitive. Be careful to specify the exact string when using programmatic row selection. Also note that the row's name (listed in the Row Tags section) is not necessarily the same as its label. In this example, I used the word Records for both the row label and its name to avoid confusion. If they are different, remember the name is used for selection, not the label.

In the form in Figure 4.8, there are five action hotspots across the top of the screen. These hotspots are Records, Books, CDs, Videos, and DVDs. Each hotspot in Figure 4.8 has a Click formula similar to one of the following:

```
FIELD $MediaTypes:=0;
@Command([RefreshHideFormulas])
```

or

```
FIELD $MediaTypes:="Books";
@Command([RefreshHideFormulas])
```

The first case uses the 0-origin index, and the second case uses the row name. Normally, you use only one type or the other, but I'm showing you both just for the sake of example. The $MediaTypes field is the special field that controls which row will be displayed. The $MediaTypes field name is constructed by prefixing the table name with a $. I use this field to control the table. The action hotspots can be used to change the value of this field. The two formula statements set the field and then refresh the display. Remember, the value you put into the $MediaTypes field is the name (as specified in Row Tags) of the row (not its label).

Finally, notice in Figure 4.8 that I have a `SaveOptions` field. This field is also a specially named field and a computed field with a value of `0`. If this specially named field contains a `0`, the document created with this form is not saved to the database. This is very useful if you do not want the document saved and you do not want the user to be prompted. You can hide both the `$MediaTypes` and the `SaveOptions` fields from the user. The user will not normally need to see these fields.

Note that in addition to using hotspots as I did in this example, you can also use outline entries to change the table's controlling field. If you use an action type outline entry, you can specify a formula to be used. This will operate in a manner similar to the hotspot actions we used in this example.

USING LAYOUT REGIONS

Layout regions provide you with a means to more precisely specify the layout of controls. When you use pages or forms, much of the layout of design elements is left up to the display program. In some ways this is good, because you can view the form from Notes clients and a variety of different Web browsers. Unfortunately, this does not give the form designer fine control over the presentation. Fields, for example, can move left or right or they can expand and cause other fields to move.

Layout regions provide control so that input fields will not change in size and you can finely tune the appearance of your form. Layout regions have one major disadvantage, however. Layout regions cannot appear in Web browsers, so anything you place in a layout region will be visible only to Notes clients. If you are developing for both Notes clients and Web browsers, you should avoid layout regions. If you will be using only Notes clients, you can use layout regions.

To create a layout region in your form, perform the following:

1. Open the form you want to use with your layout region.
2. Move your cursor to the location where you want your layout region to appear.
3. Select Create, Layout Region, New Layout Region. Your new layout region will appear (see Figure 4.9).
4. You can change the size and move the layout region with the properties box. The Left field enables you to adjust the left margin. The Width and Height properties enable you to change the size. It is usually more convenient to size the layout area with a mouse and the layout region handles. Sometimes you might want to have the size specified precisely, to the pixel. In these cases you can use the Properties box.
5. You can optionally show the border and change to 3D style. 3D style uses a gray background instead of a white one. You can also display a grid to make it easier to align controls. The Snap to Grid option automates some alignment tasks.

Figure 4.9
You can change the
size and location of a
layout region with
the properties box.

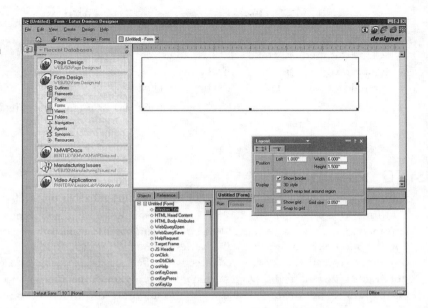

After you create the layout region, you can add elements. For all these elements, you must first highlight the layout region. The following are elements you can add to the region:

- Static text—You create static text by selecting Create, Layout Region, Text.

- Graphic—You can create a graphic image within a layout region. To do this, first copy the bitmap you want to use to the Clipboard, and then select Create, Layout Region, Graphic.

- Graphic button—You create a graphic button in a manner similar to a regular graphic. You must first copy the bitmap to the Clipboard and then select Create, Layout Region, Graphic Button. The main difference between a graphic button and a regular graphic is that the graphic button is considered a hotspot and has a Click event, and a regular graphic object does not. You can program the graphic button with a simple action, formula, LotusScript, or JavaScript. A graphic can overlay a graphic button, or vice versa within a layout region.

Note

Remember that layout regions do not work in Web browsers, so even if you create a graphic button with JavaScript, your program will still work only in the Notes client, not in Web browsers.

PART

I

CH

4

- Picture—A picture is really nothing more than another name for a graphic or graphic button. If you select Create, Picture, you can import a graphic from the file system. Using this method, you do not have to use cut and paste. After you issue Create, Picture, you will be prompted whether you want to paste your image as a graphic or a graphic button. Make your selection and click OK.

- Field—You create a field within a layout region by issuing Create, Field (with the layout region highlighted).

USING SUBFORMS

Subforms enable you to create a reusable component that can be embedded in several different forms. One typical application for a subform might be when you want to have common information (such as name and address) on a form, but also want to have additional information (such as policy information) that varies depending on the customer. In this case, the common information can be stored directly on the form, and variable information can be stored in a set of subforms. Domino can dynamically select the appropriate subform to use for the variable information. You can also use subforms for various adornments, such as headers or footers. The letterhead feature of your mail database is implemented using subforms.

On a subform, you can include any of the design elements that would normally be allowed in a form. The subform can be included in the form at the time you design the form, or the selection of the subform can be deferred until a document using the form is created. When the document is created, you can programmatically include the desired subform (as in your mail database), or you can ask the user to select a subform from a list that you provide.

To open or create a subform:

1. Open the Design pane in the database in which you want to create your subform.

2. Click on the Resources twistie in the Design pane.

3. Click on Subforms. A view showing you the existing subforms will appear in the work area on the right.

4. If you are opening an existing subform, double-click on its name in the Work Pane. If you are creating a new subform, click on the New Subform action button.

5. When your subform is open, you can use all the editing tools that were described for forms.

When you insert a subform based on a formula, it is called a computed subform. The formula is called the insert subform formula. This formula is computed when the form is opened and will not be recomputed if the document is updated and refreshed. The formula must evaluate to a subform name. If the subform name does not exist, no error message will be displayed. The subform will simply not appear.

USING SECTIONS ON FORMS

In Chapter 3 you learned how to use sections to organize the data on the page. Standard sections are also available on forms. You create a standard section on a form with the following steps:

1. Open the form to include your section.

2. Add the text and fields to be included in your section.

3. Highlight all the text and fields to be included.

4. Select Create, Section, Standard. Your section will appear. The first line of your text will appear as the default title of your section. You can modify the title by using the Section properties box.

CONTROLLED ACCESS SECTIONS

Forms also have an additional type of section called the controlled access section. Controlled access sections are typically used in workflow applications where a form may be routed but only particular individuals are allowed to approve the form. By controlling the access to these sections, and by implementing signed fields (in the Field properties Options tab), you can ensure that only authorized individuals can approve the form. An access-controlled section controls the editing, not the reading of the information within it.

To create a controlled access section:

1. Open the form that will include your controlled access section.

2. Add the text and fields to be included in your section.

3. Highlight all the text and fields to be included.

4. Select Create, Section, Controlled Access. Your section will appear. The first line of your text will appear as the default title of your section. You can modify the title by using the Form Section properties box. Notice that the Form properties box has additional tabs. In the Formula tab, you supply an access formula. There are also tabs for editors and non-editors to control whether the section is expanded.

In controlled access sections, you can define the access list as editable, which will allow the document creator to specify who can edit the section. If you want to specify ahead of time who will be able to edit the section, you can supply an access formula. The formula can be made up of user, group, or role names, or you could use an @formula, such as @DBColumn to populate the list. Being listed in the section editor list cannot confer additional rights to a user. If the user is not allowed to edit the document then being listed in the section editor list will not allow the user to edit the section. The section editor list is used to constrain the list of users who would otherwise be able to edit the document.

Here is an example of the use of a controlled access section. Suppose you have an expense account workflow application. An employee enters information about the expenses and then

PART

I

CH

4

submits it for approval by a manager. You want to ensure that only a manager can approve the form, so you include the approval within a controlled access section (see Figure 4.10).

Figure 4.10
Controlled access sections can be used for approval.

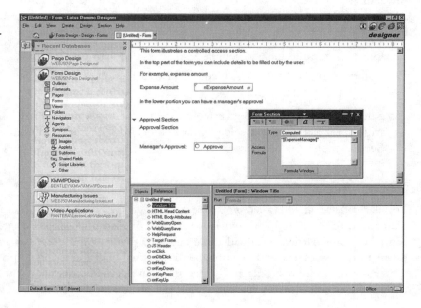

In Figure 4.10, I have shown the access formula as a computed value with the role name of ExpenseManager. You can tell this is a role name because it is enclosed in square brackets. This value for the access formula means that only users with the role ExpenseManager in the ACL will be able to access the Approval section in edit mode.

Note

Be careful with your use of controlled access sections. Note that anyone with read access can read the contents of controlled access sections. The access control applies only to the ability to edit the section. Also note that the access control applies only to databases on a Domino server unless you have specified the Enforce a Consistent ACL Across All Replicas of This Database option in the database ACL. If this option is not selected in the ACL, anyone will be able to edit the section on a local replica of the database.

You can also specify the access formula with a @DBColumn lookup or with group names.

If you require two or more separate approvals for a form, you must use a separate section for each one. A single controlled access section can have only one list of approvers. This scenario might occur, for example, if you need two levels of approval. The first level will approve in the first section and the second level will approve in the second section.

PAGES AND FORMS COMPARISON

There are many similarities between pages and forms, but there are also several differences. Both pages and forms can contain many of the same design elements, but some design characteristics are unique to each. Here is a summary of their similarities and differences.

Pages are self-contained elements that can be rendered by Domino into HTML or can hold passthru HTML formatting. They can contain graphics, tables, hotspots, text, and several other objects. You cannot, however, use fields on pages. You can create the HTML with another editor and import the HTML into Domino Designer. Pages are a design element, and as such the contents are not indexed in the full text index. Pages can be directly accessed via a URL from the Web by name.

Forms are used in conjunction with documents. Documents store data, and forms contain user interface elements called fields. This enables the user interface to be defined separately from the data. When you view a form and document combination, you are actually viewing the data items from the document filling in the fields on the form. If you enter information into the fields, they will be stored back into the document.

Forms have several design elements that cannot be used on pages. Fields, subforms, layout regions, and controlled access sections are the most important design elements that cannot be used on pages. Layout regions will not display in Web browsers, so use them only if you do not plan to access your databases via Web browsers on your intranet or the Internet.

PART

I

CH

4

SUMMARY

In this chapter, I showed you how to create forms, and we explored some additional design elements that were not covered in Chapter 3. I covered the various types of fields that you can use with forms. The most important field types are Text, Number, and Date/Time. By choosing some of the other types such as Dialog List or Radio Button, you can control the user interface for the field.

When you name your fields, be sure to develop and use a naming convention. This is very important when you develop databases that contain multiple forms, when you are developing in a group, or when you will be using multiple databases.

You can use subforms to contain portions of a form that you would like to reuse. Examples include headers and footers, corporate logos, or common fields. Controlled access sections can be used with workflow applications for approvals.

CHAPTER REVIEW

1. Explain the difference between pages, documents, and forms.
2. Layout regions allow you to nicely format fields, text, and other information for a user. What is a major drawback of using layout regions?

3. What is the difference between a table row's label and its name?

4. Create a table with programmatic control in a form. Include hotspots on your form. There should be three hotspots, labeled Small, Medium, and Large. Each hotspot should move the table to the appropriate tab. Within each of the tabs include a graphic of the appropriate size for the label.

5. What is an alias name and why should you normally include an alias name for a form?

6. What is the advantage of storing a form with a document? What is the primary disadvantage of storing forms with documents?

7. Explain the difference between the three different types of computed fields.

8. Why is it important to have a naming convention for all the objects in your database?

9. Can you code HTML directly on a form (not a page)? If so, how do you do it? Can you mix some HTML on a form with static text and regular field definitions such that the entire page is not HTML? If so, how do you do it?

10. Can you have more than one field on a form with the same name?

11. What is the difference between a save conflict and a replication conflict? What techniques can you use to minimize these conflicts?

12. What is the difference between a controlled access section and a regular section? Can you create a controlled access section to prevent read access to the section? If so, how?

CHAPTER 5

DESIGNING VIEWS AND FOLDERS

In this chapter

Views and folders are a fundamental part of Notes and Domino. They enable both the designer and user to organize documents within a Domino database. In essence, a view or folder provides a tabular display of selected fields from documents contained in a Domino database. In this chapter, I show you how to create and use views and folders in your Domino application.

ORGANIZING DOCUMENTS WITHIN YOUR DATABASE

You often see views and folders discussed at the same time because they are very similar. The major difference between views and folders is the criteria used to select documents to be shown.

Views use a formula, so the selection of documents is automatic. The formula is typically written by a designer and is generally used to filter the documents. Designers frequently use several different views in a database, each with a different formula. This enables the user to see various collections of documents, grouped and sorted in meaningful ways.

Folders don't use formulas for their selection. The documents in folders are typically moved to the folder by an end user. In the mail database, for example, a user can create and use folders to organize email. The user can decide the documents to put into each folder.

Because of the similarities in view and folder design, in this chapter I describe view design, but folder design is essentially equivalent. The difference between folders and views is mainly the method used to select documents, not differences in how they are designed.

CREATING AND OPENING A VIEW

A view is a tabular display of data extracted from a set of documents. Each row of the table represents one document, and the values in each column can be field data or can be based on a formula. Column formulas can combine data from multiple fields or use @functions to compute their result. The process of creating a view is initially creating the view itself, and then defining the data that should be included in each column.

For the purposes of this example, I'm going to create a new database from the Blank template. If you want to follow along, create a new Domino database on your local machine called View Design. Alternatively, you can find a copy of the database on the CD-ROM that reflects the final database contents. After you create your database, click on the Views line in the Design pane on the left. Your screen should be similar to Figure 5.1.

This is very interesting. Although you created a blank database, you already have a view defined in your database. Domino always requires at least one view in your database, so even when you create a blank database, an initial view is created for you. You cannot open a database that does not have at least one view. As you can see, the name of this view is untitled. This is pretty boring, and as you might imagine, the content of this initial view is pretty boring also. Let's see what Domino Designer has created for us by default.

Figure 5.1
The Domino Designer with the View Design element selected.

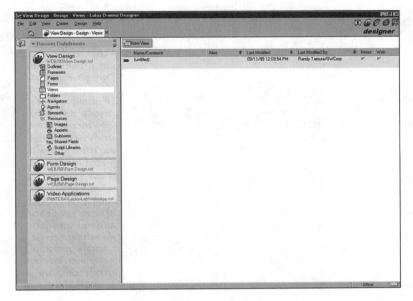

Follow these steps to open or create a view for editing:

1. Open the database that contains your view and highlight Views in the Design pane on the left.

2. To create a new view, click the New View action button. To open an existing view, double-click on the line containing the view.

3. If you double-click on the untitled line, you will see the definition of your default view (see Figure 5.2).

The default view, called untitled, contains only a single column. The column appears with the number sign (#) in the column header.

SELECTING DOCUMENTS TO INCLUDE IN A VIEW

In Figure 5.2, notice that the words View Selection appear just above the drop-down box in the Programmer's pane at the bottom of your screen. The View Selection is used to enter the formula for selecting documents that will be shown in the view. On the right half of the Programmer's pane is a drop-down list, and you can select either Easy or Formula. If you select Easy and then click the Add Condition button, you will see the Add Condition dialog box of the Search Builder feature (see Figure 5.3).

The Condition drop-down box shows the option By Field. With this option, you can choose to include documents in the view if a particular field of the document contains a specified value. For example, you could choose the field Color, and the contents could be Red. This specification shows documents in the view only if Red is contained in the Color

PART

I

CH

5

field. You can include more than one condition, so if there were a Car field, you could include a specification for the contents Ferrari. Your view selection would then show only documents with Red for Color and Ferrari for Car. This view would clearly have good taste in cars.

Figure 5.2
The untitled view as initially created by Domino Designer.

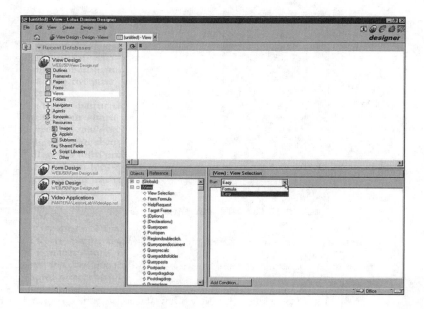

Figure 5.3
The Search Builder dialog box appears if you choose Easy for View Selection.

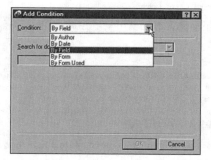

Note

The Search Builder will display only field names that exist on forms within your database. If you have not yet defined any forms (and thus no fields), you will not be able to use the Search Builder with the By Field option. To follow with this example, you need to create a form called Car with two fields: Car and Color. If you do this, they will show up in the Search Builder. Normally, in your design process, you will design and build your forms before building your views.

You can choose documents by the following keywords in the Search Builder:

- By Author—The author of the document. The author name for the document must contain text that you supply. You can alternatively indicate that the author for the document must not contain text you supply.

- By Date—You can specify the date the document was created or last modified. You can choose a specific date, older or newer than a particular date, or within or outside a date range.

- By Field—As in the example, you can enter specific text. The text must be contained in the field you name. A string comparison is made, so the field should be a text field. Alternatively, you can indicate that a field must not contain specific text you supply.

- By Form—A shorthand for multiple By Field specifications. When you select this option, a data entry field shows for all fields contained on the form. You can enter data for all the fields or some subset of them all at once. Don't confuse this option with the next one, By Form Used.

- By Form Used—You can select documents based on the form used to compose the document. This is one of the most frequently used criteria for view document selection. By using this option you can also optimize view access by using the Advanced database property: Document table bitmap optimization.

As you create your view selection, it will appear in the right side of the Programmer's pane. Each condition will appear as a small button within the pane. To edit a condition you have already entered, you can double-click on the button (see Figure 5.4).

Figure 5.4
Each condition built by the Search Builder has a separate small button in the Programmer's pane.

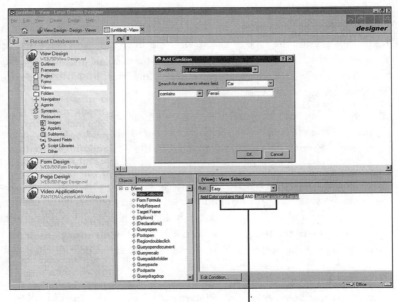

Click these buttons to edit

PART

I

CH

5

To select documents by formula, select Formula in the Run drop-down box. If you do not modify the formula, you can also switch from Easy to Formula to see the formula that Domino Designer has created for you.

If you become proficient with the @formula language, you might want to use formulas because they are much more powerful than the Search Builder functions.

TYPES OF VIEWS

As mentioned previously, to create a view, first select Views in the Design pane, and then click the New View action button. You will see the Create View dialog box (see Figure 5.5).

Figure 5.5
There are several types of shared and private views.

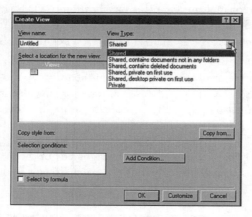

When you first create a view, you must specify the view type in addition to the view name. You cannot change the type after the view has been created. Views are generally categorized into shared views and private views. Multiple people can use shared views, but private views are restricted to a single user. Within these categories, however, there are several possibilities. Here are the view types:

- Shared—Shared views are the most common type of view. Shared views are available to users with at least Reader access to the database. Editor-level users with the privilege Create Shared Folders/Views enabled in the ACL can create shared views. Otherwise, you must have Designer- or Manager-level access to create a shared view.

- Shared, Private on First Use—These views provide an opportunity for a designer to deliver customized views to end users. For example, you could use the @UserName function in the view selection so that only a single user's data appears in the view. Each user will see different data, and after a user has used the view, it will become private. A disadvantage of this setting is that after a view becomes private, users will no longer see updates made in the shared version. If you add or delete columns or change formulas in the shared version, the user will not see the changes if the view already became private. This type of view will be stored in the database unless the Create Personal Folders/Views ACL setting for the user is disabled. In this case, the view is stored in DESKTOP.DSK.

- Shared, Desktop Private on First Use—This type of view is the same as Private on First Use except that the view is stored in the user's DESKTOP.DSK file. The reason for storing the view in DESKTOP.DSK is that if you have many users, the database could become very large if each user's private view is stored in the common database.

- Private—Users, not designers, create private views. Private views can be used to sort and organize data in a personal way without affecting the operation of the database for other users. In release 4.*x* of Notes and Domino, private views were called personal views. You might see some documentation refer to personal views, but private views and personal views are just two names for the same thing.

Note

There is a setting in the Access Control List (ACL) for a database that is called Create Personal Folders/Views. This setting can be either enabled or disabled. If you disable this setting, it does not mean that the user is prevented from creating private (personal) folders and views. A user of Reader level and above can always create a private view or folder. The ACL setting enables or disables the user from creating the private view within the database. If the setting is disabled, the private views and folders are stored in the user's DESKTOP.DSK file on the local machine.

Also note that Web browsers cannot view private views, whether they are created initially as private or they are initially shared and become private. If you want to make a customized view (similar to a shared-to-private view) accessible to Web browsers, you might be able to use a new release 5 feature called a Single Category embedded view. This feature is described later in this chapter.

The following two view types are new to release 5 of Domino. These types are available for views but not for folders. Implicit in their type is a view selection formula, so they do not have a selection formula:

- Shared, Contains Documents Not in Any Folders—A view of this type shows all the documents that have not been placed by a user in a folder. You can use this type of view for an inbox-type application where you want the document to disappear from the inbox if the user moves it to a folder. After it appears in a folder, it will automatically disappear from the inbox.

- Shared, Contains Deleted Documents—This type of view is used to support the new soft deletions. Soft deletions enable you to implement a "Trash" type of folder where documents can temporarily be stored but later recovered if desired. To use this type of folder, you must also enable soft deletions in the database properties Advanced (beanie hat) box.

Note

Soft deletions are a feature available only beginning with the release 5 database structure. If you are using the Domino Designer on a release 4.*x* database, you will not be able to select the deleted document type of view because it is not supported in the database. You can find the version of the database by looking at the Info tab of the database properties box. The ODS version should be 36 or greater to be a release 5 database.

In addition to creating views from scratch, you can also copy an existing view that is similar to the one you want to create, and modify it. To copy an existing view, you can select it from the list of views and use the copy and paste operations. After the view is created, you can rename it and modify it to suit your needs.

Another way to copy a view is to use the Copy button from the View builder. After the view has been copied you can rename the view and modify its columns.

CREATING FOLDERS

You create folders almost identically to the way you create views. Here's how:

1. Click on the Folders design element on the left; then in the right pane, click the New Folder button.

2. Give the folder a name in the dialog box that appears. Select the type of folder. The folder types are the same as the first four types of views. The new nonfolder type and soft deletion type of view cannot be specified for folders.

3. Select a location for your folder within the folder hierarchy. Do this by selecting the parent of where you want your folder to appear.

4. A default set of columns will be copied from the view/folder shown as Copy Style From. If you want to choose a different folder or view or start from a blank view, click the Copy From button. You will then see a dialog box, and you can choose your template.

5. You can click OK and your folder will be created, or you can click Customize. If you click Customize, your folder will be created, and you will be placed in edit mode on your newly created folder.

6. Customize your folder and save it.

VIEW COLUMN PROPERTIES

After you specify the documents you want selected in your view (via the View Selection formula), you must define the fields and information you want to show in your view. Each row of your view represents one document of the database, and the values in the columns are information extracted from those documents. Frequently, a column will hold the value from a single field. There are, however, other types of information that you can include. Let's go back and look at the default view of the View Design database.

VIEW COLUMN BASICS

Each view column has several attributes besides the definition of the data to be shown. Figure 5.6 shows the default view formula and properties box for the default view column.

Figure 5.6
A column can be defined by a simple function, field, or formula.

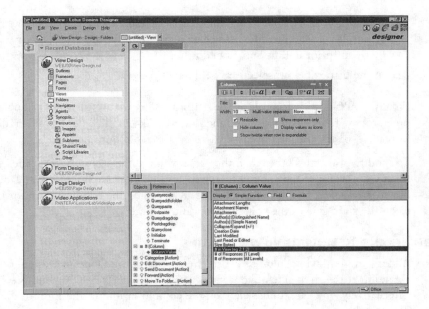

As you can see, the title of the column is found in the properties box and is a simple number sign (#). In the Programmer's pane at the bottom of the window, you see that the Column Value of the # column is highlighted in the left half of the pane, and a simple function appears in the right half of the pane.

You can define a column's contents with a simple function. The functions can be information, such as attachment lengths or names, authors, creation or modification dates, or document number within the view. Follow these steps to specify a simple function:

1. Open the view containing the column you want to modify.

2. Click on the column object's Column Value in the left half of the Programmer's pane at the bottom of the window. Alternatively, you can click on the column header of the column you want to modify in the View pane at the top of the window.

3. In the right half of the Programmer's pane, select Simple Function in the Display radio button group. If you had previously selected a different option, a warning may be displayed that your prior definition will be lost.

4. In the listbox below, select the simple function you want to use.

As an alternative to a simple function, you can define a column to contain a field value from a document. Follow these steps to use a document field as a column value:

1. Open the view containing the column you want to modify.

2. Click on the column object's Column Value in the left half of the Programmer's pane at the bottom of the window. Alternatively, you can click on the column header of the column you want to modify in the View pane at the top of the window.

PART

I

CH

5

3. In the right half of the Programmer's pane, select Field in the Display radio button group. If you had previously selected a different option, a warning may be displayed that your prior definition will be lost.

4. In the listbox below, select the field name you want to use.

Finally, you can use a formula as the definition for what to display in a column. To use a formula, follow the steps for simple function or field, but click the formula radio button instead. Type the formula in the area below the radio buttons.

To modify properties other than the value, you use the Column Properties box. You can specify the width of the column by typing a value into the Width box, by clicking the up or down arrows next to the width value, or by dragging the column separator in the view header on the right side of the column you want to modify.

ADDING AND REMOVING VIEW COLUMNS

Adding and removing columns is pretty easy within the Domino Designer. To append a column at the right side of your view, you can select Create, Append New Column. Alternatively, you can double-click on the column header to the right of the last column. This creates a new column and brings up the Properties box for the newly created column.

To insert a new column in the middle of the view, select the column to the right of the location you want the new column, and then select Create, Insert New Column. You can use this technique to insert a new column as the first column.

To delete a column, click on the header of the column and click the Delete key. Alternatively, you can click on the header of the column, and then select Edit, Clear. Either technique will prompt you with a warning that you are about to permanently delete a column. You can select multiple columns for deletion by clicking on the header of the first, and then holding down the Ctrl key and selecting the other columns. Click the Delete key or use the menus after you have selected all the columns you want to delete.

DOCUMENT TYPES AND HIERARCHIES

When I introduced forms and documents in the previous chapter, I did not discuss the different types of documents because they are a bit hard to understand until you understand the concept of views. Well, here we are in the midst of views, so let's retrace our steps a bit and talk about the different kinds of documents and how they can be displayed in views.

You can create three kinds of documents with a form:

- Document—A normal, regular, ordinary document. It can contain text fields and all the other goodies I have shown you. This is also sometimes called a *main document*.

- Response—A special kind of document that is a response to a main document. It is differentiated because within a view, a response document can appear indented under its parent main document.

- Response to Response—This is a special kind of response. It can be either a response to a main document or a response to a response.

When you create a form, you specify the type of document you want associated with the form. You make your selection in the Form properties box (see Figure 5.7).

Figure 5.7
You select the document type in the Form properties box.

When a response document is created, you can have the response document inherit values from its parent document. Typically, the parent document and the response document will both have some fields in common. By inheriting the values from the parent document at the time the response document is created, the user's job will be easier, because some fields will automatically be filled in. In addition to the inheritance fields you specify, Domino also will automatically create an additional, special field called $Ref that contains the Universal Identifier (UNID) of the parent document.

To enable inheritance of fields on response documents from the parent documents, you use the Form properties box on the Defaults tab (see Figure 5.8). After you enable inheritance on the response document, you must also create a formula on each field that you want to be inherited from the parent document. Thus, you can control inheritance for selected fields only.

To illustrate these concepts, I have created a view called CarView and three forms. The forms are for a main car document (the Car form), a response (the CarResponse form), and a response to response (the CarRtoR form). Each of the three forms has two fields: the Car field and the Color field.

In the sample CarView view, I have defined three columns. The view is shown in Figure 5.9.

Figure 5.8
You can enable inheritance by selecting an option in the response document's form properties.

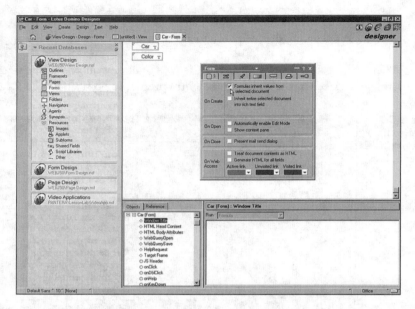

Figure 5.9
Views can show response documents below their parent document.

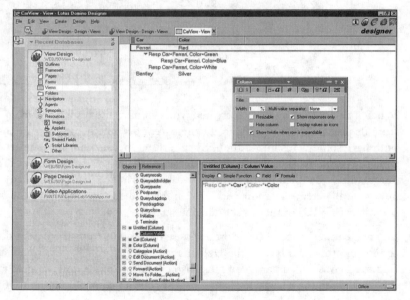

In the view, I have defined the Car column and the Color column to display fields directly from the document. In the figure, only the first and last lines in the view are main documents. The second and fourth lines are response documents and the middle line is a response to response document.

I said there were three columns, but it appears that there are only two columns, the Car and Color columns. The other column is actually the very first column of the view. The Column properties dialog box shows you the properties for this first column. Lines 2, 3, and 4 of the view in Figure 5.9 are actually shown using this column as you can see from the formula definition in the Programmer's pane. You can tell the formula is used because the lines begin with the text string Resp.

A response document displays differently from main documents because it is typically formatted via a formula contained within a single column. This is what I have shown in the example, although you would probably use a more interesting formula for your application. To display the responses as shown, you should

- Define a column (typically only width 1) to the left of your first data column. In this case, I made it the first column of the view. This column does not need to have a title. Typically, it doesn't because there is no need to show anything in the title line.

- Enable the Show Responses Only checkbox for this column. When this checkbox is enabled, the other column definitions will not apply for this row, so you must define your output for the line with a formula. The output can extend to the width of the entire view. Typically, you'll want to include summary information, such as the document author, the date, and perhaps a title field.

- Enable the Show Twistie When Row Is Expandable checkbox. This will enable the user to expand and collapse the rows of the view.

You might be wondering about the difference between regular response documents and response to response documents. Here is a little more detail. At the time you create a response document of either type, the outcome depends on two things: what type of document is selected (main or response) and the type of form used to create the new response document. If the row selected is a main document and if you create either type of response, the result is a document that shows up immediately below the selected main document. Line 2 of the view in Figure 5.9 is a response document, and it shows directly under the main document.

If the selected document is any type of response and you create a new response, you get two different results depending on the type of document you create. If you create a response to response, your new document will appear directly beneath your selected document (line 3 of the view), pretty much as you would expect.

If the selected document is any type of response and you create a regular response document, it will appear immediately below the corresponding main document, not indented from the selected document. Line 4 (the Ferrari-White line) of the view was created by highlighting line 3 (the Ferrari-Blue line) and creating a response document.

Finally, as an example of this rather hard-to-describe phenomenon, refer to Figure 5.9. In Table 5.1, I show you what happens if you have a certain document highlighted and you create a new document.

TABLE 5.1   RESPONSE AND RESPONSE TO RESPONSE

Line Selected Upon Create	Type of Document Created	Shows Up as Line
Red	Response	Green or White
Red	Response to response	Green or White
Green	Response	White
Green	Response to response	Blue
Blue	Response	White
Blue	Response to response	New under Blue

As a designer, you do not want to have to explain that table to your users. In summary, if you want your response documents to keep on indenting regardless of level, you must use response to response forms. If you want all your responses to stay only one level below the main then you need to use regular response forms. You probably won't need to use both kinds of response documents in your database. If you do, it will be pretty confusing for the users. Pick one type and just stay with it.

SORTING A VIEW COLUMN

After you define the contents of your view, you might want to sort the documents based on certain columns. Although not absolutely required, I would recommend that if you sort, you use your leftmost columns. These are the columns that people will see first, and if they are ordered, it will be more obvious. There are also certain @functions, such as @DBColumn, that work based on the first sorted column, and if you keep them to the left, remembering and maintaining these functions will be easier.

You see the sorting options in Figure 5.10. The first option is the direction of sort, either Ascending or Descending. If you sort multiple columns, they can be in different directions, the leftmost column will have the highest precedence, and the columns are sorted from left to right.

Figure 5.10
You can sort and total by column.

A Categorized column enables the documents to be sorted and grouped together by a field within the document. This field should be defined as a text field (or one of the list fields, such as a dialog list or combobox), and you might also want to enable multiple values. When a user enters a category in this field, it is used to group the documents for display.

For example, if several documents contain the value Sales in a field used in a view column, these documents will appear together if the sort column is categorized.

A user can enter two or more values into a categorized field. The user typically does this by checking multiple items in a dialog listbox. For example, suppose a user enters Sales, Contests as the two values. If the Show Multiple Values as Separate Entries checkbox is enabled, the document will show up twice within the view: once under the category Sales, and a second time under the category Contests.

When you make a Categorized view, a special category line is created automatically for each category. The documents within the category are shown underneath the appropriate category line. The categorized field itself is not shown within the document line. Sometimes, however, you want the category to appear as a regular field within the document line instead of a separate line. You can also specify more than one column that is sorted by category. New with release 5, you can check the Categorized Is Flat Version 5 or Greater option. This will show the categorized field as a regular field within the document line, even if the Show Twistie When Row Is Expandable option is enabled.

If you enable case-sensitive sorting, capital letters are sorted before lowercase letters. Accent-sensitive sorting is an option for languages other than English. Sorting will be dependent on the current language being used on the workstation.

When you enable the Click on Column Header to Sort option (see Figure 5.11), additional options become available in the properties box. You can choose Ascending, Descending, Both, or Change to View.

Figure 5.11
You can enable the user to choose the sort method.

If you choose Ascending, Descending, or Both, little triangles appear on the column header when the user uses the view. The Ascending sort is signified by a triangle pointing up. If the user clicks on this triangle, the documents will be sorted in ascending order by the values in the column. A Descending sort works similarly, and when Both is specified, the user can choose either Ascending or Descending sorting.

PART

I

CH

5

The Secondary sort column option enables you to choose another column for secondary sorting. The current column will be sorted first, and then within each identical value of the primary column, the documents will be sorted by the value contained in the secondary column.

The Change to View option implements a hyperlink to another view if the column header is clicked. For example, suppose the primary view is a summary view showing high-level information. Occasionally, users might want to see details for a particular document. Columns could contain the Change to View option, and each column could go to a different detailed view. When the user clicks a particular column heading, the view will change and the new view will show the same document (but with different fields displayed) that was selected in the primary view. This enables you to extract different, perhaps more detailed, information from the same document.

SORTING BY A HIDDEN COLUMN

Sometimes you want to display information sorted by a field that you don't want to show. For example, suppose you have a view column that contains days of the week: Sunday, Monday, Tuesday, and so forth. The typical sort for this would be in order of the days of the week, but with regular sorting, you get this list in alphabetical order, which is not particularly useful. To sort the days of the week in their weekday order, you can use a hidden column. You can put a formula within the hidden column (see Figure 5.12).

Figure 5.12
A formula and hidden column can change the sort order.

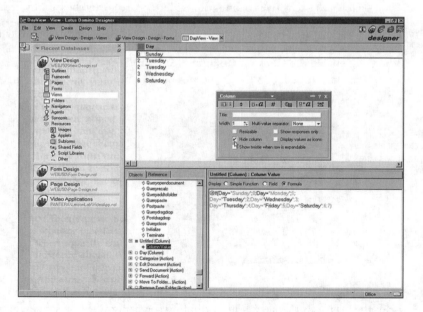

In the figure, you can see the value of the column as it is calculated by the formula. The formula is specified in the Programmer's pane at the bottom-right side of the window. It basically converts a day of the week into a number. You then specify the sorting for the hidden column and leave sorting unspecified in the actual day column. After you hide the column, the user will only see the view starting with the day column, which is sorted in the proper order by day of week.

USING ICONS IN VIEW COLUMNS

Many times, applications use icons to display status. In Figure 5.13, you see the standard mail database inbox. Notice that the highlighted line contains a paper clip. This is a fairly standard way to denote a file attachment. One of the other lines contains an exclamation point to indicate an important message.

Figure 5.13
Column icons can display status information very compactly.

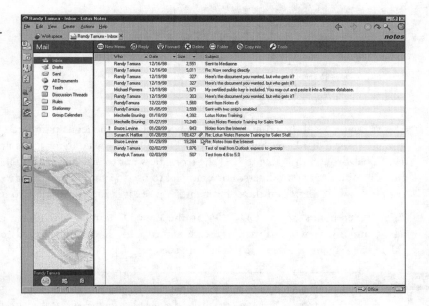

What if you could incorporate your own paper clips, exclamation points, and other icons into your own views? Wouldn't that be great? Well, it would, and I'll show you how to do it. (Okay, you don't have to get overexcited about it.)

This is all you have to do to use an icon in a column:

1. Open the view you want to contain the icon.
2. Select the column you want to contain the icon and open the Column Properties box. You can do this with the properties SmartIcon or by selecting Design, Column Properties.
3. In the Column properties box, adjust the width of the column. A width of 1 to 3 characters is probably appropriate.
4. Select the Display Values as Icons check mark.

5. As the column value, use a field or formula that evaluates to a number. You can use a number from 0 to 176. Zero will display no icon.

There are 176 valid icons in Domino release 5. You can see a table of the icons in Figure 5.14.

Figure 5.14
There are 176 valid icons in Notes/Domino release 5.

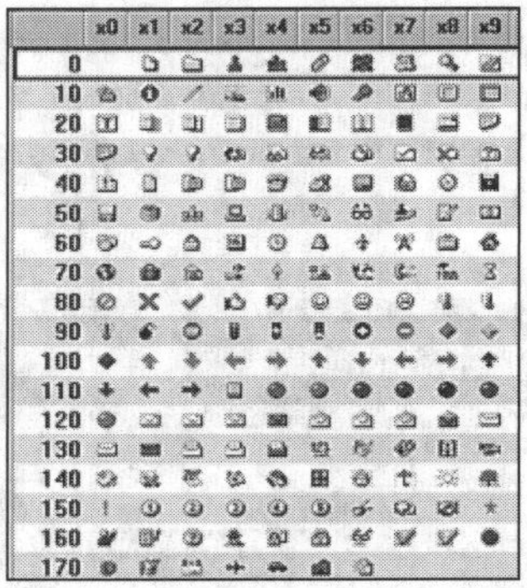

Here's how to read the table. The first row consists of the icons numbered 0 to 9. Actually, you use 0 for a blank space with no icon. The second row contains icons numbered 10 to 19. Look through the table to find the icon you want to use, and then look to the left and to the top. Add the two numbers. For example, to use the smiley face, look to the left and you see 80. Look at the top of the column and you see it is x5, so the value to use is 85.

As an added bonus, on the CD-ROM in the View Design database, there are one form, one agent, and one view that I used to create Figure 5.14. The form is called Icon, the agent is called Make Icons, and the view is called Icons.

Tip

If you have a form and an associated view, you can use the singular of a noun for the name of the form and the plural of the noun for the view. In this case, I've used the name Icon for the form and the name Icons for the view. You could use Widget and Widgets, for example, for the form and view names for entering widgets. This scheme enables you to use two different names for the form and view, but enables you to easily recognize that they are related.

FORMATTING FONTS IN A VIEW COLUMN

When you create and edit view columns, you have a lot of control over the formatting of the column. First, you have control over the fonts used within the column itself (see Figure 5.15).

Within the Font (the third) tab, you can control the fonts for the column, and within the Title (next-to-last) tab, you can control the fonts for the title line.

Figure 5.15
You can control the font face, size, and style used within view columns.

As with most windowing programs, you can control the font face (name), its size, and the style (plain, bold, italic, and so forth). You can also choose the justification within the column as left, center, or right. If you click the Apply to All button at the bottom of the dialog box, your change will apply to all the view's columns. Before you choose a wild font, however, take into consideration whether your application will be used on the Web by Web browsers. If so, you should probably choose from the generic font families that you can use with Domino. These three are Default Serif, Default Sans Serif, and Default Monospace. These translate into commonly used fonts, such as Times Roman (Times), Helvetica, and Courier. One of the most vexing problems in Web development today is the use of fonts.

When HTML was originally conceived, its purpose was to mark up the content of the Web page with the semantic meaning of the page. In other words, it was to inform the browser about titles, headers, links, and so forth. The formatting of these elements was up to the browser and the user. That's right, the user was—and is—able to control the appearance of the Web page. After the HTML author identified certain text as a heading level 1, the user could format these elements with Serif fonts or Sans Serif fonts, and make them purple if so desired.

Well, you can imagine the clash that developed because Web site developers also wanted to control the look and feel of their Web sites. The ongoing debate is still not totally resolved, although the major way for Web developers to gain back some control is with cascading style sheets (CSS). It's too far afield for me to explain this technology here, but if you are interested, pick up a current book about HTML and read about them.

Of course, if the views you developed will be used only by Notes clients, you can use fonts as you please, as long as you make sure that the fonts are available on the client machines. If you have a mixed-client environment of Mac and Windows, it is especially important to test the fonts you are using in your application.

FORMATTING NUMBERS IN A VIEW COLUMN

Figure 5.16 shows the numeric formatting tab in the Column properties box.

Figure 5.16
You can control the formatting of numbers with the Column properties box.

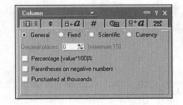

If you use general formatting for numeric formatting, the display of numbers will vary depending on how the value was input. Leading zeros will be suppressed. If you use fixed formatting, each number will be formatted with a fixed number of decimal places that you can specify. With scientific formatting, numbers will be displayed in scientific notation. Currency will display the currency symbol and two digits after the decimal.

You can also show values as percentages, which will display a value that is 100 times the numeric value. You can add parentheses on negative values by checking that box, and you can punctuate at thousands. The punctuation for the currency symbol, decimal character, and the punctuation at thousands varies, depending on the international language used.

FORMATTING DATES IN A VIEW COLUMN

Figure 5.17 shows the options for date formatting.

Figure 5.17
You can format date/time values to show both date and time or just one without the other.

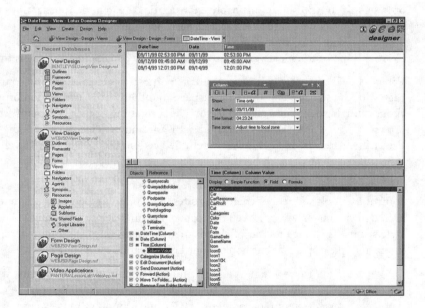

In the Show option, you can choose to show both date and time, as shown in column 1 of the view, just dates (column 2), or just times (column 3). The date format itself can be month/day, month/year, month/day/year, month/4-digit year, or month/day/4-digit year. The international settings of the operating system also affect the order of the components as well as the separator character.

Time values can be hours:minutes or hours:minutes:seconds. Time zones can automatically be adjusted to the local time zone and can show the time zone in the display.

PROGRAMMATIC COLUMN NAME

In the Advanced tab of the view Column property box, you see a section titled Programmatic Use (see Figure 5.18). In this section, you can specify a name for the column. If the column contains a field, the default value for the column name is the field name. If the view column contains an expression, the name will automatically be constructed by Notes to be of the format $n. For example, you might see names such as $0, $1, or $2.

Figure 5.18
The Column properties box enables you to change the column name and specify links.

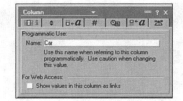

Although you can change the name for the column, you will rarely need to do so. The name you specify can be obtained in LotusScript with the ItemName property of the NotesViewColumn class. In Java, you can access the name with the getItemName method of the ViewColumn class.

The dialog box that enables you to change the name says you should use caution when changing the column name because if the column contains a field, you rarely would want another name for the column. Also, if the column contains a formula, the formula is compiled, stored internally within Domino, and may be internally referenced. Thus, the names such as $0 and $1 may be used within the database, and changing them can have unpredictable results.

SHOWING VALUES AS LINKS

When Domino displays a view in HTML to a browser, it will normally highlight the first column with tags to link to the document. Sometimes, however, you might want to highlight a column other than the first column as your link column. You can do this on the Advanced tab of the View Columns properties box.

To enable this feature, first highlight the column you want to use for linking, then in the advanced (beanie hat) tab, enable the option For Web Access: Show Values in This Column as Links. You can enable more than one column, in which case all the columns you specify will be highlighted, but they will all open the same document.

Note that this feature is not supported with the Java view applet, which is described later in this chapter in the section titled "Web Access."

VIEW PROPERTIES

In addition to the properties that can be adjusted for each column, the view itself has properties. Figure 5.19 shows the View Basics tab.

In addition to the view name, you see that the view has an alias. The alias is an important part of the view, and you should probably include one with every view you make. One thing you might find as you develop applications for Notes and Domino is that they always need to be changed and updated. As a result of these changes, the names you give to design elements can also change. When you make changes to view and form names, however, you don't want to have to go back and change all references to the new names.

Figure 5.19
The View Basics tab enables you to give an alias and a comment for a view.

> **Tip**
>
> Aliases enable you to assign a name to a view or form that can remain constant for the life of a database. You can assign the alias when the view is initially created. Typically, you use the original form or view name as the initial alias name. You make all internal references to the alias name. You can change the external name as frequently as you like, and you will not have to change any references to your view.

If you enclose the view name (not the alias) in parentheses, the view becomes hidden. You can use it for @DBColumn and @DBLookup formulas, but it will not appear to the user. Views are frequently used for looking up values, and you might sometimes need to create auxiliary views specifically for looking up information. Although these views are important to the program, they would just clutter and complicate the user interface. Thus, you should hide these views that are not directly required by end users.

The Comment field of the View Basics tab is used to enter a comment for the view. This comment will appear just below the name of the view when you are reviewing all your views in the Domino Designer.

The view style can either be Standard Outline or a Calendar view. All the views we have seen so far in this chapter are Standard Outline views. A Calendar view enables you to display a calendar, and documents that are displayed in the view can be placed on the calendar in a manner similar to the calendar found in your mail database.

Calendar views have a fairly restricted format. They typically have from two to five columns. The first two columns are mandatory, and the next three are recommended. Here is the layout you should have:

View Column	Contents
1	Date/Time, Hidden, Sorted. This contains the start date.
2	Numeric, Hidden. Duration of calendar entry, in minutes.
3	Time Value, Not Hidden. This displays the start time of the calendar entry.
4	Integer Numeric, Icon, Not Hidden. This displays an icon in the calendar. It is typically used to signify the type of calendar entry.
5	Text, Not Hidden. This is the text to display in the calendar entry.

If you create a Calendar view with these types of columns, you can display it with the Calendar view style. You might find this useful in certain applications where you want to display dates, times, and durations.

VIEW OPTIONS

Several view options can be enabled on the Options tab for the view properties (see Figure 5.20).

Figure 5.20
The view Options tab enables you to enable various options for the view.

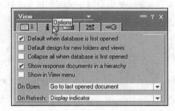

Here are the options:

- Default When Database Is First Opened—This option makes the current view the default view. In the view list, a solid arrow will indicate that this view is the default. You can have only one default view for the database. If you enable the option for one view, it will disable any previous selection on a different view.

- Default Design for New Folders and Views—When a new view is created, the current view will serve as a model for the newly created view. The newly created view will start out with the same column definitions. If you will have several similar views in a database, you can create one, set this option, and then create the others. This will save you some time in the view creation process. In addition, the default design view is used whenever a new folder is programmatically created by an agent or action.

- Collapse All When Database Is First Opened—This option will collapse any twisties that group a set of documents. By setting this option, the initial view will be more compact and perhaps easier to work with for the user.

- Show Response Documents in a Hierarchy—You previously saw how to create hierarchical response documents. For this feature to work, you must enable this option. If you do not enable the option, each column will show its own data rather than use the formula specified in the response column.

- Show in View Menu—This option displays the name of the view in the View menu for users. If you enable this option, it will give your users another way to navigate to the view. Normal navigation is via the Navigator pane, but if you are using a graphic navigator, you might want to also enable the View menu option.

PART
I

CH
5

At the bottom of the dialog box are two options, On Open and On Refresh. Here are the choices for these two options:

- On Open—The choices are Go To Last Opened Document, Go To Top Row, and Go To Bottom Row. When the view is first opened, the view will be positioned to the document you specify here.

- On Refresh—The choices are Display Indicator, Refresh Display, Refresh Display from Top Row, and Refresh Display from Bottom Row. This option controls the action taken when new documents are available for the view. These options apply only to the Notes client because Web browsers do not have an indicator.

VIEW STYLE PROPERTIES

The View Style properties are found on the third tab of the View properties (see Figure 5.21).

Figure 5.21
The View Style tab enables you to control visual aspects of the view.

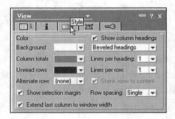

Four color options appear on the left of the dialog box:

- Background color—This is the overall background color for the view. You can choose from the 256-color palette or select from the custom color palette, and the color choice works for both Notes client and Web browsers. As usual, you should be careful choosing a color other than one found in the Web palette if your view will be displayed in Web browsers. You should generally choose white or another light color unless you have an overall color scheme that you are using for your Web site.

- Column Totals—You can choose from the 16-color palette for this option. Gray is the default color, and you typically will want to choose a color that will highlight the column total.

- Unread Rows—In the mail database, the unread documents are red. The default color for normal views is black. If you are using unread rows as a design feature of your database, you might want to choose a color that dramatically highlights them. You can choose from the 16-color palette for this option. Note that this option is not supported on the Web.

- Alternate Rows—This option enables you to specify a second color for alternating rows. You can choose to have no alternate row colors, colors from the 256-color palette, or a custom color. If you have already chosen a color and want to go back to no alternating color, you must select the leftmost icon in the top row of the color picker. This is pretty obscure, so see Figure 5.22. The middle icon enables you to choose a color from the 256-color palette, and the rightmost color circle icon enables you to select a custom color. Note that alternate row colors are not supported on the Web.

Figure 5.22
To select (none) for the alternating color, choose the leftmost icon in the top row.

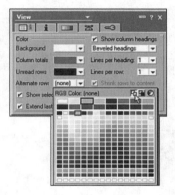

- Show Selection Margin—(Refer to Figure 5.21.) This option affects only the Notes client and Web browsers when using the Java view applet (described shortly). If you use a Web browser without the Java view applet, the option is ignored. This option enables a column for icons to the left of your view. This column displays unread marks (star), user selection (check mark), replication or save conflicts (diamond), and deleted marks (trashcans). Normally, you should leave this option enabled.

- Extend Last Column to Window Width—Enabling this option allows the contents of the rightmost column of a view to extend past the column bounds. If not enabled, the rightmost column contents will be truncated at the column bound, even if there is more room in the window.

- Show Column Headings—Checking this option displays the column titles. This option works both in the Notes client and browsers.

- Beveled or Simple Headings—This option changes the format of the displayed headings. It applies only to Notes clients and is ignored for Web browsers. Beveled headings have a gray color (and are the default); simple headings adopt the background color of the view.

- Lines Per Heading—This is the number of lines that the headings should use. This is useful if you have long headings or a lot of columns. When you have a lot of columns, you can use multiple line headers and thereby possibly make the columns narrower. You can specify up to five lines for the header.

- Lines Per Row—You can use up to nine lines for view content rows. This option would be useful if you have a lot of content to display. Domino will automatically wrap the content of a text field to fit within the column width and use as many lines as you allow.

- Shrink Rows to Content—If you use multiple content lines per row, I would recommend enabling this option. It allows each row to contain only the number of lines necessary to display its content. The number of lines is calculated separately for each row. If you use multiple lines without enabling this option, you will probably see many blank lines.

- Row Spacing—This option can be Single, 1 1/4, 1 1/2, 1 3/4, or Double. Normally, you would leave this option set for single spacing unless you want to allow extra spacing per row.

VIEW ADVANCED PROPERTIES

The View Advanced tab (with the beanie hat) enables you to change the view index settings, the handling of unread marks, the view's form formula, and ODBC and Web access options. The first two options deal with a view's index. Refer to Figure 5.23 for the next few sections.

Figure 5.23
The Advanced tab enables you to modify some important options, such as applet usage.

THE VIEW INDEX

Each view has an associated index, which is used to display the view. This index is different from a full text index. The view index options you set in the properties dialog box control when this index is created and when it is deleted. The view index has important performance and usability considerations. These considerations are

- If the view index is out of date with respect to the documents it displays, the user will see out-of-date information.
- The view index can take considerable time to build, especially for large databases, so if it is built frequently, users might have to wait a long time for it to be built before they can see the view.
- The view index takes significant space in the database, so if you build it but it is not used, you might be requiring too much space in your database for unneeded data.

Because of these important considerations, it is not possible for Domino to guess what type of refresh strategy to use for all views in all databases. This job must be left to the designer and should be based on the usage pattern of the database and the type and frequency of change of the data shown in the view.

Note that each view can have separate settings, so in some databases you might have different strategies for different views. Here are your choices:

- Auto, After First Use—In this case, no view is built until the view is used at least once. Thereafter, it is updated automatically as in the Automatic setting listed next. When you use this option, users might notice a delay when the view is first used due to the creation of the index. Use this option for databases that can be used in cycles. For example, it might be used frequently for some time, but then not used for some time. While it is being used, the index will be updated automatically, but when it isn't being used, the automatic deletion will discard the index and it won't appear until the view is used again.

- Automatic—This option always keeps the view updated. As documents are added, the view index is incrementally updated. This option updates the index even if no users are using the database. Because the index is always up-to-date, users will not notice a delay to build the index when the view is first used. Use this option for views that will be frequently used. Although views will be updated quickly, it will not be instantaneous. Domino will update the view as it has time.

- Manual—This option will not update the view until the user requests it by pressing F9 or through an equivalent programmed command. It is most useful for views containing a large number of documents that do not change frequently.

- Auto, at Most Every n Hours—With this option, you must also specify a time limit in hours. This option limits the frequency of view index updates. If you use the default—12 hours, for example—the view is updated no more frequently than 12 hours since the last update. Use this option for databases in which changes are slow. Suppose, for example, you had only one document change every 3 hours. By limiting the view index update to once every 12 hours, you can group the 4 changes into one view index update. Remember that users can also manually update the view at any time.

The Discard Index options control when the view index is deleted. This is a trade-off of space for time. The space taken by the view index is considered against the time the user must wait while the index is constructed. The discarding is actually done on the Domino server, by default at 2 a.m. by the server task UPDALL. The discard index options are

- Never—The index is permanently kept. Because this option will reserve space on the server for the index, you should use this option for views that are frequently used. If you can afford the space, you might also consider this option if the view is very large, because for large views your users might have to wait a very long time for the view index to be reconstructed. By keeping the view index permanently, users will not have to wait as long when the view is first opened.

- After Each Use—This option will flag the view as eligible to be discarded as soon as it is closed. It will not actually be discarded until the next time the UPDALL server task runs. Use this option for infrequently used views.

- If Inactive for n Days—This option is a compromise between the never and always options just described. You can specify a time limit, and if the view has not been used during that time, the view index will be discarded the next time UPDALL runs. You can use this option for views that are used cyclically. For example, an accounting view might be used only once a month. The view will be active for a short while but will then be inactive for about a month.

UNREAD MARKS IN THE VIEW

Unread marks are an aid to the user of a database so that he or she knows what information is new. The unread marks are calculated separately for each user so that if two people are viewing the same database, they will see different sets of unread marks. As you can imagine, keeping track of the unread marks causes a performance penalty, so there are several options that you, as a designer, can control.

Note

A new option in R5 is a database property called Don't Maintain Unread Marks. This enables you to completely disable unread marks for the entire database. It can be found in the Advanced (beanie hat) tab within the database properties box. To improve performance, check this box. You typically set this option when you create a database.

Note that the database property should provide much more of a performance improvement than the view options because the unread marks are not maintained. The view options control only the display of unread marks, and all the time to maintain the marks within the database is still required.

The following unread marks options control how a view displays unread marks. These options do not affect whether the unread marks information is stored, only how it is displayed. For example, you could choose two different options in different views, and the unread marks would display differently. Here are the options:

- None—This option causes the view to display faster because the unread marks are not displayed.
- Unread Documents Only—This displays unread marks only on top-level documents. It does not display unread marks for collapsed groups of documents in a view.
- Standard (compute in hierarchy)—This displays unread marks on top-level documents or on collapsed groups of documents where one of the lower-level documents is unread.

ODBC ACCESS

The next option in the Advanced tab is for ODBC access. It says Generate Unique Keys in Index. This is one of the most mysterious options for a view. First of all, this option is not for accessing ODBC databases, as it might appear. Tools that access the current Domino database via ODBC use this option.

Lotus has a product called NotesSQL that enables a Notes/Domino database to be accessed as if it were a relational database via ODBC. Other products, such as Visual Basic, Delphi, or other third-party tools, can use the NotesSQL interface. If you check the Generate Unique Keys in Index option, NotesSQL will make the view appear to other programs as if the sorted columns of the view comprise a unique key.

This option requires careful use, however. Just because you check the box does not mean that you have defined the view selection and column definitions to meet the criteria that the other program is expecting. To avoid problems, you should follow these rules if you enable this checkbox:

- Do not enable this checkbox for more than one view per form. The external system might try to update the document through more than one path, and you might get inconsistent data in your document.

- The sorted columns within the view are very important. Make sure that the column definitions for the sorted columns

  - Are defined by fields only, not formulas or expressions.

  - Taken as a group, uniquely identify a document within the database. In database terminology, this is called a *composite key*.

You should normally enable this option only if you are using NotesSQL. If so, you should refer to the NotesSQL documentation for more information.

WEB ACCESS

The section for Web access contains two options that are used when a Web browser accesses the view. The options are

- Treat View Contents as HTML—This is a great option. It enables you to specify HTML in the view column definitions. This HTML will be served to the browser. In effect, each document line of the view can contain HTML formatting that you define. I'll show you an example of this when I discuss embedded views.

- Use Applet in the Browser—Originally, the first implementation of Domino converted views to HTML and then served them to browsers. This method is still the default and works well. However, because the view is calculated on the server each time it needs to be updated, there can be many round trips from the client to the server when the user is navigating the view. For example, just opening a twistie on the view causes a round trip to the server for redisplay. New with release 5 is the capability to download a Java applet to the browser to take over some of the view functionality. If you enable this checkbox, the view will format slightly differently and will have more functionality (see Figures 5.24 and 5.25).

PART

I

CH

5

Note

When using the Java applet for views, take careful note of the performance of your application. There is usually no problem on an intranet. However, when you are using the Java applet option with a Web browser over a modem you might notice a significant performance penalty. This performance penalty occurs because the browser must download the view applet over a comparatively slow line. The view applet is relatively large, and the download time over a modem can be very significant, so be sure to test the performance of your application before deployment.

Also note that pass-thru HTML, calendar views, and link colors are not supported in the view applet.

Figure 5.24
Without the view applet, a view in the browser is relatively static.

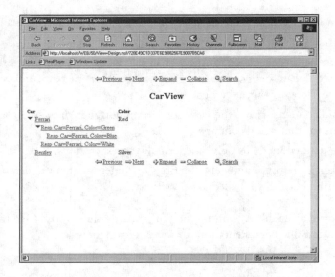

Figure 5.25
With the view applet, you can interact locally, select documents, and open and close twisties.

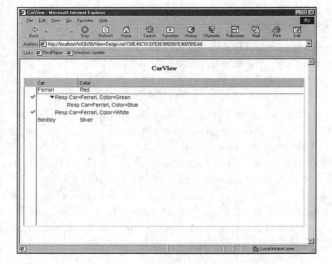

You can also change the colors for active links, unvisited links, and visited links in the view. To change one of these colors, click on the drop-down box and select the color within the color picker.

OTHER ADVANCED VIEW PROPERTIES

The following are the remaining two advanced view properties:

- Restrict Initial Index Build to Designer or Manager—This option will most likely be used with the Auto After First Usage refresh option. By selecting the restriction, you can control when the database will go into automatic index building mode.

■ Don't Show Categories Having Zero Documents—This feature enables you to suppress the display of categories when no documents are included. By enabling this option, users will not have to waste time exploring and navigating extraneous view categories. In addition, Don't Show Categories Having Zero Documents can be used when the category names themselves contain sensitive information. For example, even though sensitive documents within a category are not shown in the view, the category names might convey information. This option allows you to suppress the category names in this situation.

VIEW SECURITY PROPERTIES

You can see the Security tab (key icon) in Figure 5.26. This tab can be used to control access to the view.

Figure 5.26
With the view Security tab, you can control who can use the view.

The default is that the view can be used by all readers and above. You can enable this checkbox so you don't have to specifically list the users. If you disable the checkbox, you can specify exactly the list of users you want to be able to use the view. This list is called the view access list. This list does not override the Access Control List (ACL) for the database; it can only refine the access.

Note that the view access list is not really a security feature, only a usability feature. Although you can restrict people from using the views you create, a user could conceivably create a private view containing exactly the same columns and fields as your view. The user would then be able to view all the data in the documents. To secure the data in the documents, you should use security at the form level. You can enable form access lists and reader and author fields, and use encryption to provide security for your documents.

If you create a view access list, make sure to include servers either directly or via a group. If you do not include servers, your views might not replicate correctly.

You can enable public access by checking the Available to Public Access Users checkbox. Enabling this checkbox will allow users with No Access or Depositor access to view public documents if they have the Read Public Documents ACL setting. In addition to enabling the view for public access, you will also need to enable one or more forms for public access and create documents with a text field called $PublicAccess with a value of "1". Any document with this field set to "1" will be available for viewing in a public access view.

PROGRAMMER'S PANE VIEW PROPERTIES

Several view properties are not located in the view properties dialog box. These properties are set in the Programmer's pane at the bottom of your screen. The first option, View Selection, I have already discussed briefly, but here are some additional details.

VIEW SELECTION

The View Selection property enables you to specify a formula that is used to select documents to display in the view. The default is to select all documents in the database. If you specify a formula, the formula is evaluated for each document in the database to determine whether to show the document in the view. As you might imagine, this is potentially a time-consuming task.

There is a new performance enhancement option for release 5 to speed the display of views. The option is found in the Advanced tab of the database properties box, and you can also specify it when you create the database. The option is called Document Table Bitmap Optimization. Now, although it is fairly clear that the option optimizes something, it is not clear what, why, or how this optimization works.

Because selecting documents for a view potentially means going through every document in the database, Domino stores some (bitmap) tables to speed the process. Essentially, these tables link documents, forms, and views. The tables enable Domino to tell whether a form is used in a view. Then, by knowing whether a document uses the form, Domino can quickly determine whether a document is a candidate for a view. This optimization will work only if your view selection formula has one or more Form= conditions. If you use Form= in your view, which is fairly common, you can enable this option to improve your database performance.

When would you not want to use this optimization? Well, if you don't use Form= in your view, extra computing and storage is required, and you will not gain any benefit. The default is for this option to be turned off. You should definitely consider using it where appropriate, though, because for large databases, you might be able to improve your view performance dramatically.

THE FORM FORMULA

The form formula is a formula associated with a view that enables you to control the form used to display a document opened from within the view. The form formula is one option in the selection process Domino uses to select the form to use to display a document. Here is the sequence Domino uses:

1. If there is a form stored with the document, it is used to display the document. This option is selected in the Defaults tab of the Form properties dialog box. Use this option to enable sending a document to another database where the associated form might not exist. For example, if you are mailing a document to another person who might not have the associated form, you should enable storing the form with the document. In general, you should use this option sparingly because it uses up significantly more space in the database.

2. If no form is stored with the document, the form formula associated with the view is evaluated. The formula must evaluate to the name of a form that is available in the database. You can create or edit the form formula by highlighting the Form Formula property in the Programmer's pane under the view. You can then enter your formula in the right half of the Programmer's pane. One possible use of this option might be to select different forms based on the state of the document: (New versus Existing), (Viewing versus Editing), (Inquiry versus New Order), and so forth. Another usage would be to have one view and form used during data entry for creating documents that will be viewed on the Web. A second form and view could be used to display the document on the Web, but with graphics, different formatting, and so forth.

3. If there is no form formula in the view, the document will be displayed using the form name contained in a field called Form within the document. This field is automatically filled in with the synonym of the form name (or form name if no synonym exists) of the form used to create or most recently edit the document. Unless this field is changed, the document will be displayed using the form used to create the document. This option is the default for most documents.

4. If there is no field called Form within the document or the form cannot be found, the default form for the database is used. You can specify the database default form in the Defaults tab of the Form properties dialog box.

5. Finally, if there is no default form, you will get an error and the document will not be displayed.

VIEW ACTIONS

View actions enable you to make commonly used actions available for users via the action button bar. There are six built-in view actions: Categorize, Edit Document, Send Document, Forward, Move To Folder, and Remove From Folder. In addition, you can create your own custom actions.

The user can activate the action by clicking the action button or with the menus as a choice of the Actions menu. As a designer, you can choose to enable either menu access or button access, both, or neither.

You have four language options for programming the action. You can use the formula language, create a simple action, use LotusScript, or use JavaScript.

If you create a view action, it is unique to the particular view, and you must have separate copies for each view if you want identical function. Another option would be to create a shared action. Shared actions are new with release 5 of Domino. A shared action can be used in multiple views or forms. This is another great way to implement code once, and then use it from multiple locations within your database.

To create a shared action, click on Resources in the Design pane of your database, and then click on Other. In the work area, you can double-click on Shared Actions. An action will be created for you. You can name it, provide the code, and then save it.

EMBEDDED VIEWS

With Domino release 5, you can embed many elements on a page or form. On both pages and forms, you can embed outlines, a view, navigators, date pickers, or a Folder pane. On forms, you can embed a group scheduler or file upload control as well.

In this section, I describe how you can embed a view on a form for display in a Web browser. This capability gives you a lot of flexibility in the formatting of the view rows through the use of HTML. In addition, through the use of single category embedded views, you can create views that present customized lists to users.

Let's see how all this is accomplished. This example is comprised of one form for data entry, a view, and a second form that embeds the view. I've tried to distill this example to its simplest components to explain how to make Domino forms and views work well with the Web.

Here is the scenario. You have an online shop that sells games over the Web. There are several categories for the games, and some games can fall into more than one category. The first form you can create is the form that enables someone in your company to enter new games on your Web site (see Figure 5.27).

Figure 5.27
The sample game definition form is used to add a game and its categories.

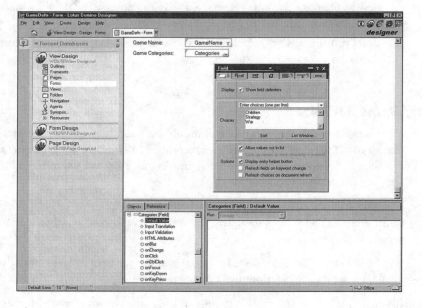

The GameDefn form is very simple; there are only two fields. When you develop your form, you'll want to include more fields and make it more attractive for data entry. Notice that there is a field called Categories. This special field name identifies the field as one to use when a view is categorized by the Categorize system action. I've also enabled the field to have multiple values on the Basics tab. This form is simple enough.

The next design element we'll create is a view. This view will eventually be embedded in a form, and I'm going to illustrate how you can use HTML to add some spice to your view and form (see Figure 5.28).

Figure 5.28
The sample GameList view has enabled Treat View Contents as HTML.

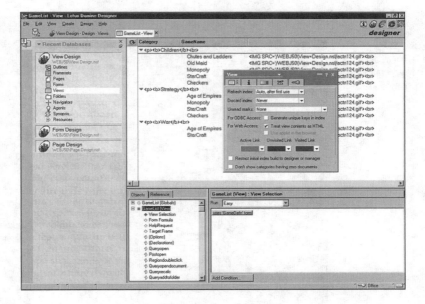

The GameList view I've created has three columns. The first column is for the category, the second is for the game name, and the third will be for an icon that will display any time we have recently listed a new game. Many Web sites use a starburst New. With Domino, we can automatically add these icons via programming.

The first column is sorted in ascending order and categorized. The contents of the column can be seen in Figure 5.28. Here is the formula for the first column:

```
"<p><b>"+Categories+"</b><br>"
```

Notice that I have included a paragraph tag, a bold tag, the Categories field, end bold, and a line-break tag. The effect of these HTML tags will be to space before the new category, and then show the category name in bold, followed by a line break so the next text will follow on the next line. If these tags are not familiar to you, refer to Chapter 7, "Using Hypertext Markup Language (HTML) for Page Design."

The second column of the view just contains the field GameName. I have not included any special formatting, although you could use the HTML tags to add features such as document linking, bold, or other characteristics. Here is the formula for the second column:

```
@Repeat(" ";5)+GameName
```

The third column formula can be seen in Figure 5.29. In this formula, the actn124.gif file is assumed to be in the image resource library. Here it is:

```
@if(@Now> @Adjust(@Created;0;0;7;0;0;0);"<br>";
"<IMG SRC=\'/"+@ReplaceSubstring(@Text(@Subset(@DbName;-1)));" "; "+")+
"/actn124.gif\'><br>"
```

Figure 5.29
The formula conditionally generates an icon using HTML.

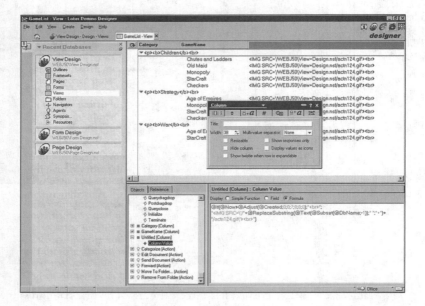

In Figure 5.29, you can see both the column value formula in the Programmer's pane and an example of the generated HTML in the view window. In essence, I am generating a reference to a GIF file that has been stored within the image library of the database. You can extract and show the image by using a URL, as shown. Using this technique is much better than having graphics stored in the file system. All the related graphics can be stored within the Domino database and will replicate automatically with the application.

The formula I've used will create conditional HTML. That is, two versions of HTML will be generated, depending on the outcome of the if statement. The first version of HTML will just generate a `<br>`, which means to break to a new line. The second version of HTML will generate a reference to an icon (GIF file) in the image library.

Note

In the URL that refers to the image file, I issue a `@ReplaceSubString` that substitutes a plus sign (+) instead of a blank space. You may not use embedded blanks within a URL string. Plus signs are used to indicate an embedded blank. This substitution is performed in case (as it is here) the database name has an embedded blank. In Figure 5.29 you can see that the embedded blank between View and Design has been changed to a plus sign to yield `View+Design`.

The essence of the formula is that an icon reference will be generated if the creation date of the document is within the last seven days. The @Adjust function takes the document creation date and adds seven days. It then compares the adjusted date to the current time. If the current time is later than the adjusted date, the document is old and we just generate a line break. If it isn't, the document's date is within the last seven days and we generate the HTML for an image with the IMG tag.

Because this view contains a reference to the @Now function, it can potentially cause the view index to be created repeatedly. If you use this technique, you can use the At Most Every 'n' Hours View Index Refresh option. This will make sure that the view is not constantly being refreshed. You can set the number of hours based on the frequency of posting to the database.

I have loaded the image resource into the image library of the database, so I do not need to enter a path for the IMG tag. If you keep the image resources within the database, they will automatically replicate with the database, and the database will be self-contained. Do you think this is cool yet?

Now we are ready to create the last design element of our example. We are now going to create the form that will embed the view that we just made. When we create an embedded view, Domino will not automatically include the navigation bars that appear when Domino natively shows a view. With embedded views, we have more control over the appearance shown to the user (see Figure 5.30).

Figure 5.30
Create an embedded view to control the view's appearance.

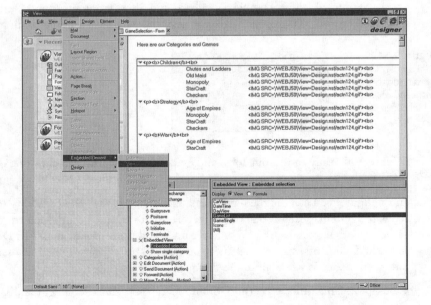

PART

I

CH

5

Follow these steps to create an embedded view:

1. First create your form. Call it GameSelection. Add some preliminary static text such as Here are our Categories and Games.

2. Select Create, Embedded Element, View. Note that you can include only one embedded view per form.

3. From the dialog box that appears, choose a particular view or check the box that says Choose a View Based on Formula. For our example, we will select the GameList view. Click OK.

4. If you selected the formula option, you must enter the formula in the Programmer's pane. The formula you enter must evaluate to the name of a view.

5. Open the properties for the embedded view by clicking the Properties icon or selecting Edit, Properties. For our example, we cannot use the view applet because it will not properly handle the formulas and dynamically generated HTML we are creating. In our example, in the Basics tab, we choose Using HTML under the Web Access Display option.

Note

The view applet is written in Java and is downloaded to the browser. This code executes in the client environment and does not use HTML to render the view. For this reason, pass-thru HTML does not work with the view applet. View applets are great for improving user interactivity and response time for standard views, but if you need to combine HTML with the view, you must use the HTML (Domino server–generated) version of views.

6. In the Display tab (the second tab) for our example, enable Fit to Window Width, Fit to Window Height, Disable Scrollbars, and Show Contents Only (Don't Show Title) (see Figure 5.31). In your form, you may choose to use different options.

Figure 5.31
In the Display tab, you can control the height and width of an embedded view.

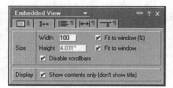

We are now ready to test our form and embedded view. You can click one of the browser icons in the upper-right corner of your screen. See Figure 5.32 for our sample output.

In the figure, you can see the dynamically generated icons. The capability to generate these icons programmatically is one of the features that makes Domino such a powerful Web server. In other systems, the Webmaster must add the icons manually. In Domino, you can just add documents, specify the rules you want to use for how long documents stay "new," and then the icons will appear and disappear automatically as they age.

I did not include other powerful Domino features, such as document and URL linking in this example, but I think you get the idea.

Figure 5.32
Icons are dynamically generated in the new document.

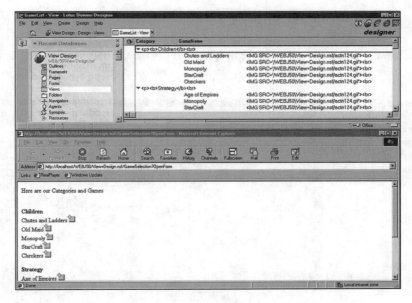

SINGLE CATEGORY EMBEDDED VIEWS

Single Category embedded views are a neat new feature of release 5. They enable you to create customized views, similar to a shared-private on first use view. The nice thing about Single Category embedded views is that they work well on the Web.

You can use a Single Category view to provide custom information to a particular user. The way it works is simple. You first create a categorized view and use as the category value some data that will distinguish one user from another. For example, you could use the user's name as the categorization value. Other sample applications are the game categories of the previous example, categories for user preferences, or just about any kind of grouping where you want to select a group of documents to customize the user's experience.

To illustrate Single Category embedded views, I am going to modify the previous games example. I will create one additional view (the Single Category view) and one form, which will contain the embedded view. First, let's do the view.

Create an additional view that is the same as the GameList view. You can do this by copying and pasting the view within the view list. Rename the new view `GameSingle`. The only change we will make to this new view is to the column formula for the first column, the `Categories` column. In GameList the formula is

```
"<p><b>"+Categories+"</b><br>"
```

Change this for the GameSingle view to

```
Categories
```

PART

I

CH

5

We want to make it the regular contents of the Categories field with no HTML formatting. Save and close the GameSingle view.

Now, create a new form and call it GameSingle also. There is no restriction on a form and view having the same name. Create a radio button field called Cat (see Figure 5.33).

Figure 5.33
Create a radio button in the GameSingle form with the Refresh Fields on Keyword Change option.

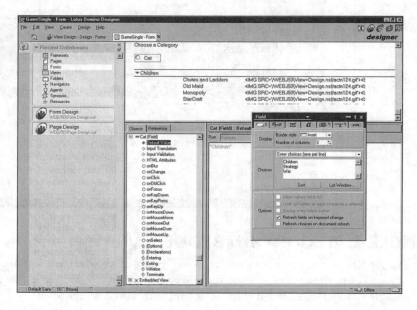

On the Control tab, enter the three options Children, Strategy, and War. Also be sure to check the Refresh Fields on Keyword Change option. This will force a re-evaluation of our Single Category view. The default value for the Cat field is Children.

Now you can embed the GameSingle view as we did in the previous example. Do this by selecting Create, Embedded Element, View. After the view is embedded within your form, choose the Show Single Category property in the Programmer's pane. Enter Cat in the formula area within the Programmer's pane (see Figure 5.34). You should also set the Display option in the Embedded View property box to Using HTML instead of the default Using Java Applet.

By specifying Cat in the formula area, we are essentially telling Domino to use the Cat field as the criterion for the Single Category. We force the option to be one of the three that we know are valid by using a radio button. After the user selects one of the radio button options, the Refresh Fields on Keyword Change option will cause the view to recalculate and display the Single Category specified in the Cat field. See Figure 5.35 for an example.

If you see the view selections followed by No Documents Found, you did not set the default value of the Cat field to Children or you have no game documents that use the Children value.

Figure 5.34
The Single Category specification can be a field name or formula.

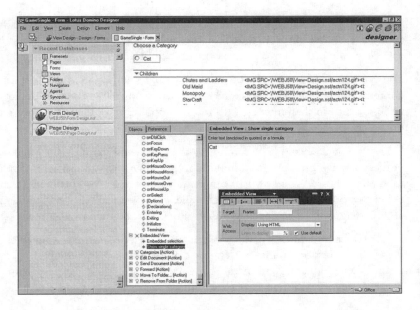

Figure 5.35
Selecting a radio button option changes the games shown.

In this example, when the user selects each of the different radio button options, the games shown will change. Each time, the "new" icon will appear automatically as before.

SUMMARY

In this chapter, I covered the fundamentals of views and folders. I showed you how to create a view or folder, how to specify its type, and how to select documents for inclusion in a view. There are two new types of views in release 5: one showing documents not in folders, and the other showing deleted documents. The deleted document feature uses the new soft deletion support of release 5 databases.

View columns display your data. You can use formulas to specify the data to be displayed, so values can be straight from a field or computed from several fields. You can sort and categorize view columns. View columns can also be hidden or used to show icons.

You can add styling to a view by modifying colors and using multiple lines for the headers or contents. New with release 5 is the capability to download the view applet to a Web browser. The user can then interact with the view applet, expand and collapse sections, and select documents.

I showed you an example of combining the power of Domino forms and views with HTML. You can use Domino programming to programmatically alter what is displayed. In the example, I showed you how you can include a new icon for documents that have been recently modified. By using this technique, all new documents will be flagged automatically, and the flags will be removed automatically when the time period expires.

Single Category embedded views is a new feature of release 5 that enables you to provide personalized information to a user. You can use a formula to compute a personalization criterion, such as a name, and then use the name to select one category within a view. This Single Category will then display only those records that have the name as the category.

CHAPTER REVIEW

1. Describe the difference between a view and a folder.

2. What is the purpose of the View Selection formula?

3. Suppose you have a database that contains information you would like to display in two different ways. The data entry form contains all the information, but when you display it to users you would like to show them a subset of the data. How could you set up two different views so that if you access the document from one view you receive all the fields, but when accessed through the second view only the subset data is shown?

4. What is the difference between a view index and a full text index?

5. Suppose you want to develop a Web application that uses a view. You don't really like the formatting provided either by the HTML rendering or the Java applet version of a view. How can you format a view so that it looks different from either the built-in HTML or Java applet formatting?

6. Where do you set the option to allow you to display an icon (such as a paperclip) within a view?

7. Suppose you want to build an e-commerce application where the user can select a category of an item, such as shoes, neckties, or shirts, and the system will display the items for sale within that category. What feature of Notes/Domino would you use to implement this capability? Could you make this work on the Web as well as within the Notes client?

8. Can you embed a view on a page as well as on a form?

9. Suppose you have a Web application where you want to display images in a list to the user. You would like to sort this list of images, however, in a particular order. How can you do this? Create a database and test your idea if you can.

CHAPTER 6

Using Outlines, Framesets, and Navigators

In this chapter

Domino provides several capabilities for organizing information and enabling users to navigate through your Web pages. This chapter gives you information about some of the navigation tools available in Domino release 5. Outlines are one mechanism you can use to enable navigation functions for your users. Framesets enable you to create several panes or frames within your window. You can control the initial number and placement of the frames. After the frameset is displayed, the user will typically be able to move the borders between the frames. Navigators are a feature from release 4 of Notes and Domino that are still available in release 5. Let's take a look at these features in more detail.

WHAT ARE OUTLINES?

An *outline* is a tool to enable you to control user navigation. Outlines can be styled vertically or horizontally, and roughly correspond to a list of destinations. Typically, you see these kinds of navigation tools on the left side of a home page, along the top or on the bottom of the page. In Notes release 4.*x*, the View Navigation pane in the upper-left corner is a kind of outline. It gives a list of the available views in the database, and by clicking on a view name, you can see the view in the upper-right pane. Outlines can perform a similar function.

You must embed an outline in either a page or form to be used. You can create as many outlines as you like, and you can embed more than one outline on a single page. You format the outline using the Embedded Outline properties box, which I'll show you later. Normally, you use outlines within pages in framesets because they can reside in one frame but control the contents of another frame. I'll cover this in the section titled "Using Frames and Framesets."

Note that there are two separate kinds of information about outlines. The first is the navigational information. You specify this information when you create and program the outline entries. The second kind of information is the display formatting for the outline. The same outline can be used in two different pages, with different formatting styles in each. Although the outline looks different on each page, the navigation for each respective entry in the outline will be the same.

USING THE OUTLINE EDITOR

If you want to follow along, you can create a new, blank, local database called Outline Design. You can open the outline editor in the Domino Designer by clicking on Outlines in the Design pane. By default, no outlines are created for you within a database. You can easily have the Designer create one for you by following these steps:

1. Open the outline editor by clicking on Outlines in the Design pane.
2. Click on the New Outline action bar button. You will see a new set of action bar buttons.
3. Click on the Generate Default Outline action button. Your new default outline will be generated for you (see Figure 6.1).

Figure 6.1
The default outline as initially created by Domino Designer.

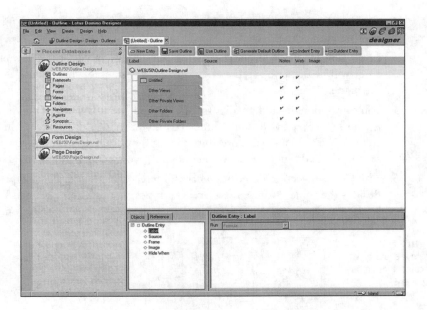

You can see from Figure 6.1 that Domino Designer will automatically create five outline entries for you: Untitled (the default view), Other Views, Other Private Views, Other Folders, and Other Private Folders. The first outline entry represents the single view of your database. If you had generated this outline after creating several views and folders, they would be included in the default outline as well.

The four additional outline entries that are created for you automatically have suggested names, but you do not have to use all these entries. You can delete some of the entries if they do not apply to your application.

If you prefer to create your entire outline from scratch, first create the outline, and then begin adding outline entries as described in the following section.

OUTLINE ENTRIES

In Figure 6.1, you can see five outline entries, each represented by a rectangular gray box. When the application executes, the user will see a text or graphic item for each outline entry. By clicking on one of these entries, the user will be able to navigate through your application. You can add, delete, move, and rename the outline entries.

To add a new entry, follow these steps:

1. Create a new outline or open an existing outline.
2. Click on the existing outline entry where you want to locate your new entry. The new entry will go below the one you select. If you want your entry to be the new first entry, click on the database line. For our example, click on the database line to create a new first entry.

PART

I

CH

6

3. Click on the New Entry action button. A new entry will be created for you under the existing entry you selected.

4. In the Outline Entry properties dialog box, enter a label for the new entry. The text you enter will be displayed to the end user. In our example, you can use the word Home for the name.

5. You can optionally add an alias for the outline entry. If you add an alias, you can refer to the outline entry by the alias name even if you change the name of the outline. This enables you to change the user interface without reprogramming your application. I recommend adding an alias. In our example, you can use the word Home for the alias.

6. The Content section describes what will happen if the user clicks on this outline entry. Besides the value (None), there are four types: Action, Link, Named Element, and URL (see Figure 6.2). These options are described in the next section.

Figure 6.2
There are four types of content for an outline entry.

7. You can optionally enter the name for an image. You can enter the name of an image within your image library, or you can specify a formula that will result in the name of an image. The image itself will be displayed as a small icon next to the label you specified previously. Note that you cannot use the image field to display a large graphic for the outline entry.

8. An outline entry has a status that is either selected (that is, has the focus) or not selected. When you click on an outline entry, the action you have specified will occur, and the focus normally changes to the clicked outline entry. You can specify that you do not want the outline entry to retain the focus by enabling the Does Not Keep Selection Focus option. Even if this option is enabled, the outline entry's action will still work.

9. After you have entered all the fields, you can close the properties box or click on another outline entry and enter its information.

OUTLINE ENTRY CONTENTS

As stated previously, the action for an outline entry can be one of four types: Action, Link, Named Element, and URL. Here is what happens with each of these types:

■ If you specify Action, you can supply an @formula to be executed when the outline entry is clicked. You specify the formula by clicking on the @ character at the right of the Value line. You will then see a dialog box where you can enter your formula.

- If you specify Link, the outline entry can be a link to a database, view, document, or anchor. Follow these steps to utilize this type of link:

  1. Go to the Notes client to set the destination of the link. Open the desired database, view, or document and select Edit, Copy As Link, followed by the type of link you want: Anchor Link, Document Link, View Link, or Database Link.

  2. In Designer, open the properties box for the outline entry.

  3. Set the Type field to Link.

  4. Click on the Paste icon. Your link will be pasted into the outline entry. For confirmation, the type of link will be displayed next to the type field. Note that the value line will contain a reference to your link, but that it will not be editable. Figure 6.3 shows you the result of a document link that has been pasted into the outline entry.

Figure 6.3
The outline entry property box after a document link has been pasted.

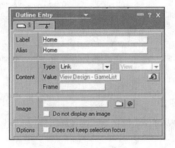

- If you specify Named Element for the outline entry type, you can provide linkage to a page, form, frameset, or view. Follow these steps to use this type of outline entry:

  1. Open the properties box for the outline entry you want to change.

  2. Set the type field to Named Element.

  3. To the right of the Named Element field, select the type of element you want to use. You can select Page, Form, Frameset, or View, Folder, or Navigator.

  4. After you select the type of named element you want to use, you can specify the actual element by selecting it directly or by supplying a formula that will evaluate to the name of the element. If you click on the folder icon, you can directly select the element, and if you click on the @ icon, you can supply a formula. Figure 6.4 shows you the result of clicking on the folder icon. You will see a second dialog box that enables you to again choose the type of object, and then select a specific object from a drop-down list.

- If you specify URL for the outline entry type, you can specify a URL in the Value field. Be sure to specify the complete URL, including the http: at the beginning of the string.

PART

I

CH

6

Figure 6.4
The outline entry
showing Named
Element selection.

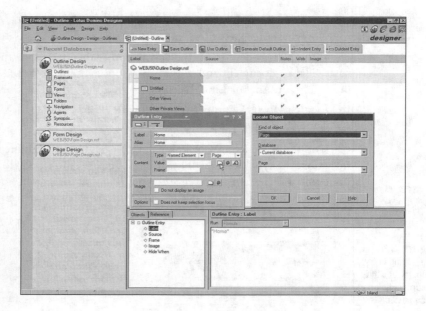

HIDING OUTLINE ENTRIES

You can optionally hide outline entries by using the Entry Hide When tab of the Outline Entry properties box (see Figure 6.5).

Figure 6.5
The Entry Hide When
tab of the Outline
Entry properties box.

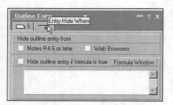

You can hide the entry from Notes 4.6 or later, or you can hide the entry from Web browsers. These options enable you to create conditionally displayed outline entries that display depending on the viewing capabilities of the user. In addition, you can supply a formula for hiding the outline entry. This type of Hide When formula is useful if you want to supply or restrict application capability based on user ID, roles, groups, or other criteria. The outline entry linkage is displayed only under the conditions you specify.

MOVING OUTLINE ENTRIES

Moving an outline entry within the hierarchy is very simple. You just click on the entry and drag it to its new location. You can move entries up or down. You can also indent entries so that they appear as a subsidiary to another outline entry. To indent an entry, click on it and click the Indent Entry action button on the top of the window. Clicking the Outdent Entry action button can outdent an entry that has already been indented.

USING FRAMES AND FRAMESETS

What are framesets, exactly? To answer that question, I'm going to give you some background by describing the HTML definitions of pages, framesets, and frames. You actually don't need all this detail to use the Domino Designer Frameset designer, but I think it will be useful for you to know what Domino is doing behind the scenes for you. After we have covered the background material, I'll return to the Domino Designer interface and show you how to use it.

HTML BACKGROUND FOR FRAMESETS

To describe framesets, let's first start with the definition of a regular HTML page without frames. I cover HTML in much more detail in Chapter 7, "Using Hypertext Markup Language (HTML) for Page Design." To display a regular HTML page, you must specify a document with the following framework:

```
<HTML>
<HEAD>
</HEAD>
<BODY>
     ... Main contents of page here ...
</BODY>
</HTML>
```

With this structure, a single page will be displayed, showing the contents contained within the <BODY> and </BODY> tags.

One of the early observations about Web pages was that frequently they contained two types of information: navigation information and content. The navigation elements are typically on the borders of the screen: left, top, bottom, or sometimes on the right. The content is typically in the middle of the window.

The two types of information have different characteristics: The page content varies from page to page, and the navigation elements are frequently similar or stay constant while the user navigates around the site. It is desirable to have the navigation elements always available, in much the same way as the top menu line of the typical Windows application is always available. From any point within the Web site, you can navigate directly to another place.

Frames and framesets were developed to combine the relatively static navigational elements and the relatively dynamic content. Framesets enable you to define separate frames, such as panes, within a window where one frame can remain visible and unchanged while the contents of the other frame changes. Here is the structure for a frameset-enabled HTML file:

```
<HTML>
<HEAD>
</HEAD>
<FRAMESET>
     ... Frame definitions here ...
</FRAMESET>
</HTML>
```

Notice that the main difference between a regular HTML page and one with frames is that we replace the <BODY> tags with <FRAMESET> tags. You cannot use both the <BODY> tag and the <FRAMESET> tag in the same document. If you include both, the browser will display the first and ignore the second.

In addition to the simple format I've shown, you can optionally include a <NOFRAMES> section for browsers that don't support frames. You can also have *nested framesets*, or framesets within frames. The frameset tag itself is used to allocate space in the window for the various frames, but without specifying the content of the frame, which will be in the <FRAME> tag.

You specify the frame layout and the orientation of a frameset by using either the ROWS or COLS attributes within the frameset. Although you can specify both parameters, it is typically not done. Typically, you will specify only one keyword for a given frameset. It is common, however, to have a column-oriented frameset within a row-oriented frameset and vice versa. Here is an example:

```
<FRAMESET ROWS="100,*,10%">
    ... Frame definitions here ...
</FRAMESET>
```

In this example, I specify three rows, which means that there will be three frames in the frameset. In this case, all the frames will take the entire width of the window because they are row-oriented. There are three separate height specifications. The first means 100 pixels, the last element means that the frame will take 10% of the remaining window height, and the middle element (the asterisk) will take whatever space remains.

Here is a more complex example:

```
<FRAMESET ROWS="100,*,10%">
   <FRAME>
   <FRAMESET COLS="200,*">
      <FRAME>
      <FRAME>
   </FRAMESET>
   <FRAME>
</FRAMESET>
```

I have enhanced the previous example by nesting one frameset within another. You can see the result of this frameset nesting in Figure 6.6.

In this case, the major orientation is row-wise with three rows. Within the middle row, however, I have defined another frameset with two columns. This type of layout, perhaps with different frame proportions, is very common on the Web. In fact, in the Domino Designer, if you indicate you want four frames, this configuration is the default configuration of the four frames.

Framesets define the layout and orientation of frames, such as panes, within a window. The content of each frame is defined with HTML as with a page. In the next section, I show you how you define the frame itself.

Figure 6.6
Nested frameset
definitions.

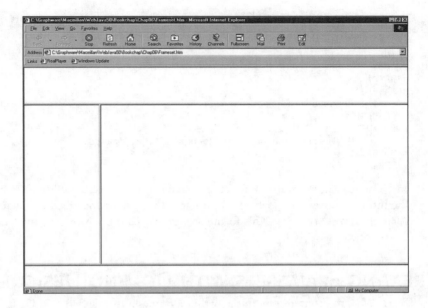

HTML BACKGROUND FOR FRAMES

After you define the structure of your Web page with the <FRAMESET> tags, you can define
the contents of the individual frames with the <FRAME> tag. If you are using regular HTML,
the simplified syntax for the <FRAME> tag is

```
<FRAME SRC="url">
```

Notice that you specify the content via a URL. In particular, the implication is that the
content of a framed page is stored separately from the frame and frameset definitions. This
contrasts with a regular page where the content and structure are stored together. You cannot supply the contents of a frame "inline" with the definition of the <FRAMESET>.

Additional attribute parameters on the <FRAME> tag are NAME, MARGINWIDTH, MARGINHEIGHT,
SCROLLING, and NORESIZE. These attributes enable you to refer to the frame and give additional information about the visible display of the frame. The NAME attribute, for example, is
required when you want to use one frame as the target of a different frame because you
refer to the target by name.

SUPPORTING BROWSERS WITHOUT FRAME CAPABILITY

Frames and framesets were not originally part of the HTML specification. During the use
of the version 3 browsers (Netscape Navigator 3 and Internet Explorer 3), it was very
important to test whether a browser was capable of displaying frames. Today, almost all
browsers support frames, but to be safe, you still might want to code defensively and test
whether the user viewing your Web site can utilize frames.

PART

I

CH

6

To code defensively in HTML, you use the <NOFRAMES> tag. The contents of this tag enable you to specify separate HTML for browsers that do not support frames.

```
<HTML>
<HEAD>
</HEAD>
<FRAMESET>
     ... Frame definitions here ...
</FRAMESET>
<NOFRAMES>
     ... HTML for browsers that do not support frames.
</NOFRAMES>
</HTML>
```

In Domino, you can use an @function called @BrowserInfo to determine whether the browser has frame capability. To use it within one of your formulas, you use @BrowserInfo("Frames"). This formula returns true if the browser supports frames, and false otherwise.

CREATING FRAMESETS WITH DOMINO DESIGNER

In HTML, the content of a frame within a frameset is specified by a URL. The URL points to a file that can contain HTML or perhaps a graphics file, such as a GIF or JPEG file. With Domino, you have many more options because in addition to specifying a simple URL, you can also specify Domino design elements, such as views or documents.

Now that you are familiar with some of the HTML theory behind framesets, let's see how you can use the Domino Designer to create your own framesets without having to drop down to the HTML level.

In Domino Designer, follow these steps to create a frameset:

1. Click on the word Framesets in the Design pane of the Domino Designer. The Work pane will show you a list of existing framesets, if you have any.

2. To create a new frameset, click on the action bar button titled New Frameset. The Create New Frameset dialog box will appear.

3. From the dialog box, first select the number of frames you want to use. You can enter 2, 3, or 4. See Figure 6.7 for a frameset using three frames. This is just an initial setting. In the unusual case that you want to use more than four frames, you can modify the initial configuration by adding and deleting frames. You should be aware, however, that most good graphic designs will not require much more than four frames. Start simply and add complexity later if needed.

4. After you select the number of frames, select the desired layout by clicking on one of the pictures across the top of the dialog box.

5. After you select the layout, click OK. Your frameset will be created (see Figure 6.8).

Figure 6.7
The Create New
Frameset dialog box
with three frames
selected.

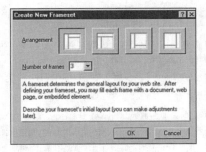

Figure 6.8
A newly created
frameset with three
frames.

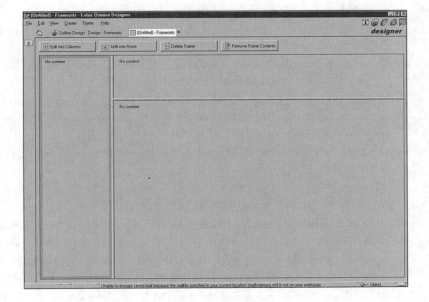

For comparison to our previous HTML introduction, here is the relevant HTML that
Domino Designer will generate for the frameset with a column on the left and two frames
on the right:

```
<FRAMESET COLS="20%,80%">
   <FRAME>
   <FRAMESET ROWS="20%,80%">
      <FRAME>
      <FRAME>
   </FRAMESET>
</FRAMESET>
```

Although Domino will not indent the HTML code, I have done it for clarity. Notice the
similarity to the hand-written HTML code you would otherwise have to write. The
HTML source generated by Domino will vary by browser and by release, so your code
might be slightly different. Also, note that although you create a single Domino frameset
with three frames, Domino will actually generate two nested HTML framesets to get the
desired layout.

PART

I

CH

6

ENHANCING AN EXISTING FRAMESET

After you create your frameset, you can edit the layout by adding or deleting frames. The result of these actions is to change the number of nested framesets and their contents. In Figure 6.8, you see that there are four action bar buttons within the frameset editor. You can use these buttons to change the layout of the frameset.

To create a new frame, you must split one of the existing frames. You can split the frame into either two columns or two rows. The first two action bar buttons accomplish these tasks. By clicking either button, you end up with one additional frame.

Follow these steps to add a frame to an existing frameset:

1. Edit the frameset by double-clicking on the frameset's name in the list of names in the Work pane.
2. After the frameset is open, click within the frame you want to split. A dark gray highlight will show you which frame is currently selected.
3. Click either the Split into Columns or Split into Rows action button. The highlighted frame will turn into two frames, either by columns or by rows. Your new frame has been added.
4. Change the split percentage by highlighting one of the borders between the frames and moving it.

Follow these steps to delete a frame of an existing frameset:

1. Edit the frameset by double-clicking on the frameset's name within the list of names in the Work pane.
2. After the frameset is open, click within the frame you want to delete. A dark gray highlight will show you which frame is currently selected.
3. Click the Delete Frame action button. The highlighted frame will be deleted and merged with one of its neighbors.

SPECIFYING FRAME CONTENTS

As mentioned, in the Domino Designer you have several options for specifying a frame's contents. This gives you a much easier, high-level design paradigm than working directly with HTML. You might want to have some frames store relatively static information and other frames store dynamic content that will vary from page to page. In addition, frames within a frameset can be linked. That is, a click on items in one frame can cause the contents of a different frame to change. This is the essence of many common frame layouts.

On the Web, you will frequently see that the frame on the left contains graphic menu items, and clicking on them causes the main frame on the right to change. In Domino, the left frame can contain an outline as you saw earlier in this chapter, and each outline element can cause a different page to display on the right.

When I was covering outlines earlier in the chapter, I did not discuss the linkage between frames. Now that you know about both framesets and outlines, let's put the concepts together.

USING AN EMBEDDED OUTLINE IN A PAGE

To use an outline, it must be embedded in a page or a form. If you haven't yet read Chapter 3, "Developing Pages with the Domino Designer," you might want to go back and read that chapter.

Most of the time, you will use an outline in conjunction with a frameset, and if so, you will normally want to embed the outline in a page. You will normally use a page rather than a form because the contents of the page containing the outline are usually static. Navigation frames containing outlines do not typically need the dynamic content that a form allows.

Creating an outline and then inserting a page is easy. Here is all you have to do:

1. Create the desired outline with the outline editor. You can use the New Entry action button to add outline entries. See Figure 6.9 for an example.

Figure 6.9
An outline with four outline entries.

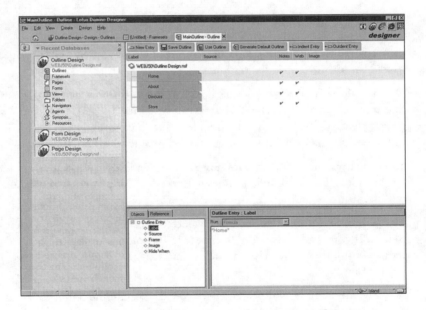

2. After your outline is created, click the Use Outline action button. A new page will be created for you with the outline already embedded. See Figure 6.10 for the resulting page from the outline.

That's it. All you have to do is click one button: A new page is created for you and the embedded outline is automatically added to this new page. Cool, eh?

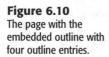

Figure 6.10
The page with the embedded outline with four outline entries.

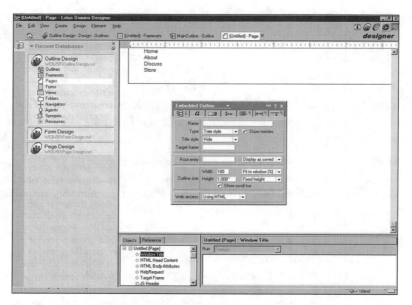

After the page is created, you can edit it normally. You also need to set the properties for your embedded outline. As you can see from the figure, there are many properties that you can adjust for the embedded outline.

On the Info page of the properties box, you should specify the name for the embedded outline control and also its type. The type can be either Tree style or Flat. When you use Tree style, you see the familiar indented folders. Flat means that when you drill down one level in the outline, the new level replaces the original level in the display.

You can check the Show Twisties box to show triangles to the left of outline entries that can be expanded. The Title style enables you to either hide or show the database title above the outline.

The Target Frame entry is one place where you can specify how you want to link your frames. If your outline is going to appear in the left frame and the contents in the right frame, within the properties box you can indicate that you want the target frame to be the right frame.

Actually, there are several places where you can specify the target frame. In addition to the Embedded Outline dialog box, you can also define the target frame within the Outline Entry properties dialog box and in the Frame properties dialog box. How does Domino reconcile these multiple definitions? The general rule is that the smallest design element will have priority. In other words, an Outline Entry's definition will override the Embedded Outline definition, which will in turn override the definition found in the Frame properties. This makes sense because you might have several links within a frame, and each one can use a different target frame.

Normally, as I've mentioned, you should start simply with just a few frames and use a consistent design. In this way, you won't have to worry about conflicting definitions. You can, for example, just define the target frame at the frame level and not use the definition of the embedded outline at all.

USING A PAGE IN A FRAMESET

After you generate your outline page, you can edit it normally as you would edit any other page. You can add other items or move the outline around on the page. After you edit the page and like the way it looks, you can then include it in your frameset. The outline page will be used to navigate and will cause the contents of linked pages to change.

Here is what you do to include your page within your frameset:

1. Click on Framesets in the Design pane to see a list of your framesets.

2. Double-click on the frameset name in the list in the work area to open the desired frameset.

3. Select the frame you want to use for your page by clicking within the frame. In our example, we use the left frame.

Tip

> You should have a naming convention for your frames so you can keep track of their contents. A very simple naming convention is to use the frame's position as its name. In my examples, I use the name `left` for the left frame, `top` for the top-right frame, and `right` for the bottom-right (main) frame. You can, of course, use different conventions, but naming the frames with some indication of their location allows you to easily remember when you see that something is going to appear in the left or right frame.

4. After you select the frame, change the content type to Named Element and Page.

5. Click on the folder icon. This brings up a dialog box, and you can choose your page from the list. Click OK. Change the default target to be the right frame (see Figure 6.11).

Now we have created a frameset with three frames. We use the left frame for navigation. In the left frame, we included a page that in turn includes an outline. When a user clicks on the outline entries in the left pane, the outline will control what will be displayed in the target (right) frame.

It seems a little complicated at first because you must be familiar with outlines, pages, and framesets. When you put them together, you can easily create framesets that work wonderfully.

Figure 6.11
An outline page set as content for the left frame with the target in the right frame.

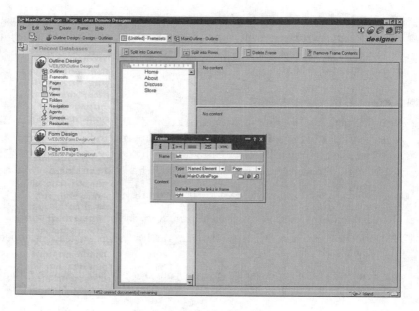

DESIGNING NAVIGATORS

Domino navigators have been around since release 4, so they should be familiar to developers who have worked with that release. If you have a Web development background, you can think of navigators as imagemaps. A typical navigator contains a background image with hotspots, and you can program the hotspots to perform various actions. There are several built-in simple actions you can use or you can program more complex actions by using either the @formula language or LotusScript. Note that JavaScript and Java are not available for use with navigators.

Here is a list of the built-in simple actions you can associate with a navigator hotspot:

- Open another navigator
- Open a view or folder
- Alias a folder
- Open a link (document, view, or database)
- Open a URL

As mentioned, you can also use the @formula language or LotusScript to program custom actions.

To create a new navigator, follow these steps:

1. Click on Navigators in the Design pane. The work area will contain a list of the existing navigators, if any.

2. Click on the New Navigator action bar button. Your new navigator is created.

3. You will then be placed in edit mode within the navigator graphical editor. In the navigator properties box, you should ensure that the checkbox Web Browser Compatible is enabled (this is the default). This property ensures that Web browsers will be able to view your navigator.

GRAPHIC BACKGROUNDS: ARE THEY FOR YOU?

Before drawing any objects onto your new navigator, decide whether you want to use a graphic background. Use a graphic background if you have at your disposal an image that contains areas that the user would immediately identify as discrete objects that may be selected to initiate an action. For example, the image of a bookcase may be used as a graphic background. Each shelf, or book, on the graphic background may be used as a link for a particular view in the database. Another obvious example of a graphic background is a map on which particular regions can be used to initiate actions.

Tip

To remove a graphic background, select Design, Remove Graphic Background.

DRAWING NAVIGATOR OBJECTS

After you choose to insert a graphic background (or decide to skip this step), you can insert navigator objects. Navigator objects include the following:

- Standard shapes, including rectangles, rounded rectangles, ellipses, lines (referred to as polylines), and polygons—All these shapes, with the exception of lines, are automatically filled with a user-defined color. Polylines are not supported on the Web.

- Hotspots, in the form of rectangles, circles, or polygons—A *hotspot* is simply an outline that can be used to identify a particular region of a graphic background. Because hotspots are only outlines, they are never filled with a color. Hotspots can be used, for example, to outline regions such as cities on a map or parts of a picture.

- Text boxes, enabling text to be displayed anywhere on a navigator—You can change the font, size, and color of the text.

- Two varieties of buttons—Graphic buttons, which are essentially rectangular pictures obtained from the Clipboard, and Hotspot buttons, which are standard buttons that contain a single line of text.

PART

I

CH

6

You can create objects using either the Create menu or the second set of SmartIcons that represent various objects that can be created. The easiest way to create an object is through the use of these SmartIcons. To enable SmartIcons, select File, Preferences, SmartIcon Settings from the menu. Enable the Icon Bar option and click OK. See Figure 6.12 for a sample navigator.

Figure 6.12
A sample navigator with a rectangle and an ellipse.

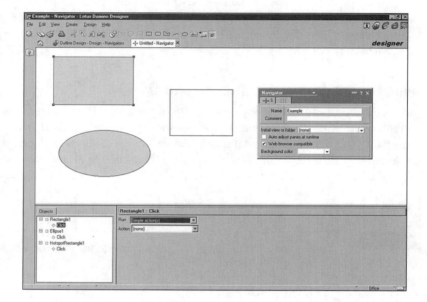

The first click of a particular object on the SmartIcon bar enables object-creation mode, represented by a crosshair cursor when the mouse pointer is over the navigator Design pane. The second click of the same SmartIcon object turns off creation mode and enables object-manipulation mode. In this mode, you may manipulate objects that have been drawn; they may be moved, resized, or deleted.

After an object has been selected, drawing it is fairly straightforward—especially to those already familiar with other drawing programs. Here are some quick drawing tips:

- To draw an ellipse, rectangle, rounded rectangle, hotspot rectangle, or hotspot circle, move the cursor to the anchor point in the navigator, and then click and hold down the mouse button. With the mouse button pressed down, move the mouse pointer to size the object. Release the mouse button to complete your drawing.

- To draw a polygon, hotspot polygon, or polyline, move the cursor to the first point, and then click once on the mouse button to begin your drawing. Each subsequent, single, mouse-button click adds a new point to your polygon. To finish drawing a polygon-type object, double-click the mouse button. For polygons, a double-click automatically draws a line from the last point to the first point, closing the bounds of the object.

- To move several objects simultaneously, hold down the Shift key and click once on each object that must be moved. When the last object is selected, continue holding the Shift key, click the left mouse button, and move the mouse to relocate all selected objects. Release the mouse button when the new positions are satisfactory.

- To draw a circle or a square, hold down the Shift key, and then begin drawing an ellipse or rectangle. The Shift key acts to constrain the object to a symmetrical pattern rather than a freely sized shape. This trick also works after an object is drawn, when one of these objects is resized.

After you draw an object, you can modify properties for each object using the properties dialog box. To make the properties box visible, click with the right mouse button over any object, and then select Object Properties.

Each object will have different properties that pertain to it. For example, a text object will enable the selection of a font and point size. However, the HiLite tab applies to all navigator objects (see Figure 6.13).

Figure 6.13
The Hotspot
Rectangle
properties box.

For objects that will trigger events, two options are available to highlight the navigator for the user. These options are not available in a Web browser. If you are using the Notes client, however, one or both of the options presented in this screen should be selected:

- Highlight When Touched—Enabling this option draws the border for the object, as specified by the Highlight Outline Width and Highlight Outline Color settings, when the user moves the mouse over the navigator object. This option should typically be selected for hotspot polygons, hotspot circles, or hotspot rectangles.

- Highlight When Clicked—Enabling this option flashes the border for the object, as specified by the Highlight Outline Width and Highlight Outline Color settings, when the user clicks on the navigator object.

PART

I

CH

6

Tip

Do you see a navigator in another database that you want to use in your database? No problem! Navigators can be cut and pasted to and from databases just like forms and views. Simply highlight the source navigator in Design Mode and select Edit, Copy (Ctrl+C). Next, open the destination database, select Navigator from the Design folder (from Design mode), and then select Edit, Paste (Ctrl+V).

PROGRAMMING THE Click EVENT

After you have drawn navigator objects, you must determine how an object will react to a Click event, the only runtime event for navigator objects.

When the user clicks on a navigator object, one of the following may occur:

- A simple action can be initiated, enabling common navigator functions, such as opening a new view, to be developed with no programming effort.

- A formula can execute, for those who are comfortable with Notes formulas.

- Script might execute, enabling simple or complex LotusScript statements to be executed. Note that you cannot choose JavaScript.

- Nothing. Objects do not necessarily have to initiate one of the previous actions. They can be included in the navigator for artistic reasons alone.

To designate an appropriate action for navigator objects, first select the object whose actions need to be defined. Next, in the Programmer's pane, select the programming method you want to use for this object (Simple Action, Formula, or LotusScript).

In many cases, simple actions are the most appropriate way to deal with navigator events. The five simple actions available for each object include the following:

- Open Another Navigator—Use this choice to link one navigator to another. When selected, a combobox will appear containing a list of available navigators.

- Open a View or Folder—This option is used to display a new view or folder in the View pane. When selected, a combobox will appear containing a list of available views.

- Alias a Folder—This particularly useful option does two things. First, it switches the View pane to the folder specified. Second, it enables objects from other views and folders to be dragged and dropped into the navigator object itself. When selected, a combobox will appear containing a list of available folders.

- Open a Link—This choice enables a document, view, or database link to be opened. When selected, a button will appear that will enable a link to be pasted. First, however, you must switch to a database, document, or view; then choose Edit, Copy as Link for the appropriate object. After a link is copied to the Clipboard, switch back to the navigator designer and click on the Paste Link button.

- Open URL—This choice links to an arbitrary URL on the World Wide Web. When you select this option, an additional button appears: Enter URL. Click this button and enter the URL that you want to link to the navigator. Be sure to remember to include the http:// at the beginning of your URL.

USING HOTSPOTS WITH AND WITHOUT NAVIGATORS

You don't have to use a navigator to use hotspots. In fact, you can create hotspots on pages and forms as well as on navigators. Hotspots created on pages and forms have slightly different capabilities than hotspots created on navigators. Here is a summary of the differences:

Navigator Hotspots

- Can open another navigator, view, or folder
- Can alias a folder (not available on the Web)
- Can open a document, view, or database link
- Can open an arbitrary URL
- Can execute an @formula or LotusScript program
- Can use only a frame's target specification

Hotspots on pages or forms

- Can open document, view, database, or anchor links
- Can open named elements: pages, forms, framesets, or views
- Can open an arbitrary URL
- Can specify a particular frame to use as a target
- Can be used for text pop-ups (not available on the Web)
- Can be displayed and used as buttons
- Can be used as formula pop-ups (not available on the Web)
- Can be used as an action hotspot, which can utilize @formulas, LotusScript, JavaScript, or simple actions (simple actions are not available on the Web)

As you can see from the two lists, hotspots directly on pages or forms are just as powerful—or perhaps more so—than hotspots that are created on navigators.

Before release 5 of Notes and Domino, there were no pages, and some items could not be placed directly on a form, so navigators were very important. With the advent of release 5, however, it might be easier to create your navigational images directly on a page or form. This will simplify your design and reduce the number of different design elements you need to use.

You can use hotspots directly on pages and forms in Domino Designer. When you use a hotspot directly on a page or form, it is associated with text. You can also directly create an image on a page or form, and then create hotspots on the image. Let's first investigate the various forms of text hotspots.

LINK HOTSPOTS

As mentioned previously, there are several different types of hotspots you can use on a page or form. The first type of hotspot is the link hotspot. This type of hotspot enables you to specify a document, view, database, or anchor. Follow these steps to create a link hotspot:

1. First, open the target of your link. For example, open the specific document, view, or database you want as the destination in the Notes client. From the menu, select Edit, Copy As Link, and then Anchor Link, Document Link, View Link, or Database Link depending on your preference. This copies the link to the Clipboard. Alternatively, you could open a design element in the Domino Designer. You can use either a named element or database link from within the designer. Again, from the menu, select Edit, Copy As Link, followed by your choice.

> **Note**
>
> Anchor links work differently than the other types of links. Anchor links cannot be created with the Domino Designer. They can be created only in the Notes client and only within documents that have been previously saved to the database. After you have created and saved the document, an anchor link can be created within a rich text field. Move the cursor to the location where you would like your anchor link, and then from the menus select Edit, Copy As Link, Anchor Link. The Copy As Link command will actually create the anchor link.

2. Return to the page or form that you want to contain the hotspot. Highlight the text you want to serve as your link.

3. From the menu, select Create, Hotspot, Link Hotspot.

4. The HotSpot Resource Link properties box should appear (see Figure 6.14).

Figure 6.14
The HotSpot Resource Link properties box.

5. If you copied a document link, the link might automatically appear. If you copied a design element, you might need to click the Paste icon, which you can do in any case. The link from the Clipboard will be pasted, and the type of your link should change to the type of link you copied to the Clipboard. Your link is complete.

You can also change some of the link properties directly from the properties box. For example, you can specify a URL rather than a document link as the hotspot destination. In this case, manually change the type of link to URL, and then type the URL into the Value field of the dialog box.

Finally, you can specify a frame where you want the result of the hotspot to appear. If you don't specify a frame, the link will appear within the same frame as the hotspot unless a frameset target frame overrides it.

HOTSPOT TEXT POP-UPS

Hotspot text pop-ups are very useful for supplying help information. You can arrange it so that helpful text will appear either when the user's mouse hovers over the hotspot or when the user clicks on the hotspot (see Figure 6.15).

Figure 6.15
The HotSpot Pop-up properties box.

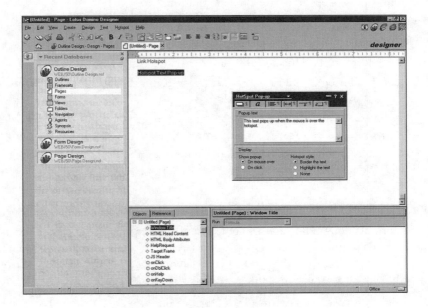

Follow these steps to create a hotspot text pop-up:

1. Add the document text to a page or form.

2. Highlight the text that will be used to trigger the hotspot.

3. Select Create, Hotspot, Text Pop-up.

4. The HotSpot Pop-up properties box will appear. Enter the pop-up text. Choose whether the text should appear on a user mouse-over or on a click by selecting the appropriate radio button.

5. Show a border around the hotspot or use a highlight color by checking the appropriate box.

Tip

Hotspot text pop-ups do not work in Web browsers, only in the Notes client.

HOTSPOT BUTTONS

Buttons that are displayed on a page or form are called *hotspot buttons*. You can program the action of the button using one of four different methods. You can use a simple action, an

@formula, a LotusScript program, or a JavaScript program. Simple actions enable you to assign values to fields, copy documents, send or reply to email, and complete many other common preprogrammed actions. If you use one of the other methods, you have the full power of the programming language at your disposal.

Follow these steps to create a hotspot button:

1. Move the cursor on the page or form to the location where you want your button to appear.

2. Select Create, Hotspot, Button.

3. The Button properties box will appear. Enter the label that you want to appear on the button in the Button label field.

4. In the Programmer's pane, select the language you want to use. The default is formula language, but you can choose Simple Action, LotusScript, or JavaScript also.

5. After you choose your language, you can use the Programmer's pane to enter your action.

FORMULA POP-UP HOTSPOTS

A formula pop-up hotspot has some characteristics of a text hotspot and a hotspot button. Formula pop-up hotspots must be associated with text on the form or page. When the user clicks on the hotspot, the formula is executed. Note that the Mouse Over option is not available for formula hotspots.

Follow these steps to create a formula hotspot:

1. Move the cursor on the page or form to the location where you want your formula hotspot to appear. Highlight the text you want to use to trigger the formula.

2. Select Create, Hotspot, Formula Pop-up.

3. The Hotspot Pop-up properties box will appear. You can change attributes of the text, such as the font or color.

4. In the Programmer's pane, the formula language is automatically selected for you. You cannot use LotusScript or JavaScript for a formula hotspot.

5. In the Programmer's pane, enter the formula that you want to execute if the user clicks on the hotspot text.

> **Note**
> Formula pop-ups do not work in Web browsers, only in the Notes client. Use an action hotspot instead.

ACTION HOTSPOTS

An action hotspot is much more powerful than a formula pop-up hotspot and also has the advantage that it works in browsers. With an action hotspot, you can specify your action with one of four different languages: Simple Action, Formula language, LotusScript, or JavaScript. When the user clicks on the hotspot, the action you supply is executed. Note that the Mouse Over option is not available for action hotspots, but if you use JavaScript, you can specify a JavaScript program for the onMouseOver event. Also, simple actions are not supported on the Web.

Follow these steps to create an action hotspot:

1. Move the cursor on the page or form to the location where you want your formula hotspot to appear. Highlight the text you want to use to trigger the formula.

2. Select Create, Hotspot, Action Hotspot.

3. The Action Hotspot properties box will appear. You can change attributes of the text, such as the font or color, and you can specify a frame for the target if required.

4. In the Programmer's pane, select the language you want to use. The default is formula language, but you can choose Simple Action, LotusScript, or JavaScript also.

5. In the Programmer's pane, enter the formula or other program that you want to execute if the user clicks on the hotspot text. If you choose JavaScript, you can program several mouse actions. I cover JavaScript in much more detail in Part II, "Programming the Client with HTML and JavaScript."

HOTSPOTS ON IMAGEMAPS

You can define hotspots on imagemaps in a manner similar to the way you work with hotspots on navigators. Imagemaps, also known as pictures, can be placed on a page in one of two ways. You can import an image file from the file system or you can use a shared image, which is an image that is already stored within a database in the shared image library. The terms *image*, *picture*, and *imagemap* are used almost synonymously. The only difference in meaning is that an image is typically called an imagemap after it has one or more hotspots on it. So you can call it either an image with hotspots or an imagemap.

Follow these steps to import an image from the file system:

1. Open the page or form you want to use. Move the cursor to the location where you want your image to appear.

2. Select Create, Picture. A dialog box showing the file system will appear.

3. You can navigate through the file system looking for the image to import. You can import the following types of files: BMP, CGM, GIF, JPEG, Lotus PIC, PCX, and TIFF 5.0.

4. Find the file you want to import and click the Import button. Your image will be imported.

Follow these steps to use an image that is already within your shared image resources:

1. Open the page or form you want to use. Move the cursor to the location where you want your image to appear.

PART
I

CH
6

2. Select Create, Image Resource. A dialog box will appear showing you all the images that are in your shared image library.

3. Select the desired image from the list of images and click OK. Your image will appear on your page or form.

After you create an image on your page or form through either of the methods, you can add a hotspot to the image. Hotspots on an image can be one of three shapes: polygon, circle, or rectangle. To create a hotspot on an image:

1. First place the image on the page or form using one of the techniques described previously.

2. Open the Picture info properties box (see Figure 6.16).

Figure 6.16
An imagemap with one circular and two rectangular hotspots.

Hotspots —

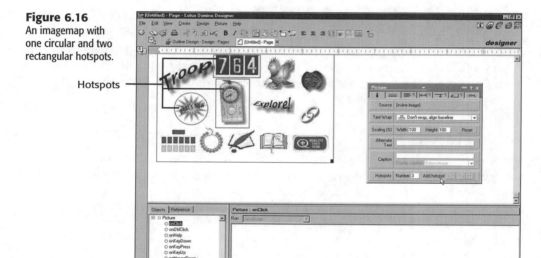

3. Click on one of the pictures in the bottom row at the right for polygon, circle, or rectangle.

4. Move your cursor into the image area. It should now appear as a cross.

5. Click on one corner of the area where you want the hotspot to be located and drag the mouse to the other corner. You will see a rubber-band shape of the hotspot area. You can adjust the location and size of the hotspot area by clicking and dragging on the handles for the shape, which look like dots. To move the hotspot shape, click and drag it.

6. After you place the hotspot on the image, you can specify an action to be taken when the user clicks on the hotspot. You can choose a link, a named element link, or a URL. A link can be a document, view, database, or anchor link. A named element will link to a design element, such as a page, form, frameset, or view. You specify the type within the Hotspot properties box.

7. You can optionally also specify an action to take in the Click event for the hotspot. The Click event can be programmed as a Simple Action, Formula, LotusScript, or JavaScript program. Simple actions are not supported on the Web.

USING EMBEDDED ELEMENTS ON A PAGE OR FORM

In defining a page, you can embed several different types of elements. In addition to outlines, which I discussed in a previous section, you can embed navigators, views, folder panes, and a date picker in pages. On forms, you can embed all those elements as well as a group scheduler and file upload control. To embed one of the following design elements, select Create, Embedded Element, and then choose one of the embedded element types. Here is a synopsis of these embedded elements:

- Embedded Outlines—These enable you to specify navigation elements for your Web site or database. Use the outline editor to edit the outline entries. Each outline entry can serve as a link to a page, form, or URL within a database. Embedded outlines are especially useful when used with framesets.

- Embedded Views—You can embed a view on a page. You embed a view so you can control the formatting of the view display. When a view is embedded on a page or form, the user will not see the standard view navigation elements. One of the important properties of an embedded view is the capability to specify the use of a Java applet for Web browsers. You can enable the Java applet in the embedded view properties box.

- Embedded Navigator—When you embed a navigator, the page or form refers to the navigator design element. Navigators can include graphics and hotspot definitions. If you change a navigator, all references to the navigator will get the changed graphics.

- Embedded Import Navigator—When you choose Import Navigator, the graphical design elements of the navigator are imported into the page. After the design elements have been imported, you can edit them directly on the page. Note that after you have imported the navigator, it is no longer linked to the original navigator definition.

- Embedded Folder Pane—The embedded folder pane enables you to have a Folder pane embedded within a page or form of your own design. The Folder pane is the pane that appears in the upper-left pane when you are looking at a view or folder. It contains a hierarchical listing of the views and folders of the database. Embedding this pane in your own page or form allows the user to navigate to one of the existing views or folders easily. Embedded Folder panes work only when the page or form is rendered to HTML (either within the Notes client or a Web browser).

- Date Picker—The Date Picker works only on the Notes client; it will not work in a Web browser. If you choose this item, it will display a calendar. This object works in conjunction with a Calendar view in another frame within the same frameset. If you insert a date picker in one frame and a Calendar view in another, they will be linked automatically. The user can choose a date on the date picker, and the Calendar view will move to that date automatically.

- Group Scheduler—The group scheduler can be embedded only on forms, not on pages. One reason is that the refresh for the group scheduler can be controlled by a reserved field named $GroupScheduleRefreshMode. Pages cannot have fields, so this option is not available. The refresh mode enables you to control what happens when the user clicks the refresh (F9) key. Because there may be many users and many databases to search for updates, you can control how much detail Domino will search upon refresh. The Group Scheduler is not available on the Web.

- File Upload Control—The file upload control enables Web users to attach files to documents. To use it, you embed the control on a form. When the form is displayed to a user, a text field and a browse button appear, and the user can enter a filename or browse for a file to be uploaded. Note that for this control to work, the Domino server administrator must define a temp directory. If a temp directory is not defined, the attachment will not be uploaded. Also, the file upload control will work only in a Web browser, not the Notes client.

NAMING CONVENTIONS FOR EMBEDDED ELEMENTS

By default, Domino will display a view to a Web browser user with a default format. You can see an example of this format in Figure 6.17.

Figure 6.17
The Default View format in a Web browser.

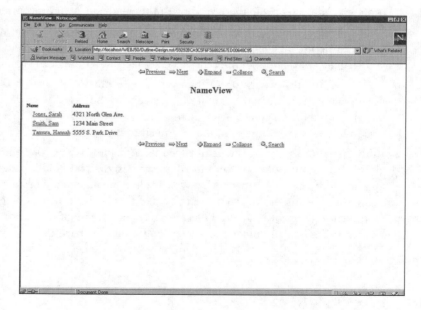

Although this formatting is functional, it is not particularly aesthetically pleasing. The top and bottom of the default view formatting allow the user to navigate, expand, collapse the view if categorized, and to display the search panel.

You might want to control the default formatting for views displayed in your application. To create this default formatting, you must first create a page or form with an embedded view. Give this page or view the name $$ViewTemplateDefault. When Domino displays any view, it will use your template instead of the standard default formatting. Note that if you override Domino's default, you must supply your own view navigational features.

To control view navigation for an embedded view, you must use the following @Commands:

@Command([ViewPageDown])

@Command([ViewPageUp])

@Command([ViewExpandAll])

@Command([ViewCollapseAll])

@Command([ViewShowSearchBar])

You can attach the commands to navigational elements of your page or form.

If you want to have even finer-grained control over your views, you can create a form or page for each view in your database. To associate a form or page with a particular view, use the following name for the form or view: $$ViewTemplate for viewname. For example, suppose you have a view named Addresses. To create an associated form, you should name it $$ViewTemplate for Addresses. Then, any reference to display the Addresses view will use the associated form and its embedded view. Any view that does not have an associated named form or page will use the default template, if one exists.

You can also associate a form or page with a navigator using naming similar to views. The default navigator page or form is called $$NavigatorTemplateDefault. When associating a specific form or view to the navigator, use the name $$NavigatorTemplate for navigatorname.

PUTTING IT ALL TOGETHER: OUTLINES, VIEWS, FRAMESETS, NAVIGATORS, AND BEYOND

Notes release 5 provides you with a rich set of tools for presenting applications to users in both the Notes client and Web browsers. It is easy to become confused about which design element to choose, so I'll try to bring all these concepts together in this section.

When you present an interface to the user, there are several important considerations, including content, layout, and navigation. These are not separate concepts; in fact, they should join seamlessly to form the user interface.

You provide basic content to the user on pages or forms. If you want to allow users to provide feedback, you must use a form. A page is a read-only design element that the user can view, but into which the user cannot enter any input (unless you manually code HTML and JavaScript). Pages are suitable if you have a small number to be displayed to the user. Forms are useful if you want to have more of a database-driven design with potentially hundreds or thousands of documents shown to the user within the form. Pages and forms are also containers that can house embedded elements, such as views, navigators, outlines, and so forth. Pages are typically used when you want to solely include outlines or navigators. You can provide basic layout within a page by just editing the content of a page and placing the elements where you want them to appear.

More complex layouts are achieved by using framesets. Frames within a frameset can contain documents, URLs, pages, forms, views, or other framesets. For most good designs, you won't need more than four or five frames, and you should typically start your frameset design simply. The content in one frame can cause changes in another frame. It is very common to have navigational elements (such as an outline in a page) in one frame, and when the user clicks in the navigation frame the content of a separate frame (the target) is changed.

The last type of design element is the navigational element. In this category are outlines, views, imagemaps, and navigators. A view is the traditional Notes navigational element, and it enables the user to navigate among documents within a database. Each outline entry within an outline performs a similar purpose but is much more powerful. With outline entries, you can navigate to URLs, pages, and forms as well as documents. A navigator is a design element that enables you to draw graphical items and create hotspots. It is a standalone design element and is typically included in a page or form. Thus, it can be created once and used in multiple locations. An imagemap is created and directly associated with a specific page or form. It is similar to a navigator but is not an independent design element. You can create hotspots on imagemaps and link them to pages, forms, or URLs.

CHAPTER REVIEW

1. Explain the purpose of an outline. Can you use the same outline on more than one page or form? Why would you want to do this?

2. Create a frameset using the Domino Designer that has four frames. There should be a top row that goes across the entire window. In the middle should be two frames, left and right. At the bottom of the window should be another frame that goes across the entire window. Examine the HTML that is generated by Domino for this frameset.

3. Create a frameset with HTML that specifies both the ROWS and COLS attribute at the same time. What kind of frameset does this generate? Why would this configuration not be typically used?

4. Create a frameset with two frames, a left frame and a right frame. In the left frame create a page with an embedded outline. Create three different outline entries for the left frame. When clicked, each outline entry in the left frame should display a different page in the right frame.

5. Create a frameset with two frames, a top frame and a bottom frame. The top frame should contain a form with an embedded outline control with three entries. Each of the three entries should be for a different URL. When the outline entry is selected, the URL will appear in the bottom frame. The top frame should also have an input field and a button. In the input field the user should be able to enter an arbitrary URL address and click the button to show the URL in the bottom frame.

6. Create a page that displays an imagemap. Select any picture you like, import it, and use it as the background. Create hotspots on the imagemap. Each hotspot should open a different URL.

7. Create a frameset with two frames, a left frame and a right frame. The left frame should contain a page with an outline. There should be four entries in the outline. Two of the entries should show URL Web pages in the right frame. One of the entries should show a view in the right frame. The final entry should link to another database and show its opening page in the right frame.

PROGRAMMING THE CLIENT WITH HTML AND JAVASCRIPT

CHAPTER 7

USING HYPERTEXT MARKUP LANGUAGE (HTML) FOR PAGE DESIGN

In this chapter

What Is Hypertext Markup Language (HTML)?

HTML has now become the *lingua-franca* of the World Wide Web, and is one of the reasons for the Web's ubiquitous nature. By standardizing on a language that can be used by a variety of Web servers and browsers, just about anyone can access information contained just about anywhere on the Internet. Basically, Web servers store or generate information using HTML and send it over the Internet, and Web browsers are able to receive HTML and display it to the end user.

HTML is a language that is used to "mark up" text. That is, it is used to add element tags around content to define the way the text is displayed. It is based on a similar language, the Standard Generalized Markup Language (SGML), which was developed originally to standardize word processing documents.

HTML has undergone several revisions, but the version most frequently used and supported on the Web now is version 4.0. Both Microsoft and Netscape support many of the features of 4.0, but there are some exceptions in each browser. In addition to supporting most of the standard's features, both browsers also support a large number of extensions. It is important to realize that the languages supported by the browsers differ because if you use some of these HTML extension features, your Web page might not display properly in all Web browsers.

Why bother studying HTML at all in this book about Domino, Java, and JavaScript? As I mentioned, HTML is used by Web servers to create and send information to Web browsers. The Domino Web server is no exception. In fact, there is a module in the Domino server that converts Domino forms, pages, and views into HTML so that it can be sent to Web browsers.

The fact that Domino database forms and views must be converted to HTML is the most fundamental reason why some features are available in the Notes client, but not in Web browsers. Fundamentally, because Web browsers are receiving and rendering HTML to the end user, any limitations of HTML will manifest themselves as restrictions on the Web to features available in the Notes client.

I want to describe HTML in enough depth in this book that you will understand its capabilities and limitations. I don't discuss every feature of HTML, but I describe the fundamentals of HTML and how Domino uses HTML to render Domino databases. In particular, I don't explain cascading style sheets (CSS), even though this is an important part of HTML. To explore HTML in more depth, you should obtain a good reference text on HTML. The topic can literally fill an entire book. For additional information, refer to *Special Edition Using HTML 4, Sixth Edition*, by Molly Holzschlag, which describes HTML, CSS, and many other HTML-related topics.

In this chapter I'll show you how to manually create your own HTML as well as give you some information on how Domino generates HTML when displaying information from a Domino database.

BASIC HTML SYNTAX

Let's first take a look at fundamental HTML syntax. HTML is made up of elements. Each element typically has a start tag, contents, and an end tag. An element's start tag and end tag are both enclosed within angle brackets, which are the less-than and greater-than symbols on the keyboard. The name within the start tag is also the element's name. The syntax for HTML elements is very simple. In its basic form the syntax is

```
<start-tag> element contents </end-tag>
```

The HTML specification defines the names of the elements and the structure of an HTML document, that is, the ways that the elements can be nested and used together. Here is an example of a header element:

```
<H1>Introduction</H1>
```

You can see in this example that the beginning and end element tags are the same except for the forward slash. A more complex tag sometimes has attributes. The syntax using attributes is

```
<start-tag attr1="value1" attr2="value2" ... attrn="valuen"> element
➥contents </end-tag>
```

The following is an example of an element with attributes:

```
<A HREF="http://www.gwcorp.com">Visit my web site by clicking here.</A>
```

In this example, you see that the attribute is called HREF and its contents are specified within the double quotes. The content for this element is shown between the beginning and ending tags. Capitalization in the tag names and attribute names is ignored and you can enter them in lower- or uppercase, although by convention, tags and attributes are usually shown in uppercase.

ELEMENTS AND TAGS

In the HTML specification, there is a distinction between elements and tags. There are two types of tags: start tags and end tags. They are the items enclosed in brackets and denote the start and end of the element. The element itself is composed of the start and end tags and the content within the tags. In an HTML document, an element can be present even if no corresponding tags are specified in the markup. For example, the HEAD element is always present, but the markup might not contain the <HEAD> or </HEAD> tags. If they are not supplied, a default element is used.

HTML DOCUMENT STRUCTURE

The basic structure of an HTML document is actually fairly simple. To conform to the standard, the document must contain the following elements:

```
<!DOCTYPE>
<HTML>
```

PART

II

CH

7

```
<HEAD>
    <TITLE> document title </TITLE>
</HEAD>
<BODY>
</BODY>
</HTML>
```

If you are defining a document that contains frames then the document structure is the following:

```
<!DOCTYPE>
<HTML>
    <HEAD>
        <TITLE> document title </TITLE>
    </HEAD>
    <FRAMESET>
    </FRAMESET>
</HTML>
```

We have just substituted the `<FRAMESET>` element for the `<BODY>` element. You can also refer to Chapter 6, "Using Outlines, Framesets, and Navigators," for more information on using framesets with Domino Designer.

HTML COMMENTS

A comment in HTML can be included anywhere in an HTML document where an element appears. You cannot include a comment inside the definition (that is, within the angle brackets) of another element. The syntax for a comment follows:

```
<!-- Your comment goes here.-->
```

Comments cannot be nested because the first occurrence of `-->` will terminate the comment.

SPECIAL CHARACTERS

The HTTP header is supplied by the server to the Web browser. In it, there are two key pieces of information: the type of content and the character set used. You might have seen an HTTP header. The following is an example:

```
Content type: text/html; charset: ISO-8859-1
```

The content type is one of many defined MIME types. The character set defines the encoding of the characters used on the Web page. To handle certain characters that are used as metacharacters within the Web pages, you can use symbolic names for characters. For example, the less-than and greater-than symbols are metacharacters used to enclose HTML tags, so if you want to use a less-than sign within your page, you must use the symbolic name. Symbolic names are officially called character entity references and begin with an ampersand (&) and end with a semicolon (;). Table 7.1 shows a few examples.

TABLE 7.1 SOME CHARACTER ENTITY REFERENCES

Symbolic Name	Character	Meaning
&lt;	<	Less-than
&gt;	>	Greater-than
&amp;	&	Ampersand
&quot;	"	Double quote
		Non-breaking space

The non-breaking space may be used to separate two words that you would like to remain together.

HTML VERSION INFORMATION

A line containing version information should be at the beginning of each HTML document. The document type is specified with a <!DOCTYPE> declaration. The document type declaration is required to be valid HTML, but it is frequently omitted. The declaration specifies that the document is, in fact, HTML as opposed to XML or some other related standard. If it is specified, it should be on the first line in the document. Here is the syntax for an HTML 4.0 document:

```
<!DOCTYPE HTML PUBLIC "-//W3C//DTD HTML 4.0 [specificationlevel]//
➥languagecode" ["specificationURI"]>
```

The *specificationlevel* is optional and can be one of the following: Strict, Transitional, and Frameset. If you omit the *specificationlevel*, Strict is assumed. The *languagecode* is used to specify the national language used. EN is used to signify English. The *specificationURI* is a Uniform Resource Identifier that identifies the document type declaration (DTD) for the document type. Here is an example:

```
<!DOCTYPE HTML PUBLIC "-//W3C//DTD HTML 4.0//EN">
```

This document declaration indicates that the document conforms to the Strict HTML 4.0 specification level and uses the English language. Here are the implications of the levels:

- Strict—Does not contain any deprecated elements. Deprecated elements are outdated and might become obsolete in future versions of HTML.

- Transitional—Includes everything at the Strict level and also includes deprecated elements. Normally if you include a DOCTYPE specification you will want to use the Transitional level unless you are using frames.

- Frameset—Includes everything at the Transitional level plus elements supporting frames.

Note that Domino does not typically generate a <!DOCTYPE> element for HTML files. <!DOCTYPE> is required for parsing XML files, however, so in the future you might see this element in wider use. An XML <!DOCTYPE> specification will be different, of course, from its HTML counterpart.

THE HTML ELEMENT

The <HTML> tag is a required element of an HTML document. Most browsers, however, are very tolerant and will properly display an HTML document even if there is no HTML element. All other elements within your document are enclosed between the <HTML> and </HTML> element tags.

THE HEAD ELEMENT

The <HEAD> element is used to contain definitions for objects that are used throughout the document. In particular, this is typically where you define JavaScript programs that are used within the document. I'll show you the use of JavaScript in much more detail later in this book. The <TITLE> element appears within the <HEAD> element.

THE TITLE ELEMENT

The <TITLE> tag of a document is important for two reasons. First, because it is displayed in the title line of the browser window, and second because this line is typically used by search engines such as AltaVista, Yahoo!, Excite, and others for indexing your Web page.

 Tip

Include keywords within your <TITLE> element that you would like to be used by the search engines for finding your page. The majority of the Web search engines place heavy emphasis on the words contained in your <TITLE> element.

Here is an example of the <TITLE> element:

```
<TITLE>Widgets by WidgeCo</TITLE>
```

THE BODY ELEMENT

The bulk of your Web page, if it does not include frames, is included within the <BODY> element. You may have only one <BODY> element within your document. Here is an example:

```
<BODY>
    Jesse, "the Body", Ventura
</BODY>
```

Of course, your <BODY> tag will probably include many more, and perhaps different elements.

THE META ELEMENT

The <META> tag is used to specify information about the document or about the document's processing. The <META> tag should be contained within the <HEAD> element. You may have more than one <META> element, and the <META> tag does not use a closing </META> tag.

The <META> element is an open-ended tag that can be used for a variety of purposes. The following are four important uses:

- Automatically transferring a user from one URL to another one.
- Forcing Web browsers to read a page from the Web server instead of using a version of the page from its cache.
- Specifying indexing information for search engines.
- Specifying a content rating for the Web page, which indicates whether the page contains, for example, sex, violence, nudity, or bad language.

Here is an example of how to use the <META> element to effect a Web browser transfer to another URL:

```
<META HTTP-EQUIV="refresh" CONTENT="5;URL=http://www.newurl.com">
```

In this example, the current page will display for five seconds prior to the transfer to the new URL. You can change this time or the destination URL. Note that support for this transfer mechanism is browser-specific, but it should work in most current versions from either Netscape or Microsoft. You should test this feature carefully, however, with all versions of browsers that might be used by your intended audience.

Web browsers usually have a cache of pages that have been visited by the user. This cache is typically stored locally on the hard disk of the user, and retrieving previously viewed pages from the local hard disk can improve performance of the browser because communication back to the Web server is minimized.

As a Web page author, however, sometimes you want to prevent cached pages from being used by the Web browser. You might want to do this, for example, if your page dynamically retrieves information from a database and cached pages might contain obsolete information. Here is an example of using the <META> tag to give an expiration date to the Web page:

```
<META HTTP-EQUIV="expires" CONTENT="0">
```

You can actually specify a date instead of "0", but using a "0" forces the browser to always retrieve the page from the server.

Here is an example of how you can specify information for Web search engines:

```
<META NAME="description"
➥CONTENT="My super duper web site. Come see all the latest widgets.">
```

The description <META> element will be used by Web search engines. Make sure to include important keywords so that Web surfers will be able to find your site. Keep the description succinct because search engines might cut off your description at a certain length. Make sure your most important information is at the beginning of your description.

In addition to the description, you can specify keywords that should be associated with your site. This allows you to add information that might not be in your <TITLE> or description. Here is how to specify keywords for your Web site:

```
<META NAME="keywords" CONTENT="widgets, California, manufacturing, WidgeCo">
```

As with your description, make sure your most important keywords are at the beginning of your list in case the search engine truncates it.

The content rating for a Web page specifies whether the page contains material that some people might find offensive. If the Web page contains a rating, certain browsers can use this information for filtering the display to the end user. For more information about this capability, see the Web pages at `http://www.w3.org/PICS` or `http://www.rsac.org/`.

SIMPLE TEXT FORMATTING

You can use many element tags to format text within an HTML document. An important fact you should keep in mind is that line breaks that appear in your HTML source are ignored. To force a new line, you must use either a `<BR>` element or a `<P>` element. Table 7.2 describes some formatting elements. Although their use in HTML 4.0 is discouraged, they are in widespread use and are still very useful.

TABLE 7.2 LEGACY SIMPLE HTML FORMATTING ELEMENTS

Element	Description
`<B></B>`	Bold. Make included text bold.
`<I></I>`	Italic. Make included text italic.
`<S></S>`	Strikethrough (deprecated). Make included text strikethrough.
`<STRIKE></STRIKE>`	Strikethrough (deprecated). Make included text strikethrough.
`<U></U>`	Underline (deprecated). Make included text underlined.
`<CENTER></CENTER>`	Center. Centers the included text (or graphics) and causes a line break before and after its use.
`<BIG></BIG>`	Big. Displays the designated text in a larger size than the current font size.
`<SMALL></SMALL>`	Small. Displays the designated text in a smaller size than the current font size.

When an element is deprecated, it means that its use is discouraged. Although the element will continue to work in most browsers, there is usually an alternative method for accomplishing the same task. HTML 4.0 is moving toward using style sheets for the formatting of text rather than using tags for formatting. The use of the other elements in the previous table is also discouraged, but they are not yet deprecated. Use of the elements in Table 7.3 is consistent with HTML 4.0.

TABLE 7.3 HTML 4.0 SIMPLE FORMATTING ELEMENTS

Element	Description
`<PRE></PRE>`	Preformatted text. Use a monospace font for the included text and offset the entry with an extra blank line before and after the text.
`<EM></EM>`	Emphasis. This element means that the enclosed text is emphasized. Most browsers will render this emphasis in an italic font.

Element	Description
<STRONG></STRONG>	Strong emphasis. This element means that the enclosed text is strongly emphasized. Most browsers will render this strong emphasis in a bold font.
 	Line break. This causes a line break, and the next line of text will start on the line below. No lines are skipped.
<P></P>	Paragraph. This breaks the current line, does an additional line break (that is, skips a line), and starts a new paragraph. The end paragraph tag is frequently omitted.

COMMON ATTRIBUTES

Several HTML attributes may be used with just about any element. Two of these attributes are the ID attribute and the CLASS attribute. The ID attribute is used to give a name to an element, while the CLASS attribute is used to assign the element to one or more classes. Typically classes are used with style sheets for formatting control. For example, you can assign all elements of a particular class a style containing the color red with a bold font. Here is an example:

```
<P ID="disclaimer" CLASS="smallprint">
```

The ID attribute can be used as the target of a hyperlink. I describe hyperlinks in more detail in the section titled "Anchors and Links."

The STYLE attribute is used to control the formatting for the element. Style information can include fonts, point sizes, color, and so forth. Most elements can contain a STYLE attribute.

Most elements also allow the TITLE attribute. The definition of this attribute can vary from browser to browser, but a common implementation is as a "tooltip" or help message that is displayed when the user places the mouse over the element.

DIV AND SPAN ELEMENTS

The DIV and SPAN elements are used to group other HTML elements or to define a context for controlling style attributes. The DIV element defines a block and can contain other elements such as, for example, paragraph elements. SPAN is used for inline content.

The direction with HTML is to separate the formatting of an HTML document from its logical markup. For example, a paragraph is a logical element, while a bold font specification is part of formatting. Netscape Navigator and Microsoft Internet Explorer have each implemented styling, positioning, and dynamic content differently. In the HTML 4.0 specification, styling uses cascading style sheets; however, neither the Microsoft nor Netscape browser supports HTML 4.0 exactly yet.

The DIV and SPAN elements can be used with style sheets to format a group of elements with a common format. For example, suppose you want to define three consecutive paragraphs in italic. You can group these paragraphs within a DIV element, and then apply a style that includes italic.

PART

II

CH

7

GRAPHICS RULE

To include an image on your Web page you use the <IMG> element. There are many possible attributes of the <IMG> element, but the following is the syntax showing the most important attributes:

```
<IMG SRC="source url" WIDTH="wpixels" HEIGHT="hpixels" BORDER="bpixels">
```

The source url specifies the filename for the graphic image. The graphic format is typically either a GIF file or a JPEG file. Width, height, and border are all specified in pixels. Here are some simple examples:

```
<IMG SRC="logo.gif" WIDTH="200" HEIGHT="100">

<IMG SRC="background.gif">
```

If you don't specify the height or width, the dimensions of the graphic file are used to display the picture.

You can also display a horizontal rule, which is another name for a horizontal line, in the browser with the <HR> element. Important parameters of the <HR> element are the SIZE and WIDTH attributes. The following is an example:

```
<HR SIZE="4" WIDTH="300">
```

In this example, the rule is four pixels in height and 300 pixels in width. You can also specify the width as a percentage of the page width. Rules are very useful for separating sections of a Web page.

ANCHORS AND LINKS

One of the most important features of HTML is the capability of one page to link to another page or another part of the same page. An *anchor* is a location within a page, usually not at the top, that can serve as the destination of a hypertext link. A *link* is the origin of the hypertext jump. Links are common in Web pages, and when you see them, they are normally displayed underlined in a color such as blue, which is different from the normal text.

In HTML, you specify both anchors and links with the same element, the <A> element. The following is an example of the <A> element when used as an anchor:

```
<A NAME="chapter2"><h1>Chapter 2</h1></A>
```

When you use <A> as an anchor, you specify a NAME attribute. This attribute will be used later when we create the link to this destination. Within the anchor, you can specify some content, which might be the name of the chapter or other information to signify a meaningful destination. Here is how you specify the link to the anchor:

```
<A HREF="#chapter2">Go to Chapter 2</A>
```

Notice that in the link we use the HREF parameter to specify the name of the anchor. We also must use the # character in front of the anchor name. This link will jump within the same page; however, if you were jumping from another page, you could specify the destination as

```
http://site/page#anchor
```

This enables you to jump into the middle of a page. If you just specify the page without the anchor, the browser will jump to the top of the page. The following is an example of a jump to the top of a page:

```
<A HREF="http://website/mypage"><IMG SRC="logo.gif"></A>
```

In this example, notice that instead of having a text link I've used an image. When you use this technique, the user can click on the graphic image and will be linked to the destination page.

You can also use the ID attribute instead of the NAME attribute to identify an anchor. However, both the ID attribute and NAME attribute share the same namespace, which means that you cannot use the same name on different tags. When deciding whether to use the ID attribute or the NAME attribute, you should realize that the ID attribute can also be used with style sheets, but NAME cannot. On the other hand, some older Web browsers recognize the NAME attribute but not the ID attribute.

Note

Don't confuse the anchor tag (<A>) with the <LINK> tag of HTML. The <LINK> tag is used primarily in the <HEAD> section of a document mainly for descriptive purposes. Its most useful function is to specify a URL to be used for including the definition of a style sheet for the document that defines the document's formatting attributes. You will mainly be using the <A> element, not the <LINK> element, for your hypertext links.

LIST FORMATTING

Most word processing programs enable you to easily create lists of items. These lists might be unordered, bulleted lists or they might be ordered and numbered lists. HTML also enables you to create lists. As with many of the other elements, the element tags are nested. You first indicate the type of list you have, and then you specify each individual list element within the list. Two common types of lists are the unordered list (<UL>) and the ordered list (<OL>). For either type of list, you specify each list item with the <LI> element. An example of an unordered list follows:

```
<UL>
    <LI>Cookies
    <LI>Crackers
    <LI>Crayons
    <LI>Castanets
    <LI>Cathedrals
</UL>
```

The following is an example of an ordered list:

```
<OL>
    <LI>Wake Up
```

```
<LI>Eat Breakfast
<LI>Work
<LI>Eat Lunch
<LI>Work
<LI>Go Home
</OL>
```

Notice that it is easy to switch from one type of list to the other by just changing the list type. It is also easy to insert or delete items from the list. The <UL> and <OL> tags act as paragraph breaks, and they cause a line to be skipped before the list begins.

Another type of list is the definition list. A *definition list* is a list of entries in which each entry consists of two parts: the term to be defined, and then the definition itself. Three elements are used to create a definition list. First is the definition list element (<DL>), second is the definition term (<DD>), and third is the definition description (<DD>). The following is an example using these three HTML elements:

```
<DL>
    <DT>Doe
    <DD>A deer, a female deer
    <DT>Ray
    <DD>A drop of golden sun
    <DT>Me
    <DD>A name I call myself
    <DT>Fa
    <DD>A long, long way to run
</DL>
```

In Figure 7.1 you can see the definition list as shown by a Web browser. I have created a Domino page and specified that the entire page should be considered HTML.

Figure 7.1
An HTML definition list displayed in a Web browser.

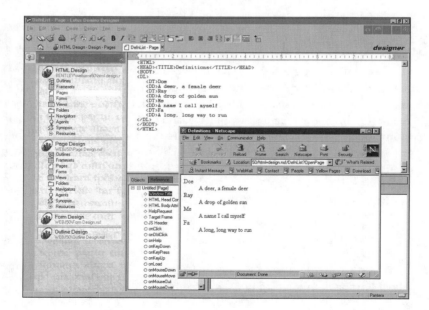

TABLES

Tables in HTML are defined through the use of several elements. Tables are an important aspect of HTML because they can be used to position text and graphics both with and without borders. When used without borders, text and graphics can be positioned on the page and create nice visual effects.

Tables are also useful when used with Domino views. For example, you can use the attribute Treat View Contents as HTML and generate HTML table element tags within the view columns. By controlling the HTML you generate, and by knowing how to use tables in HTML, you can create effects with Domino that might otherwise be difficult to obtain.

As you might expect, tables in HTML are enclosed in the element tags <TABLE> and </TABLE>. There are many attributes that you can associate with a table, including the capability to change the color of the table, the size of its border, the table alignment, and its size. Shown in the syntax are just a few of the important attributes of the <TABLE> element.

```
<TABLE BORDER="bpixels" WIDTH="wpixels" ALIGN="type" BGCOLOR="color" >
```

You can consult an HTML reference for the multitude of other attributes of a table. When you begin a table, you can define rows of the table. Each row begins with a <TR> and ends with </TR>. If your table has a heading, each column's heading is surrounded by <TH> and </TH>. Finally, each data element within the table is surrounded by <TD> and </TD>. A sample table follows:

```
<TABLE BORDER="2">
   <TR><TH>Part No.</TH><TH>Name</TH><TH>Description</TH>
   <TR><TD>00100</TD><TD>Donut Hole</TD>
   ➡<TD>Most expensive part of the donut</TD>
   <TR><TD>00200</TD><TD>Socket</TD><TD>Same as the pocket</TD>
   <TR><TD>00300</TD><TD>Bagel Hole</TD>
   ➡<TD>Most expensive part of the bagel</TD>
   <TR><TD>00400</TD><TD>Vacuum</TD><TD>Cleaned by the vacuum cleaner</TD>
   <TR><TD>00500</TD><TD>Nothing</TD>
   ➡<TD>What your son says he did in school today</TD>
</TABLE>
```

In Figure 7.2 you can see how a Web browser formats the table specified above. Also notice that each line of a table begins with <TR>, but the </TR> has been omitted. This illustrates that HTML is very forgiving and can understand the table even if the ending tag has been omitted. When I discuss XML in Part V, "Enterprise Integration Using XML, Java, and Domino," I'll show you that XML does not allow this type of abbreviation.

This is a good point to give you an example of how the same HTML can appear differently when viewed in different browsers. Although the <COL> element is defined in HTML 4.0, it is implemented by Microsoft Internet Explorer and not by Netscape Navigator 4.6. The <COL> tag enables you to specify alignment and width for a column in a table. As you can see from Figure 7.3, the display in the two browsers is quite different. You should always be sure to check your HTML code in all the target browsers you anticipate your users will use.

Figure 7.2
An HTML table shown by a Web browser.

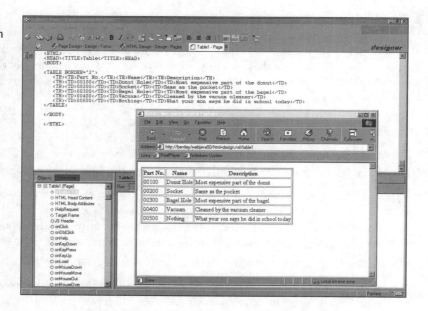

Figure 7.3
The COL element behaves differently in MS Internet Explorer and Netscape Navigator.

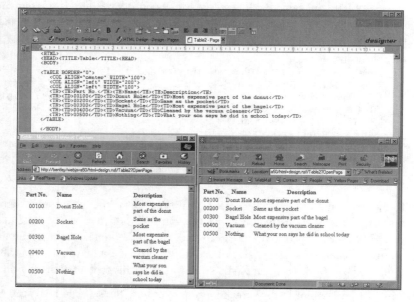

Although both browsers honor the Border="0" attribute, the column width and alignment are different. Other features are implemented in the Netscape browser but not in Internet Explorer. Both browsers support the TABLE, TH, TR, and TD elements. If you stay with these elements your tables should appear properly in both browsers.

APPLETS AND OBJECTS

The APPLET element is used to define a Java applet. It is officially deprecated, which means that it has been replaced by a newer element, the OBJECT element. Because of its widespread use, the APPLET element will probably be supported in browsers for a long time, but in your own coding you can start using the OBJECT element instead. The following is the basic syntax:

```
<APPLET CLASSID="javaclassURL" CODEBASE="URLPath" ARCHIVE="archivePath">
<PARAM NAME="p1name" VALUE="p1value">
<PARAM NAME="p2name" VALUE="p2value">
. . .
</APPLET>

<OBJECT CLASSID="javaclassURL" CODEBASE="URLPath" ARCHIVE="archivePath">
<PARAM NAME="p1name" VALUE="p1value">
<PARAM NAME="p2name" VALUE="p2value">
. . .
</OBJECT>
```

The CLASSID attribute is used to specify the Java class. You can include a CODEBASE attribute, in which case the paths for ARCHIVE and CLASSID are relative to the CODEBASE path. The ARCHIVE attribute can be used to specify JAR files that contain Java code. You can also use the OBJECT element to include OLE objects in Microsoft Internet Explorer. If you do this, the CLASSID must be the CLSID of the OLE object. Here is an example:

```
<OBJECT CLASSID="clsid:923C845F-3EFA-21CF-B3D1-110036E12333">
```

FORMS

Thus far, all the elements I've described are for displaying information, not for capturing information from the user. Within an HTML document, you can also have one or more forms, which can be used to gather information from the user. You can include input fields for text as well as other types of controls such as pushbuttons, drop-down boxes, checkboxes, and more.

An HTML form acts as the container for the controls that are displayed. Although it is possible to have more than one form within an HTML document, Domino typically generates only a single form.

Each control that is contained within the form usually has a name, which is specified by its NAME attribute. Also, the form and its controls can have associated events. Events are typically triggered by end-user actions within the browser and might occur, for example, when the user clicks on a button, presses a key, or moves the mouse over a specific control. Here is an example of a form in HTML:

```
<HTML>
<HEAD><TITLE>Form Example</TITLE></HEAD>
<BODY>
<FORM NAME="FormExample" METHOD="post">

<P>Hello, this is a form example.
```

```
<P>Please type your name here:
<INPUT TYPE="TEXT" NAME="USERNAME">

<P>Select your favorite color:<BR>
<INPUT TYPE="radio" NAME="color" value="red"> Red<BR>
<INPUT TYPE="radio" NAME="color" value="green"> Green<BR>
<INPUT TYPE="radio" NAME="color" value="blue"> Blue<BR>
<P>
<INPUT TYPE="submit" value="Send">
</FORM>
```

In Figure 7.4 you can see the display of the HTML form. Note that this is not the recommended way to generate input to be sent back to a Domino server. When Domino formats a regular Domino form or document for display, it converts it to an HTML form, wraps it with the required HTML, and sends it to the browser. Because this form was manually created with HTML, it does not necessarily follow Domino naming conventions, and Domino will not know what to do with it.

Figure 7.4
An HTML form displayed by a Web browser.

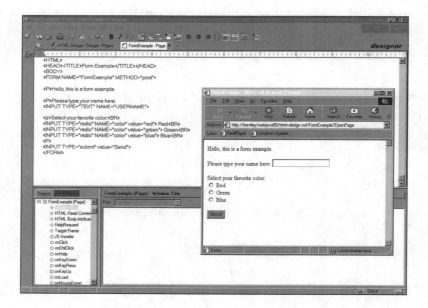

Although the HTML shown in Figure 7.4 is displayed by the browser, the input specified by the user will not be captured and sent back to the Domino database because we have not created an HTML form that Domino understands. We'll see in the next section how the Domino conventions work.

DOMINO FORMS

It is important to distinguish between an HTML form and a Domino form. The HTML <FORM> tag specifies an HTML form element. A Domino form is created in the Domino Designer. Let's see how the two are related. As a first example, I'll create a completely blank page (not a blank form) in the Domino Designer. I've also turned off the Use JavaScript When Generating Pages Database property (see Figure 7.5).

Figure 7.5
Domino generates HTML for display by a Web browser.

Domino blank form   Browser rendering of blank form

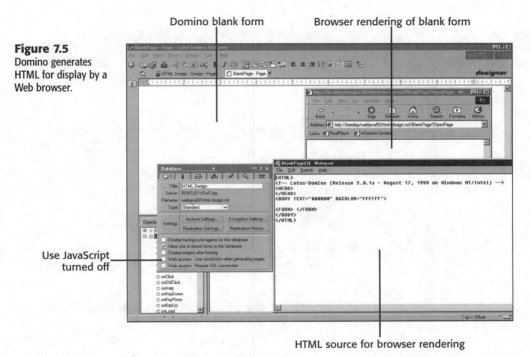

Use JavaScript turned off

HTML source for browser rendering

Whereas previously I showed you how you could use the Domino Designer to create HTML, in Figure 7.5 you can see the HTML that is automatically generated by Domino for a blank page (not a blank form). By now you know enough HTML to recognize the entire HTML document, shown in the following code:

```
<HTML>
<!-- Lotus-Domino (Release 5.0.1a - August 17, 1999 on Windows NT/Intel) -->
<HEAD>
</HEAD>
<BODY TEXT="000000" BGCOLOR="FFFFFF">

<FORM> </FORM>
</BODY>
</HTML>
```

Note

You can view the HTML source for any Web page you are viewing by using menu commands in your browser. In Microsoft Internet Explorer, you use the menu commands View, Source. In Netscape Navigator you use the commands View, Page Source. If you are viewing a framed document then those commands will show you the highest level (frameset) HTML source. To view the individual frame's source, you must right-click within the frame, and then choose View Source (Microsoft IE) or View Frame Source (Netscape Navigator).

PART
II

CH
7

Note that the HTML generated by Domino can vary from release to release and can vary depending on the options selected by the designer. In Figure 7.6 you can see the HTML that Domino generates when I enable JavaScript.

Figure 7.6
Domino generates different HTML when the JavaScript option is enabled.

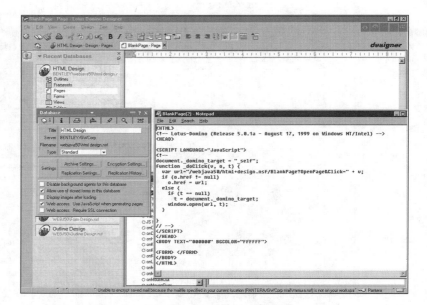

The JavaScript generated by Domino is used to handle client-side events and as mentioned can change from release to release and is not part of a documented Domino interface. It is acceptable to review the generated JavaScript to gain insight into the mechanisms used by Domino, but if you write custom code that makes assumptions about the generated JavaScript (or generated HTML), your programs might not work in a future release of Domino.

EVENTS

In Figure 7.7, you can see the Domino Designer, where I have defined a single button on a page along with a JavaScript event handler. The event is called onClick, and the JavaScript appears in the programmer's pane.

The JavaScript code follows:

```
alert("Hello world")
```

The following is the INPUT element:

```
<INPUT TYPE=button onClick="alert(&quot;Hello world&quot;)"
➥VALUE="DomButton" TITLE="Push Me.">
```

You can see that Domino has generated a form and an input field with the TYPE=button. The onClick event handler has converted the double quotes to ". When the user clicks on the button, the alert routine will display a message box with the words "Hello world."

Figure 7.7
Domino generates an
INPUT TYPE=button
to display a push-
button.

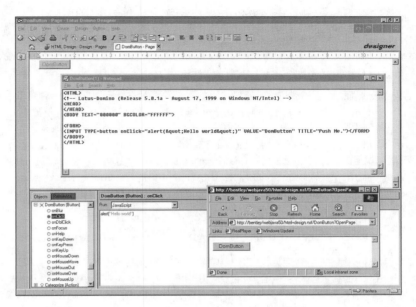

In the box on the left you can see the events that can occur with a button, including several related to the keyboard and several related to the mouse. By programming these events with JavaScript code, you can program the browser to perform tasks when the user takes certain actions. I cover these events and JavaScript in more detail in later chapters.

THE Method ATTRIBUTE

When you submit a form, you can use one of two methods: get and post. You specify the method with the METHOD attribute of the FORM element. In addition to the method, the ACTION attribute of the FORM element specifies the URL where the data will be sent.

The terms get and post are a little confusing because both actually cause data to be sent to the server. To clarify the distinction, let's first look at the get method. You can think of the get method as the way to specify a database query from the server. To issue some sort of query to the server, you will need to specify some parameters. However, the number and type of the parameters you send to a database query are usually limited. The get method only supports the ASCII character set and usually is limited in the length of the query.

If you do not specify a method, the get method is the default. Here is an example of how you would specify the FORM element using the get method:

```
<FORM NAME="Form1" METHOD="get" ACTION="http://www.mywebsite.com">
```

The get method will package the input value fields into a long URL. Here is an example. Suppose the ACTION attribute of the form is http://www.mywebsite.com and the METHOD is get. If there are two fields, FIELDA, and FIELDB on the form, the following is the effective URL that will be generated:

```
http://www.mywebsite.com?FIELDA="DATA1"&FIELDB="DATA2"
```

PART

II

CH

7

Following the Web site URL, a question mark (?) is appended, and then all the fields are appended with both the name and value of the field. Spaces are replaced by a plus sign (+), and non-ASCII characters are replaced by %HH, where HH represents the hexadecimal equivalent of the character. Each field is separated from the next with the ampersand (&) character.

You can think of the post method as a way for the user to fill out a traditional form. Unlike the get method, the post method can support various encodings other than ASCII and does not usually have length limitations on the data sent back to the server. Whereas the get method will package up the data and send it back with the URL, the post method accumulates all the data fields and sends them back as the MIME type: multipart/form-data. Because the data is sent back with this type, the data can include text, graphics, and other binary data as well as other types of files.

The following is an example of the post method with a form:

```
<FORM NAME="Form2" METHOD="post" ACTION="http://www.mywebsite.com">
```

You should be aware that you cannot just arbitrarily use the get and post methods with Domino. On the receiving side, Domino must accept data from the browser, and then interpret and convert it into data to be (potentially) stored in a Domino database. When Domino is in charge of generating the HTML that is sent to the browser, it can generate the HTML in a certain canonical form, using names and conventions so that when it receives the results back from the browser it will know how and where to store the data. If you arbitrarily generate the HTML yourself, Domino might not know what to do with it when it receives it.

After you become familiar with some of the conventions of Domino, however, you can stretch Domino's capabilities and use it in a more powerful way. That is, by knowing how HTML works, and by knowing how Domino generates and uses HTML, you can insert additional HTML coding to create interesting special effects with Domino. See the section titled "Using Domino URLs" for more information on Domino's conventions.

INPUT FIELDS AND CONTROLS

The <INPUT> element in HTML is used for many different types of user input. For example, you use <INPUT> for pushbuttons, text input fields, radio buttons, and checkboxes. All input fields must be contained within a form. To differentiate among the different types of input fields, you use the TYPE attribute on the INPUT element. The following are the available types:

- TEXT—Text box input.
- PASSWORD—Text box with characters hidden when input.
- CHECKBOX—Selection checkbox.
- RADIO—Radio button selection.
- BUTTON—Pushbutton. Similar to <INPUT TYPE="BUTTON"> but allows richer formatting such as the use of images.

- SUBMIT—Submit button. This special button causes the form to be submitted to the server.

- RESET—Reset button. This special button causes all input fields to be reset.

- IMAGE—This creates a graphical submit button.

- FILE—Enables users to select files to be submitted with a form.

- HIDDEN—A value that cannot be seen by the user but can be used to store values locally within the browser. Hidden values can be inspected and changed by JavaScript and will be transmitted to the server.

A SAMPLE INPUT FIELD

In Figure 7.8 you can see a Domino form, the generated HTML, and the visual display of the HTML. The form is very simple with just some static text and one input field. It has been generated with the Web Access: Use JavaScript option turned off.

Figure 7.8
Domino automatically generates a submit button if there is no button on the form.

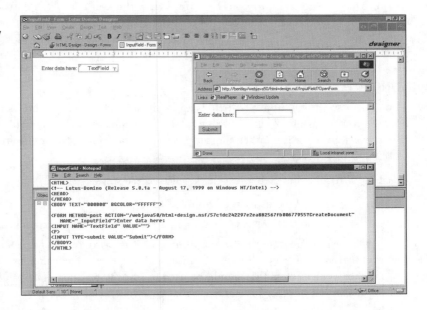

There are several points to notice about this simple form. Let's go through the generated HTML. Following the HTML, HEAD, and BODY tags, notice that the FORM tag has several attributes. The METHOD attribute specifies that it will be a post. I've already explained this attribute. The last attribute, the NAME attribute, is fairly self-explanatory. It is just the name of the form in Domino prepended with an underscore. The last attribute, the ACTION attribute, is interesting. The ACTION attribute follows:

```
ACTION="/webjava50/html+design.nsf/
➥57c1dc242297e2ea882567fb00677955?CreateDocument"
```

PART

II

CH

7

The first point to note in the ACTION attribute is the URL, which begins with a slash. Notice that it does not begin with a protocol such as http:. This URL is called a *relative URL*, and in this case it means that the specification is relative to the current base. In this instance, it means that the webjava50 directory is located beneath the default (data) directory on the Domino server. Within that directory is the html design.nsf database. Notice that the space has been replaced by a plus sign (+). Following the name of the database is the document universal identifier for the Domino form. This number tells Domino which form to use in creating a new document. Of course, the command following the question mark (?) is to create a new document.

Following the HTML FORM element you can see the static text followed by the INPUT HTML element. Because the type is not specified, a TYPE=TEXT is assumed for this element. The initial value is specified by the VALUE attribute, which in this case is empty. The name of the field is specified by the NAME attribute, and it is the same as the Domino name for the field.

The last point to notice is that the submit button is automatically generated by Domino if we don't have our own button on the form. When the user clicks this button, the contents of the form will be packaged up and sent to the URL specified in the ACTION attribute of the FORM element. As we have seen, this will cause Domino to create a new document in the database.

ADJUSTING A TEXT FIELD SIZE

The default size of an input text field is approximately 20 characters but depends on the browser you are using. Twenty characters might be suitable for many fields, but undoubtedly you will want to create either shorter or longer fields. How can you do this with HTML and Domino? It's easy.

To add HTML attributes to a text field, follow these steps:

1. First create the field using the Domino Designer.
2. Click on the HTML Attributes item in left side of the programmer's pane.
3. You can enter the following in the right side of the programmer's pane: "size=nn maxlength=mm". Include the specification within quotes. The value nn represents the number of characters that should be used to size the text box. The value mm represents the maximum number of characters that you want to allow the user to type into the text box. The length can be more or less than the size of the box that is displayed.

As an example, suppose you have an input field called TextField. If you specify "size=40 maxlength=40", the generated HTML will be

```
<INPUT NAME="TextField" VALUE="" size=40 maxlength=40>
```

Notice that when the HTML is generated the quotes surrounding the size specification are removed. The quotes actually signify a constant @formula expression. You can also use a more complex @formula to generate the attribute string.

USING RADIO BUTTONS

Figure 7.9 shows a Domino form with a radio button field and one pushbutton.

Figure 7.9
The HTML value of a radio button is the alias, if one exists.

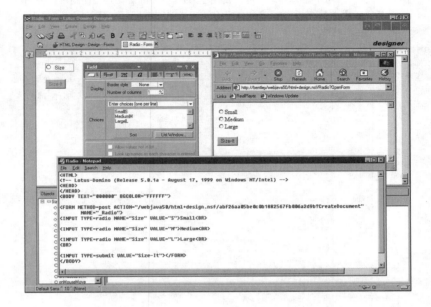

As in the previous section, the HTML, HEAD, BODY, and FORM elements are automatically generated and allow Domino to know which form to use when creating a document in the database.

A Domino radio button field translates nicely into an HTML INPUT element with TYPE=radio. In HTML, you indicate that the separate INPUT elements are tied together by virtue of their NAME field. An example of this follows:

```
<INPUT TYPE=radio NAME="Size" value="S">Small<BR>
<INPUT TYPE=radio NAME="Size" value="M">Medium<BR>
<INPUT TYPE=radio NAME="Size" value="L">Large<BR>
```

In this case, the field name is Size and is the same on each of the three INPUT elements. Radio button choices are mutually exclusive, so that selecting one choice automatically deselects all the other choices. Whichever choice is selected when the form is submitted will be used as the value of the field. Notice that the values of the fields in the HTML are S, M, and L. These are the synonyms or aliases for the values that I've specified in Domino. When the submit button is pushed, only S, M, or L will be sent back to Domino.

Finally, notice that I have included a button called Size-it. Because the form includes a button, it is automatically converted to a submit button and Domino does not generate an extra submit button for this form.

PART

II

CH

7

USING CHECKBOXES

Checkboxes are similar to radio buttons. You can create them easily with the Domino Designer. As with radio buttons, each separate checkbox entry results in its own INPUT element. The elements are tied together because they have the same name (see Figure 7.10).

Figure 7.10
Checkboxes allow the user to select multiple items.

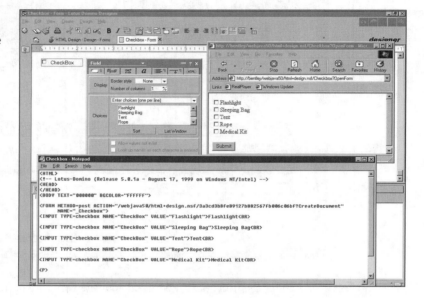

Unlike radio buttons, however, checkboxes allow the user to select multiple items. With Domino, each of the selected items represents an additional value within the checkbox field. If an item has an alias, it is used as the value. If no alias is available then the displayed value is the same as the value stored within the field.

Both radio buttons and checkboxes contain an attribute called VALUE. Note that this attribute only contains the text that is displayed or returned by the browser. In particular, the VALUE attribute does not specify whether the radio button or checkbox is checked. You must access the CHECKED attribute to determine whether the particular entry is checked. You will see the importance of this distinction when I discuss JavaScript in later chapters.

USING HIDDEN FIELDS

Hidden fields have long been available in the Notes client. A designer typically might hide a field for one of several reasons:

- Security—A particular user might not be authorized to see data stored within a field.

- Persistent auxiliary storage—A design might need to store additional information with a document, such as an audit trail, that need not be visible to the user.

- To customize general forms—You create a very general form but want to show a user only the subset of fields that apply to a particular transaction, so some fields are hidden.

Of course, there might be many other uses for hidden fields in the Notes client. When using HTML and Web browsers, there is another reason why you might want to use hidden fields. You might want to store additional information due to the "stateless" environment of the Web.

Web interactions are essentially stateless. By that I mean that each transaction from the browser to the server is independent of previous transactions. There really is no concept of a continuous session. Of course, by now there are many ways that sessions can be simulated or implemented using the stateless HTTP protocol, but the point is that the protocol itself does not handle sessions. To overcome this problem, you can use hidden fields in HTML. In essence, the server can calculate important information (such as state information), send it to the browser in the form of a hidden field, and then when the browser submits the form, the hidden information is returned to the server. The server can then use this information to determine the next step of the process.

In addition, hidden HTML fields are accessible to JavaScript programs, which can do client-side processing using this information. The JavaScript programs can read the hidden fields sent from the server, update them depending on user actions, and then the results will be sent back to the server, all without the visibility to the browser user.

In HTML, you specify a hidden field with the following syntax:

```
<INPUT TYPE="HIDDEN" NAME="fieldname" VALUE="value">
```

In the Domino Designer, follow these steps to enable hidden fields:

1. First create the text field you would like to use as a hidden field.
2. In the Field properties box, use the Paragraph Hide When tab to specify that the field should be hidden from Web browsers.
3. In the Form properties box, you must specify Generate HTML for All Fields in the On Web Access section of the Defaults (beanie hat) tab (see Figure 7.11).

Figure 7.11
You must enable Generate HTML for All Fields to use hidden fields.

You must enable the Generate HTML for All Fields option because without it, a hidden field will not be sent to the Web browser. If you were using hidden fields for security purposes, of course you would not want your hidden fields to be transmitted to the browser, even if they were not visible to the user. Remember that a user can always use the View Source capabilities of the browser to view these hidden fields. So, you should consider any field sent to the browser, even if hidden, available for the user to see.

RICH TEXT FIELDS

Rich text fields in Domino are displayed in HTML using the `<TEXTAREA>` element. This element enables the user to input several lines of text rather than just a single line. In addition to the NAME attribute for TEXTAREA, you can also specify ROWS and COLS. The default specification generated by Domino follows:

```
<TEXTAREA NAME="fieldname" ROWS=7 COLS=50>initial contents</TEXTAREA>
```

You can override the size of the field in much the same manner as you override the size in a regular text field. That is, you type values in the HTML Attributes section in the programmer's pane. Any values you type for the HTML attributes will replace the default value of `"ROWS=7 COLS=50"`.

One difference between Netscape Navigator and Microsoft Internet Explorer is the handling of text when the user types more text than will fit on a single line in the TEXTAREA. Whereas Internet Explorer will wrap the text by default, Netscape will scroll to the right and will not wrap. You can overcome this situation by adding a WRAP attribute to the TEXTAREA. The WRAP attribute is not standard in HTML 4.0, but both Netscape and Internet Explorer understand it. The form you should use is WRAP="VIRTUAL".

There are actually two places where you can add this attribute to your Rich Text field. Of course you can add it to the HTML Attributes section, just as we did for the ROWS and COLS attributes. However, as mentioned, if you put anything in that area, it will completely replace any defaults provided by Domino. Furthermore, because the HTML Attributes section in the programmer's pane defines a formula, you must enter the following:

```
"WRAP=\"VIRTUAL\" "
```

You must include the backslashes before the double quotes that are embedded within the string. If you try entering this string in the HTML Attributes section, you'll find that wrapping works fine, but because the ROWS and COLS specification defaults are gone, the TEXTAREA is very small. Is there a way to add the wrap without replacing Domino's defaults? Yes. Here's how.

To add attributes without overlaying Domino's defaults, follow these steps:

1. Click on the rich text field you want to modify.

2. Open the properties box for the field.

3. Click on the last tab, the <HTML> tab.

4. In the Other field, which is located within the HTML tags section, enter WRAP="VIRTUAL". Note: Do not add quotes around the entire string. The attributes you specify will be appended (they do not replace) to any defaults supplied by Domino. If you use both the HTML Attributes section in the programmer's pane and this field, the HTML

attributes will replace the Domino defaults, and then the attributes from the properties box will be appended.

In Figure 7.12 you can see the Field properties box for a rich text field. In it I have added the `WRAP="VIRTUAL"` attribute.

Figure 7.12
You can append HTML attributes to Domino's defaults using the Field properties box.

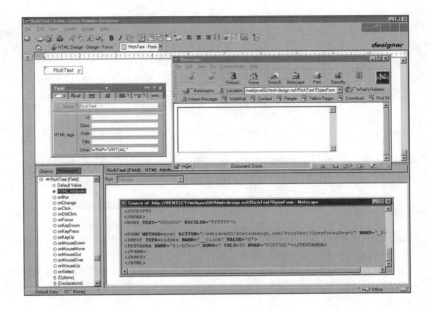

Notice that the `WRAP="VIRTUAL"` attribute is appended to the size specification that is supplied by Domino by default.

COMBOBOXES AND LISTBOXES

Although in the Notes client comboboxes and listboxes are clearly separate user interface elements, in HTML they are related. A combobox is also sometimes called a drop-down box. It is typically represented as a single field with a downward pointing arrow at the right. By clicking on this arrow, a box appears with choices that can be selected with either the mouse or keyboard. Only one selection is allowed with a combobox.

A listbox, by contrast, typically shows several lines of text choices and frequently contains a vertical scrollbar to view additional selections. A user can highlight one or sometimes more than one choice in the list. Additional choices are selected by using the Ctrl key while selecting the second and subsequent entries.

In HTML, you can create both comboboxes and listboxes with the same HTML element, the `<SELECT>` element. There is an attribute called the `MULTIPLE` attribute. Without this attribute, a combobox appears, while a listbox appears if this attribute is present (see Figure 7.13).

PART

II

CH

7

Figure 7.13
Comboboxes and listboxes both use the HTML SELECT element.

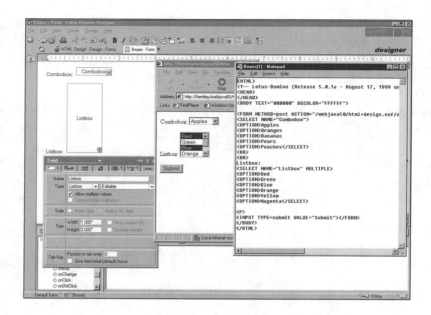

In Figure 7.13, I have created both a combobox and listbox in the Domino Designer. As you can see on the right, the choices I created for the combobox were Apples, Oranges, Bananas, Pears, and Peaches. The user can view the available selections by clicking on the arrow. Notice that HTML uses the <OPTION> element to indicate the available options within the combobox.

For the listbox, I created a listbox in the Domino Designer. Notice that I have enabled the Allow Multiple Values attribute in the Field properties box. This attribute allows multiple values to be stored in a single field. By enabling this attribute notice that the keyword MULTIPLE appears in the HTML on the right. The browser in the middle shows two rows of the listbox are selected. Note that in the Domino Designer I have made the height of the listbox two inches. This height is honored in the Designer as shown but is not supported in the Web browser.

It is important to note that if you create a listbox in the Domino Designer and you do not enable the Allow Multiple Values option, your listbox will actually appear as a combobox to the end user. The reason, of course, is that the MULTIPLE keyword will not appear on the SELECT element, and thus it will be displayed as a combobox.

In addition, there is an attribute called SIZE that enables you to specify the number of rows to be used for display. If you add a SIZE attribute to a listbox, you can change the number of rows displayed. If you add a SIZE parameter to a combobox with a value other than one, it will display as a listbox. You can add the SIZE parameter in either the HTML Attributes section of the Programmer's pane or in the Other field of the Field HTML properties box.

The following is the HTML syntax for a combobox:

```
<SELECT NAME="fieldname" SIZE="n">
<OPTION>Option1
<OPTION>Option2
<OPTION>Option3
</SELECT>
```

The following is the HTML syntax for a listbox:

```
<SELECT NAME="fieldname" MULTIPLE SIZE="n">
<OPTION>Option1
<OPTION>Option2
<OPTION>Option3
</SELECT>
```

In summary, here are some empirical rules about the display of the SELECT element with Domino. Note that these rules are not defined by any specification and may change with future releases of Web browsers or Domino.

- If you add the MULTIPLE keyword in HTML or enable the Allow Multiple Values in Domino Designer, a listbox will appear.

- If you specify the SIZE parameter in HTML, or by using the HTML Attributes section of the Domino Designer with a row count greater than one, a listbox will appear.

- If you do not add MULTIPLE and the SIZE parameter is omitted or is set to one row, a combobox will display.

USING DOMINO URLS

There are a variety of elements within a Domino database, including documents, forms, views, pages, and several others. To access these elements from a Web browser, you must specify a Uniform Resource Locator (URL). When Domino receives this URL, it examines the syntax, finds the object, converts it to HTML, and returns it, if it can. Otherwise, you will receive an error message indicating that the object cannot be found.

GENERAL DOMINO URL SYNTAX

All Domino URL requests have the following syntax:

```
http://Host/Database/ObjectSpec?Action&Arguments
```

The sections of this request represent the following:

- *Host*—Represents the IP address or name of the Domino server as specified in DNS. Note that this name is not necessarily the same as the name used within the Domino directory (name and address book). Examples include
  ```
  www.ibm.com
  www.lotus.com
  ```

PART
II

CH
7

- *Database*—Represents the directory and database name relative to the base Domino data directory (typically Domino\Data). The database name should include the NSF suffix. You can also use a database Replica ID instead of the database name. The following are examples:

  ```
  apps/expense.nsf
  public/Y1999/survey.nsf
  ```

- *ObjectSpec*—Specifies a document, page, form, view, agent, navigator, and so forth. This specification will vary depending on the type of object. The object specification can also be a universal ID (UNID) or a NoteID. The universal ID will be the same in all replicas of the database. The NoteID will vary among replicas, so its use is not recommended. A common format is to use both a viewname and a document key or UNID. The following are examples, and there are more examples with each URL:

  ```
  MyView
  ExpView/Empno
  57c1dc242297e2ea882567fb00677955
  ```

- *Action*—The action request depends on the specific object. For example, to open a database, you use OpenDatabase. To open a view, use OpenView. The following are some examples:

  ```
  OpenForm
  OpenDocument
  CreateDocument
  OpenAgent
  ```

- *Arguments*—The arguments for an action depend on the action. Many actions do not require any arguments. Some actions, such as OpenView, have several optional arguments. The following are some examples:

  ```
  Count=50
  CollapseView
  ```

SERVERS AND DATABASES

Here is how you can open servers and databases. Opening a server will request a listing of its data directory or initial database, whereas opening a database will open the design element as specified by the database designer.

```
OpenServer
```

The OpenServer command browses the Domino server's data directory.

Syntax:

```
http://Host/?OpenServer
```

Example:

```
http://www.yourserver.com/?OpenServer
```

The `OpenServer` command is used to request browsing of the Domino server's data directory. If browsing is not allowed, you will receive an error message as the result of this action. Note that for security purposes you will normally want to disable browsing of databases in the Domino directory for your server. The setting is found on the HTTP tab of the Internet Protocols tab of your server document.

OpenDatabase

The `OpenDatabase` command opens a Domino database.

Syntax:

```
http://Host/DatabaseFileName?OpenDatabase
http://Host/DatabaseReplicaID?OpenDatabase
http://Host/__DatabaseReplicaID.nsf?OpenDatabase
```

Examples:

```
http://www.yourserver.com/apps/expense.nsf?OpenDatabase
http://www.yourserver.com/y2kinfo.nsf?OpenDatabase
http://www.yourserver.com/85390FF70068BED6?OpenDatabase
http://www.yourserver.com/__85390FF70068BED6.nsf?OpenDatabase
```

Opening a database with the `OpenDatabase` URL is optional. If you use another URL such as `OpenDocument`, the database will be opened automatically. Normally you will open a database by filename. You must specify the directory path and filename relative to the Domino data directory. Remember to include the `nsf` file extension.

You might want to use the ReplicaID format for `OpenDatabase` when opening a remote database from a program. In particular, if you know the ReplicaID, you do not need to know the directory information. This can be helpful because it will insulate your program from database and directory reorganizations on another server.

Login ARGUMENT

The `Login` argument is used to force authentication with a user ID and password.

Syntax:

```
http://Host/Database/ObjectSpec?Action&Login
http://Host/?OpenServer&Login
http://Host/Database?OpenDatabase&Login
```

Examples:

```
http://www.yourserver.com/apps/expense.nsf?OpenDatabase&Login
http://www.yourserver.com/?OpenServer&Login
```

PART

II

CH

7

The Login argument can be added to any Domino URL to force user authentication, although it would typically be most useful on either the OpenDatabase or OpenServer commands. Normally, if a database access control list (ACL) contains an entry for Anonymous with No Access, this forces a login. However, if a database does not contain an entry for Anonymous, the Default ACL setting is used. The Default settings for your database might be appropriate for an internal intranet but might not be appropriate for Web access. For example, you might have a database with no ACL entry for Anonymous, but Editor access for Default. This setting would give anonymous Web users Editor access, which might be undesirable.

Use the Login argument of OpenDatabase or OpenServer (or other URL) to require a login, regardless of the ACL setting.

VIEWS AND FORMS

Opening Views enables you to provide a navigational interface to the documents within your database. Opening a form allows the user to create a new document.

OpenView

The OpenView command is used to open and display a view.

Syntax:

http://*Host*/*Database*/*ViewName*?OpenView

http://*Host*/*Database*/$defaultview?OpenView

http://*Host*/*Database*/*ViewNoteID*?OpenView

http://*Host*/*Database*/*ViewUniversalID*?OpenView

Arguments:

CollapseView	Shows the view in collapsed format.
ExpandView	Shows the view in expanded format.
Count=*n*	Specifies the number of rows to display in the view.
Start=*n*	Starts display of view at row *n*. The value can contain hierarchical values. For example, Start=7.2.3 means start at the seventh main document, second response document, then third response document.
Expand=*n*	Expands row *n* in a hierarchical view. Do not combine this argument with CollapseView or ExpandView.
Collapse=*n*	Shows row *n* in collapsed format in a hierarchical view.
RestrictToCategory= category	This option allows you to specify the category for a Show Single Category type view.
StartKey=string	Shows the view starting from the first document that matches the specified string. The string is matched to data found in the first sorted column.

Examples:

```
http://www.yourserver.com/apps/expense.nsf/
➥Trips?OpenView&ExpandView
```

```
http://www.yourserver.com/Empdata.nsf/
➥LastNames?OpenView&StartKey=Smith&Count=75
```

```
http://www.yourserver.com/Empdata.nsf/
➥Benefits?OpenView&RestrictToCategory=401K
```

```
http://www.yourserver.com/y2kinfo.nsf/Blowups?OpenView&Count=100
```

Use the OpenView command to open a Domino view. You can optionally include arguments following the OpenView command. The arguments enable you to control the display of the view. You can also include a form within the database that can be used to format the display of the view. This type of form has a name such as $$ViewTemplate for *Viewname*. Alternatively, you can have a form called $$ViewTemplateDefault. If either form is used, it should contain an embedded view. When the OpenView command is processed, the view template will be used to display the view. If there is no view template then the view will be displayed with a default format. The default format contains navigational elements at the top and bottom of the view.

The RestrictToCategory argument enables you to set the single category that will be used for a Show Single Category view.

ReadViewEntries

The ReadViewEntries command is used to return the information about a view in XML format.

Syntax:

```
http://Host/Database/ViewName?ReadViewEntries
```

```
http://Host/Database/$defaultview?ReadViewEntries
```

```
http://Host/Database/ViewNoteID?ReadViewEntries
```

```
http://Host/Database/ViewUniversalID?ReadViewEntries
```

Arguments:

PreFormat	This option causes all data to be converted to text on the server using the server's locale information. All numbers, dates, and other data types will be converted to text before being sent. Without PreFormat, the XML data will contain locale-neutral formats.
RestrictToCategory= *category*	This option enables you to specify the category for a Show Single Category type view.

Examples:

```
http://www.yourserver.com/apps/expense.nsf/
➥Trips?ReadViewEntries
```

```
http://www.yourserver.com/Empdata.nsf/
➥LastNames?ReadViewEntries&PreFormat
```

```
http://www.yourserver.com/Empdata.nsf/
➥Benefits?ReadViewEntries&RestrictToCategory=401K
```

Use the `ReadViewEntries` command to return information from a Domino view in XML format. You can optionally include arguments following the `OpenView` command. The arguments enable you to control whether the data should be preformatted to text or returned with the appropriate data types. You can also specify the category to use for a Show Single Category view.

The `RestrictToCategory` argument enables you to set the single category that will be used for a Show Single Category view.

Here is some sample output for this URL command:

```
<?xml version="1.0" encoding="UTF-8" ?>
<!-- Lotus-Domino (Release 5.0.2b - December 16, 1999
➥on Windows NT/Intel)  -->
<viewentries toplevelentries="3">
 <viewentry position="1" unid="4AD9B08B6BE05A0F88256756007E2B64"
➥noteid="8F6" siblings="3">
  <entrydata columnnumber="0" name="Form">
   <text>CtlSection</text>
  </entrydata>
 </viewentry>
 <viewentry position="2" unid="140F6C949D3993C38825687E0014DB23"
➥noteid="92E" siblings="3">
  <entrydata columnnumber="0" name="Form">
   <text>Listbox</text>
  </entrydata>
 </viewentry>
 <viewentry position="3" unid="246A24BC5CFDEECD8825687E00150BBF"
➥noteid="932" siblings="3">
  <entrydata columnnumber="0" name="Form">
   <text>Listbox</text>
  </entrydata>
 </viewentry>
</viewentries>
```

I discuss more about XML in Part V.

OpenForm

The `OpenForm` command is used to create a new document in the database.

Syntax:

```
http://Host/Database/FormName?OpenForm[&ParentUNID=UNID][&Seq=1]
```

```
http://Host/Database/$defaultform?OpenForm[&ParentUNID=UNID][&Seq=1]
```

```
http://Host/Database/FormUniversalID?OpenForm[&ParentUNID=UNID][&Seq=1]
```

```
http://Host/Database/FormNoteID?OpenForm[&ParentUNID=UNID][&Seq=1]
```

Arguments:

Seq=1
: If Seq=1 is used, the OpenForm command acts as if it is a CreateDocument command. This argument is automatically generated by Domino in the ACTION attribute of the <FORM> element in response to an OpenForm URL command.

ParentUNID=UNID
: The ParentUNID argument is used to specify the parent of the document that is about to be created. Because a document cannot be selected using the Web, this allows a parent to be selected for purposes of inheritance or for creating a response document.

Examples:

```
http://www.yourserver.com/apps/expense.nsf/Tripform?OpenForm
```

```
http://www.yourserver.com/Empdata.nsf/Employee?OpenForm
```

```
http://www.yourserver.com/y2kinfo.nsf/Problem?
➥OpenForm&ParentUNID=57c1dc242297e2ea882567fb00677955
```

```
<FORM METHOD=post ACTION="/empdata.nsf/
➥e7d5fc241897e2eb89259113f06779dd?OpenForm&Seq=1"
➥ NAME="_Employee">
```

```
http://www.yourserver.com/Empdata.nsf/$defaultform?OpenForm
```

Use the OpenForm command to create a new Domino document with the specified form. You can optionally include a UniversalID for a parent document. This parent document is used for handling inheritance and creating a response document.

When you issue the OpenForm command, Domino will prepare the HTML based on the form, and then send it to the browser. Embedded within the HTML will be a <FORM> element that contains an OpenForm&Seq=1 or CreateDocument URL command (depending on your version of Domino). The document is not actually created in the database until the CreateDocument ACTION is performed on the server. See the CreateDocument command explanation for its details. You can also see Chapter 10, "The JavaScript Form and Form Elements," in the section titled "Programming the Client with HTML and JavaScript," for additional details about creating, displaying, and editing documents.

The universal ID of the form is not easily obtained. To find it, first select the form (but don't open it) in the Domino Designer. Then open the Design Document properties box. Select the Document IDs tab (the beanie hat). You can determine the form's universal ID by combining the first two lines of the dialog box except for the first two characters and the colons of each line. The string of 32 hexadecimal digits is the form's universal ID.

You can use a feature called AutoFrame to launch a form (or page) within a frameset. You enable this feature on the Launch tab of the Form properties box. If enabled, you can specify a frameset and frame. When Domino receives the form URL, rather than just showing the form, the form will be displayed in context within the frameset you have specified.

```
ReadForm
```

The `ReadForm` command is used to open a form in read-only mode.

Syntax:

```
http://Host/Database/FormName?ReadForm
http://Host/Database/$defaultform?ReadForm
http://Host/Database/FormUniversalID?ReadForm
http://Host/Database/FormNoteID?ReadForm
```

Examples:

```
http://www.yourserver.com/apps/expense.nsf/Tripform?ReadForm
http://www.yourserver.com/Empdata.nsf/Employee?ReadForm
http://www.yourserver.com/y2kinfo.nsf/Problem?ReadForm
http://www.yourserver.com/Empdata.nsf/$defaultform?ReadForm
```

Use the `ReadForm` command to open a Domino form in read-only mode. When you use this command, input fields will not be rendered or displayed in the Web browser.

CREATING, OPENING, SAVING, AND DELETING DOCUMENTS

This section describes how you access documents within a Domino database. The easiest way will typically be to create a view, use a sorted column as a key, and then specify the key within the URL when you want to access the document. See the individual commands for details.

```
OpenDocument
```

The `OpenDocument` command is used to display a document in read-only mode. You can also open a document with an anchor link, which will typically open the document somewhere other than the top of the document.

Syntax:

```
http://Host/Database/View/DocumentKey?OpenDocument[#Anchorlabel]
http://Host/Database/View/DocUniversalID?OpenDocument[#Anchorlabel]
http://Host/Database/View/DocNoteID?OpenDocument[#Anchorlabel]
http://Host/Database/View/$first?OpenDocument[#Anchorlabel]
```

Examples:

```
http://www.yourserver.com/Empdata.nsf/LastNames/Smith?OpenDocument
http://www.yourserver.com/y2kinfo.nsf/Sites/Nuclear?OpenDocument#ThreeMile
http://www.yourserver.com/y2kinfo.nsf/e7d5fc241897e2eb89259113f06779dd/
➥57c1dc242297e2ea882567fb00677955?OpenDocument
http://www.yourserver.com/Contacts.nsf/PhoneList/$first?OpenDocument
```

Use the OpenDocument command to open a document in a Domino database. Domino will find the document, convert it along with its form into HTML, and then send it to the browser. The easiest form of this command uses a sorted view and a key to retrieve the document. The key is used to search the first sorted column in the view. A common mistake is to forget to specify that the key column is sorted. Normally it is a good practice to use the first column as your key and specify its sort attributes within the Domino Designer. If you forget to add the sort attribute to your key column, you will receive a 404-Page not found error, even though the document displays in the view in the Notes client.

The anchor label is optional, and if present is signified by the pound sign (#). The square brackets in the syntax notation mean that the anchor label is optional. Do not include the square brackets in your URL. The anchor is associated with some text found within the document. You can create anchors within the Domino Designer. You can also directly code anchors using HTML. The HTML anchor syntax is

```
<A NAME="#Anchorlabel">
```

A view is required because Domino must know which form to use when displaying the document. If the view has a form formula, it will be evaluated and used to display the document unless the document has a form stored in it.

To display the first document in the view, use the $first keyword.

EditDocument

The EditDocument command is used to display a document in edit mode.

Syntax:

```
http://Host/Database/View/DocumentKey?EditDocument[&Seq=1]

http://Host/Database/View/DocUniversalID?EditDocument[&Seq=1]

http://Host/Database/View/DocNoteID?EditDocument[&Seq=1]

http://Host/Database/View/$first?EditDocument[&Seq=1]
```

Argument:

    Seq=1   If Seq=1 is used, the EditDocument command acts as if it is a SaveDocument command. This argument is automatically generated by Domino in the ACTION attribute of the <FORM> element in response to an EditDocument URL command.

Examples:

```
http://www.yourserver.com/Empdata.nsf/LastNames/Smith?EditDocument

http://www.yourserver.com/y2kinfo.nsf/Sites/Nuclear?EditDocument

http://www.yourserver.com/y2kinfo.nsf/e7d5fc241897e2eb89259113f06779dd/
➥57c1dc242297e2ea882567fb00677955?EditDocument

<FORM METHOD=post ACTION="/y2kinfo.nsf/e7d5fc241897e2eb89259113f06779dd/
➥57c1dc242297e2ea882567fb00677955?EditDocument&Seq=1" NAME="_MyForm">

http://www.yourserver.com/Contacts.nsf/PhoneList/$first?EditDocument
```

Use the `EditDocument` command to open a document for editing from a Domino database. Domino will find the document, convert it along with its form into HTML, and then send it to the browser. The easiest form of this command uses a sorted view and a key to retrieve the document. The key is used to search the first sorted column in the view. A common mistake is to forget to specify that the key column is sorted. Normally it is a good practice to use the first column as your key and specify its sort attributes within the Domino Designer. If you forget to add the sort attribute to your key column, you will receive a 404-Page not found error, even though the document displays in the view in the Notes client.

A view is required because Domino must know which form to use when displaying the document. If the view has a form formula, it will be evaluated and used to display the document unless the document has a form included with it.

If you add the `Seq=1` argument, the `EditDocument` URL will behave as if it were a `SaveDocument` command. This URL is automatically generated by Domino in response to the `EditDocument` URL. Previously, Domino generated a `SaveDocument` command in response to an `EditDocument` URL. See the SaveDocument URL description for its details. See Chapter 10, in the section "Programming the Client with HTML and JavaScript," for more details about the `EditDocument` URL.

To display and edit the first document in the view, use the `$first` keyword.

Note that Web users with editor access will be able to view hidden text that is contained in rich text fields. Make sure you use another technique to hide information from Web users with editor access. Be sure to test your implementation.

DeleteDocument

The `DeleteDocument` command is used to delete the specified document from the database.

Syntax:

```
http://Host/Database/View/DocumentKey?DeleteDocument
```

```
http://Host/Database/View/DocUniversalID?DeleteDocument
```

```
http://Host/Database/View/DocNoteID?DeleteDocument
```

```
http://Host/Database/View/$first?DeleteDocument
```

Examples:

```
http://www.yourserver.com/Empdata.nsf/LastNames/Smith?DeleteDocument
```

```
http://www.yourserver.com/y2kinfo.nsf/Sites/Nuclear?DeleteDocument
```

```
http://www.yourserver.com/y2kinfo.nsf/e7d5fc241897e2eb89259113f06779dd/
➥57c1dc242297e2ea882567fb00677955?DeleteDocument
```

```
http://www.yourserver.com/Contacts.nsf/PhoneList/$first?DeleteDocument
```

Use the `DeleteDocument` command to delete a document from a Domino database. Domino will find and delete the document. The easiest form of this command uses a sorted view and a key to retrieve the document. The key is used to search the first sorted column in the view. A common mistake is to forget to specify that the key column is sorted. Normally it is a good practice to use the first column as your key and specify its sort attributes within the Domino Designer. If you forget to add the sort attribute to your key column, you will receive a 404-Page not found error, even though the document displays in the view in the Notes client.

To delete the first document in the view, use the $first keyword.

SaveDocument

The SaveDocument command is used in the ACTION attribute of the <FORM> HTML element when a document is displayed in edit mode. The METHOD is type post.

Syntax:

```
http://Host/Database/View/DocumentKey?SaveDocument
```

```
http://Host/Database/View/DocUniversalID?SaveDocument
```

```
http://Host/Database/View/DocNoteID?SaveDocument
```

```
http://Host/Database/View/$first?SaveDocument
```

Examples:

```
http://www.yourserver.com/Empdata.nsf/LastNames/Smith?SaveDocument
```

```
http://www.yourserver.com/y2kinfo.nsf/Sites/Nuclear?SaveDocument
```

```
http://www.yourserver.com/y2kinfo.nsf/e7d5fc241897e2eb89259113f06779dd/
➥57c1dc242297e2ea882567fb00677955?SaveDocument
```

```
http://www.yourserver.com/Contacts.nsf/PhoneList/$first?SaveDocument
```

Normally the SaveDocument command is generated by Domino and will be embedded in the HTML that is sent to the browser. Newer versions of Domino will generate EditDocument&Seq=1 instead of SaveDocument. This HTML is usually the result of the EditDocument URL command. You don't normally need to use this method. Here is an example of the URL when used in context, as generated by Domino:

```
<FORM METHOD=post ACTION="/y2kinfo.nsf/e7d5fc241897e2eb89259113f06779dd/
➥57c1dc242297e2ea882567fb00677955?SaveDocument" NAME="_MyForm">
```

In this example you see that Domino generates the command within the HTML <FORM> element. It uses the relative form of addressing so that the server name does not need to be supplied. The name found in the NAME attribute is the Domino form name prepended with an underscore (_).

To save the first document in the view, use the $first keyword.

CreateDocument

The CreateDocument command is used in the ACTION attribute of the <FORM> HTML element when a document is displayed in edit mode. The METHOD is type post.

Syntax:

```
http://Host/Database/FormName?CreateDocument
http://Host/Database/FormUniversalID?CreateDocument
http://Host/Database/FormNoteID?CreateDocument
```

Examples:

```
http://www.yourserver.com/Empdata.nsf/Employee?CreateDocument
http://www.yourserver.com/y2kinfo.nsf/MajorSite?CreateDocument
http://www.yourserver.com/y2kinfo.nsf/
➥e7d5fc241897e2eb89259113f06779dd?CreateDocument
```

Normally the CreateDocument command is generated by Domino and will be embedded in the HTML sent to the browser. Newer versions of Domino will generate OpenForm&Seq=1 instead of CreateDocument. This HTML is usually the result of an OpenForm URL command. You don't normally need to use this method. The following is an example of the URL when used in context, as generated by Domino:

```
<FORM METHOD=post ACTION="/empdata.nsf/
➥e7d5fc241897e2eb89259113f06779dd?CreateDocument"
➥ NAME="_Employee">
```

In this example you see that Domino generates the command within the HTML <FORM> element. It uses the relative form of addressing so that the server name does not need to be supplied. The name found in the NAME attribute is the Domino form name prepended with an underscore (_).

FRAMESETS, PAGES, AND NAVIGATORS

The syntax for opening framesets, pages, and navigators is similar. See the individual commands for details.

OpenFrameset

The OpenFrameset command is used to open a named Domino frameset stored within a Domino database.

Syntax:

```
http://Host/Database/FramesetName?OpenFrameset
http://Host/Database/FramesetUniversalID?OpenFrameset
http://Host/Database/FramesetNoteID?OpenFrameset
```

Examples:

```
http://www.yourserver.com/Empdata.nsf/MainFrameset?OpenFrameset
http://www.yourserver.com/y2kinfo.nsf/
➥3341697abed7d36e8825675a0064bae6?OpenFrameset
```

The `OpenFrameset` command is used to open a frameset that you have defined in a Domino database. You cannot use this URL to open a regular frameset defined in HTML. You may use either the frameset name or its UniversalID. Although you can use the NoteID for the frameset, its value will vary among replicas of the database, so its use is not recommended.

OpenPage

The `OpenPage` command is used to open a named page stored within a Domino database.

Syntax:

`http://Host/Database/PageName?OpenPage`

`http://Host/Database/PageUniversalID?OpenPage`

`http://Host/Database/PageNoteID?OpenPage`

Examples:

`http://www.yourserver.com/Empdata.nsf/MainPage?OpenPage`

`http://www.yourserver.com/y2kinfo.nsf/3341697abed7d36e8825675a0064bae6?OpenPage`

The `OpenPage` command is used to open a page within a Domino database. Pages are similar to forms but cannot contain Domino fields. You may use either the page name or its universal ID. Although you can use the NoteID for the page, its value will vary among replicas of the database, so its use is not recommended.

The universal ID of a page is not easily obtained. To find it, first select the page (but don't open it) in the Domino Designer. Then open the Design Document properties box. Select the Document IDs tab (the beanie hat). You can determine the form's universal ID by combining the first two lines of the dialog box except for the first two characters and the colons of each line. The string of 32 hexadecimal digits is the page's universal ID.

You can use a feature called AutoFrame to launch a page (or form) within a frameset. You enable this feature on the Launch tab of the Page properties box. If enabled, you can specify a frameset and frame. When Domino receives the Page URL, rather than just showing the page, the page will be displayed in context within the frameset you have specified.

OpenNavigator

The `OpenNavigator` command is used to open a named navigator stored within a Domino database.

Syntax:

`http://Host/Database/NavigatorName?OpenNavigator`

`http://Host/Database/NavigatorUniversalID?OpenNavigator`

`http://Host/Database/NavigatorNoteID?OpenNavigator`

`http://Host/Database/$defaultNav?OpenNavigator`

Examples:

```
http://www.yourserver.com/Empdata.nsf/MainNav?OpenNavigator
```

```
http://www.yourserver.com/y2kinfo.nsf/
➥3341697abed7d36e8825675a0064bae6?OpenNavigator
```

The `OpenNavigator` command is used to open a navigator within a Domino database. The `$defaultNav` option will open the default folder navigator. You may use either the navigator name or its UniversalID. Although you can use the NoteID for the navigator, its value will vary among replicas of the database, so its use is not recommended.

AGENTS

Agents can be written in either LotusScript or Java. You can invoke either type through a URL. When you invoke the agent, you don't know the language that has been used to implement the agent.

OpenAgent

The `OpenAgent` command is used to invoke an agent within a database using a URL. The agent will run on the Domino server.

Syntax:

```
http://Host/Database/AgentName?OpenAgent[&ArgString]
```

Example:

```
http://www.yourserver.com/Empdata.nsf/HelloAgent?OpenAgent&Name=Fred
```

The `OpenAgent` command is used to invoke an agent on the Domino server. When the agent runs, it uses the credentials of the last user to edit and save it. The agent can write HTML to an output stream, which will then be sent back to the browser. In LotusScript, you simply use the `Print` command in the agent. Java agents use the `getAgentOutput` method to get a `PrintWriter` object, which can be used to send output back to the client.

To access the optional argument string from within an agent, use the `DocumentContext` document. Then access the predefined field called `query_String`. This is just one of several CGI variables that may be accessed from within an agent. For more details about Java agents, see Chapter 13, "Creating Java Agents with the Domino Designer IDE."

ABOUT, HELP, ICON, AND ELEMENTS

Three special elements within a Domino database can be accessed through a URL. They are the About document, the Using document (also known as the Help document), and the Icon. You can also access file attachments, graphics, or OLE objects within a document using a URL with the `OpenElement` command.

OpenAbout, OpenHelp, AND OpenIcon

The `OpenAbout`, `OpenHelp`, and `OpenIcon` commands all have a similar syntax. They are used to open the About document, the Using (Help) document, and the Icon, respectively.

Syntax:

```
http://Host/Database/$about?OpenAbout
http://Host/Database/$help?OpenHelp
http://Host/Database/$icon?OpenIcon
```

Examples:

```
http://www.yourserver.com/Empdata.nsf/$about?OpenAbout
http://www.yourserver.com/Empdata.nsf/$help?OpenHelp
http://www.yourserver.com/Empdata.nsf/$icon?OpenIcon
```

These three commands will open and display the special document or item named in the URL.

OpenElement FOR FILE ATTACHMENTS

The OpenElement command can be used to open file attachments. A document can have several attachments, so the filename allows you to specify the correct one. You must specify the exact filename for the attached file with the following syntax.

Syntax:

```
http://Host/Database/View/Document/$File/Filename[?OpenElement]
```

Examples:

```
http://www.yourserver.com/y2kinfo.nsf/Failures/
➥thebigone/$File/readme.txt?OpenElement
```

```
http://www.yourserver.com/y2kinfo.nsf/Failures/thebigone/$File/readme.txt
```

```
http://www.yourserver.com/Empdata.nsf/Employees/
➥New/$File/resume.doc?OpenElement
```

```
http://www.yourserver.com/Empdata.nsf/Employees/New/$File/resume.doc
```

You can open a file attachment using the OpenElement URL command. Make sure that the browser can handle the type of file based on the extension of the attachment. Note that because some browsers require the type of file to be at the end of the query, Domino will treat the OpenElement as an implicit command, and it can be omitted when used with an embedded file attachment.

OpenElement FOR GRAPHIC IMAGE FILES

The OpenElement command can be used to open graphic images that have been imported into a rich text field. Use the following syntax.

Syntax:

```
http://Host/Database/View/Document/FieldName/FieldOffset
➥ ?OpenElement[&FieldElemFormat=ImageFormat]
```

PART

II

CH

7

Example:

```
http://www.yourserver.com/books.nsf/BookIDs/Book37/
➥CoverPic/0.7c?OpenElement&FieldElemFormat=GIF
```

The field offset is specified in the format *xx.yy*, where *xx* is the field number and *yy* is the byte offset into the field. In general, these offsets are difficult to determine in advance. You can import a graphic image into a rich text field, invoke a browser, and then view the page source to see the offset. The Image format may be either GIF or JPEG. If it is omitted, GIF is assumed.

OpenElement FOR OLE OBJECTS

The OpenElement command can be used to obtain OLE objects, however the syntax of the command makes it impractical to use manually. The command is included here for completeness.

Syntax:

```
http://Host/Database/View/Document/$OLEOBJINFO/FieldOffset/obj.ods?OpenElement
```

Example:

```
http://www.yourserver.com/books.nsf/BookIDs/Book37/
➥$OLEOBJINFO/0.7c/obj.ods?OpenElement
```

The field offset is specified in the format *xx.yy*, where *xx* is the field number and yy is the byte offset into the field. In general, these offsets are difficult to determine in advance. As an alternative, you can import the file as an attachment and use the $File syntax.

SEARCH

Several searches are possible using URLs. The SearchDomain command searches across an entire domain. The SearchSite command allows you to search a Domino site, while the SearchView searches an individual database view. You can either use a form that allows user input or you can programmatically perform searches.

SearchDomain

The SearchDomain command can be used to search multiple databases with a Search Site database for documents containing specified search criteria.

Syntax:

```
http://Host/Database/[TemplateForm]?SearchDomain&ArgumentList
```

Example:

```
http://www.yourserver.com/srchDom.nsf/ResultsForm?SearchDomain&Query=Smith
```

The *TemplateForm* is used to format the results of the search. If you do not supply a form name for the results, the default name of $$SearchDomainTemplate will be used. The databases to be searched must be listed in the Domain Catalog and must be marked as included for multi-database indexing. You must supply at least a query in the *ArgumentList* for this command. Other parameters of *ArgumentList* are optional. See the "Search ArgumentList" section for details. If you are especially detail oriented, examine the formula code for the Search button on the form called Search Form found within the Catalog (5.0) database template. It gives an example of the use of this URL.

SearchSite

The SearchSite command can be used to search multiple databases with a Search Site database for documents containing specified search criteria.

Syntax:

```
http://Host/Database/[$SearchForm]?SearchSite[&ArgumentList]
```

Example:

```
http://www.yourserver.com/srchsite.nsf/$SearchForm?SearchSite
```

```
http://www.yourserver.com/srchsite.nsf/
➥?SearchSite&Query=Domino+Books&SearchOrder=1
```

The database supplied in the SearchSite URL command must be a Search Site database. This is a special database that must be explicitly created. Both the $SearchForm and *ArgumentList* arguments are optional. When you specify $SearchForm, Domino will display a form that can be filled out by the user, and the *ArgumentList* is ignored. See the "Search ArgumentList" section for details.

SearchView

The SearchView command can be used to search a view within a database for documents containing specified search criteria.

Syntax:

```
http://Host/Database/View/[$SearchForm]?SearchView[&ArgumentList]
```

Example:

```
http://www.yourserver.com/books.nsf/AllBooks/$SearchForm?SearchView
```

```
http://www.yourserver.com/books.nsf/AllBooks/
➥?SearchSite&Query=Domino+Books&Count=15&SearchMax=0
```

The specified view in the given database will be searched. Make sure that the database is full text indexed or you will get an error on the Domino server. Both the $SearchForm and *ArgumentList* arguments are optional. When you specify $SearchForm, Domino will display a form that can be filled out by the user, and the *ArgumentList* is ignored. See the "Search ArgumentList" section for details.

SEARCH ArgumentList

If you specify the keyword $SearchForm, a special search form will be displayed to the user and all other arguments supplied will be ignored.

If the `ArgumentList` parameter is used then you must supply the `Query` argument. All other arguments are optional and may be included in any order. Here is a table of the arguments you can use within the ArgumentList parameter:

Argument	Description
Query=string	The `Query` argument specifies the string to be located. Embedded blanks should be converted to +.
Count=n	`Count` specifies the number of rows to return per page.
Scope=0/1/2	`Scope` specifies the scope of the search. Use 1 for Notes databases, 2 for file system, and 0 for both. The default is 0.
SearchEntry=formname	`SearchDomain` only. This form is used to format results of the search.
SearchFuzzy=TRUE/FALSE	Enable or disable fuzzy search. The default is `FALSE`. The details on this parameter are a bit fuzzy.
SearchOrder=1/2/3	1 = sort by relevance, 2 = sort by date ascending, 3 = sort by date descending. The default is 1.
SearchMax=n	The maximum number of items to return. 0 means no limit. The default value is determined by the server.
SearchThesaurus=TRUE/FALSE	Enable or disable the searching of the thesaurus for synonyms. This option is included for backward compatibility but is ignored by the Domino R5 search engine.
SearchWV=TRUE/FALSE	Enable or disable search word variants. The default is `TRUE`.
Start=n	Start display at the nth document found. This is to support paged display of secondary pages. `Start=0` means do not use paged display.

Chapter Review

1. What HTML element is used to create a drop-down box? How about a group of radio buttons?
2. What is the difference between an HTML element and an HTML tag?
3. Could the `CreateDocument` URL command be used to create a new document in a Domino database? If so, how would you specify the parameters? If not, what URL command should be used instead?
4. What is the difference between an HTML `Form` element and a Domino form? How are they related?
5. What are the primary HTML elements used to create a table in HTML? How can you create a table that does not show any borders?
6. What is a relative URL?

7. What are the three different specification levels for HTML 4.0? What do the different levels mean and how do you specify which one you want to use?

8. What is wrong with the following HTML?

```
<HTML>
<HEAD><TITLE>Hello</TITLE></HEAD>
<INPUT TYPE=button onClick="alert(&quot;Hello&quot;)">
</HTML>
```

9. How can you ensure that the browser does not use a cached version of a Web page you are creating?

10. Suppose you have a document in a Domino database with an embedded Microsoft Excel spreadsheet name Sample.xls. Give some examples of URLs that you could use to access and open the spreadsheet. Also describe the other prerequisite assumptions you would need in your database to use the URLs.

CHAPTER 8

THE JAVASCRIPT LANGUAGE AND THE DOCUMENT OBJECT MODEL

In this chapter

JAVASCRIPT FUNDAMENTALS

The JavaScript language, as I'm sure you know, is only remotely related to Java. Its name was chosen to market the language more easily by tying it to Java. JavaScript shares a few syntactic similarities to Java, which in turn is similar to C++. In this chapter I cover the basics of JavaScript and introduce its document object model (DOM).

If you are familiar with Domino, you might be aware of the relationship between the LotusScript language and Domino Objects. *Domino Objects* comprise an object model for accessing a Domino database and include classes such as NotesSession and NotesDatabase. While the object model controls the organization and access to the database, the LotusScript language describes the syntax and semantics of the program itself. That is, the LotusScript language includes constructs such as FOR/NEXT loops, assignment statements, WHILE/WEND loops, and so forth. The same relationship exists between JavaScript and the JavaScript document object model.

With JavaScript, the language describes the syntax for loops and assignment statements, while the document object model describes data, its organization, and access. The data in this case is comprised of the data found in an HTML document. Essentially, the HTML elements as they are specified in the text document describe a hierarchical structure. The browser converts this structure to an internal, object-oriented format that can then be manipulated by the JavaScript program.

Listing 8.1 shows a simple HTML page with a JavaScript program to illustrate several points. I'll explain more details about the JavaScript syntax later in this chapter. This program should be relatively easy to understand, even if you have not previously programmed with JavaScript.

LISTING 8.1   A SAMPLE HTML PAGE WITH A JAVASCRIPT PROGRAM

```
<!DOCTYPE html public "-//W3C//DTD HTML 4.0 Transitional//EN">
<HTML>
<HEAD>
<TITLE>JavaScript Test</TITLE>
<SCRIPT LANGUAGE="JavaScript">
  function CheckIt() {
    if (document.forms[0].ChkOption.checked) {
      alert("Checked");
      document.forms[0].ChkOption.checked=false;
    };
    else {
      alert("Not checked");
      document.forms[0].ChkOption.checked=true;
    }
  }
</SCRIPT>
</HEAD>
<BODY>
<FORM>
    <INPUT type="checkbox" name="ChkOption">Check Option<BR>
    <INPUT type="button" onClick="CheckIt()" value="Check It">
```

```
</FORM>
</BODY>
</HTML>
```

In this example, only two items are displayed within the HTML form. These elements are defined by the HTML <INPUT> elements between the <FORM> tags toward the bottom of the document. The first is a checkbox with the associated text of Check Option, and the second is a pushbutton with the text Check It. You can see the simple page displayed in Figure 8.1.

Figure 8.1
A simple HTML page with a checkbox and a button.

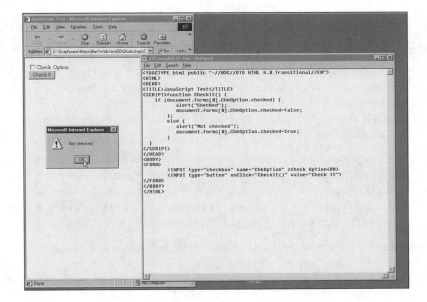

When you click the pushbutton, it will invoke the routine associated with the onClick event, which is the CheckIt function. Note that JavaScript is case sensitive, so you must capitalize all names the same way or you will introduce errors in your JavaScript program. The definition of the CheckIt function is located between the <SCRIPT> tags.

The CheckIt function will examine the status of the checkbox, display a message of the current status, and change the checkbox to the opposite status. In Figure 8.1 you see that the alert "Not Checked" has been issued. After the user clicks the OK button, the checkbox will be changed to a checked status by the script.

This illustrates a very simple example of form validation. By using JavaScript, you can examine field elements, take action depending on their status, and even change the status of these elements so they display differently to the user.

Note that the CheckIt function is declared within the <HEAD> HTML element. Even though this element occurs at the beginning of the HTML file, it will not execute unless it is invoked using the onClick event. This type of execution is sometimes called *deferred* execution. It is also possible to include JavaScript programs that will execute immediately when the page loads into the browser.

In this chapter, I show you examples primarily in HTML, as in the previous example. If you will be using JavaScript with Domino, however, one of the major advantages is in the combination of JavaScript with Domino. For example, you can use Domino to define your input fields (rather than in HTML) and you can use JavaScript for field validation tasks. Chapter 11, "JavaScript Techniques with Domino," focuses on how you can use both JavaScript and Domino together for maximum effect.

THE JAVASCRIPT LANGUAGE VERSIONS

One of the main difficulties in programming HTML and JavaScript for Web browsers is in implementation between the various browsers. There are two major vendors, Microsoft and Netscape, and within each vendor's product, there are different versions. JavaScript is supported in Netscape Navigator versions 2, 3, and 4. It is supported in Microsoft Internet Explorer versions 3, 4, and 5.

The JavaScript 1.0 language itself was initiated with Netscape Navigator 2 and Internet Explorer 3. Version 1.1 of JavaScript was used in Netscape Navigator 3. Because Internet Explorer 3 was already released, it did not support some of the JavaScript 1.1 features. Netscape Navigator 4 introduced the JavaScript 1.2 level, and when Internet Explorer 4 came out, it supported JavaScript 1.2 with additional extensions.

Meanwhile, the standardization body called the European Computer Manufacturer's Association (ECMA) was also working on a standard for the language. Due to trademark restrictions, they could not name their language JavaScript, and instead called it ECMAScript. ECMAScript is essentially the same as version 1.1 of JavaScript. Netscape Navigator 4, Microsoft Internet Explorer 4 (and 5), and the Notes client all support the ECMAScript standard. Microsoft uses the name JScript for its implementation of JavaScript.

As you might imagine, developing a robust Web application in the face of these incompatibilities is a challenge. There are essentially three approaches you can take. The first is to find out the type and version of Web browser the client is using, and then use different code depending on the browser type. This approach has the advantage that it enables you to optimize your user interface for each type of browser. The major disadvantage, of course, is that this requires a lot of work because you might have to use several different types of code and duplicate functions for each type and version of Web browser.

The second approach is to use a core subset of functions that is available in both Netscape and Internet Explorer. This approach has the advantage that it is much easier to implement, but it has the disadvantage that you might not be able to provide the latest features in one Web browser or the other.

The third approach is to support only a single vendor's browser product. Certainly Microsoft would advocate this position and encourages developers to use features that are unique to the Microsoft browser. If you are willing to disable the capability of some clients to view your Web site, you can choose this alternative. It might be appropriate, for example, within an intranet environment where you control the browser that is available on each desktop.

Getting Started with JavaScript

Now that you have an introduction to the JavaScript environment, I'll give you a quick tour of the language fundamentals. This chapter assumes you are familiar with programming languages in general and are familiar with a language such as Visual Basic, LotusScript, C++, or another similar language.

As I've mentioned several times in this book, JavaScript (and Java) are case-sensitive languages. This is perhaps one of the most important items to remember if you are converting from LotusScript, which is case insensitive. In particular, language keywords and variable names must be typed in the proper case, or they will not be recognized correctly by JavaScript.

Keywords in JavaScript are always lowercase. You should use `if`, `while`, and `for`, but not `IF`, `WHILE`, or `FOR`. Variable names are usually specified in a combination of upper- and lowercase letters, but as a programmer you can decide on your own naming conventions.

The <SCRIPT> Tag

JavaScript programs are included within an HTML page. To signify the text of the program, include it within the `<SCRIPT>` and `</SCRIPT>` tags. You can have more than one `<SCRIPT>` tag in your HTML page, and they can be included just about anywhere on the page. Normally, however, JavaScript programs are included in the `<HEAD>` section so that they are defined near the beginning of the page and can be used subsequent to their definition.

Here is the syntax for the `<SCRIPT>` element:

```
<SCRIPT LANGUAGE="language">
```

In the case of JavaScript, you specify the following:

```
<SCRIPT LANGUAGE="JavaScript">
```

Other choices for the language are VBScript, which is Microsoft's Visual Basic dialect for scripting HTML pages, or JScript, which is Microsoft's dialect of JavaScript. Microsoft browsers also allow you to specify the JavaScript keyword for compatibility. Other languages might be available for scripting, but these are the major language choices.

Comments

In JavaScript, you can add comments to your code by using two forward slashes followed by your comment text. JavaScript ignores any text until the end of the line. The following are some examples:

```
//*********************************************************
// This is the Wizbang Framis routine. It calculates the *
// number of beans within a can of pork and beans.        *
//*********************************************************
nCount = nCount + 1     // Increment the Bean counter
```

There is a special convention you can use to hide JavaScript from early browsers. Netscape Navigator version 1.0 and Internet Explorer versions 1 and 2 do not support JavaScript. In practice, you probably don't need to code this defensively anymore, but here is how to do it with the combination of HTML and JavaScript comments:

```
<SCRIPT LANGUAGE="JavaScript">
<!-- This is an HTML comment that causes early browsers to ignore.

// JavaScript program goes here
var nCount = 0          // Initialize variables

//  This is a JavaScript comment, that ends the HTML comment -->
</SCRIPT>
```

The JavaScript processor ignores the first HTML comment line and begins processing on the line following. The JavaScript processor continues processing the program up until the last comment line. Early HTML Web browsers ignore the text between <!-- and the -->.

IDENTIFIERS AND RESERVED WORDS

Identifiers are just names. You can assign names for objects and variables in your program. Identifier names must begin with a letter, an underscore (_), or a dollar sign ($). Following the initial letter, you can use a combination of letters, digits, underscore, or dollar sign characters. Identifier names in JavaScript are case sensitive, so MyVar, Myvar, and myvar represent three different identifiers.

Some identifiers in JavaScript are reserved—that is, you cannot use them as your own identifiers. Examples of reserved words are if, while, and function. These words are part of the JavaScript language itself, and if you named your own identifiers with these words, your program would be harder to process and would be confusing to human readers. Here is the list of reserved words in JavaScript:

```
break

case

continue

default

delete

do

else

export

for
```

```
function

if

import

in

new

return

switch

this

typeof

var

void

while

with
```

In addition to the words reserved by the current language, several other words are reserved for future use. They are reserved because they might be in extensions or they might be in the Java language. Most of the Java reserved words are reserved in JavaScript for possible future use. Here are these additional reserved words:

abstract	int
boolean	interface
byte	long
catch	native
char	null
class	package
const	private
debugger	protected
double	public
enum	short
extends	static
false	super
final	synchronized
finally	throw
float	throws
goto	transient
implements	true
instanceof	try
	volatile

NUMERIC AND STRING LITERALS

You will use numeric or string constants in just about any JavaScript program you create. In this section I describe some of the rules for these constants.

NUMBERS

You can specify numbers in three different bases: decimal, octal, or hexadecimal. Most numbers in your program, however, will probably use decimal. In JavaScript, all numbers are stored as floating-point values, so you can specify both a whole number part and a fractional part of a decimal number. You can optionally supply an exponent, which will scale the value by a power of 10.

Here are some examples:

```
3
3.14159
2.8147e+5
-1.82E-3
```

To specify an integer in octal, the first digit of the number must be 0. For example, 011 is actually an octal number representing 9. All digits within an octal number must be between 0 and 7.

To write hexadecimal values, precede the number with 0x. The digits can include the numbers from 0–9 and the six alphabetic characters A–F. Here are some examples:

```
031           Octal
027415        Octal
0x31          Hexadecimal
0x512247      Hexadecimal
0xCAFEBABE    Hexadecimal
```

STRINGS

Strings are an important data type within JavaScript. You will need to manipulate strings in most JavaScript programs. Creating a string constant is easy, just enclose the string within single quotes (' ') or double quotes (" "). Upper- and lowercase is maintained within your string.

In most cases, you can include a single or double quote within your string by using the opposite type of quote to enclose the string. Occasionally, however, you might need to use both types of quotes in a single string. In this case you must use an escape sequence. Escape sequences are used so that you can include characters that don't appear on the keyboard or that are otherwise difficult to include as a literal character in your string.

Escape sequences begin with a backslash (\) and are followed by a character or a set of numbers. Table 8.1 is a list of special characters you can include with escape sequences.

TABLE 8.1 JAVASCRIPT SPECIAL CHARACTER ESCAPE SEQUENCES

Escape Sequence	Represents This Character
\b	Backspace
\f	Form feed (vertical space)
\n	New line (usually form feed + carriage return)
\r	Carriage return
\t	Tab
\'	Single quote
\"	Double quote
\\	Backslash
\nnn	Character represented by the octal number nnn
\xHH	Character represented by the hex digits HH
\uHHHH	The Unicode character represented by the four hex digits HHHH

Here are some sample strings that include some special characters:

```
"He said, \"Hello, world\""
"This is the end,\ And there is no more."
"\"I can't,\" she said."
'Two quotes(\") are better than one(\')'
```

BOOLEANS

Boolean values come in two types: true and false. These types of values are used in conditional statements such as if and while. You might also want to use Boolean values to keep track of whether a status is on or off.

In JavaScript, as in C, C++, and Java, a numeric variable is considered true if it is nonzero and false if it is zero. A string variable is considered false if it is empty and true if it contains any characters.

OBJECT AND ARRAY LITERALS

At times you might need to create a literal for an object or an array. Object literals are expressed within curly brackets {}. You create a list, separated by commas, of properties and their values. For each property, you specify its name, a colon, and then its value. The following are some examples of object literals:

```
var cookie = {name:"email", value: "mailto:sam@walton.com"};
var jar = {type: "chocolate chip", count : 342 };
```

To specify an array constant, use square brackets [] and separate the elements of the array with commas. To leave a value undefined, place two commas in a row. The following are some examples:

```
var states = ["Alabama", "Alaska", "Connecticut"]
var sizes = [3.7, 2.1+5.7, 82,,, 55]
var mixed = ["First", "second", 3, 6.0 - 2.0 , "five"]
```

The values used to initialize both objects and arrays can also be expressions. Elements of the array can be of different types.

VARIABLES

JavaScript is not a strongly typed language like Java or C++. In strongly typed languages, you must declare variables to be of a particular type, and this type cannot change within the program. In LotusScript (and Visual Basic) you can declare a variable to be of type VARIANT. This type of variable can hold different sorts of values at different times. For example, you can assign a number to a variable and then later assign a text string to the same variable. This is similar to a JavaScript variable. In JavaScript, any variable can hold any type of data.

In JavaScript, seven types of data can be assigned to a variable. Table 8.2 shows the list of the valid data types.

TABLE 8.2   JAVASCRIPT DATA TYPES

Type	Example	Description
Boolean	true or false	True or false. Can be used in if/then types of expressions.
Number	3.14	A numeric value can be used for calculations.
String	"Hello, world"	A string of characters.
Null	null	Used to signify no value.
Object	document	An instance of a class. An object contains properties and methods.
Array	[1,3,5]	An array holds multiple values. Each element of the array can be a different type.
Function	alert()	The definition of a function.

Variable names, and in fact all names in JavaScript, are case sensitive. It is very important to develop a naming convention for your variables and use it rigorously. Most JavaScript variable names use a combination of upper- and lowercase. Some programmers like to include a prefix to the variable that indicates its normal type. For example, nCount is a numeric variable. The variable strName might contain a string value for a name of some sort.

To declare a variable, use the var statement. You can also include an initialization when you declare the variable. Finally, you can declare multiple variables in a single statement. Here are some examples:

```
var nHits = 0;
var strLabel = "Frozen Foods";
var strAddress, strName;
var bStatus = true, nCount = 0;
```

If you forget to declare a variable, your program might work anyway because JavaScript will automatically define a global variable for you. However, within functions you normally want to define local variables, so an automatic reference to a global variable is typically not what you want.

Note

> Using two different types of capitalization for a single variable name is a common mistake. For example, the variables NCount and nCount are two different variable names. If you have declared nCount, for example, but somewhere within your program you use Ncount or NCount, JavaScript will automatically create a global variable. This is almost certainly not what you had in mind. If your program acts like it is ignoring your assignment to a variable, check its capitalization.

FUNCTIONS

Functions are program routines that you create to perform operations and optionally return a result. When you create a function, you typically give it a name and define the parameters that should be passed to the function. You can use the return statement to exit a function and optionally return a result to the calling program.

The following is the syntax to declare a function:

```
function funcname([parm1], [parm2], . . ., [parmn]) {
    function body
}
```

Here is an example function:

```
function errmsg(code, msg) {
    alert("Error " + code + ". " + msg);
}
```

This routine receives two parameters, a code and a message. It displays an alert message box with both the code and the message text. Note that in JavaScript parameters are passed by value. That means that the arguments in the calling routine are evaluated, the values are assigned to the parameter variables, and then the function routine is invoked. The original arguments are not modified from within the function.

JavaScript does not check the number or type of arguments passed. If extra arguments are supplied they are ignored, and if too few are supplied, any additional parameters are set to undefined. You can make use of this fact within your function if you want to handle a variable number of arguments.

VARIABLE SCOPE

Variables in JavaScript can be either local or global in scope. By default, variables that you have not declared with a var statement are global. In general, avoid using global variables if possible. If you must use global variables, highlight them in some way so that you know they are global. I typically use a prefix g_, as in g_UserID, to signify that a variable is global.

The scope of a variable dictates which routines are aware of the variable and how naming conflicts are resolved when more than one variable has the same name. JavaScript uses static scoping, which allows you to look at the source code for a program and determine which variable will be used. Here is an example:

```
var x = "global"        // the global version of x

function f() {
   var x = "x local f"        // a local version of x
   g();
}
function g() {
   alert (x);              // the global version of x is used.
}

f();                    // invoke the function f.
```

This case shows two versions of the variable x. One is global, and the other is contained within function f. The program invokes function f on the last line. When it does so, the local version of x is defined within f. At this point, function g is called. Within g is a reference to the variable x. Which x is used? The rule is that you look first within the routine itself for the variable. If it is not found, look outside the routine in the source code for the enclosing code. In this case, it is the global x. We don't use the calling program's version of the variable. We can determine which variable is used by looking at the declarations within the program.

Notice how the use of global variable x makes this program confusing. A much better method for implementing this routine would be to use a parameter in the inner program and pass the value to the function. Here is how you would code the function g with a parameter:

```
function g(msg) {
  alert(msg);     // Parameter for message
}
```

I have made two modifications. First, I've modified the function to use a parameter, and second I've changed the name to a meaningful variable name. Both these techniques will aid you in avoiding errors over the long term and do not require the use of global variables. Again, try to use local variables and function parameters whenever possible. Avoid global variables.

OBJECTS

An object is similar to an array in that it is an aggregate. That is, it can hold several separate named values. In addition, objects can contain subroutines that are called *methods*. The methods typically operate on the internal values, which are called *properties*.

As an example, suppose you wanted to create an object called employee with several attributes. Here is how you might do it:

```
var employee = new Object();
employee.Name = "Fred Smith";
```

```
employee.Address = "1234 Main Street";
employee.Serial = 567890;
```

Objects can contain other objects. For example, you could modify the previous example to the following:

```
var employee = new Object();
employee.Name = "Fred Smith";
employee.Address = new Object();
employee.Address.First = "Federal Expressions";
employee.Address.Second = "1234 Main Street";
employee.Address.Third = "San Francisco, CA 91234";
employee.Address.Fourth = "USA";
employee.Serial = 567890;
```

In this case, the Address property of the employee object is itself an object. It contains its own properties, which are the different lines of the address.

As I show later in this chapter, the JavaScript Document Object Model (DOM) contains a hierarchy of elements similar to the nested address example.

ARRAYS

You can use arrays to hold aggregates of data; that is, many items of data grouped together with just a single variable name. Unlike some other languages, arrays in JavaScript can contain values of different types. For example, the first element of an array might be a number, while the second value is a string. To access arrays, use the square brackets [ ] operator and supply an index. Array subscripts begin with 0, so a subscript of 1 is the second element of the array.

To create a new array, use the new operator with the keyword Array(). Here is an example:

```
var MyArray = new Array();
MyArray[0] = true;
MyArray[1] = 3.14159;
MyArray[2] = "The cat with the hat";
```

You can also specify a length when you create the array. Here is an array with 10 elements.

```
var Size10 = new Array(10);
```

The array has 10 elements that can be indexed from 0–9. Specifying a size, however, does not limit the array to that size. In fact, to add an element to the array, you can assign a value to an element. Here is an example:

```
var BigOne = new Array(10);
BigOne[1000] = "Hello";
```

In this case, we defined the array to be 10 elements long (from 0–9), but then assigned a value to index 1000. In JavaScript, arrays are stored sparsely, which means that space for items with index numbers 10–999 is not actually allocated. In this case, space is allocated for only 11 total elements, from 0–9 and 1000. If you access an array item that has not actually been allocated, you will get the value undefined.

You can specify an array literal by using square brackets and separating elements with commas. Here is an example:

```
var AnotherArray = [3.14159, "Hot cat", false];
```

As you can imagine, the looping construct is very useful when combined with arrays:

```
for (i = 1; i <= 10; ++i)
  cNames[i] = "Name" + i;    // concatenate "Name" and the number
```

You can also use the square bracket syntax to access an object's properties. This is called an *associative* array. You supply one value, and the associated value is returned. As an example, suppose you have a single frame in a frameset that has the name `"left"`. You can access the frame by specifying the following:

```
frames["left"]
```

This is much more meaningful than trying to access the frame by a numeric index. The same type of syntax can be used with forms.

```
forms["mainform"]
```

EXPRESSIONS

Expressions in JavaScript are similar to those found in C, C++, or Java. Of course there are the standard mathematical operations of addition (+), subtraction (-), multiplication (*), division (/), and remainder (%). There are the standard comparison operators less than (<), less than or equal (<=), greater than (>), and greater than or equal (>=).

Equality in JavaScript is denoted by ==, two consecutive equal signs. This is familiar to C, C++, and Java programmers but might not be familiar to BASIC programmers. Inequality is signified by !=, the exclamation point and the equal sign.

The assignment symbol is a single equal sign (=), as in

```
a = 2;
```

Note

LotusScript and Visual Basic programmers must beware of the improper use of the assignment statement in an `if` statement. Here is an example:

```
var a = 1;
if (a=2) alert("It is 2");
```

Improbable as it might seem, this code will display the message saying `"It is 2"`. The reason, of course, is that the `if` statement causes an assignment, not a compare. A non-zero value for a condition evaluates to `true`, which then causes the alert to display the message. Here is what you should use:

```
var a = 1;
if (a==2) alert("It is 2");
```

This will not display the alert message because the `if` statement contains a comparison, not an assignment.

INCREMENT AND DECREMENT

JavaScript contains a special operator for incrementing and decrementing variables. The following two constructs are very common in programs:

```
variable = variable + 1
variable = variable - 1
```

There is a special syntax for these two operations. Use two plus signs (++) to indicate increment, and two minus signs (--) to indicate decrement. Here is an example:

```
++nCount;
```

This means to take the value of nCount, increment by one, and store the result back in nCount. In addition, you can use this compact notation within the middle of an expression and access either the value before or after it is incremented.

```
preIncr = 1;
value = ++preIncr    // Increment first, value contains 2
```

If the plus signs (++) appear before the variable name, the variable is incremented first, and the incremented value is the result of the expression. Our example of preIncr gives a value of 2. In the following example of postIncr, the resulting value is 1:

```
postIncr = 1;
value = postIncr++    // Increment after use, value contains 1
```

Use the decrement operator (--) in a similar fashion.

LOGICAL OPERATORS

The logical operators work with the Boolean values of true and false. You typically use comparison operations that result in a Boolean value. When you have Boolean values, you can combine them with the three logical operations of AND, OR, and NOT. Here is the syntax to use for these three operations:

```
&&    AND

||    OR

!     NOT
```

Here are some examples of how you use the operations:

```
bRetired = false
if ((nAge > 65) && (! bRetired)) { alert("Still working!"); }
if ((cType == "police") || (nSpeed <= 65) ) { alert("Speed OK") }
```

When you combine operations using &&, the result is true if both operands are true. If you use ||, the result is true if either operand is true. The NOT operator (!) result is the opposite of the operand. For example, if the variable bRetired is false, the result of !bRetired is true.

Be careful not to confuse the logical operators with their bitwise counterparts, bitwise AND (&), bitwise OR (|), and bitwise NOT (~). Normally you will not need to use the bitwise versions. When you use the bitwise versions, the operation converts the values to 32-bit integers, and then performs the operations on the integers in a bitwise, or bit-by-bit, manner. In other words, the operation is performed on each bit of one operand paired with the corresponding bit of the other operand. Thus, a bitwise AND operation actually results in 32 separate answers contained in a 32-bit integer. This is almost never what you intended to do.

STRING OPERATORS

Strings are a very important part of JavaScript. Strings are important because you will frequently want to manipulate them to produce the desired effect in the Web browser. With the JavaScript language you can concatenate and compare strings to one another. In addition, there is a powerful String class, with which you can extensively manipulate, combine, and split apart strings.

In JavaScript, use the concatenate operator (+) to combine two strings. The result of the operation is a combined string, taking the left and right operands and combining them into a single string. Here is an example:

```
"mother" + " in law"
```

results in

```
"mother in law"
```

If you use the plus sign when either operand is a string, the other operand is first converted to a string and then the two operands are concatenated. Here is an example:

```
3 + "5"
```

results in

```
"35"
```

Note that this is quite different from the result you would expect if you were adding the two values. Only when both operands are numeric is addition performed.

SIMPLE STATEMENTS

JavaScript ignores spaces, tabs, and line breaks in your program. This means that you can have a single statement on one line or on multiple lines. You can also include several statements on a single line.

Statements in JavaScript are terminated by an optional semicolon. If you omit the semicolon then JavaScript will try to automatically insert it where appropriate. Normally this will not cause a problem, but occasionally JavaScript might assume a semicolon at the end of a line if it appears to be a complete statement.

To avoid most problems, and to make your programs more readable

- Generally include one statement per input line.
- End all your statements with an explicit semicolon.

One of the simplest and most common types of statements is the assignment statement. It uses the equal (=) sign as the assignment operator. Here are some examples:

```
nCount = 0;
cName = "Mary Smith";
```

The assignment operator can also be used in conjunction with another operation, such as addition or multiplication. Here are some examples:

```
nOdd += 2;          // equivalent to:  nOdd = nOdd + 2;
nTriple *= 3;       // equivalent to:  nTriple = nTriple * 3;
strHW = "Hello";
strHW += ", world"  // equivalent to:  strHW = strHW + ", world"
```

The first example takes the variable nOdd, adds 2, and then places the value back into the variable. The second example takes the value nTriple, multiplies by 3, and then stores the result back in the variable. The third example appends the value ", world" onto the existing value in the strHW variable.

SELECTION STATEMENTS

The if statement in JavaScript is similar to the one found in Java, C, C++, and most other programming languages. Unlike Visual Basic or LotusScript, there is no keyword THEN. You must enclose the condition within parentheses. You can also specify an else clause, but it is optional. Here is the syntax for the if statement:

```
if (condition)
   statement
```

Here is an example:

```
if (cUserID = "admin")
   bAuthorized = true;
```

Here is the syntax when you include the else clause:

```
if (condition)
   statement
else
   statement
```

Note that when you use more than one nested level of if statement, the else clause is always paired with the closest if statement.

You can supply a group of statements rather than just a single statement by including the group of statements within curly brackets {}. Although this grouping can occur anywhere within your program, it is frequently used within an `if` statement. Here is an example:

```
if (cRadioButton=="red" && cType=="fruit") {
   cItem = "apple";
   cVariety = "delicious";
}
else {
   cItem = "food";
   cVariety = "generic";
}
```

The `if` statement can choose between only two alternatives. The `switch` statement can be used to select among several different choices rather than just two. Here is the syntax:

```
switch (expression) {
case n1:        // execute if expression == n1
   statements
   break;
case n2:        // execute if expression == n2
   statements
   break;
case n2:        // execute if expression == n3
   statements
   break;
default:        // execute if no previous match
   statements
   break;
}
```

The `switch` statement is the same as the corresponding statement in C, C++, or Java. You supply an expression that is evaluated. The value is compared to the values found in each of the cases. When a match is found, the corresponding group of statements will be executed. Note that each group ends with a `break` statement. The `break` statement ends the group of statements and will jump to the next statement following the `switch` statement. If you omit the `break` statement, control will fall through to the next case. Although this might be useful on rare occasions, you should normally always use the `break` statement. If you forget to put `break` statements in each case, control will continue through each subsequent statement until either a `break` statement is encountered or the `switch` statement ends. This operation is significantly different from the `select/case` statement in LotusScript.

LOOPING STATEMENTS

The `for` statement in JavaScript provides a method to easily loop through a group of statements. You can provide an initialization, an ending condition, and an incrementing expression. Here is the syntax:

```
for (initialize; endcondition; incrementexpr)
 statement
```

Here is a very typical usage:

```
for (i = 0; i < 10; ++i)
  myarray[i] = 0;
```

In this case, the variable is set to 0 initially, and then the ending condition test is performed. If the test is true, the statement is executed. By using curly brackets, you can use a group of statements instead of a single statement. If it is false, the loop terminates. Following the execution of the statement, the incrementing expression is executed. In this case, the variable i is incremented. The loop in this case will be executed exactly 10 times, with the variable i containing each of the values 0, 1, 2, …, to 9. Note that the loop starts at 0 because arrays are indexed from 0, not 1.

Another important use of the for keyword is to loop through all the properties of an object. You can use this statement to process all the properties of a particular object without knowing ahead of time the names of the properties. Here is the syntax of this type of for statement:

```
for (prop in object)
  statement
```

Here is an example of a typical usage of this type of for statement:

```
for (p in obj) {
  alert(p + " = " + eval("obj." + p) );
}
```

This loop will cycle through all the properties of the variable obj, will display the name and an equal sign, and will evaluate and display the value of the property.

The while loop enables you to specify a condition that is tested, and if true, it will repeatedly execute a single statement. If you have a group of statements, you can use the curly brackets to group them together. In this case, the condition is tested at the beginning of the group of statements. If the condition is true, the group of statements is executed. The cycle repeats with the testing of the condition and execution of the statements until the condition evaluates to false. At that point, the loop will terminate and move on to the next statement. If the condition is initially false, the loop will not execute at all. Here is the syntax:

```
while (expression)
  statement
```

Here is an example:

```
bObjectFell = false;
bJuggling = true;
while (bJuggling) {
   if (bObjectFell) {
      bJuggling = false;
   }
   else {
      // Sing and dance
      bObjectFell = didItFall(); // Random events
   }
}
```

This loop will repeatedly cycle until a call to the `didItFall` routine returns `true`. The next time through the loop, it will set `bJuggling` to `false`, and the loop will terminate.

THE break AND continue STATEMENTS

The `break` statement is used to leave an existing control structure and go to another location in the program. I have shown you the typical usage within a `switch` statement. You will typically use a `break` at the end of each `case` within the `switch` statement. When the `break` statement is executed, control will continue with the statement following the `switch` statement.

You can also use the `break` statement within loops. When used in this manner, the `break` statement causes the loop to terminate and moves to the statement beyond the loop. Here is the syntax for the `break` statement:

```
break [labelname];
```

You can optionally include the name of a label for an enclosing statement. You will typically need to supply this label only if you have nested loops or `switch` statements.

The `continue` statement is used within a loop. Typically this statement will be associated with a condition and will appear in the middle of the loop. The purpose of the `continue` statement is to bypass the remaining code for the current iteration of the loop. When the `continue` statement is executed, control will move to the portion of the loop that tests whether the loop should continue. It increments or tests the appropriate values and then will continue with the next iteration of the loop.

THE return STATEMENT

The `return` statement can be included within a function to exit the function and optionally return a value. Here is the syntax of the `return` statement:

```
return [expression];
```

If you omit the *expression*, no value is returned. If you include the *expression*, it will be evaluated and returned as the value of the function. Here is an example of a very simple function that adds two numbers and returns the result:

```
function add(a, b) {
    var sum = a + b;
    return sum;
}
```

THE String OBJECT

The `String` object is used to manipulate strings. When you use string literals, they are special cases of `String` objects. You can create `String` variables with the new keyword. Here is how to create your own `String` variable:

```
var strName = new String();
```

After you have created a String, you can use the methods and properties of the String object. The primary property you'll use with the String object is the length property. You can determine the length of a string this way:

```
iLen = strName.length;
```

The methods of the String object can be broken into two categories: routines that return the string enclosed in HTML tags and routines that manipulate the string itself. The String object methods are listed in Tables 8.3 and 8.4.

TABLE 8.3   STRING OBJECT METHODS THAT RETURN TAGS

Method Name	Description
anchor(*name*)	Returns the string enclosed in `<A NAME="name">` and `</A>`. If *name* is not supplied, the value undefined is used.
big()	Returns the string enclosed in `<BIG>` tags.
blink()	Returns the string enclosed in `<BLINK>` tags.
bold()	Returns the string enclosed in `<B>` tags.
fixed()	Returns the string enclosed in `<TT>` tags.
fontcolor(*color*)	Returns the string enclosed in `<FONT COLOR="color">` and `</FONT>`. If *color* is not supplied, the value undefined is used.
fontsize(*size*)	Returns the string enclosed in `<FONT SIZE="size">` and `</FONT>`. If *size* is not supplied, the value undefined is used.
italics()	Returns the string enclosed in `<I>` tags.
link(*href*)	Returns the string enclosed in `<A HREF="href">` and `</A>`. If *href* is not supplied, the value undefined is used.
small()	Returns the string enclosed in `<SMALL>` tags.
strike()	Returns the string enclosed in `<STRIKE>` tags.
sub()	Returns the string enclosed in `<SUB>` tags. The `<SUB>` tags create a subscript.
sup()	Returns the string enclosed in `<SUP>` tags. The `<SUP>` tags create a superscript.

TABLE 8.4   STRING OBJECT METHODS THAT QUERY AND MANIPULATE

Method Name	Description
charAt(*index*)	Returns the character at the specified index.
charCodeAt(*index*)	Returns the ISO-Latin-1 number of the character at the specified index.
concat(*str1, str2, . . .*)	Concatenates one or more strings onto the current string.

continues

TABLE 8.4 CONTINUED

Method Name	Description
fromCharCode(*n1*, *n2*, . . .)	Creates a string from the numeric code points specified. This is a special method. It can only be called with the syntax: String.fromCharCode(). It cannot be called from an existing string object.
indexOf(*substring* [,*start*])	Searches the current string for the first occurrence of *substring*. You can optionally specify a starting position from 0 to the length minus 1. It returns the index of the first character of the first occurrence of the substring. If not found, -1 is returned.
lastIndexOf(*substring* [,*position*])	Searches the current string for the last occurrence of *substring*. You can optionally specify a position with a value from 0 to the length minus 1. If you specify the position, the search will only search from the beginning of the string to the specified position. It returns the index of the first character of the last occurrence of the substring. If not found, -1 is returned.
match(*regexp*)	Returns an array of strings that match the supplied regular expression.
replace(*regexp*, *replacement*)	Replaces the first occurrence or all occurrences of substrings that match the regular expression.
search(*regexp*)	Returns the index of the first substring that matches the supplied regular expression. If not found, -1 is returned.
slice(*start*, *end*)	Extracts a substring from the current string from the *start* position to the character just before the *end* position. Similar to substring, but slice allows negative numbers. Negative numbers represent positions starting from the end of the string.
split(*delimiter*)	Returns an array of substrings. Splits the current string at each occurrence of the specified delimiter. The delimiter is not included in the returned string array. This method is the inverse of the Array.join method.
substr(*from*, *length*)	Extracts a substring from the current string from the *from* position for the specified length.
substring(*start*, *end*)	Extracts a substring from the current string from the *start* position to the character just before the *end* position. Similar to slice, but substring does not allow negative numbers.
toLowerCase()	Converts the current string to lowercase.
toUpperCase()	Converts the current string to uppercase.

THE Date OBJECT

The Date object is used to create and manipulate dates within JavaScript.

Caution

Be very careful with the Date object. Some of its functions are not Year 2000-compliant but depend on the browser and version being used. In particular, do not use the getYear() method. In some browsers this method assumes a century of 1900. Use the getFullYear() method instead. The getFullYear() method always returns a four-digit year.

With the Date object, you can create a date object, set its date and time components, parse strings into date objects, and convert dates into strings for display.

ARRAY OBJECTS

When you create an array, you are actually creating an Array object. As such, the array you create has properties and methods. In addition to the standard accessing of array elements, you can invoke the Array methods. The single Array property is the length property. It normally returns the number of elements in the array. If the array is not contiguous, it returns a number one larger than the index of the last element of the array. Table 8.5 gives you a list of the available methods for Array objects.

TABLE 8.5 ARRAY METHODS

Method Name	Description
concat(*elem1, elem2, . . .*)	Creates a new copy of the current array and concatenates the specified elements at the end. This method does not modify the current array.
join([*separator*])	Joins the elements of an array into a single string. If a separator is specified, it is used in between each element. This method is the inverse of the String.split method.
pop()	Removes and returns the last element of the array.
push(*elem1, elem2, . . .*)	Appends the specified elements, in order, at the end of the current array. Contrast with Array.concat, which does not modify the current array.
reverse()	Reverses the order of the elements in the array.

continues

TABLE 8.5   CONTINUED

Method Name	Description
shift()	Removes and returns the first element of the array. It then shifts the remaining elements down by one position.
slice(*start*, *end*)	Extracts a subset of the items from the array. The *start* position is the index of the first item to return, and the *end* position is one greater than the last position to use. This method creates a new array to return and does not modify the current array.
sort([*function*])	Sorts the array in ascending sequence. If a function is supplied, it should be a comparison function that will return -1, 0, or 1 depending on whether the first argument is less than, equal to, or greater than the second.
splice(*start*, *delNum*, *elem1*, *elem2*, . . .)	From the array index specified by *start*, first deletes *delNum* items, then appends the given elements at that location. If *delNum* is not specified, deletes all remaining items before appending.
toString()	Converts the current array to the string with items separated by commas.
unshift(*elem1*, *elem2*, . . .)	Shifts the existing array and adds the supplied elements at the front of the array. (Netscape Navigator 3/4 only.)

THE JAVASCRIPT DOCUMENT OBJECT MODEL (DOM)

If you are familiar with the Domino Object hierarchy, the JavaScript Document Object Model should be easy for you to conceptually understand. It is similar in function and purpose, but the model itself is different from the Domino Object Model.

In Figure 8.2, you see the hierarchical layout of the JavaScript Document Object Model (DOM). Think of each box as a container, with the items shown below a particular item as being contained within it. For example, the location object is contained within the window object. The document object is also contained within the window object, and the document object is a container itself.

Figure 8.2
The hierarchical
Document Object
Model for JavaScript.

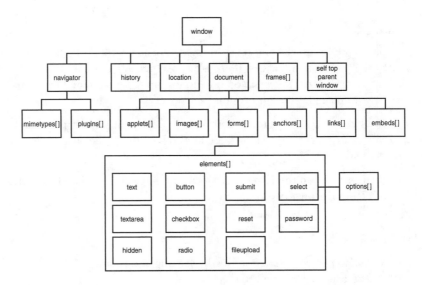

Although the containment hierarchy shows you which types of objects are contained within others, it does not reflect any particular document. The data for any particular document is usually found by examining the HTML. For example, suppose you have the following HTML:

```
<HTML>
<HEAD>
<TITLE>This is a test</TITLE>
</HEAD>
<BODY>
<IMG SRC="http://www.acme.com/sample.gif">
<FORM>
<INPUT TYPE="button" NAME="BTN1">
<A HREF="http://www.gosomewhere.com">Go Somewhere</A>
</FORM>
</BODY>
</HTML>
```

As the browser parses the text, it creates a data structure in memory. The data structure can be accessed and manipulated by JavaScript programs. The window object is at the top of the hierarchy. This means that the object is the outermost container. The window object contains other objects such as the document object. The document object, in turn, contains images, forms, links, and so on.

In Chapter 9, "The JavaScript Window and Document Objects," I show more details about the hierarchy and these two important objects in particular. Chapter 10, "The JavaScript Form and Form Elements," covers the form and its components.

SUMMARY

In this chapter I showed you the basic syntactic elements of the JavaScript language. As in most programming languages, there are constants, variables, and flow of control statements such as `if` or `while`. I showed you how to use these fundamental elements of JavaScript and also how to place JavaScript programs on an HTML page.

I showed you a few of the important built-in objects of JavaScript such as the `String` object and the `Array` object. You can use the methods of these objects to manipulate the data elements of your program.

Finally, I introduced the JavaScript Document Object Model. I show you some details of this model in the next two chapters.

CHAPTER REVIEW

1. Write a JavaScript function to trim leading and trailing blanks from a string parameter and return the modified string.

2. Write a JavaScript function that accepts two parameters, an array, and a string. The routine should search the array for the string and return the index if it is found in the array. If it is not found, return -1.

3. Where should you normally include your JavaScript programs in an HTML page?

4. If you are familiar with the Domino functions @Explode and @Implode, which JavaScript functions correspond to these @functions?

5. What is wrong with the following program fragment? Why?

```
var switch = true;
if (switch) {alert("Switch is true")}
else {alert("Switch is false")}
```

6. Write a JavaScript function that takes three string parameters with the following function declaration:

```
function replaceSubstring(Source, Findstring, Replacestring)
```

Your routine should search the Source string for the first occurrence of the Findstring and replace it with the Replacestring. Hint: Use indexOf.

7. Write a JavaScript function that takes a single string parameter. It should return the ProperCase of the string. The ProperCase of a string means that the first letter of each word should be capitalized.

THE JAVASCRIPT WINDOW AND DOCUMENT OBJECTS

In this chapter, I describe two of the most important objects in the JavaScript Document Object Model (DOM): the window object and the document object. The window object represents the browser window and the document object represents the contents of the window. Each object has various properties and methods that you can use to manipulate it. You can also use these objects to navigate through the DOM hierarchy. Before we examine the window and document objects, let's take a more detailed look at the differences between the Web Document Object Model and the Notes Document Object Model.

THE WEB DOM AND THE NOTES DOM

At the end of Chapter 8, "The JavaScript Language and the Document Object Model," I showed you the DOM hierarchy of objects. You can consider that hierarchy the generic JavaScript hierarchy. In truth, each Web browser's implementation of JavaScript varies slightly from this conceptual model. Now that we're going to explore the details of the objects, it is important to understand the distinctions between the various models.

The Notes implementation of the DOM is a subset of the W3C DOM specification, but it also adds features of both the Netscape Navigator and Microsoft Internet Explorer browser models. It is not identical to the Netscape or Microsoft implementation, but because it was licensed from Netscape, it is closer to the Netscape implementation. Fortunately, if you stick to the subset supported by Lotus, your JavaScript programs are likely to work with both the Netscape and Microsoft browsers as well as with the Lotus browser.

An important point is that in order for the Notes client to recognize JavaScript, you must code it in the programmer's pane in one of the appropriate events. For example, a common location would be in the JSHeader event of the form. If you code your JavaScript program in passthru HTML, it will work in Web browsers, but it will not work in the Notes client.

Let's take another look at the generic DOM hierarchy. At the top of the hierarchy is the window object. I've reproduced the hierarchy chart in Figure 9.1.

Let's begin by examining the window object.

Figure 9.1
The generic hierarchical Document Object Model for JavaScript.

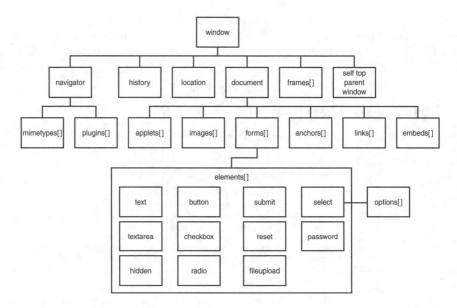

THE window OBJECT

In a non-framed page, the window object represents the current browser window. When you use frames, each frame has its own window object. I discuss frames in greater detail later in this chapter, so for now let's concentrate on a single window object.

As you can see, the window object contains several objects, such as the navigator object, the history object, the document object, and so on. In addition, the window object contains some properties that you can use to query the status or to navigate the window hierarchy.

To access a property of the window object, use the dot notation as follows:

```
nav = window.navigator      // Access the navigator property of window
```

In the example, I've extracted the navigator property and assigned it into a variable called nav. The nav variable now refers to the navigator object. The navigator object has its own properties and methods, as I'll show you shortly.

Before moving on, I'd like to distinguish between the DOM hierarchy that is shown in Figure 9.1 and the window hierarchy that exists on a particular Web page. The DOM hierarchy is static and represents a model of the containment of the various objects, but the window hierarchy represents the containment of windows and frames during program execution.

At runtime it is possible to have a containment hierarchy of framesets and windows. This containment hierarchy consists of window objects at runtime. I'll discuss both the static DOM hierarchy and the runtime window hierarchy, but please keep in mind the distinction. This distinction will become clearer as we examine framesets later in this chapter.

WINDOW PROPERTIES

Table 9.1 lists the properties found in the window object.

TABLE 9.1 THE window OBJECT PROPERTIES

Property	Description
closed	true if the window object has been closed. Do not attempt to manipulate the window object after it has been closed.
defaultStatus	The default message to display on the window's status bar.
document	The document object. This object contains methods and properties relating to the text displayed within the window.
frames	This is an array containing a window object for each frame within the frameset contained in this window. If the window does not use frames then this array will be empty.
history	The history object enables you to navigate through the list of Web sites that the browser has displayed. You can use methods such as back and forward.
innerHeight	Supported only in Navigator 4 and above. This is the height of the document, in pixels, within the browser. It does not contain any of the toolbars or status bars.
InnerWidth	Supported only in Navigator 4 and above. This is the width of the document, in pixels, within the browser. It does not contain any of the toolbars or status bars.
Length	The number of frames in the frames array.
Location	The location object Represents the current Web location displayed by the Web browser. You can find the host server name, port number, and complete URL from this object.
name	The name property returns the name of the window (or frame). You can specify the name with the NAME= attribute.
navigator	The navigator object contains information about the browser being used to display the Web page.
opener	The opener property returns the window object of the window that opened the current window. For child windows, it returns the parent window.
outerHeight	Supported only in Navigator 4 and above. This is the height of the browser's window, including any toolbars and status bars.
outerWidth	Supported only in Navigator 4 and above. This is the width of the browser's window, including any toolbars and status bars.
pageXOffset	Supported only in Navigator 4 and above. The pageXOffset property returns the offset, in pixels, that the page is scrolled horizontally. A value of 0 represents the left-most position. Internet Explorer has a similar, but incompatible, property called scrollLeft.

Property	Description
pageYOffset	Supported only in Navigator 4 and above. The pageYOffset property returns the offset, in pixels, that the page is scrolled vertically. A value of 0 represents the top-most position. Internet Explorer has a similar, but incompatible, property called scrollTop.
parent	The parent property represents the window object of the parent of the current frame. You can navigate through the frameset hierarchy using this property.
screen	The screen object enables you to obtain information about the current screen resolution and size.
self	The self property refers to the current window.
status	The status property contains the message shown in the status line of the browser.
top	The top property represents the window object at the top of the frameset hierarchy.
window	The window property refers to the current window. It is a synonym for self.

THE window OBJECT METHODS

Because of JavaScript's object-oriented heritage, there are no standalone subroutines in a library. Each built-in subroutine is actually a method of an object. The window object in particular is where many of the commonly used routines reside. For example, the alert and prompt routines are actually methods of the window object. Table 9.2 shows the portable methods associated with the window object.

TABLE 9.2   THE window OBJECT METHODS

Method	Description
alert(*string*)	The alert method displays a message in a dialog box.
blur()	The blur method removes focus from the current window. Typically, the browser window will place itself behind any other windows. This is the opposite of the focus method.
clearInterval(*id*)	Clears the periodic interval time specified by the *id* returned from the setInterval method.
clearTimeout(*id*)	Cancels the pending execution of code that was set with setTimeout. You must specify the *id* that was returned from setTimeout.
close()	Closes the current window object. In JavaScript 1.1 and later, only windows opened by JavaScript can be closed by this method. You should use this method only on top-level windows, not on frames within windows. You can query the closed property to see if a window has already been closed.

continues

TABLE 9.2 CONTINUED

Method	Description
confirm(string)	Displays a dialog box with a question that can be answered by yes or no. The dialog box actually displays OK and Cancel. It will return true if OK is pressed and false otherwise.
focus()	Brings the browser window to the front of any other windows. It is the opposite of the blur method.
moveBy(hpix,vpix)	Moves the current window by a relative number of horizontal and vertical pixels.
moveTo(hpos,vpos)	Moves the current window's upper-left corner to the absolute horizontal and vertical position. The 0,0 value is the upper-left corner of the screen.
open(URL,name,attribs,rep)	Opens a new window. All the parameters are optional. If URL is not specified, a blank window will be opened. If specified, the name parameter can be used as the target of links. The attribs parameter can be used to specify properties of the new window such as its size, location, and any toolbars to display. If the rep parameter is true, the URL should replace the current entry in the browsing history and will not create a new one. This method returns a window object.
prompt(msg,default)	The prompt method displays a message in a dialog box and allows the user to enter a string. The default parameter will be displayed in the input area. If you don't supply a default, the word undefined will be used as the default value. Typically, you will want to use "" as the default. The method will return either the string typed by the user or null if the user clicked the Cancel button.
resizeBy(hpix,vpix)	Resizes the window by the number of pixels specified. Positive values increase the size of the window, and negative values decrease the size.
resizeTo(width,height)	Resizes the window to the absolute size, specified in pixels.
scroll(hpos,vpos)	In JavaScript 1.1, scrolls the window object contents to the specified position. This routine is deprecated (that is, should not be used in new code). You should use scrollTo instead.
scrollBy(hpix,vpix)	Scrolls the window relatively from the current position by the number of horizontal and vertical pixels specified.
scrollTo(hpos,vpos)	Scrolls the window so that the horizontal and vertical positions specified are moved to the window's 0,0 (upper-left) position.
setInterval(expr,ms)_	Sets an interval timer, specified in milliseconds, and some JavaScript code to execute periodically.
setTimeout(expr,ms)	Sets a timeout value, specified in milliseconds, and some JavaScript code to execute once when the timeout value is reached.

USER INTERFACE METHODS

You can use three major user interface methods in JavaScript. These three methods are the `alert`, `prompt`, and `confirm` methods of the `window` object. In this book there are many examples that use these methods. In JavaScript, because the window object and its methods are used everywhere, the window prefix can be omitted and is assumed. This is the reason why, for example, you can use

```
alert("Hello, world");
```

rather than the more lengthy and formal

PART

II

CH

9

```
window.alert("Hello, world");
```

Of course, you are free to use the longer version if you like. Here is an example using the prompt method:

```
cUserName = prompt("Please enter your name", "");
if (null == cUserName) {
  alert("Null name");     // User pressed Cancel
}
else {
  if ("" == cUserName) {
    alert("Empty name");  // User pressed OK with empty field
  }
  else {
    alert("Hello, " + cUserName)
  }
}
```

This code distinguishes between the user clicking the Cancel button and clicking OK, but with an empty field. As a side note, notice that I have coded the comparisons with the constant on the left rather than on the right. This will highlight errors if I inadvertently use a single equal instead of the double equals. For example,

```
if ("" = cUserName)
```

will generate a runtime error. On the other hand,

```
if (cUserName = "")
```

will not generate any error. In both of these cases I really meant to use the comparison operator ==, but I made a simple error. In the second case, the program will continue executing, will probably give erroneous results, and you might not know about the error until after you have spent a lot of time debugging. Figure 9.2 shows you an example of the error generated by Netscape Navigator. Internet Explorer will also generate an error message.

As you can see in Figure 9.2, Netscape Navigator highlights the error. To show the console, you must type the following in the location field of the browser and press the Enter key:

```
javascript:
```

When you do, the console window will open. If you do not have the console window open, the browser will not report any errors and will not display any output.

Figure 9.2
The extra JavaScript window of Netscape Navigator shows you errors.

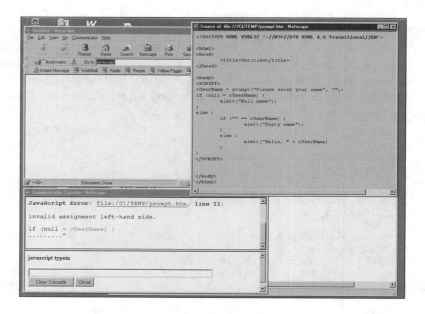

The final user interface method is the `confirm` method of the window object. Its usage is similar to the `prompt` method. Use it as follows:

```
bDelete = confirm("Delete all specified files?");
if (bDelete) {
    // Handle deletion
}
```

If the user clicks Cancel or closes the dialog box without clicking either button, the method will return `false`. It will return `true` only if the OK button is clicked.

TIMER METHODS

Two pairs of routines are related to timers. These routines are the `setInterval`/ `clearInterval` and the `setTimeout`/`clearTimeout` methods. The main difference between these pairs of routines is that the `setTimeout` method will cause a one-time execution of an expression, whereas the `setInterval` method will repeat the execution of the expression at periodic intervals.

Here is an example of how you might use the `setTimeout` method:

```
<BODY>
In 5 seconds you will be transported to the Lotus web site.
<SCRIPT>
window.setTimeout("window.location='http://www.lotus.com'", 5000)
</SCRIPT>
</BODY>
```

In this example, I set the timeout to 5000 milliseconds (five seconds). At the end of this time, I set the `window.location` property to the Lotus Web site URL. The browser will execute the expression at the end of five seconds, which will then cause the browser to display the Lotus Web site.

You use the `setInterval` method in a manner similar to `setTimeout`. After you set the timer interval, the code you specify will be executed periodically. One reason why you might want to use the interval timer is to update a counter based on time. Keep in mind, however, that the interval timer is probably not precise. Although you specify the interval time, it is just approximate. The code might not run exactly at the time specified because of other activities and programs being used on the computer at the same time.

Another use for the `setInterval` method is to initialize frames within a frameset. The precise ordering of the loading of frames is not defined. The order in which the frames of a frameset are initialized depends on computer load factors, communications delays, and so forth. What if the frames of a frameset need to refer to each other? How can one frame refer to another frame when you don't know the order in which they will be loaded?

One way to solve this dilemma is to have a JavaScript variable act as a type of flag. If the variable is present and set to the known, initial value, then a referring frame can be sure that the referenced frame is loaded and available. In this case, the referencing frame would use the `setInterval` method to periodically query the referenced frame to see whether the variable is available. It could check, say, every 500 milliseconds (one half second) or other appropriate interval. When the flag variable is available, the referencing frame can stop the interval timer and begin using information from the referenced frame.

WINDOW MANIPULATION METHODS

You can use several methods to manipulate a user's view of window objects. You can open new windows; close windows you have opened; and move, resize, and scroll the windows. In this section I'll give you some examples of these methods.

THE open METHOD

To open a new window, use the `open` method. Here is its syntax:

```
winobj = window.open(url, name, attributes, replace)
```

- *url*—The *url* parameter specifies the URL to be opened in the new window. It is optional, and if not specified, a blank, new window will be opened. Remember to include the protocol, `http:`.

- *name*—The *name* parameter specifies the name of the new or existing window. If it names an existing window, the window is opened and the existing `window` object is returned from the method. This parameter is optional, but if you will be using the window as the target of links, you should give the window a name.

- *attributes*—The *attributes* parameter of the `open` method is a string of values. The attributes enable you to specify the size and adornments of the browser window. For example, you can choose whether to show the toolbar, menu bar, or status line in the window. If you are opening an existing window with the `open` method, the attributes are ignored. If you do not specify the attributes on the open method, the browser defaults are used. When you specify one of the attributes, however, all other attributes are considered omitted unless you explicitly include them in your list. Here is a list of some of the common attributes. Use a comma to separate each item in the list and do not include any blanks.

- location—Show an input field so the user can enter a new URL.
- menubar—Show the menu bar. This is the line that contains the text commands, such as File and Edit.
- scollbars—Show horizontal and vertical scrollbars if necessary.
- status—Show the status line. This is the line at the bottom of the browser that displays status messages.
- toolbar—Show the toolbar line. This is the line with the back and forward buttons.

Netscape and Microsoft also have proprietary (and incompatible) attributes that you can use if you know the browser type. In particular, sizing and specifying the initial location of the browser window are incompatible between Netscape and Microsoft. In addition, the Netscape security model requires the UniversalBrowserWrite security privilege in order to specify some attributes.

■ replace—Use the replace parameter for existing windows. If it is true, the new page should replace the current item in the browser's history list.

Here are some examples of the open method:

```
window.open();                    // open a new, blank window.
open("http://www.lotus.com");          // open a specific URL
open("http://www.gwcorp.com", "Mysite"); // open a URL and assign it a name
window.open("", "MyWin", "location,menubar"); //open with location and menubar
```

THE close METHOD

The close method is used to close an open window. In JavaScript 1.1 and later, this method can only be used to close a window that was opened with JavaScript. This restriction is to prevent a malicious script from causing the user's browser to exit. Here is an example of closing a window:

```
aWin = window.open("http://www.gwcorp.com"); // Open the window
//
// Add your code here to manipulate the window
//
aWin.close();          // and close it.
```

Because the window prefix is assumed for the current window, a window can close itself by issuing close(). You could also use window.close() or self.close().

THE moveBy AND moveTo METHODS

The moveBy method is used to move a window a certain number of pixels from its current position. This is sometimes called a *relative move*. The moveTo method is used to move to an absolute location on the screen. Here is an example you can easily try with your browser:

```
moveTo(30,30)          // Move to an absolute position
for(i=0;i<20;i++) {
   moveBy(10,10);      // Move down and to the right
}
```

This example will move the current window to the absolute screen location 30,30, and then will move the window successively down and to the right. You should be able to see the movement of the window on your screen.

THE resizeBy AND resizeTo METHODS

The resizeBy and resizeTo methods are used to change the size of the browser window. You use resizeBy with negative values to decrease the size of the current window and positive values to make the window bigger. The resizeTo method can be used to set the browser to a fixed size. Here is an example:

```
resizeTo(300,300);      // Size to an absolute size
for(i=0;i<20;i++) {
   resizeBy(-10,-10);   // Get small
}

for(i=0;i<20;i++) {
   resizeBy(10,10);     // Get large
}
```

THE scrollBy AND scrollTo METHODS

The scrollBy and scrollTo methods are used to scroll the current browser contents by the number of pixels specified. You can use scrollBy for relative scrolling and scrollTo for absolute scrolling. In the example that follows, I'll also show you the setInterval method because scrolling the window is such a fast operation that if you do it in a loop, you will not be able to visually see any movement. You will only be able to see the end result of all the scrolling. Here is the example:

```
resizeTo(300,300);     // Set the window to an absolute size

for(i=0;i<50;i++) {
   document.write("blah  " + i + " <BR>"); // Lots of blahs
}
setInterval("scrollBy(0,10)",200);   // Every 200 ms., scroll by 10 pixels
```

In this example, I have set an interval timer. The timer is set for 200 milliseconds, or 0.2 seconds. Five times every second, the interval timer will cause the scrollBy method to run. This will cause the browser to scroll by 10 pixels. You should be able to see the browser scroll. You can play with the time interval and the number of pixels to get various scrolling effects. I don't recommend that you necessarily include this type of coding in your Web page, but it makes an interesting demonstration.

PART

II

CH

9

WINDOW EVENTS

The event mechanism enables you to write code that will be invoked when certain key events occur in the browser. These events are typically triggered by user interactions with the browser. You can specify the event handlers in HTML when you create the window or by modifying the appropriate window property for a dynamically created window. Here are some examples of the syntax for event handlers:

```
<BODY onBlur="handleblur()">
<BODY onLoad="doLoad()">
<FRAMESET onLoad="fsLoad()">
```

Table 9.3 shows the major window object events and their descriptions.

TABLE 9.3   THE window OBJECT EVENTS

Event	Description
onBlur	The onBlur event is executed when the window loses focus. You might want to suspend animation or other user interface effects because the window might not even be visible.
onFocus	The onFocus event is executed when the window gains the user focus.
onLoad	The onLoad event occurs when the window has been fully loaded. You can use this method to set a status variable that indicates the document has been fully loaded and is available.
OnResize	The onResize event occurs when the window is resized.
OnUnload	The onUnload event occurs when the window is being closed or when the user has given a command to the browser to view a new page.

Note

The onLoad event of the <FRAMESET> tag should fire when all the included frames have been loaded. This might not work reliably in all versions of browsers. Code your frames using status variables that you can check to make sure that all your frames have actually been loaded.

THE STATUS LINE

The *status line* is the line at the bottom of the browser that can contain a message. It may contain the security icons, the loading status, and other information as well. You can use two window properties to change the text message contained in the status line.

The defaultStatus property of the window object allows you to assign a string that will be displayed when the status line is not otherwise in use. Each frame of a frameset can have a separate defaultStatus value. In a multiple-frame environment, the defaultStatus for the frame containing the mouse will be displayed. You could use this feature, for example, to display information about the current frame.

The status property of the window object enables you to change the message in a transient way. When you assign a value to the status property, it will be displayed in the status line, but only until another message is displayed in its place. As the user moves the mouse, the message may rapidly change.

Here is an example of how you can set these two properties:

```
window.defaultStatus = "Have a nice day"
window.status="Processing. . ."
```

THE navigator OBJECT

You access the navigator object using a property of the window object. It describes characteristics of the browser being used. Table 9.4 shows the major properties of the navigator object and the values returned for the Notes client, Netscape Navigator, and Microsoft Internet Explorer for recent versions of each program. These are just examples. You might obtain different results depending on your browser version.

TABLE 9.4 SAMPLE PROPERTIES OF THE navigator OBJECT

Property	Notes Client	Netscape Navigator	Internet Explorer
appCodeName	Domino	Mozilla	Mozilla
appMinorVersion			;3283;
appName	Lotus Notes	Netscape	Microsoft Internet Explorer
appVersion	4.0 (compatible; Lotus-Notes/5.0; Windows NT)	4.7[en](WinNT;U)	4.0 (compatible; MSIE 5.0; Windows NT; DigExt)
cookieEnabled			true
language		en	
mimeTypes	[object mimeTypeArray]	[mimeTypeArray]	[mimeTypeArray]
platform		Win32	Win32
plugins	[object PluginArray]	[PluginArray]	[PluginArray]
systemLanguage			en-us
userAgent	Mozilla/4.0 (compatible; Lotus-Notes/5.0; Windows NT)	Mozilla/4.7 [en](WinNT; U)	Mozilla/4.0 (compatible; MSIE 5.0; Windows NT; DigExt)
userLanguage			en-us

Notice that some properties are not available in some browsers and your results may vary even with different versions of the same browser. When you develop JavaScript programs, you can first determine the browser type and use this information to provide different actions depending on the type (and possibly version) of the browser.

Here is some simple JavaScript code that you can use to find out all the properties associated with the navigator object. You can modify this program to find out the attributes for any built-in object. Note that this same program will produce different results depending on the browser you use.

```
nav = window.navigator
for (p in nav) {
    alert(p + " = " + eval("nav."+p))
}
```

To use this program from a Domino database, follow these steps:

1. In the Domino Designer, open the database you want to use for your test.
2. Create a new page.
3. In the JSHeader event for the page, enter the preceding code.
4. Click one of the browser test buttons in the upper-right corner of the Domino Designer.

Essentially, the code will loop through each attribute found in the navigator object and display its name and value. Notice that the eval function is used to evaluate a string that is dynamically created. The property name is concatenated to the right of the string "nav.". For each property, a string such as "nav.appName" is created and then evaluated by the eval function. The result is then used for display by the alert function.

I have supplied a slightly more sophisticated version of this program on the CD-ROM in a database titled JavaScript DOM. You can open this database in the Domino Designer to see how it has been constructed. In Figure 9.3, you see the output of Netscape Navigator version 4.7, Internet Explorer version 5, and the Notes client.

The Notes client implementation is slightly different from the browser versions because with JavaScript for the Notes client you cannot overwrite the currently displayed document. Instead, I created a rich text field and added the contents to the field dynamically.

Here is the source code for the JavaScript display routine:

```
// Show all properties for the object whose name is passed in.
function showProp (objName) {
    var win = window
    var obj = eval(objName)     // Turn the name into an actual object reference
    // We must handle Notes client differently from browser.
    if ("Domino" == window.navigator.appCodeName) {
        document.forms[0].JSValues.value = "Properties for the " +
            objName + " object in " +
            win.navigator.appName + " "+ win.navigator.appVersion + "\n"
        for (p in obj) {
```

```
            // Note the "+=" below appends the text string to the field.
            document.forms[0].JSValues.value += p + " = " +eval("obj."+p)+"\n"
        }
    }
    else { // It is a browser
        win.document.write("Properties for the " + objName + " object in " +
            win.navigator.appName + " "+ win.navigator.appVersion + "<br>")
        for (p in obj) {
            win.document.write(p + " = " + eval("obj."+p) + "<br>")
        }
        win.document.close();
    }
}
```

Figure 9.3
The navigator
properties for Notes,
Navigator, and
Internet Explorer.

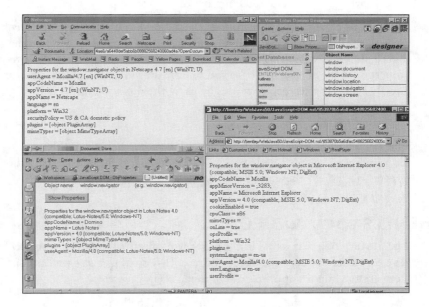

In this routine, the Notes client must be handled differently from the browser because it does not currently support dynamically changing the page. Instead, a rich text field named JSValues was created on the form. This field is populated with the property values.

THE screen OBJECT

You access the screen object using a property of the window object. It describes characteristics of the screen being used. Here are the major properties of the screen object:

availHeight   The number of vertical pixels available after subtracting any permanent toolbars or other permanent objects.

availLeft   Available only in Netscape Navigator. The absolute offset, in pixels, from the left of the screen to the first available pixel after permanent toolbars or other permanent objects.

availTop	Available only in Netscape Navigator. The absolute offset, in pixels, from the top of the screen to the first available pixel after permanent toolbars or other permanent objects.
availWidth	The number of horizontal pixels available after subtracting any permanent toolbars or other permanent objects.
colorDepth	The number of bits available for color lookups.
height	The total number of vertical pixels on the screen.
pixelDepth	Not available in Internet Explorer. The number of bits available for color lookups.
width	The total number of horizontal pixels on the screen.

In Netscape Navigator and the Notes client, you can use the for .. in construct to loop through the screen properties. Internet Explorer versions 4 and 5 treat the screen object slightly differently from other objects. You cannot use a for .. in loop to access all the properties of the screen object as you can for the navigator object. You can, however, directly access the screen properties by using the dot notation, as in

```
scr = window.screen
wid = scr.width
```

The availTop and availLeft properties of the screen object enable you to compensate for the Windows 95/98/NT start toolbar. If the toolbar is located on the left or top of the screen, you can use these properties to determine the offset.

THE history OBJECT

The history object is found in the history property of the window object. You can use the history object to query the history of recently visited pages as well as control navigation. Here are the important properties of the history object:

- length—The number of items contained in the history list.
- current—Supported only in Navigator 4+. URL of the current page. Requires UniversalBrowserRead security setting enabled.
- next—Supported only in Navigator 4+. URL of the next page. Requires UniversalBrowserRead security setting enabled.
- previous—Supported only in Navigator 4+. URL of the previous page. Requires UniversalBrowserRead security setting enabled.

Here are the important methods of the history object:

- back()—Move the browser to the URL that was viewed immediately before the current one. This is equivalent to clicking the Back button in the browser.

- forward()—Move the browser to the URL that was viewed immediately after the current one. This is equivalent to clicking the Forward button in the browser.

- go(*n* | *target*)—If *n* is positive, move the browser forward *n* entries in the history list. If *n* is negative, move it back *n* entries in the history list. You can also specify a target, which is a relative URL.

Here is an example of how you can move the browser back to the previous URL:

```
his = window.history;
his.back();
```

This is equivalent to

```
his = window.history;
his.go(-1);
```

THE location OBJECT

The location object can be obtained from the location property of the window object. The location object enables you to extract components of the current URL and to modify the entire URL or its components. If you modify the location object, the browser will display the contents of the newly constructed URL.

To understand the methods of this object, let's review the component parts of a URL:

protocol://hostname:port/pathname?search#hash

For example, in the following URL:

```
http://www.somehost.com:80/ecommerce/buyit.nsf/catview/p123?opendocument#price
```

The URL would be parsed as follows:

protocol	http:
hostname	www.somehost.com
host	www.somehost.com:80
port	80
pathname	/ecommerce/buyit.nsf/catview/p123
search	?opendocument
hash	#price

Here are the properties of the location object:

- hash—Returns the hash portion of the URL, including the #. This represents the name of an anchor link.

- host—The hostname and port portion of the URL. In the preceding example, the host value would be www.somehost.com:80.

- hostname—Returns the hostname portion of the URL.

- href—Returns the complete URL.

- `pathname`—Returns just the pathname portion of the URL.
- `port`—Returns the port number of the URL.
- `protocol`—Returns the protocol of the URL. For Web browsers, this is `http:` and for the Notes client it is `Notes:`.
- `search`—Returns the part of the URL beginning with the question mark and before the hash.

There are two methods for the `location` object:

- `reload()`—Reloads the current URL. It operates the same as the Reload (Navigator) and Refresh (Internet Explorer) buttons.
- `replace(newURL)`—Used to replace the current page with the one found at the new URL. It replaces the current page in the history list.

Here is a simple example of how you might use the `replace` method:

```
url = prompt("Enter new URL");
window.location.replace(url);
```

The preceding code will prompt for a new URL, and then it will replace the current page with the one that was typed.

USING FRAMESETS AND MULTIPLE WINDOWS

When you use framesets with HTML and JavaScript, each frame within the frameset is a `window` object. Thus, you are actually dealing with multiple `window` objects when you work with frames. The windows in a frameset follow a hierarchical pattern, and from one frame you can get to the contents of another frame.

Chapter 6, "Using Outlines, Framesets, and Navigators," gave an overview of the syntax for using framesets within HTML. As you'll recall, when you create a frameset, you will normally specify that it is either a row-oriented or column-oriented frameset (but not both). To obtain more complex arrangements, you can nest a column-oriented frameset within a row-oriented frameset (or vice versa). Here is a column-oriented frameset embedded within a row-oriented frameset:

```
<FRAMESET ROWS="20%,*,20%" FRAMEBORDER="yes">
   <FRAME NAME="AFrame" SRC="AFrame.html">
   <FRAMESET COLS="20%,80%" FRAMEBORDER="yes">
     <FRAME NAME="BFrame" SRC="BFrame.html">
     <FRAME NAME="CFrame" SRC="CFrame.html">
   </FRAMESET>
   <FRAME NAME="DFrame" SRC="DFrame.html">
</FRAMESET>
```

This specification will result in three rows of the frameset, and the middle row will have two columns (see Figure 9.4).

Figure 9.4
Four frames arranged in a single, nested frameset.

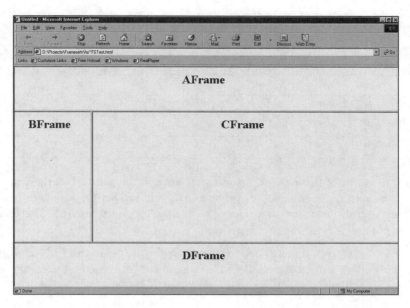

FRAME NAMING AND ACCESS

Frame naming and access can be very confusing because the way you access information in one frame from another depends not only on how the frames are nested, but also on how the files are nested. Let me start from the simplest concepts.

To refer to outermost, sometimes called the topmost, windows, you can use the window object named `top`. Any window can refer to itself using one of the two keywords `self` and `window`. To refer to a window's parent, you can use the `parent` window property. The definition of a window's parent in a frameset context can be the confusing part, so let me defer that discussion.

Each window has a property called `frames` containing an array that lists all the frames that are contained within that particular `window` object. In addition, the `window` object has a property called `length`, which represents the number of frames stored in the `frames` array.

Refer to Figure 9.4 and its source. If you were to query `self.length` in the file `AFrame.html`, you would find its value to be `0`. However, the value `parent.length` would be 4. The reason, of course, is that there are four frames in the frameset. The interesting point is that if you were to query `self.length` and `parent.length` from the `Bframe.html` file, you would find the same values. In particular, notice that the value of `parent.length` would be 4, not 2.

Table 9.5 lists the values for the length of the `frames` array for each of the frames.

TABLE 9.5	LENGTH OF frames ARRAYS FOR SINGLE-FILE FRAMESET	
	self.length	**parent.length**
top	4	4
AFrame	0	4
BFrame	0	4
CFrame	0	4
DFrame	0	4

If the value of the window's length attribute is 4, this means that there are four objects in the frames array. The frames array, like all arrays in JavaScript, is indexed from 0, so the values in the array are frames[0], frames[1], frames[2], and frames[3]. These four objects are the window objects for the four frames.

Suppose you are writing code for the AFrame.html file. In this file you would like to refer to the window named DFrame. Because you know that DFrame is at index position 3, you could use the following syntax:

```
dwin = parent.frames[3];   // Access the DFrame window object
```

You can see right away, however, that this might be very prone to error if you change the layout or embedding of the frames. If you have assigned a name attribute for the frame as I have done, you can refer to the frame with the following alternative notation:

```
dwin = parent.DFrame;      // Access the DFrame window object by name
```

This is obviously much better and will be less prone to error. Of course, you'll probably want to assign your frames more meaningful names based on the content you'd like to use for them.

For the two frames BFrame and CFrame, the frames array contains the same content. For example, you can use the same syntax—parent.BFrame to access the BFrame. The general principle at work here is that *the frames array (and the length property) will contain one entry for each <FRAME> tag found within a given HTML file, regardless of the depth of nesting of <FRAMESET> tags.*

FRAMESETS WITHIN FRAMESETS

So far, it seems that the access from one frame to another is pretty straightforward. Let's now see how it can become more complicated. Consider the following frameset HTML:

```
<FRAMESET ROWS="20%,*,20%" FRAMEBORDER="yes">
    <FRAME NAME="AFrame" SRC="AFrame.html">
    <FRAME NAME="MidFrame" SRC="MidFrame.html">
    <FRAME NAME="DFrame" SRC="DFrame.html">
</FRAMESET>
```

Consider also the following definition for `MidFrame.html`:

```
<FRAMESET COLS="20%,80%" FRAMEBORDER="yes">
  <FRAME NAME="BFrame" SRC="BFrame.html">
  <FRAME NAME="CFrame" SRC="CFrame.html">
</FRAMESET>
```

When you display this pair of HTML files along with the original HTML files, you will see that the resulting page appears identical to Figure 9.4 in the browser. There are, however, some major differences on how the frames are now referenced.

If you were to refer to the variable `parent.length` from within the `AFrame.html` file, you would find that it now has the value 3 rather than 4. In addition, if you refer to the variable `parent.length` in the `BFrame.html` file, you will find that it is now 2 instead of 4. The value of `self.length` would still be 0 for each of the individual frame HTML files.

Table 9.6 lists the values you would find for the length of the `frames` array for each of the frames.

TABLE 9.6 LENGTH OF `frames` ARRAYS FOR NESTED FILE FRAMESET

	self.length	parent.length
`top`	3	3
`AFrame`	0	3
`Midframe`	2	3
`BFrame`	0	2
`CFrame`	0	2
`DFrame`	0	3

Because we have now separated the frameset into two different files, we have altered the structure of the tree hierarchy (see Figure 9.5).

Suppose you want to refer to the window called `DFrame`. From the `AFrame.html` file, you would still use `parent.DFrame`. However, from the `BFrame.html` file, you would need to change your reference to `parent.parent.Dframe`.

You might wonder about using a reference such as `top.DFrame`. In fact, for this example, the two references would both work. However, as a general rule, you should avoid using an absolute reference such as `top`. The main reason is that you might want to change the layout of your page or include the entire page in a new, higher-level frameset. If you code absolute references such as `top` within your JavaScript, your code might not work as intended if you later make changes.

One suggestion to make relative references a little easier is to use local variables. You can include the following at the beginning of your JavaScript routine:

```
var dwin = parent.parent.DFframe    // assign local variable
```

Figure 9.5
A nested frameset using two files has different naming from a frameset using a single file.

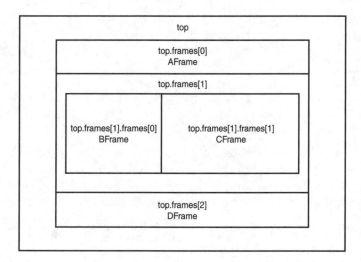

Now, in your code you can refer to the local variable dwin, which will contain the window object for the DFrame window. By using this technique, you might have to change only a few local variables at the beginning of your code rather than making changes throughout.

THE document OBJECT

The document object of JavaScript is an important container. You will use the document object frequently because it contains the forms and data elements such as fields. When you use JavaScript with Domino, the JavaScript document object also corresponds to one Domino document. You can access the JavaScript document using the document property of a window object.

DOCUMENT PROPERTIES

Table 9.7 lists the major properties of the document object.

TABLE 9.7   THE MAJOR document OBJECT PROPERTIES

Property	Description
alinkColor	The alinkColor property is the color of a link while it is active (that is, has the focus). This property corresponds to the ALINK attribute of the <BODY> tag. The link colors (alinkColor, linkColor, and vlinkColor) all use a string of the format #RRGGBB, where RR, GG, and BB represent hexadecimal numbers. For example, #00FF00 represents pure green.
anchors	The anchors property is an array of all the anchors within the document. Anchors use the <A NAME="*name*"> tag as a destination. You can find the length of this array with anchors.length.
applets	The applets property is an array that contains all the applets found within the document. You can find the length of this array with applets.length.

Property	Description
bgColor	bgColor is the background color of the document. It corresponds to the BGCOLOR attribute of the <BODY> tag.
cookie	The cookie property allows a JavaScript program to read and write cookies. Cookies are special variables that facilitate communication between a Web client and the server.
domain	The domain property contains the hostname of the server from which the document originated. The domain property is used to control some aspects of document security. Its use enables collaborating servers within the same domain to share certain information.
embeds	The embeds property contains an array of all the objects that are embedded on the page. Embedded objects include ActiveX controls and Netscape plug-ins. You can obtain the length of this array with embeds.length.
fgColor	The fgColor property is the default foreground text color of the document. You can also set this value using the TEXT property of the <BODY> tag.
forms	The forms property of the document object contains an array of all the forms contained in the document. Unlike Domino, JavaScript forms are contained with a document object, and you can have more than one form contained in the document. In general, however, when Domino is generating the HTML, it will create only one form within the document. You create forms in HTML with the <FORM> tag. Forms are important because elements such as fields and buttons can appear only within the context of a form in a document. These input elements cannot appear elsewhere within the document. I cover forms and their elements in Chapter 10, "The JavaScript Form and Form Elements." You can find out how many forms are in the document using the forms.length property.
images	The images property is an array of all the images in the document. You create an image using the <IMG> tag in HTML. You can find out the number of images using the images.length property. You can use the images array to implement mouse rollover effects with JavaScript.
lastModified	The lastModified property of the document object contains a string with the date and time the document was last modified. Web servers are not required to maintain this property, however, so be careful when using it.
linkColor	The linkColor property contains the color of links that have not yet been visited.
links	The links property is an array of all the links within the document. Links use the <A HREF="url"> tag to link to other locations. You can find the length of this array with links.length.
referrer	The referrer property contains the URL of the document that was used to link to the current document.
title	The title property contains a string that represents the title for the document. You can create the title with the <TITLE> tag in HTML.
URL	The URL property is a string corresponding to the URL of the current document.
vlinkColor	The vlinkColor property is the color to be used for links that have been visited.

PART

II

CH

9

DOCUMENT METHODS

Only a few methods are associated with the document object. The important methods deal with the dynamic generation of HTML from JavaScript. I show you how this is done shortly. First, let's take a look at the major document object methods shown in Table 9.8.

TABLE 9.8   THE MAJOR document OBJECT METHODS

Method	Description
close	The close method closes the output stream for the document.
open	The open method opens an output stream into which you can write HTML.
write	The write method writes one or more strings into the output stream.
writeln	The writeln method writes one or more strings into the output stream and appends a newline character to the end of the line.

To write HTML into the current document, you will use an output stream. You can write HTML source text to the stream and the browser will render it. It is not necessary to open the stream; you can begin writing with the write method. However, when you are finished, you should close the stream because this will force any buffered output to be displayed.

Note

As of version 5.0.1, the Web browser that is part of the Notes client does not implement the document.write method when using the preview feature. If you attempt to use it, you will get the message This feature is not yet implemented. If you use the Notes Web browser and preview with the Domino server, the document.write is properly handled.

Let's take a look at a very simple script that creates HTML.

```
<HTML>
<SCRIPT LANGUAGE="JAVASCRIPT">
  document.write("<H1>Hello, doc!</H1>")    // write the HTML
  document.close();    // close the output stream
</SCRIPT>
</HTML>
```

This simple HTML file will write the HTML H1 string to the output stream and close it. The browser will then display the hello message. The actual syntax for the write and writeln methods is

```
document.write(value1, value2, . . . )

document.writeln(value1, value2, . . . )
```

Each of the values can be an expression, variable, or constant. The values will just be concatenated for output. With writeln, after the last value has been output, a newline character will be appended. Note that newline characters are typically ignored by browsers, so write and writeln will usually behave similarly. To force the browser to move to a new line, you should use the <BR> tag in the HTML you send to the output stream.

If you issue an open method, any existing text in the document is cleared and will behave as if it were a new document. The syntax for the open method is

```
document.open([mimetype])
```

If you do not specify the *mimetype*, it will default to text/html.

As the HTML for the page is received and processed by the browser, you can generally continue to create and append content to the page. Once the page loading has completed and awaits user input, you can no longer append to the page. If you issue a document.write after the page has already downloaded, the page will be completely cleared and the new text will replace the existing page.

PART

II

CH

9

Here is an example:

```
<HTML>
<SCRIPT LANGUAGE="JAVASCRIPT">
function test() {
    document.write("Overlay?<BR>");
}
</SCRIPT>
<BODY>

THIS IS MY STATIC TEXT<BR>
<SCRIPT LANGUAGE="JAVASCRIPT">
   test();
</SCRIPT>
<FORM>
<INPUT type="button" value="Do Test" onClick="test()">
</FORM>
</BODY>
</HTML>
```

In this example, the JavaScript routine called test is invoked from two different places. In the first case it is invoked just after the line of static text. It is invoked inline and will output the string Overlay? just below the static text. An input button with the label Do Test will appear just below the output of the routine. Thus, the initial display will have three lines:

```
THIS IS MY STATIC TEXT
Overlay?
Do Test  (Button)
```

If the button is clicked, the test routine will be invoked, the page will be completely cleared, and only the text Overlay? will appear on the page.

This example illustrates that a single JavaScript routine might display its output in context or might clear the page before displaying its output. If you issue a document.write after the page has been rendered, as in the onClick example, the page will be cleared. If the document.write is issued during the process of initially rendering the page, then the page will not be cleared.

NOTES CLIENT WITH INTERNET EXPLORER

If you are using the Notes client, one option you can specify in your Personal Address book in the location document is your choice of browser. You can choose from Notes, Netscape Navigator, Microsoft Internet Explorer, or an option called Notes with Internet Explorer. Although it might seem obvious that this option combines both the Notes client and Microsoft Internet Explorer, there are nuances that are important. This section describes this feature of the Notes client.

Microsoft has implemented its Internet Explorer as a component. That means that other application programs can use and control IE within their user interfaces. Lotus has implemented this facility in its Notes client. In addition, however, Lotus has its own Web browser that is implemented in the Notes client. When you choose the option Notes with Internet Explorer, the Notes client will seamlessly choose between the two implementations depending on the data to be shown.

In particular, Notes does not always use Internet Explorer. When you use URLs that display forms, views, or framesets the Notes browser is used. For example, suppose the following URL is issued from the Notes client:

```
http://server/db.nsf/Myview?OpenView
```

In this case, the Notes browser will be used. One way to tell whether the Notes browser is in use is by issuing the menu command View, Show, HTML Source. If the Notes browser is in use, the command will be enabled and you can see the HTML source that the Notes browser is using. If Internet Explorer is in use, the HTML Source menu option will not be available.

The Notes browser is similarly used to view pages, forms, and framesets. However, when you are viewing a document, the embedded Internet Explorer browser is invoked. For example, the following URL causes Internet Explorer to render the page:

```
http://server/db.nsf/Myview/Doc123?Opendocument
```

Knowing which browser will be used to render the page is important because the HTML that is accepted is different and the JavaScript objects, methods, and properties are different in Internet Explorer from what they are in the Notes browser.

To experiment with these options, in the Domino Designer open the JavaScript DOM database. Highlight the ObjProperties view, then click on the various browser preview buttons in the upper-right corner of the screen. Have fun.

CHAPTER REVIEW

1. Create a page in the Domino Designer that contains JavaScript to display the browser type (also known as the userAgent).

2. This chapter focused mainly on properties and methods that are available in most of the common browsers. Suppose you wanted to take advantage of features that were

available only in a particular browser. How could you do this? Why would you want to do this? What might be some problems associated with optimizing for a particular browser?

3. Create a page in the Domino Designer that has one text input field and three buttons. One button should implement the browser BACK function, the second should implement the FORWARD function, and the third button should go to the URL specified in the text input field. Because you are using a Domino page, you will not be able to use Domino fields. You must create your input field and buttons using HTML.

4. Write a JavaScript program that will take the current window and center it both vertically and horizontally within the screen.

5. What are the implications of naming frames when framesets are included in the same file as opposed to different files?

6. Explain the difference between the document object in the Document Object Model and a Domino document.

7. Using the Domino Designer, create various configurations of framesets. Display these framesets with a Web browser, and then view the HTML source using the browser View Source menu command. What type of embedded framesets does Domino generate? Use the frameset designer and split some frames and see the HTML that is generated. Now, using a frameset with, say, two or three frames, embed another frameset within one of the frames. View the HTML source. What have you learned about how Domino generates frames and what implication would this have for accessing one frame from another?

8. Write a JavaScript program that will display a message in the status area and scroll it to the left at a rate of five characters a second. When it reaches the left edge it should stop. (Hint: The initial message may have many leading blanks.) How would you change the program so that it will scroll to the right?

9. Create an HTML page that uses a frameset with two side-by-side frames. In the left frame, create an input field with a button. Write a JavaScript program that is activated when the button is clicked. The program should read a URL that has been entered in the input field and should populate the right frame with the contents of the specified Web page.

THE JAVASCRIPT FORM AND FORM ELEMENTS

THE RELATIONSHIP BETWEEN DOMINO AND DOM DOCUMENTS AND FORMS

The previous chapter described the `window` and `document` objects of the document object model (DOM). This chapter describes the `form` object and its elements. The terms *document* and *form* in the context of the JavaScript DOM have different meanings from their Domino counterparts. I start this chapter by describing the relationship between Domino and DOM documents and forms.

In Domino, a *form* is like a template that contains text constants, graphics, input fields, and controls. A *document* is a container for data, much like a record in a relational database. A document contains no formatting information but can be viewed through a form. That is, the information in the document is combined with the display elements of the form for presentation to the user. A given document can be viewed through different forms for different users or for different business purposes. Put simply, the document contains the data and the form contains the visual formatting.

In the JavaScript DOM, a document represents the contents of a window that is displayed to the user. In a frameset, each frame of the frameset is actually a window and therefore contains a `document` object. Documents in the DOM can contain text, graphics, and essentially any kind of formatting available in HTML. Forms are used to capture information from the user to send back to the server. Forms contain input elements such as fields, buttons, drop-down lists, and other controls. Forms are contained within a document, and a document can contain more than one form. The list of forms is found in a property of the `document` object that is appropriately called the `forms` property.

How, then, do we reconcile the two different models and how do they work together? Two scenarios exist for combining Domino with the JavaScript DOM. The first is when the developer uses passthru HTML and essentially codes a Web page directly. In this case, because the developer is creating the HTML, the mapping between Domino objects and the HTML is up to the developer. This is a tricky technique and might depend on particular implementation conventions in Domino; therefore, it is not recommended. You should definitely avoid your own HTML mapping until you are thoroughly familiar with how HTML, Domino, and JavaScript all work together. Fortunately, this technique is usually not required.

The more interesting case is the mapping between Domino objects and HTML when the Domino server performs it. In this case, Domino form design elements such as buttons, fields, and other controls are converted to their HTML equivalents. Domino's operation depends on the URL used to display the Web page. This means, for example, that a field and its contents can generate different HTML depending on the URL that is used to access it. Three similar, but different, URLs are used to display, create, and edit Domino documents from a Web browser.

Displaying a Domino Document and Its Form

The first type of URL is specified by the suffix ?OpenDocument. The document can be selected from a view, as in

```
http://server/db.nsf/viewname/documentkey?OpenDocument
```

In this version of URL, Domino finds the view, looks up the key in the first sorted column, and displays the document and its associated form. When Domino converts the document and form to HTML, it will create a single HTML <FORM> within the document. This <FORM> element in HTML will create a form object in the DOM object hierarchy. The DOM form object will be contained in the forms array property of the document object.

Note that because we are displaying a Domino document and its associated form, any fields that are in the form will be filled in with the information from the document. The field information from the document will be converted to text constants and will not appear as an input field to the user. The information will be displayed as read-only to the browser client.

Creating a Domino Document

To display a Web page that is used to create a new Domino document in the database, use a URL with the suffix ?OpenForm. This URL does not actually create the document, but displays the form to be filled out by the user. Here is the syntax for this type of URL:

```
http://server/db.nsf/formname?OpenForm
```

When this type of URL is used, only a Domino form is involved, not a Domino document. When you use the ?OpenForm version of a URL, the fields of the Domino form are converted to HTML <INPUT> elements. The generated HTML is sent to the Web browser, and the browser user can then fill in the fields with information.

You might wonder, "What happens after the form has been displayed to the browser user and the user has filled in the fields?" That's a good question. Of course, we would like the answer to be that the information that the user entered into the HTML form is packaged up, sent back to Domino, and a new Domino document is created. This is exactly what happens, but the interesting part is how this is accomplished.

To create that new document in the Domino database, an additional, Domino-generated URL is required. This URL uses the suffix ?OpenForm&Seq=1. This URL is embedded by Domino within the HTML that was sent in response to the ?OpenForm. The ?OpenForm&Seq=1 URL is found in the ACTION attribute of the HTML <FORM> element. Here is an example of the HTML that is generated:

```
<FORM METHOD=post ACTION="/empdata.nsf/e7d5fc241897e2eb89259113f06779dd
➡?OpenForm&Seq=1"NAME="_Employee">
```

To recap, the preceding <FORM> element HTML is part of the HTML that is generated and sent in response to the original ?OpenForm URL. When the user submits that form, the browser sends the ?OpenForm&Seq=1 URL back to the server. Note that in previous releases, a ?CreateDocument was generated instead of the newer, modified version of ?OpenForm. You can still also use ?CreateDocument for the action field.

In this example, the post method is used, which is a specific instruction to the Web browser on how to package the fields and send them back to the server. The ACTION attribute specifies where to send the data. In this case, the long hexadecimal string is the universal ID of the Domino form to be used to create the document. Finally, the name attribute is the Domino form name, prepended with an underscore.

When this form is submitted, Domino will receive the universal ID and the name of the form that should be used to create the document. It will also receive the field content information from the browser, and will happily create the new document.

EDITING AN EXISTING DOMINO DOCUMENT

We have now seen how to display (in read-only mode) Domino documents and how to create new ones. Let's see how we can edit an existing document. To edit an existing document, use the ?EditDocument version of a URL. Here is the syntax:

```
http://server/db.nsf/viewname/documentkey?EditDocument
```

This URL is similar to the ?OpenDocument format. However, rather than opening the document in read-only mode, the ?EditDocument will generate HTML for the Domino document and form so that document fields are specified as <INPUT> elements rather than text constants. This will allow the browser user to edit the data and resubmit it.

To send back the updated data, Domino generates another URL. This URL is the counterpart of the ?OpenForm&Seq=1 URL that was used for the creation of new documents. When editing an existing document, Domino will generate the ?EditDocument&Seq=1 URL. Here is an example:

```
<FORM METHOD=post ACTION="/y2kinfo.nsf/e7d5fc241897e2eb89259113f06779dd/
➡57c1dc242297e2ea882567fb00677955?EditDocument&Seq=1" NAME="_MyForm">
```

In this example, two universal IDs are specified in the ACTION attribute URL. These universal IDs are for the view and document to be updated. Notice also that the form name is specified in the NAME attribute of the <FORM> element. In previous releases, a ?SaveDocument URL was issued rather than the newer URL with the Seq=1 parameter. You can still use the ?SaveDocument URL.

We have the following pairs of URL commands:

Function	To Display Form and/or Document	To Submit New or Updated Data (Generated by Domino)
New document	?OpenForm	?OpenForm&Seq=1 ?CreateDocument
Edit existing document	?EditDocument	?EditDocument&Seq=1 ?SaveDocument

Other commands, such as ?ReadForm, display a form in read-only mode, and ?DeleteDocument deletes documents. These are described in Chapter 7.

USING PURE HTML TO CREATE A DOMINO DOCUMENT

I've described the way you can use URLs and HTML with Domino. Is it possible to create (and edit) Domino documents by coding HTML directly? The answer is a qualified yes. You must use the Domino Designer to create a form, but after the form is created, you can create documents with the form using native HTML. Although you can create documents in this manner, it is not necessarily recommended. Mainly, for most standard operations it is much easier and simpler to use the Domino Designer to design your Web pages and then have Domino serve the forms directly. The user interface in the Designer makes it much easier to add fields, text, and the graphics that make up your page.

However, with that said, if you have a special programming situation, you might want to create Domino documents using passthru HTML. The following is an example.

As mentioned, you must first create a form in the Domino designer that contains the field definitions you will be using. For our example, suppose you create a Domino form called DomDoc with two fields, cName and cComment. These fields are both text fields. Here is the HTML that can be used to create a new DomDoc document. This example can be found on the CD-ROM in the database for this chapter, DOM form Design.

```
<html>
<body>
<form method="post" action="http://server/database.nsf/DomDoc?CreateDocument">
<input type="text" name="cName" value="John Doe">
<input type="text" name="cComment" value="This is great!">
<input type="submit">
</form>
</body>
</html>
```

This HTML will display the two fields and a submit button. When the submit button is clicked, the document will be posted to the Domino server and a new document will be created in the database. Note that the NAME attribute of the <FORM> element is not absolutely necessary. The form name is found in the URL.

THE form OBJECT

A form object in the DOM is always contained in a document object. In the DOM, a document can contain several form objects; each form corresponds to a <FORM> element in HTML. Domino will generate only a single form, but there might be occasions where you will find multiple forms useful, and you can directly code HTML to implement multiple forms. Any input element that you want to display on your page must be included within a <FORM> element. So, for example, to display a button, you could use the following HTML:

```
<HTML>
<HEAD>
<TITLE>Button Example</TITLE>
<SCRIPT LANGUAGE="JavaScript">
function DoIt() {
    alert("Thank you");
}
</SCRIPT>
</HEAD>
<BODY>
<FORM>
<INPUT TYPE="button" VALUE="Push This" onClick="DoIt()">
</FORM>
</BODY>
</HTML>
```

Notice in this example that I have not given the form or button a name because I am not submitting any information to be stored back on the server. Let's now take a look at the properties and methods of the DOM form object.

THE form PROPERTIES

Table 10.1 lists the properties found in the form object.

TABLE 10.1   THE form OBJECT PROPERTIES

Property	Description
action	The action property contains the contents of the ACTION attribute of the <FORM> tag. This property specifies the URL to which the form data is sent when the form is submitted.
elements	The elements property is an array of the entire input element objects within the form.
elements.length	elements.length is the length of the elements array.
encoding	The encoding property corresponds to the ENCTYPE attribute of the <FORM> tag.
length	The length property contains the number of elements in the form. This is the same as the elements.length property.
method	The method property corresponds to the METHOD attribute of the <FORM> tag. The method may be either GET or POST.

Property	Description
name	The name property corresponds to the NAME attribute of the <FORM> tag. If Domino generates the HTML, this corresponds to the name of the Domino form, prepended with an underscore.
OnReset	The onReset property contains the JavaScript event handler code to execute just before a form is reset (input fields are reset to their default state). The routine should return false to prevent the reset from occurring.
OnSubmit	The onSubmit property contains the JavaScript event handler code to execute just before a form is submitted. This routine is a good location to incorporate form field validation. If this routine returns false, the form is not submitted.
target	The target property corresponds to the TARGET attribute of the <FORM> tag. The target specifies the window or frame that should be used to display the result from submitting the form.

THE FORM SUBMISSION PROCESS

The attributes of the <FORM> element tag are parsed and stored as properties of the form DOM object. These properties control the process that is used to submit the form back to the server. This is a generic process and is used for all form submissions, but Domino uses it in a stylized manner as I've described. Here is the more generic process that is used for all HTML servers and browsers.

1. The server sends the HTML containing a <FORM> to the Web browser client. If the form contains fields that will be filled in by the user and will be submitted, the <FORM> element will contain additional attributes. The ACTION attribute specifies the URL that is used as the destination for the submission. It normally contains a relative URL (that is, on the same server that originally sent the HTML document). In the case of Domino, it contains a database name, some universal IDs, and a command such as ?OpenForm&Seq=1 (?CreateDocument) or ?EditDocument&Seq=1 (?SaveDocument).

2. The <FORM> also contains a METHOD attribute. The two methods are GET and POST. The GET method is the default and is normally used for simple query type operations. The information from the form is converted to a string, appended to the URL specified in the ACTION attribute, and submitted to the server. The POST method is usually used when there is a lot of data to submit, such as when a form is filled out. In this case, the form data is packaged up and sent in the request body. The server can read the form data from the standard input stream. The POST method is used by Domino to create and edit Domino documents.

3. After the server has received the data and processed it, the server sends a response back to the browser client. If a target attribute was specified in the <FORM> tag then the response might be shown in a different window from the original request. Normally Domino does not use this attribute.

THE form METHODS

Table 10.2 lists the methods found in the form object.

TABLE 10.2	THE form OBJECT METHODS	
Method	**Description**
reset()	Calling the reset method simulates a user clicking the reset button. The onReset event handler is called, and if it returns false, the form will not actually be reset.
submit()	Calling the submit method simulates a user clicking the submit button. Note that the onSubmit handler is not called when you invoke the submit method. If you want to perform validation, you will need to invoke it yourself before invoking the submit method.

Here is an example of how you might use the submit method:

```
<SCRIPT LANGUAGE="JavaScript">
function validate() {
   if ("" == document.forms[0].UserName.value) {
      alert("You must enter a value for the User Name field.");
      return false;  // Fails validation
   }
   return true;  // Succeeds validation
}

function autosubmit() {
   // . . . Processing here . . .
   if (validate()) {
      document.forms[0].submit();   // submit the form
   }
}
</SCRIPT>
<FORM>
<INPUT TYPE="Text" NAME="UserName">
<INPUT TYPE="button" VALUE="Submit it" onClick="autosubmit()">
</FORM>
```

In this example, there is one input field called UserName and one button. Notice that, within the code to handle the button, I validate the contents of the UserName field. Because of the way the validation routine is written, it can be used as an onSubmit event handler and also as a standalone validation routine. Your routine should return true if the validation was successful and false if the validation fails.

Note also that I have accessed the form by indexing the forms array of the document object. This array contains all the form objects. In this case, because we have only a single form (the normal case), you can access it through index 0. By using the forms array, you don't need to give your form a name, and if you have only a single form, you know that it will be at index 0.

Sometimes, however, you will want to work with more than one form. In this case, it is probably a good idea to assign each form its own unique name. If you give the form a name, you can access it using its name with the following syntax:

```
[window.]document.formname
```

For example, suppose you have the following HTML:

```
<FORM NAME="EmpData">
<INPUT TYPE="Text" NAME="FirstName">
</FORM>
```

You can access the form with the syntax

```
document.EmpData
```

or (if there are no other forms)

```
document.forms[0]
```

THE form ELEMENTS

Most elements within a <FORM> element use the HTML <INPUT> element. The exceptions are the <SELECT>, <OPTION>, and <TEXTAREA> elements. There are 11 types of input elements:

- Button—This is a standard pushbutton.
- Checkbox—A checkbox enables the user to selectively enable or disable an option.
- FileUpload—The fileupload control enables an end user to upload a file to the server.
- Hidden—Hidden fields are useful for storing temporary JavaScript variables and for sending computed values back to the server without being visible to the end user.
- Password—A password field allows the user to enter text, and a mask character will be displayed.
- Radio—A radio button is used to enable the user to select only one option from a group.
- Reset—A reset control is a button that clears all input fields.
- Select and Option—The select control is used to implement drop-down boxes, list-boxes, and comboboxes in the user interface.
- Submit—The submit button submits the form to the server.
- Text—A text input element displays as a single-line input field.
- TextArea—A text area is used for multiline text input. Domino rich text fields are displayed in HTML as text areas.

For each of the various types of input fields, use the following syntax:

```
<INPUT TYPE="type" [NAME="name"] [VALUE="value"] other-attributes>
```

Here is an example:

```
<INPUT TYPE="button" NAME="BT" VALUE="Click Here" onClick="DoIt()">
```

Notice that the type is not case sensitive. In the sections that follow, I describe the major attributes to use for each of the various input types. I will not cover every attribute for every input element type.

REFERENCING form ELEMENTS

There are several ways to reference form elements such as buttons or text input fields. First, each form element can be obtained from the form property elements. The elements property of the form object is an array that may be subscripted starting from 0. The array length can be found in the form property length. Here is an example of a routine that loops through each of the form elements:

```
<SCRIPT LANGUAGE="JavaScript">
function listall() {
  alert("There are " + document.forms[0].length + " elements")
  for (i=0; i < document.forms[0].length; ++i) {
     alert("element: " + document.forms[0].elements[i].name);
  }
}

</SCRIPT>
<FORM>
<INPUT type="button" name="fred">
<INPUT type="text" name="t1">
<INPUT type="text" name="t2">
<INPUT type="text" name="t3">
<INPUT type="button" name="list" value="list" onclick="listall()">
</FORM>
```

If used within an HTML file, this routine will show the number of elements and will display the name of each element.

Referencing input objects using the elements array works well if your purpose is to go through the entire list and operate on each one. However, this is not normally how you will use input text fields or buttons. Normally, you will want to get or set the value of a text field directly from your JavaScript program.

You can give each input element a name and then refer to the element by that name. This syntax is just an extension of the naming convention we used when we were accessing the form itself. For example, to refer to the button named list in the preceding HTML, you would use the following name:

```
document.forms[0].list
```

If you have the following HTML:

```
<FORM NAME="Registration">
<INPUT TYPE="button" NAME="DoReg" Value="Register" onClick="DoReg()">
</FORM>
```

you could refer to the button with the following name:

```
document.Registration.DoReg
```

The value property of this button would be accessed with

```
document.Registration.DoReg.value
```

Notice that if the form also has a name, it makes your references much easier to understand. You can also assign intermediate names for objects that you will use frequently. Here is an example:

```
var regForm = document.forms[0]
```

or

```
var regForm = document.Registration
```

After you have assigned a name for the form, you can refer to its elements using the variable you just created. You could now refer to the button within the form as

```
regForm.DoReg
```

If you use this technique, you should create these variables at the top of your JavaScript program. Then, you can refer to them throughout the code. An additional advantage is that if you create additional forms or other elements, it can be much easier to change your single definition rather than change references throughout your code. This is especially important if you are using multiple frames because the number and arrangement of your frames can change frequently.

THE button INPUT TYPE

You've seen several examples of buttons. You can create a button with the following HTML syntax:

```
<INPUT TYPE="button" [NAME="name"] [VALUE="button label"] [onClick="handler"]>
```

The VALUE attribute of the button is used to specify the label that will be displayed. The onClick attribute is used to specify JavaScript code that should execute when the button is clicked.

Domino generates a button element when you have created a hotspot button in a Domino form or page. If you specify JavaScript code in the Domino designer for the onClick event, Domino will generate the HTML to execute the JavaScript code at the browser.

THE checkbox INPUT TYPE

A checkbox input element is specified in HTML with the following syntax:

```
<INPUT TYPE="checkbox" NAME="name" VALUE="submission value" [CHECKED]
➥[onClick="handler"]>
```

Checkboxes allow the user to optionally enable or disable an option. The checkbox input type only displays the box itself, it does not display the label. You display the label text on either the left or right depending on where you position the text. Here is an example with the text displayed to the right of the checkbox:

```
<INPUT TYPE="checkbox" NAME="expedite" VALUE="expedite">Expedite Shipping<BR>
```

The CHECKED attribute is used to set the default for the checkbox. If you include this attribute, the checkbox will be checked by default. You can also query whether the checkbox is checked by accessing the checked property of the checkbox. Here are some examples:

```
document.forms[0].expedite.checked = true   // Check the box

if (document.forms[0].expedite.checked) { . . . }
```

One common source of error with the checkbox element is to use the value property rather than the checked property. The value property is used as the submission value for the input element, but it will not tell you whether the checkbox is checked. The value property is used with text input fields. The checked property is used for both checkboxes and radio input elements.

If you use Domino to generate your checkbox, the VALUE attribute will be set to the alias of the value displayed.

THE fileUpload INPUT TYPE

The fileUpload input element type is used to upload files from a client to the server. Here is the syntax:

```
<INPUT TYPE="file">
```

Although this control is called the fileUpload object in most HTML documentation, notice that you use the type file rather than fileUpload.

When this input element is used in a form, it will display a text entry field and a browse button. If pressed, the browse button will allow the user to navigate through the local file system to find the file to be uploaded.

You can have Domino generate this HTML element by issuing the following command from the menus: Create, Embedded Element, File Upload Control from within the form designer. Notice that you cannot embed a file upload control in a Domino page, only in a Domino form.

THE hidden INPUT TYPE

The hidden input type is useful for storing temporary values, intermediate results, or other information that you do not want the user to see. Although hidden input fields will not appear in the Web page, they will be visible if the user views the HTML source, so do not use hidden fields for any type of security. Hidden input elements are useful for results that are calculated and should be sent back to the server without the user's intervention. Here is how you can create a hidden input field with HTML:

```
<INPUT TYPE="hidden" NAME="name" [VALUE="submission value"]>
```

Although the value is hidden, you can reference and change the value from JavaScript in a manner similar to a text field. Here is an example of how you can change a hidden field's value:

```
<SCRIPT LANGUAGE="JavaScript">
function AssignValue(newVal) {
   document.forms[0].theField.value = newVal
}
function ShowValue(newVal) {
   alert("The field's value is " + document.forms[0].theField.value )
}
</SCRIPT>
<FORM>
<INPUT TYPE="hidden" NAME="theField" VALUE="Initial">
<INPUT TYPE="Button" VALUE="SetField" onClick="AssignValue('Test')">
<INPUT TYPE="Button" VALUE="ShowField" onClick="ShowValue()">
</FORM>
```

You can also create hidden fields by using the Domino Designer. You can use the Designer to create the field within a form and add the hidden attribute within the field's property box. However, in addition, you must specify the Generate HTML for All Fields attribute in the On Web Access section of the Defaults (beanie hat) tab of the form's property box. Without enabling this box, hidden fields will not be generated in HTML. The HTML will simply not include them.

After you have created hidden fields on forms with the Domino Designer, you can refer to them in your JavaScript programs as I have just illustrated.

THE password INPUT TYPE

The password input element type is used like a text input element but will display a mask character so that no one can see which characters are typed. Here is the syntax for this element:

```
<INPUT TYPE="password" [NAME="name"] [SIZE="size"] [MAXLENGTH="maxlen"]
➥[onClick="handler"]>
```

You access the value of a password field in the same manner as a text field. In addition, you can supply other TEXT attributes such as SIZE or MAXLENGTH. See "The text Input Type" for more details.

THE radio INPUT TYPE

A radio input element is specified in HTML with the following syntax:

```
<INPUT TYPE="radio" NAME="name" VALUE="submission value" [CHECKED]
➥[onClick="handler"]>
```

A radio button is used to allow the user to select a single option from a group. The radio input type displays only the circular icon itself, not the label. You display the label text on either the left or right, depending on where you position the text. Here is an example with the text displayed to the left of the radio button:

```
Regular Shipping <INPUT TYPE="radio" NAME="shipping" VALUE="regular"> <BR>
Expedite Shipping <INPUT TYPE="radio" NAME="shipping" VALUE="expedite"> <BR>
```

Radio buttons are displayed in groups. Only one of the buttons within the group is checked at a time. Selecting a new button will deselect the existing selection. The grouping is specified by the NAME attribute. All radio buttons with the same name are considered to be grouped together, even if they are not physically grouped in the same area.

The CHECKED attribute is used to set the default for the radio button. If you include this attribute, the radio button will be checked by default. You can also query whether the radio button is checked by accessing the checked property. Here are some examples:

```
document.forms[0].shipping[1].checked = true  // Check the button

if (document.forms[0].shipping[0].checked) { . . . }
```

One common source of error with the radio element is using the value property rather than the checked property. The value property is used as the submission value for the input element, but it will not tell you whether the button is checked. The checked property is used for both checkboxes and radio input elements.

If you use Domino to generate your radio button, the VALUE attribute will be set to the alias of the value displayed.

Here is an example showing how to loop through all the radio buttons in a single group:

```
function radioDisplay() {
 var rg = document.forms[0].shipping   // Get the radio group in an array
 for (var i=0; i < rg.length; i++) {   // Loop through each one
   alert("rg["+i+"]=" + rg[i].value + " and checked is " + rg[i].checked);
 }
}
```

THE reset INPUT TYPE

A reset button is similar to a regular button object but has some special characteristics. When clicked, the reset button will invoke the onReset event handler method of the form object, if one exists. If the return code from the onReset event handler is true, all the input fields of the form will be reset to their initial state. If it is false, the operation will abort and the fields will not be cleared. Here is the syntax for a reset button:

```
<INPUT TYPE="reset" [NAME="name"] [VALUE="button label"] [onClick="handler"]>
```

If you provide both an onClick handler for the button and an onReset handler for the form, the onClick handler will be invoked first. If it returns true (continue with processing) then the form's onReset handler will be invoked. If either handler returns false, the reset will be aborted. Note in the following example that the text field has an initial value of "Reset?". If the reset is not aborted, the value of this field will be reset to this initial value; the field will not be cleared.

```
<HTML>
<BODY>
<SCRIPT LANGUAGE="JavaScript">
function formreset() {
  alert("form.reset");
  return true;    // true to reset the form
}
</SCRIPT>
<FORM onReset="formreset()">
<INPUT type="text" value="Reset?">
<INPUT type="reset" onclick="alert('onclick');return true">
</FORM>
<BODY>
</HTML>
```

THE select AND option OBJECTS

The select object contains and works with an array of option objects. This object is used to make a selection from a list of possible choices. To create select and option objects in HTML, use the following syntax:

```
<SELECT NAME="name" [MULTIPLE] [SIZE="rows"] onChange="handler">
<OPTION [VALUE="returnValue"] [SELECTED] >OptionText1
<OPTION [VALUE="returnValue"] [SELECTED] >OptionText2
<OPTION [VALUE="returnValue"] [SELECTED] >OptionText3
   . . .
<OPTION [VALUE="returnValue"] [SELECTED] >OptionTextn
</SELECT>
```

The SIZE attribute of the <SELECT> element specifies the number of rows to display for the element. Microsoft Internet Explorer allows JavaScript to change the size attribute of the select object, but Netscape Navigator does not. If it is greater than one or if the MULTIPLE attribute is included, the <SELECT> element will appear as a listbox. If SIZE is one and MULTIPLE is not selected, the element will appear as a combobox.

The onChange attribute specifies an event handler you can supply that will be invoked when the selection changes within the <SELECT> element.

Table 10.3 lists the properties found in the select object.

TABLE 10.3 THE select OBJECT PROPERTIES

Property	Description
Length	The read-only length property contains the number of elements in the options array.
OnChange	The onChange property contains the handler code to invoke when the selected item changes.
options	The options property contains an array of option objects. Each object represents one item that can be selected. The number of options and the options themselves can be changed by JavaScript code.

continues

PART

II

CH

10

TABLE 10.3   CONTINUED

Property	Description
selectedIndex	The integer index of the selected option. If MULTIPLE is selected, this property just has the value of the first one. If no option is selected, this property will contain -1.
size	Internet Explorer only. You can change the number of rows that the object occupies. This property corresponds to the HTML <SIZE> attribute.
type	The type property contains select-one if only a single option is allowed or select-multiple if multiple selections are allowed.

The option object contains information pertaining to a single option that can be selected from the select list. option objects are typically created using HTML, but JavaScript can also dynamically create them.

The VALUE attribute is used as the value to be returned if the option is selected. If you don't provide a return value, the value of the option text is used as the return value. Keep in mind that the value returned is the value of the <SELECT> element. For example, suppose the name of the <SELECT> element is COLOR. If the value attribute of the selected option is RED then the browser will return COLOR=RED.

Table 10.4 lists the properties found in the option object.

TABLE 10.4   THE option OBJECT PROPERTIES

Property	Description
defaultSelected	The read-only defaultSelected property contains true if the current option is the default option, false otherwise.
index	The index property contains a zero-origin integer representing the index of this option in the options array.
selected	The selected property is a Boolean value that represents whether the current option is selected. You can read or write this property. If you set the property, the option will be selected but the onChange handler will not be invoked.
text	The text property represents the text string that is displayed to the user.
value	The value property is the string that will be sent back to the server if this option is selected at the time the form is submitted.

You can create a new option object with the following constructor in JavaScript:

```
var opt = new Option(text, value, defaultSelected, selected)
```

The *text*, *value*, *defaultSelected*, and *selected* arguments to the constructor represent the corresponding parameter values. When you dynamically create an option, you must first increase the length of the options array using the property options.length. The following is an example:

```
<HTML>
<HEAD>
<SCRIPT LANGUAGE="JavaScript">
function AddOpt(optstring) {
 // First, create the new option
 var nopt = new Option(optstring, optstring, false, false)
 // Assign an alias for the options array
 olist = document.forms[0].OptList.options
 olist.length += 1                  // Increase the length of the array
 olist[olist.length-1] = nopt     // Add the new option
}
</SCRIPT>
<BODY>
<FORM>
<SELECT NAME="OptList" SIZE=5 MULTIPLE>
<OPTION VALUE="RetValue1">Test1
<OPTION>Test2
</SELECT>
New Option:<INPUT TYPE="text" NAME="NewOpt"><BR>

<INPUT TYPE="button" VALUE="AddOption"
➥onClick="AddOpt(document.forms[0].NewOpt.value)">
</FORM>
</BODY>
</HTML>
```

PART
II
CH
10

In this example, there is a selection list, which is displayed as a listbox, an input field where you can type a new option, and a button. When the button is clicked, a new option will be added to the selection list (see Figure 10.1).

Figure 10.1
A simple HTML program to add an option to an option list.

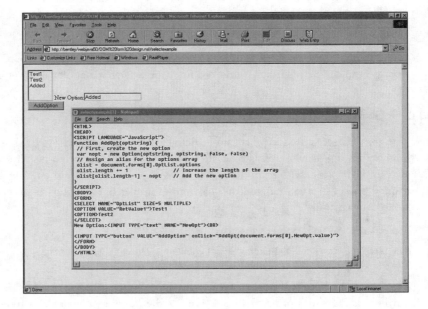

THE submit INPUT TYPE

A submit button is similar to a regular button object but has some special characteristics. When clicked, the submit button will attempt to package up the information of the current form and send it to the server. The method used will be either GET or POST, as specified on the <FORM> element or with the method property of the form object. The ACTION attribute of the <FORM> tag will be used as the destination. Here is the syntax for a submit button:

```
<INPUT TYPE="submit" [NAME="name"] [VALUE="button label"] [onClick="handler"]>
```

The VALUE attribute, if specified, will be used for the button label. Note that both the button's onClick handler and the form's onSubmit event handler will be invoked, if they exist. The button's onClick handler will be invoked first. If the return code from both event handlers is true, the fields will be sent to the server. If either handler returns false, the operation will abort and the fields will not be sent. Also, if both event handlers are specified and the onClick handler returns false, the form's onSubmit handler will not be invoked. Here is an example:

```
<HTML>
<BODY>
<SCRIPT LANGUAGE="JavaScript">
function formsub() {
  alert("form.submit");
  return true;   // true to submit the form
}
</SCRIPT>
<FORM onSubmit="formsub()">
<INPUT type="submit" onclick="alert('onclick');return false">
</FORM>
<BODY>
</HTML>
```

In the example, the onClick handler returns false, while the onSubmit handler returns true. Because the onClick handler is invoked first, the onSubmit handler is never called.

THE text INPUT TYPE

The text object is used for most input fields in HTML. It appears as a single-line input field within the browser. This type of object is used by Domino to display fields of types text and datetime, and for numbers. In HTML you can specify the number of characters to display (the SIZE attribute) and the maximum number of characters to accept as input (the MAXLENGTH attribute).

Here is the HTML syntax for a text field:

```
<INPUT TYPE="text" [NAME="name"] [VALUE="default"] [SIZE="size"]
➥[MAXLENGTH="maxlen"] [onChange="handler"]>
```

The VALUE attribute will be displayed as the initial value within the input field. The SIZE attribute is the width of the field, specified as the number of characters to be displayed in the browser. The MAXLENGTH attribute is the maximum number of characters that the browser will allow the user to type into the field. This value may be more or less than the SIZE attribute. The onChange handler will be invoked when the user moves the focus away from the field. It will not be invoked for every keystroke input into the field.

For field validation you have two choices; one is to validate using the onChange handler of the text object. This will be invoked only when the user changes the field. The second choice, usually preferable, is to use the onSubmit handler of the form object. This handler will be invoked automatically when the form is submitted unless you invoke the form.submit() method directly.

In the Domino Designer, you can specify the SIZE and MAXLENGTH attributes for a field in the HTML Attributes event for the field (see Figure 10.2).

Figure 10.2
Specify the SIZE and MAXLENGTH attributes in the HTML Attributes event in Domino Designer.

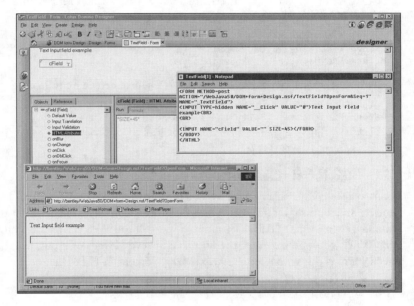

In Figure 10.2, notice that the HTML Attributes event is specified by a Domino formula. For this reason, you must use quotes around the expression you use. In this example, I have specified a SIZE attribute but not a MAXLENGTH attribute. You can see the HTML that has been generated by Domino includes the SIZE=45 specification that I included.

After you have created a field either with the Domino Designer or by using HTML directly, you can change the value of the field by using the value property of the text object. One common mistake is to forget that you must use the value property; you cannot just assign a value to the text object directly. Here is an example:

```
<SCRIPT LANGUAGE="JavaScript">
function AssignValue(newVal) {
    document.forms[0].InField.value = newVal
}
</SCRIPT>
```

```
<FORM>
<INPUT TYPE="text" NAME="InField" VALUE="">
<INPUT TYPE="Button" VALUE="SetTest" onClick="AssignValue('Test')">
</FORM>
```

If the button is clicked in this example, the input field's value will change. To refer to an input field in another frame, the name must also include the navigation to the other window. Here is an example.

Suppose you have two frames, left and right, within a frameset. Here is how code within the left frame could change a variable in the right frame:

```
parent.right.document.forms[0].FirstName.value = "Sally";
```

You can assign the form to an intermediate object for ease in referencing. Here is an example:

```
var rightform = parent.right.document.forms[0];
rightform.FirstName.value = "Sally";
rightform.LastName.value = "Smith";
```

As mentioned, make sure that you use the value property. The following is incorrect:

```
var rightform = parent.right.document.forms[0];
rightform.FirstName = "Sally";    // INCORRECT!!
rightform.LastName = "Smith";     // INCORRECT!!
```

THE Textarea ELEMENT

The Textarea element can be created directly from HTML using the HTML <TEXTAREA> element. In addition, Domino also generates the <TEXTAREA> element for any rich text fields contained on a form. Textarea elements appear in the Web browser as multiline edit controls. When you want to allow the user to edit several lines of input, use the Textarea object. Here is the syntax for the <TEXTAREA> element in HTML:

```
<TEXTAREA [NAME="name"] [ROWS="rows"] [COLS="rows"]
➥[WRAP="off|virtual|physical"] [onChange="handler"]>
```

The ROWS attribute controls the number of rows to display, and the COLS attribute is the number of columns. The default values are 2 rows and 20 columns. You should normally include explicit specifications for the number of rows and columns because 2 rows and 20 characters are usually not enough space for a typical <TEXTAREA> element.

You can control whether text automatically wraps within the control. If you set WRAP to off, no wrapping is done, and text will appear in a single line and scroll left and right. If you set WRAP to virtual, the wrapping will occur on the screen, but CR-LF characters will not appear in the data. If you set WRAP to physical, CR-LF will appear in the data.

Note that Netscape Navigator and Microsoft Internet Explorer have different defaults for the WRAP attribute of this element. Navigator uses a default of WRAP="off", while Internet Explorer uses a default of WRAP="virtual". This means that your <TEXTAREA> element will behave differently in the two browsers if you do not explicitly set the WRAP attribute. In addition, because Domino rich text fields are displayed as `<TEXTAREA>` elements, they are affected as well. My recommendation is to explicitly add a `WRAP="virtual"` attribute to this element. There is not much value in using a `<TEXTAREA>` element if the text does not wrap to several lines.

The `onChange` event handler for `<TEXTAREA>` operates as it does for the `<INPUT TYPE="text">` element. That is, the event occurs when the focus shifts to another control. In particular, the `onChange` event does not fire for each keystroke. You can use the `onChange` event to do field validation of the `<TEXTAREA>` element.

Mapping Domino Design Elements to DOM Elements

Table 10.5 lists the mapping of Domino Design elements to DOM elements. Note that this mapping represents version 5.0.1 of Domino, but might be changed in future versions. The mapping might also vary in the future based on other factors such as the browser type. Use this table as a starting point, but test your code thoroughly in various browsers (including different versions of the same browser).

PART
II
CH
10

TABLE 10.5   DOMINO DESIGN ELEMENT MAPPING TO DOM ELEMENTS

Domino	DOM	HTML
Text field	text	`<INPUT TYPE="text" NAME="fldname">`
Date/Time field	text	`<INPUT TYPE="text" NAME="fldname">`
Number field	text	`<INPUT TYPE="text" NAME="fldname">`
Dialog list	select	`<SELECT><OPTION> </SELECT>`
Checkbox	checkbox	`<INPUT TYPE="checkbox" NAME="fldname">`
Radio button	radio	`<INPUT TYPE="radio" NAME="fldname">`
Listbox	select	`<SELECT><OPTION> </SELECT>`
Combobox	select	`<SELECT><OPTION> </SELECT>`
Rich Text field	textarea	`<TEXTAREA NAME="fldname">`
Authors, Names, or Readers field	text	`<INPUT TYPE="text" NAME="fldname">`
Password field	password	`<INPUT TYPE="password" NAME="fldname">`
Formula field	text	`<INPUT TYPE="text" NAME="fldname">`
Action	link	`<A HREF="" onClick="handler">label</A>`
Computed text	N/A	Computed on the server, result rendered as regular inline text.

continues

TABLE 10.5 CONTINUED

Domino	DOM	HTML
Link Hotspot	link	`<A HREF="url">label</A>`
Text Pop-up Hotspot	N/A	Rendered as regular inline text. Pop-up will not work in browser.
Button Hotspot	button	`<INPUT TYPE="button" onClick="handler" VALUE="label">`
Formula Pop-up Hotspot	N/A	Rendered as regular inline text. Pop-up will not work in browser.
Action Hotspot	link	`<A HREF="" onClick="handler">label</A>`
Picture	image	`<IMG SRC="..?OpenElement">`
Image Resource	image	`<IMG SRC="..?OpenImageResource">`
Hotspot on image resource or Picture	area	`<MAP><AREA SHAPE="shape" COORDS="coords" HREF="url"></MAP>`

ANCHORS AND LINKS

The Anchor tag, `<A>`, is used both for defining a destination and for defining a link to a destination. In Chapter 7, I showed you how to use the tag for both purposes. After you have defined anchors and links in your HTML document, you can reference them with two different arrays in the DOM.

The `links` array and the `anchors` array are both properties of the `document` object. By accessing these arrays, you can query the properties of links and anchors.

An `anchor` object has a name property along with coordinate specifications of its location. Netscape Navigator uses `x` and `y` as the location properties, while Internet Explorer uses `offsetLeft` and `offsetTop`. Fortunately, you will not normally need to query or set the location of an anchor.

A `link` object contains several useful properties. Links are much more common in HTML documents than anchors. Here is the syntax for a link:

```
<A HREF="url" [TARGET="windowname"]
    [onClick="handler" ]
    [onMouseOver="handler" ]
    [onMouseOut="handler"]
> text or image to display </A>
```

To understand the properties of this object, let's review the component parts of a URL:

```
protocol://hostname:port/pathname?search#hash
```

For example, in the following URL:

```
http://www.somehost.com:80/ecommerce/buyit.nsf/catview/p123?opendocument#price
```

the URL would be parsed as follows:

```
protocol    http:
hostname    www.somehost.com
port        80
pathname    /ecommerce/buyit.nsf/catview/p123
search      ?opendocument
hash        #price
```

Here are the properties of the link object:

- hash—Specifies the hash portion of the URL, including the #. This represents the name of an anchor link.

- host—The hostname and port portion of the URL. In the preceding example, the host value would be www.somehost.com:80.

- hostname—The hostname property specifies the hostname portion of the URL.

- href—The href property specifies the complete URL.

- pathname—The pathname property specifies just the pathname portion of the URL.

- port—The port property specifies the port number of the URL.

- protocol—The protocol property specifies the protocol of the URL. For Web browsers, this will be http: and for the Notes client it will be Notes:.

- search—The search property specifies the part of the URL beginning with the question mark and prior to the hash.

- target—The target property specifies the name of the window that should be used to display the link.

THE area AND map ELEMENTS

The area and map elements are used together. The <MAP> HTML element is a container used to hold one or more <AREA> elements. Each area defines an area of the browser window and behaves like a link object.

The <MAP> element is primarily used to name the group of <AREA> elements. The syntax of the <MAP> element is very simple:

```
<MAP NAME="name">
```

The <AREA> element syntax is

```
<AREA SHAPE="shape" COORDS="coords" [ID="identifier"] [HREF="url"]
➥[ALT="message"] >
```

The SHAPE attribute can be circle, polygon, or rect. The default is rect, for a rectangular shape. The COORDS attribute specifies the coordinates for the shape; the number of

PART

II

CH

10

coordinates depends on the type of shape. ID is used to name the area. HREF specifies a link destination, and ALT specifies an alternative text message to display for the area. The alternative message is displayed if the user hovers the mouse over the area.

If you use the Domino Designer to specify a hotspot over a graphic image such as a picture or image resource, Domino will convert the reference to a <MAP> and a set of <AREA> elements when it serves the image to a Web browser.

In the DOM model, <AREA> tags generate links and are found within the links array of the document object. You can use the link properties for a link object as described in the section titled "Anchors and Links."

USING IMAGES

Images are specified with the use of the <IMG> element tag. You can use images anywhere in your Web page, including within text elements. A popular use for images is within a hypertext link. If displayed in this manner, the user can click on the image and it will behave as a hypertext link. Here is the HTML syntax for the <IMG> element:

```
<IMG SRC="url" WIDTH="width" HEIGHT="height"
    [NAME="name"] [BORDER="borderwidth"]
    [HSPACE="horizsize"] [VSPACE="vertsize"]
    [USEMAP="mapname"]>
```

The SRC attribute of the <IMG> tag specifies a URL that is used to locate the image. If you code this tag yourself, notice that the <A> tag uses the HREF attribute, while the <IMG> tag uses the SRC attribute. I'm not sure why they are different, but it is probably historical. At any rate, use the appropriate attribute for the HTML element.

The WIDTH and HEIGHT attributes specify the size of the image, in pixels. The location of the image is not specified in the tag. The location of the image is determined by the placement of the <IMG> tag within the HTML file itself. A common technique for positioning graphics is to use an HTML table.

The NAME attribute allows you to specify a name for the image. The BORDER attribute is a number and if it is greater than zero, it will draw a border around the image. To eliminate the border, specify the BORDER attribute as zero. HSPACE and VSPACE are specified in pixels and represent extra spacing in the horizontal and vertical directions around the image.

The USEMAP attribute is used to specify an image map. An image map is created with the <MAP> and <AREA> tags as previously described. Domino will generate a USEMAP attribute for hotspots over graphical images such as pictures or image resources.

Probably the most important runtime feature of an image element is the capability to dynamically change the content of the image. This is the core feature that enables mouse rollovers. I describe mouse rollovers in Chapter 11.

THE \<Applet\> TAG

The \<APPLET\> tag is used to specify a Java applet that should be loaded in the browser. The \<APPLET\> tag is usually used in conjunction with the \<PARAM\> tag, which is used to specify parameters to the Java applet. Here is the syntax for the \<APPLET\> tag:

```
<APPLET CODE="classname" WIDTH="width" HEIGHT="height"
    [CODEBASE="pathurl"] [ARCHIVE="zipfile"]
    [NAME="name"] [BORDER="borderwidth"]
    [HSPACE="horizsize"] [VSPACE="vertsize"]
    [ALT="message"]>
```

You can access an array containing all the applets within a document using the applets property of the document object. In the \<APPLET\> tag, specify the name of the base class for the applet, the width and height you would like it to use within the browser window, and several other optional attributes. The WIDTH and HEIGHT attributes specify the amount of space, in pixels, that the applet should take.

The CODE attribute specifies the main class file of the applet. An applet can be made up of several class files incorporated within an archive file. However, one of them must be designated as the main file. The ARCHIVE parameter specifies the name of the ZIP or jar file that contains all the Java classes that make up the applet. The CODEBASE attribute specifies a URL which contains a directory path to the directory that contains both the main class file and the archive file.

The NAME attribute allows you to specify a name for the applet. The BORDER attribute is a number, and if it is greater than zero, it will draw a border around the applet. To eliminate the border, specify the BORDER attribute as zero. HSPACE and VSPACE are specified in pixels and represent extra spacing in the horizontal and vertical directions around the applet.

The ALT attribute is the alternative text to display in case the applet fails to load or otherwise has a problem.

The \<PARAM\> tag allows you to specify parameters that you would like to send to the applet. The two significant attributes for the \<PARAM\> tag are NAME and VALUE. For each \<PARAM\> tag, you specify a name and value. Within the Java applet, you can obtain the value attribute for each parameter. Here is an example showing you the \<APPLET\> and \<PARAM\> tags:

```
<APPLET CODE="Calendar.class" NAME="Cal"
    CODEBASE="applets\cal\" ARCHIVE="JavaCal.jar"
    WIDTH="400" HEIGHT="300" >
<PARAM NAME="year" VALUE="2000">
<PARAM NAME="month" VALUE="November">
<PARAM NAME="day" VALUE="27">
<PARAM NAME="style" VALUE="monthly">
</APPLET>
```

CHAPTER REVIEW

1. Explain the difference between a Domino form and document and the Document Object Model (DOM) form and document.

2. What is the difference between the GET method and the POST method when submitting an HTML page? Where do you specify this parameter?

3. Create a page in the Domino Designer using passthru HTML. On the page, include two text input fields, a checkbox, and a button. Write JavaScript routines to do the following: When the button is clicked, check to see whether the checkbox is checked. If so, copy the information from the first input field to the second input field. If the first input field is blank, display an error message. If the checkbox is not checked then display a message indicating that no copying will take place.

4. Create a form in the Domino Designer with two input fields, a checkbox, and a button. Make it operate just as in exercise 3. Use a browser to view the page, and compare the HTML and JavaScript with the HTML and JavaScript you created manually.

5. When you create a hidden field in the Domino Designer, what option must you enable so that the field is generated as an HTML hidden field? Create a form with a hidden field in the Domino Designer and experiment with the option enabled and disabled to see the results in your browser.

6. Why is it a good idea to use the WRAP attribute with the <TEXTAREA> HTML element?

7. If you don't explicitly set attributes, how large will a Domino rich text field display in the browser? What HTML element is used to display a rich text field and what HTML attributes must you use to change the size?

8. How do the <SELECT> and <OPTION> HTML elements display in a Web browser? Which three Domino user interface elements use these two HTML elements for display? What rules determine how these user interface elements are displayed in the browser? What is the purpose of the MULTIPLE attribute?

9. What does the VALUE attribute do for the <INPUT TYPE="button"> element? If you use Domino to generate a checkbox or radio button, what does it use for the VALUE attribute in the HTML it generates?

10. What are the <MAP> and <AREA> HTML elements used for? What feature of Domino generates these HTML elements? What kinds of shapes can you use for an <AREA>?

11. Radio buttons usually appear in groups. Clicking one of the radio buttons deselects whichever button was previously selected. Only one button of the group can be selected at a time. What HTML feature do you use to specify the grouping for the radio buttons? Can you have more than one group of radio buttons within a single Web page, and if so, how?

CHAPTER 11

JavaScript Techniques with Domino

In this chapter I describe some techniques that you can use with JavaScript and Domino. You can use these techniques to improve the user interface of your Web application, to increase the integrity of your data by performing validation, and to improve performance by moving some processing to the Web client instead of to the server.

There is no single theme to the techniques I show in this chapter. They are meant to form a cross section of various methods to perform commonly required tasks at the Web client. Let's start with one of the most important tasks: validating user input.

FORM VALIDATION

When you validate user input at the Web client in JavaScript, errors are caught earlier and the user experience is improved because he or she will not have to wait for communication to the server. There are several types of user input validation, but here are some common requirements:

- Fields should not be left blank.
- The data type of user input should be checked: Numeric fields should not contain letters.
- Fields should contain semantically correct information: Date fields should contain a valid date. Phone numbers should contain the correct number of digits.
- Credit card numbers should be checked to see that the checksum is valid.
- Choices for a field should come from a predefined list of valid choices. Examples of predefined lists might be department names, colors, localities, and so forth.

CHECKING FOR BLANK FIELDS

Let's start with a simple validation. This one checks to make sure that the user has entered values for specific fields. Here is some code that performs validation of the UserName field. In it, the validate routine checks that the field's value is non-blank. It displays a message and returns false if the field fails validation. If the field contains a value, it returns true.

```
<SCRIPT LANGUAGE="JavaScript">
function validate() {
   if ("" == document.forms[0].UserName.value) {
      alert("You must enter a value for the User Name field.");
      return false;  // Fails validation
   }
   return true;  // Succeeds validation
}
</SCRIPT>
```

Although functional, this routine suffers from a few problems. First, the routine is hard coded to use the UserName field. If your form has only a single field, this might be acceptable, but most likely your form will contain several input fields. If you wanted to extend this approach to multiple fields on the form, you would need to code many similar validation routines. The name validate is also overly broad and might not fit your validation needs for other occasions.

Let's see how to take the core from this program and recast it in a more reusable format. Look at the following JavaScript program:

```
<SCRIPT LANGUAGE="JavaScript">
function nonBlank(field) {
   if ("" == field.value) {
      alert("You must enter a value for the " + field.name + " field.");
      return false;  // Fails validation
   }
   return true;  // Succeeds validation
}
</SCRIPT>
```

In this routine, I have passed a field object to the nonBlank routine. This routine will then check the field to make sure that it is non-blank, conditionally issue a message, and return false if validation fails and true if it succeeds. Notice that the field object is used to access both the value property and the name property. Remember that when you access a field's value, you must add the .value suffix. Here is an example of how this routine might be used in a Web page:

```
<SCRIPT LANGUAGE="JavaScript">
function autosubmit() {
   // . . . Processing here . . .
   if (nonBlank(document.forms[0].FirstName) &&
       nonBlank(document.forms[0].LastName)
       ) {
      document.forms[0].submit();   // submit the form
   }
}
</SCRIPT>
<FORM>
First Name: <INPUT TYPE="Text" NAME="FirstName"><BR>
Last Name:  <INPUT TYPE="Text" NAME="LastName"><BR>
<INPUT TYPE="button" VALUE="Submit it" onClick="autosubmit()">
</FORM>
```

In this example, the nonBlank routine is called twice, once to check the FirstName field and once to check the LastName field. When I invoke the nonBlank routine here, I do not include the .value suffix because I am passing the field object itself, not a string value. I will access the value within the subroutine. I pass the field object itself because, within the subroutine, I want to access not only the field's value, but its name as well.

If you call the submit method of the form object, remember that the form's onSubmit handler will not automatically be invoked. Therefore, you will be responsible for calling any validation routines yourself as I have done in the previous example. If you use an <INPUT type="submit"> button, the onSubmit routine of the form will be invoked automatically.

CHECKING FOR PATTERNS

You can use a validation routine to check whether a field contains all numbers or certain punctuation (such as a phone number) or represents a valid date. To perform more sophisticated pattern checking, you might want to use regular expressions.

Regular expressions specify a pattern. After you have specified the pattern, you can search a string for the pattern, find one or more matches within a string, or replace the pattern with another string.

A complete discussion of the regular expression language is outside the scope of this book, but I provide you with some of the basics and simple rules surrounding their use. Literal regular expressions begin and end with a forward slash (/) and can contain some modification characters after the final slash. Here are some examples:

```
/Name/              Literal string "Name"
/[abc]/               'a', 'b', or 'c'
/[0-9]+/          A string of one or more digits
/[^0-9]/          Any character other than a digit
/\s/              Any whitespace [\t\n\r\f\v]
/(first|last)/        The string "first" or "last"
/[a-zA-Z]/        Any upper- or lowercase letter
/[A-Z][a-z]*/       An initial capital followed by 0 or more lowercase letters
```

You can have repetition modifiers that can match sequences of characters. Here are the repetition modifiers:

```
{n,m}       Match the previous item at least n times, but at most m times.
{n,m}       Match the previous item at least n times.
{n}         Match the previous item exactly n times.
?           Match the previous item zero or one time. Equivalent to {0,1}.
+           Match the previous item one or more times. Equivalent to {1,}.
*           Match the previous item zero or more times. Equivalent to {0,}.
```

If you want your string to match special characters, you must include an escape (backslash) character before the character. For example, to match a left parenthesis, you must use \(within your string. Here is a list of the special characters that must be escaped:

```
/ \ . * + ? | ( ) [ ] { }
```

You can also use octal or hexadecimal escape codes. For octal, use a backslash followed by three digits. A hexadecimal number is a backslash, an x, and two hex digits. Here are examples:

```
\102    Octal for the decimal value 66
\x2F    Hexadecimal for the decimal value 47
```

Certain non-printing characters have special symbols:

```
\f    Form feed - Equivalent to \x0C
\n    Newline - Sometimes called linefeed. Equivalent to \x0A
\r    Carriage return - Equivalent to \x0D
\t    Tab - Equivalent to \x09
```

If you enter a literal string, the pattern will match that string. If you enter a bracketed set of letters, the pattern will match any single character within the brackets. If you add a plus sign after a character, the pattern will match one or more of that character. A caret (^) means any character except the character following the ^. The vertical bar (|) means or. The pattern will match the string on the left or right of the vertical bar. You can concatenate patterns by placing them one after the other.

The String object contains three methods that utilize regular expressions. They are match(), replace(), and search(). The match method matches a string with a regular expression and returns an array if there is at least one match. The first element of the array is the matched string; the other elements are the substrings that match any parenthesized expressions within the pattern. The replace method will replace the first match or all matches of a pattern with a replacement string. The search method will search a string for a pattern and will return the index of the match or -1 if there was no match.

Here is a routine that will validate that a field contains only numeric characters:

```
function IsDigits(field) {
   var v = field.value    // The string value to be searched
   var m = v.match(/[0-9]+/) // One or more digit characters
   if (null != m) {       // if we matched something
      // if we match the entire string, the lengths will match
      if (m[0].length == v.length ) {
         return true;      // Succeeds validation
      }
      // We only matched a substring. Fall through to error report
   }
   alert("You must enter only numbers for the " + field.name + " field.");
   return false;  // Fails validation
}
```

In the IsDigits validation routine, we use a pattern of [0-9]+, which means we must match one or more digit characters. By using different patterns for the regular expression, you can match phone numbers, dates, Social Security numbers, credit card numbers, and so forth.

VALIDATING CREDIT CARD NUMBERS

Almost all credit cards carry a checksum digit as the last digit of the card. With the advent of so much e-commerce, you might need to check the validity of a credit card number. This algorithm will check whether the digits of the card correspond correctly to the checksum. This routine obviously will not check whether the number has been validly assigned to an individual. Also, it is possible, although unlikely, that an invalid number might appear as valid. For these reasons, you should use the credit card checking algorithm only as a preliminary, first check to assist the user. This method should catch most of the common typing errors, transposed digits, single-digit errors, omitted numbers, and so on.

The JavaScript code presented in Listing 11.1 is also included in the JavaScript library database that is on the CD-ROM.

LISTING 11.1 SAMPLE CODE TO VERIFY A CREDIT CARD NUMBER: CredCard.js (1.0) IN JSLib.nsf

```
// Credit Card Validity Check
// Copyright (c) 1999,2000 Randy Tamura

function isCCValid(cInputCardNo) {
   var cCardNo = ""; // Only digits allowed
   var i;             // Temporary variable
   var nCheckSum;     // Build the checksum here
   var nMult;          // 1 or 2
   var nDigit;        // Value of digit * mult
   // First delete any non-numbers
   for (i=0; i < cInputCardNo.length; i++) {
      if (-1 != "0123456789".indexOf(cInputCardNo.charAt(i))) {
       cCardNo += cInputCardNo.charAt(i); // append to card no
       }
   }
   if ("" == cCardNo) return false; // Empty: Not valid
   // If length is odd append a zero to the left
   if (1 == cCardNo.length % 2) cCardNo = "0" + cCardNo;

   // cCardNo should now be an even number of characters
   nCheckSum = 0;
   // Start from the first character
   nMult = 2;          // First multiplier is 2
   for (i=0; i < cCardNo.length; i++) {
      nDigit = parseInt(cCardNo.charAt(i)); // Get the digit value
      // Every other digit is multiplied by 2. We shift left to multiply
      if (2 == nMult) nDigit = nDigit << 1; // Multiply by 2
      // If the digit value is now greater than 9, reduce to single digit
      if (nDigit > 9) nDigit = nDigit - 9;  // Single digit answer
      nCheckSum += nDigit; // Add to the checksum
      // Switch the multiplier
      if (2 == nMult) {nMult = 1} else nMult = 2;
   }
   // If the final answer is divisible by 10 it is valid
   if (0 == nCheckSum % 10) {
      return true;  // Valid credit card number
   }
   else {
      return false; // Invalid number
   }
}
```

The isCCValid routine will return true if the credit card number is valid and false otherwise. After declaring some variables, this routine goes through a loop eliminating any extraneous characters such as spaces or hyphens. The rest of the algorithm will work with a string of digits only.

If the credit card string does not contain any digits, it will return false, signaling that the number is not valid. The main algorithm assumes that the string has an even number of digits, so if it has an odd number, a zero is appended to the left of the string.

The checksum works by weighting every other digit by multiplying it by 2. If the result is more than a single digit (that is, more than 9), it is reduced to a single digit by subtracting 9. The sum of these digits is added together. If the final result is a multiple of 10, the credit card number is assumed to be valid. Notice that by chance, a person could type an incorrect credit card number and it might possibly result in a valid number (a different multiple of 10). However, an error in a single digit cannot result in a valid number, and transposing two digits should also be caught because of the even/odd weighting of the digits of the number.

The JavaScript library contained on the CD-ROM contains a copy of the credit card validating program as well as a small sample Web page that invokes it. If you decide to use this program, test it thoroughly because it might or might not work for your particular application. As I mentioned, you also need to do further checking of the credit card number for validity before you use the value for processing. This check is designed to be performed at the Web client to aid the user in spotting typographical errors that can be fixed without a message to the server.

ROLLOVERS

Rollovers are a great user interface device. A *rollover* is a mouse effect that occurs when you move your mouse over a graphic area of a Web page. As you roll your mouse over the area, the graphic changes. The main use for the rollover is to give the user feedback about the currently selected item.

Rollovers have been a useful device for just about as long as the mouse has been around. Think about what happens when you move the mouse to the edge of a window in Microsoft Windows. As your mouse moves to the edge or corner of a window, the cursor icon changes its shape to indicate that you can drag the edge or corner to change the size of your window. That's similar to a Web rollover.

In today's Web world, rollovers are used within menus, to create pop-ups, and in a variety of other creative ways. In all cases, the rollover is used to give the user feedback about the object that is currently selected or what will happen if the current object is clicked.

In Chapter 3, "Developing Pages with the Domino Designer," I showed you how to use image resources in the Domino Designer to automatically create image rollovers. The capabilities within Domino are restricted, however, and there might be occasions when you want to "roll your own," so to speak.

Creating your own rollovers is pretty easy. Most custom designed rollovers depend on these JavaScript capabilities: the <IMG> event handler attributes of onMouseOver and onMouseOut and a general subroutine to swap images.

In implementing a mouse rollover, we are going to use two images: a normal image and a second image that will display when the mouse is over the image. We can call this second image the highlighted image. In addition, we must make sure that the performance is very fast when we swap these two images back and forth. We cannot afford to go back to a server to retrieve the images, so the images must be preloaded before they are needed.

Here is our strategy:

1. At the time the page is loaded, download all images that will be required for our rollovers. These images will be stored using a naming convention so we can access them later.

2. Both the normal and highlighted versions of each rollover must be downloaded, but the highlighted versions should not be displayed.

3. When the mouse moves over the image, swap out the normal image and display the highlighted image. If the browser does not support images and swapping, there should be no ill effects.

4. When the mouse moves out of the image, swap out the highlighted image and display the normal image again.

That's it; it really isn't too complicated. The real issues in implementation are more bookkeeping than difficult coding. We have bookkeeping issues because we are likely to have many, perhaps dozens, of images, and they can be scattered throughout our Web page. How can we deal with this plethora of pictures? It's simple. We just use naming conventions and a subroutine. Here's how.

The first part of the naming convention is to realize that our pictures come in pairs. That is, there is a normal version of the image and a highlighted version. We give each pair a name, but also give each picture a unique suffix. For example, I like to use the suffixes in and out. The out picture is the normal picture, and the in picture is used when the mouse is in the image.

Suppose I have a graphic menu that has a home button. My two images would be named homein.gif and homeout.gif. A button labeled about would result in the image names aboutin.gif and aboutout.gif. This convention is easy to understand. In addition to the names of the files, I dynamically construct variable names within the program. For these names, I include an underscore within the name to indicate that the name is constructed. For example, I use the base name home, but with a suffix of either _in or _out to create a variable name such as home_in or home_out.

Here is an example of some JavaScript code:

```
<SCRIPT LANGUAGE="JavaScript">
<!--Hide script from older browsers
   // First check to see if the browser supports images.
   // This code will be executed when the page loads
   if (document.images)      {
       // Yes. Images supported. Load the images
       var home_in = new Image()
       home_in.src = "HomeIn.gif"
       var home_out = new Image()
       home_out.src = "HomeOut.gif"

       var about_in = new Image()
       about_in.src = "AboutIn.gif"
```

```
        var about_out = new Image()
        about_out.src = "AboutOut.gif"
  }
// Invoked when the mouse moves out of given image.
function out(imgName)
  {   if (document.images)
      eval('document.'+imgName+'.src ='+imgName+'_out.src')
      // example: document.home.src = home_out.src
  }

// Invoked when the mouse moves over of given image.
function over(imgName)
  {   if (document.images)
      eval('document.'+imgName+'.src ='+imgName+'_in.src')
      // example: document.home.src = home_in.src
  }
// End hiding script -->
</SCRIPT>
```

The sample code consists of three major parts. The first part is executed when the Web page loads because it is not part of a JavaScript function. We check whether the document.images property exists because some early browsers do not support images. All current browsers support images, but it probably doesn't cost much performance to keep the safety check in the code.

The code creates four new image objects. The src property of each object is set to a URL that identifies the graphic file. The second two parts of the JavaScript are the two routines out and over. The out routine will be invoked when the mouse moves out of a given image, and the over routine will be invoked when the mouse is over the image.

In both the out and over routines, the src property of the displayed image is overwritten with a new value, either the out or in image object. Here is the HTML that is used on the page to define the displayed image:

```
<A HREF="home.htm" onMouseOver="over('home')" onMouseOut="out('home')">
<IMG NAME="home" HEIGHT=24 WIDTH=120 SRC="HomeOut.gif" BORDER=0>
</A>
<A HREF="about.htm" onMouseOver="over('about')" onMouseOut="out('about')">
<IMG NAME="about" HEIGHT=24 WIDTH=120 SRC="AboutOut.gif" BORDER=0>
</A>
```

Remember that JavaScript is case sensitive. In this example, both the over and out routines are passed strings that are used to construct variable names. This means that if your capitalization is incorrect, the eval routine will not be able to find the proper image. For this example, there are three image locations for each graphic. These are the two original images used to store the in and out versions as well as the current version, which will contain one of the two original images at any given time. The current version is created with the <IMG> tag in the HTML. Notice in the <IMG> tag that I have used the NAME attribute. The NAME of the <IMG> is the name used within the eval expression in both the in and out routines.

Note that the graphic images themselves can be stored in the Domino Image Resources library. When they are there, you can refer to them by name. The JavaScript library database on the CD-ROM illustrates the use of images stored in the image library for this example.

SHARED JAVASCRIPT LIBRARIES

After you have created a lot of useful JavaScript code, you might want to reuse it. In fact, if you are not reusing your JavaScript code, you are probably wasting time reinventing code. Domino now has features that enable you to share LotusScript and Java code in Script libraries, to reuse graphic images using an image library, and to share fields and subforms within your database. However, there are no facilities for sharing JavaScript in your database or across databases.

In this section I show you how to use features that are part of the core Domino capabilities to implement your own JavaScript libraries. I include many of the examples of this chapter in the JavaScript library database on the CD-ROM.

There are several methods for creating JavaScript libraries, each with their own pros and cons. I show you how to create libraries with subforms and by using Domino documents, forms, and views.

USING SUBFORMS

The first method to create a JavaScript library is by using Domino subforms. Using subforms takes advantage of the fact that each subform has its own JSHeader event. When you include one or more subforms together on a main form, all the JSHeader elements of all the subforms and the main form are executed. This enables you to define a subform for a set of functions and then mix and match the functions as you require.

When you use subforms to implement a JavaScript library, you really only utilize the JSHeader event of the subform. The formatting part of the subform is not required. I suggest, however, that you include at least a single line that names or describes the capabilities of the JavaScript routines defined in the JSHeader. Make sure that the line of description is hidden from Web browsers. That way, the comment will be visible during your design phase but will not be transmitted to the Web clients. You can also include other information about the routines on the form, such as the version and date. If the information is extensive, you might want to use some hide-when features so that the comments are visible only to the designer, not to the end user.

In the JavaScript library (JSLib.nsf) database for this chapter, I have included a sample subform that includes some string-handling routines in JavaScript. You can see how the subform is implemented and use the same methodology for your own databases.

USING A FORM, DOCUMENTS, AND A VIEW

One benefit of using a design element such as a subform for your JavaScript routines is that you can use the built-in editor for JavaScript. This editor includes color coding and syntax checking. One drawback of using this approach, however, is that you have limited flexibility in keeping additional management information about your programs. For example, it is difficult to maintain multiple versions and store information such as the name of the person who last modified the code.

You can add these features and more by using Domino capabilities with a form, documents, and a view. Figure 11.1 shows a sample form that can be used to store a JavaScript routine. In this form, I've included the name, a version, a short synopsis, and a longer description of the function. Finally, there is a field reserved for the JavaScript code itself.

Figure 11.1
A sample Domino form to hold JavaScript.

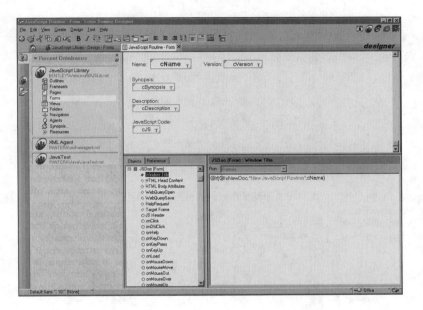

In the sample form, I've hidden all the fields and labels from Web browsers except for the JavaScript field (cJS). That way, the extra management information will display in a Notes client but will not be used when the JavaScript is sent to a Web browser.

Figure 11.2 shows a sample document within the JavaScript library database. This module happens to contain several string-handling utility routines that are patterned after the LotusScript equivalents.

From the sample form and document shown in Figures 11.1 and 11.2, it is clear that you can include other information in your own forms such as dates, times, programmer names, check-in and check-out history, and so forth. This information can be used to organize your JavaScript libraries.

In Figure 11.3 you can see the JS view of the database. In this view, the name of the module, its version, and its description are shown. If you add other information, you can include it here as well. This view is important not only because it is a management summary of your JavaScript programs, but because it also serves a purpose in accessing the JavaScript routines.

Figure 11.2
A JavaScript document in `JSLib.nsf`.

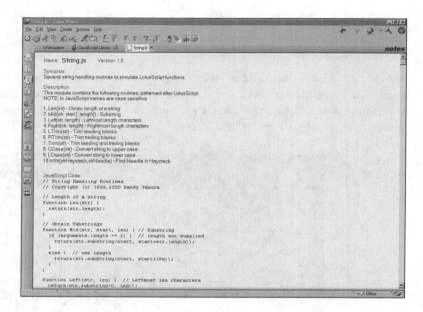

Figure 11.3
A JS view shows all the JavaScript documents in `JSLib.nsf`.

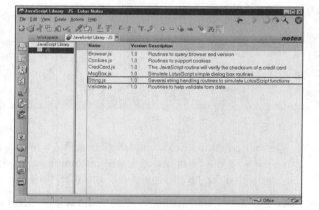

Now that I've shown you an example of how you might set up a JavaScript library, let's take a look at how you might refer to the code you've stored in the library.

Two different methods are available for accessing the code. The method to use depends on whether you will refer to the JavaScript code from within the same database or from a different database. Let me start with the case where you have an application database and you want to store your JavaScript code in a separate Domino database. For the purposes of illustration, suppose your Domino JavaScript library has the name `JSLib.NSF`.

To refer to JavaScript code within the library, use a URL in the `<SCRIPT>` HTML element. If you want to refer to the `String.js` module, here is the syntax:

```
<SCRIPT SRC="http://server/directory/JSLib.NSF/JS/String.js">
</SCRIPT>
```

You must fill in the appropriate server and directory for your JavaScript library. You might place this URL on a page or form as passthru HTML. In essence, this URL will access the database, then the JS view, and then use String.js as the key within the view. The first column of the view, which contains the module names, must be sorted so the view lookup will work properly. Also, note that I have given the routine a name with .js as a suffix. This is because some browsers might not allow an arbitrary file to be used for JavaScript. The .js suffix will enable the browser to know that the content is JavaScript.

To use this technique, a user must be enabled within the JSLIB.NSF access control list (ACL). Depending on your application, you might want to enable users by group, by the default setting, or by the anonymous setting.

That's all there is to it. With this methodology, you can create and update your JavaScript library and use the code throughout your databases. This is a great way to produce standardized JavaScript routines and make them available throughout your organization.

One disadvantage of having a centralized library is that if you change a shared JavaScript routine, you must test it with all the applications that use that function. It is quite possible to modify a shared JavaScript routine, and then an application that has not been modified will stop working. It is therefore very powerful, but also somewhat dangerous, to use a central, shared library. When you use this technique, you must have a development infrastructure that can support the development, testing, and promotion of JavaScript routines.

I mentioned that there are two methods for using Domino forms, views, and documents as a JavaScript library. The second method involves copying the JavaScript forms, views, and documents to your application database. The reason you might want to copy the JavaScript documents to your application database is to avoid potential problems with a centralized, shared database. When the documents are stored within the database, you have more control over when and how they get updated. You can test with a known set of JavaScript routines and they will not change unless you, as a designer, want them changed.

With this methodology, you can create a centralized JavaScript library, but implement it more as a Domino template rather than a shared database. That is, some of the design elements of the centralized repository can be replicated into your applications. By using replication technology, you can control when the design elements are updated. They can be updated automatically or manually.

This template style approach can also be used with subforms to implement your JavaScript library. Using subforms might be slightly preferable because you must deal with only a single design element rather than using a form, documents, and a view.

PART
II

CH
11

CLIENT/SERVER COMMUNICATION WITH HTTP

You know that when you specify that you want to retrieve a Web page in your browser, you use the protocol HTTP. You probably also know that HTTP stands for Hypertext Transfer

Protocol. But do you really know how this protocol works? What messages are sent between the client and server? Why should you care? In this section I'm going to describe HTTP and how it works. You should understand how HTTP works because many aspects of it are important to designing programs for the Web. Understanding HTTP headers will be important when I discuss Java agents as well as XML. I'll explain what the 404 code means as well as many others that you probably have not seen. After I've discussed how HTTP works, I'll show you how HTTP headers are used to implement cookies.

THE HTTP PROTOCOL

Although it might seem that HTTP is arcane, it is really fairly simple. In fact, its simplicity is what makes it so powerful. The current specification level for HTTP is 1.1, but many clients and servers still use the 1.0-level specification.

Communication using HTTP is between a client, also called a user agent, and a server. You can think of communication using HTTP as a four-stage process. Here are the steps:

1. Connection is established. The client initiates the connection with the server. HTTP does not specify the actual communications protocol, but in nearly all cases on the Internet the protocol will be TCP/IP. The default port for HTTP is port 80.

2. The client issues a request. The client sends a request to the server. The request can use one of several methods, such as GET or POST, and will typically also contain additional information. The request is made up of a header as well as a body. A GET request is typically used to retrieve information, and a POST is used to send information from the client to the server.

3. The server sends a response to the request. The response, of course, will depend on the type of request that was made. When the response is sent, it will contain both a header and a body. The first line of the response header contains the HTTP version of the server as well as a numeric response code. This is where the ubiquitous 404 status code appears. Also contained in the header is an important field called Content-Type. I'll explain this shortly.

4. The connection is closed. Either the client or server can close the connection. In HTTP 1.0 the connection is typically closed for each transaction. In HTTP 1.1, the connection can stay open for multiple request/response exchanges.

HTTP REQUEST

Now that you have an overview of how the protocol works, let's take a look at the messages that are sent using HTTP. As mentioned, both the request and response have a header and a body. After a connection has been established, the user agent (client) sends the HTTP request to the server. The general syntax of the HTTP request consists of the following four components, in order:

- The HTTP request line
- One or more header lines

- A blank line
- An optional body

Here is the syntax for the HTTP request line:

```
Method Request-URI HTTP-Version
```

The *HTTP-Version* is either HTTP/1.0 or HTTP/1.1. The *Request-URI* is the uniform resource identifier. This is just another name for a URL. Web terminology is moving toward using URI instead of URL for many cases. Although there are some official differences, for practical purposes you can consider them as synonyms. Here is an example that uses the GET method:

```
GET http://www.gwcorp.com HTTP/1.1
```

Table 11.1 lists all available methods that can be used with HTTP.

TABLE 11.1   THE HTTP METHODS

Method	Description
OPTIONS	The OPTIONS method requests the server to respond with the communications options that are available from the server. Domino returns the answer in a response header field called Public. The field will contain a list of the available (enabled) HTTP methods.
GET	The GET method requests the information specified by the request URI. This method is the most common method for retrieving Web pages.
HEAD	The HEAD method is the same as a GET request except that the server does not return the body of the response, only the header.
POST	The POST request method is used to post or store information back on the server. This is the method used by the Domino server to store information in a Domino database.
PUT	The PUT method is used to store information on the server. The main difference between POST and PUT is that the URI in the POST method is used to identify a resource or process that knows how to handle the enclosed data. The PUT method URI identifies the enclosed data. The server is assumed to know how to process the enclosed data. The PUT method is not used by Domino.
DELETE	The DELETE method is used to delete the resource specified by the URI. DELETE is not used by Domino. Domino uses its own URI commands to delete Domino documents.
TRACE	The TRACE method is used to invoke a loop-back with the server. The server will respond with a message that contains the original request in the body section of the response.
CONNECT	The CONNECT method is a reserved name for use with a proxy that can dynamically switch to being a tunnel.
user-extension method	Extensions can be defined if the client and server agree on conventions. Servers should ignore unknown method requests.

Note that every Web server might not implement every method or might restrict their use. In particular, the default configuration of the Domino server allows only the GET, POST, and HEAD methods. Any other methods are disabled. The enabling and disabling of these methods are found in the HTTPD.CNF file in the Data directory of the Domino server.

The GET Method Request

The GET method is used to retrieve data, typically a Web page, from a server. Here is an actual example of a GET request from Microsoft Internet Explorer:

```
GET / HTTP/1.1
Accept: image/gif, image/x-xbitmap, image/jpeg, image/pjpeg,
➥application/vnd.ms-powerpoint, application/vnd.ms-excel,
➥application/msword, application/x-comet, */*
Accept-Language: en-us
Accept-Encoding: gzip, deflate
User-Agent: Mozilla/4.0 (compatible; MSIE 5.01; Windows 98)
Host: porsche
Connection: Keep-Alive
```

In this example, the first line is the request line. It contains the method, which is GET, followed by a single slash. The single slash represents the home page of the server. The HTTP version supported by the client is specified by HTTP/1.1.

The second line of the request begins the request header. Each line of the request header is a keyword followed by a colon, followed by a space, followed by the value for the header field. The line is terminated by a carriage return and a line feed. Each line of the header uses this same syntax.

The first line following the request line of Internet Explorer is an Accept line and indicates the MIME types of the response that are acceptable to the browser. It would not fit on a single line for this book, so it has been artificially split into several lines. Notice that the Accept line ends with */*, which means that it will accept all media types. A typical response type would be text/html.

The Accept-Language field contains the languages that are preferred as a response; en-us is U.S. English. Accept-Encoding specifies compression schemes that are understood by the user agent. By sending the User-Agent field from the client to the server, the server has access to the client type. Note that this is just a string passed in the header. There is nothing to prevent a program from providing false information. The Host field is used to send the name of the client's machine, and the Connection field tells the server whether it should close or keep the connection alive.

Here for comparison is the GET header sent by Netscape Navigator 4.61:

```
GET / HTTP/1.0
Connection: Keep-Alive
User-Agent: Mozilla/4.61 [en] (Win98; U)
Host: porsche
Accept: image/gif, image/x-xbitmap, image/jpeg, image/pjpeg, image/png, */*
```

```
Accept-Encoding: gzip
Accept-Language: en
Accept-Charset: iso-8859-1,*,utf-8
```

It has most of the same fields, but in a different order. The Netscape browser indicates that it supports HTTP 1.0, not 1.1. The values are clearly different, and there is one additional field called the `Accept-Charset` field. This is used to indicate which character sets are acceptable in the server's response.

If you use a `?OpenDocument` URL with Domino, you are using the `GET` method. In this case, the request line will contain something like the following:

```
GET http://server/database.nsf/view/key?OpenDocument HTTP/1.0
```

When the Domino server receives a request such as this, it retrieves the input document and sends it back to the client. If you submit a form with parameters, the parameters are appended to the end of the URI in the format &*name=value*. Here is an example of the invocation of an agent with parameters:

```
GET http://server/database.nsf/agent?OpenAgent&Fname=John&Lname=Smith HTTP/1.0
```

The drawback to this approach is that some clients or servers have a limitation of 255 characters for URIs. The reason the `GET` request is normally recommended only for queries is that usually queries have a small number of fields and the contents are also typically short. A large form, or a form with a large field, could easily exceed the 255-character limitation. The `POST` method can overcome this length limitation.

THE POST METHOD REQUEST

The `POST` method is the second major request type of HTTP. The `POST` method is used to create new documents in a Domino database and to update existing documents. Its use is similar to the `GET` method. Here is an example from Microsoft Internet Explorer of a `POST` request:

```
POST / HTTP/1.1
Accept: image/gif, image/x-xbitmap, image/jpeg, image/pjpeg,
➥application/vnd.ms-powerpoint, application/vnd.ms-excel,
➥application/msword, application/x-comet, */*
Accept-Language: en-us
Content-Type: application/x-www-form-urlencoded
Accept-Encoding: gzip, deflate
User-Agent: Mozilla/4.0 (compatible; MSIE 5.01; Windows 98)
Host: porsche
Content-Length: 39
Connection: Keep-Alive

field1=This+is+field1&field2=Now+field2
```

As you can see, the request line contains the `POST` method. The `Accept` lines are the same as they were for the `GET` method. Notice that the `Content-Type` is now specified as `application/x-www-form-urlencoded`. This `Content-Type` indicates to the server that the content (body) represents an HTML form. The `Content-Length` field contains the length of the body of the request. The header is terminated by a blank line and the body begins on the next line. In the example, the last header line is the Connection field line. There are 39 characters in the body. Blanks have been converted to plus (+). The two fields on this form are field1 and field2. The contents of each field are specified with an equal sign and separated by an ampersand. Notice that because fields and their contents are stored in the message body, there is essentially no length limitation when you use the POST method.

The character stream you have just seen is the type of data that is transmitted when you submit a form to a Web server. Let's take a look now at how Netscape sends this same form.

```
POST / HTTP/1.0
Connection: Keep-Alive
User-Agent: Mozilla/4.61 [en] (Win98; U)
Host: porsche
Accept: image/gif, image/x-xbitmap, image/jpeg, image/pjpeg, image/png, */*
Accept-Encoding: gzip
Accept-Language: en
Accept-Charset: iso-8859-1,*,utf-8
Content-type: application/x-www-form-urlencoded
Content-length: 39

field1=This+is+field1&field2=Now+field2
```

The data sent by Netscape closely mirrors the data sent by Microsoft Internet Explorer. There are obvious differences, for example, in the User-Agent field, and the Accept lines are different as they were with the GET request. Notice, however, that the Content-Type with Netscape is also specified by application/x-www-form-urlencoded, just as it was with Internet Explorer. The length of the data is the same at 39 characters. Also note that a blank line still separates the body from the header.

HTTP RESPONSE

After the server receives the request, it must process the request and prepare a response. The response can just be the header if a HEAD request was received, or the response can contain a body if, say, a GET request was sent. The response to the GET will typically be an HTML page, which the browser will then use for display to the end user.

The format of the HTTP response is similar to the format for the request. The response begins with a status line, a sequence of header lines, a blank line, and finally an optional body.

The format of the status line is

```
HTTP-Version Status-Code Reason-Phrase
```

For example, a common successful status code is

```
HTTP/1.0 200 OK
```

This status indicates that the server's version is HTTP 1.0, and the return code is 200, which means that the operation was successful. Here is a complete header and the first few lines of a retrieval from a Web server:

```
HTTP/1.0 200 OK
Server: Microsoft-IIS/3.0
Date: Thu, 02 Dec 1999 02:32:52 GMT
Content-Type: text/html
Accept-Ranges: bytes
Last-Modified: Mon, 14 Jun 1999 08:56:50 GMT
Content-Length: 8402

<!DOCTYPE HTML PUBLIC "-//W3C//DTD HTML 3.2 FINAL//EN">
<HTML>
<HEAD>
<META HTTP-EQUIV="Content-Type" CONTENT="text/html; charset=ISO-8859-1">
<META NAME="Generator" CONTENT="NetObjects Fusion 4.0 for Windows">
<TITLE>Lotus Notes and Domino Consulting : Graphware Corporation</TITLE>
```

In this example, you can see that the header is similar in syntax to the request header. Although Content-Type and Content-Length are the same as their request counterparts, all the other headers are different in the response from the request. The Server field gives you the name of the Web server. The Date field is the date and time that the message originated. Accept-Ranges is used to inform the client that the server accepts requests for ranges of bytes. In other words, the client can request partial information for a file. This is most useful in restarting an aborted download. As an example, during one session a very large file is partially transmitted. If the server accepts range requests, the client can inform the server that it wants to download only the last part of the file rather than restart it. The Last-Modified field gives the date and time that the server believes the resource was last modified. Programs that cache the contents from the Web server use this information.

HTTP RESPONSE STATUS CODES

Information about the status codes defined by HTTP follows. Status codes are returned on the first line of the response sent from the server to the client. Status codes are three-digit codes grouped into five categories. The categories are

- 1XX: Informational—The request was received and the process is continuing.
- 2XX: Success—The requested action was received and processed.
- 3XX: Redirection—Further action is required to complete this request. The server might respond with a new URI, for example, and the user Agent must request the new URI.
- 4XX: Client Error—The request contains invalid syntax or cannot be processed.
- 5XX: Server Error—The server was not able to fulfill a request that appeared to be valid.

Table 11.2 is a complete list of status codes for HTTP 1.1.

TABLE 11.2   THE HTTP STATUS CODES

Code	Description
100	Continue. This is sent by the server to acknowledge receipt of an initial part of a request. The client can complete it by sending the remainder of the request.
101	Switching Protocols. The server is able to comply with a client request to change protocols.
200	OK. The normal response code. The request has succeeded.
201	Created. The request to create a new resource was completed successfully.
202	Accepted. The request for processing was accepted for processing but has not been completed. This reply might be in response to a batch-oriented request.
203	Non-Authoritative Information. Information might be from a cache or other third-party source. Only used in place of code 200.
204	No Content. Used when no body is sent with the response message.
205	Reset Content. The server fulfilled the request and the user agent should reset the document view.
206	Partial Content. The server has successfully fulfilled a request that included a Range header.
300	Multiple Choices. The supplied URI could correspond to several different resources.
301	Moved Permanently. The requested URI has been assigned a new location. If possible, relink references to the new location. The new location should be specified in the Location field of the response header.
302	Found. The resource has temporarily moved to a new location. The Location field should contain the new location.
303	See Other. The resource can be found under a different URI, and the client should request the URI at the new address.
304	Not Modified. The client has issued a conditional request and the resource has not been modified. Normally the client can use the cached copy.
305	Use Proxy. The resource must be accessed through the proxy given in the Location field.
306	(Unused). This code was previously used but is no longer used. It is now reserved.
307	Temporary Redirect. The resource temporarily resides under a different URI. The temporary URI should be specified in the Location field.
400	Bad Request. The request could not be understood by the server.
401	Unauthorized. The request requires authentication. If no authentication credentials were provided, the user agent can prompt the user and resubmit the request. If credentials were supplied, a 401 indicates that authorization was refused.
402	Payment Required. Reserved for future use.

Code	Description
403	Forbidden. The server understood the request but is refusing to satisfy it. Authorization will not help and the request should not be repeated.
404	Not Found. The server cannot find the requested URI or wants to refuse the request for an undisclosed reason.
405	Method Not Allowed. The method supplied is not allowed for the requested URI.
406	Not Acceptable. The resource requested can only generate responses that are not acceptable to the client according to the client's `Accept` headers.
407	Proxy Authentication Required. Similar to 401 but indicates the user must authenticate with the proxy.
408	Request Time-out. The client did not produce a request within the time that the server was willing to wait.
409	Conflict. The request could not be satisfied because of a conflict with the current state of the resource.
410	Gone. The requested resource is no longer located at the specified URI, and no forwarding address is known. The U.S. Postal service calls these dead letters.
411	Length Required. The server does not accept the request without a `Content-Length` header.
412	Precondition Failed. A precondition given in the request header evaluated to `false` and prevented the request to be satisfied.
413	Request Entity Too Large. The request entity is larger than the server is able or willing to process. If it is a temporary problem, the server can include a `Retry-After` header.
414	Request-URI Too Large. The URI is larger than the server is able or willing to process.
415	Unsupported Media Type. The entity of the request body is in a format that cannot be handled by the requested resource.
416	Requested Range not satisfiable. The `Range` specified in the request header cannot be processed by the server.
417	Expectation Failed. The expectation given by the client in the request header could not be met by the server.
500	Internal Server Error. The server encountered an unspecified problem and cannot complete the request.
501	Not Implemented. The server does not support the requested method or functionality.
502	Bad Gateway. The server, while acting as a gateway or proxy, received an invalid response from the upstream server.
503	Service Unavailable. The server is currently unable to handle the request due to a temporary overloading or maintenance of the server.
504	Gateway Time-out. The server, while acting as a gateway or proxy, did not receive a timely response from the upstream server.
505	HTTP Version Not Supported. The server is not able or willing to support the HTTP protocol version that was used in the request message.

PART

II

CH

11

Whew, there are probably more HTTP status codes than you imagined. I hope you found this section interesting. If you want more information about HTTP, you can find the current specification on the Web at http://www.w3c.org. The HTTP/1.1 specification is called RFC 2616 and is dated June, 1999.

In addition to understanding the overall flow of HTTP, it is important to understand both the request and response headers. Normally when you view Web pages, you never see these headers, but they are an important part of the communication between client and server.

DOMINO GENERATION OF HTTP HEADERS

When you use Domino forms, views, and documents, you don't usually need to worry about HTTP headers or HTML. However, when you are generating your own HTML, having complete control over the HTTP headers as well as the HTML is frequently a necessity.

When you write Domino agents in either Java or LotusScript, you can control not only the HTML that is generated, but also the HTTP response headers. The default, however, is for Domino to generate all the headers as well as some "boilerplate" HTML around your agent output. Here is an example of the HTML that is automatically generated for you:

```
<HTML>
<!-- Lotus-Domino (Release 5.0.1a - August 17, 1999 on Windows NT/Intel) -->
<HEAD>
</HEAD>
<BODY TEXT="000000">
    . . Your Agent's Output Here . .
</BODY>
</HTML>
```

In addition, the HTTP response headers are also generated. One obvious problem with the generation of this structure is that you cannot use framesets because the <BODY> tags are already created automatically. You can avoid having Domino generate this structure. Here is a sample agent in Java that will not generate the boilerplate:

```
import lotus.domino.*;

import java.io.*;
public class JavaAgent extends AgentBase {
    public void NotesMain() {
        try {
            Session session = getSession();
            AgentContext agentContext = session.getAgentContext();
            PrintWriter out = getAgentOutput();
            out.println("Content-Type: text/html");
            out.println("<HTML><HEAD></HEAD><BODY>");
            out.println("<H1>Hello World</H1>");
            out.println("</BODY></HTML>");
        } catch(Exception e) {
            e.printStackTrace();
        }
    }
}
```

The key to this example is the `println` statement that outputs the `Content-Type` header. Domino looks at the first output you write to the `PrintWriter`. If the first token ends with a colon, it assumes that it is a response header. Because you are creating your own response header, Domino does not include any of the boilerplate HTML around your output. Domino still creates some of its own response header lines. Each time you issue a `println`, Domino inspects it to see if the first token ends with a colon. It continues outputting the headers as long as it sees that they are in the proper format.

> **Note**
>
> Domino looks at your first line of output carefully. A header requires a token without any blanks followed immediately by a colon. For example, `Content-Type:` does not contain any blanks. If your first line contains `Content-Type :` (with a blank), Domino will not recognize it as a header, will include the boilerplate, and will treat your output as HTML text. You can have as many headers as you like, but each must follow the header format. The first output line that does not appear to be a header will be treated as HTML text and will cause all the other lines to be treated as HTML.

In the example, the output that begins with `<HTML>` does not follow the convention, and therefore cannot be a header. Thus, Domino terminates the header section and starts outputting the body. Here are the actual header and body generated by the sample Java agent:

```
HTTP/1.1 200 OK
Server: Lotus-Domino/5.0.1
Date: Mon, 06 Dec 1999 00:18:09 GMT
Connection: close
Content-Type: text/html
Content-Length: 61
<HTML><HEAD></HEAD><BODY>
<H1>Hello World</H1>
</BODY></HTML>
```

Notice that I did not have to output the blank line that separates the header from the body. Domino knows to insert this blank line automatically. The `Connection` header field value of `close` tells the client that this connection will be terminated after this response. A Web client would need to open a new connection to send another request.

COOKIES

Cookies are a feature you might want to exploit with Domino and JavaScript. *Cookies* are used to store state information on the client. Cookies originate at the server, are sent to the client, and later can be sent from the client back to the server. In this section I describe how cookies work and how you can take advantage of them with JavaScript and Domino.

Cookies are implemented by sending information in the response and request headers. The server issues a `Set-Cookie` header in a response to the client. The client then sends the cookie back to the server in a request header when a match occurs with a domain and path.

Four attributes that control the lifetime and accessibility of the cookie information are associated with each cookie. The syntax of the Set-Cookie response header is

```
Set-Cookie: Name=Value[;expires=Date] [;domain=Domain_Name]
➡[;path=Path] [;secure]
```

When the user agent (browser) interprets this response header, it saves the value internally. Cookies are transient by default. That is, they expire at the end of the current browser session unless an expires clause is included in the Set-Cookie header. The date format for the expires clause is in the format

```
Weekday, DD-Mon-YYYY HH:MM:SS GMT
```

and is based on various Internet standards. The domain name is used to allow a cookie to be shared among servers in the same domain. For example, if the domain is specified as lotus.com, the following names would be allowed: java.lotus.com and shopping.partners.lotus.com.

The pathname is used to define a subset of URLs in the domain that is valid. The most general path is a single slash (/). A path of /main would match /mainstore and /main/Web/site.htm.

The final attribute is a Boolean flag called secure. If included, the cookie will be transmitted only if the communications channel is a secure channel such as one that uses SSL.

ACCESSING COOKIES FROM JAVASCRIPT

You can set and access cookies from JavaScript. They are available using a special property of the document object called cookie. The property does not behave exactly as other properties, however. You assign a name/value pair with attributes to the cookie property. Assigning a new value to the cookie property causes the browser to actually parse and process the string. If you assign a new string, previous name/value pairs are not lost. Consider the following example:

```
<script language="JavaScript">
document.cookie="First=Fvalue";
document.cookie="Second=Svalue";
document.cookie="First=" + escape("New First");
alert(document.cookie)

</script>
```

The first assignment statement initializes the first cookie. The assignment to the cookie named Second adds an additional cookie value. The next assignment to the cookie named First overlays the original assignment. Finally, the alert statement produces the following result:

```
First=New%20First; Second=Svalue
```

In the alert statement, Microsoft Internet Explorer 5.0 will end the string with a semicolon, while Netscape Navigator 4.6 will not. Each browser and version can vary slightly in the output produced. Notice that I have used the escape function to convert the embedded blank to its hexadecimal equivalent. You should not use spaces in cookie values, so using `escape` and `unescape` is an easy way to manage special characters.

To delete a cookie, use the `expires` clause with a date that has already expired. This method is not particularly intuitive, but once you know how to do it, it is not very hard.

Sending Cookies Back to the Server

After the cookies have been sent and potentially modified with JavaScript, the browser automatically sends them back to the server. The browser checks the active cookies and the Web pages involved. When a match is found between the current Web page domain and path, the browser sends a request header that has the following syntax:

```
Cookie: Name1=value1; Name2=Value2; . . .
```

Notice that this format is similar to the format we obtain when we access the `document.cookie` property after we have assigned some values.

The server can access the cookies by locating the appropriate request header and reading the values. I'll show you how to do this with agents in Chapter 13, "Creating Java Agents with the Domino Designer IDE."

Cookie Limitations

Cookies are designed to store small amounts of information, so you should not use them to store large quantities of data. The Netscape cookie specification defines the minimum number of cookies that a client should support, but the limitations are shared among all applications accessed by the Web browser. Here are the minimum specifications:

- 300 total cookies.
- 4KB per cookie, where the name and the value combine to form the 4KB limit.
- 20 cookies per server or domain. Completely specified hosts and domains are treated as separate entities, and each has a 20-cookie limitation.

These are minimum specifications, so a browser must support at least these resource quantities. There are no maximum specifications, and a browser is free to support many more resources. However, in your programming, you should assume that a browser supports only the minimum number of resources.

Because of the 20-cookie limitation per server it is a good idea to combine all the values you want to save into a single cookie name/value pair. Within the value string you can encode further name/value pairs. You then need to be careful about running into the 4KB limitation per cookie value.

I have included some routines on the CD-ROM to support the packing and unpacking of strings so that you can save them to cookies. They are stored in the `JSLib.NSF` (JavaScript library) database on the CD-ROM. In Listing 11.2 you can see the cookie-handling routines.

```javascript
// Cookie Support
// Copyright (c) 1999,2000 Randy Tamura


// appendCookie: Append a name/value pair to a CookieVal string
// cCookieVal - The CookieVal string to which the name/value pair should
➥be appended.
// cName - The name of the name/value pair. Duplicate name checking not
➥performed.
// cValue - The value of the name/value pair.
// returns - new CookieVal
function appendCookie(cCookieVal, cName, cValue) {
    // We concatenate a new name/value pair to the Cookie value.
    // This is stored in string format
    return cCookieVal + "&" + cName + ":" + escape(cValue);
}


// extractCookie: Given the name, extract a value from a CookieVal string
// cCookieVal - The CookieVal string from which the value should be extracted.
// cName - The name of the name/value pair.
// returns - value or empty string if not found.
function extractCookie(cCookieVal, cName) {
    // We look for the specified name and return its value
    // The CookieVal is stored in string format
    var cReturn;    // The return value
    if ("" == cCookieVal) return "";    // No values

    // Now find the specific cStoreName cookie in the string
    var nStart = cCookieVal.indexOf("&" + cName + ":");
    if (-1 == nStart) return "";   // cName not found
    nStart += cName.length + 2;    // Point at first data char
    var nEnd = cCookieVal.indexOf("&", nStart); // Find the end
    if (-1 == nEnd) {
        nEnd = cCookieVal.length; // Point at last char
    }
    cReturn = cCookieVal.substring(nStart, nEnd); // Extract the Cookie
    return cReturn;   // and return it
}


// saveCookie: Save a CookieVal - Save to Web browser. It may have several
➥name/value pairs
// doc - The document object that should be used for the save.
// cStoreName - The actual cookie name that will be known by the browser.
// cCookieVal - The CookieVal string to save.
// nSeconds - (optional) (integer) The duration that the cookie should live,
➥in seconds.
// cDomain - (optional) The domain name.
// cPath - (optional) The path associated with the cookie.
// bSecure - (optional) (boolean) The secure option
// returns - void
function saveCookie(doc, cStoreName, cCookieVal, nSeconds, cDomain, cPath,
➥bSecure ) {
    var cCooking;   // Used to store intermediate strings
    var dtExpires; // Date this cookie expires
    cCooking = cStoreName + "=" + cCookieVal // The name=value
```

```
    if (nSeconds) {
        // Calculate expiration date
        dtExpires = new Date((new Date()).getTime() + 1000 * nSeconds);
        cCooking += "; expires=" + dtExpires.toGMTString();
    }
    if (cDomain) { // If the domain was supplied
        cCooking += "; domain=" + cDomain;
    }
    if (cPath) {   // If the path was supplied
        cCooking += "; path=" + cPath;
    }
    if (bSecure) { // If the secure parameter was supplied
        cCooking += "; secure";
    }
    // Done cooking, now assign the cookie
    doc.cookie = cCooking;
}

// loadCookie: Load a CookieVal - It may contain several name/value pairs.
// doc - The document object that should be used for the load
// cStoreName - The actual cookie name that will be known by the browser.
// returns - The CookieVal string or empty string if not found.
function loadCookie(doc, cStoreName) {
    var cCooking;  // Used to store intermediate strings
    var cReturn;   // The return value
    cCooking = doc.cookie; // Get all the Cookie name/values
    if ("" == cCooking) return "";    // No values

    // Now find the specific cStoreName cookie in the string
    var nStart = cCooking.indexOf(cStoreName + "=");
    if (-1 == nStart) return "";  // cStoreName not found
    nStart += cStoreName.length + 1; // Point at first data char
    var nEnd = cCooking.indexOf(";", nStart); // Find the end
    if (-1 == nEnd) {
        nEnd = cCooking.length; // Point at last char
    }
    cReturn = cCooking.substring(nStart, nEnd); // Extract the CookieVal
    return cReturn;  // and return it
}
```

Four routines are supplied in the Cookies.js module. These routines can be used to manipulate a string called a CookieVal. The CookieVal contains name/value pairs. Each name/value pair is separated from the others with the & character. A name is separated from its value with :. You can add and extract values from this string using these routines and also save the CookieVal to the browser. You can use these routines as they are, or you can add additional features. They don't check for the 4KB limitation, there is no duplicate name checking, and so forth.

- appendCookie—Add a name/value pair to a CookieVal.
- extractCookie—Given a name, extract the value from a CookieVal.
- saveCookie—Save a CookieVal to the browser.
- loadCookie—Load a CookieVal from the browser.

You can use more than one CookieVal, but you must give each one a unique name when you give it to the browser. When you call saveCookie, the CookieVal is saved to the browser. In order for the cookie to be persistent, however, you must supply a lifetime, specified in seconds, to the saveCookie routine. If you do not specify a lifetime, the cookie will expire at the end of the current browser session. If you do specify a lifetime, the cookie will be persistent until that time limit expires.

I've given you the source code for these routines, but I do not explain in detail how they operate because they are fairly self-explanatory. Review the comments within the code for more information. There is also a sample HTML page in the JSLib.nsf database that illustrates how to use the Cookies.js module.

CHAPTER REVIEW

1. What is the difference between using the onSubmit event of the form and directly calling form.submit()? How and when does the onSubmit event of the form get invoked?

2. Write an HTML page with several fields and one hidden field. The initial contents of the hidden field should be a list of input field names, separated by commas. Write a JavaScript routine that will read the hidden field, create an array from the values stored there, and then will validate each of the named fields to ensure that it is non-blank.

3. Write a JavaScript routine that will check the value of a text input field against a list of valid values that are stored in a hidden field. If the user enters a wrong value, issue an alert. What other kind of user interface element might be easier for a user to use?

4. Write a JavaScript routine that will match a decimal number. The pattern should allow a number in the U.S. format n[.[n]]. There are one or more digits before the decimal. The decimal point is optional. If it is present, there can be more digits after the decimal. The routine should return true if the string passes validation, false otherwise. How might you extend this so that a number like .5 would be accepted? How might you extend this so that an optional plus or minus would be accepted? How might you extend this so that you could include a different decimal separator such as a comma for other countries?

5. Write a JavaScript routine that will parse a proposed phone number as input. Use a U.S.-style phone number that should match the 10-digit number with the format (nnn)nnn-nnnn. Your routine should return true if it is a valid phone number, false otherwise. How might you extend this to another phone pattern such as nn.nn.nn.nn, which is commonly used in France?

6. Create an HTML page with an input field and a button. In the onClick event of the button, call the credit card validation routine. Check some of your credit card numbers. Does it accurately check them? Try inputting common typographical mistakes to see whether they are caught.

7. What JavaScript events are used to implement rollovers? In the example, I used several individual variables with a naming convention to implement the rollovers. Implement the rollovers using an associative array instead of individual variables. An associative array uses names for subscripts instead of numbers. For example, you could have an array called `MyImages` with subscripts `"Home_In"` and `"Home_Out"`. You would reference array elements as in `MyImages["Home_In"]` and `MyImages["Home_Out"]`.

8. List several ways to implement a JavaScript library. Which method do you prefer and why? Write a set of JavaScript routines that could be used to format numbers. Store these routines in a JavaScript library, and refer to them from a Web page to test them.

9. What are the purposes of the `GET` and `POST` methods of HTTP? How do they differ and when would you use each? What is the difference between the `POST` and `PUT` methods of HTTP? List the four basic steps of an HTTP communication transaction.

10. What is the format of an HTTP header field? What is the format and purpose of the first line of a response message? What are the five categories of status codes for HTTP responses?

11. If you want to prevent Domino from generating HTML boilerplate coding around agent output, how can you do it? How does Domino know that it should not generate the boilerplate coding?

12. How and where (within the messages) are cookie values sent back and forth between a Web server and its client? What prevents a malicious JavaScript program from a random Web site from reading your credit card information that is stored in a cookie from a different Web site? Why is it a good idea to pack several name/value pairs together when storing cookie values?

PART

II

CH

11

PART III

USING JAVA WITH NOTES AND DOMINO

CHAPTER 12

JAVA AGENTS, APPLETS, AND APPLICATIONS

In this chapter

In this chapter, I present some important information about Java and some specific Java classes such as the `Applet` class, and show how Domino relates to these classes. This is an important chapter to read and understand before you read the rest of the chapters in Part III, "Using Java with Notes and Domino" as well as before Part IV, "The Domino Objects for Java." Both Part III and Part IV assume you understand the concepts in this chapter.

SETTING UP THE JAVA ENVIRONMENT

If you are serious about using Java with Domino, you should consider a separate third-party development environment for Java. Although Lotus has made great strides with release 5, Java support in Domino is suitable only for developing agents. To develop applets, servlets, or many other Java programs, you will need a third-party IDE. In Chapter 14, "Using the Domino Designer and Third-Party IDEs with Java," I describe two specific development tools: IBM's Visual Age for Java and Symantec's Visual Café.

There are many Java development environments, and you can probably choose any of them. Here are a few: IBM Visual Age for Java, Inprise (the company formerly known as Borland) Jbuilder, Symantec Visual Café, and Java Workshop from Sun. There are probably hundreds of other options, and you can even download Sun's Java Development Kit (JDK) free from the Web at `http://www.java.sun.com`. Sun's JDK package is extremely minimal, however, and you'll probably want a real development environment for serious work.

A JAVA OVERVIEW

Java was originally conceived by Sun Microsystems as a language for embedded controllers (for example, a device such as the one in your microwave oven). This language became extremely popular with the advent of the Web and because Netscape included it in its browser. It has quickly evolved, however, and now there are probably millions of Java programmers around the world.

Of course, you know that one of the main advantages of Java is that it is operating system–independent and hardware platform–independent. Sun's mantra is "write once, run anywhere." But how, exactly, does Java achieve this feat technically? The answer lies in another term that you might have heard: the Java Virtual Machine, or JVM. The JVM is a software program that simulates a real machine. The JVM accepts, as input, binary opcodes in files that have been prepared by a Java compiler. This set of binary opcodes corresponds to the machine-language codes that are used by traditional hardware, such as the Intel Pentium.

The binary codes are stored in files on the host operating system in class files. Groups of class files can be stored in a directory in the operating system, or they can be collected in a single file called an archive. Several kinds of archive files are available: JAR files, CAB files, and ZIP files. ZIP is a standard format for compressing a group of files and saving them as a single file. This extension is not normally used anymore, however, because it was confusing for some users who thought the ZIP files needed to be uncompressed. JAR files are the standard format for Java archives and are stored internally with the same format as ZIP files.

CAB files (short for cabinet) were created by Microsoft and are used by its Internet Explorer and the Microsoft JVM.

Java achieves its machine and operating system independence by specifying the standardized format for class files, archives, and the machine operations contained in the class files. There are several implementations of Java Virtual Machines. Each of the major Web browsers, as well as Notes and Domino, contains a JVM, and you can run standalone JVMs as well. A standalone JVM comes with Sun's JDK. With a standalone JVM, you can write a Java application that does not depend on a Web browser.

Note

Here is a tidbit for those of you interested in Java trivia that you can use to impress your friends. The creators of Java used a hexadecimal magic number in the first four bytes of a Java class file. This is so the JVM can do an integrity check on the file before trying to execute it. Because the magic number is an arbitrary number, they used the hexadecimal value CAFEBABE. Although this is a valid hexadecimal value, it's also pretty cute. Use a hexadecimal editor to look at a Java class file sometime. Then you can go impress your friends.

THE CLASSPATH

So now we have a JVM and a class file that contains binary opcodes. Is there anything else we need? Well, yes, of course. The class file that you have developed probably needs to allocate and manage resources, such as memory and data. It probably needs to interact with a user through a user interface. There should be some capability of communicating over a network, and you must have security programs. You probably don't want to write all this kind of code. Normally, these types of services are provided by an operating system. Well, we're in luck.

An entire library of programs has been written in Java, and the programs are included in archive files that are distributed with the Java environment. They perform many of the routine tasks that are normally provided by any operating system environment. There is only one problem: How does the JVM find these files? The answer is the CLASSPATH environment variable.

PART

III

CH

12

Note

This section describing the CLASSPATH environment variable applies to version 1.1.x of the Java Development Kit. This is the version that ships with Notes and Domino. In Java version 2.0, class files are treated differently, as described in the next section.

The CLASSPATH environment variable is actually similar in concept to the PATH variable that you might remember from the old days. The CLASSPATH variable tells the JVM where to find additional classes that are not included in the currently running class. Standard classes for user interface and many other functions are included in these libraries. In addition to the standard libraries, you can write your own Java programs, store them in archives, and include them in the CLASSPATH. Lotus, in fact, has done this for many of the support functions required for Notes and Domino. Thus, to use these Lotus-written Java programs, you must include the Lotus archives in your CLASSPATH (for the Java development tool's use).

When Notes or Domino JVM is running, it actually uses an internal CLASSPATH variable. Notes and Domino do not use the CLASSPATH environment variable. Domino is automatically capable of finding its own Java programs, such as those that implement the Java Domino Objects. In addition, it is capable of automatically finding Java programs that are stored as agents within databases.

For your own custom classes that are not agents, however, Domino uses its own internal CLASSPATH variable. The internal class path is specified in the Notes.ini file and has the name JavaUserClasses. In order for Notes or Domino to be able to find any custom classes you write that are not stored within a database, you must be sure to modify the JavaUserClasses variable in Notes.ini. Here is an example:

```
JavaUserClasses=c:\Development\MyJavaClasses\Util.jar
```

You can specify more than one directory and separate them with semicolons.

If you get an error message during development that your classes cannot be found, check to make sure that you have set the JavaUserClasses variable in Notes.ini. Setting the regular CLASSPATH environment variable, although probably required for your Java IDE, will not be sufficient for Notes and Domino.

JAVA DEVELOPMENT KIT VERSIONS

If you program a Windows application in C++, there are three separate and distinct concepts to work with: the programming language itself (C++), the compiler tool, and the Windows Application Programming Interface (API). These same three concepts apply to Java programming. You need to know the Java programming language, you must have a particular Java programming/compiler tool, and you need a programming API. The programming API is supplied by Sun Microsystems in the Java Development Kit (JDK), but it is almost always also supplied by the Java tool vendor when you purchase a Java programming tool.

The Java Development Kit provides an API that contains many of the programming features of a windowing operating system such as Windows. This is perhaps one of the reasons why Microsoft wants to portray Java as just a programming language. Although Java is a language, the JDK supplies the capability to create windows and buttons, use networking, access databases, and many of the other features that we take for granted in Microsoft Windows. In addition, you can use the JDK on top of Windows, UNIX, Macintosh, or any other platform that supports the JVM. This includes Notes and Domino.

The JDK from Sun has undergone many revisions. At the time this is being written, two versions are available: JDK 1.1.x and JDK 2.0. The 1.1.x version is shipped with Notes and Domino due to the cycle of testing and quality assurance that goes into Domino before release. Java version 2.0 was announced by Sun on December 8, 1998, so there was not enough time to certify the Domino code with Java version 2.0, but I expect that it will be supported soon after it can be tested. Release 5.0.2 of Domino supported JDK 1.1.8, but this will definitely change over time, so refer to the release notes for your particular version of Domino for the current JDK version.

Many new capabilities are in version 2.0, including security enhancements and the inclusion of the Java Foundation Classes (JFC). The JFC includes the Swing components, the Java 2D graphics interfaces, drag-and-drop, accessibility, and many other application services. The Swing user interface components are an enhancement to the original Abstract Windowing Toolkit (AWT) found in version 1.1 of the JDK. Although the AWT still works for compatibility, the Swing set of components is essentially a replacement.

As mentioned, in version 2.0, the CLASSPATH environment variable holds a less prominent role. In version 1.1.x, the setting of this variable caused a lot of setup problems (and is why I described it in the previous section). With version 2.0, system classes are found automatically by the JVM.

JAVA CLASSES, PACKAGES, AND ARCHIVES

All programs in Java are a part of some class. Classes, as we have seen, are written in the Java source code language and then are translated to class files. Class files consist of machine-independent byte codes. The class file byte codes essentially represent machine operations to the Java Virtual Machine and are the instructions that get executed by the JVM.

As you might imagine, when you are doing large-scale development, you will quickly find that you need some methods to organize your class files, because you can quickly get hundreds of files to organize and manage.

Packages are hierarchical groupings of class files. They are logical groupings and can be implemented physically in different ways. One simple and common way to organize the files in a package is with an operating system file directory structure. You simply use the hierarchical nature of file folders (directories) containing other nested folders to implement a hierarchical structure.

In Java, names are specified by a combination of identifiers and periods. The rightmost name represents the classname. All the other qualifiers in the name represent the package. For example, in java.lang.Object, java.lang represents the package name, and the name Object represents the classname. In the name java.awt.event.ActionEvent, the name ActionEvent is the classname and java.awt.event is the package name. The Java naming convention uses an initial capital letter for class names and all lowercase letters for package names.

PART

III

CH

12

If you have the packages `java.awt`, `java.awt.datatransfer`, `java.awt.event`, `java.awt.image`, and `java.awt.peer`, you can imagine a directory folder structure that could accommodate this:

```
java
    awt
        datatransfer
        event
        image
        peer
```

In this case, there can also be other packages below the `java` level, such as `java.io`, `java.lang`, and `java.net`. When you have such a directory structure, all the classes in the `java.awt.event` package, for example, are stored in the directory that corresponds to that package.

When you are working by yourself on a small project, this structure is probably fine. You have everything you need, and it is all visible and easily accessible. However, suppose you are developing a large system and there are hundreds of components. It soon becomes much harder to manage multiple user access to hundreds of different files. Because of this, archive files were developed.

The original archive file format for Java was a ZIP file. This type of file was a de facto standard around the Internet, and many or most PC users have some sort of program, such as pkzip, pkunzip, or winzip, to create and extract files from ZIP files. By using a ZIP format, all the class files can be incorporated in a single file in the operating system. Also, the directory structure within the file can be preserved so that you can still have the hierarchical nature of the packages.

It was soon discovered, however, that users of these ZIP files did not realize that you could use the files within the ZIP archive and that you did not need to unzip the files for them to be used by Java. So a new format was created called the Java Archive (JAR) file. This essentially was just another name for a ZIP file, and all the ZIP file utilities can be used to create and extract from these files also. The only difference is that a JAR file should also contain a manifest file, which is like a table of contents and enables the members of the JAR file to have attributes. The attributes are stored within the manifest file in the JAR.

Finally, Microsoft decided that it wanted a format that was unique to its products. It already had a format called CAB, which stands for cabinet. It incorporated the CAB file format with its Internet Explorer. CAB files have an advantage in that they have a better compression algorithm, so the files are smaller. They have a disadvantage in that the files are in a Microsoft proprietary standard format and might not be supported on platforms other than Windows. If a product does support the CAB file format, it probably provides the same functionality as the JAR format.

For package files that are widely distributed, the packages should follow a naming convention outlined in the Java language specification. If two packages from different sources by chance have the same name, a user might have a very limited ability to fix the problem because the source code might not be available. As a result, the following naming convention is used to name Java classes. If the company producing the Java code has an Internet domain name, the first two levels of the package name should use them in reverse order. For example:

```
com.ibm.CORBA.iiop
```

```
com.lotus.esuite.util
```

```
com.sun.java.swing
```

```
uk.acme.widgets.starter
```

```
gov.whitehouse.shredder.docs
```

The highest-level qualifiers of Java and Javax are reserved by JavaSoft for standard libraries and extensions, so you should never name your classes beginning with these names. If you do not want to follow the standard naming convention and your packages do not begin with the domain type, you should probably at least use your company name as the high-level qualifier, as in

```
lotus.chart
```

```
lotus.notes.addins
```

```
sun.net.ftp
```

Sun recommends that if you are creating packages, the first letter of your package should be lowercase. Classes, on the other hand, should typically begin with an uppercase letter. Thus, in the package java.applet, you find the class Applet. The fully qualified name of the class is java.applet.Applet.

There are no #include statements in Java. In C and C++, you use the #include statement to include additional source code modules. In Java, you use the import statement to accomplish a similar effect. The purpose of the Java import statement is slightly different than the #include statement of C++, however. The purpose of the Java import statement is to allow your programs to use a shorthand notation.

You can import a single class or an entire package. Here are some examples:

```
import java.awt.Graphics;
import java.applet.*;
import lotus.domino.*;
```

The first import statement is importing a single class, and the second two statements are importing entire packages. The last two import statements allow a shorthand for all the classes in the respective packages.

PART

III

CH

12

You could refer to the `Applet` class as

```
public class MyApplet extends java.applet.Applet
```

or, if you have done the import, you can refer to the class as

```
public class MyApplet extends Applet
```

You can always refer to classes by their fully qualified names, so importing classes is not strictly required in any program, but it can make the program much more legible. You do not need to import the `java.lang` package, because all methods in that package are imported by default. The controlling factor on whether a class is found is the class path.

JAVA EXCEPTION HANDLING

Like C++, Java uses exception handling to handle runtime errors that occur in programs. In C++, exceptions were added as an innovation after the language was already in use, and as a result, many C++ programs do not use exceptions. In contrast, Java has had exceptions since its origin, so you will probably find that most—if not all—Java programs use the exception-handling model. In fact, Java compilers will complain if an exception is possible but there is no code to handle the exception.

Exception handling involves the use of several different statements and objects. The essence of exception handling is that you group statements that might potentially cause an exception (including within called subroutines), and then if one occurs, you can catch it and handle it. Syntactically you use the `try-catch` statement for grouping. Here is the full syntax:

```
try {
    // This is the try block. Normal program statements are here
    // If an exception occurs, this block may be left early.
}
catch (Exceptiontype1 e1) {
    // This block catches exceptions of type Exceptiontype1
}
catch (Exceptiontype2 e2) {
    // This block catches exceptions of type Exceptiontype2
}

// More catch clauses can appear here

finally {
    // Here are statements that will be executed in all cases.
    // This block will execute whether or not there is an exception.
}
```

`Exceptiontype1` and `Exceptiontype2` represent classes that are derived from (that is, they extend either directly or indirectly) the `Throwable` class. I'll explain shortly how they are used.

You can have as many different types of exceptions as you want to handle. The `finally` clause does not appear within C++. This is a very useful clause for cleaning up anything you initialize in the `try` clause. It is better to clean up in the `finally` clause than a `catch` clause, because then the cleanup will occur in both the error and nonerror cases. In the error case, the `finally` clause will be executed after the `catch` clause.

An exception is created with the `throw` statement. The syntax for the throw statement is

```
throw expression;
```

The *expression* must result in an object of the class `Throwable`. All exceptions are extended from this class. You can create your own exception classes, and throw and catch the exceptions. This technique is useful whenever you have a program that might detect an error situation several levels deep within subroutines, but if an error occurs, you want the program to "unwind" to a higher-level routine for processing. Java provides a language mechanism to do this gracefully without resorting to return codes.

Any exceptions that are generated by Notes or Domino use the `NotesException` class. This class extends the `java.lang.Exception` class and contains two fields: `id` and `text`. You can refer to these fields within the exception handler (the `catch` block). Here is an example:

```
try {
    ... Statements ...
}
catch (NotesException e) {
    System.out.println("NotesException: " + e.id + " ... " + e.text);
    e.printStackTrace();
}
catch (Exception e) {
    e.printStackTrace();
}
```

This code prints out the Notes error code and message along with the standard Java stack trace. For exceptions other than a `NotesException`, only the stack trace is printed.

> **Note**
>
> In release 4.6 of Notes and Domino, you used the `getErrorCode` method to extract the error code from the `NotesException` class. This method is no longer available. In release 5, you must use the `id` and `text` fields. Symbolic names for the codes may be found in the `NotesError` class.

JAVA STANDALONE APPLICATIONS

With Java, unlike LotusScript, you can create standalone applications that you can run from a command-line prompt. In Windows, this is similar to the concept of an EXE program module. Java standalone applications have a `main` routine that is invoked by the runtime environment.

I'll be using some standalone applications to illustrate some concepts in this chapter and elsewhere, so I'd like to show you how to create a simple Java standalone application. Here it is:

```
public class MyMain0 {
    public static void main(String args[]) {
        System.out.println("Hello, Java");
    } // end main
} // end class
```

This routine will print out "Hello, Java" to the Java debugging console. The key point to observe about the example is that you must have a `public static void` method called `main` with a single parameter that represents an array of `String` objects.

You need a Java compiler to convert the source code into a class file. You can use any Java IDE such as IBM's Visual Age for Java, Symantec's Visual Café, or some other compiler. If you are using the Sun JDK, the compiler is called javac. Here is the command line to compile the program to produce the class file:

```
javac MyMain0.java
```

When you have this class file, you can run the program by passing the class filename to the Java executable, as in

```
Java MyMain0
```

This will run the compiled class file and display the output. Some Java compilers might be able to actually compile the class file into an executable.

JAVA APPLICATIONS AND MULTITHREADING

Multithreading is a method of concurrent programming. Multithreading allows two or more programs to work at the same time, cooperatively. When run on a computer with only a single CPU, the system divides the CPU's time among the threads that are ready to run. By sharing the processor time, programs can be written to improve response time or provide more throughput for a given CPU.

In Java, multithreading is built into the language. This feature is one of the reasons why you might want to consider Java rather than LotusScript for certain agents. Some types of programs lend themselves more easily to multithreading than others. If multithreading is one of the requirements of your application, Java is a good choice.

The Java language provides a built-in class called, remarkably enough, Thread. The fully qualified name of this class is java.lang.Thread, so it exists in the java.lang package. Notes provides an important extension to this class called NotesThread. Let's take a look at both of these classes. I'll first describe Thread and then the extensions provided by NotesThread.

The Thread class is used to implement all threads in Java. You can implement your thread in two ways using the Thread class (there is one additional way with NotesThread). The first method is to write your own class that extends the Thread class. In this case, your class actually is a special case of a thread. You write your own class method called run() that overrides the base class method.

The second way to implement a thread involves two separate classes. With this approach, you create your own class that does not extend the Thread class. Instead, you implement an interface called the Runnable interface. This interface defines only one method, the run() method. You create an instance of your class, and then create an instance of the Thread class and pass your class to the Thread constructor. At the appropriate time, your run() method will be called.

You now know that the code of your thread will exist within the run method. When does the code in the run method get invoked? You might think that it would start up as soon as your object is created, but it does not. If that were to happen, you wouldn't get much of a chance to initialize or set things up for your thread before it got off and running. So the creation of your thread and the running of it are separated. To start the code found in your run() method, you invoke the start() method of the thread. This gives you a chance to do some initialization before you invoke the start method. It also means that if you forget to invoke start, your thread will never run.

The start method is located in the Thread class. If your class extends the Thread class, then the start method will be a part of your own class because it is inherited from Thread. If you implemented the Runnable interface, you invoke start from the Thread object, not your own object.

Here is an application showing the first method of implementing threads:

```
public class MyMain1 {
   public static void main(String args[]) {
     try {
       ExtendedThread etMyThread = new ExtendedThread(); // My Thread
       etMyThread.start();  // This will eventually invoke my run();
       etMyThread.join();   // Wait for thread to finish
     }
     catch(InterruptedException e) {
     }
   }
}
public class ExtendedThread extends Thread {
   public void run() {
      System.out.println("ExtendedThread Running!");
   }
}
```

Note

I've shown the main Java program and the ExtendedThread classes as separate classes to make it easier to understand. It would be typical in Java to combine these two routines into the same class instead of two different classes. This is because for the javac compiler each separate class must be stored in a separate file with the class name as the filename. If you want to compile with the javac compiler, you'll need to separate the classes into separate files before compiling.

PART
III

CH
12

In this example, the ExtendedThread object is created with the new statement. The thread does not actually start until the start method is called. At that time, the start method initializes the thread and invokes its run method. Meanwhile, the original thread returns from the call to start and continues. At this point, it executes the join method, which causes the main thread to wait until the second thread has finished execution. When it does, the main thread wakes up again and finishes the program.

Here is an example of the second method of implementing threads:

```
public class MyMain2 {
    public static void main(String args[]) {
        try {
            RunnableThread rtMyThread = new RunnableThread(); // My Thread
            Thread theThread = new Thread(rtMyThread);  // java.lang.Thread
            theThread.start();  // This will eventually invoke my run();
            theThread.join();   // Wait for thread to finish
        }
        catch(InterruptedException e) {
        }
    }
}
class RunnableThread implements Runnable {
    public void run() {
        System.out.println("RunnableThread Running!");
    }
}
```

In this second example, note that the class RunnableThread is not really a Thread class object; it just runs on a separate thread from the main thread. You can think of the run method in this case as if it were a main program entry point.

In both of these examples, the join method is used to synchronize the main thread with the newly created thread. It would normally be considered a good programming practice for the main thread to wait until the subsidiary threads have finished before it finishes itself.

You might be asking when you should extend the Thread class and when you should use the Runnable interface. If you have complete control over all your classes, it doesn't matter too much which method you use. You can use either. Sometimes, however, you don't have complete control because you might be using some existing classes. In this case, you might not be able to take a class and have it extend the Thread class because you can use only single inheritance in Java, and the class you are working with might already be extending something else. In this situation, you should use the Runnable interface on your existing class because you will then not need to extend the Thread class. You need only to add the run method. Here is an example of the declaration:

```
public class MyClass extends MyBaseClass implements Runnable {
    // Here is your MyClass stuff

    public void run() {
        // Thread code here
    }
}
```

In this case, you don't need to modify any code in the MyBaseClass class. In fact, you might not even have the source code for that class. You just need to implement your extensions to the base class, implement one additional method (the run method), and pass your class to the Thread constructor. After that, the base class, as well as your extensions, will be run on a separate thread.

NOTES AND DOMINO MULTITHREADING USING JAVA

You can use the threading mechanisms I described in the previous section within Notes and Domino. However, if you use them, you will not be able to access any Notes or Domino data. You can use the standard Java threading classes only if you are going to use them for animation or other standard Web kinds of processing in, for example, a standard Java applet. If you want to use threading and access Domino databases or services, you must use the NotesThread class.

Now that you've seen the two ways to implement threads with the standard Java libraries, let me show you the modifications necessary to use threads within Notes and Domino. Because NotesThread extends the standard Java Thread class, the first method you can use to create your thread is to extend NotesThread. It works similarly to regular Java, but rather than implementing a run() method, you must implement a runNotes() method. The second way to implement threading with Notes is to implement a Runnable interface. In this case, you still implement a run() method, not a runNotes method. Here are the previous two examples, slightly modified for the Notes and Domino environment. As mentioned, you must supply a runNotes method for this approach to work. In NotesThread, the run method is specified as final, so you will not be allowed to override the run method even if you want to. You will get a compile-time error message if you attempt to use run instead of runNotes. Here is an example of the first method of implementing threads within Notes and Domino:

```
import lotus.domino.*;

public class MyNotesMain1 {
   public static void main(String args[]) {
     try {
       ExtendedThread etMyThread = new ExtendedThread(); // My Thread
       etMyThread.start();  // This will eventually invoke my runNotes();
       etMyThread.join();   // Wait for thread to finish
     }
     catch(InterruptedException e) {
     }
   }
}
public class ExtendedThread extends NotesThread {
   public void runNotes() {
      System.out.println("ExtendedThread Running!");
   }
}
```

Notice that the main program is essentially identical to the version that we created for regular Java threading. The only changes are found in the ExtendedThread class, where it extends NotesThread instead of Thread and contains a runNotes method instead of a run method.

Note

You might see some Domino examples and documentation combine the two classes I've shown previously into a single class. This single class extends `NotesThread` (as in the `ExtendedThread`) and also has a `static main` method as well.

I use two classes to illustrate that the `main` method is called on the caller's thread. The `runNotes` method is running on a newly created, separate thread. If you combine both the `main` and `runNotes` methods in one class, make sure you understand that `main` and `runNotes` will be running on separate threads, even though they are defined in the same class.

The same note applies to combining the two classes in the following example.

Here is an example of the second method of implementing threads within Notes and Domino:

```
import lotus.domino.*;

public class MyNotesMain2 {
   public static void main(String args[]) {
      try {
         RunnableThread rtMyThread = new RunnableThread(); // My Thread
         // NotesThread extends java.lang.Thread
         NotesThread theThread = new NotesThread(rtMyThread);
         theThread.start();  // This will eventually invoke my run();
         theThread.join();   // Wait for thread to finish
      }
      catch(InterruptedException e) {
      }
   }
}
class RunnableThread implements Runnable {
   public void run() {
      System.out.println("RunnableThread Running!");
   }
}
```

You can easily see by comparing the Notes/Domino version with the previous version that the interfaces are very similar. In the Notes version of the applications, it is even more critical for the main routine to wait until the secondary threads have finished (via the `join` method). This is because Notes or Domino will automatically terminate all the subsidiary threads when the main thread finishes. So the subsidiary threads cannot run longer than the main thread.

It should be apparent from the examples why the `NotesThread` version uses `runNotes` and the `Runnable` version uses the `run` method. When you extend `NotesThread`, your class is a `NotesThread`, which in turn is a `Thread` class. In the `NotesThread` class, Lotus has implemented the run method, which will be invoked by Java. The Lotus code within `run` eventually calls your `runNotes` method after it initializes the Notes environment. On the other hand, when you implement the `Runnable` interface, your code is in a separate class, and your run method does not conflict with the Lotus version of the run method. By the time your run method is called, the `NotesThread` class has already set up the Notes environment. Here is the sequence of calls upon startup of a `Runnable` class:

1. `java.lang.Thread:start` initializes the new thread environment and calls the thread's run method on the new thread.
2. `NotesThread:run` initializes Notes environment and calls the `run` method of your `Runnable` class. This method call is made on the `NotesThread`'s thread.
3. `YourClass:run` is your thread code in the run method.

There is a third way to create a `NotesThread` in addition to the two that are normally available for all threads. This approach uses static methods within the `NotesThread` class to initialize Notes on the currently running thread. You use this approach if your program is invoked on a thread over which you have no control. In essence, rather than create a new `NotesThread` object, this approach initializes Notes without creating a separate `NotesThread` and turns the currently running thread into a pseudo-`NotesThread`.

This approach to initializing Notes can also be used if you write a standalone Java application that will use Domino Objects classes. The static initialization might also be required when you are writing event handlers for Java events. Sometimes your methods will be invoked on one of Java's runtime threads (not your own). If you want to call the Domino Objects on your event handler's thread, you will need to statically initialize and terminate during the event handler's operation.

If you do need to initialize Notes on the currently running thread, first you must call `NotesThread.sinitThread()` before using any other Notes/Domino classes. When you are finished with the Notes classes, you must call `NotesThread.stermThread()`. These two calls must be balanced. In particular, even if exceptions occur, you must be sure to call `stermThread` before your routine exits. Here is some sample code:

```
import lotus.domino.*;

public class MyNotesMain3 {
   public static void main(String args[]) {
     try {
       // Initialize Notes on the currently running thread
       NotesThread.sinitThread();
       // Here you can place any Java code
     }
     catch(Exception e) {
       e.printStackTrace();        // Print a stack trace
     }
     finally {
       NotesThread.stermThread(); // This will be called in all cases
     }
   }
}
```

Notice that in this code, I used the `finally` clause to house the `stermThread` call. By implementing the termination this way, the thread Notes environment will be terminated whether or not there is an exception. If you fail to properly terminate the Notes environment, your program can hang or cause an abnormal termination.

THE Session CLASS

We've seen so far how Notes and Domino use the NotesThread class to implement the start-up and shutdown of the Notes and Domino environment. After this environment is set up, however, one additional class must be used to initiate access to Domino. This class is the Session class, which corresponds to the NotesSession class of LotusScript. I introduce the Session class in this section, but you can find more details in Chapter 16, "The NotesThread, NotesFactory, NotesException, Session, and Agent Classes."

The Session class is at the top of the Domino Object Model hierarchy. All other classes are obtained via the Session, either directly or indirectly. For example, from a Session object, you can get a DbDirectory object, through which you can access Domino databases. You can also obtain an AgentContext object (in an agent) from the Session, which gives you information about the current agent's context.

Okay, if the Session class is so important, how do you create one? Good question. There are two ways to get a Session object. You can either create one from scratch or you can obtain one from another class that happens to have one. When you are writing an agent, Notes will create a Session object for you, and you can just obtain it. When you are writing any other type of Java program, you must create it from scratch. Creating a new Session in Java from scratch is similar to using the LotusScript statement Dim session As New NotesSession. In Java, you use the CreateSession method of the NotesFactory class. Here is how you do it with Java:

```
Session s = NotesFactory.CreateSession();
```

Note

In release 4.6 of Notes and Domino, you used the static Session.newInstance method to create a new Session variable from scratch. The NotesFactory method now takes the place of Session.newInstance.

I mentioned that when you are writing code for an agent, you can obtain the Session object that was created for you. Within an agent context, you must do two things. First, your agent must extend the AgentBase class, and then you must have a NotesMain method. Within the NotesMain method, you use

```
Session s = this.getSession();
```

I describe this in more detail in the next section.

JAVA AGENTS, SERVLETS, APPLETS, AND APPLICATIONS

The Java language can be used in several different contexts with Notes and Domino. In particular, you can use Java in agents, servlets, applets, and applications. Each of these different contexts interacts differently with the Domino environment, so let me explain these contexts. In Chapter 2, "Domino Designer and the Integrated Development Environment (IDE)," I told you about the differences between these types of programs and when each language could be used. I'd like to examine each of the Java contexts now in more detail.

Some of the main characteristics of these different types of programs are how they are created, how they are invoked, and how they are terminated. I'll describe these characteristics in each section.

DOMINO JAVA AGENTS

Java agents in Domino are really just special cases of the `NotesThread` class that we saw earlier. To create an agent, you extend the `AgentBase` class. However, the `AgentBase` class itself is just an extension of the `NotesThread` class, so without necessarily knowing it, your agent is also a `NotesThread`.

When I showed you how a `NotesThread` is started, I said that you need to provide only one routine, the `runNotes` method. When the `NotesThread` is started, the `runNotes` method is invoked automatically. In the special case of agents, however, the Notes system has some additional housekeeping chores to perform before it can start your code. So, in the case of agents, Notes commandeers the `runNotes` method, declares it final so you cannot use it, and substitutes the `NotesMain` method for your code. Here is how a Notes Java agent actually starts up:

1. `java.lang.Thread:start` initializes the new thread environment and calls the thread's run method on the new thread.

2. `NotesThread:run` initializes the Notes environment and calls `AgentBase:runNotes`.

3. `AgentBase:runNotes` initializes the agent environment and calls your agent's `NotesMain` method.

4. `YourAgent:NotesMain` is your agent code.

The `AgentBase runNotes` method sets up an `AgentContext` object and creates a `Session` object. Because your agent extends the `AgentBase` class, you can use `this.getSession` to get the `Session` object that was created by `runNotes`.

If we look at the code that is automatically produced by the Domino Designer IDE for a Java agent, it should now be very clear. Notice that the `getSession` call omits the `this` qualifier. You can use either `this.getSession` or just plain `getSession`. It is important to understand the shorthand and why you don't need to use the `this` qualifier. (It's because `getSession` is defined in `AgentBase` and your agent extends `AgentBase`, so in effect your agent is an `AgentBase`.) Here's the code:

```
import lotus.domino.*;
public class JavaAgent extends AgentBase {
    public void NotesMain() {
        try {
            Session session = getSession();
            AgentContext agentContext = session.getAgentContext();
```

```
        // (Your code goes here)
    } catch(Exception e) {
        e.printStackTrace();
    }
  }
}
```

Your Java agent automatically terminates when your `NotesMain` method ends. After it ends, control is returned in the reverse order to `AgentBase:runNotes` and then `NotesThread:run`. When `run` finishes, the thread itself is finished.

Also notice in the automatically generated code that an `AgentContext` is obtained. The `AgentContext` includes information such as the effective username, the current database, and the set of unprocessed documents that the agent should handle, along with several other agent properties.

Remember that an agent can run on either the Notes client or a Domino server. When the agent is running on the Notes client, the effective user is the current workstation user ID. However, when the agent is running on the server, the effective user is the user who last signed the agent. In addition, via the agent properties, you can also set up the agent to run with the identity of a Web user.

You can run a Java agent on a Domino server via a URL. You do this from a Web browser with the following syntax:

```
http://server/database.nsf/agentname
```

The database must exist, of course, and the specified agent must be a shared agent within the database. To send output back to the Web user, you must create a `PrintWriter` object by getting it from the `AgentBase` object. Here is how you do that:

```
Session s = getSession();
AgentContext ac = s.getAgentContext();
PrintWriter pw = getAgentOutput();  // Get AgentOutput
pw.println("<h1>Hello World</h1>");    // Send output back to browser
```

For this to work, make sure that your agent is declared as a shared agent. Note that you can specify this choice only when the agent is created. After it's created, you cannot turn a non-shared agent into a shared agent. You make an agent shared by checking the checkbox directly beneath the agent's name in the Create Agent dialog box.

The capability to run an agent on the server is similar to the servlet capability. There are a few differences, however. First, an agent is stored within a Domino database. Because of this, it can be replicated and can travel along with the database to another server. In addition, Java agents use the Domino security model and are more secure than servlets. Agents are written by extending `AgentBase` as previously described, and you use a `NotesMain` method for your agent code.

JAVA SERVLETS

Java servlets are stored as Java class files and archive (JAR) files within a directory on the server. Servlets can be initialized and stay active within the Domino server. When resident, a servlet can process many requests in a multithreaded manner from several Web clients at once. The capability to remain in memory can provide servlets with an important performance advantage for certain applications. Because servlets might be handling many requests simultaneously, it is critical that servlets be threadsafe.

One common use for servlets is to access non-Domino databases via JDBC. You can also access Domino databases using the Java techniques described in previous sections. Servlets are an industry standard for server-side Java programming, whereas agents are Domino-specific. Servlets are typically implemented as extensions of the `javax.servlet.http.HttpServlet` class. There is a full discussion of servlets in Chapter 27, "Using IBM WebSphere for Java Servlets and Java Server Pages (JSP)."

JAVA APPLETS

An *applet* is a set of one or more Java classes that is downloaded to a Web browser and executed within the context of the JVM in the Web browser itself. Regular Java applets are independent of Notes and Domino. You can have Java applets that are created and served by a Web server, such as Domino or any other Web server.

Just as Domino Java agents are special cases of the Java `Thread` class, with release 5 of Notes and Domino you can have specialized Domino applets as well. Let me first describe a regular Java applet, and then I'll explain how Domino Java applets are different.

An applet in Java is actually invoked by the Web browser. There is no main method in a Java applet. In fact, there are four important methods in a Java applet: `init`, `start`, `stop`, and `destroy`. Here are their definitions:

- `void init()`—This method is invoked when the applet is first loaded. It is called only once.
- `void start()`—This method is invoked after the `init` method. It is also invoked when the page comes into view or the browser is restored from an icon view.
- `void stop()`—This method is invoked when the page is left or when the browser is minimized into an icon.
- `void destroy()`—This method is invoked when the applet is no longer required. It is called after the `stop` method.

For completeness, I should mention that a Java applet is not actually a base class. As a matter of fact, it is four layers down in the hierarchy. The upper layers are `Component`, `Container`, `Panel`, and `Applet`. In other words, `Applet` extends `Panel`, which extends `Container`, which extends `Component`. These classes can be found in the `java.awt` package.

If you are using the Java Swing classes, an additional class called `JApplet` is available. This is similar to the `Applet` class but uses the Swing classes rather than the standard user interface classes.

PART

III

CH

12

It is beyond my scope here to explain all these other classes, but you should be aware of them. Suffice it to say that these other classes deal with user-interface characteristics, such as layout and the graphical appearance of the applet. For more information on applets, see Chapter 15, "Developing Java Applets for Use with Domino."

DOMINO JAVA APPLETS

What exactly is a Domino Java applet? A regular applet that is served by a Domino server to a Web browser might qualify, but that is not what I mean by a Domino Java applet. A Domino Java applet is an applet that has the capability to access Domino objects. In other words, it can do everything that a normal applet can do, but it can also access Domino.

What does it mean to access Domino? This is an important question. Remember that a regular applet is a Java program running within the JVM in the Web browser. Consider this hypothetical case. Suppose you have the newest gadget, a Web-enabled television set. This TV is a pure Java machine. It has a Java Virtual Machine (JVM) installed and can download and execute Java programs, but it certainly isn't a personal computer. Can you execute a Domino Java applet? Yes. In your Web television set, you can access Domino databases, traverse views, and use a Java program to perform functions that you might have used LotusScript for previously.

It is important to understand the capabilities of a Domino Java applet and to understand how this type of applet differs from a regular, ordinary Java applet. Let's take a look at a Domino Java applet.

A Domino Java applet is similar in concept and implementation to a Domino Java agent. If we want to create a Domino Java applet, we must extend the `AppletBase` class. This is analogous to extending the `AgentBase` class for agents. After we have extended `AppletBase`, there are four important methods for our Domino Java applet:

- `void notesAppletInit()`—This method is invoked when the applet is first loaded. It is called only once.
- `void notesAppletStart()`—This method is invoked after the `notesAppletInit` method. It is also invoked when the page comes into view or the browser is restored from an icon view.
- `void notesAppletStop()`—This method is invoked when the page is left or when the browser is minimized into an icon.
- `void notesAppletDestroy()`—This method is invoked when the applet is no longer required. This method is called after the `notesAppletStop` method.

I'm sure that you can see the immediate similarity to the four methods that are defined for a regular applet. Just as in the case for agents, the four `notesApplet` methods correspond to the underlying methods. I should also mention that the regular `init`, `start`, `stop`, and `destroy` methods are declared final within `AppletBase`, so you are not allowed to override them, and you should not call them directly.

A few additional methods are in the `AppletBase` class. These methods are `openSession`, `closeSession`, and `getSession`. `openSession` calls `getSession`, and I don't think there is any additional function performed in `openSession` that does not also occur in `getSession`. Thus, you can probably consider them synonyms, but `openSession` and its counterpart `closeSession` are the preferred methods.

The `openSession` (and `getSession`) method is similar to the `getSession` method found in `AgentBase`. Remember that we need to have a `Session` object to access the Domino objects. After we have this `Session` object, we can pretty much traverse the entire object model hierarchy. There are two forms for `openSession` within `AppletBase`:

```
Session s = openSession();     // Anonymous access

Session s = openSession(String userid, String password);
```

The first of these methods is used for anonymous access, and in the second method, you pass the user ID and password strings.

When you are finished with the `Session` object, you can close it with `closeSession`.

```
closeSession(s);     // Close the previously opened Session.
```

The last method in `AppletBase` is the `IsNotesLocal` method. This routine returns true if the applet is running within a Notes client and is accessing a local database. It returns false if you are accessing a remote server.

If you are using the Java Swing classes, you can extend your applet from the `JAppletBase` class rather than the `AppletBase` class. The `JAppletBase` class supports an identical set of methods to the `AppletBase` class.

I have not described, until now, the magic that is used to implement Domino access from a Web-enabled television set. Hold on to your hats, here come the acronyms: CORBA and IIOP. These two technologies are important because they basically enable you to perform client/server computing, using Web browsers and Java over the Internet. The client can be any Java-enabled Web browser, and the server is Domino. I describe these technologies in more detail in Chapter 15.

PART
III

CH
12

ACCESSING DOMINO DATABASES FROM JAVA APPLICATIONS

There are a couple of scenarios for accessing Domino from standalone Java applications. First, you can access local Domino databases if you have Java and the Notes executable files present on your computer. This will typically be the configuration on your desktop or laptop computer if you are using the Notes client.

Second, with those magic components CORBA and IIOP, you can create a standalone Java application that runs on your desktop but accesses a remote Domino server. In this case, all you need to have present on your local computer is a JVM and the appropriate archive files. You do not need to have the Notes executable files present.

In the earlier section, "Java Applications and Multithreading," I showed you the basics of standalone Java applications and how to initialize the Notes/Domino environment. As mentioned, a standalone application can extend NotesThread, or you can create a class that implements the Runnable interface. In either case, you must also have a static main routine. This main routine is invoked by the JVM machine. Here is an example of a Java program that extends NotesThread. This is an example that must run locally. It does not use CORBA or IIOP.

```
import lotus.domino.*;

public class MyNotesMain4 {
   public static void main(String args[]) {
     try {
       ExtendedThread etMyThread = new ExtendedThread(); // My Thread
       etMyThread.start();  // This will eventually invoke my runNotes();
       etMyThread.join();   // Wait for thread to finish
     }
     catch(InterruptedException e) {
     }
   }
}
public class ExtendedThread extends NotesThread {
   public void runNotes() {
     try {
        Session s = NotesFactory.createSession(); // Create a new Session
        String v = s.getNotesVersion();  // Notes version
        String p = s.getPlatform();       // Platform
        System.out.println("Running version " + v + " on platform " + p);
     }
     catch (Exception e) {
        e.printStackTrace();
     }
   }
}
```

Here is how this routine starts up:

1. JVM calls MyNotesMain4:main, which creates an ExtendedThread, which extends NotesThread. The main then calls ExtendedThread:start (which is actually implemented in Thread:start).

2. Thread:start (ExtendedThread:start) initializes the thread and calls ExtendedThread:run. Because ExtendedThread extends NotesThread, the run method is actually implemented in NotesThread:run.

3. The NotesThread:run routine initializes the NotesThread environment and calls the ExtendedThread:runNotes method. This is where your code resides.

> **Note**
>
> Do not confuse the Thread:start routine with the Applet:start routine. Although they have the same method name, they are completely different methods. Thread:start is a system routine that starts a thread; Applet:start is an optional user-written routine invoked by a browser when an applet starts.

The following example uses CORBA and IIOP. This main program can run on a client that does not have the Notes executables locally.

```
import lotus.domino.*;

public class MyNotesMain5 {
   public static void main(String args[]) {
      try {
         RunnableThread rtMyThread = new RunnableThread(); // My Thread
         // NotesThread extends java.lang.Thread
         NotesThread theThread = new NotesThread(rtMyThread);
         theThread.start();   // This will eventually invoke my run();
         theThread.join();    // Wait for thread to finish
      }
      catch(InterruptedException e) {
      }
   }
}
class RunnableThread implements Runnable {
   public void run() {
      try {
         String IOR = lotus.domino.NotesFactory.getIOR("ACMESERVER");
         System.out.println("IOR='" + IOR + "'");
         Session s = NotesFactory.createSessionwithIOR(IOR,
         ➥"John Doe/AcmeCorp", "secretpassword");
         String v = s.getNotesVersion();  // Notes version
         String p = s.getPlatform();      // Platform
         System.out.println("Running version " + v + " on platform " + p);
      }
      catch (Exception e) {
         e.printStackTrace();
      }
   }
}
```

This code is an example of the Runnable interface. The major point to notice in this example is the fact that we have a new variable called IOR. IOR stands for Interoperable Object Reference. The IOR is specified as a string. If you print it out, you'll notice that it is a huge hexadecimal string. This string is used to set up the CORBA communication between the client and the server. If you are debugging online, you'll also notice a fairly long delay when you create the Session because of all the CORBA initialization. After the CORBA initialization has finished, however, the application will run fairly quickly.

If you want to eliminate the need for the IOR, you can use the createSession method with the three parameters host, userid, and password. Here is the syntax:

```
Session s = NotesFactory.createSession(hostname, userid, password);
```

Hostname is the same parameter you pass to the getIOR method. The regular createSession method will obtain the IOR for you, making it a little easier to use.

The two examples MyNotesMain4 and MyNotesMain5 showed two different ways to create a standalone application. MyNotesMain4 created an inherited thread, and MyNotesMain5 created a Runnable class. You can use CORBA via either method.

One final note about this example: If you want to try this example yourself, you must substitute your server name, your user ID, and your password at the appropriate points in the program.

SUMMARY

In this chapter I described the differences between Domino Java agents, applets, and applications. I showed you how to initialize these various environments.

I introduced you to using each of the various types of programs you might want to create. I give you more detailed information in later chapters. To learn more about agents, see Chapter 13, "Creating Java Agents with the Domino Designer IDE," and Chapter 14, "Using the Domino Designer and Third-Party IDEs with Java." To find out more about applets, read Chapter 15, "Developing Java Applets for Use with Domino." To discover more about Java servlets, read Chapter 27, "Using IBM WebSphere for Java Servlets and Java Server Pages."

CHAPTER REVIEW

1. What entry point is required if you want to create a Java application? Is this same entry point required for a Java agent? How about an applet?

2. Is it possible to create a Java Domino agent that will run in both a Web browser and the Notes client? How about an applet that runs in both?

3. What entry points are used for a regular Java applet? Are these same entry points used if you create an applet that will be using the Domino Objects classes, and if not, what are they?

4. What is the difference between extending the `java.lang.Thread` class and implementing the `runnable` interface?

5. How does the Java Virtual Machine (JVM) know where to look for classes that it must load at runtime?

6. If you have a ZIP file that contains a set of Java class files, do you need to unzip it before it can be used with the JVM?

7. If you want to create an applet that will access the Domino Objects classes, what class must you extend when you are creating your applet?

8. Describe the naming convention, including capitalization, that you should use when creating your own Java classes, packages, and method names. If you have your own Internet domain name and expect to be sharing, selling, or otherwise distributing your classes, what prefix should you use on your package names?

9. Describe the difference between the `NotesThread` class and the built-in Java `Thread` class. When should you use each one?

10. Describe a scenario where you might have to implement the `runnable` interface rather than extend `NotesThread`.

11. Create a standalone Java application that creates three threads. Have each thread print a unique message to the debug console and then exit.

CHAPTER 13

CREATING JAVA AGENTS WITH THE DOMINO DESIGNER IDE

In this chapter

WHAT IS A JAVA AGENT?

If you are already familiar with Notes and Domino, you might already know about LotusScript agents or agents written with the @formula language. You can also write agents using Java as well as with simple actions. An agent that is written in any of these languages is really just a program that has the following characteristics:

- An execution location (client or server) where the agent will run.
- A database in which the agent resides. An agent can access and modify other databases as well as the one in which it resides.
- An event that triggers the agent to run.
- A set of documents on which to operate.
- An agent can be personal or shared. Only the person who created the personal agent can run it. Any authorized user can run shared agents.
- The program itself, written in one of several languages.

The first five characteristics are common to all agents, regardless of which language is used for implementation. The last item, which is the program itself, is the part that can be written in Java or any of the other languages.

NOTES CLIENT VERSUS DOMINO SERVER AGENTS

Agents can run either in the Notes client or on the Domino server. Agents cannot be run in a Web browser. In a browser you can run applets, of course, but applets are a fruit of an entirely different color.

When using the Notes client, agents can be run in either the foreground or the background. Background agents in the Notes client can be invoked on a scheduled basis, or when events, such as new mail arriving, occur. Whether the agent runs in the foreground or background, it runs with the security identity of the user that is using the Notes client. To run scheduled background agents in the Notes client, you must enable the option Enable Scheduled Local Agents in the Startup Options section in the Basics tab of the User Preferences dialog box. Open this box from the menus with File, Preferences, User Preferences.

A background server agent running on Domino can be triggered from scheduled events, such as arriving mail or a request from a Web browser. A scheduled background agent does not have an associated user at a workstation, so another security mechanism is required. The *effective user ID* of a background agent is the user who created or last modified the agent. An agent triggered using a URL on the Web can be run either with the last modifier's credentials or the credentials of the Web user. You can make this selection in the Agent properties box at the bottom of the Design tab.

AGENT SECURITY

The effective user (or actual user) determines the security authorization for an agent. Any user with at least Reader access to a database can normally execute personal agents. When an agent runs in the Notes client, typically no security checks are enforced because the user is considered a manager. To enforce agent security on a local database, you must enable the option Enforce a Consistent ACL Across All Replicas of This Database. This option can be found on the Advanced tab of the Access Control List dialog box.

Five settings in the Domino public directory (formerly Name and Address book) can be used to control access to server agents. Three options deal with regular Notes/Domino agents, and two options relate to IIOP restrictions. The basic Agent Restriction settings can be found in the Domino Directory on the Security tab of the Server document. The Agent Restrictions section contains the following three settings:

- Run Personal Agents—Dictates who can run personal agents on the server. If left blank, anyone can run personal agents. If you want to restrict personal agents, you should create a group called Personal Agents in the directory. This will make maintenance of the group easier.
- Run Restricted LotusScript/Java Agents—If this field is left blank (the default) then no one can run restricted agents on the server. Restricted agents are allowed to do only a subset of the normal functions of the LotusScript and Java languages. For example, a restricted agent cannot access the server's file system. If you want to allow agents to be run on the server, you should create a group called Restricted Agents in your directory. You should minimize the number of people allowed to run agents on the server for both security and performance reasons.
- Run Unrestricted LotusScript/Java Agents—If this field is left blank (the default) then no one can run unrestricted agents on the server. Unrestricted agents are allowed complete access to the Domino server's resources and all features of the LotusScript and Java languages. For example, an unrestricted agent can access the server's file system, can call external ("C" language) programs, and perform other operations that could potentially be damaging to the server. If you want to allow agents to be run on the server, you should create a group called Unrestricted Agents in your directory. You should minimize the number of people allowed to run agents (especially unrestricted agents) on the server for both security and performance reasons.

The two IIOP settings correspond to the Restricted/Unrestricted settings for regular agents. The IIOP settings control access to agents from Web browsers.

CREATING A JAVA AGENT

The minimum access level you need to create a personal agent is Reader if you have the option Create LotusScript/Java Agent enabled within the database's ACL. To create a shared Java agent, you need at least Designer access to the database, and you need the Create LotusScript/Java Agent option enabled within the database's ACL. If you have Designer access but do not have the Create LotusScript/Java Agent option enabled in the ACL, you can still create agents using formulas or simple actions.

After you have the proper authorizations enabled, you can create a Java agent. There are a few different scenarios for Java agents. One scenario is to use a Java agent to perform periodic or on-demand manipulation of Domino databases. In this case, you'll need to access the Domino Objects back-end classes. A slightly different scenario is to use Java agents to respond to users on the Web. You can dynamically create HTML with your Java agent and send it back to the Web user. Of course, this type of agent might also need to access the back-end classes as well. Another possible scenario is to use a Java agent to manipulate XML (Extensible Markup Language) data and send it to a Web browser or even to a mobile user on a cell phone using WML (Wireless Markup Language) and WAP (Wireless Access Protocol).

You can create Java agents in either the Domino IDE or with a third-party development tool. When you use the Domino IDE, you specify the language Java in the Run box of the Programmer's pane. If you use a third-party tool to create your Java class files, you use Imported Java in the Run box of the Programmer's pane. I explain the Imported Java option in Chapter 14, "Using the Domino Designer and Third-Party IDEs with Java."

USING THE DOMINO IDE TO CREATE A JAVA AGENT

Let's start our tour of Java agents by creating a simple agent. We'll begin by creating a simple program that prints "Hello, Java" to the Java debugging console.

> **Note**
>
> The origin of this simple example is from Kernighan and Ritchie's classic book, *The C Programming Language*. The first example given in this book to learn C was a program to print the words "Hello, world". Many books since that time have used this example to honor "K&R" and because it is one of the easiest programs to write and understand.

In Figure 13.1 you can see our Hello agent as well as the Java Console.

To create the Java agent, follow these steps:

1. Click on the word Agents in the Design pane.
2. Click the New Agent action button.
3. When the new agent appears in the work area, enter the name `Hello` and click the Shared Agent checkbox.
4. Use the value All documents in the database for the set of documents to act on.
5. Add the following line just below the import `lotus.domino.*`; statement:
   ```
   import java.io.*;
   ```
6. Add the following two lines below the comment (`Your code goes here`):
   ```
   PrintWriter out = getAgentOutput();
   out.println("Hello, Java");
   ```

Here is the complete text of the agent:

```
import lotus.domino.*;
import java.io.*;
public class JavaAgent extends AgentBase {
```

```
public void NotesMain() {
    try {
        Session session = getSession();
        AgentContext agentContext = session.getAgentContext();
        // (Your code goes here)
        PrintWriter out = getAgentOutput();
        out.println("Hello, Java");
    } catch(Exception e) {
        e.printStackTrace();
    }
}
```

Figure 13.1
A sample Domino agent to print "Hello, Java".

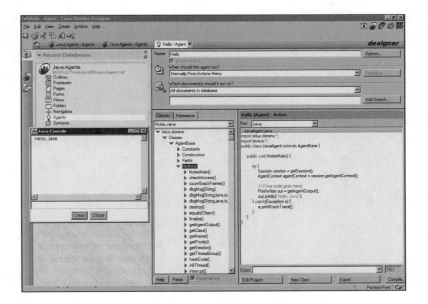

After you have created the agent, you can save it and execute it from the Actions menu. You will see the output in the Java debug console. To display the Java debug console, issue File, Tools, Show Java Debug Console from the menus.

Here is an explanation of what we have just done. We needed the import java.io.* statement because the input/output classes are not implicitly included in our Java program. In particular, we need the definition of the PrintWriter class, which is included in the java.io package. We obtain the PrintWriter object by calling the getAgentOutput method, which is a method of AgentBase. Because our agent extends AgentBase, the getAgentOutput method is always available to agents. After we have obtained the PrintWriter, we use the println method to output a string of characters.

In Java, a hierarchy of input/output classes exists. Each level of the hierarchy has several classes. At the lowest, most basic level are the Stream classes. Stream classes deal with input and output of streams of bytes. On the Stream classes, you can build filtering streams, data streams, memory streams, compression streams, and cryptographic streams.

Another group of classes for performing input and output are the Reader and Writer classes. These classes deal with characters instead of bytes. You might be thinking, "But isn't a character the same thing as a byte?" The answer is that in ASCII, a character is represented as a single byte, but in UNICODE, a character is multiple bytes. So, because Readers and Writers deal with characters, they can be dealing with multibyte characters. Examples of Readers and Writers include the InputStreamReader and the OutputStreamWriter classes. These classes use the Stream classes for their basic input and output functions. The PrintWriter class I've shown you in this example also produces character output. By default, as in our example, this output will go to the Java debug console.

As an added bonus, if we invoke this agent from a Web browser, the output from this agent running on the server will be sent back to the Web browser in HTML format. That's because the PrintWriter class determines the invocation method and if invoked from the Web, it redirects its output back to the Web. To invoke the agent from a Web browser, use the following syntax in your browser:

```
http://server/database.nsf/Hello[?OpenAgent]
```

The square brackets indicate that the ?OpenAgent parameter is optional if you don't have more than one design element called Hello within your database. If you have, for example, a Hello page and a Hello agent, you should probably include the Domino command ?OpenPage or ?OpenAgent so that your intention is not ambiguous.

TRIGGERING A JAVA AGENT

An agent can be invoked in several ways. I've already mentioned two. You can manually run an agent, or an agent can be invoked by a URL that includes an ?OpenAgent command. In addition to these methods, an agent can be invoked on a regular, scheduled basis or it can be invoked when an event occurs, such as when new mail arrives in a database.

These triggering mechanisms are used regardless of the language you choose for your agent. Java, Imported Java, and LotusScript all have the same triggering model.

You select the triggering method when you create the agent. The following are the options you can choose in the agent editor that cause the agent to be triggered:

- Manually From Actions Menu
- Manually From Agent List
- Before New Mail Arrives
- After New Mail Has Arrived
- If Documents Have Been Created or Modified
- If Documents Have Been Pasted
- On Schedule More Than Once A Day
- On Schedule Daily
- On Schedule Weekly

- On Schedule Monthly
- On Schedule Never

THE DOCUMENTS ON WHICH THE JAVA AGENT WILL ACT

After you have selected the trigger for the agent, you can select the set of documents on which to act. When you first create an agent, the default value is Selected Documents. This option works only for agents that are triggered within views or when a particular document is open. For many agents this will not be the appropriate setting. In fact, you will get an error message if you try to invoke this type of agent in an improper context. When you have an agent that is invoked manually or by using the Web, you should set the documents to All Documents in the Database to avoid receiving the error message.

The following are the available settings for the documents:

- All Documents in Database
- All New and Modified Documents Since Last Run
- All Unread Documents in View
- All Documents in View
- Selected Documents
- Run Once (@Commands may be used)

Although there can be many possible ways to identify the specific documents on which to act, within the agent the group of documents is called "unprocessed." There are two important methods of the AgentContext class: getUnprocessedDocuments and updateProcessedDoc. The getUnprocessedDocuments method returns a DocumentCollection that contains Document objects for all the documents that need to be processed. If you have selected All Documents in Database then this collection will contain all the documents of the database.

When you work with new mail or All New and Modified Documents Since Last Run, you need a method to determine which documents are new and which have already been processed. To flag a document as having been processed, you pass the Document object to the updateProcessedDoc method. If you do not flag the document as having been processed, it will continue to be identified as unprocessed.

CREATING A SIMPLE SPAM FILTER

While I was writing this chapter, I received an email from an anonymous source with the following subject line: "Lose 5–15 Inches in One Hour! Introducing Non-Surgical Liposuction!" Now, I'm not sure whether I could really lose that 5–15 inches, and I don't think I want to try non-surgical liposuction. However, it did give me a good idea for an example: a simple email spam filter. In this case, I'm going to filter out any email messages that I receive that have "liposuction" in the subject field. I'm reasonably sure that if I receive any email with that particular word, it isn't going to be from a professional colleague.

Because this agent will be a filter, you should set this agent to run on All New and Modified Documents since last run. This will cause the unprocessed document collection to contain only the new and modified documents in the email database.

Let's see how we could construct our filter in Java. In this example, I'm going to show you not only the specifics of this agent, but some programming techniques as well. For example, we'll take a look at how you can debug your agent. Here is a listing of the agent, including code to aid in debugging:

```java
import lotus.domino.*;
import java.util.*;

public class JavaAgent extends AgentBase {
    public void NotesMain() {
        try {
            Session session = getSession();
            AgentContext agentContext = session.getAgentContext();

            setDebug(true); // Debugging mode on for dbgMsg
            // Obtain the set of documents to work with
            DocumentCollection dc = agentContext.getUnprocessedDocuments();
            Document doc = dc.getFirstDocument(); // Get the first document
            StringTokenizer st; // java.util.StringTokenizer utility object
            String token; // A single token
            while (doc != null) { // While there are more unprocessed documents
            dbgMsg("doc != null");
                // We have a document, now tokenize subject field
                st = new StringTokenizer(doc.getItemValueString("Subject"));
                while (st.hasMoreTokens()) {
                    dbgMsg("st.hasMoreTokens");
                    token = st.nextToken(); // Get the next token from the tokenizer
                    dbgMsg("Token: " + token);
                    if (token.equalsIgnoreCase("liposuction")) {
                        dbgMsg("put in folder");
                        // Put the document in the Trash folder
                        doc.putInFolder("Trash");
                        // Put the document in the Trash folder
                        // Indicate this one processed
                        agentContext.updateProcessedDoc(doc);
                        // Indicate this one processed
                    }
                }
                doc = dc.getNextDocument();  // Get the next Domino Document
            }
            dbgMsg("Done");  // Completed
        } catch(Exception e) {
            e.printStackTrace();
        }
    }
}
```

The first point to notice is a new import statement in this routine. I've imported java.util.*. This import is for the StringTokenizer class. By using the import, I can refer to the class without its packaging prefix. For example, without the `import` statement, I would need to refer to the class as `java.util.StringTokenizer` throughout the program. With the `import` statement, I can refer to the `StringTokenizer` class without `java.util` prefix.

After the standard agent initialization, you'll notice the `setDebug(true)` method call. This call enables the logging of output from the `dbgMsg` routine. Both the `setDebug` and `dbgMsg` methods are part of the `AgentBase` class. When `setDebug` is `true`, any calls to `dbgMsg` will result in output to the Java debug console. If it is `false`, the debugging messages are suppressed. Sometimes when you include many of the debugging messages, the output can be quite voluminous. By setting the flag to `true` or `false` in different parts of your code, you can selectively enable debugging messages.

After the flag has been set, I obtain the unprocessed document collection. The program will loop through each of these documents, and for each document it will inspect the subject line. If it finds the word *liposuction* within the subject line, it will put the document in the trash folder.

I have included a Domino database on the CD-ROM with the agent, a simulated email form, and associated documents. I first created a single document for testing purposes. In the subject field I put the following: `Test Liposuction`. Here is the output that appeared in the Java debug console:

```
dbg: doc != null
dbg: st.hasMoreTokens
dbg: Token: Test
dbg: st.hasMoreTokens
dbg: Token: Liposuction
dbg: put in folder
dbg: Done
```

I ran the agent a second time and here is the resulting output:

```
dbg: Done
```

As you can see, the second time the agent ran, the document collection was empty because I had flagged each document with the `updateProcessedDoc` method of the `AgentContext` object. You can obtain the Java Agents database from the CD-ROM and try creating your own documents and observe the results.

Using Java Agents to Create Web Pages

One of the more powerful features of agents is that they can be used to produce dynamic Web pages. A dynamic page differs from a static page in that a program is generating the HTML rather than having static HTML delivered from a file. A dynamic page is powerful because the program can do lookups and personalize the Web page for the particular viewer.

You can also pass parameters to your agent using the URL. The parameters passed to the agent can be used as keys for lookups in Domino views or even relational database systems. In combination with JavaScript on the client, you can create very powerful applications that work cooperatively on the client (JavaScript) and on the server (in a Java agent).

COMMON GATEWAY INTERFACE (CGI) CONVENTIONS

The Common Gateway Interface (CGI) was one of the original ways to produce programmable output for the Web. This interface is supported on almost all the current Web servers, but its use is diminishing because there are other, better alternatives today. Nevertheless, CGI is important because some of the conventions that were developed for CGI have influenced how server programs access data from and about the client.

CGI programs are usually written in a programming language such as C, C++, or PERL. There is no specific language requirement because a CGI program is actually an executable program that runs on the Web server. In Windows NT, for example, you can write the CGI program in any language that generates an EXE file. One of the advantages of CGI programs is that they can be written in any language. One of the disadvantages, however, is that because the program is an executable, it must be loaded and deleted by the operating system for every request to the CGI program. This can entail a large overhead if the Web server is very busy. As I'll show you in Chapter 27, "Using IBM WebSphere for Java Servlets and Java Server Pages (JSP)," Java servlets can provide much of the same functionality with much less overhead because they can stay resident in the server's memory.

Several pieces of information must be passed to the CGI program. Some information describes the client, such as the user agent name, the MIME types that the user agent supports, and so forth. Other information can be considered parameters of the request. For example, Query_String represents the information following the question mark (?) in the URL.

Because of the number of variables that need to be passed to the CGI routine, the CGI specification uses operating system environment variables. These are variables that can be set or read outside a program as well as from within the program. Commonly used environment variables in Windows include the PATH variable and the CLASSPATH variable for Java classes.

To make it easy for the CGI program, the Web server consolidates information from several sources and places the values all in environment variables for CGI. In particular, the following are some locations where the Web server gathers information:

- The Web server internal values—For example, the client's IP address, the TCP/IP port used for communication, and the version of the CGI specification supported by the Web server.

- The HTTP request header—For example, the User agent name, the MIME types accepted, the request method (GET or POST), the Content MIME type, and the Content length. For GET requests, the Query string is contained in the request header.

- The HTTP request body—For a POST request this contains the Query string.

For more information on the HTTP protocol and HTTP headers, see Chapter 11, "JavaScript Techniques with Domino."

For Domino agents, conventions similar to CGI are used. However, instead of using environment variables, Domino creates a special document. The special document provides the environment or context for the actual operation requested. In Domino, this special document is called the DocumentContext document. You access the DocumentContext from the AgentContext object with the getDocumentContext method.

USING THE DocumentContext DOCUMENT

Let's look at how you can use the DocumentContext object to get the CGI variables. Here is a sample program:

```
import lotus.domino.*;
import java.io.*;
import java.util.*;

public class JavaAgent extends AgentBase {
    public void NotesMain() {
        try {
            Session session = getSession();
            AgentContext agentContext = session.getAgentContext();

            PrintWriter out = getAgentOutput();
            Document doc = agentContext.getDocumentContext();
            out.println("<H1>CGI Variables Received by Agent</H1>");
            out.println("<TABLE><TR><TH>Name</TH><TH>Value</TH></TR>");
            // Get the CGI variables
            Vector items = doc.getItems();
            for (int iItem = 0; iItem < items.size(); iItem++) {
                Item item = (Item)items.elementAt(iItem);
                out.println("<TR><TD>" + item.getName() + "</TD><TD>" +
                ➥item.getText() + "</TD></TR>");
            }
            out.println("</TABLE>");
        } catch(Exception e) {
            e.printStackTrace();
        }
    }
}
```

In Figure 13.2 you can see the output of the agent program as displayed by Microsoft Internet Explorer. Basically, the program works by getting the DocumentContext object, and then getting all the item values from the Document Context. I created an HTML table, formatting the name and value in each row of the table.

For fun, I ran the same agent from Netscape Navigator. All the CGI values were the same except for the ones that were prefixed with HTTP_ (for example HTTP_ACCEPT, HTTP_USER_AGENT, and so on). Not only were these values different, but the actual set of variables was different. Why? In Chapter 11, in the section "Client/Server Communication with HTTP," I described the HTTP headers and showed you how they vary from browser to browser. The CGI variables that are prefixed HTTP_ are the ones that Domino finds in the HTTP request header, and they vary depending not only on the browser, but on the version of the browser as well. So, the moral of the story is to be careful when you are using any CGI variables that begin with HTTP_ because they might not even exist if the user uses an old browser or a different browser than you've tested.

Figure 13.2
CGI variables contained in the DocumentContext object.

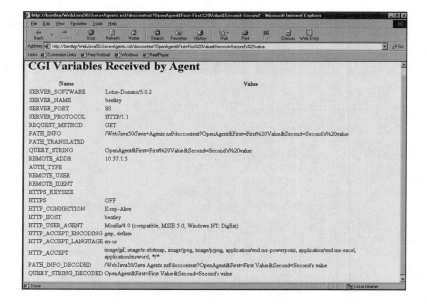

Probably the three HTTP_ variables you can count on are HTTP_ACCEPT, HTTP_HOST, and HTTP_USER_AGENT. Fortunately, the host and user agent variables are the HTTP_ variables that you are most likely to need. Other CGI variables that you might find useful are the Query_String and the Query_String_Decoded variables. I normally use only the Query_String_Decoded variable because it is just the Query_String value, but has had all the escape characters resolved back to their character equivalents. Notice in Figure 13.2 that the Query_String variable has embedded %20 (blank) characters while the decoded version has resolved these to actual blank characters. Be careful, though, because if there is no query string, the Query_String_Decoded variable will not exist.

A UTILITY CLASS FOR HANDLING PARAMETERS

Now that you know how to retrieve the CGI variables, you can find out information about the client. In addition, the user can add parameters to the URL when invoking the agent. The syntax for the string passed to the agent can be up to you; Domino or HTTP does not dictate it. If you follow HTTP conventions, however, you can make processing the string a little easier. Here is an example of syntax you can use:

```
?OpenAgent&Var1=value1&Var2=value2 . . .
```

This syntax is consistent with the spirit of HTTP syntax. To make processing easier, we can create a library that will parse the URL as previously done and combine the variables found with the CGI variables into a single table. That way, you can access either the CGI variables or the URL variables with one set of utility routines.

In the Java Agents Domino database on the CD-ROM, I have included a class called AgentParameters in a Java shared library. This library is based on a sample that was originally written by Ned Batchelder of Iris and made available on www.Notes.net. I have modified and enhanced the code. Here is an overview of this class:

```
class AgentParameters extends Hashtable{
    public AgentParameters();
    public void parseParameters(Session session);
    public void parseQueryString(String cQueryString);
    public String getString(key);
    public void printTable(PrintWriter out);
}
```

Four methods are in this class in addition to the constructor. Of these, you probably only need two: parseParameters and getString. The printTable method is a utility routine to format and output the table in HTML. Here is a sample agent that uses the AgentParameters class:

```
import lotus.domino.*;
import java.io.*;

public class JavaAgent extends AgentBase {
    public void NotesMain() {
        try {
            Session session = getSession();
            PrintWriter out = getAgentOutput();

            AgentParameters pt = new AgentParameters();
            pt.parseParameters(session);
            // Retrieve and print out a couple of selected variables
            out.println("http_user_agent=" +
                        pt.getString("http_user_Agent") + "<BR>");
            out.println("request_method=" +
                        pt.getString("request_method") + "<BR>");
            // Now print the whole table
            out.println("<H1>CGI Variables Received by Agent</H1>");
            pt.printTable(out);

        } catch(Exception e) {
            e.printStackTrace(getAgentOutput());
        }
    }
}
```

As you can see from this example, we create a new AgentParameters object, which is a specialized Hashtable. After we have created it, we parse the CGI variables as well as any URL parameters and place them into a table. After this has been accomplished, we can just retrieve the variables by name. The example shows how to extract the http_user_Agent and request_method variables.

In Figure 13.3 you can see the output from running the sample agent. Notice that the first two lines are printed directly from the agent, whereas the main table is the result of the `printTable` method. Also notice that two variables have been specified in the URL, namely `MyVar` and `Second`. Both of these variables have been inserted into the `AgentParameters` object that is displayed in the figure.

Figure 13.3
A sample Domino agent that processes parameters.

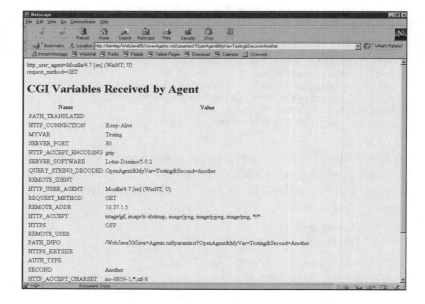

Here is the class definition for the `AgentParameters` class. (The Java source for this class is in the `AgentParameters` shared Java library in the Java Agents database on the CD-ROM.)

```java
import java.util.*;
import java.io.*;


// AgentParameters - Parse and Store agent CGI and URL parameters
// Randy Tamura
// Based on sample routine posted on Iris Sandbox at  www.notes.net.
// Parts originally written by Ned Batchelder of Iris.
public class AgentParameters extends Hashtable {
   public AgentParameters () {}

   // Add CGI variables and URL parameters to hash table.
   public void parseParameters(Session session)
      throws lotus.domino.NotesException
   {
      AgentContext agentContext = session.getAgentContext();
      Document doc = agentContext.getDocumentContext();

      // First add all of the CGI variables. They are in the document context.
      Vector items = doc.getItems();

      for (int iItem = 0; iItem < items.size(); iItem++) {
         Item item = (Item)items.elementAt(iItem); // Get next CGI variable
         // and store into hash table
         put(item.getName().toUpperCase(), item.getText());
```

```
          // and store into hash table
    }

    // If there was no query sting, the DECODED variable will not exist.
    String qs = doc.getItemValueString("QUERY_STRING_DECODED");
    if (null  != qs) {
      // Now parse the URL Query String
      parseQueryString(qs);   // We know we have one.
    }
}

// Parse and add the URL parameters to the Hashtable
public void parseQueryString(String cQueryString) {
    // Query string:    OpenAgent&var1=value1&var2=value2
    // Third parameter true=return separator tokens
    StringTokenizer toks = new StringTokenizer(cQueryString, "&=", true);
    // first token is command: skip it. (ie. OpenAgent)
    String tok = toks.nextToken();
    // first token is command: skip it. (ie. OpenAgent)
    String key = null;       // No current key value
    boolean bKeyNext = true; // Next token is a key
    // Note: bKeyNext stays true until after we have seen the "="

    while (toks.hasMoreTokens()) {
        tok = toks.nextToken();         // Get the next token
        // Check for next keyword beginning marker
        if (tok.equals("&")) {                  // Do we have &
           if (bKeyNext && (key != null)) {  // Is this  &Key& situation?
              // Yes. Use null value
              put(key, "");   // Store the name, w/Null value
           }
           // We've finished with the previous key/value reinitialize
           key = null;                // No current key value
           bKeyNext = true;   // Next token is a key
        }
        else if (tok.equals("=")) {
           bKeyNext = false;    // We have seen =, Next token is value
        }
        else { // It is not a separator, must be name or value
           if (bKeyNext) {      // If we're looking for a name,
              // Canonicalize: Make all keys upper case
              key = new String(tok).toUpperCase(); // Set the name
           }
           else { // We're looking for the value
              if (key != null) { // If the key was seen,
                 put(key, tok);  // Groovy, use both the name and value
              }
              key = null;  // Now done with this key
           }
        }
    }
    // We have to special-case a valueless argument at the end.
    if (bKeyNext && (key != null)) {
       // Null value
       put(key, "");
    }
}
```

```
// A simple accessor to make casts unnecessary.
public String getString(String key) {
   return (String) get(key.toUpperCase());
}

// Print out the table in HTML format
public void printTable(PrintWriter out) {
   Object key;

   out.println("<TABLE><TR><TH>Name</TH><TH>Value</TH></TR>");
   Enumeration e = keys();
   while (e.hasMoreElements()) {
      key = e.nextElement();    // Get next key
      out.println("<TR><TD>" + key.toString() + "</TD><TD>" +
         get(key).toString() + "</TD></TR>");
   }
   out.println("</TABLE>");
   }
}

// end of class AgentParameters
```

The main method for the AgentParameters class is the parseParameters method. It will add all the CGI variables to the hash table, and then it will call the parseQueryString method. The parseQueryString uses the StringTokenizer class found in java.util to tokenize the query string. For each parameter found, it will add the name and value to the hash table. To ensure that improper capitalization does not hamper retrieval, all keys are converted to uppercase before being stored in the hash table.

After the table has been constructed, two methods can be used to access the table. The getString method retrieves a value from the table for a given name. If the key is not found, the method will return null. The printTable method prints out the table by using HTML. This method is similar to the routine we saw for outputting the CGI variables.

WORKING WITH A JAVA SHARED LIBRARY

You can use a Java shared library with any Java agents that are stored in the same database. Java shared libraries are actually found in the Script Libraries item within the Resources section in the design pane. I'm sure that they're called Java shared libraries because the name Java Script libraries would be too easily confused with JavaScript libraries, which would be an entirely different kind of library.

To create a new Java shared library, follow these steps:

1. Click the Script Libraries name in the design pane, and then click the New Script Library action button.

2. In the Run drop-down box, the default is LotusScript. Change this option and select Java.

3. Your screen should now appear as in Figure 13.4.

Figure 13.4
Classes in a Java shared library are available to agents in the same database.

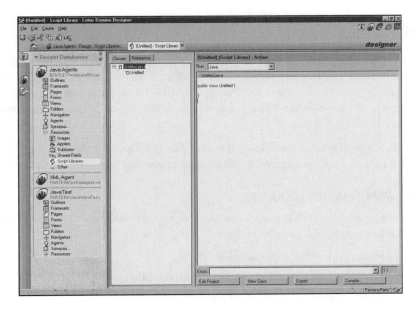

A Java shared library can contain not only Java code, but classes and other files as well. To add additional files to your shared library, click the Edit Project button at the bottom of the screen. You will see a dialog box like the one in Figure 13.5.

Figure 13.5
You can add more files to your Java shared library.

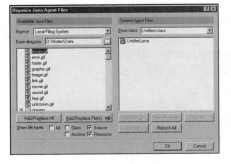

To add more files, select the files in the left pane that you would like to add to your project, and click the Add/Replace Files button below. To add all the files shown in the left pane, click the Add/Replace All button. You can selectively display files in the left pane by checking the checkboxes at the bottom of the dialog box. After files have been added to the project, if you make changes outside Domino, you can refresh the contents in your Domino database by clicking the Refresh button. When you have finished adding your files, click the OK button to close the dialog box.

You can create more than one class and store it in your Java library. Click the New Class button at the bottom of the screen. A gray bar will appear, and you can edit your new class.

PART
III

CH
13

You can edit any of the classes displayed just by scrolling the window and editing the appropriate class.

After you have created your Java library, you can export the contents to the file system. This will enable you to compile the routines with another compiler, store them in another database, or process them any other way you'd like. Click the Export key at the bottom of the screen and you will see a file dialog box. Pick the directory where you'd like your files to be saved, and click OK.

The Compile button enables you to compile the Java code displayed in the editing window. Code is also automatically compiled when you try to save the Java shared library.

USING JAVA SHARED LIBRARIES

When the shared library has been created, you can easily use it within your Java agent. Here is how to add the library to an agent:

1. First create your Java shared library.
2. Create/edit the agent that will refer to the library.
3. At the bottom of the Design pane, click the Edit Project button. You will see a dialog box similar to Figure 13.6.
4. In the Browse drop-down box, select Shared Java Libraries.
5. Pick the Java library you want to use.
6. Click the Add/Replace File(s) button in the dialog box. Your library will appear in the right side of the dialog box, as shown in Figure 13.6.
7. You can now refer to all the classes in the Java shared library within your agent.

Figure 13.6
Browse shared Java libraries to add a library to an agent.

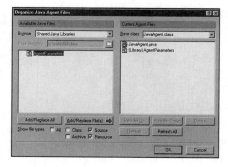

After you have included the Java shared library in your agent's project, the classes behave as if they are on the CLASSPATH when the library has been added to the project.

GENERATING AN XML DOCUMENT WITH A DOMINO AGENT

Normally when you produce output from an agent to be returned to the Web client, Domino will produce boilerplate HTML surrounding your output. This usually makes it very convenient to quickly write an agent that will return results to the user. On occasion, however, the boilerplate HTML will get in your way. On these occasions, you must override the generated HTML. In Chapter 11 I gave a detailed explanation of how to override Domino's automatic HTML. In short, the first string you write out must conform to the syntax for an HTTP header, which is a token followed by a colon as in the following:

```
Content-Type: text/html
```

For some specialized applications, you might want to override the header not only to eliminate the generated HTML, but also to return a different MIME type other than HTML. In particular, you might want to return XML instead of HTML. The MIME type for XML is text/xml, and you would specify it in HTTP as

```
Content-Type: text/xml
```

A special dialect of XML called Wireless Markup Language (WML) is part of a protocol that can be used for wireless phones called WAP. This dialect of XML uses a content type of text/vnd.wap.wml. The appropriate HTTP header is

```
Content-Type: text/vnd.wap.wml
```

In the next example, I'll show you how to generate and send XML to the Web browser. As I'm writing this, Microsoft Internet Explorer 5 is the only major browser that will display XML, but others are sure to follow soon.

I explain XML in much greater detail in Chapter 22, "Introduction to Extensible Markup Language (XML)." For now, it is only important to know that XML is a language that appears similar to HTML. XML elements are enclosed in angle brackets, and a document's elements are stored hierarchically. The power of XML lies in the fact that you can define your own hierarchical structure and semantics for data while using the XML syntax. This enables XML to be used for a variety of applications in diverse areas. One of the main uses for XML is for the storage of data in a canonical format and for the exchange of data between dissimilar systems.

Here is an example of an XML document:

```
<?xml version="1.0"?>
<note>
<item name="UserName">
<text>JJones</text>
</item>
<item name="Password">
<text>secret</text>
</item>
</note>
```

PART

III

CH

13

This simple example is a model for a document with two items. The first item is named UserName and its value is JJones. The second item is called Password and its value is secret. The next example illustrates how you might use XML to describe some of the characteristics of a database. In the following example, I use the shared Java program for processing parameters. With the parameters, you can specify input to the agent. The resulting output will be an XML file that I display using Internet Explorer 5.

Here is the syntax of the URL that the agent will accept:

```
http://database.nsf/DbXML[?OpenAgent[&filepath=path][&managers]]
```

With this syntax, if you omit all the parameters, the agent will display information about the current database. If you include a path, it will be used to locate a different database. If you include the managers parameter, the XML will include a list of the managers for the database.

Figure 13.7 shows you an example of the output of the program when run with the following parameters:

```
?Openagent&filepath=help/help5_designer.nsf&managers
```

Figure 13.7
A Java agent can produce dynamic XML output.

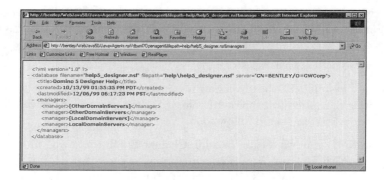

As you can see from the output, the XML includes the database name, path, title, and other information. Because the managers parameter was included in the URL, the list of managers for the database was also included.

Here is the Java Agent that produced the output:

```java
import lotus.domino.*;
import java.io.*;
import java.util.*;

public class JavaAgent extends AgentBase {
    public void NotesMain() {
        PrintWriter out = getAgentOutput();
        try {
            Session session = getSession();
            AgentContext agentContext = session.getAgentContext();
```

```
        AgentParameters pt = new AgentParameters();
        pt.parseParameters(session);

        // Get the requested db name
        String filepath = pt.getString("filepath");
        if (null == filepath) {
            // If none supplied, use this database
            filepath = agentContext.getCurrentDatabase().getFilePath();
        }
        // dbname should now have a valid value

        String server = session.getServerName();

        DbDirectory  dbd = session.getDbDirectory(server);
        if (null == dbd) {
            out.println("Error - Unable to get DbDirectory");
            throw new Exception();
        }

        Database db = dbd.openDatabase(filepath);
        printDBXML(db, out, pt);    // Output the xml

    } catch(NotesException e) {
        out.println(e.id + "  " + e.text);
        e.printStackTrace(out);
    } catch(Exception e) {
        e.printStackTrace(out);
    }
    finally {
        out.flush();
        out.close();
    }
}

void printDBXML(Database db, PrintWriter out, AgentParameters pt) {
    try {
        out.println("Content-Type: text/xml");
        out.println("<?xml version='1.0'?>");
        out.println("<database filename='" + db.getFileName() +
                    "' filepath='" + db.getFilePath() +
                    "' server='" + db.getServer() + "'>");
        out.println("<title>" + db.getTitle() + "</title>");
        out.println("<created>" + db.getCreated().toString() + "</created>");
        out.println("<lastmodified>" + db.getLastModified().toString() +
                "</lastmodified>");
        if (db.isFTIndexed()) {
            out.println("<ftindexed>" + db.getLastFTIndexed().toString() +
                    "</ftindexed>");
        }
        if (null != pt.getString("managers")) {
            out.println("<managers>");
            Vector vMgr = db.getManagers();
            for (int iMgr=0; iMgr < vMgr.size(); iMgr++) {
                out.println("<manager>" + vMgr.elementAt(iMgr).toString() +
                        "</manager>");
            }
            out.println("</managers>");
        }
```

PART

III

CH

13

```
        out.println("</database>");
    } catch(NotesException e) {
        out.println(e.id + " " + e.text);
        e.printStackTrace(out);
    } catch(Exception e) {
        e.printStackTrace(out);
    }
  }
}
```

The two methods in this agent are the NotesMain method and the printDBXML method. The main method parses the parameters and accesses the database to be processed. It then calls the printDBXML method to actually output the XML. The main routine determines the database to use, opens up a database directory, and finally opens the database object. The database, the output (PrintWriter) class, and the parameters (AgentParameters) class are passed to the printDBXML method.

It isn't necessary for you to completely understand the XML syntax at this point. I've used this example to give you a little introduction to the syntax of XML. The output should be very easy and obvious to understand.

Notice that because the first line output is the MIME Content-Type, Domino does not automatically generate the Content-Type header or the boilerplate HTML. In this case, we don't need any HTML at all because the entire file is XML.

Study the code for this routine and the output. It should be very obvious how you could modify this routine to add additional XML elements or update the existing ones.

CHAPTER REVIEW

1. What are the ways in which an agent can be triggered?

2. To produce HTML output from an agent that will be sent back to the Web browser, an object of what Java class must be used? What import statement must be used to access this class? What method do you use to obtain this object and where does the method reside?

3. What is the difference between the Stream I/O classes in Java and the Reader/Writer classes in Java?

4. The current Domino IDE for Java does not have a built-in debugger. What is one programming technique you can use to debug programs in the IDE? What methods are available in the AgentBase class to assist you?

5. What are CGI environment variables? What are they used for? How can you access them within Domino?

6. What is special about CGI variables that begin with HTTP_?

7. Review the `AgentParameters` class shown in the text of this chapter. It references two routines, `get` and `put`. They are not declared within the program. Where are these routines declared and to what class do they belong? Why don't they need to be declared? (Hint: The answer is not explicitly given in the chapter. This question will test your understanding of the Java language and its class libraries.)

8. What is a Java shared library? How can you refer to code in a shared library from an agent you create?

9. Modify the agent that produces XML output about a database. Your modifications should be as follows:

   a. Add an extra `<replicaid>` element just below the `<title>` line. It should contain the Replica ID for the database.

   b. Check for a `forms` keyword and a `views` keyword similar to the existing `managers` keyword. If `forms` has been included, display a list of forms, and if `views` has been supplied, display a list of the views.

CHAPTER 14

Using the Domino Designer and Third-Party IDEs with Java

In this chapter

In this chapter, I show you how to use two Java integrated development environments (IDEs) with Domino. These two Java IDEs are representative of the types of Java development environments available and have been chosen because they are both very popular. Symantec's VisualCafé IDE is now in its fourth version and is one of the most popular Java IDEs. IBM's Visual Age for Java is in its third major release and, because it comes from IBM, it has some Domino-specific support right out of the box.

In addition to these two development environments, many others are available. After you understand the techniques that you can use with these two environments, you should be able to work with just about any Java development environment. Let's get started with Symantec's VisualCafé.

SYMANTEC VISUALCAFÉ

As I write this, Symantec has just released version 4 of its VisualCafé Java development environment. It is available in three different editions: Standard Edition, Expert Edition, and the Enterprise Suite. Each product is targeted to a different audience and has progressively more features as you move from the Standard Edition to the Enterprise Suite.

The screen shots in this book are from VisualCafé Expert Edition, version 4. If you are using a different version or different edition, your screen shots might be slightly different.

CREATING AND RUNNING A SIMPLE APPLICATION

One major advantage of using VisualCafé or IBM's Visual Age for Java (or one of the other Java IDEs) is that these development environments have extensive debugging tools. When you use Domino's built-in Java editor, no debugging capability is available other than the capability to write out messages as the program executes.

The ability to use debugging breakpoints and to inspect variables in the middle of execution can be a great aid to your development and can shorten your development cycle. As a first example, I'll show you how to build a standalone Java application. In later examples I'll show you how you can use the debugging features of VisualCafé and how to use it with Domino.

I'll assume that you have obtained a copy of VisualCafé and have installed it. Before you can create your first application, you must set the Java Virtual Machine version. The default for Symantec's VisualCafé is Version 1.2 of Java. However, at this time Domino only supports version 1.1 of Java.

Note

Writing about specific versions of Domino and third-party products is always tricky because the industry moves so fast. For example, release 5.0 and 5.0.1 of Domino support Java 1.1.6. Release 5.0.2 supports Java 1.1.8. As you read this, your release of Domino might support Java 1.2. If so, adjust your IDE for the version you want to use.

To set the version, do the following:

1. From the menu, select Tools, Environment options. You will see the Environment options dialog box.

2. Click the Virtual Machines tab.

3. In the Use VM drop-down box, select Java JDK 1.1.7a. Your version might have a different revision of 1.1, such as 1.1.8. This should be okay. Just about any 1.1.x version of Java should be compatible with Domino (see Figure 14.1).

4. You will receive a warning message that your change will not take effect until you restart VisualCafé. Click OK and then restart VisualCafé to make the change take effect.

Figure 14.1
The Environment Options box enables you to select the Java version.

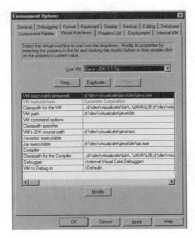

In VisualCafé, all Java programs, whether they are applets, applications, or other kinds of programs, are created in the context of a project. In Café, a project can hold Java source files and other resources associated with your project.

To create a new project:

1. From the menu select File, New Project.

2. A dialog box will appear with many different kinds of projects, including JFC Application, JFC Applet, and others. For our example, pick Empty Project, which will give us complete control. Click OK (see Figure 14.2).

Figure 14.2
The New Project box in VisualCafé.

After you have created the project, add the first source file.

3. First issue File, New File from the menus.

4. When the new file opens, type the following code into the window (see Figure 14.3):

```
public class Hello {
    public static void main(String args[]) {
        System.out.println("Hello, Java");
    }
}
```

Figure 14.3
The first step of a
Java application in
VisualCafé.

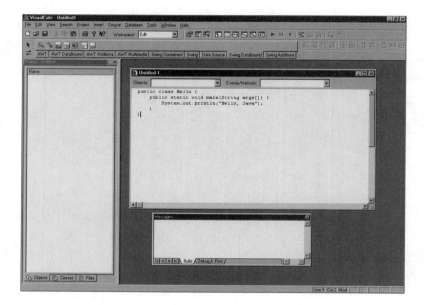

5. Now save your file by clicking File, Save As. You will see a dialog box. Enter the filename Hello and click Save.

6. You also need to save your project. Do so by using the File, Save All menu command. You will see a dialog box offering to save the project with a .vep extension. Name your project Hello.vep and click Save.

7. You are now ready to test your program. Click the Run in Debugger button on the toolbar (it looks like a triangular play button). You can also issue the menu command Project, Run in Debugger (or you can press F5). Your output should appear similar to Figure 14.4.

Figure 14.4
The Hello, Java pro-
gram output.

Notice that the output of your program appears in the Messages box. The first message says `Hello.class successfully loaded`, and the second is the output of your program. After you have reviewed the output, you can close this project.

What happened when you clicked the Run in Debugger button? First, your Java routine was compiled. If you click the Build tab in the Messages box, you'll see the messages generated when the program was compiled. The last line is key. It should say `Build Successful`. Of course, if it doesn't then you might have made a typographical error in your program and it couldn't compile.

The output of the Java compiler is a class file. Unlike some typical languages that require a linkage edit step, the Java Virtual Machine (JVM) can directly interpret Java class files. These class files are binary files, similar to object code for a particular computer. The JVM interprets these class files in a manner similar to a real hardware CPU executing machine instructions.

The Symantec Java compiler, unlike some other IDEs, also has the capability to generate Intel x86 object code that can be used to create Windows EXE files or DLL modules. If your program will be run repetitively, you might want to consider generating an executable module rather than Java class files. Executable modules have an advantage in performance, but their disadvantage is that they are not portable. Java class files can be executed on any Java platform, which makes them ideal for use as an applet within a client Web browser.

Now that you have mastered the basics of creating a project and editing a file in the Symantec IDE, let's take a look at how we could use the Symantec IDE with a more interesting example with Domino.

Debugging with VisualCafé

For this next example, you are going to create a Java application that accesses a Notes database on your client workstation. To try this example, make sure your workstation has the proper prerequisites:

- I'm assuming you're working on a Win32 (95/98/NT) Intel workstation.
- You must have Symantec VisualCafé installed on your workstation.
- You must have the Notes client installed on your workstation so that all the system code and DLLs are available.
- The directory containing the Notes/Domino DLL files is in your PATH environment variable. On Windows NT this is set using the Environment tab of the System Properties dialog box. You can access this dialog box by using the System icon in the Control Panel or by right-clicking the My Computer icon on the desktop. The DLL files are often in the `lotus/notes` directory. Make sure this directory is in your PATH. If you omit this step, you might get a runtime Java error indicating that Java cannot find the DLL named `nlsxbe`.

- You must have the `notes.jar` file in your `CLASSPATH` environment. `notes.jar` is typically found in the same directory as the Notes/Domino executables. The Symantec IDE enables you to set the `CLASSPATH` for your project within the IDE, and I'll show you how to do this shortly. Other IDEs can require you to set this environment variable outside the IDE, so be careful to check the requirements of your development environment.

Assuming that you have set up your environment, you can get started with your first Domino application:

1. Create a new project by issuing File, New Project from the menus. Again use the Empty Project.

2. You are going to access the `notes.jar` file in your project, so to allow Café to find it, you need to add the path to the `notes.jar` file to your project. Do this by issuing Project, Options. You'll see the Project Options dialog box. Click the Directories tab. Select the Input Class Files option in the Show Directories For input box. Your initial list of directories will be blank. Click the New icon (it is the leftmost of the four icons and looks like an arrow between two lines) to add a directory to the list. Add the path to the `notes.jar` file. On my system, it is located in the directory `D:\Lotus\notes`, so the full path is `D:\Lotus\notes\notes.jar` (see Figure 14.5). Note that you must include the full path for `notes.jar`, not just the directory where `notes.jar` is located. Obviously, your path might be something different.

Figure 14.5
The VisualCafé Project Options dialog box.

3. From the menu, select File, New and enter the following program into the IDE or find the source code on the CD-ROM:

```
import lotus.domino.*;

public class NotesVersion {
   public static void main(String args[]) {
```

```
    try {
        // Initialize Notes on the current thread
        NotesThread.sinitThread();
        // (Your code goes here)
        // Create a session
        Session s = NotesFactory.createSession();
        System.out.println(s.getNotesVersion()); // print version
    }
    catch (NotesException e) {
        // A Notes specific exception occurred
        System.err.println(e.id + " " + e.text);
        e.printStackTrace(System.err);
    }
    catch (Exception e) {
        e.printStackTrace(System.err); // Generic error,print trace
    }
    finally {
        // Always shut down the Notes thread
        NotesThread.stermThread();
    }
  }
}
```

4. Save the file with the name NotesVersion.java, and save the project with the name NotesVersion.vep.

5. You are now ready to test your project. First press F7, which is the build key. Make sure that you are able to build the program without error. If you get a compile-time error, check to make sure that you have properly included the notes.jar file as described in step 2 and that you don't have any typographical errors in your program. Watch out especially for problems with upper- and lowercase. Java is case sensitive, so if you type the wrong case, it might not recognize a name.

6. From the menus, select Project, Step Into. This will start the program and the debugger and will step into your program. The debugger will stop at the first executable statement in your main routine, as you see in Figure 14.6.

7. As you can see from Figure 14.6, you have access to a wealth of information in the debugger. You can configure the types of information you view and their locations onscreen. In the lower-left corner of the figure, you can see the variables and their current values. At the first statement, no variables have values yet. On the left you can see a hierarchical view of the classes and source code for the project. The call stack and message windows are also visible.

8. Three buttons that are useful within the debugger are on the toolbar on the right side. They are the step into, step over, and step out buttons. You can use these to control the execution of your program. These functions also appear as menu options of the Debug menu.

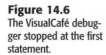

Figure 14.6
The VisualCafé debugger stopped at the first statement.

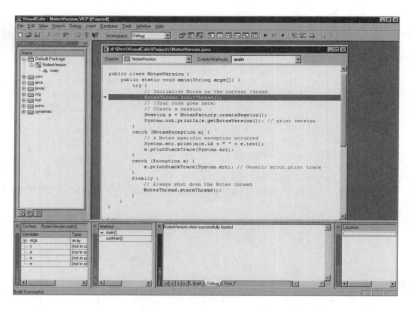

The `NotesThread.sinitThread` method initializes the Notes environment on the current thread. This is one of several ways to initialize the environment. For additional information on initializing the Notes environment, see Chapter 12, "Java Agents, Applets, and Applications." For now, click the step over button.

9. You see the red highlight that indicates the next line to execute has moved to the line that will create a session object.

   The Notes environment has been initialized. You are working with the local copies of the Notes executable libraries (that is, not with a server). Click the step over button again.

10. Now notice in the lower-left corner that the variable s contains an object. This is the session object we have just created. Finally, click the step over button again to execute the `println` statement. You'll see the Notes version number appear in the debug output window and the highlight move to the `try` statement. This is because you have reached the end of the `try` block. Click the step over button again.

11. The highlight now moves to the `finally` statement, which will terminate the `NotesThread`. Notice that I have included it in the finally clause so that even if an exception is anywhere in the main program, the thread will be terminated after the exception is handled. You must always make sure you match an `stermThread` method call for every `sinitThread` call (see Figure 14.7).

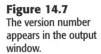

Figure 14.7
The version number appears in the output window.

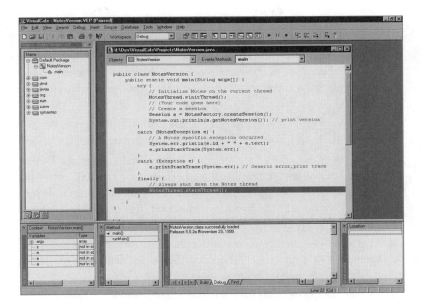

CREATING A CORBA JAVA APPLICATION

I've now shown you how you can create an application that uses the Notes DLLs that reside on your workstation. In this section, I show you how you can use VisualCafé to create a CORBA application that will communicate with a Domino server. Getting CORBA applications to work requires a bit of configuration, and you'll need administrative privileges for Domino. For these reasons, if you have a Domino server that you can use for testing other than your production server, it would be a good idea to use it for these tests.

CONFIGURING DOMINO FOR USE WITH CORBA APPLICATIONS

Let me first describe the setup and configuration you need to perform. You can use the Domino Administrator program or you can modify the Domino Directory (Public Name and Address book) directly.

- In the Notes.ini file for the server, make sure that you include both HTTP and DIIOP in the ServerTasks line. For example:
  ServerTasks=[other tasks],http,diiop
- In the server document for the server you will be using, click the Security tab. In release 5.0.2 (or later), a section is titled Java/COM Restrictions. You must enter the name of the user ID that you will be using for testing into either the restricted or unrestricted entry. Restricted Java programs will not be able to access files on the server and have other restrictions. Unrestricted Java programs can perform more operations, but potentially pose a greater security risk. In release 5.0 and 5.0.1 the section is

PART

III

CH

14

titled IIOP Restrictions rather than Java/COM Restrictions. If you will be using anonymous connections (without username or password), you must enter the name anonymous in one of the fields. If a name is in both fields, it will behave as if it were unrestricted. Finally, the values in these fields are not immediately picked up by the DIIOP task. After you make any changes to these fields, you must issue `tell diiop refresh` on the Domino server console.

■ You'll need to review the Server Access section and potentially update the Access Server, Not Access Server, Create New Databases, and Create Replica Databases fields.

■ In the Ports tab, under the Internet Ports subtab, under the IIOP sub-subtab, you find the port numbers used by IIOP for both normal and SSL use. The default is port 63148 for regular IIOP and 63149 for SSL use. If you will attempt to use CORBA through a firewall, you might need to adjust these settings or enable these port numbers to pass through your firewall. Otherwise the defaults should work fine.

■ In the Internet Protocols tab under the IIOP subtab, you can specify the number of threads. The default is 10. This is sufficient for our testing, but you might want to modify this value for production use.

■ On the client side, you must include NCSO.jar in your CLASSPATH variable. This jar file contains the client-side classes required for remote CORBA access. If you will also need local access to Notes databases, you will need to include notes.jar. In VisualCafé, the CLASSPATH is set in the Project Options dialog box. For Café, add the NCSO jar file on a line by itself above the notes.jar line. Other IDEs can use an environment variable. Here is an example:

```
set CLASSPATH=[other files];D:\Notes\Data\domino\java\ncso.jar;D:\lotus\
➥Notes\notes.jar
```

DEVELOPING A SIMPLE CORBA APPLICATION

A CORBA application is one that has both client and server components. These components can run on the same machine (say for testing), but typically reside on separate machines. The client and server components communicate using the Internet Inter-Orb Protocol (IIOP). In the case of Domino, you don't have to write the server component because Domino has a built-in task called DIIOP that will communicate with your application.

I'll show you a variation of the NotesVersion program that will print out both the server's name and the Notes version. Here is the program:

```
import lotus.domino.*;

// This is a CORBA Java application
public class NotesServerVersion {
    public static void main(String args[]) {
        try {
            // Don't need to initialize Notes on the current thread
            // (Your code goes here)
            // Create a session
```

```
            Session s = NotesFactory.createSession("<your server here>");
            System.out.println(s.getServerName()); // print server
            System.out.println(s.getNotesVersion()); // print version
        }
        catch (NotesException e) {
            // A Notes specific exception occurred
            System.err.println(e.id + " " + e.text);
            e.printStackTrace(System.err);
        }
        catch (Exception e) {
            e.printStackTrace(System.err); // Generic error,print trace
        }
        finally {
            // Don't need to shut down the Notes thread
        }
    }
}
```

To run this program with VisualCafé, you must first make sure you have configured Domino as outlined in the previous section. Create a new project called NotesServerVersion. Include the source code and make sure you update the Project Options dialog box. The Directories tab should contain the path to the NCSO.jar file. In my system the path is D:\notes\data\domino\java\ncso.jar. As you enter the code, make sure that you replace the text <your server here> with the name of your Domino server.

NCSO stands for *Notes Client Side Objects*. This jar file contains classes that determine whether you are running Notes locally or you must use CORBA and IIOP. It automatically enables the code you need to communicate with the server if you are running remotely.

Notice in the sample code that you no longer have to initialize a NotesThread object. Why? When you are running locally, your program calls the Notes executable (DLL) files on the local machine. These executable files must be initialized per thread. When you run remotely, your Java program does not need to have the Notes executable (DLL) files on your machine. When you manufacture a Session object through the NotesFactory class, the Java classes will remotely call routines located on the server. This fact is very important for applets because they will run on machines that typically do not have the Notes executable files.

To execute the code as written in the example, you must enter the name anonymous in the Java/COM Restrictions section of the Security tab of the server document. This section was renamed at Domino release 5.0.2, and in your version of Domino you might see its previous name: IIOP Restrictions. Alternatively, you can add a username (the Internet short name) and password as additional parameters following the server name. This will provide an authenticated session instead of an anonymous session. Here is the code to create a session with a specific user ID:

```
Session s = NotesFactory.createSession("<your server here>",
➥"<user name>", "<password>");
```

Of course, you should substitute your server's name, the username, and the password in the statement. If you use this format, the Java application will have authorization to access anything the given user could access.

After you have configured your Domino directory, created your VisualCafé project, and entered the source code, you are ready to compile it. Make sure that you also substitute the name of your Domino server in the source code where it says <your server here>. Compile and run the program. It should print the name of your server and the version of Domino that you are running.

If your code does not run, check the following:

- If you are getting error messages about security exceptions or that you are not authorized, recheck all the Domino directory configurations. You can also try to use an authenticated session rather than an anonymous session.

- If you are getting errors at compile time, make sure that you have included NCSO.jar in the Project Options dialog box.

- Make sure that you are running the correct version of the JDK. In VisualCafé you set the version in the Tools, Environment Options dialog box. Click the Virtual Machines tab. Make sure you are using JDK 1.1.x and not JDK 1.2.x. The CORBA routines are not supported with JDK 1.2, and this is the default for Symantec VisualCafé. Domino 5.0.2 ships with Java version 1.1.8, and previous Domino versions shipped with Java 1.1.6 or earlier.

DOMINO AGENTRUNNER

The AgentRunner tool ships with Domino to assist you in debugging agents when you use third-party IDEs such as VisualCafé. In release 4.x, AgentRunner was a separate tool that was used in conjunction with Notes and Domino. In R5, the AgentRunner tool is more integrated.

For R5, the AgentRunner tool consists of these components: the AgentRunner.nsf Domino database and a set of debugging classes that are found in notes.jar. Strictly speaking, all you need to run Java programs with AgentRunner is included with Domino R5.

In addition, however, Lotus has a product called the Lotus Domino Toolkit for Java/CORBA. I recommend that you get a copy of this toolkit. The current version of the toolkit for Domino R5 as I'm writing this is version 2.0. The toolkit contains documentation, tools, and sample programs for using Java and CORBA with Domino. You should be able to download a copy of this toolkit from the Lotus Web site at http://www.lotus.com. Click the Developer's section.

The main advantage of using AgentRunner to debug your Domino agents is that you can use the interactive debugger of your IDE. Although the Domino Designer has the capability to edit, compile, and save your agents, it does not have an interactive debugger.

Unlike Java applications, agents in Domino require a context. That is, agents are housed within a Domino database. Agents have security attributes and they are associated with various types of triggering mechanisms that imply a set of documents that should be used with the agent. For example, a user might run an agent with certain documents that have been selected from a view, or an agent might be run when new documents are added to a database. This contextual information is important both when running and debugging the agent.

Because we'll be compiling and debugging the agent outside the Domino environment, outside a Domino database, how exactly does AgentRunner work? Good question. Essentially, the AgentRunner classes and database are used to simulate the context for your agent. The context information is captured and stored in the AgentRunner.nsf database and then used during debugging of the agent. Here are the overall steps to using the AgentRunner:

1. You edit and create your Java agent code in a text editor or Java IDE such as Symantec VisualCafé. When you create your agent, you extend the DebugAgentBase class instead of the normal AgentBase class. Use your Java IDE to create class files for your agent and save them in the file system.

2. Open the database that will be used to house your agent. Create a new agent and set the type to Imported Java. Import the class files you created with your IDE.

3. Set the agent-triggering specifications and the documents on which it should act. Run the agent from within the database. When you run the agent, the DebugAgentBase class will capture the current agent context and write the information into the AgentRunner.nsf database file on your local workstation. Note that the getSession method will return null, and any use of the Session object within your agent can cause a null pointer exception. This exception can be ignored because the purpose of running the agent is to capture the context, not to actually run the agent.

4. The context information for running your agent has now been captured to the AgentRunner database. You should now open this database and examine and edit the context information for your agent. You must change the Agent Runs On field and the Search Criteria field because these fields cannot be automatically generated. The context also includes information such as the agent name, the database where the agent resides, the server, and a list of Note IDs for documents that are "unprocessed."

5. You can now go back to your Java IDE and start the debugging process for your agent. When you start execution of your agent, the DebugAgentBase class will create a simulated environment. It will actually start up the Notes environment, access the AgentRunner database, find the context information, and start your agent code. This is the clever part of the AgentRunner scheme. The DebugAgentBase class is initialized differently when run within the Notes client than when it is run from the outside. When running inside the environment, its purpose is to capture the context. When running outside, for example in the IDE, its purpose is to use the previously captured context and simulate it for your agent code.

PART

III

CH

14

6. While your agent is running in this debug environment, if it makes calls to access certain context information, the simulated information will be accessed and returned. You can step through your code, examine your variables, and find your logic errors through the interactive debugging process.

7. When you've finished your debugging, set the parent class back to AgentBase instead of DebugAgentBase, recompile your Java agent, and reimport your classes into your database. You should test that your agent behaves properly in the real database, but any problems you encounter should be minor.

CONFIGURING DOMINO AGENTRUNNER

I want to give you some pointers on configuring AgentRunner because everything must be set up properly or your agent will not run. Individually, each of these factors is very simple, but they are not well documented, so it is easy to overlook something.

Our first consideration is the AgentRunner.nsf database. You will potentially have two versions of this database, one installed on the Domino server and one on your workstation. Which is used? You will normally always be using the local (client) copy of the AgentRunner.nsf file. That's because when you run your agent manually to trigger the capture of the agent context document, the agent will run locally and you won't be specifying any server name. Thus, the context document will be stored in the local copy of AgentRunner.nsf. This is especially important to understand if you have both the client and server installed on the same machine for testing.

In addition, you should make sure that your AgentRunner.nsf file is in the root data directory for Notes. This directory is typically called d:\Notes\Data. That's because when the class files look up the database, they don't use any directory path and you can't configure the location. This is the default location when Notes is installed, but you should be aware that you cannot move the AgentRunner.nsf database to another directory.

The next consideration is that the Notes executable files must be in the path because the Java classes will be opening up Notes sessions to read AgentRunner.nsf. If you are testing on a machine that has both the Notes client and the Domino server installed on the same machine, make sure that you're using the executables for the Notes client.

The Notes executables will be looking for the Notes.ini file because it contains the data directory location. Thus, the Notes.ini file must be found in the path and you should be careful if you have multiple Notes.ini files. If you keep the Notes.ini file in the same directory as the executables, by setting the path to include the executables, the corresponding Notes.ini file will be found also.

The AgentRunner.main program takes three parameters: the agent name, the full path to the database, and the server name. It uses these parameters to look up the context in the AgentRunner.nsf database. Capitalization does not matter when you specify these names. If you omit the server name, it will default to local. You should always use a local database. Debugging a remote (server) database with your local IDE does not seem to work.

If you take a look at the `AgentContext` form in the `AgentRunner.nsf` database, you'll see several fields. Three fields of this form are important for starting your agent. The passed-in parameters are matched against the following fields in the `AgentContext` form. The agent name uses the field `CurrentAgent`. The database name parameter matches to `CurrentDatabase_FilePath`, and the server name is matched to `CurrentDatabase_Server`. Remember, when starting to debug the agent, the database name must be specified with the full path and filename.

The net result of these configuration factors is that if the `AgentRunner` classes cannot find the correct `AgentRunner.nsf` database and context documents, you will get the cryptic message, "No AgentContext document found for agent." If you get this message, here is what you should do:

- First check your path. Make sure that you have the Notes client executables in the path along with the location for `Notes.ini`. I recommend keeping `Notes.ini` in the executable directory.

- Check that you are passing command-line parameters to your main routine and that they are in the right order.

- Check the `AgentRunner.nsf` database and make sure that there really is a context document in the database. You create the context document by running the agent in your database. It will create the document in the AgentRunner database.

- Check the exact spelling of the parameters you pass to the main routine. You can find out exactly what your AgentRunner is looking for by opening up the document in the `AgentRunner.nsf` file and examining the appropriate fields.

USING DOMINO AGENTRUNNER WITH VISUALCAFÉ

Next, I'm going to show you a concrete example of constructing an agent with VisualCafé and running the debugger. You can follow along with VisualCafé by creating a new project called AccessAgent. Here is the code for AccessAgent:

```
import lotus.domino.*;
import java.io.*;

// AccessAgent: Print user name and access to current database
// For Debugging: extend DebugAgentBase instead of AgentBase
public class AccessAgent extends DebugAgentBase {
    public void NotesMain() {
        PrintWriter out = getAgentOutput(); // For output
        // The printable list of ACL level names.
        // Must be defined in this order
        String aclnames[] = {
            "No Access",  // LEVEL_NOACCESS  == 0
            "Depositor",  // LEVEL_DEPOSITOR == 1
            "Reader",     // LEVEL_READER   == 2
            "Author",     // LEVEL_AUTHOR   == 3
            "Editor",     // LEVEL_EDITOR   == 4
```

```
            "Designer",  // LEVEL_DESIGNER == 5
            "Manager"} ; // LEVEL_MANAGER == 6

    try {
        // Get the session and agent context
        Session session = getSession();
        AgentContext agentContext = session.getAgentContext();
        // Create a Name object from the UserName
        Name user = session.createName(session.getUserName());
        // Extract the common name and the organization
        String cn = user.getCommon();
        String org = user.getOrganization();
        out.println("Hello " + cn + " of the " +
                    org + " organization!");
        // Now get the database from the context
        Database db = agentContext.getCurrentDatabase();
        ACL acl = db.getACL();  // and the ACL object
        // Get the ACL entry for this user
        ACLEntry acle = acl.getEntry(user.toString());
        // Display the user's access
        out.println("You have " + aclnames[acle.getLevel()] +
            " access to the " + db.getFileName() + " database.");
        out.flush(); // Make sure output is flushed out.
    }
    catch (NotesException e) {
        out.println(e.id + " " + e.text);
        e.printStackTrace(out);
    }
    catch (Exception e) {
        e.printStackTrace(out);
    }
  }
}
```

After you have created your agent in VisualCafé, compile it and note the location of the
generated AccessAgent.class file. Now open the Domino Designer to the database that
you would like to house your agent. I have created a database called TPIDE Agents
(TPIDEAge.nsf), which stands for Third Party IDE Agents. Follow these steps to import and
run your agent with Domino:

1. After you have created or opened your Domino database for the agent, click the word
   Agents in the design pane on the left.

2. Click the New Agent action button to create your new agent.

3. Give the agent the name AccessAgent and make it a shared agent. Specify that it should
   operate on all documents in the database.

4. Set the Run drop-down box to Imported Java, and click the Import Class Files button
   at the bottom of the window.

5. Locate your class file in the local filing system in the left pane and click Add/Replace
   File(s). Your class file will appear in the right window. Note that after you have imported the files once, you must reimport them any time you make a change in your IDE. At
   that time, the button and dialog box will be identical except for the title that indicates
   that you are reimporting instead of importing for the first time (see Figure 14.8).

Figure 14.8
You must import or reimport your Java any time you make a change to the source in the Java IDE.

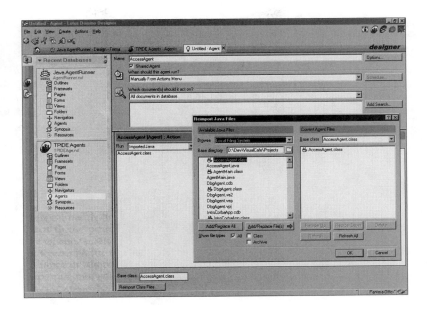

6. Click OK to close the window. Close and save your agent.

7. Now run your agent by clicking Actions, AccessAgent from the menus in your database. If you open the Java Console by issuing File, Tools, Show Java Debug Console, you will see a message confirming that the context was saved in the `AgentRunner.nsf` database. Your agent will not produce any other visible output. By running the agent, a document is created in the Java AgentRunner database (`AgentRunner.nsf`) in your data directory. This is the document that contains your agent's context information.

8. Open the `AgentRunner.nsf` database. You should see the name of your database and agent listed under the Local server. Open the document for editing by clicking the Edit Document view action button.

9. You should now see the AgentContext document for your agent. This is the document that will be used by the IDE to retrieve simulated information for your agent while it is running outside the actual Notes environment. You can add a descriptive comment for the agent if you like.

10. You must change the Agent Runs On field in the agent context document. The agent could not determine this field when you ran it, so you must set the field manually. In our case, we're going to change the field to All documents in the database (see Figure 14.9).

11. If you had search criteria, you would also set this field manually. In our case, we can leave the default blank field.

12. Save and close the agent context document. You are now ready to go back to the VisualCafé IDE and test your agent. You can close the `AgentRunner.nsf` database.

Figure 14.9
You must set the Agent Runs On and Search Criteria fields manually.

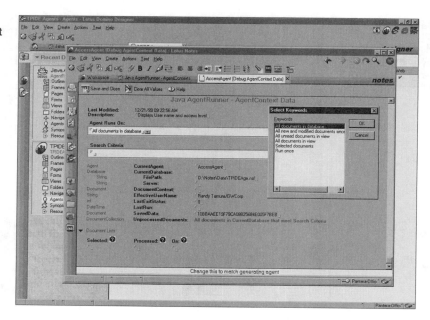

To complete our agent, we must add a main program. When the agent runs in the Notes context, it does not need a Java main program because the Notes environment initializes Java and just calls the agent's `NotesMain` routine. In the VisualCafé environment, however, we have a normal Java application so we must provide a Java main program. Here is the listing for the `AgentMain` class and main routine:

```
import lotus.domino.*;

public class AgentMain
{
    public static void main (String[] args) {
        try {
            AgentRunner.main(args);
        }
        catch (Exception e) {
            e.printStackTrace();
        }
    }
}
```

The `AgentMain` class is very simple; it just invokes the `AgentRunner.main` routine, passing it the arguments that were passed in from outside Java. Create this class and add it to your project.

Finally, we must set the project options so that it invokes our main routine with the proper runtime arguments. In VisualCafé, click the Project, Options menu items. You will see the Project Options dialog box. Click the Project tab, as you see in Figure 14.10. Make sure that your Project Type is Application and your main class is `AgentMain`. The program arguments should contain the name of the agent (`AccessAgent`) and the full path to the database.

Figure 14.10
Use Project Options to set the project type, main class, and program arguments.

Click OK to close the dialog box. Before we start our agent, let's add a breakpoint, which will cause the IDE to stop so we can examine the program as it runs. To set a breakpoint, follow these steps:

1. Open the Java source file in the VisualCafé IDE. In our example, open the `AccessAgent.java` file.

2. Click the cursor on the line where you want to stop. In our case, click on the line
   `PrintWriter out = getAgentOutput();`

3. After you have clicked the line to move the cursor, press F9. This will set the breakpoint. Alternatively, you could right-click the line and use the Set Breakpoint menu item. A red diamond will appear to the left of the line.

We're now ready to start debugging. Click the Run in Debugger arrow on the toolbar at the top of the screen. VisualCafé will compile and load your program and run it until it reaches your breakpoint. Three debugging buttons are on the toolbar to the right of the Stop button. These debugging buttons are called Step Into, Step Over, and Step Out. They enable you to selectively step into method calls, step over them, or continue until the current method returns to its caller.

For now, use the Step Over button and step until you get to the following line:

`Session session = getSession();`

You can see the results of my debugging session so far in Figure 14.11.

In the frames within your window you can see the call stack and variables. If your window does not appear exactly as in Figure 14.11, don't worry. You can control the appearance of your window with the View menu item. You can add various informational frames including variable values, call stack, messages, and so forth.

PART
III

CH
14

Figure 14.11
Use the Step Into, Step Over, and Step Out buttons to control program execution.

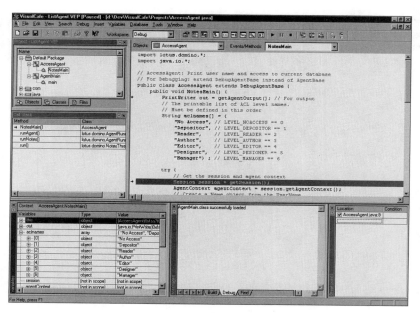

At this point you can let the agent complete by clicking the Run in Debugger (play) button. Your output should appear in the Messages window.

TESTING YOUR AGENT IN THE DATABASE

After you have finished testing your agent with AgentRunner, you can do the following to test it within the Notes environment:

1. Within the Java IDE, such as VisualCafé, change the base class of your agent from DebugAgentBase to AgentBase. Compile your program and note the location of your new class file.

2. In the Domino Designer, open the database that contains your agent. In our example it is TPIDE Agents.

3. Open the agent and click the Reimport Class Files button at the bottom of the window.

4. Click the Refresh All button. Your class name should turn red in the right pane to indicate that it was reimported. Close the dialog box by clicking OK.

5. Save and close your agent. You can now test the real agent within your Notes environment.

IBM VISUAL AGE FOR JAVA

Using IBM's Visual Age for Java (VA Java) with Domino is similar in many respects to using Symantec's VisualCafé. In both cases you are using a third-party IDE to develop and test your application or agent. When completed, you can import the final code back into Domino for final testing.

VA Java has some unique characteristics, however, because the development model is different from many other IDEs. For example, in most development environments, the fundamental unit of development is a file. For example, you edit a Java text file and create a class file. VA Java, however, does not work directly with files. It stores your programs and associated information in a database called the *repository*. The database is organized into entities such as projects, packages, and classes.

When you want to use VA Java with another system such as Domino, however, the compiled Java classes must be exported to files. These files can then be imported into the Domino environment. Let's see how the process works with VA Java.

The version of VA Java I'll be using for the examples is IBM Visual Age for Java, version 2.0, Enterprise Edition. As I'm writing this, version 3.0 has just become available, but the screens will be very similar to the illustrations I'm using from version 2.0.

PROJECTS AND PACKAGES

In VA Java, all your Java code plus any libraries that you use must be stored in the VA Java repository. The repository can store both class files and Java source code files. You might have just class files, for example, for the Sun JDK or for the Lotus Domino back-end class library. You will typically have both source files and class files for any Java programs that you create yourself.

The highest level of organization within VA Java is called the project. A project can consist of one or more packages. A package is the unit of grouping within Java. Typically when you use an import statement in your Java program, you are importing a Java package. Package names use the dot notation.

Each package is made up of one or more classes or interfaces. In Java, you can define a class to be part of a default, unnamed package. Symantec's VisualCafé can easily deal with this unnamed package, and in fact each of the examples I showed in the previous section used an unnamed package. IBM's VA Java, on the other hand, stores all your classes in the repository, and having a "free-floating" class that does not belong to an explicit package is not easily created or managed.

To create a class, you must first create both a project and a package to house your Java code. If you would like to follow along, install IBM's Visual Age for Java. You can use either version 2.0 or 3.0; the screens are very similar.

If you are using VA Java 3.0, the Domino 5.0 libraries are included with the package. With VA Java 2.0, the Domino 4.6 libraries are included, so we must load the Domino 5.0 libraries manually. Therefore, if you're using VA Java 2.0, don't install the Domino libraries shipped with the product. Use the procedure described in the next section to add the Domino 5.0 libraries to your installation.

IMPORTING THE DOMINO 5.0 LIBRARIES TO VA JAVA

Before you can develop for Domino with VA Java, you must ensure that you have imported the Lotus Domino Java libraries into the VA Java IDE. First I will explain how to add the Domino 5.0 libraries to Visual Age for Java 3.0 and then how to add them to version 2.0. With VA Java 3.0, the 5.0 libraries are shipped with the product. You can enable these libraries in VA Java 3.0 with the following steps:

1. From the menus select File, Quick Start (or press F2).
2. Select Features in the left pane, and then double-click Add Feature in the right pane.
3. Select Lotus Domino Java Library 5.0 and install the feature.

If you are using a newer version of Domino, say 5.0.x rather than 5.0, you might want to use newer Domino libraries than the ones shipped with VA Java 3.0. Lotus does add features in the "point" releases, so if you want to take advantage of these new features, you'll need to access the latest Domino Java classes. You can also use the following procedure with VA Java 2.0 to add the current Domino libraries to your VA Java environment:

1. From the menus, select File, Quick Start (or press F2).
2. In the left pane select Basic and in the right pane select Create Project. Click OK.
3. Give the project the name Lotus Domino Java Library and click Finish.
4. In the workspace, click the Projects tab and then select the newly created project. From the menus, issue Selected, Import.
5. In the Import dialog box choose Jar File. We are going to import the notes.jar and NCSO.jar files into VA Java. Click Next.
6. In the Import from jar/zip file dialog box, enter the full path to the notes.jar file. A typical path might be D:\Lotus\Notes\notes.jar. Check the class and resource check boxes. Make sure that the project is called Lotus Domino Java Library. You can leave the versioning options off. Click Finish. If you see error messages asking you to override existing files, go ahead and override them. This will ensure that the code shipped with Domino will be used rather than a potentially older version shipped with VA Java.
7. Repeat the import process by selecting the Lotus Domino Java Library project in the Projects tab and issuing Select, Import. Choose the Jar file option again and click Next.
8. This time, select the NCSO.jar file, which is located in the Notes Data directory. It has a path similar to the following: d:\Notes\Data\domino\java\NCSO.jar. You can use the Browse button to navigate to this directory and file. Click Open to store the name in the Filename field. Use the same dialog box settings as before and click Finish.
9. If you are using Domino 5.0.3 or later, repeat the import process with the xml4j.jar file. This will resolve references to the org.w3c.dom and org.sax packages.

We needed to import the two (or three) jar files because the notes.jar file contains the domino.local implementation of the Domino library, whereas the NCSO.jar file contains the

CORBA client-side implementation of the classes. The `xml4j.jar` file contains XML-related classes.

CREATING AND RUNNING A SIMPLE APPLICATION

After you have imported the Domino Java library, you can begin to develop applications using VA Java. In this section, we'll create and run our first simple application using VA Java. Before we can create our program, however, we must first create a project.

To create a new project, package, and class in VA Java, do the following:

1. Click the folder icon in the toolbar, which is called Add New or Existing Project to Workspace.

2. In the dialog box, enter the project name: `Domino Examples`. Click Finish.

3. With the Domino Examples project selected, click the C button in the toolbar. This button is used to create a class. You will see the Create Class dialog box. The project should be Domino Examples; make the package name `test`. By convention, package names are all lowercase. Class names begin with an initial capital letter.

4. The class name should be `NotesVersion` and the Superclass should be blank, as you see in Figure 14.12. Click Finish to create the class.

Figure 14.12
Use the Create Class button to create a new class.

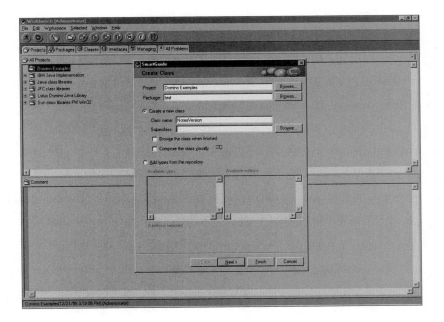

5. VA Java will create the class and the constructor for the class automatically for you. You don't need to modify the constructor.

6. Now add the `main` method. You create a method by first highlighting the `NotesVersion` class and then clicking the M (for method) button in the toolbar. Because we're creating a `main` method, select the Create a New Main Method radio button. Click Finish. An empty `main` method will be created for you.

7. Double-click the `main` method to open up an editing window. Here is the code for the main method:

```
public static void main(String args[]) {
    try {
        // Initialize Notes on the current thread
        NotesThread.sinitThread();
        // (Your code goes here)
        // Create a session
        Session s = NotesFactory.createSession();
        System.out.println(s.getNotesVersion()); // print version
    }
    catch (NotesException e) {
        // A Notes specific exception occurred
        System.err.println(e.id + " " + e.text);
        e.printStackTrace(System.err);
    }
    catch (Exception e) {
        e.printStackTrace(System.err); // Generic error,print trace
    }
    finally {
        // Always shut down the Notes thread
        NotesThread.stermThread();
    }
}
```

8. You can copy and paste the code from the CD-ROM or you can type the code from the text. When you have finished editing the text, close the window and save your file.

9. When you attempt to save the file, you'll see some compile errors as shown in Figure 14.13. Click the Save button to save the method anyway.

10. You get the compile errors because you have not entered the Java import statement for the Domino classes. Here is how to fix this problem. In the workspace, click the `NotesVersion` class. This line has a C next to the `NotesVersion` class name and has two methods indented underneath. In the source window at the bottom of the screen, add the following line above the class declaration:

```
import lotus.domino.*;
```

This line imports all the Domino classes. After adding this line, the error indicators should disappear.

11. Before you can run this program, you must set the equivalent of the `CLASSPATH` variable so that the Notes classes can be found at runtime. Do this by right-clicking the class name in the workspace. Select Properties. The Properties for NotesVersion dialog box will appear. Select the Class Path tab (see Figure 14.14).

Figure 14.13
Compile errors caused by lack of import statements.

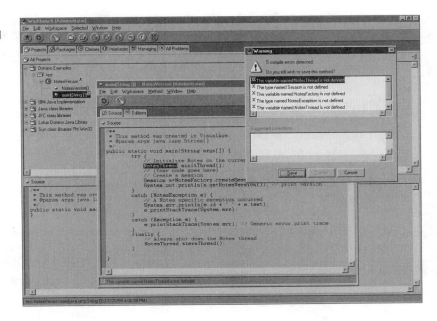

Figure 14.14
Set the execution class path in the main class's Properties box.

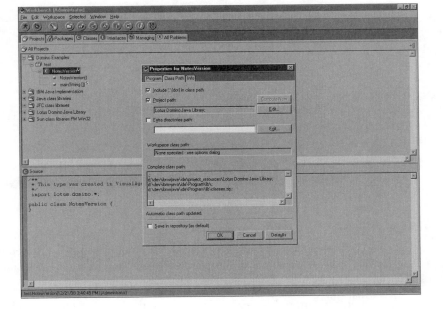

12. Enable the first two checkboxes in the dialog box. The Compute Now button is used to dynamically find all the classes that are imported from your class. VA Java will look in the repository and resolve all the references it can find. Click the Compute Now button and notice that the Lotus Domino Java Library is found and added to the list of classes at the bottom of the dialog box. Click OK to close the dialog box.

13. You are now ready to test your Java application. Click the runner icon in the toolbar. This will run your application. Figure 14.15 shows the console window where you can see the output of the program. Note that, depending on the speed of your computer, it might take a significant amount of time to execute your program because you are initializing the entire Notes system from within your application. During the initialization your system might seem to be locked up, but it is actually running. Just let the system run.

Figure 14.15
The Console window displays the program's output.

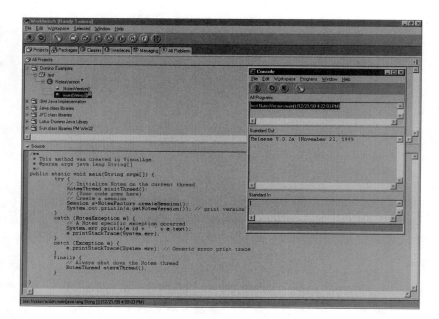

DEBUGGING WITH VA JAVA

Debugging an application with VA Java is fairly straightforward. The debugger has the capability to set breakpoints and inspect variables. You can try the debugger with the NotesVersion application we have created.

To set a breakpoint, right-click the gray area to the left of the line of code where you want the debugger to stop. Select the Add item, which will add the line to the list of breakpoints. After the breakpoint is set, you will see a circular icon to the left of the line. This is your indication that a breakpoint is on the line.

To try this with the `NotesVersion` application, follow these steps:

1. Right-click in the far left gray area of the line of the `sinitThread` method call statement. Select Add to create the breakpoint. A circular icon should appear to the left of the line.

2. Click the runner symbol in the toolbar. This will start the program. It will stop in the debugger at the breakpoint you have specified.

3. After the breakpoint is reached, the debug window appears. The debugger has a different toolbar than the workbench. In the debugging toolbar are three buttons with functions similar to those found in the Symantec IDE. The three buttons enable you to Step Into, Step Over, and Run to Return.

4. For our example, after the breakpoint has been reached, click the Step Over button. This initializes the `NotesThread`. The right side of the `createSession` assignment statement is highlighted, indicating that this is the next expression that will be evaluated, as you see in Figure 14.16.

Figure 14.16
You can step through your application with the VA Java debugger.

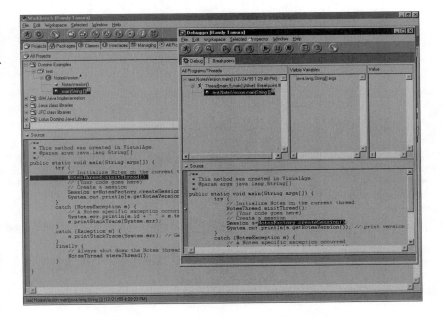

5. You can continue to step through the program or just click the Resume button (which looks like a Play button). This will resume execution of the program. Because you don't have any other breakpoints, the program will continue until the end of the program. The program's output will appear in the Console window of VA Java.

CREATING AN AGENT WITH VA JAVA

I described the general characteristics of AgentRunner in the section "Domino AgentRunner," previously in this chapter. If you haven't already read that section, do so before proceeding here. In this section I show you how to create an agent and then test it with AgentRunner.

Using AgentRunner with VA Java is similar to its use with Symantec's VisualCafé. Let me show you how to use AgentRunner to run the same agent (AccessAgent) we used with VisualCafé.

To create your Agent with VA Java, do the following:

1. Highlight the test package in the Domino Examples project we created. We'll use this same package because it is handy, but you can also create a new project or package if you would like. Normally you won't include arbitrary programs within the same package; they should be grouped by functionality.

   After you have highlighted the name test, create a new class by clicking the C button in the toolbar. The Create Class dialog box will appear.

2. In the dialog box, the project should be Domino Examples, and the package name is test. Enter AccessAgent for the Class name.

3. Click the Browse button next to the Superclass line. Scroll to the DebugAgentBase class. You can also start typing the name DebugAgentBase in the Pattern field. After you find DebugAgentBase, highlight the lotus.domino entry in the bottom pane of the Superclass dialog box (see Figure 14.17). Click OK to close the Superclass dialog box.

Figure 14.17
Your agent will extend the lotus.domino.DebugAgentBase class.

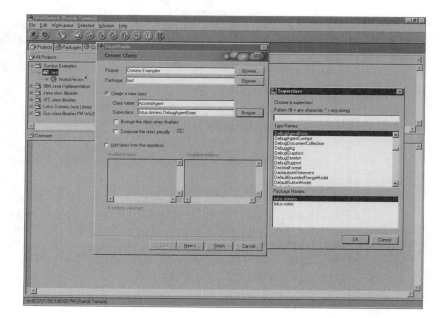

4. Click Next to see the Attributes dialog box. Click the Add Package button. We want to add the `lotus.domino` package, so start typing `lotus.domino` in the pattern field. When you find it, click the Add button. The import statement `import lotus.domino.*;` should appear in the Attributes dialog box, shown in Figure 14.18.

Figure 14.18
VA Java can automatically add import statements to your Java program.

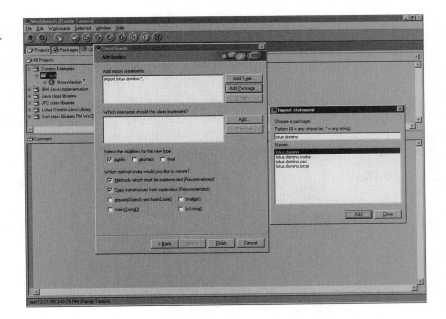

5. Find the `java.io` package in the same way. Click the Add button to add the import statement. Click the Close button to close the Import statement dialog box. Click the Finish button to create the class.

6. With the `AccessAgent` class line highlighted, click the M button in the toolbar. This will add a new method to our `AccessAgent` class. You will see the Create Method dialog box.

7. Leave the Create a New Method radio button selected. In the line that contains the method's prototype header, change it to the following:
   `void NotesMain()`

8. Note that you do not specify the public attribute (see Figure 14.19). If you try, VA Java will give you an error message. You only specify the return type of the method. You can click the Types button to change the type of object that the method will return.

9. Click the Next button. You will see the Attributes dialog box. You can specify any attributes for the method in this box. In our case, we want the method to be a public method, so leave the public access modifier enabled (see Figure 14.20).

PART

III

CH

14

Figure 14.19
Don't specify any
method modifiers on
the header line.

Figure 14.20
Specify the modifiers
in the Attributes dia-
log box.

10. We're going to capture all exceptions within the NotesMain method, so no exceptions
    will be thrown outside the class. Click the Finish button to create the class. You will see
    a dialog box telling you that Java conventions use an initial lowercase letter for method
    names. The name NotesMain is required by Notes but begins with a capital letter.
    Because we must have the capitalization, click the Proceed button. Do not click the
    Lower Case and Proceed button. Your method will be created.

11. Highlight the NotesMain method of your AccessAgent class. You can either type the
    AccessAgent class into the editor or open the Java program from the CD with Notepad
    and cut and paste the text into the VA Java IDE.

Here is the code for the NotesMain method of the AccessAgent class:

```
public void NotesMain() {
    PrintWriter out = getAgentOutput(); // For output
    // The printable list of ACL level names.
    // Must be defined in this order
    String aclnames[] = {
        "No Access", // LEVEL_NOACCESS == 0
        "Depositor", // LEVEL_DEPOSITOR == 1
        "Reader",    // LEVEL_READER == 2
```

```
            "Author",    // LEVEL_AUTHOR == 3
            "Editor",    // LEVEL_EDITOR == 4
            "Designer",  // LEVEL_DESIGNER == 5
            "Manager"} ; // LEVEL_MANAGER == 6

    try {
        // Get the session and agent context
        Session session = getSession();
        AgentContext agentContext = session.getAgentContext();
        // Create a Name object from the UserName
        Name user = session.createName(session.getUserName());
        // Extract the common name and the organization
        String cn = user.getCommon();
        String org = user.getOrganization();
        out.println("Hello " + cn + " of the " +
                    org + " organization!");
        // Now get the database from the context
        Database db = agentContext.getCurrentDatabase();
        ACL acl = db.getACL();  // and the ACL object
        // Get the ACL entry for this user
        ACLEntry acle = acl.getEntry(user.toString());
        // Display the user's access
        out.println("You have " + aclnames[acle.getLevel()] +
            " access to the " + db.getFileName() + " database.");
        out.flush(); // Make sure output is flushed out.
    }
    catch (NotesException e) {
        out.println(e.id + " " + e.text);
        e.printStackTrace(out);
    }
    catch (Exception e) {
        e.printStackTrace(out);
    }
}
```

ADDING A Main METHOD AND EXPORTING THE CLASS FILE

The different pieces of your program are stored separately in VA Java. Notice that the import statements and the class definition are found by highlighting the class line in the workbench. Each method is stored separately, and in the source code for the NotesMain method we don't see the class definition or import statements. As you make changes to your source code, remember that to add import statements you must modify the class definition, not the source code for an individual method.

Let me point out a couple of the icons that appear in your workspace. Look at the NotesVersion class that you created earlier. On the class line you can see that it contains a little runner icon. That means that the class can be run as an application. Also on the main method, an S appears. This indicates that the method is a static method. Our AccessAgent does not have a runner icon yet because it does not qualify as a full-fledged application at this point.

To be a valid application, the Java program must contain a static, public method returning void called main. It should accept one argument, which is an array of strings. Because the

NotesVersion class meets these qualifications, it has the runner icon and can be run. To enable our AccessAgent to be run, we must add our main method.

Here is how you can add the main method:

1. Highlight the AccessAgent class line. Click the M button on the toolbar to create a new method.

2. Select the Create a New main Method radio button. The string corresponding to the method's header is changed to the appropriate value. Click the Finish button to create your new main method.

3. Notice that your agent is now runnable and has the runner icon next to the class name. It won't do much, however, until you add some code to the main method. Here is the code to add to the main method:

```
public static void main (String[] args) {
    try  {
        AgentRunner.main(args);
    }
    catch (Exception e) {
        e.printStackTrace();
    }
}
```

4. You must now export the class files so that you can send them to your Domino database. Highlight the AccessAgent line and then select File, Export. Select the Directory option and click Next. This will export files to a specified file directory.

5. In the directory field, enter the name of the directory where you would like to export your class files. For the What Do You Want to Export field, select Class and deselect Java and Resource. Click Finish to export the classes.

6. In the Domino designer, open the database where you'd like to house the agent. Create a new agent by clicking the word Agents in the Design pane and then clicking the new Agent action button.

7. Give the agent the name AccessAgentVAJ to indicate that it is the VA Java version of AccessAgent. Make the agent a shared agent and it will act on all documents in the database. The Run Type should be Imported Java. Click the Import Class Files button at the bottom of the window.

8. A dialog box will open that enables you to import your class file. Navigate to the directory you specified for export. At that location, you'll notice that you have a subdirectory called test. This is because the package we created was called test. Do not open up the test package. Instead, make the export directory your base directory and leave the test directory showing in the left pane.

9. Highlight the test directory in the left pane and click the Add/Replace File(s) button. Your class should appear in the right pane. In the Base Class drop-down menu on the top right of the dialog box, make sure that test\AccessAgent.class has been specified as the base class, as you see in Figure 14.21.

Figure 14.21
With VA Java, you'll typically have package names in addition to your class name.

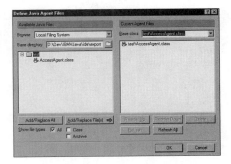

10. Click OK to close the dialog box. Save and close the agent.

11. Run the agent using the menus with Actions, AccessAgentVAJ. Running the agent will create a document in your AgentRunner database.

TESTING A VISUAL AGE FOR JAVA AGENT WITH AGENTRUNNER

Now that you have created your agent and have run it within the database context to capture the AgentContext document, you're just about ready to test your agent. You only have a little more configuration to do with the IDE and you'll be ready to roll.

In the Visual Age for Java IDE you must specify the parameters to the main program (for AgentRunner) and you must adjust the CLASSPATH so that VA Java can find not only your classes, but all the Domino classes as well. Here is what you should do in the VA Java IDE:

1. Right-click the AccessAgent class line. Select Properties. This will open the Properties for AgentAccess dialog box, see Figure 14.22. Note that if the Java class is not runnable (that is, it does not have a little runner icon and does not have a static main method), you will not be able to set the command-line arguments.

Figure 14.22
Right-click and select properties of a runnable class to set the command-line arguments.

2. The first tab is called Program and enables you to specify the command-line parameters. To run AgentRunner, you must pass in Domino's name for the agent (not necessarily the class name as you'll see), the database where the agent resides, and optionally the server. For this example, use the agent name AccessAgentVAJ. The database path for my database is d:\notes\data\tpideage.nsf. Your database name and path can be different. Omit any entry for the server name.

3. After you have entered the command-line arguments, click the Class Path tab. As with your first VA Java program, you must make sure that VA Java is able to find the Notes classes. If you don't, you'll get a runtime error indicating that it cannot find a class. Click the Compute Now button to have VA Java automatically find the appropriate classes and add them to the class path. After they have been found, click OK.

4. Click the NotesMain method line in the workspace. This will show you the source code for the method in the preview pane. Right-click in the gray area to the far left of a line where you'd like to set a breakpoint. The entire line will appear, highlighted. Select Add. A circular icon should appear indicating that a breakpoint has been set on the line.

5. Click the runner button in the toolbar. The program should run until it hits your breakpoint. Use the Step Into, Step Over, and Run to Return buttons to control execution. You can also examine variable values by clicking the variable name in the Visible Variables pane.

6. After you have finished exploring, click the Resume key to finish the program execution.

CHAPTER REVIEW

1. What is the primary advantage of using a third-party Java IDE with Domino? Domino has its own Java IDE. What can you do with the Domino IDE and what can't you do with it?

2. What is the difference between a Java application and a Java agent? What is the difference between a Java application that uses the Notes executables locally and a Java application that uses CORBA?

3. Why is it unnecessary to initialize a NotesThread when you are writing the client side of a Java CORBA application for Domino?

4. Write a Domino application in Java that prints out names using the following routines from the Session class: getCommonUserName, getServerName, getUserName, and getUserNameObject. It should also use getEffectiveUserName from the AgentContext class. What happens if you use the NotesFactory class with and without usernames? Is there a difference when you run your application using CORBA to a server as opposed to running using the local Notes executables? What can you conclude, and can you explain the differences in output with the various conditions?

5. Write a Domino Java application that opens the DbDirectory and prints the name, title, and full path for each database in the directory. Debug the application using your Java IDE.

6. What type of error would you expect to get if the CLASSPATH variable were not set properly while you debug a Domino Java application? Suppose, for example, that it did not contain any of the Domino jar files.

7. Suppose you are using AgentRunner with Domino and you get the error message "No AgentContext document found for Agent." What are some of the configuration problems that can cause this?

8. Suppose you are using IBM's Visual Age for Java to create an agent for a Domino database. You have created and tested your initial code, but you found a problem. What steps must you to take to change your code, recompile it, and retest it with VA Java? How about with Symantec's VisualCafé?

9. What do you think might be some advantages to IBM's repository approach with VA Java? Why might a repository be beneficial, especially if you are developing in a team environment?

10. What is the difference between a project and a package with VA Java? Suppose you were using another third-party tool that supplied you with jar files. How would you integrate these files into the VA Java development environment?

11. How do you specify command-line parameters in Symantec's VisualCafé? How do you do so with VA Java?

CHAPTER 15

DEVELOPING JAVA APPLETS FOR USE WITH DOMINO

In this chapter

WHAT IS A JAVA APPLET?

In previous chapters I've shown you how to create Java applications and Domino Java agents. In this chapter we'll explore Java applets. I describe applets, show how they differ from applications, and give you some examples of how to create applets that work with Domino.

The word *applet* is used to describe a program that is intended to be smaller than a complete application. Just as a booklet is a small book, an applet is a smaller version of an application. An applet also reminds me of a character named Mini-me in a certain Austin Powers movie, but that's another story entirely.

Applets normally cannot operate on their own as applications; they exist in a host environment, typically a Web browser. Applets don't require a main program; they are invoked at certain key points in the life cycle of the Web page that is their home. In addition, because applets are downloaded from a server to a Web browser, they have very strict security requirements. Applets operate in a secure environment known as the *sandbox* and cannot access the user's local file system or Web servers other than the one from which they are downloaded. Applications, on the other hand, are typically invoked from the local file system and typically do not have access restrictions.

Four methods are invoked by the browser at key points in the life cycle of an applet:

- init()—This method is invoked when the Web page containing the applet is first loaded. The init method is called just once during the life cycle of the page.

- start()—This method is called just after the init method to indicate that the applet should start processing. It is also called to start processing after a previous call to stop.

- stop()—This method is called when the browser wants the applet to stop processing. It is typically called just before destroy, but might also be called when a browser is minimized or when an applet scrolls out of view.

- destroy()—This method is called just before the page is unloaded. The applet should clean up and prepare to be terminated.

The browser also calls a fifth method, the paint method, when the applet should repaint its user interface. If your applet does not have a user interface, you do not need to provide code for the paint method. Most applets do provide some sort of user interface, however, so you will normally need to use paint.

You use slightly different techniques to write an applet as opposed to an application. Typically, in an application your main program is in charge and when you want to perform certain processing, you call methods of objects you create. An applet, however, is designed to operate in an existing browser environment. The browser is in charge, and your applet provides services when called upon.

For example, if you want to provide a user interface in an application, your application would prepare the user interface and show it to the user. The paint method, on the other hand, is called by the browser to repaint the screen. You should not normally call the paint method yourself from the init or start methods. Let's see how these concepts work in a concrete example.

BUILDING YOUR FIRST JAVA APPLET

In developing this example, I'm going to show you first a simple applet and then gradually add features to it. I'm going to use Symantec's VisualCafé for development. If you have another Java IDE, you should be able to follow along as well. In the next section, I'll show you how to create a very simple graphic application that draws a rectangle and fills it with a random color.

THE INITIAL RANDOM RECTANGLE

If you would like to follow along, start your Java IDE and create a new project called RandRect, which stands for Random Rectangle. In VisualCafé, you can start by creating an AWT applet. Give your new Java source file the name RandRect0.java with the following contents:

```java
import java.awt.*;
import java.applet.*;

public class RandRect0 extends Applet
{
    public void init()    {
        // This code is automatically generated by VisualCafé when you add
        // components to the visual environment. It instantiates and initializes
        // the components. To modify the code, only use code syntax that matches
        // what VisualCafé can generate, or VisualCafé may be unable to back
        // parse your Java file into its visual environment.
        //{{INIT_CONTROLS
            setLayout(null);
            setSize(426,266);
        //}}
    }

    // paint is automatically invoked by the browser
    public void paint(Graphics g) {
        g.setColor(getRandomColor()); // Pick a random color
        g.fillRect(0, 0, 100, 100);   // Fill fixed size rectangle w/color
    }

    // This is a static array of color values that will be randomly sampled.
    public final static Color randColors[] = {
        Color.white, Color.lightGray, Color.gray, Color.darkGray,
        Color.black, Color.red, Color.pink, Color.orange,
        Color.yellow, Color.green, Color.magenta, Color.cyan,
        Color.blue};

    // Pick a random color from the color array. Returns a Color object
    public Color getRandomColor() {
```

```
            // The array index begins at 0. Max value is length-1.
            int iColor = (int) ((randColors.length-1) * Math.random());
            return(randColors[iColor]); // Return a color value
      }
}
```

In this first example, I've defined only two of the applet methods: init and paint. Let's first look at init. All the code in this routine was automatically generated by VisualCafé. Notice that following the long explanatory text, a special comment called INIT_CONTROLS is listed. VisualCafé automatically generates the code within this section, and you don't normally need to modify the Java source code. Notice the size is specified as 426 pixels wide by 266 pixels high. This is just the size that applet had within the Java IDE. If I had changed the size with the user interface, Café would have generated different numbers.

The setLayout method is used to control the layout of controls within the applet. The Abstract Windowing Toolkit (AWT) defines several layouts, but the default will work fine for our example.

The paint method is where we actually generate output to display. The paint method is invoked automatically by the browser when the applet is first initialized and whenever part of the applet's area within the browser is covered and then exposed by the movement of other windows. Notice that the paint method takes one parameter, a Graphics context object. All output must be placed in a Graphics context. In our case, we're just going to set the color and draw a fixed-size rectangle. The rectangle's upper-left corner should be at 0,0 and the width and height will be 100 pixels each. Note that the third and fourth parameters are the width and height, not the coordinates of another corner of the rectangle.

The randColors array holds predefined Color object values. This array will be accessed by the getRandomColor method. In getRandomColor, the Math.random method is used to generate a number between 0.0 and 1.0. I then scale the value to produce an index into the color array. Because the array indices start at 0, the maximum value is one less than the number of elements in the array. Thus, when scaling the index value, you must first subtract 1.

You can now compile the applet in the Java IDE. This will generate a class file. In VisualCafé, make sure that the project options indicate that the project type is Applet. Do this by selecting Project, Options from the menu. In the dialog box, set the project type to Applet—a program that runs inside a Web Page. In the Debugger tab, select the appropriate browser for your machine.

After you have set the type to Applet, you can test it by clicking the Run in Debugger (Play) button. This will automatically generate an HTML file and run the default Web browser. Here is a sample HTML file that was automatically generated by VisualCafé:

```
<HTML>
<HEAD>
<TITLE>Autogenerated HTML</TITLE>
</HEAD>
<BODY>
<APPLET CODE="RandRect0.class" WIDTH=426 HEIGHT=266></APPLET>
</BODY>
</HTML>
```

Run the program now. Your applet should generate a random color and paint a 100 pixel by 100 pixel square. If you use another window and drag it over the applet's square, you'll find that it redraws portions of the square in different colors. This effect is caused because, as you move the other window over the square, the browser is repeatedly calling the applet's paint method. Try this for a while and notice the effects you can create.

CHANGING THE LOCATION AND SHAPE

You might have noticed that although the color was random, the size and shape of the rectangle were fixed. In fact, the size restricted the rectangle to be a square. Let's now enhance our applet to include both a random size and shape to the color. We'll also throw in some graphic text as well. To do this, we only need to modify one routine and add one routine. Here are the changes.

First, change the name of the class to RandRect1. The name of the Java file should be RandRect1.java. Do this by modifying the class line to read as follows:

```
public class RandRect1 extends Applet
```

Here is the additional method that should be added to the class:

```
public Rectangle getRandomRect() {
    Rectangle b = getBounds();         // Get applet bounds
    Dimension size = b.getSize();
    int iX = (int) ((size.width-1) * Math.random()); // Pos x
    int iY = (int) ((size.height-1) * Math.random()); // Pos y
    int iWidth = (int) ((size.width - iX) * Math.random());
    int iHeight = (int) ((size.height - iY) * Math.random());
    return(new Rectangle(iX,iY, iWidth, iHeight));
}
```

The getRandomRect method first obtains the applet bounds through the getBounds method. The getBounds method is actually a method of the Component class, which is a hierarchical parent of an applet. The Applet class hierarchy is as follows: Object→Component→Container→Panel→Applet. Any methods of any parent of the Applet class can be used within an applet.

After the bounds of the applet have been obtained, the size of the rectangle is obtained through the getSize method. A Dimension object holds just two values, a width and height. I use the width and height to generate a random upper-left corner of the rectangle. After the position has been established, I calculate the maximum width and height that should be used with the Math.random method so that the size of the random rectangle will not exceed the bounds of the applet. Finally, the rectangle is created and returned to the caller.

One more method must be modified to use our new getRandomRect method. The paint method must be updated as follows:

```
public void paint(Graphics g) {
    Rectangle r;
    g.setColor(getRandomColor());
    r = getRandomRect();
```

```
        g.fillRect(r.x, r.y, r.width, r.height);
        Font font = new Font("SanSerif", Font.BOLD, 24);
        g.setFont(font);
        g.setColor(getRandomColor());
        g.drawString("Lotus Domino", r.x, r.y);
}
```

The paint method now generates a random color and a random rectangle. The fillRect routine fills the random rectangle with the random color. After the rectangle has been created, I create a new font so that the message Lotus Domino can be painted at the same coordinate as the upper-left corner of the rectangle. Note that the coordinate of the string is specified as the lower-left corner of the text string, so that the text will appear on top of the rectangle (see Figure 15.1).

Figure 15.1
Lotus Domino atop a random rectangle.

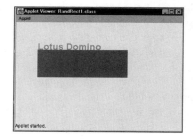

Although you cannot tell from the black-and-white picture in this book, the Lotus Domino is a lovely pink and the rectangle is magenta. If you try this and minimize and open the AppletViewer a few times, the color and shape of the rectangle changes each time. By this fact you can verify that start is being called each time the browser opens because a new color and size are selected.

ADDING ANIMATION TO THE APPLET

One advantage of applets within Web browsers is that applets can provide animation. If the browser is in charge and giving commands such as init and start to the applet, how can it do the animation? In a word: multithreading. Java has many multithreading capabilities built into the language, and you can use these features for graphical animation.

For this example, I will be using a single class, a single RandRect2 object, but two threads. Remember that RandRect2 extends Applet, so it is just a specialized version of an applet. The first thread is the one that is our normal applet thread. On this first thread, the browser will invoke the init, start, stop, destroy, and paint methods. During the init call, I will create a second thread that will be used for painting. By using multiple threads, the first thread can be responsive to requests that come from the browser, and the second can repaint on its own schedule. The only tricky part comes when it is time to shut down both threads. I'll use a shared variable to communicate between the threads. Listing 15.1 shows you the complete code for the applet.

LISTING 15.1   RandRect2 SHOWS MULTITHREADED ANIMATION IN AN APPLET

```java
import java.awt.*;
import java.applet.*;

public class RandRect2 extends Applet implements Runnable
{
    Thread paintThread;
    private volatile boolean keepRunning;

    public void init()
    {
      // This code is automatically generated by VisualCafé when you add
      // components to the visual environment. It instantiates and initializes
      // the components. To modify the code, only use code syntax that matches
      // what VisualCafé can generate, or VisualCafé may be unable to back
      // parse your Java file into its visual environment.
        //{{INIT_CONTROLS
        setLayout(null);
        setSize(426,266);
        //}}
        paintThread = new Thread(this);
        paintThread.start();
    }

    public void stop() {
        System.out.println("stop called");
        keepRunning = false;
    }

    public void destroy() {
        keepRunning = false;
    }

    public void run() {
        long sleepTime = 100;
        keepRunning = true;

        while (keepRunning) {
            try {
                Thread.sleep(sleepTime);
            }
            catch (InterruptedException e) {
                // ignore
            }
            repaint();
        } // end while
        // We've finished
        System.out.println("run thread finished.");
    }

    public void paint(Graphics g) {
        Rectangle r;
        g.setColor(getRandomColor());
        r = getRandomRect();
```

continues

LISTING 15.1   CONTINUED

```java
                g.fillRect(r.x, r.y, r.width, r.height);
                Font font = new Font("SanSerif", Font.BOLD, 24);
                g.setFont(font);
                g.setColor(getRandomColor());
                g.drawString("Lotus Domino", r.x, r.y);
        }

        public final static Color randColors[] = {
                Color.white, Color.lightGray, Color.gray, Color.darkGray,
                Color.black, Color.red, Color.pink, Color.orange,
                Color.yellow, Color.green, Color.magenta, Color.cyan,
                Color.blue};

        public Color getRandomColor() {
                int iColor = (int) ((randColors.length-1) * Math.random());
                return(randColors[iColor]);
        }

        public Rectangle getRandomRect() {
                Rectangle b = getBounds();           // Get applet bounds
                Dimension size = b.getSize();
                int iX = (int) ((size.width-1) * Math.random()); // Pos x
                int iY = (int) ((size.height-1) * Math.random()); // Pos y
                int iWidth = (int) ((size.width - iX) * Math.random());
                int iHeight = (int) ((size.height - iY) * Math.random());
                return(new Rectangle(iX,iY, iWidth, iHeight));
        }
}
```

Although the size of the applet has grown, the majority of it contains pieces that we have already seen. As a matter of fact, the paint routine, the randColors array, the getRandomColor method, and the getRandRect methods have not changed at all from our previous version.

Let's focus on the changes introduced in this version of the applet. The first change is on the class definition line. In addition to the change in name, you'll notice the clause implements Runnable. This means that the applet implements the Runnable interface, which contains the single method run.

To create a multithreaded applet, you cannot extend the Thread class because you must extend the Applet class. The Java language does not allow multiple inheritance, so you can extend only a single class. Implementing the Runnable interface, however, is the preferable alternative to multiple inheritance. I'll show you in a moment how the run method is used.

On the first line within the class, I've declared a new Thread object called the paintThread. This Thread object will repaint the applet's area of the window on a scheduled basis. The keepRunning variable is declared private and volatile. It is private so that other classes cannot access it, and it is declared volatile because this variable will be used for communication between our two threads. The paintThread will inspect the keepRunning variable and keep painting until it is false. The variable must be declared `volatile` because otherwise Java code optimization can generate code that ignores a change to the variable from another thread. Normally Java is not expecting a variable on one thread to be modified by another thread, so we must inform the compiler through the `volatile` modifier.

Two additional lines are in the `init` method:

```
paintThread = new Thread(this);
paintThread.start();
```

The first line creates a new `Thread` object, passing the applet as a parameter. The object passed to the `Thread` constructor must be `Runnable`. That is, it must implement the `Runnable` interface and have a `run` method. The `this` parameter represents the `RandRect2` applet object, so it satisfies the requirement because it implements `Runnable`.

The second line invokes the `Thread` object's `start` method. This method is not the applet's `start` method. Make sure you understand the distinction. Although the names are the same, the `Thread.start` method is used to start a new thread and has nothing to do with applets. The `Thread.start` method will create the new thread and call the `run` method for the object that was passed to the constructor. This `run` method will be invoked on the new thread (see Figure 15.2).

Figure 15.2
Two threads with the same object are used to implement animation.

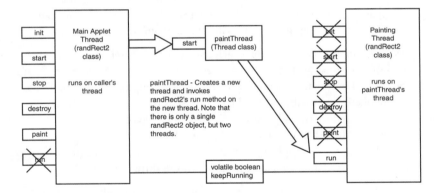

In Figure 15.2 you can see the threading model for the two threads. The main applet thread appears on the left. It runs on the caller (Browser's) thread. The `Thread` object in the middle, called `paintThread`, was created with the `new Thread` statement. Notice that, in the constructor for `paintThread`, the `this` object is passed as a parameter. The `this` object is the applet itself, which is an object of the `randRect2` class. The diagram is a bit misleading because the thread shown on the left and the thread on the right are actually using the same object! We have two threads, but only a single applet object. The thread on the left (on the browser's thread) will never call the `run` method of our object. The thread on the right, however, will only call the `run` method. Our secondary thread on the right will never use the applet's methods.

Also, because we have only a single object, the sharing of the keepRunning variable is automatic. Only one version of the variable exists, but two different threads of execution are accessing the same variable.

If all this seems a bit confusing, keep in mind that only one applet object exists. Objects are created only when we use a new keyword. Because we never created any secondary randRect2 class objects, only one is possible Two threads of execution are running through our single object, and as you can imagine, you must be careful when multiple threads are accessing the same class variables (as in the keepRunning variable).

Let's now go back and look at what happens on our main thread after the call to Thread.start. The main applet thread that called paintThread.start continues execution and then returns from the init call. At this point in the main thread, the browser would typically call the applet's start method. I have specifically left this method undefined to highlight the difference between the applet's start method and the Thread.start method. Because the applet does not have a start method, the browser has finished the applet's initialization.

On our newly created secondary thread, the Thread class invokes the run method. The run method initializes the keepRunning variable and begins a while loop. If you look at the while loop, you can see that it appears to be an endless loop. We can exit this loop only if keepRunning changes to false, but this thread never changes the value. Don't worry, though, because our main applet thread will save us from the endless loop.

Within the try block, the thread sleeps for 100 milliseconds (one tenth of a second). At the end of that time, an InterruptedException occurs, but we just ignore it and call the repaint method. The repaint method sets a flag indicating that our applet's paint method needs to be invoked. Eventually, when the system sees the flag, it will invoke the paint method (on the main applet's thread). Notice that we don't invoke the paint method ourselves on the secondary thread. We just set the flag and let the system invoke paint automatically because it will occur on the applet's main thread. Look again at Figure 15.2 to see the relationship of the run method and the paint method on the different threads.

Finally, when either the stop or destroy methods are called, the keepRunning flag is set to false. This will terminate the while loop in the run method. After the loop has finished, the run method will complete and when it returns, the secondary thread will complete.

PASSING PARAMETERS TO APPLETS WITH HTML

You can pass parameters to an applet from HTML. You do this by using the <PARAM> element. This HTML element has the following syntax:

```
<PARAM NAME="name" VALUE="value">
```

You place <PARAM> tags between the <APPLET> tags in HTML. You can have several <PARAM> tags if you need to pass several parameters to your Java applet. To access the parameters from Java, you must use the getParameter method.

To continue with our example, suppose you would like the user to be able to vary the amount of time that the applet sleeps between each repainting. The default value is one tenth of a second, but the user might want either faster or slower repainting. We will create a parameter with the name `sleepms`. Here is an example of using the applet with a 15-millisecond sleep time:

```
<APPLET CODE="RandRect3.class" WIDTH=500 HEIGHT=400>
<PARAM NAME="sleepms" VALUE="15">
</APPLET>
```

In this example, I've also changed the width and height of the applet's area. How can we code the Java applet to read the parameter? Here is some sample code that can be used during initialization to set the `sleepTime` variable. After it is set, the main body of the `run` method can use the `sleepTime` variable.

```
long sleepTime;
String strSleepMs = getParameter("sleepms");
sleepTime = 100; // Default
if (null != strSleepMs) {
    try {
        long lparm = Long.parseLong(strSleepMs);
        sleepTime = lparm;
    }
    catch (Exception e) {
        // ignore
    }
}
```

In this example, if we get a parameter, we try to parse it into a long value. If we're successful, we assign the sleep time. If not, we just ignore it and use the default.

The source code, class files, and HTML files for the examples I've shown you are on the CD-ROM. You can load them in your browser and experiment with them.

CREATING A PASSWORD BOX APPLET

For our next example, I'm going to show you how to create a password dialog box. As before, I'll start with a very simple example, and we'll enhance it with features as the project expands. Our password box will contain two input fields: one for the user ID and the second for the password. It will also contain two buttons, an OK button and a Reset button. The OK button will process the user ID and password, and the Reset button will clear the input fields.

I used the Abstract Windowing Toolkit (AWT) in our random rectangle applet. The AWT uses the class `Applet` as the base class for applets. Thus, our random rectangle classes all extended the class `Applet`. For this applet, I'm going to show you how you can use the Swing applet base class called `JApplet`. The Swing classes are included as an add-on to the Java Development Kit (JDK) 1.x. In Java 2, the Swing classes are built in. Some early versions of the Swing classes used packages with the prefix `com.sun.java.swing`. In version 1.1 of the Swing classes and later, the package prefix is `javax.swing`.

If your Java IDE uses the com.sun.java.swing prefix, try to obtain a newer version of the library so that your code will be compatible with future releases of Java. In the examples shown here, I use the javax.swing version.

In Figure 15.3 you can see the JPwdApplet0 applet in the Symantec VisualCafé form designer. You can see the component palette toolbar above the editing window. In the toolbar you can find icons for the JLabel class, JTextField class, JPasswordField class, and JButton class. These are the elements that make up the items in the dialog box.

On the left of the screen you can see the list of elements that are contained within the applet. I have used names such as lblUserID for the name of the label field for the user ID, fldUserID for the name of the user ID field, and btnOK for the name of the OK button.

Figure 15.3
The Symantec VisualCafé Form designer automatically generates Java code.

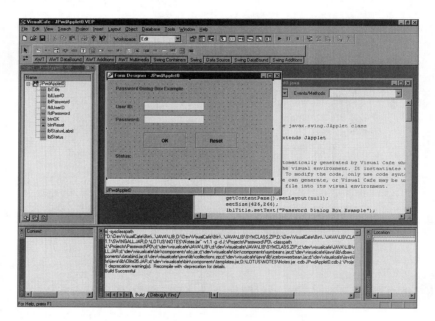

In Listing 15.2 you can see the source code for the JApplet. VisualCafé has generated the majority of this code automatically. I have modified it slightly and included a little bit of extra code. The initialization code that is found in the constructor was originally in the init method. I moved it into a constructor so that when we later modify the init method, Symantec Café will not complain. The code in the constructor creates all the user interface objects, such as the input fields, labels, and buttons. The bounds for each element are automatically generated based on the location in the form designer.

VisualCafé also creates an object of class SymAction. This is a utility class and object used to handle events that occur within the user interface.

The init method is very small. It just calls the doClear method to clear the input fields. The doPasswordChk routine does nothing at this point except display the values that the user has entered. They will be displayed in the dialog box in a status field. The two action_Performed methods are automatically invoked when the user clicks one of the two buttons.

LISTING 15.2 JPwdApplet0 SHOWS AN APPLET BASED ON THE SWING JApplet CLASS

```java
import java.awt.*;
import javax.swing.*;

/**
 * A basic extension of the javax.swing.JApplet class
 */
public class JPwdApplet0 extends JApplet
{
    public JPwdApplet0() {
        // This code is automatically generated by VisualCafé when you add
        // components to the visual environment. It instantiates and initializes
        // the components. To modify the code, only use code syntax that matches
        // what VisualCafé can generate, or VisualCafé may be unable to back
        // parse your Java file into its visual environment.
        //{{INIT_CONTROLS
        getContentPane().setLayout(null);
        setSize(426,266);
        lblTitle.setText("Password Dialog Box Example");
        getContentPane().add(lblTitle);
        lblTitle.setBounds(24,12,264,24);
        lblUserID.setText("User ID:");
        getContentPane().add(lblUserID);
        lblUserID.setBounds(24,60,72,24);
        lblPassword.setText("Password:");
        getContentPane().add(lblPassword);
        lblPassword.setBounds(24,96,72,24);
        getContentPane().add(fldUserID);
        fldUserID.setBounds(96,60,156,24);
        getContentPane().add(fldPassword);
        fldPassword.setBounds(96,96,156,24);
        btnOK.setText("OK");
        btnOK.setActionCommand("OK");
        getContentPane().add(btnOK);
        btnOK.setBounds(96,144,108,40);
        btnReset.setText("Reset");
        btnReset.setActionCommand("Reset");
        getContentPane().add(btnReset);
        btnReset.setBounds(228,144,108,40);
        lblStatusLabel.setText("Status:");
        getContentPane().add(lblStatusLabel);
        lblStatusLabel.setBounds(24,192,72,24);
        getContentPane().add(lblStatus);
        lblStatus.setBounds(24,216,384,24);
        //}}

        //{{REGISTER_LISTENERS
        SymAction lSymAction = new SymAction();
        btnReset.addActionListener(lSymAction);
```

continues

LISTING 15.2   CONTINUED

```
        btnOK.addActionListener(lSymAction);
        //}}
    }

    //{{DECLARE_CONTROLS
    javax.swing.JLabel lblTitle = new javax.swing.JLabel();
    javax.swing.JLabel lblUserID = new javax.swing.JLabel();
    javax.swing.JLabel lblPassword = new javax.swing.JLabel();
    javax.swing.JTextField fldUserID = new javax.swing.JTextField();
    javax.swing.JPasswordField fldPassword = new javax.swing.JPasswordField();
    javax.swing.JButton btnOK = new javax.swing.JButton();
    javax.swing.JButton btnReset = new javax.swing.JButton();
    javax.swing.JLabel lblStatusLabel = new javax.swing.JLabel();
    javax.swing.JLabel lblStatus = new javax.swing.JLabel();
    //}}

    public void init() {
        doClear();
    }


    class SymAction implements java.awt.event.ActionListener {
        public void actionPerformed(java.awt.event.ActionEvent event) {
            Object object = event.getSource();
            if (object == btnReset)
                btnReset_actionPerformed(event);
            else if (object == btnOK)
                btnOK_actionPerformed(event);
        }
    }

    void doPasswordChk() {
        lblStatus.setText("User:" + fldUserID.getText() +
                "; 	Password:" + fldPassword.getText());
    }

    void doClear() {
        fldUserID.setText("");
        fldPassword.setText("");
        lblStatus.setText("");
        fldUserID.requestFocus();
    }

    void btnReset_actionPerformed(java.awt.event.ActionEvent event) {
        System.out.println("clear action performed");
        doClear();
    }

    void btnOK_actionPerformed(java.awt.event.ActionEvent event) {
        System.out.println("ok action performed");
        doPasswordChk();
    }
}
```

In Figure 15.4 you can see the dialog box as displayed by the Applet viewer of VisualCafé. Notice that a user ID and password have been entered into the dialog box. The OK button was clicked, and you can see the user ID and password displayed on the status line.

Figure 15.4
The Password dialog box with the secret exposed.

This password example so far has involved a lot of code, but its processing is really not too interesting. When the OK button is clicked, the doPasswordChk method is called, and it just displays the information gathered from the user. In addition, the user interface of the applet is rather hard to use.

For example, if the user presses Enter after entering the user ID, the cursor does not move to the next field. Also, after the password has been entered, the OK button function should automatically be invoked. Finally, no accelerator keys are available to the user. We'll fix all these user interface problems in our next enhancement to this applet.

IMPROVING THE USER INTERFACE OF THE PASSWORD APPLET

The first change we'll make to the applet is to add accelerator keys for each field and for the two buttons. Java has a nice feature that enables you to specify that a label is associated with a particular input field. For example, the prompt User ID: is a label, but it is actually associated with the field called fldUserID. In Symantec's VisualCafé you can associate the label by filling in the LabelFor property in the property box (see Figure 15.5).

Also notice in the source code window that I have added a line of code to highlight the mnemonic in the label. Here is the code:

```
lblUserID.setDisplayedMnemonic((int)'U');
```

This line of code will underline the U of the User ID label. In addition, because we have called the setLabelFor method, this mnemonic will be associated with the input field. Unfortunately, you cannot set the mnemonic for a label in the property box; you must manually add the Java code in the source code window. Use similar code to highlight the P of the Password label.

Figure 15.5
Use the
setDisplayed-
Mnemonic method of
JLabel to underline a
mnemonic in a label.

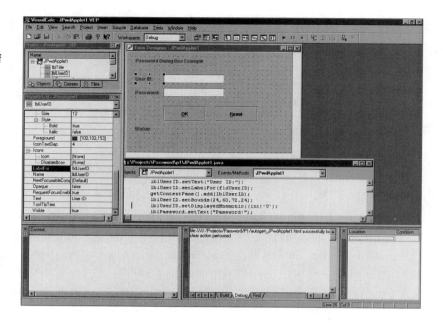

Mnemonics for buttons can be set directly with the property box. In the property box for the OK button, enter the character O as the value for the Mnemonic property. Use R for the Reset button. Here is the code generated by VisualCafé for the Reset button:

```
btnReset.setMnemonic((int)'R');
```

This takes care of the four accelerators for the fields and buttons. Now let's turn our attention to the Enter key. When the user types text into a text field and presses the Enter key, an action event will occur for the field. We can use VisualCafé structure to handle the event for us; we just need to code the event handlers for the two fields. Here are the methods to handle the actionPerformed events for the two input fields:

```
void fldUserID_actionPerformed(java.awt.event.ActionEvent event) {
    fldPassword.requestFocus();
}

void fldPassword_actionPerformed(java.awt.event.ActionEvent event) {
    if (fldUserID.getText().equals("")) {
        fldUserID.requestFocus();
    } else {
        // process password.
        doPasswordChk();
    }
}
```

In the event handler for the User ID field, I set the focus to the password field, so as soon as the user types the user ID and presses Enter, the focus will move to the password field. When the user finishes the password field and presses Enter, the event handler will check to make sure that the User ID field has a value and then will process the password with `doPasswordChk`. If the User ID field is blank, the focus is set back to the User ID field. The rest of the applet is substantially the same.

You can obtain the source code and class files for the `JPwdApplet1` applet from the CD-ROM. You can experiment with it and verify that you can use the accelerator keys as well as the Enter key. The visual display is the same as our `JPwdApplet0` except that the accelerator keys are underlined in our dialog box. Next I'll show you how to use this applet from within a Domino database.

INCORPORATING A JAVA APPLET IN A DOMINO DATABASE

You can use Java applets in Domino pages, forms, and documents. To use the applets in the Domino designer, follow these steps:

1. Create the page or form that you want to use to house your applet. Open this page or form for editing.

2. After adding any static text or graphics to the page or form, move the cursor to the location where you would like to place your applet. You can use tables to position your applet on the page.

3. From the menus, select Create, Java Applet. You will see the Create Java Applet dialog box (see Figure 15.6).

Figure 15.6
The Create Java Applet dialog box enables you to import an applet.

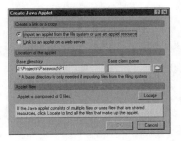

4. Normally you will be importing your applet from the file system or an applet resource, so leave the first radio button selected. If you have only a single class file, you can import it by typing the directory and class name. You can also locate it by using the folder icon. Our sample password applet has two class files, a main applet class file and an auxiliary class file generated by VisualCafé. Because we have two class files, click the Locate button.

5. After you click the Locate button, you will see the Locate Java Applet Files dialog box, shown in Figure 15.7. In the left pane you can navigate through the file system or shared applet file resources. After you have found the class files required for your applet, highlight them in the left pane and click the Add/Replace File(s) button underneath the left pane. If you want to add all the files from the left pane, you can click Add/Replace All.

Figure 15.7
The Locate Java Applet Files dialog box enables you to select Java files to be imported.

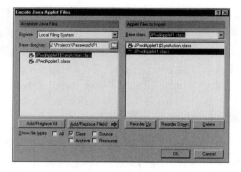

6. After the class files have been specified in the right pane, select the base class file from the drop-down box at the top of the right pane.

7. To finish your selection, click the OK button. Make sure your base class file is properly specified in the Create Java Applet dialog box and click OK to close it.

8. On your page or form, you can resize the applet by dragging the lower-right corner of the gray box that represents the applet's display area (see Figure 15.8).

Figure 15.8
You can size the applet by dragging the lower-right corner of the gray box.

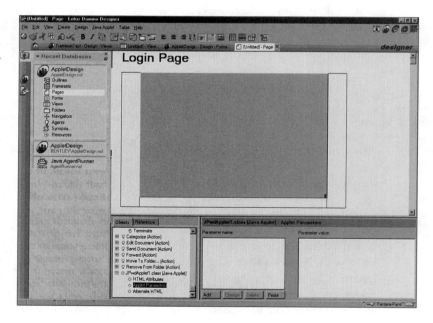

In Figure 15.8, I have used a table to locate my applet on the page. I have left the borders of the table visible for the illustration, but you will normally want to turn off all the borders of the table. Figure 15.9 shows you the result of clicking the IE Preview button in the upper-right corner of the display.

Figure 15.9
Internet Explorer displays the Password applet and Domino page.

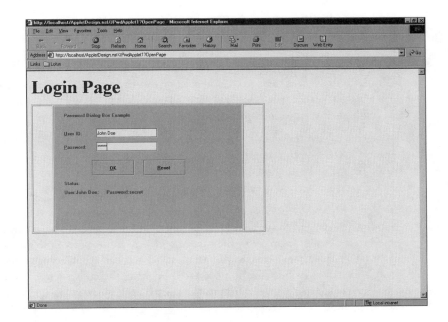

Because I did not specify a font for the text Login Page, it uses the default browser font. The table borders are also displayed around the applet.

CREATING A CORBA DOMINO JAVA APPLET

I've now shown you how to create a regular Java applet, how to add animation and multi-threading, and how to store it within a Domino database. Our next task will be to add CORBA features to our password applet. By using CORBA, the applet can communicate with the Domino server and use the Java Domino Objects classes. You could test all the previous examples on a standalone workstation, but this section will require the use of a Domino server. You can, however, use a single computer with both the server and client running on the same machine.

To compile the password applet for CORBA, we must make a few changes. Surprisingly, very few changes are required.

First, you must include a new `import` statement:

```
import lotus.domino.*;
```

Second, you must change the name of the applet base class. Instead of `JApplet`, you must use `JAppletBase`.

Note   You can also use `AppletBase` instead of `JAppletBase`. `AppletBase` is used if you are using the AWT style user interface instead of the Swing classes.

I've also changed the name of the applet to `JPwdApplet2`:

```
public class JPwdApplet2 extends JAppletBase
```

Third, you must change the name of the init method. `JAppletBase` overrides the four applet methods: init, start, stop, and destroy. In their place, `JAppletBase` provides these four: `notesAppletInit`, `notesAppletStart`, `notesAppletStop`, and `notesAppletDestroy`. Use these methods instead of the normal methods.

`JAppletBase` needs to override the normal applet methods because it must initialize the Domino CORBA environment. This essentially means that it must create a Domino Session. In the init method defined in `JAppletBase`, a Session is created, and then your `notesAppletInit` method is called.

Note that with Symantec VisualCafé, if your control initialization was done in the init method instead of the constructor, the compiler will complain if you rename the init method to `notesAppletInit`. On the other hand, you cannot leave the initialization method called init because `JAppletBase` will not allow it. You can resolve this quandary because VisualCafé enables its initialization code within either the constructor or the init method. By moving the control initialization to the constructor, you can rename your init method to `notesAppletInit`.

That's all we need to do in our Java code to make our applet a CORBA applet. These changes affect only a few lines of code. Of course, just changing it to a CORBA applet will not be very interesting if we cannot take advantage of the power of CORBA. So, here is a redefinition of our `doPasswordChk` routine. This routine will now do an actual authentication with the Domino server using the supplied user ID and password. If the authentication passes, the name will be displayed; otherwise, an error message will be issued.

```
void doPasswordChk() {
    try {
        Session session = getSession(fldUserID.getText(),
                                     fldPassword.getText());
        lblStatus.setText("Authenticated:" + session.getUserName());
    }
    catch (NotesException e) {
        lblStatus.setText("Notes error:" + e.id + " " + e.text);
        System.out.println(e.id + " " + e.text);
        e.printStackTrace();
    }
    catch (Exception e) {
        lblStatus.setText("Unidentified error during authentication");
        e.printStackTrace();
    }
}
```

In this example, I retrieve the user ID and password, use them for the getSession (of `JAppletBase`), and then display the message. If the user is not authenticated, a NotesException will be thrown. The catch statement will display the error and message.

Listing 15.3 shows the complete authentication applet.

LISTING 15.3   JPwdApplet2 PERFORMS ACTUAL DOMINO AUTHENTICATION

```java
import java.awt.*;
import javax.swing.*;
import lotus.domino.*;

/**
 * A basic extension of the javax.swing.JApplet class
 */
public class JPwdApplet2 extends JAppletBase
{
    public JPwdApplet2()
    {
        // This code is automatically generated by VisualCafé when you add
        // components to the visual environment. It instantiates and initializes
        // the components. To modify the code, only use code syntax that matches
        // what VisualCafé can generate, or VisualCafé may be unable to back
        // parse your Java file into its visual environment.
        //{{INIT_CONTROLS
        getContentPane().setLayout(null);
        setSize(426,266);
        lblTitle.setText("Password Dialog Box Example");
        getContentPane().add(lblTitle);
        lblTitle.setBounds(24,12,264,24);
        lblUserID.setText("User ID:");
        lblUserID.setLabelFor(fldUserID);
        getContentPane().add(lblUserID);
        lblUserID.setBounds(24,60,84,24);
        lblUserID.setDisplayedMnemonic((int)'U');
        lblPassword.setText("Password:");
        lblPassword.setLabelFor(fldPassword);
        getContentPane().add(lblPassword);
        lblPassword.setBounds(24,96,84,24);
        lblPassword.setDisplayedMnemonic((int)'P');
        getContentPane().add(fldUserID);
        fldUserID.setBounds(108,60,156,24);
        getContentPane().add(fldPassword);
        fldPassword.setBounds(108,96,156,24);
        btnOK.setText("OK");
        btnOK.setActionCommand("OK");
        btnOK.setMnemonic((int)'O');
        getContentPane().add(btnOK);
        btnOK.setBounds(96,144,108,40);
        btnReset.setText("Reset");
        btnReset.setActionCommand("Reset");
        btnReset.setMnemonic((int)'R');
        getContentPane().add(btnReset);
        btnReset.setBounds(228,144,108,40);
        lblStatusLabel.setText("Status:");
        getContentPane().add(lblStatusLabel);
        lblStatusLabel.setBounds(24,192,72,24);
```

continues

LISTING 15.3 CONTINUED

```java
        getContentPane().add(lblStatus);
        lblStatus.setBounds(24,216,384,24);
        //}}

        //{{REGISTER_LISTENERS
        SymAction lSymAction = new SymAction();
        fldUserID.addActionListener(lSymAction);
        fldPassword.addActionListener(lSymAction);
        btnReset.addActionListener(lSymAction);
        btnOK.addActionListener(lSymAction);
        //}}
    }

    //{{DECLARE_CONTROLS
    javax.swing.JLabel lblTitle = new javax.swing.JLabel();
    javax.swing.JLabel lblUserID = new javax.swing.JLabel();
    javax.swing.JLabel lblPassword = new javax.swing.JLabel();
    javax.swing.JTextField fldUserID = new javax.swing.JTextField();
    javax.swing.JPasswordField fldPassword = new javax.swing.JPasswordField();
    javax.swing.JButton btnOK = new javax.swing.JButton();
    javax.swing.JButton btnReset = new javax.swing.JButton();
    javax.swing.JLabel lblStatusLabel = new javax.swing.JLabel();
    javax.swing.JLabel lblStatus = new javax.swing.JLabel();
    //}}

    public void notesAppletInit() {
    // public void init() {
        doClear();
    }


    class SymAction implements java.awt.event.ActionListener
    {
        public void actionPerformed(java.awt.event.ActionEvent event)
        {
            Object object = event.getSource();
            if (object == fldUserID)
                fldUserID_actionPerformed(event);
            else if (object == fldPassword)
                fldPassword_actionPerformed(event);
            else if (object == btnReset)
                btnReset_actionPerformed(event);
            else if (object == btnOK)
                btnOK_actionPerformed(event);
        }
    }

    void fldUserID_actionPerformed(java.awt.event.ActionEvent event)
    {
```

```
        fldPassword.requestFocus();
    }

    void fldPassword_actionPerformed(java.awt.event.ActionEvent event)
    {
        if (fldUserID.getText().equals("")) {
            fldUserID.requestFocus();
        }else {
            // process password.
            doPasswordChk();
        }

    }

    void doPasswordChk() {
        try {
            Session session = getSession(fldUserID.getText(),
                                    fldPassword.getText());
            lblStatus.setText("Authenticated:" + session.getUserName());
        }
        catch (NotesException e) {
            lblStatus.setText("Notes error:" + e.id + " " + e.text);
            System.out.println(e.id + " " + e.text);
            e.printStackTrace();
        }
        catch (Exception e) {
            lblStatus.setText("Unidentified error during authentication");
            e.printStackTrace();
        }
    }

    void doClear() {
        fldUserID.setText("");
        fldPassword.setText("");
        lblStatus.setText("");
        fldUserID.requestFocus();
    }

    void btnReset_actionPerformed(java.awt.event.ActionEvent event)
    {
        System.out.println("clear action performed");
        doClear();
    }

    void btnOK_actionPerformed(java.awt.event.ActionEvent event)
    {
        System.out.println("ok action performed");
        doPasswordChk();
    }
}
```

Although it seems like a lot of code for the applet is here, VisualCafé automatically generates most of it. The actual code for obtaining the user ID and password and authenticating with Domino is fairly small.

To execute this applet from Domino, we must design a page or form to house the applet. You can follow the procedure from the previous section to create your page or form. I've created a page called JPwdApplet2 in the Domino designer. On my page I just have a page title and the applet itself.

For CORBA applets, you must also perform one extra step, which is very important. You must enable the Applet uses Notes CORBA classes option in the Java Applet properties box, as you see in Figure 15.10.

Figure 15.10
You must enable
CORBA classes for
CORBA applets.

You can open the Java Applet properties box by right-clicking the applet in the designer and then selecting Java Applet Properties. If you forget to enable this property, you might receive a Class Not Found exception.

You say you want to see this program? Okay, we're just about ready. Here are some final items to check before we run the program:

- Your database should reside on a Domino server. The server and Web browser can be on the same machine, but you cannot test it simply using a standalone Notes client.
- Make sure that the user you are going to authenticate is enabled to use CORBA. You do this in the Domino Directory (Public Name and Address book). Open the server document and select the Security tab. The section will be titled Java/COM Restrictions for Domino 5.0.2 or Greater and will be titled IIOP Restrictions for 5.0 or 5.0.1. For this test, add the user ID name to the Run restricted field. If you add the name Anonymous, you will be able to authenticate with a blank user ID. If your server is running while you make a change to this field, make sure that you issue tell diiop refresh on the server console after you have saved your changes.

You can now test the applet from a browser through the following URL:

```
http://<your server>/AppletDesign.nsf/JPwdApplet2?OpenPage
```

Of course, if your database or page is named something else, substitute your values. Figure 15.11 shows the output of this applet in the browser.

Congratulations! You've now created an applet that has been authenticated with a Domino server. You can use this applet as the basis of a more interesting application that uses the Java Domino Objects classes.

Figure 15.11
You can use a CORBA
applet to authenticate
with Domino.

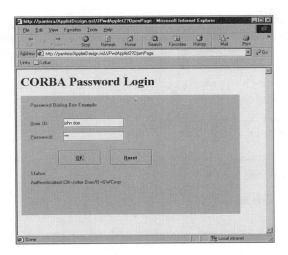

WHAT IS A JAVABEAN?

JavaBeans is the name for the application programming interface (API) for the component model for Java. A JavaBean is a component that conforms to certain standardized calling conventions. By using these conventions, graphical user interface (GUI) builders can use beans and connect them without the need for user programming.

For example, an event such as pushing a button can trigger an event in another bean. The connection of the events can be shown graphically in the user interface for the IDE. If you are familiar with Microsoft Visual Basic controls, JavaBeans is a similar component model for Java.

JavaBeans have the following characteristics:

- Introspection—This capability enables tools such as Java IDEs to inspect the properties, methods, and events of a class. The tool can then present options, property lists, and graphical operations to the user.

- Properties—Although the Java language does not have built-in capabilities to support object properties, the JavaBeans specification defines accessor functions to get and set property values. Thus with beans, a Java IDE can display a property attribute box with property names and values.

- Events—The event-handling mechanism for JavaBeans enables a JavaBean designer to create code that will fire events and can listen for events from other components. Because of the standardized naming conventions, the connections between components can be arranged by a user without the need to have access to the source code for the beans.

- Persistence—JavaBeans implement the `Serializable` interface. This enables the bean to store its state information to an external medium such as a file. Persistence enables a JavaBean user to change property values and have the new values retained.

To turn your class variables into properties, make sure that you use the following naming convention for access routines:

```
public void set<Property>(<PropType> p);
<PropType> get<Property();
```

Examples:

```
public void setName(String name);
String getName();
public void setLevel(int level);
int getLevel();
```

You can create JavaBeans with both Symantec VisualCafé and IBM's Visual Age for Java. After you have created a bean, you can modify the source code. After all, a bean is just a Java program that follows the naming conventions.

CHAPTER REVIEW

1. Name some differences between Java applets and applications. Is it possible for a Java program to be both an applet and application at the same time? If so, how?

2. Why is it desirable to have applet animation running on a separate thread from the main applet thread?

3. Explain the difference between `Applet.start()` and `Thread.start()`.

4. Modify the Password applet so that the user ID and password are passed in to the applet as <PARAM> elements from HTML. You should use two <PARAM> tags: <PARAM NAME="userid" VALUE="*value*"> and <PARAM NAME="password" VALUE="*value*">.

5. Write an applet that simulates a banner advertisement. The applet's display area should change color every five seconds. Each time it changes color, it should display a different message. The messages should be passed to the applet in <PARAM> tags. They should be of the format <PARAM NAME="msg0" VALUE="*messagetext0*">, <PARAM NAME="msg1" VALUE="*messagetext1*">, . . . <PARAM NAME="*msgnnn*" VALUE="*messagetextnnn*">.

6. How can you associate a mnemonic hotkey with an input field? (Assume that the field has a label associated with it.)

7. What can you do with a Domino CORBA applet that you cannot do with a regular applet? To use CORBA features in your applet, what option must you enable and where is it located? If you get a security exception while trying to execute a Domino CORBA applet, where would you look to see if the authorizations are set properly?

8. Which four applet methods are not used when you design a Domino CORBA applet? Which four methods do you use instead? You can use two different alternatives for a base class for your Domino CORBA applet. What are they?

9. Write a Domino CORBA applet that requests a user ID and password and, if authorized, produces a list of the names of all the databases in the DbDirectory. If you know the AWT or Swing, you can output the list in the applet's browser area. If you don't, you can just output the list to the Java Debug console.

10. Write a Domino CORBA applet that requests a user ID and password and, if authorized, produces a list of all the names in the ACL for the NAMES.NSF database. Enhance the program by allowing the user to pass in the database name by using a <PARAM> element in HTML.

PART IV

THE DOMINO OBJECTS FOR JAVA

CHAPTER 16

THE NotesThread, NotesFactory, NotesException, Session, AND Agent CLASSES

In this chapter

This chapter and the following five chapters of Part IV, "The Domino Objects for Java," are designed to provide you with a reference for all the Java classes for the Domino Objects. Each class, method, and property is defined along with a short explanation or example. In this chapter, I cover the important classes that provide the initialization, termination, and other environment for the rest of the Domino Java classes.

THE NotesThread CLASS

Class Definition

```
public class NotesThread extends java.lang.Thread
```

Methods

- initThread
- runNotes
- sinitThread
- stermThread
- termThread

The NotesThread class is used any time you need to access the Domino Objects locally. This class provides the environment for the Notes/Domino executables. You must initialize a NotesThread object for each Java thread of execution that will access the Domino object classes. You cannot use this class for objects that make remote calls.

The following are three ways to initialize the local Notes environment:

1. Create a class that extends NotesThread, and then implement the runNotes method. Your runNotes method will be invoked after the Notes environment has been established. The runNotes method will be invoked on a new thread when you invoke the Thread.start method of your class.

2. Use static initialization and termination through the sinitThread and stermThread methods. This causes the currently running thread to be initialized for calls to the Notes environment. An extra thread is not created. You must call stermThread once for each call to sinitThread. Failure to call the stermThread method is a serious error.

3. Create your own class that implements the Java Runnable interface. Pass an object of this class to one of the NotesThread constructors. The run method of your class will be invoked after the Notes environment has been initialized.

If you use AgentBase or AppletBase for your Domino agents and applets, you do not need to initialize NotesThread because these classes handle it for you. For additional examples and information, see Chapter 12, "Java Agents, Applets, and Applications."

COMMON METHODS TO CREATE

Objects of this class are created directly with Java. There are three ways to initialize the Notes environment. In the first, you extend `NotesThread` with your own class; in the second you don't actually create a `NotesThread` object, you just use static methods. The third way is to create a `NotesThread` object and pass your own `Runnable` class to it.

```
public NotesThread()

public NotesThread(Runnable runClass)

public NotesThread(String name)

public NotesThread(Runnable runClass, String name)

public NotesThread(ThreadGroup group, String name)

public NotesThread(ThreadGroup group, Runnable runClass, String name)

public NotesThread(ThreadGroup group, Runnable runClass)
```

You can use one of several constructors to create an object of the `NotesThread` class.

METHODS

```
public void initThread()
```

Notes calls this routine before the invocation of `runNotes`. If you want to perform initialization before `runNotes`, you can override this routine. If you do override it, however, be sure to call `super.initThread` (the base class routine) within your code. There is very little Lotus documentation on this method, so it borders on the undocumented. This routine is not declared `final` by Lotus, so as long as you make a call to the base class routine, you shouldn't have any problems. Normally you shouldn't need to use this method, but it is available for you just in case you have special requirements.

```
public void runNotes() throws NotesException
```

The `NotesThread` class invokes the `runNotes` method when the Notes environment has been initialized. Note that this method is called only when your class extends the `NotesThread` class. If you use static initialization or the `Runnable` interface, the `runNotes` method will not be invoked. Here is an example that extends `NotesThread`:

```
public class ExampleNT0 extends NotesThread {
    public static void main(String args[]) {
        try {
          ExampleClass0 myThread;
          myThread = new ExampleNT0(); //Initialize the current thread for Notes
          myThread.start();   // Start it. runNotes will be called.
          myThread.join();    // Wait for it.
        }
```

```
      catch(Exception e) {
         e.printStackTrace();
      }
   }
   public void runNotes() {
      // Your code goes here.
      System.out.println("Hello, world");
   }
}
```

```
public void sinitThread()
```

```
public void stermThread()
```

The sinitThread and stermThread methods are used to initialize the current thread for the Notes environment. Here is a sample Domino application:

```
public class ExampleNT1 {
   public static void main(String args[]) {
      try {
         // Initialize the current thread for Notes
         NotesThread.sinitThread();
         // Your code goes here.
      }
      catch(Exception e) {
         e.printStackTrace();
      }
      finally {
         // Use finally clause to clean up
         NotesThread.stermThread();
      }
   }
}
```

You must use NotesThread methods to initialize any thread that will be making calls to Domino Objects. If you are creating all the threads in your application, these locations are fairly obvious. In the special case of applets, however, be careful because the browser might call some of your methods on threads that it owns, not your own threads. This can occur, for example, with event handling routines that respond to dynamic events such as button pushes. In these cases, if you will be making calls to the Domino Objects, you must use the static initialization and termination routines (sinitThread and stermThread) on these threads.

```
public void termThread()
```

Notes calls this routine after the invocation of runNotes. If you want to perform termination and free resources after the call to runNotes, you can override this routine. If you do override it, however, be sure to call super.termThread (the base class routine) within your code. There is very little Lotus documentation on this method, so it borders on the undocumented. This routine is not declared final by Lotus, so as long as you make a call to the base class routine, you shouldn't have any problems. A final method means that you cannot override the method in a subclass. Normally you shouldn't need to use this method, but it is available just in case you have special requirements.

THE NotesFactory CLASS

Class Definition

`public class NotesFactory`

Property

■ getIOR

Methods

■ createSession

■ createSessionWithIOR

The NotesFactory class is used to manufacture either a local or remote Session object. A local Session object will access databases on the current machine; a remote Session object will use CORBA and IIOP to access a Domino server remotely. If you will be using local classes, be sure to initialize the Notes environment before creating the session. Remote sessions do not need to initialize the local Notes environment.

COMMON METHODS TO CREATE

All the methods of NotesFactory are static methods. This means that there is no need to actually create a NotesFactory object. You can call all the methods directly, and you typically do not create a NotesFactory object.

PROPERTIES

`static public String getIOR(String server) throws Exception;`

IOR stands for Interoperable Object Reference. This is a CORBA term that describes a string that can be used to identify an object on a remote machine. On the Domino server, a file stores the IOR. This file is called `dioop_ior.txt` and is located in the `domino\html` subdirectory of the Domino data directory. Normally as a programmer you do not need to worry about the contents of this file, but if you're curious, it contains an extremely long hexadecimal string. The contents of the string are standardized by CORBA.

The server parameter specifies the server to be used. The server should be running the Domino diiop task. The server name should be specified as the network name of the Domino server.

Normally you will not need to use the IOR, but if you have the IOR, you can create a session by using the createSessionWithIOR method of the NotesFactory class. The IOR is used only in the process of creating CORBA/IIOP Domino sessions.

PART
IV
CH
16

METHODS

```
static public Session createSession() throws NotesException

static public Session createSession(String server) throws NotesException

static public Session createSession(String server, String userID, String
password) throws NotesException

static public Session createSession(String server, String args[], String
userID, String password) throws NotesException

static public Session createSession(java.applet.Applet app, String userID,
String password) throws NotesException

static public Session createSession(java.applet.Applet app, org.omg.CORBA.ORB
orb, String userID, String password) throws NotesException
```

The createSession method without arguments creates a local Session object. The three createSession methods with a server parameter create remote sessions. Internally, the remote createSession methods first obtain the IOR and then call createSessionWithIOR to actually create the Session. For local sessions, make sure you have initialized the Notes runtime environment using the NotesThread class.

The two methods that use a java.applet.Applet parameter are to be used with Java applets. These two calls enable you to control the creation of a session. Normally, you should make your applet extend AppletBase (or JAppletBase), and then you will not need to call the createSession method directly. AppletBase will take care of this for you. See Chapter 15, "Developing Java Applets for Use with Domino."

Remote session security is controlled in the Domino directory (Name and Address book) for the Domino server. Make sure you enable Java remote access for the specified user (or Anonymous).

To enable SSL security, use the method with the args parameter and specify -ORBEnableSSLSecurity for args[0].

The following is an example of creating a local session:

```
public class ExampleNF0 extends NotesThread {
    public static void main(String args[]) {
        try {
            ExampleClass0 myThread;
            myThread = new ExampleNF0(); //Initialize the current thread for Notes
            myThread.start();   // Start it. runNotes will be called.
            myThread.join();    // Wait for it.
        }
        catch(Exception e) {
        }
    }
```

```
    public void runNotes() {
        try {
            Session session = NotesFactory.createSession();
            System.out.println("Notes Version: " + session.getNotesVersion());
        }
        catch(Exception e) {
            e.printStackTrace();
        }
    }
}
```

```
static public Session createSessionWithIOR(String IOR) throws NotesException
```

```
static public Session createSessionWithIOR (String IOR, String userID,
String password) throws NotesException
```

```
static public Session createSessionWithIOR (String IOR, String args[],
String userID, String password) throws NotesException
```

The createSessionWithIOR methods all create remote sessions. The thread creating these remote sessions should not use NotesThread. Remote session security is controlled in the Domino directory (Name and Address book) for the Domino server. Make sure you enable Java remote access for the specified user (or Anonymous).

To enable SSL security, use the method with the args parameter and specify -ORBEnableSSLSecurity for args[0].

THE NotesException CLASS

Class Definition

```
public class NotesException extends org.omg.CORBA.UserException
```

Properties

- id
- text

When the Domino Objects detect an error and throw an exception they use the NotesException class. Two public properties can be accessed from the exception object: id and text. These store the integer code and error message, respectively, for the exception.

COMMON METHODS TO CREATE

Objects of this class are not typically created by a user program but are created by the Domino Objects directly with Java.

PROPERTIES

```
public int id;
```

The id variable can be accessed directly from a NotesException object because it is public. It contains the NotesException error code. Notes error codes begin with 4001. The user-readable error codes are defined in the NotesError class, where you will find named error codes such as NOTES_ERR_DETACH_FAILED.

```
public String text;
```

The text variable contains the error message that corresponds to the error code.

Here is an example of the use of the NotesException class:

```
try {
    // Your code here
}
catch (NotesException e) {
    System.out.println("Notes error " + e.id + ". " + e.text);
    e.printStackTrace();
}
```

THE Base CLASS INTERFACE

Class Definition

```
public interface Base
```

Method

■ recycle

Most of the Domino object classes extend the Base class interface. The Base class interface contains only two versions of the recycle method. By extending this class, future extensions and enhancements that apply to all Domino object classes can be easily implemented. This class is not created directly; it serves only as a base for other classes.

The Base class also facilitates the implementation of the CORBA support. Through multiple implementations of the Base class interface, both local and CORBA versions of the Domino object classes can be implemented without requiring any changes to the users of the classes.

METHODS

```
public abstract void recycle() throws NotesException
```

```
public abstract void recycle(java.util.Vector objVect) throws NotesException
```

The recycle method enables you to reclaim space for Java Domino Objects that have been freed but not yet reclaimed by the Java garbage collector. The version of recycle without a parameter recycles the current object. Make sure you have finished using the current object before calling `recycle`. You can also call `recycle` on the `Session` object with a `Vector` of objects. If you have several objects that you want to recycle simultaneously, this is a more efficient way to recycle them.

THE Session CLASS

Class Definition

```
public class Session extends lotus.domino.Base
```

Properties

- getAddressBooks
- getAgentContext
- getCommonUserName
- getInternational
- getNotesVersion
- getPlatform
- getServerName
- getURL
- getURLDatabase
- getUserName
- getUserNameList
- getUserNameObject
- isConvertMime/setConvertMime
- isOnServer

Methods

- createDateRange
- createDateTime
- createLog
- createName
- createNewsletter
- createRegistration
- createRichTextParagraphStyle
- createRichTextStyle
- evaluate
- freeTimeSearch

- getDatabase
- getDbDirectory
- getEnvironmentString
- getEnvironmentValue
- resolve
- setEnvironmentVar

The Session class represents a Notes session. Each session is typically associated with a user ID, although it is also possible to have anonymous sessions. The Session class is at the top of the hierarchy of Domino Objects that are typically used to access Domino databases. You can obtain a session by creating it with a NotesFactory method call or by obtaining it using getSession in either an agent or an applet.

When you have obtained a Session object, you can obtain other subsidiary objects such as a DbDirectory, or you can access attributes of the current session such as the user or server information.

COMMON METHODS TO CREATE

AgentBase.getSession, NotesFactory.createSession, NotesFactory.createSessionWithIOR, AppletBase.getSession, AppletBase.openSession

PROPERTIES

`public java.util.Vector getAddressBooks() throws NotesException`

The getAddressBooks property routine returns a Vector of Database objects, one per address book. Both Domino directories and personal address books are returned. To access one of the returned Database objects, you must first open the database.

`public AgentContext getAgentContext() throws NotesException`

The getAgentContext property routine returns the AgentContext object. The result of this method is defined only if it is running within a Domino agent. If it is used outside a Domino agent, the routine will throw an exception. See Chapter 13, "Creating Java Agents with the Domino Designer IDE," for more information on agents.

`public String getCommonUserName() throws NotesException`

The getCommonUserName property routine returns the common username for the user ID that created the Session.

`public International getInternational() throws NotesException`

The International object contains information about the current regional settings. These settings include information such as the date format, time zone, currency formatting, and so on. The getInternational property routine accesses the International object.

```
public String getNotesVersion() throws NotesException
```

This property returns the release number and date for the version of Notes/Domino that is running the session.

```
public String getPlatform() throws NotesException
```

The `getPlatform` property returns a `String` description of the operating system platform that is currently running the session.

```
public String getServerName() throws NotesException
```

The `getServerName` property routine returns a string containing the fully distinguished name for the server that is currently running the session. If the session is not running on a server, this property returns `null`.

```
public String getURL() throws NotesException
```

The `getURL` property routine returns a string containing the URL associated with the current session. It returns an empty string if called locally.

```
public Database getURLDatabase() throws NotesException
```

The `getURLDatabase` property routine returns a `Database` object that represents the default Web Navigator database. The returned database is also opened.

```
public String getUserName() throws NotesException
```

The `getUserName` property returns a string containing the fully distinguished name for the user or server that created the session.

```
public java.util.Vector getUserNameList() throws NotesException
```

The `getUserNameList` property routine returns a `Vector` of `Name` objects. The first `Name` object is the regular username object and the second, if it exists, is the `Name` object for the alternative name. As of release 5.0.2, this class is not implemented for CORBA/IIOP sessions and will throw a "not implemented" exception.

```
public Name getUserNameObject() throws NotesException
```

This property returns a `Name` object that represents the user or server that created the session.

```
public boolean isConvertMime() throws NotesException
```

```
public void setConvertMime(boolean) throws NotesException
```

These properties specify whether `TYPE_MIME_PART` items should be converted to rich text when instantiated. Set the value to `false` to prevent conversion and to `true` to force conversion to rich text before instantiating the items. For example, you must set the value before issuing a `Document.getFirstItem("Body")`. The default value is `true`. See Chapter 20, "Working with the Item and Formatting Classes," for more details.

```
public boolean isOnServer() throws NotesException
```

The `isOnServer` property routine returns `true` if the session is on a Domino server and `false` otherwise.

METHODS

```
public DateRange createDateRange() throws NotesException
```

```
public DateRange createDateRange(DateTime startTime, DateTime endTime) throws
NotesException
```

```
public DateRange createDateRange(java.util.Date startTime, java.util.Date
endTime) throws NotesException
```

The `createDateRange` method creates a new `DateRange` object. You can create a `DateRange` object with an explicit start and end date/time, or you can change either the start or end time after it has been created.

```
public DateTime createDateTime(String date) throws NotesException
```

```
public DateTime createDateTime(java.util.Date date) throws NotesException
```

The `createDateTime` method creates a new `DateTime` object. You can pass either a string representation of the date and time or a Java `Date` object representation.

```
public Log createLog(String name) throws NotesException
```

The `createLog` method creates a new `Log` object with the specified name. The method returns the newly created `Log` object.

```
public Name createName(String name) throws NotesException
```

```
public Name createName(String name, String language) throws NotesException
```

The `createName` method creates a `Name` object from the specified name string. This string should be specified as an abbreviated or fully distinguished name. If not, it will be interpreted as a flat name. You can also specify a language to be associated with the name. For primary names the language should be `null`, but for alternative names you can specify the language.

```
public Newsletter createNewsletter(DocumentCollection doccoll) throws
NotesException
```

The createNewsletter method takes the specified DocumentCollection and creates a
Newsletter object. When you have created the Newsletter object, you can format it with the
Newsletter methods.

```
public Registration createRegistration() throws NotesException
```

The createRegistration method creates a new Registration object. The Registration
object can then be used for administration functions such as cross-certifying, registering new
users and servers, and many other administrative functions. See Chapter 21, "The
Registration, Newsletter, and Log Classes," for more information.

```
public RichTextParagraphStyle createRichTextParagraphStyle() throws
NotesException
```

The createRichTextParagraphStyle method creates a new RichTextParagraphStyle object.
This object can then be used to format a rich text paragraph.

```
public RichTextStyle createRichTextStyle() throws NotesException
```

The createRichTextStyle method is used to create a RichTextStyle object. A
RichTextStyle object can be used to set attributes for rich text such as the font, color, and
other attributes.

```
public java.util.Vector evaluate(String formula) throws NotesException
```

```
public java.util.Vector evaluate(String formula, Document doc) throws
NotesException
```

The evaluate method is used to evaluate a Domino @formula. You specify the @formula as
the parameter and the result is returned in the Vector. If there is only a scalar result, it is
returned as the first element of the Vector. If the @formula references a field, you must
specify a document in the second parameter. The @formula cannot be used to change values
of the document; only back-end methods can be used to modify the document. For example,
you can use the replaceItemValue method of the Document class. Remember to include
java.util.* to obtain the Vector class.

The following is an example:

```
try {
    Session session = getSession();
    AgentContext agentContext = session.getAgentContext();
    DocumentCollection dc = agentContext.getUnprocessedDocuments();
    Document doc = dc.getFirstDocument();
    Double dResult;
    // Formulas return a numeric 1.0 for true, 0.0 for false
    Double dTrue = new Double(1.0);
    Vector v;
```

```
      // Go through each document in the unprocessed set.
      while (null != doc) {
         // See if the name is Homer
         v =session.evaluate("@Contains(Name; \"Homer\")", doc);
         dResult = (Double) v.elementAt(0); // Extract result
         if (dResult.equals(dTrue)) {System.out.println("Name is Homer");}
         else  {System.out.println("Name is not Homer");}
         agentContext.updateProcessedDoc(doc); // Mark as completed
         doc = dc.getNextDocument();  // Now get the next document
      }
      System.out.println("Done.");
} catch(NotesException e) {
   System.out.println(e.id + ". " + e.text);
   e.printStackTrace();
} catch(Exception e) {
   e.printStackTrace();
}
```

public java.util.Vector freeTimeSearch(DateRange timeWindow, int duration, Object names, boolean firstfit) throws NotesException

The freeTimeSearch method searches for available free time slots within a specified time window. The duration is specified in minutes, and you include either a String or a Vector of Strings that represents the list of names to include in the search. The firstfit parameter should be true to return just the first free time slot and false to return all free time slots within the time window.

public Database getDatabase(String server, String db) throws NotesException

public Database getDatabase(String server, String db, boolean createonfail) throws NotesException

The getDatabase method creates a Database object for the database and server you specify. You should use an empty string for the local environment or IIOP calls and the canonical or abbreviated name of the server otherwise. If you specify createonfail as true, the Database object will be created even if the database is not found. If createonfail is not specified or is false, the method will return null.

public DbDirectory getDbDirectory(String server) throws NotesException

The getDbDirectory method returns a DbDirectory object for the server you specify. If the server is null, the current session's environment is used. You must use null for a CORBA remote session.

public String getEnvironmentString(String varname) throws NotesException

public String getEnvironmentString(String varname, boolean systemvar) throws NotesException

The getEnvironmentString method returns the string value of the specified environment variable. The varname parameter represents the name of the variable. If systemvar is false or omitted, varname is prepended by a $ before obtaining the value. If systemvar is true, then varname is not modified and is used directly to obtain the value. The value is obtained from the notes.ini file for the session. This method can be used for string or numeric values.

```
public Object getEnvironmentValue(String varname) throws NotesException
```

```
public Object getEnvironmentValue(String varname, boolean systemvar) throws
NotesException
```

The getEnvironmentValue method returns the value of the specified numeric environment variable. The varname parameter represents the name of the numeric variable. If systemvar is false or omitted then varname is prepended by a $ before obtaining the value. If systemvar is true then varname is not modified and is used directly to obtain the value. The value is obtained from the notes.ini file for the session. Do not use this method for string values; use getEnvironmentString instead.

```
public Base resolve(String url) throws NotesException
```

The resolve method returns the Domino object referenced by a URL. This method will return a Database, View, Form, Document, or Agent object, and you must supply a cast to the appropriate type.

The following is an example:

```
Database db = (Database) session.resolve("http://server/name.nsf");
```

```
public void setEnvironmentVar(String varname, Object value) throws
NotesException
```

```
public void setEnvironmentVar(String varname, Object value, boolean system-
var) throws NotesException
```

The setEnvironmentVar method sets the value of the specified environment variable. The varname parameter represents the name of the variable. The value Object can be either a string or numeric value. If systemvar is false or omitted, varname is prepended by a $ before setting the value. If systemvar is true then varname is not modified and is used directly as the name. The value is stored in the notes.ini file for the session. If the environment variable already exists, its value is changed to the new value, and if it doesn't exist it will be created.

THE AgentContext CLASS

Class Definition

```
public class AgentContext extends Base
```

Properties

- getCurrentAgent
- getCurrentDatabase
- getEffectiveUserName
- getLastExitStatus
- getLastRun
- getSavedData
- getUnprocessedDocuments

Methods

- unprocessedFTSearch
- unprocessedSearch
- updateProcessedDoc

The AgentContext object contains information about the current context for a Domino agent. Agents run within a database and are associated with an effective user ID. The AgentContext object contains this information as well as other contextual information. You can obtain the AgentContext object from the Session object by using the getAgentContext method. For more information about the AgentContext, see Chapter 13.

COMMON METHODS TO CREATE

Session.getAgentContext

PROPERTIES

public Agent getCurrentAgent() throws NotesException

The getCurrentAgent property routine returns an Agent object that represents the currently running agent.

public Database getCurrentDatabase() throws NotesException

The getCurrentDatabase property routine returns a Database object for the database that contains the current agent.

public Document getDocumentContext() throws NotesException

The document context is a special document called the *in-memory document*. An external program can create it before the agent is run to provide communication from the program to the agent. If the agent is activated in a view in the user interface, the in-memory document is the currently highlighted document of the view. If the agent is triggered from the Web, the in-memory document contains information about the CGI variables and HTTP headers.

Use the `getDocumentContext` property routine to retrieve the document context object. The following example of an agent can be invoked by a URL and will display all the CGI variables and HTTP headers back to the user.

Example:

```
import lotus.domino.*;
import java.io.*;
import java.util.*;

public class JavaAgent extends AgentBase {
   public void NotesMain() {
      try {
         Session session = getSession();
         AgentContext agentContext = session.getAgentContext();

         PrintWriter out = getAgentOutput();
         Document doc = agentContext.getDocumentContext();
         out.println("<H1>CGI Variables Received by Agent</H1>");
         out.println("<TABLE><TR><TH>Name</TH><TH>Value</TH></TR>");
         // Get the CGI variables
         Vector items = doc.getItems();
         for (int iItem = 0; iItem < items.size(); iItem++) {
            Item item = (Item)items.elementAt(iItem);
            out.println("<TR><TD>" + item.getName() + "</TD><TD>" +
                   item.getText() + "</TD></TR>");
         }
         out.println("</TABLE>");
      } catch(Exception e) {
         e.printStackTrace();
      }
   }
}
```

public String getEffectiveUserName() throws NotesException

The *effective* username is the username used for security and identification purposes for the agent. When running on a workstation, `Session.getUserName` and `AgentContext.getEffectiveUserName` are the same. When running on a server, the `EffectiveUserName` is the name of the agent's owner (the person who previously modified and saved the agent), whereas the `UserName` is the name of the server itself.

public int getLastExitStatus() throws NotesException

Use the `getLastExitStatus` property routine to obtain the status code returned by the Agent Manager the last time the current agent ran.

public DateTime getLastRun() throws NotesException

The `getLastRun` property routine returns the date and time the current agent was last executed. If the agent has never been run before, this property returns `null`.

```
public Document getSavedData() throws NotesException
```

A special document called the SavedData document is associated with each agent. Each time an agent is modified and saved, the SavedData document is deleted and re-created. The agent can use this document to store information between invocations. The SavedData document is replicated with the database, but is only visible to the agent and cannot be seen in regular views. If the agent is deleted, the SavedData document is also deleted.

```
public DocumentCollection getUnprocessedDocuments() throws NotesException
```

When you create an agent, you can specify the set of documents on which you want the agent to run. The choices include all documents in the database, new and modified documents, all documents in a view, and so on. The documents you select are collectively called the *unprocessed* documents. When you get the getUnprocessedDocuments property, you receive the collection of documents that the agent should process. After a document has been processed, you must call the updateProcessedDoc method to mark the document as processed and to make sure that the document is processed only once. If you do not call the updateProcessedDoc method, the document will appear again in the UnprocessedDocuments collection on a subsequent run of the agent. You can mark all documents in a document collection as processed by using the updateAll method of the DocumentCollection class. The processed mark is kept for each agent and each document. That is, marking a document as processed in one agent will not affect the mark for another agent. See the description of the Session.evaluate routine for an example of the use of getUnprocessedDocuments.

METHODS

```
public DocumentCollection unprocessedFTSearch(String query, int maxdocs)
throws NotesException
```

```
public DocumentCollection unprocessedFTSearch(String query, int maxdocs, int
sortoptions, int otheroptions) throws NotesException
```

The unprocessedFTSearch method searches the unprocessed document collection for documents that match the full-text query string. The maxdocs parameter contains a count of the maximum number of documents to return. A zero value for maxdocs means that all matching documents should be returned. The sortoptions parameter can contain Database.FT_SCORES, Database.FT_DATE_DES, or Database.FT_DATE_ASC. These values indicate that the documents should be sorted by relevance, descending date order, or ascending date order, respectively. The otheroptions parameter can contain Database.FT_FUZZY for a fuzzy search or Database.FT_STEMS to use stem words as the basis for the search.

Example:

```
DocumentCollection dc = agentContext.unprocessedFTSearch("scouting", 0,
         ➥Database.FT_SCORES, Database.FT_STEMS);
```

```
public DocumentCollection unprocessedSearch(String formula, DateTime
afterDate, int maxdocs) throws NotesException
```

The unprocessedSearch method returns a collection of documents from the unprocessed set of documents that match a specified formula and have been modified or created after a specified date. The maxdocs parameter specifies the maximum number of documents to return or zero, which means return all matching documents.

Example:

```
DateTime dt = session.createDateTime("12/31/1999");
DocumentCollection dc = agentContext.unprocessedSearch("@Contains(Body;
➥\"Y2K\")", dt, 0);
```

The example will search for all unprocessed documents with a Body field that contains the string Y2K that have been created or modified after December 31, 1999.

```
public void updateProcessedDoc(Document doc) throws NotesException
```

The updateProcessedDoc method marks a particular document as having been processed. You use this method to prevent an agent from retrieving the same document more than one time during subsequent runs of the same agent. Marking a document as processed in one agent does not affect other agents, and a particular document can be processed by one agent but unprocessed by another.

Example:

```
DocumentCollection dc = agentContext.getUnprocessedDocuments();
Document doc = dc.getFirstDocument();
while (doc != null) {
    // Your code here
    agentContext.updateProcessedDoc(doc);
    doc = dc.getNextDocument();
}
```

The example will loop through the collection of unprocessed documents; after each document has been processed, it will mark it and then get the next document.

THE AgentBase CLASS

Class Definition

```
public class AgentBase extends lotus.domino.NotesThread
```

Properties

- getAgentOutput
- getSession
- isRestricted
- setDebug

Methods

- dbgMsg
- NotesMain

The AgentBase class serves as a base class for Java agents that you develop. It extends NotesThread and initializes the Notes environment for your agent. You must provide a NotesMain method as part of your class that will be called by the runtime system. For more information, see Chapter 13.

COMMON METHODS TO CREATE

This class is not usually created in a standalone manner. When you create a Java agent, your source code should extend the AgentBase class.

PROPERTIES

```
public java.io.PrintWriter getAgentOutput()
```

The getAgentOutput property routine returns a java.io.PrintWriter object that can be used to output information from the agent. When the agent is running on a workstation, the output will be directed to the Java debug console. The output is buffered, so be sure to flush the PrintWriter so that all the output will appear. You flush the PrintWriter with the flush method of the PrintWriter class.

In a server environment, the output will appear on the Domino console. If the agent is invoked from the Web, the PrintWriter represents the HTML stream that will be sent back to the Web client.

Note that if you want to abbreviate java.io.PrintWriter to just PrintWriter, you must use import java.io.*.

```
public Session getSession()
```

The getSession property routine will return the Session that has been initialized for the agent. After you have obtained the Session object, you can traverse the object hierarchy to obtain further information.

```
public boolean isRestricted()
```

The isRestricted property routine returns true if the agent is a restricted agent. The agent is restricted if the owner (the last person who modified and saved the agent) is listed in the Restricted Users section in the Security tab for the Domino server. Restricted agents are prevented from performing certain operations on the server.

```
public void setDebug(boolean msgon)
```

The `setDebug` property routine is a write-only property that controls whether the `dbgMsg` method will produce output. If it is `false` then any calls to `dbgMsg` will not produce output. If it is `true` then calls to `dbgMsg` will produce output on the Java debug console.

METHODS

```
public void dbgMsg(String message)
```

```
public void dbgMsg(String message, java.io.PrintStream ps)
```

```
public void dbgMsg(String message, java.io.PrintWriter pw)
```

The `dbgMsg` method will output the message string to the Java debug console or to the provided `PrintStream` or `PrintWriter`. The output is controlled by the `Debug` property. The `Debug` property can be turned on or off using the `setDebug` method.

```
public void NotesMain()
```

The `NotesMain` method is called by the `AgentBase` class after the Notes environment has been initialized. This is the method that you should provide when writing a Java agent. If you use the Domino Designer IDE, a skeleton version of the `NotesMain` method is provided. Typically, the `NotesMain` method will obtain the `Session` and `AgentContext` objects, but accessing these objects is not required.

THE DebugAgentBase CLASS

The `DebugAgentBase` class is provided as a mechanism to debug Domino agents outside the Domino environment. While you are debugging, you use the `DebugAgentBase` class rather than the normal `AgentBase` class. `DebugAgentBase` is used in two modes. The first mode is used within the Domino environment, captures context information, and stores it in the `AgentRunner` database. A Java program outside the Domino environment uses the second mode. In this mode, the `DebugAgentBase` reads the previously saved context information and simulates the context for the Java program, allowing it to be debugged in a Java IDE outside the Domino environment. For more details and examples, see Chapter 13, "Creating Java Agents with the Domino Designer IDE," and Chapter 14, "Using the Domino Designer and Third-Party IDEs with Java."

COMMON METHODS TO CREATE

This class is not usually created in a standalone manner. When you create a Java agent, your source code should extend the `DebugAgentBase` class. During the debugging phase of your development, you can substitute `DebugAgentBase` for `AgentBase` and test your application outside the Domino environment.

SuperClass

AgentBase

Properties and Methods

The properties and methods of the DebugAgentBase class are the same as those provided by the AgentBase class.

The Agent Class

Class Definition

public class Agent extends Base

Properties

- getComment
- getCommonOwner
- getLastRun
- getName
- getOwner
- getParameterDocID
- getParent
- getQuery
- getServerName/setServerName
- getTarget
- getTrigger
- getURL
- isEnabled/setEnabled
- isNotesAgent
- isPublic
- isWebAgent

Methods

- remove
- run
- runOnServer
- save

The Agent class is used to obtain information about an agent stored in a Domino database. You can find out the name, owner, time and date the agent was last run, and many other attributes of the agent. In addition, you can run the agent locally or request that the agent be run on the Domino server that contains the database.

COMMON METHODS TO CREATE

`Database.getAgent, Database.getAgents, AgentContext.getCurrentAgent`

PROPERTIES

`public String getComment() throws NotesException`

The `getComment` property routine returns the comment that describes the agent. The designer of the agent specifies this comment.

`public String getCommonOwner() throws NotesException`

Use the `getCommonOwner` property routine to access the common name of the person who last modified and saved the agent. The owner's authorization level is used when access to database items is checked against the database ACL.

`public DateTime getLastRun() throws NotesException`

The `getLastRun` property routine returns the date and time the current agent was last executed. If the agent has never been run before, this property returns `null`.

`public String getName() throws NotesException`

Use the `getName` property routine to access the name of the current agent. The agent's name is specified by the designer at the time the agent is created or modified.

`public String getOwner() throws NotesException`

The `getOwner` property routine accesses the fully distinguished name of the owner of the agent. The owner is the person who last modified and saved the agent.

`public String getParameterDocID() throws NotesException`

The `getParameterDocID` property access routine is used to implement parameter passing from an agent running on a Notes client to an agent running on a Domino server. The client agent creates a document and saves it in the database. It then obtains the document ID, also known as the Note ID, for the document and passes it to the `runOnServer` method. The `getParameterDocID` method can be used within the server agent to retrieve the document ID and subsequently obtain the document and the stored parameters. The `getParameterDocID` routine is available on Domino release 5.0.2 and later.

`public Database getParent() throws NotesException`

Use the `getParent` property to obtain a `Database` object for the database that contains the agent.

```
public String getQuery() throws NotesException
```

The getQuery property routine returns the query string that was specified in the Domino designer using the Add Search button.

```
public String getServerName() throws NotesException
```

```
public void setServerName(String serverName) throws NotesException
```

You can retrieve or set the name of the server on which the current agent should run. If the string is null or the empty string, it indicates the local workstation. If the agent is scheduled, the getServerName property routine will return the name of the server on which the agent is scheduled. If the agent is not scheduled, the routine will return the name of the parent database's server.

You can set the serverName to an asterisk (*) to indicate that the agent can run on any server.

```
public int getTarget() throws NotesException
```

The getTarget property access routine returns a code that indicates the set of documents on which the current agent acts. Here are the valid values:

- Agent.TARGET_ALL_DOCS
- Agent.TARGET_ALL_DOCS_IN_VIEW
- Agent.TARGET_NEW_DOCS
- Agent.TARGET_NEW_OR_MODIFIED_DOCS
- Agent.TARGET_NONE
- Agent.TARGET_RUN_ONCE (Release 5.0.2 and later)
- Agent.TARGET_SELECTED_DOCS
- Agent.TARGET_UNREAD_DOCS_IN_VIEW

```
public int getTrigger() throws NotesException
```

The getTrigger property access routine returns a code that indicates the type of trigger that will run the current agent. Here are the valid values:

- Agent.TRIGGER_AFTER_MAIL_DELIVERY
- Agent.TRIGGER_BEFORE_MAIL_DELIVERY
- Agent.TRIGGER_DOC_PASTED
- Agent.TRIGGER_DOC_UPDATE
- Agent.TRIGGER_MANUAL
- Agent.TRIGGER_NONE
- Agent.TRIGGER_SCHEDULED

```
public String getURL() throws NotesException
```

The getURL property routine returns a string containing the URL associated with the current agent.

```
public boolean isEnabled() throws NotesException
```

```
public void setEnabled(boolean enable) throws NotesException
```

The Enabled property is true if the agent is enabled to run and false if it is currently disabled. If you call setEnabled with false, the agent will be disabled. The isEnabled and setEnabled property routines only affect scheduled agents. They do not have an effect on other agents.

```
public boolean isNotesAgent() throws NotesException
```

The isNotesAgent property access routine returns true if the current agent can run in a Notes client environment and false if not.

```
public boolean isPublic() throws NotesException
```

The isPublic property routine returns true if the current agent is a shared (public) agent. It returns false if it is a personal agent. Personal agents are stored in the owner's desktop file and are accessible only to the owner.

```
public boolean isWebAgent() throws NotesException
```

The isWebAgent property access routine returns true if the current agent can run in a Web browser environment and false if not.

METHODS

```
public void remove() throws NotesException
```

The remove method permanently deletes the current agent from the database.

```
public void run() throws NotesException
```

```
public void run(String noteid) throws NotesException
```

The run method enables an agent to be dynamically called from another program. This method works with CORBA, so the calling program can be a Java application on a client machine. The second syntax was introduced with version 5.0.2 of Notes and Domino. This syntax enables you to pass data from the calling program to the called program as described in the next paragraph.

To use this mechanism, the calling program creates a document in the database, updates fields with values to be passed, saves the document, and obtains the note ID for the document. The calling program then obtains the Agent object for the agent to be called and invokes the run method, passing the Note ID. The called agent can retrieve the parameter using the getParameterDocID method. The called agent can then inspect and update the values passed in the document before returning. After control returns to the calling program, the updated values can be retrieved.

```
public void runOnServer() throws NotesException
```

```
public void runOnServer(String noteid) throws NotesException
```

The runOnServer method is similar to the run method, but it enables a program to invoke an agent that resides on a Domino server. This method works with CORBA, so the calling program can be a Java application on a client machine. The second syntax was introduced with version 5.0.2 of Notes and Domino. This syntax enables you to pass a data from the calling program to the called program as described in the next paragraph.

To use this mechanism, the calling program creates a document in the database, updates fields with values to be passed, saves the document, and obtains the Note ID for the document. The calling program then obtains the Agent object for the agent to be called and invokes the runOnServer method, passing the Note ID. The called agent can retrieve the parameter using the getParameterDocID method. The called agent can then inspect and update the values passed in the document before returning. When control returns to the calling program, the updated values can be retrieved.

Two agents are involved in the following example: the calling agent (JavaCaller) and the called agent (JavaOutput).

Example:

```
// This is the first agent - JavaCaller
import lotus.domino.*;

public class JavaCaller extends AgentBase {

    public void NotesMain() {

        try {
            Session session = getSession();
            AgentContext agentContext = session.getAgentContext();

            Database db = agentContext.getCurrentDatabase();
            Agent agentToCall = db.getAgent("JavaOutput");
            if (session.isOnServer()) {
                System.out.println("JavaCaller is on server");
            }
            else {
                System.out.println("JavaCaller is on workstation");
            }
            // Create the document to be used to pass values
            Document doc = db.createDocument();
            String origname = session.getUserName(); // Pass the user name
            doc.replaceItemValue("Name", origname);  // in the "Name" field.
            System.out.println("Name in document: " + origname);
            doc.save(true,true);  // Be sure to save document
```

```
            String docid = doc.getNoteID(); // Get the document (note) ID
            System.out.println("JavaCaller: Calling agent, docid=" + docid);
            agentToCall.runOnServer( docid); // Now invoke on the server
            System.out.println("JavaCaller: Returned from call
        ➥to secondary agent");

            doc.recycle(); // Remove from cache
            doc = db.getDocumentByID(docid); // get updated value
            String newname = doc.getItemValueString("Name");
            System.out.println("Name in document: " + newname);


        } catch(Exception e) {
            e.printStackTrace();
        }
    }
}

// This is the called agent - JavaOutput
import lotus.domino.*;

public class JavaOutput extends AgentBase {

    public void NotesMain() {

        try {
            Session session = getSession();
            AgentContext agentContext = session.getAgentContext();

            Agent agent = agentContext.getCurrentAgent();
            if (session.isOnServer()) {
                System.out.println("JavaOutput is on server");
            }
            else {
                System.out.println("JavaOutput is on workstation");
            }
            // Get the document ID that was passed by caller
            String paramdocid = agent.getParameterDocID();
            if (null != paramdocid) {
                System.out.println("ParamDocid = '" + paramdocid + "' ");
                Database db = agentContext.getCurrentDatabase();
                // Now get the document (by docid) saved by our caller.
                Document doc = db.getDocumentByID(paramdocid);
                // Extract out the saved value
                String callername = doc.getItemValueString("Name");
                System.out.println("Name in document: " + callername);
                String servername = session.getServerName();
                // Replace the value so that the caller sees something new
                doc.replaceItemValue("Name", servername);
                System.out.println("Replacing Name in document: with " +
                ➥servername);
                doc.save(true,true); // Save it for the caller
                doc.recycle(); // Free document from cache
            }
            else {
                System.out.println("ParamDocid = null");
            }
```

```
        } catch(Exception e) {
          e.printStackTrace();
        }
    }
}
```

The example illustrates the use of the parameter passing mechanism for agents. The calling agent creates a document, saves a value in a field, saves the document, obtains the document (note) ID, and calls the secondary agent on the server.

The called agent obtains the document ID, then retrieves the document itself, and inspects the contents of the field. It also then updates the field so that it can be passed back to the calling agent.

Here is sample output from the caller in the sample program:

```
JavaCaller is on workstation
Name in document: CN=Randy Tamura/O=GWCorp
JavaCaller: Calling agent, docid=92A
JavaCaller: Returned from call to secondary agent
Name in document: CN=BENTLEY/O=GWCorp
```

Because the JavaOutput called program is running on the server, the console output goes to the Domino console. Here is the console output that appears for this agent:

```
01/04/2000 12:21:43 PM  Addin: Agent printing: JavaOutput is on server
01/04/2000 12:21:43 PM  Addin: Agent printing: ParamDocid = '92A'
01/04/2000 12:21:43 PM  Addin: Agent printing: Name in document:
➥CN=Randy Tamura/O=GWCorp
01/04/2000 12:21:43 PM  Addin: Agent printing: Replacing Name in document:
➥with CN=BENTLEY/O=GWCorp
```

```
public void save() throws NotesException
```

The save method is used to save changes that were made to the agent. You must call the save method after calling either setServerName or setEnabled. If you do not call save, your changes will be lost.

THE AppletBase AND JAppletBase CLASSES

Class Definitions

```
public class AppletBase extends java.applet.Applet
```

```
public class JAppletBase extends javax.swing.JApplet
```

Properties

- getSession
- isNotesLocal

Methods

- `closeSession`
- `notesAppletInit`
- `notesAppletStart`
- `notesAppletStop`
- `notesAppletDestroy`
- `openSession`

The `AppletBase` and `JAppletBase` classes are the base classes you should use when creating applets that will use CORBA and IIOP to access Domino Objects on the server. These classes will initialize the CORBA environment and the communication with the Domino server. Note that the Domino server must be running the DIIOP task and you must set the security attributes in the Domino directory to allow access to the server using IIOP. For more detailed information, see Chapter 15, "Developing Java Applets for Use with Domino."

COMMON METHODS TO CREATE

This class is not usually created in a standalone manner. When you create a Java applet, your source code should extend the `AppletBase` class or the `JAppletBase` class.

PROPERTIES

```
public Session getSession() throws NotesException
```

```
public Session getSession(String userID, String password) throws
NotesException
```

The `getSession` property routine will return the session that has been initialized for the applet. When you have obtained the `Session` object, you can traverse the object hierarchy to obtain further information. You can get an authenticated session by specifying the user ID and password or you can get an anonymous session.

```
public boolean isNotesLocal()
```

The `isNotesLocal` property routine will return `true` if the session is running locally and `false` if it is running on a Domino server.

METHODS

```
public Session closeSession(Session session) throws NotesException
```

The `closeSession` method is used to close a session that has been opened with either `getSession` or `openSession`.

```
public void notesAppletInit()
```

```
public void notesAppletStart()
```

```
public void notesAppletStop()
```

```
public void notesAppletDestroy()
```

These four methods should be used in place of the standard Applet init, start, stop, and destroy methods. Because of the CORBA environment, the AppletBase class must perform some preprocessing at each of the regular Applet methods before passing control to your code.

```
public Session openSession() throws NotesException
```

```
public Session openSession(String userID, String password) throws
NotesException
```

The openSession method routine will return the session that has been initialized for the applet. After you have obtained the Session object, you can traverse the object hierarchy to obtain further information. You can get an authenticated session by specifying the user ID and password or you can get an anonymous session.

CHAPTER REVIEW

1. Describe the three ways that you can initialize the Notes environment. Do you always need to create a NotesThread object to utilize local Domino classes? If not, how do you do it?

2. Describe a situation in which you would have to implement the Runnable interface on your class in order to initialize the Notes environment.

3. What is the purpose of the NotesFactory class, and how do you create a NotesFactory object?

4. What does the Session class represent? How do you create a Session object?

5. What are the two levels of superclass immediately above the AgentBase class? Describe the initialization of the AgentBase class, starting with the class two levels above. Trace through the two levels above AgentBase and finish with the invocation of the NotesMain method.

6. Suppose you wanted to keep track of the number of times that a particular agent has been run. In addition, you want to know the cumulative elapsed time that the agent has used during its runs. What feature could you use to implement this? Write the agent and test it.

7. Write a CORBA Java application that takes as command-line parameters the following information: server, user, password, and database name. The application should log on to the server with the user and password and then print the following information for the database: the database title, its filename, and the size.

8. Write an agent that will be invoked any time a document is updated in a database. Each time it is run, it should check the value of the Name field and change the field so that the value is in proper case. That is, the initial letter of each word of the field should be capitalized. Make sure that documents are not processed more than once. (Hint: Review the evaluate method of the Session class.)

9. Explain the purpose of the DebugAgentBase class and how you use it. (Hint: See Chapter 14, "Using the Domino Designer and Third-Party IDEs with Java.") Use the DebugAgentBase class with a third-party IDE to develop and test an agent.

10. Write an agent that produces a list of all the agents that are found in the same database. For each agent, it should list the agent's name, the owner's common name, and the date when the agent was last run.

CHAPTER 17

THE Database, DbDirectory, AND ACL CLASSES

In this chapter

In Chapter 16, "The NotesThread, NotesFactory, NotesException, Session, and Agent Classes," I described the important classes that handle the Java Domino Objects infrastructure. In this chapter, I describe the Database, DbDirectory, ACL, and Replication classes. These classes enable you to find and manipulate databases.

THE Database CLASS

Class Definition

```
public class Database extends Base
```

Properties

- getACL
- getAgents
- getAllDocuments
- getCategories/setCategories
- getCreated
- getCurrentAccessLevel
- getDesignTemplateName
- getFileName
- getFilePath
- getFolderReferencesEnabled/setFolderReferencesEnabled
- getForms
- getLastFTIndexed
- getLastModified
- getManagers
- getMaxSize
- getParent
- getPercentUsed
- getReplicaID
- getReplicationInfo
- getServer
- getSize
- getSizeQuota/setSizeQuota
- getTemplateName
- getTitle/setTitle
- getURL
- getViews

- isDelayUpdates/setDelayUpdates
- isFTIndexed
- isMultiDbSearch
- isOpen
- isPrivateAddressBook
- isPublicAddressBook

Methods

- compact
- createCopy
- createDocument
- createFromTemplate
- createOutline
- createReplica
- enableFolder
- FTDomainSearch
- FTSearch
- getAgent
- getDocumentByID
- getDocumentByUNID
- getDocumentByURL
- getForm
- getOutline
- getProfileDocCollection
- getProfileDocument
- getURLHeaderInfo
- getView
- grantAccess
- open
- queryAccess
- remove
- replicate
- revokeAccess
- search
- updateFTIndex

The Database class is one of the major Domino Object classes and represents a Domino database. You can use it to obtain information about the database, such as its name, the last time it was modified, documents within the database, its forms, views, and much more information. Many ways to obtain a Database object exist. If you know the server and filename, you can open it directly. In addition, many other objects enable you to access the Database object using the getParent property routine.

COMMON METHODS TO CREATE

Session.getDatabase, Session.getURLDatabase, DbDirectory.createDatabase, DbDirectory.getFirstDatabase, DbDirectory.getNextDatabase, DbDirectory.openDatabase, DbDirectory.openDatabaseByReplicaID, DbDirectory.openDatabaseIfModified, DbDirectory.openMailDatabase, Database.createCopy, Database.createFromTemplate, Database.createReplica, AgentContext.getCurrentDatabase, Agent.getParent, Document.getParentDatabase, View.getParent, Form.getParent, DocumentCollection.getParent, ACL.getParent

PROPERTIES

public ACL getACL() throws NotesException

The getACL property access routine returns an object that represents the Access Control List (ACL) for the database. You can use the ACL object to control who has access and the type of access allowed.

public java.util.Vector getAgents() throws NotesException

The getAgents property routine returns a Vector of all the agents in the database. Each element of the Vector is an Agent object.

public DocumentCollection getAllDocuments() throws NotesException

The getAllDocuments property routine returns an unsorted DocumentCollection object that contains a Document object for each document in the database.

public String getCategories() throws NotesException

public void setCategories(String categories) throws NotesException

The getCategories and setCategories property methods are used to obtain and set the categories that are used for this database in the database catalog. The database catalog is typically called CATALOG.NSF and is found on the server. If you retrieve the Database object from DbDirectory.getFirstDatabase or DbDirectory.getNextDatabase, you can access the categories without opening the database. Otherwise, you must first open the database. When setting the categories, you separate multiple categories with a comma or semicolon within the string.

```
public DateTime getCreated() throws NotesException
```

The `getCreated` property returns the date and time that the database was created. It is returned in a Domino `DateTime` object.

```
public int getCurrentAccessLevel() throws NotesException
```

The `getCurrentAccessLevel` property routine returns an integer code representing the user's access level to the database as dictated by the ACL. The current user's access level is returned if the program is running locally or using remote CORBA/IIOP. If an agent is running on a server, the access level of the agent's owner (the person who last saved the agent) is returned. The valid values range from 0 (no access) to 6 (manager access). Seven constants are defined in the ACL class that can be used:

- `ACL.LEVEL_NOACCESS`
- `ACL.LEVEL_DEPOSITOR`
- `ACL.LEVEL_READER`
- `ACL.LEVEL_AUTHOR`
- `ACL.LEVEL_EDITOR`
- `ACL.LEVEL_DESIGNER`
- `ACL.LEVEL_MANAGER`

```
public String getDesignTemplateName() throws NotesException
```

If the current database inherits its design from a template database, the `getDesignTemplateName` returns the name of that template. If the current database inherits only some design elements (such as forms or views) from a template or if it does not inherit from a template, the property returns an empty string.

```
public String getFileName() throws NotesException
```

The `getFileName` property returns the name of the current database, excluding the path.

```
public String getFilePath() throws NotesException
```

The `getFilePath` property returns the name of the current database, including the path. If the database is located locally, the returned path is the full path, including the drive letter. If the database file is located on a Domino server, the returned path is relative to the data directory. For example, suppose the full path on the Domino server is `D:\Domino\Data\eCommerce\Contact.nsf`. The `getFilePath` routine returns `eCommerce\Contact.nsf`. Java programs running on a client and using CORBA/IIOP to access a server return the server format for the path.

```
public boolean getFolderReferencesEnabled() throws NotesException
```

```
public void setFolderReferencesEnabled(boolean enable) throws NotesException
```

A new feature included with Release 5 of Notes and Domino is the capability to track folder references, listing the folders in which a particular document appears. The getFolderReferencesEnabled property routine enables you to query whether this feature is currently enabled or disabled. The setFolderReferencesEnabled property routine enables you to turn this feature on and off. To use this feature, however, you must create a hidden view in the database called ($FolderRef) or ($FolderRefInfo). Without one of these views, attempting to call the setFolderReferencesEnabled property routine causes an exception. The setFolderReferencesEnabled will not automatically create the view for you; you must create it from the Domino designer. You can copy the design for one of these views from the Mail template database.

After the view is available in the database, you can turn on this property to track folder references. Note that tracking folder references causes a performance penalty. Tracking the folders for documents is done only while the setFolderReferencesEnabled property is enabled. If you disable it, add documents to folders, and subsequently re-enable the property, any document movement while the property was disabled is not available.

Example:

```
import lotus.domino.*;
import java.util.*;

public class FolderTest {
   public static void main(String args[]) {
      try {
         // Use Local Notes executables
         NotesThread.sinitThread(); // Static initialization

         Session session = NotesFactory.createSession();
         if (null == session) { System.out.println("session is null");}
         else {
            Database db = session.getDatabase("", "TempTest.nsf");
            // Get the initial setting of the flag
            boolean fre = db.getFolderReferencesEnabled();
            System.out.println("before FRE: " + (fre?"Enabled":"Disabled"));
            // Enable the folder reference flag, regardless of previous setting
            db.setFolderReferencesEnabled(true);
            fre = db.getFolderReferencesEnabled();
            System.out.println("after FRE: " + (fre?"Enabled":"Disabled"));
            DocumentCollection dc = db.getAllDocuments();
            // Obtain just the first document of the database
            Document doc = dc.getFirstDocument();
            // Find the folder references for the first document
            Vector v = doc.getFolderReferences();
            System.out.print("Refs:");
            for (int i=0; i < v.size(); i++) {
               System.out.print( (String) v.elementAt(i) + ", ");
            }
```

```
            System.out.println("");
        }
    }
    catch (NotesException e) {
        System.out.println("Notes error: " + e.id + ". " + e.text);
        e.printStackTrace();
    }
    catch (Exception e) {
        e.printStackTrace();
    }
    finally {
        NotesThread.stermThread();
    }
  }
}
```

The sample program opens a test database and queries and prints the folder references flag. At that point it forces the flag to be true and prints the folder references for the first document in the database. Note that if there is no ($FolderRef) or ($FolderRefInfo) view in the database, attempting to enable folder references causes a NotesException. In this sample you will also get a null pointer exception if there are no documents in the folder. Be sure to account for these cases in your own program.

public java.util.Vector getForms() throws NotesException

The getForms property routine returns a Vector of Form objects containing all the forms in the database.

public DateTime getLastFTIndexed() throws NotesException

The getLastFTIndexed property routine returns a Domino DateTime object that indicates the date and time the database was last full-text indexed. If the database does not have a full-text index, this routine returns null.

public DateTime getLastModified() throws NotesException

The getLastModified property routine returns a Domino DateTime object that indicates the date and time the database was modified.

public java.util.Vector getManagers() throws NotesException

The getManagers property routine returns a Vector of String objects containing the names of all people, servers, and groups that have manager access to the database. The names are returned in canonical format for hierarchical names and as flat names for groups and Web users.

public long getMaxSize() throws NotesException

The getMaxSize property routine returns the maximum size of the database in kilobytes. This is the size, in kilobytes, to which the database can expand. R5 databases have a 4-terabyte limitation, which does not usually impose a limitation on most current databases. R4 databases have a 4GB limit, so this property is most useful with R4 databases.

```
public Session getParent() throws NotesException
```

The getParent property returns the Session object that contains the current database.

```
public double getPercentUsed() throws NotesException
```

As documents are added to and deleted from a database, some of the space within the database file becomes unused. The getPercentUsed property returns a numeric value that represents the percentage of the database that is occupied by real data.

```
public String getReplicaID() throws NotesException
```

A database's replica ID is a 16-digit hexadecimal string. This string is the same for all replica copies of the same database. The getReplicaID property access routine returns the database's replica ID.

```
public Replication getReplicationInfo() throws NotesException
```

The getReplicationInfo property routine returns a Domino Replication object. The Replication object contains various properties and status information about the replication characteristics of the database.

```
public String getServer() throws NotesException
```

The getServer property access routine returns the fully distinguished name of the server where the database is located. If the database is on a local machine, an empty string is returned. If you use this method from a client with a CORBA session, the fully distinguished server's name is returned.

```
public double getSize() throws NotesException
```

The getSize property returns the file size of the current database, in bytes. Note that this routine returns the number of bytes, while the getMaxSize routine and the SizeQuota routines work with kilobytes.

```
public int getSizeQuota() throws NotesException
```

```
public void setSizeQuota(int quota) throws NotesException
```

Use the getSizeQuota property routine to get the database's size quota. The size quota for a database is typically specified by a system administrator and represents the maximum amount of space that can be used before triggering special handling. In contrast to the MaxSize property, which reflects an absolute maximum size (for R4 databases), the size quota is somewhat softer. For example, when a size quota is associated with a mail database, the router can still add mail to the database. The user is prevented from adding documents or views to the database but can still read mail that has been sent. You can use the setSizeQuota routine to change the quota for the current database.

```
public String getTemplateName() throws NotesException
```

If the database is a template, the `getTemplateName` property returns its template name. Note that this name might be different from the current database name. If the current database is not a template, it returns an empty string.

Refer also to the `getDesignTemplateName` property, which returns the name of the design template from which the current database inherits its design elements.

```
public String getTitle() throws NotesException
```

```
public void setTitle(String title) throws NotesException
```

The `getTitle` property routine returns the title of the database. The `setTitle` routine will change the title. If you change the title of the database in which the program currently runs, the title will not change until the database is closed.

```
public String getURL() throws NotesException
```

The `getURL` property routine returns a string containing the URL associated with the current database object.

```
public java.util.Vector getViews() throws NotesException
```

The `getViews` property routine returns a `Vector` of `View` objects representing all the views and folders in the database.

```
public boolean isDelayUpdates() throws NotesException
```

```
public void setDelayUpdates(boolean delayflag) throws NotesException
```

The `DelayUpdates` flag is used to determine whether certain operations are batched to the server for improved performance. If the flag is `false`, operations to the server are synchronous, and the client waits until the server operation is complete before proceeding. If you issue `setDelayUpdates(true)`, updates from calls such as `save` and `remove` are delayed and sent as a batch. Although delayed updates improve performance, they increase the chance that some data might be lost if there is a crash while some updates are cached but not yet sent to the server.

The default for this property is `true`. This flag is not persistent and if you want to change it, you must change it each time you open a database.

```
public boolean isFTIndexed() throws NotesException
```
The `isFTIndexed` property indicates whether the database has a full-text index.

```
public boolean isMultiDbSearch() throws NotesException
```
The `isMultiDbSearch` property indicates whether the database is a multi-database search index database. This type of database is a special database that consolidates index information

from other databases. A multi-database query will search this special database to find the answer to the query.

```
public boolean isOpen() throws NotesException
```

The isOpen property indicates whether the database is open. It returns true if the database is open and false otherwise. It is sometimes important to use the isOpen method because certain routines that return a Database object also open the database, while others do not. The following methods do not open the database object. You must explicitly use the Database.open method.

- Dbdirectory.getFirstDatabase
- Dbdirectory.getNextDatabase
- Session.getAddressBooks

The following Database properties and methods can be used on a Database object without opening it. See the property or method description for more information.

- Database.getCategories
- Database.isDelayUpdates
- Database.getDesignTemplateName
- Database.getFileName
- Database.getFilePath
- Database.isOpen
- Database.isPrivateAddressBook
- Database.isPublicAddressBook
- Database.getParent
- Database.getReplicaID
- Database.getServer
- Database.getSizeQuota
- Database.getTemplateName
- Database.getTitle

```
public boolean isPrivateAddressBook() throws NotesException
```

If the database object has been retrieved using Session.getAddressBooks, the isPrivateAddressBook property indicates whether the current database is a personal address book. If the database was not accessed using getAddressBooks, this property will be false.

```
public boolean isPublicAddressBook() throws NotesException
```

If the database object has been retrieved using Session.getAddressBooks, the isPublicAddressBook property indicates whether the current database is a Domino directory (public address book). If the database was not accessed using getAddressBooks, this property will be false.

METHODS

public int compact() throws NotesException

The compact method of the database object compacts the database. The database must be local or the method will throw an exception. It returns an integer that represents the difference, in bytes, in the size of the database before and after compaction.

public Database createCopy(String server, String dbfilename) throws NotesException

The createCopy method creates a copy of the current database on the specified server with the specified filename. The new database is not a replica copy of the original database. The copy will contain a copy of all the design elements, the ACL, and the database title. The new database will not contain any documents. If the database with the specified filename already exists, an exception will be thrown. Specify an empty string for the server name to create a local copy. You must be authorized to create new databases for this method to succeed. Programs that are running on a server or via remote (IIOP) methods cannot create a database on another server.

public Document createDocument() throws NotesException

The createDocument method creates a new document in the current database. You must call the document's save method if you want the document to be saved permanently in the database. It is also a good idea to create a field within the document named Form and to populate this field with the name of the form that should be used to display the document in the user interface.

public Database createFromTemplate(String server, String dbfilename, boolean inherit) throws NotesException

createFromTemplate creates a new database on the specified server with the specified filename. If the current database object is a template, it will be used as the basis for the new database. The inherit flag should be true if you want the new database to inherit future changes from the template database. If the current database is not a template, the createFromTemplate method will create a new, blank database like the DbDirectory.createDatabase method. You must be authorized in the Domino directory to create a new database.

If you use this call from a CORBA Java program, the server specification must match the CORBA session server. You can also use an empty string for the server specification, which will cause the database to be created on the session server.

```
public Outline createOutline(String name) throws NotesException
```

```
public Outline createOutline(String name, boolean defaultOutline) throws
NotesException
```

The createOutline method creates a new outline with the specified name in the database. If you set defaultOutline to true, a default outline will be created. If you set it to false or if you omit the defaultOutline parameter, an empty outline will be created. After you have created your outline, be sure to call the Outline.save method to permanently save your outline to the database.

```
public Database createReplica(String server, String dbfilename) throws
NotesException
```

The createReplica method creates a replica copy of the current database on the specified server with the specified filename. If the database with the specified filename already exists, an exception will be thrown. Specify an empty string for the server name to create a local copy. You must be authorized to create replica databases for this method to succeed. Programs that are running on a server or by using remote (IIOP) methods cannot create a database on another server.

```
public void enableFolder(String folder) throws NotesException
```

The enableFolder method ensures that the specified folder exists. If it doesn't then it will be created.

```
public Document FTDomainSearch(String query, int maxdocs, int sortoptions,
int otheroptions, int start, int count, String entryForm) throws
NotesException
```

The FTDomainSearch method performs a domain-wide search. It searches all the databases that are listed in the Domain Catalog and that are marked for multi-database indexing. The current Database object must represent a Domain Catalog. The maxdocs parameter specifies the maximum number of documents to return. A zero means to return all documents. The sortoptions parameter can contain Database.FT_SCORES, Database.FT_DATE_DES, or Database.FT_DATE_ASC. These values indicate to sort the documents by relevance, descending date order, or ascending date order, respectively. The otheroptions parameter can contain Database.FT_DATABASE to include Domino databases in the search, Database.FT_FILESYSTEM to include files other than Domino databases, Database.FT_FUZZY for a fuzzy search, or Database.FT_STEMS to use stem words as the basis for the search. Any keywords in the query string must be quoted and you might need to escape the quotes.

The start parameter indicates the starting page to return, and the count parameter is the number of pages to return. The entryForm is the name of the search form in the Domain Catalog.

The return value is a document that contains the result of the query.

```
public DocumentCollection FTSearch(String query) throws NotesException
```

```
public DocumentCollection FTSearch(String query, int maxdocs) throws
NotesException
```

```
public DocumentCollection FTSearch(String query, int maxdocs, int
sortoptions, int otheroptions) throws NotesException
```

The FTSearch method performs a full-text search of all the documents in the database. It returns a DocumentCollection of the documents that match the query, and is sorted by the sortoptions.

The maxdocs parameter specifies the maximum number of documents to return. A zero means to return all documents. The sortoptions parameter can contain Database.FT_SCORES, Database.FT_DATE_DES, or Database.FT_DATE_ASC. These values indicate that the documents should be sorted by relevance, descending date order, or ascending date order, respectively. The default is FT_SCORES. The otheroptions parameter can contain Database.FT_DATABASE to include Domino databases in the search, Database.FT_FILESYSTEM to include files other than Domino databases, Database.FT_FUZZY for a fuzzy search, or Database.FT_STEMS to use stem words as the basis for the search.

The database does not need to be full-text indexed for this method to work, but if it is, the search will be more efficient. You can programmatically test whether the database is full-text indexed with the IsFTIndexed property, and you can create or update the index with the updateFTIndex method (for local databases only).

This FTSearch method searches the entire database, but you can also use View.FTSearch or DocumentCollection.FTSearch to search these collections if you require a more refined search.

```
public Agent getAgent(String name) throws NotesException
```

The getAgent method gets an Agent object with the specified name. If the specified agent is private and the current user is not the owner, or if the agent cannot be found, then null will be returned.

```
public Document getDocumentByID(String noteid) throws NotesException
```

The getDocumentByID obtains the document with the specified document note ID from the database. The NoteID is a hexadecimal string of up to eight characters and uniquely identifies the document within the current database. The NoteID will vary among different replicas of the same database, so in general you should use getDocumentByUNID instead.

```
public Document getDocumentByUNID(String noteid) throws NotesException
```

The getDocumentByUNID obtains the document with the specified universal ID (UNID) from the database. The UNID is a hexadecimal string of up to 32 characters and uniquely identifies the document within all replicas of the database. If a document has the same UNID as another document in a replica database, the documents are replicas of one another.

```
public Document getDocumentByURL(String url, Boolean reload) throws
NotesException
```

```
public Document getDocumentByURL(String url, boolean reload, boolean
reloadifmod, boolean urllist, String charset, String webuser, String
webpassword, String proxyuser, String proxypassword, boolean nowait) throws
NotesException
```

The getDocumentByURL returns a document from the Web Navigator database. The database can be either the personal Web Navigator database or the server Web Navigator database. This method can also be used to go back to the Internet to obtain the document before returning it.

The url parameter specifies the uniform resource locator to be used. It should start with http:. Use true for the reload parameter if you want the method to reload the page from its Internet server. False will load it from the Internet only if it is not already in the database. The reloadifmod parameter is similar to reload but indicates you want the page reloaded only if it has been modified on the Internet server.

If you specify true for the urllist parameter, the list of URL links found on the page will be stored in fields called URLLinksn. That is, URLLinks1, URLLinks2, and so forth will be used as each field reaches 64KB. The charset option is the name of the MIME character set to use for processing the Web page. webuser and webpassword can be specified if the URL is password protected. proxyuser and proxypassword can be required if you use a proxy server that requires authentication. Specify nowait to be true if you do not need the Document object and if you want your program to proceed without waiting for the retrieval of the page.

```
public Form getForm(String formname) throws NotesException
```

The getForm method is used to get a Form object with the specified name. You can supply the actual name or an alias.

```
public Outline getOutline(String outlinename) throws NotesException
```

The getOutline method is used to get an Outline object with the specified name. You can supply the actual name or an alias. If you modify the outline after you have retrieved it, make sure to call the Outline.save method to save it permanently back in the database.

```
public DocumentCollection getProfileDocCollection(String profileName) throws
NotesException
```

Profile documents are special documents that do not appear in user views. They are typically used to store configuration information and can be used to personalize a user's experience. Profile documents are stored within a database in a two-level hierarchy. You can specify a profile name, and within that profile you can specify a set of keys or users of the profile. Profile documents are cached on the server, so they have fast performance, but as a result you should be judicious in their use.

Use the `getProfileDocCollection` to obtain a `DocumentCollection` of all the profile documents for a particular profile name. Typically there is one for each user, but actually you can use any string for the key.

```
public Document getProfileDocument(String profileName, String profileUser)
throws NotesException
```

Use the `getProfileDocument` method to retrieve or create a profile document. Profile documents are different from regular documents. The act of getting the document with the given keys will actually create the document if it does not exist.

```
public String getURLHeaderInfo(String url, String header, String webuser,
String webpassword, String proxyuser, String proxypassword) throws
NotesException
```

The `getURLHeaderInfo` can be used to obtain an HTTP response header value for a particular URL. See the section titled "Client/Server Communication with HTTP" in Chapter 11, "JavaScript Techniques with Domino," for an in-depth description of the HTTP protocol and the usage of headers in HTTP.

The `url` parameter is the Web page to obtain. It should begin with the string `http:`. The header parameter specifies the particular field name that you would like extracted from the server's response header. Some common response header field names include `Server`, `Date`, `Content-Type`, `Last-Modified`, and `Content-Length`.

The `webuser` and `webpassword` parameters can be used if the Web page requires authentication. If not, you can pass `null` values. The `proxyuser` and `proxypassword` parameters can be used if you are using a proxy server that requires authentication.

```
public View getView(String viewname) throws NotesException
```

The `getView` method is used to get a `View` object with the specified name. You can supply the actual name or an alias. The `getView` method is used for public views or public folders. When it is invoked in a local database, it can also access personal views or folders.

```
public void grantAccess(String name, int level) throws NotesException
```

Use the `grantAccess` method to add or change the ACL specification for a particular user, group, or server. You supply the name of the user, group, or server as well as a code that indicates the level of access. The valid levels range from 0 (no access) to 6 (manager access). The ACL class defines the following seven constants that can be used:

- `ACL.LEVEL_NOACCESS`
- `ACL.LEVEL_DEPOSITOR`
- `ACL.LEVEL_READER`
- `ACL.LEVEL_AUTHOR`
- `ACL.LEVEL_EDITOR`

- ACL.LEVEL_DESIGNER
- ACL.LEVEL_MANAGER

Do not use this method at the same time you are using an ACL object for the database because you might get inconsistent results.

public boolean open() throws NotesException

The open method opens a database. Some operations that create a Database object also open the database. In these cases you do not need to open the database, and you can get an error if you try to reopen it. Also, some Database methods, such as getFileName or getTitle, do not require you to open the database. You can use the property isOpen to test whether a database is open before trying to open it.

public int queryAccess(String name) throws NotesException

The queryAccess method returns the access level for the person, group, or server specified by the name string. The return value is an integer code. The return levels range from 0 (no access) to 6 (manager access). The ACL class defines seven constants that can be used:

- ACL.LEVEL_NOACCESS
- ACL.LEVEL_DEPOSITOR
- ACL.LEVEL_READER
- ACL.LEVEL_AUTHOR
- ACL.LEVEL_EDITOR
- ACL.LEVEL_DESIGNER
- ACL.LEVEL_MANAGER

public void remove() throws NotesException

The remove method permanently deletes the database associated with the current Database object. Obviously, you should use this method with care. Normal ACL access rights are enforced. You can remove a database only if you have manager access rights. Typically you will have manager access rights to local databases unless the Enforce Consistent ACLs for All Replicas advanced option is enabled in the ACL and you do not have manager rights.

public boolean replicate(String server) throws NotesException

The replicate method replicates the current database with one or more replicas on the specified server. The return value is true if the database was replicated without errors and false if there were errors. The Database object must be local or an exception will be thrown.

```
public void revokeAccess(String name) throws NotesException
```

The revokeAccess method removes the specified name from the ACL. This has the effect of restoring default access for the person, group, or server specified by the name. Note that issuing revokeAccess is not the same as specifying ACL.LEVEL_NOACCESS for the user. If the name is included in the database ACL with No Access, the user is totally prevented from accessing the database.

```
public DocumentCollection search(String formula) throws NotesException
```

```
public DocumentCollection search(String formula, DateTime sinceDate) throws
NotesException
```

```
public DocumentCollection search(String formula, DateTime sinceDate, int
maxdocs) throws NotesException
```

The search method uses the specified @formula as a selection criterion. Its use is similar to a view selection formula (but does not use the keyword SELECT). If the sinceDate parameter is specified, only documents newer than the given date are returned. You can use null if you do not want to filter the documents by date. The maxdocs parameter represents the maximum number of documents to return. Specify 0 if you want to retrieve all documents.

Note that this method does not do a full-text search. The specified formula is used to control the selection of the documents.

```
public void updateFTIndex(boolean create) throws NotesException
```

The updateFTIndex method creates or updates the full-text index for a database. Full-text indexes speed up full-text searches but are not required to execute a full-text search. For local databases, specify true for the create parameter to create the index. Specify false to update the existing database. If you attempt to create an index on a remote database, an exception is thrown. To create an index on a server, you must manually create it by using the user interface and you must have designer or manager access to the database.

THE DbDirectory CLASS

Class Definition

```
public class DbDirectory extends Base
```

Properties

- getName
- getParent

Methods

- createDatabase
- getFirstDatabase
- getNextDatabase
- openDatabase
- openDatabaseByReplicaID
- openDatabaseIfModified
- openMailDatabase

In the Java Domino Objects classes, the DbDirectory class is significantly different from the LotusScript equivalent. I haven't described the LotusScript objects in this book, but because the DbDirectory functions are packaged differently, I do provide some cross-reference information in case you work with both LotusScript and Java.

In LotusScript, the NotesDbDirectory class has only two methods (GetFirstDatabase and GetNextDatabase) and is used primarily to traverse the available databases. In Java, however, the DbDirectory class is much more powerful and useful. In Java, the functions of creating and opening a database are within the DbDirectory class, rather than the Database class itself. The Java Database class is used to access data within the database, not to open it.

Here is the beginning of a Java agent:

```
public void NotesMain() {
   try {
      Session session = getSession();
      AgentContext agentContext = session.getAgentContext();
      // (Your code goes here)
      DbDirectory dbd = session.getDbDirectory("");
      dbd.createDatabase("MyJavaDb");
```

Notice that in this Java version we must first get a Session and a DbDirectory object before we can use createDatabase. The AgentContext object is not required for this example, but the IDE gives it to us free.

The DbDirectory class contains the createDatabase, openDatabase, openByReplicaID, and openIfModified methods that are found in the NotesDatabase class of LotusScript. The createCopy, createFromTemplate, and createReplica methods are contained in the Java Database class.

Table 17.1 shows the correspondence of the LotusScript and Java classes for databases. The first three columns contain LotusScript methods and the last three are Java methods.

TABLE 17.1 LOTUSSCRIPT AND JAVA DATABASE CLASSES

LotusScript	Java				
NotesSession	NotesDbDirectory	NotesDatabase	Session	DbDirectory	Database
GetDatabase			getDatabase		
GetDbDirectory			getDbDirectory		
	GetFirstDatabase			getFirstDatabase	
	GetNextDatabase			getNextDatabase	
		Create		createDatabase	
		CreateCopy			createCopy
		CreateFromTemplate			createFromTemplate
		CreateReplica			createReplica
		Open		openDatabase	
		OpenByReplicaID		openDatabaseByReplicaID	
		OpenIfModified		openDatabaseIfModified	
		OpenMail		openMailDatabase	
		OpenURLDb	getURLDatabase		
		OpenWithFailover		openDatabase (with failover)	

COMMON METHODS TO CREATE

```
Session.getDbDirectory
```

PROPERTIES

```
public String getName() throws NotesException
```

The getName property access routine returns the name of the server on which the DbDirectory resides. If the DbDirectory is on a local machine, the property is null.

```
public Session getParent() throws NotesException
```

The getParent property routine returns the Session object that contains the DbDirectory object.

METHODS

```
public Database createDatabase(String dbfilename) throws NotesException
```

```
public Database createDatabase(String dbfilename, boolean open) throws
NotesException
```

The createDatabase method creates a database on the server associated with the session. You specify the filename relative to the server's data directory. If the Boolean flag open is true, the Database object will be opened for you.

```
public Database getFirstDatabase(int type) throws NotesException
```

The getFirstDatabase method returns a Database object for the first database of the type specified. The returned Database object is closed. The Type value can be one of the following values:

- DbDirectory.DATABASE—Any database (.nsf, .ns4, .ns3, .nsg, or .nsh)
- DbDirectory.TEMPLATE—Any template (.ntf)
- DbDirectory.REPLICA_CANDIDATE—Any database not disabled for replication
- DbDirectory.TEMPLATE_CANDIDATE—Any database or template

The first database of the specified type will be returned and null will be returned if there are no matching databases.

```
public Database getNextDatabase() throws NotesException
```

This method returns the next database of the same type specified in the getFirstDatabase call or null if there are no more. You must issue getFirstDatabase before calling getNextDatabase.

```
public Database openDatabase(String dbfilename) throws NotesException
```

```
public Database openDatabase(String dbfilename, boolean failover) throws
NotesException
```

The openDatabase method opens the specified database on the session's current server. If the database cannot be opened and failover is not specified, the method returns null. If failover is true, an attempt is made to open the database on another server in the same cluster. You cannot use failover for remote (IIOP) databases.

```
public Database openDatabaseByReplicaID(String replicaid) throws
NotesException
```

The openDatabaseByReplicaID method opens the database with the specified replica ID on the DbDirectory's server. Here is an example of how you might use openByReplicaID.

```
Session session = getSession();
AgentContext agentContext = session.getAgentContext();
// (Your code goes here)
DbDirectory dbDirLocal = session.getDbDirectory("");  // Local db directory
// First open the server database
DbDirectory dbDirServer = session.getDbDirectory("<your server>");
Database dbLocal  = dbDirLocal.openDatabase("MyJavaDb"); // Open the local db
// Now open the server replica of my local database
Database dbServer=dbDirServer.openDatabaseByReplicaID(dbLocal.getReplicaID());
// Now you can manipulate dbLocal and dbServer replica databases
System.out.println("Local title="+dbLocal.getTitle());    //Print out the title
System.out.println("Server title="+dbServer.getTitle()); //Print out the title
```

In this example, I first open a local copy of a database. After the local copy is opened, I get the replica ID and use this to open the server replica of the same database. This is useful because it works even if the server copy has a different filename, different directory, and different database title. I don't need to know any of these properties of the server database as long as I know my local copy is a replica of the server version.

```
public Database openDatabaseIfModified(String dbfilename, DateTime sinceDate)
throws NotesException
```

The openDatabaseIfModified method opens the specified database if one or more documents have been modified since the sinceDate. The method returns null if the database has not been modified since the date.

```
public Database openMailDatabase() throws NotesException
```

The openMailDatabase method opens the current user's mail database. This method must be executed on a workstation or on the agent owner's mail server because a server cannot open a database on another server.

This method returns null if the database cannot be opened.

THE ACL CLASS

Class Definition

```
public class ACL extends Base
```

Properties

- getInternetLevel/setInternetLevel
- getParent
- getRoles
- isUniformAccess/setUniformAccess

Methods

- addRole
- createACLEntry
- deleteRole
- getEntry
- getFirstEntry
- getNextEntry
- removeACLEntry
- renameRole
- save

The ACL class represents the access control list for a database. There is only one ACL object per database. The ACL object has several properties and methods and is a container for ACLEntry objects. There is one ACLEntry object per name in the ACL. The name can be a reference to a person, group, server, or a wildcard entry such as */orgname. You can use the ACL object to traverse through the ACLEntry objects.

COMMON METHODS TO CREATE

```
Database.getACL, ACLEntry.getParent
```

PROPERTIES

```
public int getInternetLevel() throws NotesException

public void setInternetLevel(int level) throws NotesException
```

The getInternetLevel retrieves the maximum Internet access level for the database. The setInternetLevel can be used to set the access level. The valid levels range from 0 (no access) to 6 (manager access). The ACL class defines the following seven constants that can be used:

- ACL.LEVEL_NOACCESS
- ACL.LEVEL_DEPOSITOR
- ACL.LEVEL_READER
- ACL.LEVEL_AUTHOR
- ACL.LEVEL_EDITOR
- ACL.LEVEL_DESIGNER
- ACL.LEVEL_MANAGER

```
public Database getParent() throws NotesException
```

The getParent property returns the Database object that contains the ACL object.

```
public java.util.Vector getRoles() throws NotesException
```

The getRoles property returns a Vector of String elements representing all the roles in the ACL object. Each role name is enclosed in square brackets.

```
public boolean isUniformAccess() throws NotesException
```

```
public void setUniformAccess(boolean uniform) throws NotesException
```

Use the isUniformAccess property routine to query whether uniform access is set for the database. Change the uniform access property using the setUniformAccess method. If uniform access is enabled, a consistent ACL is enforced across all replicas of the database, including local copies.

METHODS

```
public void addRole(String name) throws NotesException
```

The specified name is added as a role in the ACL. Do not enclose the name in square brackets. Remember to call the ACL.save method to permanently save your changes to the ACL.

```
public ACLEntry createACLEntry(String name, int level) throws NotesException
```

The createACLEntry method creates a new ACLEntry with the specified name and level. You must supply the complete hierarchical name, but you can use the abbreviated format. Remember to call the ACL.save routine to permanently save your changes to the database.

The valid levels range from 0 (no access) to 6 (manager access). The ACL class defines the following seven constants that can be used:

- ACL.LEVEL_NOACCESS
- ACL.LEVEL_DEPOSITOR

PART

IV

CH

17

- ACL.LEVEL_READER
- ACL.LEVEL_AUTHOR
- ACL.LEVEL_EDITOR
- ACL.LEVEL_DESIGNER
- ACL.LEVEL_MANAGER

The newly created ACLEntry object is returned. Note that this method is functionally equivalent to the Database.grantAccess method. However, you should not mix the use of these two methods because you might get inconsistent results in your ACL.

public void deleteRole(String name) throws NotesException

The deleteRole method deletes the specified role name from the ACL object. Do not include brackets around the name. Remember to call the ACL.save routine to permanently save your changes to the database.

public ACLEntry getEntry(String name) throws NotesException

The getEntry method retrieves the ACLEntry that corresponds to the name specified. You must supply the complete hierarchical name, but you can use the abbreviated format. If the name is not found, null is returned.

public ACLEntry getFirstEntry() throws NotesException

The getFirstEntry method retrieves the first ACLEntry in the ACL object. The first entry is typically the -Default- entry. The getFirstEntry method is usually used in conjunction with the getNextEntry method to access each of the ACLEntry objects.

public ACLEntry getNextEntry() throws NotesException

public ACLEntry getNextEntry(ACLEntry entry) throws NotesException

Without a parameter, the getNextEntry method retrieves the next ACLEntry in the ACL object following the last one received. If a parameter is specified, getNextEntry retrieves the entry following the one given. The version without a parameter works more efficiently for remote operations because the ACL object is cached.

public void removeACLEntry(String name) throws NotesException

The removeACLEntry removes the specified entry from the ACL object. The name can be for a person, group, or server. You must supply the complete hierarchical name, but you can use the abbreviated format. Remember to call the ACL.save routine to permanently save your changes to the database. Note that this method is functionally equivalent to the Database.revokeAccess method; however, you should not use both of these methods at the same time because you might get inconsistent results in your ACL.

Removing an entry from the ACL resets the access to the database default. This is not functionally equivalent to setting the entry to No access.

```
public void renameRole(String oldname, String newname) throws NotesException
```
The renameRole changes the name of a role in the ACL. Do not specify brackets on either the old or new name. Any entries in the ACL object that were assigned to the old role name are assigned the new role name. Remember to call the ACL.save routine to permanently save your changes to the database.

```
public void save() throws NotesException
```
The save method permanently saves changes that have been made to the ACL. If you make changes to the ACL object but don't call save, the changes are lost and do not take effect.

THE ACLEntry CLASS

Class Definition

```
public class ACLEntry extends Base
```

Properties

- getLevel/setLevel
- getName/setName
- getNameObject
- getParent
- getRoles
- getUserType/setUserType
- isAdminReaderAuthor/setAdminReaderAuthor
- isAdminServer/setAdminServer
- isCanCreateDocuments/setCanCreateDocuments
- isCanCreateLSOrJavaAgent/setCanCreateLSOrJavaAgent
- isCanCreatePersonalAgent/setCanCreatePersonalAgent
- isCanCreatePersonalFolder/setCanCreatePersonalFolder
- isCanCreateSharedFolder/setCanCreateSharedFolder
- isCanDeleteDocuments/setCanDeleteDocuments
- isGroup/setGroup
- isPerson/setPerson
- isPublicReader/setPublicReader
- isPublicWriter/setPublicWriter
- isServer/setServer

Methods

- `disableRole`
- `enableRole`
- `isRoleEnabled`
- `remove`

The `ACLEntry` class represents a single-name entry in the `ACL`. The entry could represent a person, group, or server. An `ACLEntry` is not created for roles. You can obtain the roles using the `ACL.getRoles` property.

To refine the `ACL` privileges for an individual, you can enable or disable certain privileges using `ACLEntry` property routines. Table 17.2 indicates which privileges are automatically available (X), optional (O), or not available (blank) for the different levels of access. The optional privileges can be turned on or off.

TABLE 17.2   PRIVILEGES (✓) AND OPTIONAL PRIVILEGES (O) FOR DIFFERENT LEVELS OF ACCESS

Privilege	Manager	Designer	Editor	Author	Reader	Depositor	No Access
Create documents	✓	✓	✓	O	-	✓	-
Delete documents	O	O	O	O	-	-	-
Create personal agents	✓	✓	O	O	O	-	-
Create personal folders/views	✓	✓	O	O	O	-	-
Create shared folders/views	✓	✓	O	-	-	-	-
Create LotusScript/Java agents	✓	O	O	O	O	-	-
Read public documents	✓	✓	✓	✓	✓	O	O
Write public documents	✓	✓	✓	O	O	O	O

COMMON METHODS TO CREATE

`ACL.createACLEntry, ACL.getEntry, ACL.getFirstEntry, ACL.getNextEntry`

PROPERTIES

```
public int getLevel() throws NotesException
```

```
public void setLevel(int level) throws NotesException
```

The getLevel method returns the access level for the current ACLEntry. The return value is an integer code. The return levels range from 0 (no access) to 6 (manager access). Seven constants defined in the ACL class can be used:

- ACL.LEVEL_NOACCESS
- ACL.LEVEL_DEPOSITOR
- ACL.LEVEL_READER
- ACL.LEVEL_AUTHOR
- ACL.LEVEL_EDITOR
- ACL.LEVEL_DESIGNER
- ACL.LEVEL_MANAGER

You use the setLevel method to set the level of the current entry. Be sure to call ACL.save if you change the level so that your changes are permanently stored in the database.

```
public String getName() throws NotesException
```

```
public void setName(String name) throws NotesException
```

```
public void setName(Name name) throws NotesException
```

Use the getName property to get the name of the current ACLEntry as a string. There are two versions of the setName property routine. You can set the name of the current entry with either a String or a Name object. If you change the name of the current entry, you must call ACL.save so that your changes are permanently stored in the database.

```
public Name getNameObject() throws NotesException
```

The getNameObject property method obtains the current ACLEntry name as a name object rather than a string. There is no setNameObject method. Use setName with a Name object instead.

```
public ACL getParent() throws NotesException
```

The getParent property routine returns the ACL object that contains the current ACLEntry.

```
public java.util.Vector getRoles() throws NotesException
```

The getRoles property routine returns a Vector of String elements representing all the roles that are enabled for this ACLEntry. Each string is a role name, enclosed in square brackets. For example, one role might be [Supervisor].

```
public int getUserType() throws NotesException
```

```
public void setUserType(int usertype) throws NotesException
```

The getUserType property routine returns a code representing the type of user for this ACLEntry. The valid values are

- ACLEntry.TYPE_MIXED_GROUP
- ACLEntry.TYPE_PERSON
- ACLEntry.TYPE_PERSON_GROUP
- ACLEntry.TYPE_SERVER
- ACLEntry.TYPE_SERVER_GROUP
- ACLEntry.TYPE_UNSPECIFIED

If you change the UserType, be sure to call ACL.save to permanently store your changes in the database.

```
public boolean isAdminReaderAuthor() throws NotesException
```

```
public void setAdminReaderAuthor(boolean flag) throws NotesException
```

The isAdminReaderAuthor property indicates whether the administration server can modify reader and author fields. This property corresponds to a similar option on the Advanced tab of the Access Control List dialog box. The setAdminReaderAuthor property routine can change the value of the property. Specify true to enable the administration server to modify reader and author fields.

The isAdminReaderAuthor property applies only if the current entry is the administration server entry (see isAdminServer). If you use setAdminReaderAuthor(true) for an entry other than the administration server, it is ignored and will not throw an exception.

```
public boolean isAdminServer() throws NotesException
```

```
public void setAdminServer(boolean flag) throws NotesException
```

The isAdminServer property is true if the current ACLEntry represents the administration server for the database. The setAdminServer property routine can be used to mark the current entry as the administration server. Remember to call the ACL.save routine to permanently save your changes to the database.

Note

You can have only one administration server defined for a database. However, when you use setAdminServer(true) to set an administration server, Domino does not automatically go through and disable any previous administration server setting. Thus, you will end up with two administration servers, which is an undefined condition. If you are changing the administration server, you must be sure to call setAdminServer(false) on any previous administration server entry as well as setting the new one.

```
public boolean isCanCreateDocuments() throws NotesException
```

```
public void setCanCreateDocuments(boolean flag) throws NotesException
```

The isCanCreateDocuments property is true if the current entry can create new documents. It is always true for Depositor, Editor, Designer, or Manager access. It is always false for Reader or No Access. For Author level access, the capability to create documents is conditional. When you create a new entry with Author access, this property is false by default. To enable it, use the setCanCreateDocuments property routine with the value true. Be sure to call the ACL.save routine to permanently save your changes to the database.

```
public boolean isCanCreateLSOrJavaAgent() throws NotesException
```

```
public void setCanCreateLSOrJavaAgent(boolean flag) throws NotesException
```

The isCanCreateLSOrJavaAgent property is true if the current entry can create LotusScript or Java agents. It is always true for Manager access. It is always false for Depositor or No Access. For Reader, Author, Editor, or Designer level access, the capability to create agents is conditional. When you create a new entry with Reader, Author, Editor, or Designer access, this property is false by default. To enable it, use the setCanCreateLSOrJavaAgent property routine with the value true. Be sure to call the ACL.save routine to permanently save your changes to the database.

```
public boolean isCanCreatePersonalAgent() throws NotesException
```

```
public void setCanCreatePersonalAgent(boolean flag) throws NotesException
```

The isCanCreatePersonalAgent property is true if the current entry can create personal agents. It is always true for Designer or Manager access. It is always false for Depositor or No Access. For Reader, Author, or Editor level access, the capability to create personal agents is conditional. When you create a new entry with Reader, Author, Editor, or Designer access, this property is false by default. To enable it, use the setCanCreatePersonalAgent property routine with the value true. Be sure to call the ACL.save routine to permanently save your changes to the database.

```
public boolean isCanCreatePersonalFolder() throws NotesException
```

```
public void setCanCreatePersonalFolder(boolean flag) throws NotesException
```

The isCanCreatePersonalFolder property is true if the current entry can create personal folders. It is always true for Designer or Manager access. It is always false for Depositor or No Access. For Reader, Author, or Editor level access, the capability to create personal folders is conditional. When you create a new entry with Reader, Author, or Editor access, this property is false by default. To enable it, use the setCanCreatePersonalFolder property routine with the value true. Be sure to call the ACL.save routine to permanently save your changes to the database.

```
public boolean isCanCreateSharedFolder() throws NotesException
```

```
public void setCanCreateSharedFolder(boolean flag) throws NotesException
```

The isCanCreateSharedFolder property is true if the current entry can create shared folders. It is always true for Designer or Manager access. It is always false for Author, Reader, Depositor, or No Access. For Editor level access, the capability to create shared folders is conditional. When you create a new entry with Editor access, this property is false by default. To enable it, use the setCanCreateSharedFolder property routine with the value true. Be sure to call the ACL.save routine to permanently save your changes to the database.

```
public boolean isCanDeleteDocuments() throws NotesException
```

```
public void setCanDeleteDocuments(boolean flag) throws NotesException
```

The isCanDeleteDocuments property is true if the current entry can delete documents. It is always false for Reader, Depositor, or No Access. For Author, Editor, Designer, or Manager level access, the capability to delete documents is conditional. When you create a new entry with Author, Editor, Designer, or Manager access, this property is false by default. To enable it, use the setCanDeleteDocuments property routine with the value true. Be sure to call the ACL.save routine to permanently save your changes to the database.

```
public boolean isGroup() throws NotesException
```

```
public void setGroup(boolean flag) throws NotesException
```

The isGroup property indicates whether the current ACLEntry object represents a group. The property is true if the ACLEntry is one of the following types: ACLEntry.TYPE_MIXED_GROUP, ACLEntry.TYPE_PERSON_GROUP, or ACLEntry.TYPE_SERVER_GROUP. See the setUserType and getUserType property routines for more details. Be sure to call the ACL.save routine to permanently save your changes to the database.

```
public boolean isPerson() throws NotesException
```

```
public void setPerson(boolean flag) throws NotesException
```

The isPerson property indicates whether the current ACLEntry object represents a person. The property is true if the ACLEntry is one of the following types: ACLEntry.TYPE_PERSON, ACLEntry.TYPE_PERSON_GROUP, or ACLEntry.TYPE_MIXED_GROUP. See the setUserType and getUserType property routines for more details. Be sure to call the ACL.save routine to permanently save your changes to the database.

```
public boolean isPublicReader() throws NotesException
```

```
public void setPublicReader(boolean flag) throws NotesException
```

The isPublicReader property is true if the current entry has public reader access to a database. The setting has no effect unless the regular access is Depositor or No Access. Other types of access will always be able to read the database and will return `true`. For Depositor and No Access level access, the capability to read public documents is conditional. When you create a new entry with Depositor or No Access level access, this property is `false` by default. To enable it, use the `setPublicReader` property routine with the value `true`. Be sure to call the `ACL.save` routine to permanently save your changes to the database.

```
public boolean isPublicWriter() throws NotesException
```

```
public void setPublicWriter(boolean flag) throws NotesException
```

The `isPublicWriter` property is true if the current entry has public writer access to a database. It is always `true` for Editor, Designer, or Manager access. For Author, Reader, Depositor, and No Access level access, the capability to write public documents is conditional. When you create a new entry with Author, Reader, Depositor, or No Access level access, this property is `false` by default. To enable it, use the `setPublicWriter` property routine with the value `true`. Be sure to call the `ACL.save` routine to permanently save your changes to the database.

```
public boolean isServer() throws NotesException
```

```
public void setServer(boolean flag) throws NotesException
```

The `isServer` property indicates whether the current `ACLEntry` object represents a server. The property is true if the `ACLEntry` is one of the following types: `ACLEntry.TYPE_SERVER`, `ACLEntry.TYPE_MIXED_GROUP`, or `ACLEntry.TYPE_SERVER_GROUP`. See the `setUserType` and `getUserType` property routines for more details. Be sure to call the `ACL.save` routine to permanently save your changes to the database.

METHODS

```
public void disableRole(String role) throws NotesException
```

The `disableRole` method disables the specified role for the current `ACLEntry`. Do not include the brackets when specifying the role name. The role must exist in the database. Be sure to call `ACL.save` to save your changes back to the database.

```
public void enableRole(String role) throws NotesException
```

The `enableRole` method enables the specified role for the current `ACLEntry`. Do not include the brackets when specifying the role name. The role must exist in the database. Be sure to call `ACL.save` to save your changes back to the database.

```
public boolean isRoleEnabled(String role) throws NotesException
```

The `isRoleEnabled` method returns true if the specified role is enabled for the current `ACLEntry`. Do not include the brackets when specifying the role name. The role must exist in the database.

```
public void remove() throws NotesException
```
The remove method removes the current ACLEntry from the ACL object. Be sure to call ACL.save to permanently save your changes back in the database.

THE Replication CLASS

Class Definition

```
public class Replication extends Base
```

Properties

- getCutoffDate
- getCutoffInterval/setCutoffInterval
- getPriority/setPriority
- isAbstract/setAbstract
- isCutoffDelete/setCutoffDelete
- isDisabled/setDisabled
- isIgnoreDeletes/setIgnoreDeletes
- isIgnoreDestDeletes/setIgnoreDestDeletes

Methods

- clearHistory
- reset
- save

The Replication class controls the replication properties of the current database. There is only one Replication object per database, and it is obtained using the Database.getReplicationInfo property. The Replication object enables you to enable and disable replication, control cutoff dates, control deletions, and control many other replication parameters. You must call the save method after you make any changes to the Replication properties for the properties to be permanently saved in the database.

COMMON METHODS TO CREATE

```
Database.getReplicationInfo
```

PROPERTIES

```
public DateTime getCutoffDate() throws NotesException

public long getCutoffInterval() throws NotesException

public void setCutoffInterval(long interval) throws NotesException
```

```
public boolean isCutoffDelete() throws NotesException

public void setCutoffDelete(boolean cutoff) throws NotesException
```

The getCutoffDate, getCutoffInterval, and isCutoffDelete methods work together to control two different, but related features of Domino. The first feature is the automatic purging of deletion stubs, and the second is the automatic deletion of unchanged documents. Here is how they work.

The CutoffDate is the current date minus the CutoffInterval number of days. With one of these values and the current date, you can easily calculate the other. Notice that you cannot change the CutoffDate because it is automatically calculated based on the CutoffInterval.

When a document is deleted from a Domino database, it is not completely removed from the database. Instead, the data from the document is removed and the document is turned into a deletion stub. When the database replicates, the deletion stub is sent to the replica database and causes deletion of the document in the replica. Because these deletion stubs take space in the database, if left unchecked, they would grow and waste space. Therefore, after some amount of time, these deletion stubs should be removed from the database.

The deletion stubs should not be removed prematurely, however, because once a deletion stub is gone, there is no record that the document was ever in the database because both it and the original document have been removed. If the database replicates with a replica copy that still has the original document, the document migrates back from the replica and would reappear even though it was deleted. So, the document must be deleted in all replica copies of the database before the deletion stubs are removed from a database.

The CutoffInterval controls the window of time during which it is expected that all replica copies of the database will have deleted the document. After the CutoffInterval has elapsed, deletion stubs are automatically purged. You cannot turn this automatic deletion on or off; you can only change the number of days in the CutoffInterval. It is performed automatically by the Updall task, which is scheduled by default to run at 2:00 AM every night.

To reduce the amount of processing time required for the removal of deletion stubs, the deletion stubs for a given database are processed only three times during the cutoff interval. For example, if the cutoff interval is set to the default 90 days for a particular database, deletion stubs are removed only every 30 days, or three times during the 90 days. It isn't critical to process these deletion stubs every day. So when Updall looks at a particular database, if it has been greater than one third of the CutoffInterval since the deletion stubs were purged, it will process the deletion stubs for the database.

At the same time that the Updall task is processing the deletion stubs, it can check for documents that have not changed during the cutoff interval and can purge these documents as well. You can enable this purging of unchanged documents with the setCutoffDelete property for the database, and you can query it with the isCutoffDelete property routine. This property is off by default. This feature uses the same cutoff interval as the deletion stub processing, and you can turn it on and off, but you cannot turn off deletion stub processing.

Documents that are purged by the setCutoffDelete flag do not use deletion stubs; they are completely deleted from the database so that the automatically deleted documents do not propagate the deletion to other replica copies of the database. If the document exists in other replica copies and is edited, the document will replicate back into the current database because there is no deletion stub.

You can update the CutoffInterval and the setCutoffDelete values in the Notes user interface in the Replication Settings dialog box under the Space Savers tab.

If you change the property, be sure to call the Replication.save method to permanently save your changes to the database.

```
public int getPriority() throws NotesException
```

```
public void setPriority(int priority) throws NotesException
```

You can associate a replication priority with each database. The getPriority and setPriority property routines can be used to obtain and set the replication priority. The priority values are set as an integer code. Here are the valid codes:

- Replication.CNOTES_REPLCONST_PRIORITYLOW   (1547)
- Replication.CNOTES_REPLCONST_PRIORITYMED   (1548)
- Replication.CNOTES_REPLCONST_PRIORITYLOW   (1549)
- Replication.CNOTES_REPLCONST_PRIORITYNOTSET (1565)

The low, medium, and high replication settings do not actually by themselves change the replication schedule. In the Domino directory, a set of connection records dictates the timing of the replication. The administrator has control over the replication schedule and it is even possible (say by mistake) that high-priority databases are replicated less frequently than low-priority databases. All the setPriority property does is assign a label to the database that tells the replicator that this database is a low-, medium-, or high-priority database. It is up to the administrator to assign replication schedules for low-, medium-, and high-priority databases.

If you change the property, be sure to call the Replication.save method to permanently save your changes to the database.

```
public boolean isAbstract() throws NotesException
```

```
public void setAbstract(boolean abstract) throws NotesException
```

The isAbstract and setAbstract property routines control whether large documents should be truncated and attachments removed during replication. The purpose of Abstract property is to enable local replica copies (especially of mail databases) to replicate a summary of the information while leaving the complete document on the server copy.

If you change the property, be sure to call the Replication.save method to permanently save your changes to the database.

```
public boolean isDisabled() throws NotesException
```

```
public void setDisabled(boolean disabled) throws NotesException
```

The isDisabled and setDisabled property routines enable you to control whether replication is enabled or disabled. Use setDisabled with a value of true to disable replication. You can change the disable replication property in the Notes user interface in the Replication Settings dialog box on the Other tab.

If you change the property, be sure to call the Replication.save method to permanently save your changes to the database.

```
public boolean isIgnoreDeletes() throws NotesException
```

```
public void setIgnoreDeletes(boolean ignoredel) throws NotesException
```

The isIgnoreDeletes and setIgnoreDeletes property routines enable you to control whether the deletion stubs of the current database are propagated out of the database to other replicas. Use setIgnoreDeletes with a value of true to indicate that the database should not replicate any deletion stubs to other databases. You can change this setting in the user interface in the Replication Settings dialog box under the Send tab. If you enable the Do Not Send Deletions Made in This Replica to Other Replicas option, isIgnoreDeletes returns true.

If you change the property, be sure to call the Replication.save method to permanently save your changes to the database.

```
public boolean isIgnoreDestDeletes() throws NotesException
```

```
public void setIgnoreDestDeletes(boolean ignoredel) throws NotesException
```

The isIgnoreDestDeletes and setIgnoreDestDeletes property routines enable you to control whether the deletion stubs of other replicas will be replicated into the current database. Use setIgnoreDestDeletes with a value of true to indicate that deletion stubs in other replicas should not be replicated into the current database. You can change this setting in the user interface in the Replication Settings dialog box under the Advanced tab. If you disable the Replicate Incoming Deletions option, isIgnoreDestDeletes returns true.

If you change the property, be sure to call the Replication.save method to permanently save your changes to the database.

Properties Not Implemented

Apparently, after the Lotus R5 documentation was completed, but before shipment, there were some changes. The following property routines of the Replication class appear in the Lotus printed documentation but are actually not implemented (as of release 5.0.3) in the Replication class. These methods also appear on the Domino Objects for Java and CORBA wall poster provided by Lotus, although some of the property routine names are prefixed by get rather than is.

The online help documentation has been updated, and these routines do not appear in the online help.

```
public boolean isDoNotBrowse() throws NotesException

public void setDoNotBrowse(boolean nobrowse) throws NotesException

public boolean isDoNotCatalog() throws NotesException

public void setDoNotCatlog(boolean nocatalog) throws NotesException

public boolean isHideDesign() throws NotesException

public void setHideDesign(boolean hideit) throws NotesException

public boolean isMultiDbIndex() throws NotesException

public void setMultiDbIndex(boolean dbi) throws NotesException

public boolean isNeverReplicate() throws NotesException

public void setNeverReplicate(boolean nr) throws NotesException

public boolean isNoChronos() throws NotesException

public void setNoChronos(boolean nc) throws NotesException
```

METHODS

```
public int clearHistory() throws NotesException
```
The clearHistory method clears the replication history.

```
public int reset() throws NotesException
```
The reset method resets the replication properties to their last saved values.

```
public int save() throws NotesException
```
The save method permanently saves changes to the Replication properties. If you do not call save, your changes to the properties are not stored in the database.

CHAPTER REVIEW

1. Write a Java application (local or remote) that accesses the DbDirectory and loops through each Database object in the directory. For each Database object, print the filename and path and the last date/time that the database was modified.

2. Explain the differences between the Database.createCopy, the Database.createFromTemplate, the Database.createReplica, and the DbDirectory.createDatabase methods. Why do you think the createDatabase method is in the DbDirectory class rather than the Database class?

3. Explain the differences between the Database.FTDomainSearch, the Database.FTSearch, and the Database.search methods. How is the Database.updateFTIndex method different from any of the search methods?

4. Write an audit routine agent that will inspect the ACL for the Domino directory (names.nsf) database. The agent should check to make sure that every user in the ACL that has the [ServerModifier] role has Manager-level access. If the person does not have Manager-level access, write an error message with System.out.println.

5. What is the CutoffInterval used for in the Replication object? What is the relationship between the CutoffInterval and the CutoffDate?

6. What is the difference between the getMaxSize, getSize, and getSizeQuota properties of the Database object?

7. What is the purpose of a deletion stub and how is one created? What is the relationship between deletion stubs and the Updall task?

8. Is it possible for someone listed with No Access in the ACL for a database to read and or write certain kinds of documents within that database? If so, what do you need to do with the ACL to enable it?

9. A user sets the Database replication priority for a database to High priority. However, the database does not seem to be replicating at all. Is this possible? How and why?

10. What are the differences between a document ID, a replica ID, and a universal ID?

11. Write a Java agent or application that will go through each database in the DbDirectory, find out whether the database is full-text indexed, and find out the last time it was indexed. For any database where the index has not been updated in the last 30 days, update the index. Print out the status for each database with System.out.println.

12. Write a Java agent or application that will go through each database in the mail directory on your server and print out (with System.out.println) the database name and size quota for the database. Suppose you wanted to implement a particular size quota for all the mail databases. How would you modify the program?

PART

IV

CH

17

THE DOCUMENT COLLECTION CLASSES

This chapter covers the document collection classes. Included within this group are the DocumentCollection class and classes relating to views. The View class represents a view or folder, whereas the ViewColumn class represents a single column. Three classes were introduced with R5. These are the ViewEntry class, the ViewEntryCollection class, and the ViewNavigator class.

THE DocumentCollection CLASS

Class Definition

public class DocumentCollection extends Base

Properties

- getCount
- getParent
- getQuery
- isSorted

Methods

- addDocument
- deleteDocument
- FTSearch
- getDocument
- getFirstDocument
- getLastDocument
- getNextDocument
- getNthDocument
- getPrevDocument
- putAllInFolder
- removeAll
- removeAllFromFolder
- stampAll
- updateAll

The DocumentCollection class represents a collection of documents. The documents are not sorted unless they are the result of a search. The View and ViewEntryCollection classes also provide access to collections of documents. Views are indexed in the database and can provide more efficient access. However, you might need to work with a collection of documents that has no view so you can use a `DocumentCollection` for this purpose. The elements of a `Document` collection are `Document` objects, which are discussed Chapter 19, "The `Document`, `Outline`, and `Form` Classes."

The `DocumentCollection` class has its own navigational methods; it is not an extension of the `java.util.Vector` class. Each collection maintains a current document pointer, and many of the methods will move this pointer from one document to another.

The `DocumentCollection` methods can return a deletion stub. A *deletion stub* represents a document that has been deleted, but not yet permanently removed from the database. It is kept so that replica copies will recognize that the document has been deleted from the database. You can use the `Document.isValid` method to determine whether a document is a deletion stub. Deletion stubs occur only if a document is deleted after the collection is defined.

COMMON METHODS TO CREATE

You obtain a `DocumentCollection` through many of the searching routines, or routines that access documents by a key.

`Database.FTSearch, Database.getAllDocuments, Database.getProfileDocCollection, Document.search, AgentContext.getUnprocessedDocuments, AgentContext.unprocessedFTSearch, AgentContext.unprocessedSearch, View.getAllDocumentsByKey, Document.getResponses`

PROPERTIES

`public int getCount() throws NotesException`

The `getCount` property returns the number of documents in the collection.

`public Database getParent() throws NotesException`

The `getParent` property routine returns the `Database` object that contains the `DocumentCollection`.

`public String getQuery() throws NotesException`

The `getQuery` property access routine returns the text of the query that produced the document collection if it was the result of a search. For collections that were not produced from a search, this property returns an empty string.

`public boolean isSorted() throws NotesException`

The `isSorted` property returns `true` if the `DocumentCollection` is sorted and `false` if not. The documents will be sorted as the result of one of the search methods. The sorting will be based on a relevance score with the most relevant documents ordered first.

METHODS

```
public void addDocument(Document doc) throws NotesException
```

```
public void addDocument(Document doc, boolean checkDups) throws
NotesException
```

The addDocument method adds the specified document to the document collection. The checkDups parameter only applies to remote calls. If it is true, then an immediate check for duplicates will take place rather than deferring to the next method that calls the server. If the document is a duplicate of one already in the collection, an exception is thrown. You cannot add a document to a collection that is the result of a multi-database search.

The addDocument method can be used to create custom collections that cannot be created by standard Domino search methods. You can use it to combine the results of multiple collections into a single collection.

```
public void deleteDocument(Document doc) throws NotesException
```

The deleteDocument method deletes a document from a document collection. If the document does not exist or is already deleted, an exception will be thrown. You cannot delete a document from a collection that is the result of a multi-database search.

Deleting a document from a collection is not the same as deleting it from the database. After a document is deleted from a collection, it still remains in the database. You must use the Document.remove method to remove a document from a database.

```
public void FTSearch(String query) throws NotesException
```

```
public void FTSearch(String query, int maxdocs) throws NotesException
```

The FTSearch method performs a full-text search of the documents in the document collection. It reduces the subset of documents in the DocumentCollection to those that match the query. The resulting documents are sorted by relevance with the most relevant first.

The maxdocs parameter specifies the maximum number of documents to return. A 0 means to return all documents.

The database does not need to be full-text indexed for this method to work, but if it is, the search will be more efficient. You can programmatically test whether the database is full-text indexed with the IsFTIndexed property, and you can create or update the index with the updateFTIndex method.

```
public Document getDocument(Document doc) throws NotesException
```

The getDocument method returns the document object that matches the input document. If it does not exist in the collection, a null will be returned.

At first this method seems rather strange because if you already have the document, why are you trying to access it from the collection? The answer is that this method is really most useful as a membership test within a document collection. For example, suppose you have two collections, and you want to know which documents in the first collection are also in the second collection. You can iterate through the first collection, calling getDocument on the second collection. If the result is null, the document does not appear in the second collection.

public Document getFirstDocument() throws NotesException

The getFirstDocument method returns the first document in the collection. If the documents are the result of a search, the first document is the one that has the highest relevance score. If no documents are in the collection, this method returns a null.

public Document getLastDocument() throws NotesException

The getLastDocument method returns the last document in the collection. If the documents are the result of a search, the last document is the one that has the lowest relevance score. If there are no documents in the collection, this method returns a null.

public Document getNextDocument() throws NotesException

public Document getNextDocument(Document doc) throws NotesException

The getNextDocument method returns the document that follows the current document or the one supplied as a parameter.

The implementation of CORBA/IIOP remote support locally caches documents from the server. When you use getNextDocument without a parameter, the cache can be used. When you use getNextDocument with the Document parameter, however, the cache is invalidated and new information must be retrieved from the server. Therefore, try to avoid using this construct for remote applications. Instead, use a loop with getFirstDocument() and getNextDocument().

public Document getNthDocument(int n) throws NotesException

The getNthDocument method returns the document based on its position within the collection. To retrieve the first document, use a parameter value of 1 (not 0). The second document uses a parameter of 2, and so forth.

Domino is not internally capable of randomly accessing documents in the collection, so using this routine causes sequential access of the previous documents in the collection. Thus, to access the 1000th document of a collection, Domino will count through all the previous 999 documents. If you access documents in a loop with getNthDocument, the loop time will get successively longer and longer.

The implementation of CORBA/IIOP remote support locally caches documents from the server. When you use getNextDocument without a parameter, the cache can be used. When you use getNthDocument, however, the cache is invalidated and new information must be retrieved from the server. Therefore, try to avoid using getNthDocument for remote applications. Instead, use a loop with getFirstDocument() and getNextDocument().

```
public Document getPrevDocument() throws NotesException
```

```
public Document getPrevDocument(Document doc) throws NotesException
```

The getPrevDocument method returns the document that precedes the current document or the one supplied as a parameter.

The implementation of CORBA/IIOP remote support locally caches documents from the server. When you use getPrevDocument without a parameter, the cache can be used. When you use getPrevDocument with the Document parameter, however, the cache is invalidated and new information must be retrieved from the server. Therefore, try to avoid using this construct for remote applications. Instead, use a loop with getLastDocument() and getPrevDocument().

```
public void putAllInFolder(String foldername) throws NotesException
```

```
public void putAllInFolder(String foldername, boolean createonfail) throws
NotesException
```

The putAllInFolder method puts all the documents in the current DocumentCollection into the specified folder. If you specify createonfail to be false, an exception will be thrown if the folder does not exist. If you do not specify createonfail, the default value is true, so a folder will be created if it does not exist.

You can specify nested folders by using backslashes in the name, such as "Basketball\\Lakers". You must use two slashes to represent a single slash in the name.

Example:

```
import lotus.domino.*;

public class JavaAgent extends AgentBase {
    public void NotesMain() {
        try {
            Session session = getSession();
            AgentContext agentContext = session.getAgentContext();
            Database db = agentContext.getCurrentDatabase();
            DocumentCollection dc = db.FTSearch("record");
            int count =dc.getCount();
            System.out.println("Collection has " + count  + " elements.");
            if (count > 0) {
                dc.putAllInFolder("NewFolder"); // created if doesn't exist
                View v= db.getView("NewFolder");
                if (null != v) {
                    System.out.println(v.getName() + " exists.");
```

```
                }
            }
        } catch(Exception e) {
            e.printStackTrace();
        }
    }
}
```

public void removeAll(boolean force) throws NotesException

The removeAll method removes from the database all the documents that are contained in the document collection. There is special handling of documents that are modified by other users after the creation of the current collection, but prior to the execution of removeAll. If the force parameter is false, these special documents are not deleted from the database. If force is true, all documents in the collection are deleted regardless of what other users might have done to the same documents.

After completion of the method, all documents that were successfully removed from the database are removed from the document collection.

Contrast this method with removeAllFromFolder. The removeAll method deletes the documents completely from the database, whereas the removeAllFromFolder just removes the documents from the folder and leaves them in the database.

public void removeAllFromFolder(String foldername) throws NotesException

The removeAllFromFolder method removes all documents that are in the document collection from the specified folder. Note that this method does not actually delete the documents from the database; it just removes them from the folder. You can include nested folders by using backslashes in the folder name.

public void stampAll(String itemname, Object value) throws NotesException

The stampAll method enables you to perform a mass change on the entire collection of documents. You can specify a field name and a new value. The new value will replace the field's value in all the documents. If the field does not exist in a document, it will be created.

Note that this method works directly on the disk versions of the documents. Any in-memory Document objects are not affected by this routine. Thus, you must save any pending document changes prior to using this routine so that your changes will be reflected in the disk copy of the document. Also, after execution of the method, you must refresh the value of any in-memory Document objects to see the changes that were made using stampAll.

public void updateAll() throws NotesException

The updateAll method is similar to the AgentContext.updateProcessedDoc method, except that updateAll marks all documents in the collection as having been processed. Your method does not apply to remote (CORBA) calls because it must be invoked within an agent.

This method does not actually change any values within each document. It modifies the flag that indicates that a particular agent has processed the document. Contrast this method with the stampAll method, which updates a field within each document. The updateAll method will not cause a document to be a replication candidate, whereas the stampAll method will.

THE View CLASS

Class Definition

```
public class View extends Base
```

Properties

- getAliases
- getAllEntries
- getBackgroundColor
- getColumnCount
- getColumnNames
- getColumns
- getCreated
- getHeaderLines
- getLastModified
- getName
- getParent
- getReaders/setReaders
- getRowLines
- getSpacing
- getTopLevelEntryCount
- getUniversalID
- isAutoUpdate/setAutoUpdate
- isCalendar
- isCategorized
- isConflict
- isDefaultView
- isFolder
- isHierarchical
- isModified
- isPrivate
- isProtectedReaders/setProtectedReaders

Methods

- clear
- createViewNav
- createViewNavFrom
- createViewNavFromCategory
- createViewNavFromChildren
- createViewNavFromDescendants
- createViewNavMaxLevel
- FTSearch
- getAllDocumentsByKey
- getAllEntriesByKey
- getChild
- getColumn
- getDocumentByKey
- getEntryByKey
- getFirstDocument
- getLastDocument
- getNextDocument
- getNextSibling
- getNthDocument
- getParentDocument
- getPrevDocument
- getPrevSibling
- refresh
- remove

PART
IV
CH
18

The View class represents a view or folder in the database. The View class provides an ordering of the documents and enables progression through the documents shown in the view. From the View class, you can access a ViewEntryCollection, which is a collection of ViewEntry objects. Each ViewEntry represents one row of the view. A ViewNavigator object enables you to navigate through the ViewEntry elements. You can also access a DocumentCollection for a view; however, a DocumentCollection will not enable you to access non-document rows such as totals. A ViewNavigator enables you to access total and category rows as well as document rows.

COMMON METHODS TO CREATE

Database.getView, Database.getViews, ViewColumn.getParent,
ViewNavigator.getParentView, ViewEntryCollection.getParent, Document.getParentView,
ViewEntry.getParent

PROPERTIES

`public java.util.Vector getAliases() throws NotesException`

The getAliases property routine enables you to access the list of aliases for the view. It does not return the view's name. To access the view name, use the View.getName property routine.

`public ViewEntryCollection getAllEntries() throws NotesException`

The getAllEntries property routine returns a ViewEntryCollection that represents all document entries in the view. Elements of a ViewEntryCollection represent only documents, not total or category rows. You can use a ViewNavigator to navigate to total and category rows.

`public int getBackgroundColor() throws NotesException`

The getBackgroundColor property routine returns a code that represents one of the 16 valid background colors. You can use one of the following RichTextStyle color constants for the color:

- RichTextStyle.COLOR_BLACK
- RichTextStyle.COLOR_WHITE
- RichTextStyle.COLOR_RED
- RichTextStyle.COLOR_GREEN
- RichTextStyle.COLOR_BLUE
- RichTextStyle.COLOR_CYAN
- RichTextStyle.COLOR_YELLOW
- RichTextStyle.COLOR_MAGENTA
- RichTextStyle.COLOR_DARK_RED
- RichTextStyle.COLOR_DARK_GREEN
- RichTextStyle.COLOR_DARK_BLUE
- RichTextStyle.COLOR_DARK_CYAN
- RichTextStyle.COLOR_DARK_YELLOW
- RichTextStyle.COLOR_DARK_MAGENTA
- RichTextStyle.COLOR_GRAY
- RichTextStyle.COLOR_LIGHT_GRAY

```
public int getColumnCount() throws NotesException
```

The `getColumnCount` property routine returns the number of columns in the view.

```
public java.util.Vector getColumnNames() throws NotesException
```

The `getColumnNames` property returns a vector of `String` objects, each representing one column of the view. The names are returned in the order in which they appear in the view from left to right.

```
public java.util.Vector getColumns() throws NotesException
```

The `getColumns` property returns a vector of `ViewColumn` objects. The objects are returned in the order in which they appear in the view from left to right.

```
public DateTime getCreated() throws NotesException
```

The `getCreated` property routine returns the date and time that the view was first created. See also the `getLastModified` property, which returns the date and time that the view was last modified.

```
public int getHeaderLines() throws NotesException
```

The `getHeaderLines` property routine returns the number of lines allocated the view's header. See also the `getRowLines` property.

```
public DateTime getLastModified() throws NotesException
```

The `getLastModified` property returns the date and time that the design of the view was last modified. See also the `getCreated` property routine, which returns the date and time that the view was first created.

```
public String getName() throws NotesException
```

The `getName` property returns the name of the view. Use the `getAliases` property to get the aliases for the view.

```
public Database getParent() throws NotesException
```

The `getParent` property routine returns the `Database` object for the database that contains the view.

```
public java.util.Vector getReaders() throws NotesException
```

```
public void setReaders(java.util.Vector readers) throws NotesException
```

When you design a view with the Domino Designer, you can control who has access to a view on the Security tab of the View properties dialog box. By default, all readers and above have access to the view. You can designate specific users or groups to be allowed to use the view in the dialog box. In Java, you can access the list using the getReaders and setReaders property methods. The list of readers can also include role names enclosed in square brackets.

If the default has not been changed and all readers are allowed to read the view, the getReaders routine will return a vector with zero elements.

When setting the value, you create a Vector of String elements. Each element represents one name. To remove the reader restrictions and allow all readers to access the view, use setReaders with a null parameter.

Example:

```java
import lotus.domino.*;
import java.util.*;

public class JavaAgent extends AgentBase {
    public void NotesMain() {
        try {
            Session session = getSession();
            AgentContext agentContext = session.getAgentContext();
            Database db = agentContext.getCurrentDatabase();
            View v = db.getView("View1");
            Vector vr = v.getReaders();
            // Print out the current readers
            System.out.print("Readers: ");
            if (null == vr) {
                System.out.println("null");
            }
            else {
                System.out.println(vr.size() + " elements.");
                for (int i = 0; i < vr.size() ; i++) {
                    System.out.print(vr.elementAt(i) + "\n");
                }
            }
            System.out.println("");
            Vector newvr = new Vector(2);
            newvr.addElement("John Doe/Acme");
            newvr.addElement("Anonymous");
            v.setReaders(newvr);

        } catch(Exception e) {
            e.printStackTrace();
        }
    }
}
```

The example will print out the current reader list and then change it to a list with two elements, John Doe and Anonymous.

public int getRowLines() throws NotesException

The getRowLines property returns the number of lines in each row of the view. See also the getHeaderLines property.

```
public int getSpacing() throws NotesException
```

The getSpacing property returns a code that indicates the amount of spacing that should be placed between rows of a view. Here are the valid values:

- View.SPACING_SINGLE
- View.SPACING_ONE_POINT_25
- View.SPACING_ONE_POINT_50
- View.SPACING_ONE_POINT_75
- View.SPACING_DOUBLE

```
public int getTopLevelEntryCount() throws NotesException
```

The getTopLevelEntryCount property returns the number of top-level entries in a view. If the view is categorized or includes totals, only these lines are included in the count. When the view is not categorized, a count of all the main documents is returned.

```
public String getUniversalID() throws NotesException
```

The getUniversalID property returns the universal ID of the view. A universal ID is a 32-character hexadecimal string that uniquely identifies the view in all replicas of a database.

```
public boolean isAutoUpdate() throws NotesException
```

```
public void setAutoUpdate(boolean update) throws NotesException
```

The isAutoUpdate property routine returns a flag that indicates whether the view should be automatically updated before a navigation operation if the view has changed. The setAutoUpdate property routine allows you to set the flag. For local operations, the default is true, which means that the view will be automatically refreshed if it has changed since the database was opened or since the last refresh.

For remote operations (CORBA), the default value is false. Setting this value to true will turn off caching for remote operations.

```
public boolean isCalendar() throws NotesException
```

The isCalendar property returns true if the view represents a calendar view and false otherwise.

```
public boolean isCategorized() throws NotesException
```

The isCategorized property routine returns true if the view is categorized.

```
public boolean isConflict() throws NotesException
```

The isConflict property is true if the view is enabled for conflict checking and false otherwise.

```
public boolean isDefaultView() throws NotesException
```

The isDefaultView property is true if the current view is the default view for the database.

```
public boolean isFolder() throws NotesException
```

The View class represents both folders and views. You can determine whether a View object is a folder or view by checking the isFolder property. It is true for folders and false for views.

```
public boolean isHierarchical() throws NotesException
```

The isHierarchical property is true if the view shows response documents in a hierarchy. You can set this property in the user interface on the Options tab of the View properties box. Enable the Show response documents in a hierarchy checkbox option.

```
public boolean isModified() throws NotesException
```

The isModified property returns true if the view has been modified since it was retrieved. This property works in conjunction with the isAutoUpdate property. If AutoUpdate is true then the View is automatically updated after documents change, so isModified returns false because the view is up-to-date. If AutoUpdate is false then isModified returns true if documents change. Here is an example agent that illustrates the relationship between isModified and isAutoUpdate.

```java
import lotus.domino.*;

public class JavaAgent extends AgentBase {
    public void NotesMain() {
        try {
            Session session = getSession();
            AgentContext agentContext = session.getAgentContext();
            Database db = agentContext.getCurrentDatabase();
            View v= db.getView("View1");
            System.out.println("* * * First Test * * *");
            System.out.println("View1 AutoUpdate: " + v.isAutoUpdate());
            System.out.println("View1 Before IsModified: " + v.isModified());
            Document doc = v.getFirstDocument();
            doc.replaceItemValue("Field1", "Modify Field1");
            doc.save();
            System.out.println("View1 After IsModified: " + v.isModified());

            System.out.println("\n* * * Second Test * * *");
            v.setAutoUpdate(false);
            System.out.println("View1 AutoUpdate: " + v.isAutoUpdate());
            System.out.println("View1 Before IsModified: " + v.isModified());
            doc.replaceItemValue("Field1", "Modify Field1 Again");
            doc.save();
            System.out.println("View1 After IsModified: " + v.isModified());

        } catch(Exception e) {
            e.printStackTrace();
        }
    }
}
```

Here is the sample output generated by this agent:

```
* * * First Test * * *
View1 AutoUpdate: true
View1 Before IsModified: false
View1 After IsModified: false
* * * Second Test * * *
View1 AutoUpdate: false
View1 Before IsModified: false
View1 After IsModified: true
```

In the first test, isAutoUpdate is set to false. Notice isModified returns false before and after modifying a document. In the second test, isModified returns true after the document has been modified.

```
public boolean isPrivate() throws NotesException
```

The isPrivate property returns true if the view is a private (personal) view or is a private-on-first-use view. Lotus uses the term private in the creation of views, but the term personal views in conjunction with ACLs. The terms private view and personal view are synonymous.

```
public boolean isProtectReaders() throws NotesException
```

```
public void setProtectReaders(boolean protect) throws NotesException
```

When you design a view with the Domino Designer, you can control who has access to a view on the Security tab of the View properties dialog box. By default, all readers and above have access to the view. You can designate specific users or groups to be allowed to use the view in the dialog box. In Java, you can access the list using the getReaders and setReaders property methods.

The isProtectReaders flag controls whether this list of readers is protected during replication. If the value is true, the list of readers for the view will not be changed by replication. If it is false, the list can be overwritten by replication. You can set this flag with the setProtectReaders property routine.

The ProtectReaders property cannot be set from the Domino Designer user interface. The only way to set this property is by using these property routines. Domino stores the list of readers in an internal item called $Readers. When you protect the $Readers item, another internal item is created called $RetainFields and its content is set to "$Readers". This prevents replication from overwriting the $Readers field.

METHODS

```
public void clear() throws NotesException
```

The clear method clears any full-text search filtering for a view. Any calls to getDocument methods will reference all documents of the view, not just the results of the search.

```
public ViewNavigator createViewNav() throws NotesException
```

```
public ViewNavigator createViewNav(int cacheSize) throws NotesException
```

The `createViewNav` method creates a view navigator for the view. The view navigator contains all the entries of the view, even if a full-text search has been performed. Use a `ViewEntryCollection` to navigate a full-text search filtered view. You can specify a cache size for remote (CORBA) sessions. The value of the cache size can be from 0–128, which is the default size. A cache improves the performance of navigating sequentially through the view.

```
public ViewNavigator createViewNavFrom(Object entry) throws NotesException
```

```
public ViewNavigator createViewNavFrom(Object entry, int cacheSize) throws
NotesException
```

The `createViewNavFrom` method creates a view navigator starting from a particular document or view entry. The entry parameter should be either a `Document` object or a `ViewEntry` object. The `cacheSize` specifies the number of entries to save and can be an integer from 0–128, but only applies to remote (CORBA) sessions.

```
public ViewNavigator createViewNavFromCategory(String categoryname) throws
NotesException
```

```
public ViewNavigator createViewNavFromCategory(String categoryname, int
cacheSize) throws NotesException
```

The `createViewNavFromCategory` method creates a view navigator for the entries that are shown under the specified category. The `cacheSize` specifies the number of entries to save and can be an integer from 0–128, but only applies to remote (CORBA) sessions. You can use subcategories by including backslashes in the category name. For example, `"Accounts\\Western"` would indicate a subcategory.

```
public ViewNavigator createViewNavFromChildren(Object entry) throws
NotesException
```

```
public ViewNavigator createViewNavFromChildren(Object entry, int cacheSize)
throws NotesException
```

The `createViewNavFromChildren` method creates a view navigator for the entries that are immediate children of the specified document or View entry. The entry parameter should be either a `Document` object or a `ViewEntry` object and cannot be `null`. The `cacheSize` specifies the number of entries to save and can be an integer from 0–128, but only applies to remote (CORBA) sessions.

```
public ViewNavigator createViewNavFromDescendants(Object entry) throws
NotesException
```

```
public ViewNavigator createViewNavFromDescendants(Object entry, int
cacheSize) throws NotesException
```

The `createViewNavFromDescendants` method creates a view navigator for the entries that are descendants of the specified document or View entry. The `entry` parameter should be either a `Document` object or a `ViewEntry` object and cannot be `null`. The `cacheSize` specifies the number of entries to save and can be an integer from 0–128, but only applies to remote (CORBA) sessions.

```
public ViewNavigator createViewNavMaxLevel(int level) throws NotesException
```

```
public ViewNavigator createViewNavMaxLevel(int level, int cacheSize) throws
NotesException
```

The `createViewNavMaxLevel` method creates a view navigator for the entries that are within a certain number of levels from the top level. The level parameter can range from 0 (top level only) to 30 (default). The `cacheSize` specifies the number of entries to save and can be an integer from 0–128, but only applies to remote (CORBA) sessions.

```
public int FTSearch(String query) throws NotesException
```

```
public int FTSearch(String query, int maxdocs) throws NotesException
```

The `FTSearch` method performs a full-text search of the documents in the view. It filters the documents in the `View` to those that match the query.

The `maxdocs` parameter specifies the maximum number of documents to return. A 0 means to return all documents. The return value represents the number of documents in the view following the search.

The database does not need to be full-text indexed for this method to work, but if it is, the search will be more efficient. You can programmatically test whether the database is full-text indexed with the `IsFTIndexed` property, and you can create or update the index with the `updateFTIndex` method.

After you have executed the `FTSearch` method, the view navigation and access routines apply only to the filtered subset. For example, `getAllEntries` returns only the entries in the filtered subset. Navigation methods such as `getNextDocument` access only filtered documents.

If you execute the `clear` method, the full-text search filter is removed and the original documents of the view will be restored.

```
public DocumentCollection getAllDocumentsByKey(java.util.Vector keys) throws
NotesException
```

```
public DocumentCollection getAllDocumentsByKey(Object key) throws
NotesException
```

```
public DocumentCollection getAllDocumentsByKey(java.util.Vector keys, boolean
exact) throws NotesException
```

```
public DocumentCollection getAllDocumentsByKey(Object key, boolean exact)
throws NotesException
```

The getAllDocumentsByKey method enables you to search a view for documents that match one or more keys. The key(s) will be compared to sorted columns of the view. Each key in the Vector represents one column to search. The key values can be String, Number, DateTime, or DateRange objects and are compared to the keys found in the sorted columns. If you specify the exact parameter as true, only exact matches will be included in the result. The default is to allow partial matches.

The return value is an unsorted DocumentCollection of all the documents that match the keys. If no documents match the key(s), the DocumentCollection will be empty. If you want to preserve the order of the matched documents or access column values, use the getAllEntriesByKey method.

A common mistake is to forget to turn on sorting for your search columns. If your result set is empty, be sure to check whether you have turned on sorting for the columns you are using as keys.

```
public ViewEntryCollection getAllEntriesByKey(java.util.Vector keys) throws
NotesException
```

```
public ViewEntryCollection getAllEntriesByKey(Object key) throws
NotesException
```

```
public ViewEntryCollection getAllEntriesByKey(java.util.Vector keys, boolean
exact) throws NotesException
```

```
public ViewEntryCollection getAllEntriesByKey(Object key, boolean exact)
throws NotesException
```

The getAllEntriesByKey method enables you to search a view for documents that match one or more keys. The key(s) will be compared to sorted columns of the view. Each key in the Vector represents one column to search. The key values can be String, Number, DateTime, or DateRange objects and are compared to the keys found in the sorted columns. If you specify the exact parameter as true, only exact matches will be included in the result. The default is to allow partial matches.

The return value is a ViewEntryCollection in view order of all the documents that match the keys. If no documents match the key(s), the ViewEntryCollection will be empty. With a ViewEntryCollection you can access view column values, which is not necessarily possible with a DocumentCollection.

A common mistake is to forget to turn on sorting for your search columns. If your result set is empty, be sure to check whether you have turned on sorting for the columns you are using as keys.

public Document getChild(Document doc) throws NotesException

The getChild method returns the first response document to the specified document in the view. The method returns null if there are no responses to the document. If you have called FTSearch, the getChild method returns the next document in the view, whether it is a child or not.

public ViewColumn getColumn(int columnNumber) throws NotesException

The getColumn method returns a ViewColumn object that represents the specified column. The columnNumber must be greater than or equal to one, which represents the first column. The ViewColumn object can be used to retrieve various formatting characteristics about the column.

public Document getDocumentByKey(java.util.Vector keys) throws NotesException

public Document getDocumentByKey(Object key) throws NotesException

public Document getDocumentByKey(java.util.Vector keys, boolean exact) throws NotesException

public Document getDocumentByKey(Object key, boolean exact) throws NotesException

The getDocumentByKey method enables you to search a view for a document that matches one or more keys. The key(s) will be compared to sorted columns of the view. Each key in the Vector represents one column to search. The key values can be String, Number, DateTime, or DateRange objects and are compared to the keys found in the sorted columns. If you specify the exact parameter as true, only exact matches will be included in the result. The default is to allow partial matches.

The return value is the first document that matches the keys. If no documents match the key(s), the result is null.

A common mistake is to forget to turn on sorting for your search columns. If your result set is empty, be sure to check whether you have turned on sorting for the columns you are using as keys.

PART

IV

CH

18

```
public ViewEntry getEntryByKey(java.util.Vector keys) throws NotesException
```

```
public ViewEntry getEntryByKey(Object key) throws NotesException
```

```
public ViewEntry getEntryByKey(java.util.Vector keys, boolean exact) throws
NotesException
```

```
public ViewEntry getEntryByKey(Object key, boolean exact) throws
NotesException
```

The getEntryByKey method enables you to search a view for a document that matches one or more keys. The return result is a ViewEntry for the matching document, if one exists. The key(s) will be compared to sorted columns of the view. Each key in the Vector represents one column to search. The key values can be String, Number, DateTime, or DateRange objects and are compared to the keys found in the sorted columns. If you specify the exact parameter as true, only exact matches will be included in the result. The default is to allow partial matches.

The return value is a ViewEntry for the first document that matches the keys. If no documents match the key(s), the result is null.

A common mistake is to forget to turn on sorting for your search columns. If your result set is empty, be sure to check whether you have turned on sorting for the columns you are using as keys.

public Document getFirstDocument() throws NotesException

The getFirstDocument method returns the first document of the view. It returns null if there are no documents in the view. If the view is filtered by FTSearch, only documents matching the search criteria are returned. The ViewNavigator and ViewEntryCollection classes can provide more efficient methods for navigating through views, especially on remote (CORBA) sessions because of caching support.

public Document getLastDocument() throws NotesException

The getLastDocument method returns the last document of the view. It returns null if there are no documents in the view. If the view is filtered by FTSearch, only documents matching the search criteria are returned. The ViewNavigator and ViewEntryCollection classes can provide more efficient methods for navigating through views, especially on remote (CORBA) sessions because of caching support.

public Document getNextDocument(Document doc) throws NotesException

The getNextDocument method returns the document that follows the specified document of the view. It returns null if there are no more documents in the view. If the view is filtered by FTSearch, only documents matching the search criteria are returned. The ViewNavigator and ViewEntryCollection classes can provide more efficient methods for navigating through views, especially on remote (CORBA) sessions because of caching support.

`public Document getNextSibling(Document doc) throws NotesException`

The `getNextSibling` method returns the document that follows the specified document at the same level in the view. If the specified document is a main document, the returned document will be a main document. If the specified document is a response document or a document within a category, the resulting document will be also. The method returns `null` if there are no more siblings in the view. If the view is filtered by `FTSearch`, only documents matching the search criteria are returned. The `ViewNavigator` and `ViewEntryCollection` classes can provide more efficient methods for navigating through views, especially on remote (CORBA) sessions because of caching support.

`public Document getNthDocument(int n) throws NotesException`

The `getNthDocument` method returns the Nth main document in the view. To retrieve the first document, use a value of 1. Only main documents are returned; response documents are skipped. The method returns `null` if there is no document at the specified location. If the view is filtered by `FTSearch`, only documents matching the search criteria are returned. The `ViewNavigator` and `ViewEntryCollection` classes can provide more efficient methods for navigating through views, especially on remote (CORBA) sessions because of caching support.

`public Document getParentDocument(Document doc) throws NotesException`

The `getParentDocument` method returns the parent document for the specified document of the view. It returns `null` if the specified document is a main document. If the view is filtered by `FTSearch`, the previous document in the view is returned, regardless of level.

`public Document getPrevDocument(Document doc) throws NotesException`

The `getPrevDocument` method returns the document that precedes the specified document of the view. It returns `null` if there are no preceding documents in the view. If the view is filtered by `FTSearch`, only documents matching the search criteria are returned. The `ViewNavigator` and `ViewEntryCollection` classes can provide more efficient methods for navigating through views, especially on remote (CORBA) sessions because of caching support.

`public Document getPrevSibling(Document doc) throws NotesException`

The `getPrevSibling` method returns the document that precedes the specified document at the same level in the view. If the specified document is a main document, the returned document will be a main document. If the specified document is a response document or a document within a category, the resulting document will be also. The method returns `null` if there are no previous siblings in the view. If the view is filtered by `FTSearch`, only documents matching the search criteria are returned. The `ViewNavigator` and `ViewEntryCollection` classes can provide more efficient methods for navigating through views, especially on remote (CORBA) sessions because of caching support.

```
public void refresh() throws NotesException
```

The View object represents a snapshot of the contents of the view at a particular point in time. Additions and deletions that occur subsequent to the snapshot do not affect view navigation until the refresh method is called. The refresh method updates the contents of the view with any changes since the last refresh or since the view was created. If isAutoUpdate is true, the view will be refreshed automatically on every view navigation.

After a refresh, existing ViewEntry objects might no longer be valid because the documents might have changed or might have been deleted. Do not use these ViewEntry objects after you have performed a refresh.

```
public void remove() throws NotesException
```

The remove method removes the current view from the database. Because this operation works with the back-end classes, the view might be visible in the Notes user interface. If possible, avoid removing a view that is currently visible to the user. When the user closes and opens the database, the view will no longer be visible. After a view has been removed from the database, any further references to the view will cause an exception.

THE ViewColumn CLASS

Class Definition

```
public class ViewColumn extends Base
```

Properties

- getAlignment
- getDateFmt
- getFontColor
- getFontFace
- getFontPointSize
- getFontStyle
- getFormula
- getHeaderAlignment
- getItemName
- getListSep
- getNumberAttrib
- getNumberDigits
- getNumberFormat
- getParent
- getPosition
- getTimeDateFmt
- getTimeFmt

- getTimeZoneFmt
- getTitle
- getWidth
- isAccentSensitiveSort
- isCaseSensitiveSort
- isCategory
- isField
- isFormula
- isHidden
- isHideDetail
- isIcon
- isResize
- isResortAscending
- isResortDescending
- isResortToView
- isResponse
- isSecondaryResort
- isSecondaryResortDescending
- isShowTwistie
- isSortDescending
- isSorted

The ViewColumn class represents a column in a view or folder. It is used mainly to inquire about the column formatting.

COMMON METHODS TO CREATE

View.getColumn, View.getColumns

PROPERTIES

```
public int getAlignment() throws NotesException
```

The getAlignment property routine returns a code that represents the data alignment within the column. The valid values are

- ViewColumn.ALIGN_LEFT—(Value 0)
- ViewColumn.ALIGN_RIGHT—(Value 1)
- ViewColumn.ALIGN_CENTER—(Value 2)

The Alignment code values cannot be combined. Only a single value is returned.

```
public int getDateFmt() throws NotesException
```

The getDateFmt property routine returns a code that represents the formatting of dates within the column. The valid values are

- ViewColumn.FMT_YMD—(Value 0) (Year, month, and day)
- ViewColumn.FMT_MD—(Value 2) (Month and day)
- ViewColumn.FMT_YM—(Value 3) (Year and month)
- ViewColumn.FMT_Y4M—(Value 6) (4-digit year and month)

The DateFmt code values cannot be combined. Only a single value is returned.

```
public int getFontColor() throws NotesException
```

The getFontColor property access routine returns the color for the text displayed within the view column. The valid values are

- RichTextStyle.COLOR_BLACK
- RichTextStyle.COLOR_WHITE
- RichTextStyle.COLOR_RED
- RichTextStyle.COLOR_GREEN
- RichTextStyle.COLOR_BLUE
- RichTextStyle.COLOR_CYAN
- RichTextStyle.COLOR_YELLOW
- RichTextStyle.COLOR_MAGENTA
- RichTextStyle.COLOR_DARK_RED
- RichTextStyle.COLOR_DARK_GREEN
- RichTextStyle.COLOR_DARK_BLUE
- RichTextStyle.COLOR_DARK_CYAN
- RichTextStyle.COLOR_DARK_YELLOW
- RichTextStyle.COLOR_DARK_MAGENTA
- RichTextStyle.COLOR_GRAY
- RichTextStyle.COLOR_LIGHT_GRAY

The FontColor code values cannot be combined. Only a single value is returned.

```
public String getFontFace() throws NotesException
```

The getFontFace property routine returns the name of the font face for the data within the column.

```
public int getFontPointSize() throws NotesException
```
The getFontPointSize property routine returns the point size of the font for the data within the column.

```
public int getFontStyle() throws NotesException
```
The getFontStyle property routine returns a code that represents the style of the font of the column. Here are the valid values:

- ViewColumn.FONT_BOLD—(Value 1)
- ViewColumn.FONT_ITALIC—(Value 2)
- ViewColumn.FONT_UNDERLINE—(Value 4)
- ViewColumn.FONT_STRIKEOUT—(Value 8)

The returned value can consist of multiple values. For example, the font style might be both bold and italic. In the code that follows, I use the bitwise AND operator (&) to test whether the flag is on or off. The result will be nonzero only if the specified flag is on. The bitwise AND is used to ignore other flags that might be contained within the same variable.

Example:
```
import lotus.domino.*;

public class JavaAgent extends AgentBase {
    public void NotesMain() {
        try {
            Session session = getSession();
            AgentContext agentContext = session.getAgentContext();
            Database db = agentContext.getCurrentDatabase();
            View view = db.getView("View1");        // Get the view
            ViewColumn vc = view.getColumn(1);       // Get the first column
            String fontface = vc.getFontFace();      // Get the Font face name
            int fontsize = vc.getFontPointSize();    // Get the point size
            int fontstyle = vc.getFontStyle();       // Get the styles
            System.out.println("Column1 Font: " + fontface + " " + fontsize +
            ➥" points");
            if (0 != (fontstyle & ViewColumn.FONT_BOLD))
            ➥{System.out.println("Bold");}
            if (0 != (fontstyle & ViewColumn.FONT_ITALIC))
            ➥{System.out.println("Italic");}
            if (0 != (fontstyle & ViewColumn.FONT_UNDERLINE))
            ➥{System.out.println("Underline");}
            if (0 != (fontstyle & ViewColumn.FONT_STRIKEOUT))
            ➥{System.out.println("Strikeout");}
        } catch(Exception e) {
            e.printStackTrace();
        }
    }
}
```

The example gets the first view column in the view named View1. It prints out the name of the font face and the point size. Following this, it prints out one line for each style attribute that is turned on for the view column.

`public String getFormula() throws NotesException`

The getFormula property returns the View column's formula. If the view column represents a single field, the property might return an empty string or a string containing just the field name. If the View column's value represents a field, use the getItemName property routine to get the name of the item. You can use the isFormula property routine to determine whether the formula represents a formula or single field.

`public int getHeaderAlignment() throws NotesException`

The getHeaderAlignment property routine returns a code that represents the alignment for the header of the column. The valid values are

- ViewColumn.ALIGN_LEFT—(Value 0)
- ViewColumn.ALIGN_RIGHT—(Value 1)
- ViewColumn.ALIGN_CENTER—(Value 2)

The HeaderAlignment code values cannot be combined. Only a single value is returned.

`public String getItemName() throws NotesException`

The getItemName property routine returns the name of the field that is used for display in the column. If the value of the column is specified by a formula, this property returns the name of an internal name. You can access the formula by using getFormula. You can use isField to test whether the formula represents a single field.

`public int getListSep() throws NotesException`

The getListSep property returns a code that represents the separator used for multiple-value (List) fields. Here are the valid codes:

- ViewColumn.SEP_SPACE—(Value 1)
- ViewColumn.SEP_COMMA—(Value 2)
- ViewColumn.SEP_SEMICOLON—(Value 3)
- ViewColumn.SEP_NEWLINE—(Value 4)

The ListSep code values cannot be combined. Only a single value is returned.

`public int getNumberAttrib() throws NotesException`

The getNumberAttrib property returns a code that represents the formatting attributes used for numeric fields. Here are the valid codes:

- ViewColumn.ATTR_PUNCTUATED—(Value 1) (Punctuated at thousands)
- ViewColumn.ATTR_PARENS—(Value 2) (Parentheses for negative numbers)
- ViewColumn.ATTR_PERCENT—(Value 4) (Format as percentage)

Note that the NumberAttribute can have multiple values, which are represented by adding the codes. The formatting attributes can be extracted by using a bitwise AND technique similar to the one found in the getFontStyle example.

public int getNumberDigits() throws NotesException

The getNumberDigits method returns the number of decimal places for a numeric value in the column.

public int getNumberFormat() throws NotesException

The getNumberFormat property returns an integer code that represents the type of formatting that should be used for numeric values in the column. Here are the valid codes:

- ViewColumn.FMT_GENERAL—(Value 0)
- ViewColumn.FMT_FIXED—(Value 1)
- ViewColumn.FMT_SCIENTIFIC—(Value 2)
- ViewColumn.FMT_CURRENCY—(Value 3)

The NumberFormat code values cannot be combined. Only a single value is returned.

public View getParent() throws NotesException

The getParent property returns a View object for the view that contains the view column.

public int getPosition() throws NotesException

The getPosition property returns the column number, or position, within the view. Columns are numbered starting from 1 for the leftmost column.

public int getTimeDateFmt() throws NotesException

The getTimeDateFmt property returns an integer code that represents the type of format used for a time-date value within the column. Here are the valid values:

- ViewColumn.FMT_DATE—(Value 0)
- ViewColumn.FMT_TIME—(Value 1)
- ViewColumn.FMT_DATETIME—(Value 2)
- ViewColumn.FMT_TODAYTIME—(Value 3)

The TimeDateFmt code values cannot be combined. Only a single value is returned.

```
public int getTimeFmt() throws NotesException
```

The getTimeFmt property returns an integer code that represents the type of format used for a time value within the column. Here are the valid values:

- ViewColumn.FMT_HMS—(Value 0) (Hours, Minutes, Seconds)
- ViewColumn.FMT_HM—(Value 1) (Hours and Minutes)

The TimeFmt code values cannot be combined. Only a single value is returned.

```
public int getTimeZoneFmt() throws NotesException
```

The getTimeZoneFmt property returns an integer code that represents the formatting used for the time zone of a date-time value within the column. Here are the valid values:

- ViewColumn.FMT_NEVER—(Value 0) (Never show it)
- ViewColumn.FMT_SOMETIMES—(Value 1) (Only if non-local)
- ViewColumn.FMT_ALWAYS—(Value 2) (Always show it)

The TimeZoneFmt code values cannot be combined. Only a single value is returned.

```
public String getTitle() throws NotesException
```

The getTitle property returns the title of the view column. If there is no title, it will return an empty string.

```
public int getWidth() throws NotesException
```

The getWidth property returns the width of the column.

```
public boolean isAccentSensitiveSort() throws NotesException
```

The isAccentSensitiveSort property returns true if the view column uses accent-sensitive sorting. In the Domino Designer, you can enable this property in the Column properties box on the Sorting tab.

```
public boolean isCaseSensitiveSort() throws NotesException
```

The isCaseSensitiveSort property returns true if the view column uses case-sensitive sorting. In the Domino Designer, you can enable this property in the Column properties box on the Sorting tab.

```
public boolean isCategory() throws NotesException
```

The isCategory property returns true if the view column is categorized.

```
public boolean isField() throws NotesException
```

The isField property returns true if the view column value is based on a field. You can use getItemName to retrieve the field's name.

`public boolean isFormula() throws NotesException`

The `isFormula` property returns `true` if the view column value is based on a formula. Note that in some cases, a single field name can also return `true` for `isFormula`. You can use `getFormula` to retrieve the formula's value.

`public boolean isHidden() throws NotesException`

The `isHidden` property returns `true` if the view column is hidden. In the Domino Designer, you can enable this property in the Column properties box.

`public boolean isHideDetail() throws NotesException`

The `isHideDetail` property returns `true` if the details for the view column totals are hidden.

`public boolean isIcon() throws NotesException`

The `isIcon` property returns `true` if the view column should be rendered as icons rather than text or numbers. In the Domino Designer, you can enable this property in the Column properties box. The option is called `Display values as icons`.

`public boolean isResize() throws NotesException`

The `isResize` property returns `true` if the column is resizable. In the Domino Designer, you can enable this property in the Column properties box.

`public boolean isResortAscending() throws NotesException`

The `IsResortAscending` property is not about a ski resort. If the column can be re-sorted in ascending sequence, this property is `true`. That is, if the column has the `Click on column header to sort` option, and ascending sorting is enabled, this property will return `true`. Note that this property is separate from the `isSorted` and `isSortDescending` properties, which return the status of the regular sorting of the column.

`public boolean isResortDescending() throws NotesException`

The `IsResortDescending` property is not about a Florida resort. If the column can be re-sorted in descending sequence, this property is `true`. That is, if the column has the `Click on column header to sort` option, and descending sorting is enabled, this property will return `true`. Note that this property is separate from the `isSorted` and `isSortDescending` properties, which return the status of the regular sorting of the column.

`public boolean isResortToView() throws NotesException`

If the column can be re-sorted by the user clicking on the column header, the `isResortToView` property is `true`. In the Domino Designer, you can enable this property in the Column properties box on the Sorting tab. The option is titled `Click on column header to sort`.

```
public boolean isResponse() throws NotesException
```

The isResponse property is true if the column contains only response documents. In the Domino Designer, you can enable this property in the Column properties box. The option is called Show responses only.

```
public boolean isSecondaryResort() throws NotesException
```

The isSecondaryResort property routine returns true if the column has a secondary re-sortable column. In the Domino Designer, when you enable the Click on column header to sort, the column is sortable by the user. Enabling this option makes another checkbox available called Secondary sort column. The secondary sort column is used if the user clicks on the column header to sort the view in a different order than the default. If you enable the Secondary Sort column checkbox, the isSecondaryResort property will return true, indicating that the current column has a secondary column that will be used for sorting. In the Domino Designer you can specify which other column is used for secondary sorting. As far as I can tell, however, there is no way to programmatically determine which column is the secondary sort column.

Note

Contrary to what the property name implies, and what you might find in some documentation, this property does not return true if the current column is a secondary column. It returns true if the current column is user sortable and it specifies that another column should be used for secondary sorting.

```
public boolean isSecondaryResortDescending() throws NotesException
```

A secondary re-sortable column can be enabled when a column has the Click on column header to sort option specified. If you indicate that you want a secondary sort column (for example, isSecondaryResort is true), you can also specify whether you want the secondary column sorted in ascending or descending order. If the isSecondaryResortDescending property returns true, the secondary sort is descending. If this property returns false, the secondary sort is ascending. If the isSecondaryResort property is false, the result of this property is not meaningful.

Note

Contrary to what the property name implies, and what you might find in some documentation, this property does not reflect the sorting status of the current column. It reflects the direction of the sort of the separate column that is used for secondary sorting.

Also note that there is no complementary ascending property value. Only the descending version of this property is available. A false return value indicates an ascending secondary sort.

```
public boolean isShowTwistie() throws NotesException
```

The isShowTwistie property returns true if twisties are enabled for a column. That is, if the column can be expanded and contracted, this property will be true. In the Domino

Designer, you can enable this property in the Column properties box. The option is Show twistie when row is expandable.

`public boolean isSortDescending() throws NotesException`

The isSortDescending property is only meaningful if the isSorted property is true. If isSorted is false, the column is not sorted and the direction of sort is not meaningful. The isSortDescending property returns true if the column is sorted in descending order and false if the column is sorted in ascending order.

`public boolean isSorted() throws NotesException`

The isSorted property returns true if the column is sorted and false if it is not. Sorted columns are important for view lookups. If you forget to enable sorting, your lookups will not work properly.

THE ViewEntry CLASS

Class Definition

`public class ViewEntry extends Base`

Properties

- getChildCount
- getColumnIndentLevel
- getColumnValues
- getDescendantCount
- getDocument
- getFTSearchScore
- getIndentLevel
- getNoteID
- getParent
- getSiblingCount
- getUniversalID
- getPosition
- isCategory
- isConflict
- isDocument
- isTotal
- isValid

PART

IV

CH

18

The ViewEntry class represents a single row of a view. You can access a ViewEntry object using the ViewNavigator class or the ViewEntryCollection class. Usually a ViewEntry corresponds to a document, but it doesn't always refer to a document. For example, some rows of a view represent category lines and others represent totals. The properties of a ViewEntry object let you know what kind of data the entry represents.

COMMON METHODS TO CREATE

View.getEntryByKey, ViewNavigator.getChild, ViewNavigator.getCurrent, ViewNavigator.getFirst, ViewNavigator.getFirstDocument, ViewNavigator.getLast, ViewNavigator.getLastDocument, ViewNavigator.getNext, ViewNavigator.getNextCategory, ViewNavigator.getNextDocument, ViewNavigator.getNextSibling, ViewNavigator.getNth, ViewNavigator.Parent, ViewNavigator.getPos, ViewNavigator.getPrev, ViewNavigator.getPrevCategory, ViewNavigator.getPrevDocument, ViewNavigator.getPrevSibling, ViewEntryCollection.getEntry, ViewEntryCollection.getFirstEntry, ViewEntryCollection.getLastEntry, ViewEntryCollection.getNextEntry, ViewEntryCollection.getNthEntry, ViewEntryCollection.getPrevEntry

PROPERTIES

```
public int getChildCount() throws NotesException
```
The getChildCount property routine returns the number of immediate children of the current view entry.

```
public int getColumnIndentLevel() throws NotesException
```
The getColumnIndentLevel property returns the indention level of a view entry within its column. The indent level of a main document is 0, the first level response document is level 1, the second level is 2, and so forth.

The difference between getColumnIndentLevel and getIndentLevel is that getColumnIndentLevel represents the level of main, response, and response-to-response levels, whereas getIndentLevel is the nesting level of categories.

```
public java.util.Vector getColumnValues() throws NotesException
```
The getColumnValues property returns a Vector that contains the values in each of the columns. The type of the element in the Vector depends on the data type shown within the column. The valid return types are Double, DateTime, or String.

```
public int getDescendantCount() throws NotesException
```
The getDescendantCount property returns the count of all descendants of the current view entry.

```
public Document getDocument() throws NotesException
```

The getDocument property returns the document associated with the current view entry. It returns null if the current view entry is not associated with a document. If you retrieve a Document object using a ViewEntry, the document will not have these properties: FTSearchScore, ColumnValues, or ParentView. Use the corresponding properties with the same names in the ViewEntry object.

```
public int getFTSearchScore() throws NotesException
```

The getFTSearchScore is valid if the view entry was retrieved from a full-text search. If the FTSearch was performed on a database without a full-text index, this routine will return an arbitrary number. The score is based on the number of search words that are found in the document and the weighting assigned. Do not use the value returned if the database is not full-text indexed.

```
public int getIndentLevel() throws NotesException
```

The getIndentLevel returns the indention level for the view entry within the view. A main document is level 0, a response document is level 1, and so forth.

The difference between getColumnIndentLevel and getIndentLevel is that getColumnIndentLevel represents the level of main, response, and response-to-response levels, whereas getIndentLevel is the nesting level of categories.

```
public String getNoteID() throws NotesException
```

The getNoteID property returns a String that represents the Note ID (also sometimes called the Document ID) for a view entry if it represents a document. If the ViewEntry represents a category or total, the getNoteID property routine returns an empty string. The Note ID represents the note uniquely within a given database. Replica copies of the same note in different replica databases will most likely have different Note IDs. Use the getUniversalID property routine to get the UNID, which is the same for all replica copies of the same document in all databases.

```
public Object getParent() throws NotesException
```

The getParent property returns an Object of type ViewEntryCollection, ViewNavigator, or View, depending on the container for the ViewEntry. You must properly cast the returned Object to the proper type in Java.

```
public int getSiblingCount() throws NotesException
```

The getSiblingCount property routine returns the number of siblings to the current ViewEntry. The count includes itself, unless it is a total.

```
public String getUniversalID() throws NotesException
```

Every document in a Notes database has a universal ID. The universal ID is a 32-character hexadecimal string and uniquely identifies the document within all replica copies of the database. That is, every replica copy of the note has the same universal ID, regardless of the replica database in which it appears.

```
public String getPosition() throws NotesException
```

The getPosition property returns a string that represents the position of the entry within the view hierarchy. A position is a set of numbers separated by decimal points. For example, position 2.4.1 represents the first document in the fourth category within the second category.

```
public boolean isCategory() throws NotesException
```

The isCategory property returns true if the view entry is a category line within the view and false if not.

```
public boolean isConflict() throws NotesException
```

The isConflict property returns true if the view entry represents a document that has a save conflict or a replication conflict. These documents are highlighted in the view with a diamond.

```
public boolean isDocument() throws NotesException
```

The isDocument property is true if the view entry represents a document.

```
public boolean isTotal() throws NotesException
```

The isTotal property is true if the view entry represents a line that contains a total.

```
public boolean isValid() throws NotesException
```

The isValid property returns true if the view entry does not represent a deletion stub. When a document is deleted, it is not immediately removed from the database. Instead, a deletion stub replaces the valid document. This is so that future replications with other databases will realize that the document has been deleted. Valid documents are those that are not deletion stubs.

THE ViewEntryCollection CLASS

Class Definition

```
public class ViewEntryCollection extends Base
```

Properties

- getCount
- getParent
- getQuery

Methods

- addEntry
- deleteEntry
- FTSearch
- getEntry
- getFirstEntry
- getLastEntry
- getNextEntry
- getNthEntry
- getPrevEntry
- putAllInFolder
- removeAll
- removeAllFromFolder
- stampAll
- updateAll

PART

IV

CH

18

The ViewEntryCollection class represents a collection of ViewEntries, all of which represent documents. ViewEntryCollections do not contain any entries that represent categories or totals. The collection maintains a current pointer. Navigation methods such as getNext use and modify the current pointer.

COMMON METHODS TO CREATE

View.getAllEntriesByKey, View.getAllEntries, ViewEntry.getParent

PROPERTIES

`public int getCount() throws NotesException`

The getCount property returns the number of entries in the ViewEntryCollection object.

`public View getParent() throws NotesException`

The getParent property routine returns the View object that is the parent of the ViewEntryCollection.

```
public String getQuery() throws NotesException
```

The getQuery property routine returns the query string that was used to create the ViewEntryCollection if the collection was the result of a full-text search. If the collection was not the result of a full-text search, this property returns an empty string.

METHODS

```
public void addEntry(Object obj) throws NotesException
```

```
public void addEntry(Object obj, boolean checkDups) throws NotesException
```

The obj parameter can be either a Document object or a ViewEntry object and cannot be null. The addEntry method adds the specified object to the view entry collection. The checkDups parameter only applies to remote calls. If it is true, an immediate check for duplicates will take place rather than deferring to the next method that calls the server. If the document is a duplicate of one already in the collection, an exception is thrown. You cannot add a document to a collection that is the result of a multi-database search.

```
public void deleteEntry(ViewEntry entry) throws NotesException
```

The deleteEntry method deletes a ViewEntry from a ViewEntryCollection. The ViewEntry must represent a document, not a category or total. If the ViewEntry does not exist or is already deleted, an exception will be thrown. You cannot delete a ViewEntry from a different collection. After a ViewEntry is deleted it cannot be used for navigation.

When you delete a ViewEntry from the collection, it does not remove the document from the database, nor from the folder represented by the ViewEntryCollection.

```
public void FTSearch(String query) throws NotesException
```

```
public void FTSearch(String query, int maxdocs) throws NotesException
```

The FTSearch method performs a full-text search of the documents in the ViewEntryCollection. It reduces the subset of documents in the ViewEntryCollection to those that match the query. The resulting documents are sorted by relevance with the most relevant first.

The maxdocs parameter specifies the maximum number of documents to return. A 0 means to return all documents.

The database does not need to be full-text indexed for this method to work, but if it is, the search will be more efficient. You can programmatically test whether the database is full-text indexed with the IsFTIndexed property, and you can create or update the index with the updateFTIndex method.

```
public ViewEntry getEntry(Object entry) throws NotesException
```

The getEntry method returns the ViewEntry object that matches the input ViewEntry. If it does not exist in the collection, a null will be returned.

At first this method seems rather strange because if you already have the ViewEntry, why are you trying to remove it from the collection? The answer is that this method is really most useful as a membership test within a ViewEntry collection. For example, suppose you have two collections, and you want to know which documents in the first collection are also in the second collection. You can iterate through the first collection, calling getEntry on the second collection. If the result is null, the document does not appear in the second collection.

```
public ViewEntry getFirstEntry() throws NotesException
```

The getFirstEntry method returns the first view entry in the collection. If the view entries are the result of a search, the first document is the one that has the highest relevance score.

```
public ViewEntry getLastEntry() throws NotesException
```

The getLastEntry method returns the last view entry in the collection. If the view entries are the result of a search, the last view entry is the one that has the lowest relevance score.

```
public ViewEntry getNextEntry() throws NotesException
```

```
public ViewEntry getNextEntry(ViewEntry entry) throws NotesException
```

The getNextEntry method returns the document that follows the current document or the one supplied as a parameter.

The implementation of CORBA/IIOP remote support locally caches documents from the server. When you use getNextEntry without a parameter, the cache can be used. When you use getNextEntry with the ViewEntry parameter, however, the cache is invalidated and new information must be retrieved from the server. Therefore, try to avoid using this construct for remote applications. Instead, use a loop with getFirstEntry() and getNextEntry().

```
public ViewEntry getNthEntry(int n) throws NotesException
```

The getNthEntry method returns the document based on its position within the collection. To retrieve the first ViewEntry, use a parameter value of 1 (not 0). The second document uses a parameter of 2, and so forth.

The implementation of CORBA/IIOP remote support locally caches documents from the server. When you use getNextEntry without a parameter, the cache can be used. When you use getNthEntry, however, the cache is invalidated and new information must be retrieved from the server. Therefore, avoid using this construct for remote applications. Instead, use a loop with getFirstEntry() and getNextEntry().

```
public ViewEntry getPrevEntry() throws NotesException
```

```
public ViewEntry getPrevEntry(ViewEntry entry) throws NotesException
```

The getPrevEntry method returns the document that precedes the current document or the one supplied as a parameter.

The implementation of CORBA/IIOP remote support locally caches documents from the server. When you use getPrevEntry without a parameter, the cache can be used. When you use getPrevEntry with the ViewEntry parameter, however, the cache is invalidated and new information must be retrieved from the server. Therefore, avoid using this construct for remote applications. Instead, use a loop with getLastEntry() and getPrevEntry().

```
public void putAllInFolder(String foldername) throws NotesException
```

```
public void putAllInFolder(String foldername, boolean createonfail) throws
NotesException
```

The putAllInFolder method puts all the documents in the current ViewEntryCollection into the specified folder. If you specify createonfail to be false, an exception will be thrown if the folder does not exist. If you do not specify createonfail, the default value is true, so a folder will be created if it does not exist.

You can specify nested folders by using backslashes in the name, such as "Basketball\\Lakers". You must use two slashes to represent a single slash in the name.

Example:

```
import lotus.domino.*;

public class JavaAgent extends AgentBase {
    public void NotesMain() {
        try {
            Session session = getSession();
            AgentContext agentContext = session.getAgentContext();
            Database db = agentContext.getCurrentDatabase();
            View view = db.getView("View1");
            ViewEntryCollection vec = view.getAllEntriesByKey("record", false);
            int count = vec.getCount();
            System.out.println("Collection has " + count + " elements.");
            if (count > 0) {
                vec.putAllInFolder("NewFolder"); // created if doesn't exist
                View v= db.getView("NewFolder");
                if (null != v) {
                    System.out.println(v.getName() + " exists.");
                }
            }
        } catch(Exception e) {
            e.printStackTrace();
        }
    }
}
```

```
public void removeAll(boolean force) throws NotesException
```

The removeAll method removes from the database all the documents that are contained in the ViewEntry collection. There is special handling of view entries associated with documents that are modified by other users after the creation of the current collection, but prior to the execution of `removeAll`. If the `force` parameter is `false`, these special documents are not deleted from the database. If `force` is `true`, all view entries in the collection are deleted regardless of what other users might have done to the same documents.

After completion of the method, all view entries that were successfully removed from the database are removed from the collection.

Contrast this method with `removeAllFromFolder`. The `removeAll` method deletes the documents completely from the database, whereas the `removeAllFromFolder` just removes the documents from the folder and leaves them in the database.

```
public void removeAllFromFolder(String foldername) throws NotesException
```

The `removeAllFromFolder` removes all documents associated with entries in a view entry collection from the specified folder. This method does not actually delete the documents from the database; it just removes them from the folder. You can include nested folders by using backslashes in the folder name, as in `"Account\\Pacific"`.

```
public void stampAll(String itemname, Object value) throws NotesException
```

The `stampAll` method enables you to perform a mass change on the entire collection of documents that are associated with view entries. You can specify a field name and a new value. The new value will replace the field's value in all the documents. If the field does not exist in a document, it will be created.

This method works directly on the disk versions of the documents. Any in-memory `Document` objects are not affected by this routine. Thus, you must save any pending document changes prior to using this routine so that your changes will be reflected in the disk copy of the document. Also, after execution of the method, you must refresh the value of any in-memory `Document` objects to see the changes that were made using `stampAll`.

```
public void updateAll() throws NotesException
```

The `updateAll` method is similar to the `AgentContext.updateProcessedDoc` method, except that `updateAll` marks all documents in the collection as having been processed. This method does not apply to remote (CORBA) calls because it must be invoked within an agent.

This method does not actually change any values within each document. It modifies the flag that indicates that a particular agent has processed the document. Contrast this method with the `stampAll` method, which updates a field within each document. The `updateAll` method will not cause a document to be a replication candidate, whereas the `stampAll` method will.

THE ViewNavigator CLASS

Class Definition

```
public class ViewNavigator extends Base
```

Properties

- getCacheSize
- getMaxLevel
- getParentView

Methods

- getChild
- getCurrent
- getFirst
- getFirstDocument
- getLast
- getLastDocument
- getNext
- getNextCategory
- getNextDocument
- getNextSibling
- getNth
- getParent
- getPos
- getPrev
- getPrevCategory
- getPrevDocument
- getPrevSibling
- gotoChild
- gotoEntry
- gotoFirst
- gotoFirstDocument
- gotoLast
- gotoLastDocument
- gotoNext
- gotoNextCategory
- gotoNextDocument
- gotoNextSibling
- gotoParent
- gotoPos

- gotoPrev
- gotoPrevCategory
- gotoPrevDocument
- gotoPrevSibling

The ViewNavigator class allows your Java program to traverse the set of ViewEntries in a view or a subset of a view.

A ViewNavigator is similar to a ViewEntryCollection in that both are collections of ViewEntry elements. Both enable you to navigate through the collection and maintain a current pointer. ViewNavigators, however, enable you to access totals and categories, while ViewEntryCollection objects do not. With a ViewNavigator you can create a subset collection of the view such as all children or all descendants of a particular object.

The ViewNavigator contains a set of goto methods that are preferred to the get methods because goto methods do not need to create a ViewEntry object.

For remote (CORBA) operation, the ViewNavigator caches information. If you use the current pointer, the cache will be used. If you go directly to a ViewEntry without using the current pointer, the cache must be flushed. Caching is only available when AutoUpdate is set to false.

COMMON METHODS TO CREATE

View.createViewNav, View.createViewNavFrom, View.createViewNavFromCategory, View.createViewNavFromChildren, View.createViewNavFromDescendants, View.createViewNavMaxLevel, ViewEntry.getParent

PROPERTIES

```
public int getCacheSize() throws NotesException
```

```
public void setCacheSize(int numEntries) throws NotesException
```
The getCacheSize property routine returns the current cache size for the ViewNavigator, expressed in the number of entries. The setCacheSize property routine can be used to change the setting. The valid values are from 0 (no caching) to 128, the default.

```
public int getMaxLevel() throws NotesException
```

```
public void setMaxLevel(int level) throws NotesException
```
The getMaxLevel and setMaxLevel property routines are used to get and set the maximum nesting level for the view entries. The valid values are from 0–30.

```
public View getParentView() throws NotesException
```
The getParentView property routine gets the view that contains the current ViewNavigator.

METHODS

```
public ViewEntry getChild() throws NotesException
```

```
public ViewEntry getChild(ViewEntry entry) throws NotesException
```
The getChild method returns the first child of the current entry or of the specified ViewEntry. If the ViewNavigator is empty, this routine will return null.

```
public ViewEntry getCurrent() throws NotesException
```
The getCurrent method returns the current ViewEntry. You typically use getCurrent after navigating with one of the goto methods. If the ViewNavigator is empty, this routine will return null.

```
public ViewEntry getFirst() throws NotesException
```
The getFirst method returns the first ViewEntry in the ViewNavigator. If the ViewNavigator is empty, this routine will return null.

```
public ViewEntry getFirstDocument() throws NotesException
```
The getFirstDocument method returns the first ViewEntry in the ViewNavigator that corresponds to a document. ViewEntry elements that represent categories or totals are skipped. If the ViewNavigator is empty, this routine will return null.

```
public ViewEntry getLast() throws NotesException
```
The getLast method returns the last ViewEntry in the ViewNavigator. If the ViewNavigator is empty, this routine will return null. When there are totals, this method returns the ViewEntry with the grand total value.

```
public ViewEntry getLastDocument() throws NotesException
```
The getLastDocument method returns the last ViewEntry in the ViewNavigator that corresponds to a document. ViewEntry elements that represent categories or totals are skipped. If the ViewNavigator is empty, this routine will return null.

```
public ViewEntry getNext() throws NotesException
```

```
public ViewEntry getNext(ViewEntry entry) throws NotesException
```
The getNext method returns the next ViewEntry following the current entry or the specified ViewEntry in the ViewNavigator. If the ViewNavigator is empty, this routine will return null.

```
public ViewEntry getNextCategory() throws NotesException
```
The getNextCategory method returns the next ViewEntry in the ViewNavigator that corresponds to a category or total. If your view contains both categories and totals, you should

test further for the type of `ViewEntry`. If the `ViewNavigator` is empty, this routine will return `null`.

`public ViewEntry getNextDocument() throws NotesException`

The `getNextDocument` property returns the next `ViewEntry` in the `ViewNavigator` that corresponds to a document. `ViewEntry` elements that represent categories or totals are skipped. If the `ViewNavigator` is empty, this routine will return `null`.

`public ViewEntry getNextSibling() throws NotesException`

`public ViewEntry getNextSibling(ViewEntry entry) throws NotesException`

The `getNextSibling` method returns the next sibling `ViewEntry` to the current entry or of the specified `ViewEntry`. If the `ViewNavigator` is empty or if there are no more siblings, this routine will return `null`.

`public ViewEntry getNth(int n) throws NotesException`

The `getNth` method returns the entry at the specified index in the top level of the view. The first entry is considered index number 1. If the `ViewNavigator` is empty or the requested entry does not exist, this routine will return `null`.

This method has special behavior when the caller does not have reader access to some documents within the database. When the caller does not have read access to a document, the method will return the next document for which the caller has reader access. This can result in the same document being returned multiple times. For example, suppose you have reader access to documents 1–3 and 9–11. If you request document 4, you will get document 9. If you request document 5, you will also get document 9. So, as you can see, all the documents within the gap will return document 9.

`public ViewEntry getParent() throws NotesException`

`public ViewEntry getParent(ViewEntry entry) throws NotesException`

The `getParent` method routine returns the `ViewEntry` that is the parent of the current or specified view entry within the `ViewNavigator`.

`public ViewEntry getPos(String pos, char separator) throws NotesException`

The `getPos` method accesses a `ViewEntry` based on its position string. A position string is one like `"2.4.1"`, which represents the first child within the fourth child within the second `ViewEntry`. The separator is the character used to separate the numbers, such as a period (.). If the `ViewNavigator` is empty or if there is no document at the specified position, this routine will return `null`.

```
public ViewEntry getPrev() throws NotesException
```

```
public ViewEntry getPrev(ViewEntry entry) throws NotesException
```

The getPrev method returns the previous ViewEntry prior to the current entry or the specified ViewEntry in the ViewNavigator. If the ViewNavigator is empty, this routine will return null.

```
public ViewEntry getPrevCategory() throws NotesException
```

The getPrevCategory method returns the previous ViewEntry in the ViewNavigator that corresponds to a category or total. If your view contains both categories and totals, you should test further for the type of ViewEntry. If the ViewNavigator is empty, this routine will return null.

```
public ViewEntry getPrevDocument() throws NotesException
```

The getPrevDocument property returns the previous ViewEntry in the ViewNavigator that corresponds to a document. ViewEntry elements that represent categories or totals are skipped. If the ViewNavigator is empty, this routine will return null.

```
public ViewEntry getPrevSibling() throws NotesException
```

```
public ViewEntry getPrevSibling(ViewEntry entry) throws NotesException
```

The getNextSibling method returns the previous sibling ViewEntry to the current entry or of the specified ViewEntry. If the ViewNavigator is empty or if there are no more siblings, this routine will return null.

```
public boolean gotoChild() throws NotesException
```

```
public boolean gotoChild(ViewEntry entry) throws NotesException
```

The gotoChild method moves the current pointer to the first child of the current entry or to the first child of the specified entry. It returns true if the move was successful and false otherwise.

```
public boolean gotoEntry(Object entry) throws NotesException
```

The entry parameter of the gotoEntry method can be either a ViewEntry or a Document object. The gotoEntry method moves the current pointer to the specified document or view entry. It returns true if the move was successful and false otherwise.

```
public boolean gotoFirst() throws NotesException
```

The gotoFirst method moves the current pointer to the first ViewEntry within the ViewNavigator. It returns true if the move was successful and false otherwise.

```
public boolean gotoFirstDocument() throws NotesException
```

The gotoFirstDocument method moves the current pointer to the first ViewEntry in the ViewNavigator that corresponds to a document. ViewEntry elements that represent categories or totals are skipped. It returns true if the move was successful and false otherwise.

```
public boolean gotoLast() throws NotesException
```

The gotoLast method moves the current pointer to the last ViewEntry in the ViewNavigator. It returns true if the move was successful and false otherwise.

```
public boolean gotoLastDocument() throws NotesException
```

The gotoLastDocument method moves the current pointer to the last ViewEntry in the ViewNavigator that corresponds to a document. ViewEntry elements that represent categories or totals are skipped. It returns true if the move was successful and false otherwise.

```
public boolean gotoNext() throws NotesException
```

```
public boolean gotoNext(ViewEntry entry) throws NotesException
```

The gotoNext method moves the current pointer to the next ViewEntry following the current entry or the specified ViewEntry in the ViewNavigator. It returns true if the move was successful and false otherwise.

```
public boolean gotoNextCategory() throws NotesException
```

The gotoNextCategory method moves the current pointer to the next ViewEntry in the ViewNavigator that corresponds to a category or total. It returns true if the move was successful and false otherwise.

```
public boolean gotoNextDocument() throws NotesException
```

The gotoNextDocument property moves the current pointer to the next ViewEntry in the ViewNavigator that corresponds to a document. ViewEntry elements that represent categories or totals are skipped. It returns true if the move was successful and false otherwise.

```
public boolean gotoNextSibling() throws NotesException
```

```
public boolean gotoNextSibling(ViewEntry entry) throws NotesException
```

The gotoNextSibling method moves the current pointer to the next sibling ViewEntry to the current entry or of the specified ViewEntry. It returns true if the move was successful and false otherwise.

```
public boolean gotoParent() throws NotesException
```

```
public boolean gotoParent(ViewEntry entry) throws NotesException
```

The gotoParent method routine moves the current pointer to the ViewEntry that is the parent of the current or specified view entry within the ViewNavigator. It returns true if the move was successful and false otherwise.

```
public boolean gotoPos(String pos, char separator) throws NotesException
```

The gotoPos method moves the current pointer to a ViewEntry based on its position string. A position string is one like "2.4.1", which represents the first child within the fourth child within the second ViewEntry. The separator is the character used to separate the numbers, such as a period (.). It returns true if the move was successful and false otherwise.

```
public boolean gotoPrev() throws NotesException
```

```
public boolean gotoPrev(ViewEntry entry) throws NotesException
```

The gotoPrev method moves the current pointer to the previous ViewEntry prior to the current entry or the specified ViewEntry in the ViewNavigator. It returns true if the move was successful and false otherwise.

```
public boolean gotoPrevCategory() throws NotesException
```

The gotoPrevCategory method moves the current pointer to the previous ViewEntry in the ViewNavigator that corresponds to a category or total. It returns true if the move was successful and false otherwise.

```
public boolean gotoPrevDocument() throws NotesException
```

The gotoPrevDocument property moves the current pointer to the previous ViewEntry in the ViewNavigator that corresponds to a document. ViewEntry elements that represent categories or totals are skipped. It returns true if the move was successful and false otherwise.

```
public boolean gotoPrevSibling() throws NotesException
```

```
public boolean gotoPrevSibling(ViewEntry entry) throws NotesException
```

The gotoNextSibling method moves the current pointer to the previous sibling ViewEntry to the current entry or of the specified ViewEntry. It returns true if the move was successful and false otherwise.

CHAPTER REVIEW

1. Write a Java agent that finds the first document in a view that contains the word Java in the first sorted column of the view.

2. Explain the difference between a ViewNavigator and a ViewEntryCollection.

3. Why is it generally preferable to use the getNext sequential type methods rather than using getNth type methods when looping through a collection?

4. The routines getFTSearchScore, getColumnValues, and getParentView appear in the Document object. Why is it a better idea to use the equivalent routines in the ViewEntry object instead of the Document object? Hint: Think about what happens if the document appears in more than one view.

5. What is the advantage of using the goto routines of the ViewNavigator instead of the get routines?

6. Is it possible for different rows of a view or folder to have different fonts? If so, how do you specify it programmatically? If not, why not?

7. Write a Java agent that will search through the first column of a view for all documents that contain the word Blue in the column. For these documents only, add up the contents of the second column, which contains a numeric value. Write out the total with System.out.println.

8. Suppose you are give a database with three folders, FolderIn, FolderOut1, and FolderOut2. Write a Java agent that will search through each of the documents in FolderIn and place them in FolderOut1 if the date field in the first column is less than January 1, 2000. Place the document in FolderOut2 if the date is greater than or equal to January 1, 2000. Remove the document from FolderIn when it has been moved. What kinds of errors can occur?

9. What is the purpose of AutoUpdate for a View? What are the relative merits of turning this flag on or off?

THE Document, Outline, AND Form CLASSES

THE Document CLASS

Class Definition

public class Document extends Base

Properties

- getAuthors
- getColumnValues
- getCreated
- getEmbeddedObjects
- getEncryptionKeys/setEncryptionKeys
- getFolderReferences
- getFTSearchScore
- getItems
- getKey
- getLastAccessed
- getLastModified
- getNameOfProfile
- getNoteID
- getParentDatabase
- getParentDocumentUNID
- getParentView
- getResponses
- getSigner
- getSize
- getUniversalID/setUniversalID
- getURL
- getVerifier
- hasEmbedded
- isDeleted
- isEncryptOnSend/setEncryptOnSend
- isNewNote
- isProfile
- isResponse
- isSaveMessageOnSend/setSaveMessageOnSend
- isSentByAgent
- isSigned

- isSignOnSend/setSignOnSend

- isValid

Methods

- appendItemValue

- computeWithForm

- copyAllItems

- copyItem

- copyToDatabase

- createReplyMessage

- createRichTextItem

- encrypt

- generateXML

- getAttachment

- getFirstItem

- getItemValue

- getItemValueDouble

- getItemValueInteger

- getItemValueString

- hasItem

- makeResponse

- putInFolder

- remove

- removeFromFolder

- removeItem

- renderToRTItem

- replaceItemValue

- save

- send

- sign

PART

IV

CH

19

The Document class represents a single document in a Domino database. Documents store information in elements called *items*, which are stored within the document. You can access documents by navigating through a view or one of the other document collection type objects.

In the Notes client, a user creates a document when filling out a form. In Java, you can create a document without using a form. *Forms* display text and graphics and provide fields for user interaction. If you create a document with Java, create an item within the document to store the name of the form to be used with the document in the user interface. The name of this item should be Form. Set the contents of the Form item in the document to the name of the document's form. Otherwise, a user might not be able to see or edit the document.

If you create or modify a document, you must call the save method for the changes to be stored in the database. If you forget to call save, any changes you make to the Document object will be lost. When you save a document, a special field called $UpdatedBy is created and added to your document, even if no other items are in the document. This field contains your user ID name.

A deletion stub represents a document that has been deleted but not yet permanently removed from the database. It is kept so that replica copies will recognize that the document has been deleted from the database. You can use the Document.isValid method to determine whether a document is a deletion stub.

Normally, documents represent user data, but special documents are also in a Domino database. For example, design elements are actually stored in Domino documents. If you obtain the Note ID for a view, for example, you can get a Document object that corresponds to the view.

COMMON METHODS TO CREATE

You obtain a Document using many of the collection classes or directly by one of the routines that access documents by a key.

```
AgentContext.getSavedDocument, Database.createDocument, Database.FTDomainSearch,
Database.getDocumentByID, Database.getDocumentByUNID, Database.getDocumentByURL,
Database.getProfileDocument, Newsletter.formatDocument,
Newsletter,formatMsgWithDoclinks, Document.copyToDatabase,
Document.createReplyMessage, AgentContext.getDocumentContext,
DocumentCollection.getDocument, DocumentCollection.getFirstDocument,
DocumentCollection.getLastDocument, DocumentCollection.getNextDocument,
DocumentCollection.getNthDocument, DocumentCollection.getPrevDocument,
Item.getParent, View.getChild, View.getDocumentByKey, View.getFirstDocument,
View.getLastDocument, View.getNextDocument, View.getNextSibling, View.getNthDocument,
View.ParentDocument, View.PrevDocument, View.getPrevSibling, ViewEntry.getDocument
```

PROPERTIES

```
public java.util.Vector getAuthors() throws NotesException
```

The getAuthors property returns a Vector of String elements where each element represents a name of a user who has edited and saved the document. In the document, this list is kept in the item called $UpdatedBy. You can limit the number of entries in the $UpdatedBy item with one of the advanced Database properties.

This routine does not return a list of the people with Author access.

`public java.util.Vector getColumnValues() throws NotesException`

The `getColumnValues` routine returns a `Vector` of elements, where each element represents one column's value from the view. This property will have a value and be meaningful only if the document was obtained from a view. Otherwise, the return value is `null`.

In the `Vector` return value, the first item represents the value in the first column of the view in the row that represents the current document.

`public DateTime getCreated() throws NotesException`

The `getCreated` property access routine returns the time and date that the document was created.

`public java.util.Vector getEmbeddedObjects() throws NotesException`

The `getEmbeddedObjects` routine in the `Document` class returns a `Vector` of `EmbeddedObject` objects. Each `EmbeddedObject` corresponds to an OLE/2 or OLE/1 embedded object. If no objects are there, the `Vector` is empty. This property is not supported on OS/2, UNIX, or the Macintosh.

Note that a `getEmbeddedObjects` routine is also in the `RichTextItem` class. Although they have the same name, they operate slightly differently. At the document level, the `getEmbeddedObjects` property includes OLE/1 and OLE/2 objects created in release 4 or higher; however, it does not return file attachments or OLE/1 objects created in Notes release 3. Use `RichTextItem.getEmbeddedObjects` to perform this function.

`public java.util.Vector getEncryptionKeys() throws NotesException`

`public void setEncryptionKeys(java.util.Vector keys) throws NotesException`

The `getEncryptionKeys` property routine is used to retrieve the set of names of the encryption keys used to encrypt the document. These keys are used by the `encrypt` method. `setEncryptionKeys` sets the names of the encryption keys to be used to encrypt the document.

After setting the encryption keys, the `encrypt` and `save` methods must be called in order to actually encrypt the document. The values specified in the `setEncryptionKeys` routine are stored in a text item within the document named `SecretEncryptionKeys`.

`public java.util.Vector getFolderReferences() throws NotesException`

A new feature included with release 5 of Notes and Domino is the capability to track folder references; that is, the folders in which a particular document appears. The `getFolderReferences` property access routine returns a `Vector` of `String` objects that represent the Universal IDs for the folders that contain the current document. You cannot obtain folder references for any arbitrary database, however. Folder references must first be enabled.

The getFolderReferencesEnabled property routine queries whether this feature is currently enabled or disabled. The setFolderReferencesEnabled property routine enables you to turn this feature on and off. To use this feature, however, you must create a hidden view in the database called ($FolderRef) or ($FolderRefInfo). Without one of these views, attempting to call the setFolderReferencesEnabled property routine will cause an exception. The setFolderReferencesEnabled property routine will not automatically create the view for you; you must create it from the Domino designer. You can copy the design for one of these views from the Mail template database.

After the view is available in the database, you can turn on this property to track folder references. Note that tracking folder references causes a performance penalty. Tracking the folders for documents is done only while the setFolderReferencesEnabled property is enabled. If you disable it, add documents to folders, and subsequently re-enable the property, any document movement while the property was disabled is not available.

For example,

```java
import lotus.domino.*;
import java.util.*;

public class FolderTest {
    public static void main(String args[]) {
        try {
            // Use Local Notes executables
            NotesThread.sinitThread(); // Static initialization

            Session session = NotesFactory.createSession();
            if (null == session) { System.out.println("session is null");}
            else {
                Database db = session.getDatabase("", "TempTest.nsf");
                // Get the initial setting of the flag
                boolean fre = db.getFolderReferencesEnabled();
                System.out.println("before FRE: " + (fre?"Enabled":"Disabled"));
                // Enable the folder reference flag, regardless of previous setting
                db.setFolderReferencesEnabled(true);
                fre = db.getFolderReferencesEnabled();
                System.out.println("after FRE: " + (fre?"Enabled":"Disabled"));
                DocumentCollection dc = db.getAllDocuments();
                // Obtain just the first document of the database
                Document doc = dc.getFirstDocument();
                // Find the folder references for the first document
                Vector v = doc.getFolderReferences();
                System.out.print("Refs:");
                for (int i=0; i < v.size(); i++) {
                    System.out.print( (String) v.elementAt(i) + ", ");
                }
                System.out.println("");
            }
        }
        catch (NotesException e) {
            System.out.println("Notes error: " + e.id + ". " + e.text);
            e.printStackTrace();
        }
```

```
      catch (Exception e) {
         e.printStackTrace();
      }
      finally {
         NotesThread.stermThread();
      }
   }
}
```

The sample program will open a test database, query, and print the folder references flag. At that point it will force the flag to be true and will print the folder references for the first document in the database. Note that if no ($FolderRef) or ($FolderRefInfo) view is in the database, attempting to enable folder references will cause a NotesException.

public int getFTSearchScore() throws NotesException

If the document was retrieved from a full-text search and the database is full-text indexed, the getFTSearchScore property routine returns the full-text search score. If it was not the result of a full-text search, the property will return 0, and if the database does not have a full-text index, the result is undefined. The score is based on the number of search words that are found in the document and the weighting assigned. Because the result of this property routine is unpredictable if the database is not full-text indexed, be sure that your database is full-text indexed before using the value returned by this property routine.

public java.util.Vector getItems() throws NotesException

The getItems property returns a Vector of Item objects that represent all the items stored in the document.

public String getKey() throws NotesException

The getKey property returns the key for a profile document. This can be any string, but when profiles are used on a per-user basis, the string is typically a username. The Database.getProfileDocument method is used to get and create profile documents. getProfileDocument is rather unusual because a profile document will be created if one does not exist. Normally retrieval routines such as getProfileDocument are read-only and do not create any data. However, for profile documents, attempting to read the profile document will create it if it does not exist.

public DateTime getLastAccessed() throws NotesException

The getLastAccessed property routine returns the date and time that the document was last modified or read. This property is affected by one of the advanced database properties called Maintain LastAccessed Property. The default for this option is false, so unless you change the default, this property routine will not return meaningful information. If you want to use this document property, you must make sure to enable the Maintain LastAccessed Property in the Domino user interface for the database. As of release 5.0.2 of Domino, no way to programmatically enable this option exists.

```
public DateTime getLastModified() throws NotesException
```

The getLastModified property routine returns the date and time that the document was last modified. In contrast to getLastAccessed, Domino always records the date of last modification.

```
public String getNameOfProfile() throws NotesException
```

The getNameOfProfile property returns the name of a profile document. This can be any string, but typically serves to provide a category for a set of profile documents. For example, profile documents might be used for user preferences for a particular database. The name of the profile might be Preferences. The Database.getProfileDocument method is used to get and create profile documents. getProfileDocument is rather unusual because a profile document will be created if one does not exist. Normally, retrieval routines such as getProfileDocument are read-only and do not create any data. However, for profile documents, attempting to read the profile document will create it if it does not exist.

```
public String getNoteID() throws NotesException
```

The getNoteID property returns a String that represents the Note ID (also sometimes called the Document ID) for the document. The Note ID is a hexadecimal string of up to eight characters and represents the note (document) uniquely within a given database. Replica copies of the same note in different replica databases will most likely have different Note IDs.

Because Note IDs for the same note will vary in different databases, you should typically use Universal IDs (UNIDs) to refer to documents rather than Note IDs. You can get the UNID for a document with the getUniversalID property.

```
public Database getParentDatabase() throws NotesException
```

The getParentDatabase property returns a Database object that represents the database in which the current document resides.

```
public String getParentDocumentUNID() throws NotesException
```

If the current document is a response document, the getParentDocumentUNID property routine returns the Universal ID of the parent document. If the current document is not a response then this property returns null.

```
public View getParentView() throws NotesException
```

If the current document was obtained from a view, the getParentView property will return a View object for that parent view. If the document was not retrieved from a view, this routine returns a null.

```
public DocumentCollection getResponses() throws NotesException
```

The getResponses property returns a DocumentCollection that contains Document objects that represent the immediate children of the current document. The returned collection does not traverse the hierarchy and does not return all descendants, such as response-to-responses.

```
public String getSigner() throws NotesException
```

The getSigner property routine returns a string containing the name of the person who has signed the document, if the document contains a signature. If the document is not signed, the property will return null.

```
public int getSize() throws NotesException
```

The getSize property returns the document size, in bytes. The size includes the size of any attachments to the document.

```
public String getUniversalID() throws NotesException
```

```
public void setUniversalID(String unid) throws NotesException
```

The getUniversalID returns the Universal ID (UNID) for the current document. The *UNID* is a hexadecimal string of up to 32 characters and uniquely identifies the document within all replicas of the database. If a document has the same UNID as another document in a replica database, the documents are replicas of one another.

If you modify the UNID for an existing document, it behaves as if it were a new, different document. That is, it will no longer replicate with copies of the original document in other databases. You cannot change the UNID to a value that is the same as another document within the database. If you attempt to do this, you will get a runtime error.

```
public String getURL() throws NotesException
```

The getURL property routine returns the Domino URL for the document object.

```
public String getVerifier() throws NotesException
```

The getVerifier property routine returns a string that contains the name of the user who verified the signature on the current document. If the document is not signed, this property will return null.

```
public boolean hasEmbedded() throws NotesException
```

The hasEmbedded property routine returns true if the document contains one or more embedded objects, file attachments, or object links. The hasEmbedded property is not supported on OS/2, UNIX, or Macintosh platforms.

```
public boolean isDeleted() throws NotesException
```

The isDeleted property routine returns true if the current document is deleted and false otherwise.

```
public boolean isEncryptOnSend() throws NotesException
```

```
public void setEncryptOnSend(boolean flag) throws NotesException
```

The isEncryptOnSend property routine returns true if the document will be encrypted when it is mailed. Domino will search for the public key of each recipient, whether a main or copy recipient. If the key for the recipient is found, the document will be encrypted for that recipient using the recipient's public key. If the public key is not found, the document will be sent to that recipient unencrypted.

This flag does not affect encryption when saving the document to a database, only when being sent using email.

Use the setEncryptOnSend property routine to set the encryption on (if true) or off (if false).

To encrypt a document other than a mail document, use the encrypt method, which will encrypt the document when it is saved.

```
public boolean isNewNote() throws NotesException
```

The isNewNote property access routine returns true if the document is new and has not yet been saved to the database.

```
public boolean isProfile() throws NotesException
```

Profile documents are special documents that do not appear in user views. They are typically used to store configuration information and can be used to personalize a user's experience. Profile documents are stored within a database in a two-level hierarchy. You can specify a profile name, and then within that profile you can specify a set of keys or users of the profile. Profile documents are cached on the server, so they have fast performance, but as a result you should be judicious in their use.

The isProfile property returns true if the Document object is a profile document. See also the getKey and getNameOfProfile property routine descriptions.

```
public boolean isResponse() throws NotesException
```

The isResponse property returns true if the current document is a response to another document.

```
public boolean isSaveMessageOnSend() throws NotesException
```

```
public void setSaveMessageOnSend(boolean flag) throws NotesException
```

When you create a new message, you have the option of saving the message to the mail database when it is mailed. If you call setSaveMessageOnSend with the parameter true, the message will be saved when sent. You can query the status of this flag by calling isSaveMessageOnSend.

When you are creating unattended agents that send messages or create logs, you might find it useful to call setSaveMessageOnSend with a value of false so that the message is mailed but not saved.

```
public boolean isSentByAgent() throws NotesException
```

This property routine will return true if James Bond sent the message. Not. Just checking to see if you're still with me. The isSentByAgent property will actually return true if a Notes/Domino agent sent the message. The purpose of this property is to enable you to avoid infinite mail loops, where an agent is sending responses to another agent, which is sending responses. If an agent sent a message, the document will contain a special field called $AssistMail with a value of 1. When your agent is sending an automatic response to an email message, you should first check to see whether an agent sent it. If so, you don't need to send a response.

```
public boolean isSigned() throws NotesException
```

The isSigned property is true if the document contains one or more digital signatures. At the time the document is sent, the sender can digitally sign it to verify that it is from whom it says it's from. See the isSignOnSend property for additional information.

```
public boolean isSignOnSend() throws NotesException
```

```
public void setSignOnSend(boolean flag) throws NotesException
```

The isSignOnSend property is true if the document will be signed when it is sent. The process of signing the document involves the following steps:

- Notes generates a hash code from the data that comprises the email message.
- The hash code is encrypted using the sender's private key. This encrypted hash code is the signature for the mail message.
- The signature, the sender's public key, and the sender's certificates are sent along with the email.
- When the receiver receives the message, Domino tries to decrypt the signature with the sender's public key. If the decryption is successful, the origin of the message is authenticated and you can be sure that the message has not been tampered with. This is because no one should have a copy of the sender's private key except the authentic sender and because the hash code was generated from the message content.

Although the sender's public and private keys are used to generate and decrypt the signature, this encryption is independent of encryption of the message itself. You can send a signature along with an unencrypted email message, for example. Use the setEncryptOnSend property to encrypt the message itself.

```
public boolean isValid() throws NotesException
```

The isValid property returns true if the document does not represent a deletion stub. When a document is deleted, it is not immediately removed from the database. Instead, a deletion stub replaces the valid document. This is so that future replications with other databases will realize that the document has been deleted. Valid documents are those that are not deletion stubs.

The isValid property is the opposite of the isDeleted property, so when one is true, the other is false.

METHODS

```
public Item appendItemValue(String itemname) throws NotesException

public Item appendItemValue(String itemname, int value) throws NotesException

public Item appendItemValue(String itemname, double value) throws
NotesException

public Item appendItemValue(String itemname, Object value) throws
NotesException
```

The appendItemValue method creates a new item in a document and, if a value is specified, sets the value. If a value is not specified, a text field will be created with an initial value of the empty string. Both integers and doubles will create a number field in the database. If you pass a DateTime object, a date/time value is created in the database. To create a multi-valued item, you should specify a java.util.Vector that contains String, Integer, Double, or DateTime elements.

When you use the appendItemValue method to create an item in a document, a special flag called the SUMMARY flag is also turned on for the item. The SUMMARY flag must be on for the item to be available for use in a view.

The method returns the new Item object.

Note

In a document it is possible, though not normally desirable, to have two items with the same name. It is not desirable because some properties or methods only work with the first item with a given name. The appendItemValue routine will always create a new item with the specified name. That is, if an item with the name already exists then appendItemValue will create an additional item with the same name.

> For this reason, you should normally use the `replaceItemValue` method instead of the `appendItemValue` method. The `replaceItemValue` method will not create a new item if one exists with the specified name. The `replaceItemValue` method will also work even if the item does not exist in the document. If the item does not exist, `replaceItemValue` will create it. You can safely use `appendItemValue` if you have just created a new document.

```
public boolean computeWithForm(boolean ignore, boolean throwexcp) throws
NotesException
```

The `computeWithForm` method enables you to validate a document by executing the default value, translation, and validation formulas in the form. The first parameter is ignored. If you specify `true` for the `throwexcp` parameter, an exception will be thrown if validation fails. If you specify `false` for `throwexcp`, the method will return `false` on an error but an exception will not be thrown. In either case, if validation succeeds, a `true` will be returned from the method.

For example,

```
try {
    Document doc = db.createDocument(); // Create new document
    doc.replaceItemValue("Form", "Expense Report");
    // Don't throw exception
    if (doc.computeWithForm(false, false)) {
        // Save the document if we pass validation
        doc.save(true, true);
    } else {
        System.out.println("Document fails validation, not saved.");
        // Any other error handling here
    } catch(Exception e) {
        e.printStackTrace();
    }
}
```

```
public void copyAllItems(Document destdoc, boolean replace) throws
NotesException
```

The `copyAllItems` method copies all items of the current document into the destination document. If the replace parameter is `true`, items in the destination document are replaced. If it is `false`, the items are appended in the destination document. Normally you should specify `true` for the replace parameter. See the note under the `appendItemValue` method.

Here is a sample code fragment:

```
try {
    DocumentCollection dc = agentContext.getUnprocessedDocuments();//Documents
    Document docOriginal = dc.getFirstDocument(); // Get just the first one
    Document doc = db.createDocument(); // Create new document
    docOriginal.copyAllItems(doc, true); // Copy to destination
    doc.save(true, true);  // and save destination document
} catch(Exception e) {
```

```
          e.printStackTrace();
      }
  }
```

```
public Item copyItem(Item item) throws NotesException
```

```
public Item copyItem(Item item, String newname) throws NotesException
```

The copyItem method is used to copy an item into the current document and can optionally assign a new name to the item. This method returns the newly created item. If you don't specify a new name, the item retains its existing name.

If an item with the same name already exists in the document, it will be replaced by the copyItem method.

```
public Document copyToDatabase(Database db) throws NotesException
```

The copyToDatabase method copies the current document into another database. The return value is the new document in the specified database.

```
public Document createReplyMessage(boolean toall) throws NotesException
```

The createReplyMessage method creates a new document intended as a reply to the current document. If you specify the toall parameter as true, the reply document will be addressed to all recipients.

For example,

```
import lotus.domino.*;

public class JavaAgent extends AgentBase {
    public void NotesMain() {
        try {
            System.out.println("CreateReply Started");
            Session session = getSession();
            AgentContext agentContext = session.getAgentContext();
            Database db = agentContext.getCurrentDatabase();
            DocumentCollection dc = agentContext.getUnprocessedDocuments();
            Document doc = dc.getFirstDocument();
            Document reply;
            String subject;
            while (null != doc) {
                System.out.println("Processing next doc");
                reply = doc.createReplyMessage(false);
                subject = doc.getItemValueString("Subject");
                // if there was an original subject
                if ("" != subject) {
                    subject = "Re: " + subject; // regarding original subject
                    reply.replaceItemValue("Subject", subject);
                } else {
                    reply.replaceItemValue("Subject", "Received your query");
                }
                reply.replaceItemValue("Body", "Your request is being processed.");
                reply.setSaveMessageOnSend(true);
```

```
        // email response to sender
        reply.send(doc.getItemValueString("From"));
        doc = dc.getNextDocument();
      }
    } catch(Exception e) {
      e.printStackTrace();
    }
    System.out.println("CreateReply Finished");
  }
}
```

The example will reply to the set of unprocessed documents. If you specify the agent trigger to be After New Mail Has Arrived, the set of documents will be the new mail documents. This example could be modified for use as a very simple out-of-office agent, or it could be modified for a workflow mail-in database.

`public RichTextItem createRichTextItem(String rtItemname) throws`
`NotesException`

The `createRichTextItem` method is used to create a new rich-text item within the document. The `rtItemname` parameter specifies the item's name, and the method returns the newly created item.

`public void encrypt() throws NotesException`

The `encrypt` method indicates that a document should be encrypted when it is saved. Encryption occurs for a document on a field-by-field basis. All items for which `Item.isEncrypted` is `true` will be encrypted, whereas all other items will remain visible to all users. Note that encrypted fields do not have the SUMMARY flag, which means that they cannot be used in views. (They can be, but the contents of the field will not be visible, so they aren't very useful.)

You use `setEncryptionKeys` to set the encryption keys that should be used for the document. Any user who has any one of the encryption keys can decrypt all encrypted fields of the document. You cannot set the keys separately for each field.

If no encryption keys are associated with the document, the current user's public key will be used to encrypt the document, and only this user will be able to decrypt the document with his or her private key.

Mail encryption works differently from encrypting documents because it involves the public keys of the recipients. If you want to encrypt mail, use the `setEncryptOnSend` property routine and the `send` method to encrypt mail.

When using the `encrypt` method, be sure to issue the `save` method. Otherwise, the encryption will not take effect.

For example,

```
import lotus.domino.*;
import java.util.Vector;
```

```
public class JavaAgent extends AgentBase {
    public void NotesMain() {
        try {
            Session session = getSession();
            AgentContext agentContext = session.getAgentContext();
            // Select the document(s) to be encrypted in the view and run agent
            DocumentCollection dc = agentContext.getUnprocessedDocuments();
            // Get the first document
            Document doc = dc.getFirstDocument();
            // Create a vector to hold encryption key names
            Vector vKeys = new Vector(1);
            vKeys.addElement("Enlightenment"); // Key to enlightenment
            while (null != doc) {
                // For each document, set the Encryption keys
                doc.setEncryptionKeys(vKeys);
                // Get the item named "Field1" and enable encryption.
                Item item = doc.getFirstItem("Field1");
                if (null != item) item.setEncrypted(true);
                // Now flag that encryptable fields should be encrypted
                doc.encrypt(); // encrypt it
                // Encrypt the fields and save the document
                doc.save();
                doc = dc.getNextDocument(); // Get the next document
            }
        } catch(Exception e) {
            e.printStackTrace();
        }
    }
}
```

In the example, the agent gets the unprocessed documents from the view and encrypts a field called Field1 in each selected document. To run this example, you will need to have an encryption key called Enlightenment stored in your User ID file. You easily can create one in the Notes client in the Tools, User ID dialog box. Select the Encryption button, and then click New to create the key.

Note

Encrypting an item within a document is not the same as enabling encryption for a field of a form. When you enable encryption for a form field in the Advanced Tab's Security Options section and you specify Enable Encryption for This Field, encryption will be used with all documents created or edited with the form. In contrast, encrypting a document with Java only encrypts the specified item within the specified document. Other documents are not affected. Furthermore, if you encrypt a document with Java, and then edit it with a form that does not specify encryption for the field, a warning will be displayed and the data will be saved as plain text.

```
public String generateXML() throws NotesException

public void generateXML(XSLTResultTarget xsltRT) throws NotesException,
java.io.IOException, org.xml.sax.SAXException
```

`public void generateXML(java.io.Writer wr) throws NotesException, java.io.IOException`

The `generateXML` method creates a Domino XML (DXL) representation of the current document and returns it in the specified format. Without parameters, the `generateXML` method will return a string containing the generated XML. If a `XSLTResultTarget` object is used, the result can be sent to a variety of output types. See Chapter 23, "Understanding the Extensible Stylesheet Language (XSL)," in the section titled "`XSLTResultTarget`" for more information on that object type. Finally, if you pass a `Writer` object, the results will be sent to that type of output.

The following example obtains the first document from a personal address book, generates the corresponding XML, and then prints it to the Java console.

```
public void NotesMain() {

    try {
        Session session = getSession();
        AgentContext agentContext = session.getAgentContext();
        DbDirectory dbdir = session.getDbDirectory("");
        Database db = dbdir.openDatabase("Names.nsf");
        DocumentCollection dc = db.getAllDocuments();
        // Just pick up the first document of the database
        Document doc = dc.getFirstDocument();
        // Generate some XML from the personal address book.
        String sXml = doc.generateXML();
        System.out.println(sXml);  // Display the XML source
    } catch(Exception e) {
        e.printStackTrace();
    }
}
```

`public EmbeddedObject getAttachment(String filename) throws NotesException`

The `getAttachment` method can be used to obtain an `EmbeddedObject` that represents an attachment stored at the `Document` level rather than within a rich-text item. The method can also be used to obtain attachments within rich-text items. The `filename` specifies the filename of the attachment.

`public Item getFirstItem(String itemname) throws NotesException`

Documents can contain multiple items with the same name. The `getFirstItem` method returns the first item with the given name. Normally you should avoid having more than one item with a given name in a document. Multiple items with the same name can occur through the use of the `appendItemValue` method. You should use the `replaceItemValue` method instead.

If you have more than one item with a given name, use the `getItems` property routine and cycle through the items until you find the one you want.

If a form field is defined as a `Computed for Display` value, no item representation is stored in the document.

> **Note**
> I've mentioned in several places in this chapter that it is possible to have multiple items with the same name, but it is not a good idea to use this capability. Why does Lotus provide this feature? Lotus uses multiple items with the same name to implement rich-text fields that can grow to any arbitrary length. The same technique is used for embedded objects or file attachments. Although this is a general capability of the system, user programs typically should not use it.

```
public java.util.Vector getItemValue(String itemname) throws NotesException
```

The `getItemValue` method is similar to the `getFirstItem` method, but the `getItemValue` method returns the value of the first item rather than the `Item` object itself. If multiple items exist with the same name, only the value of the first item is returned.

The method returns a `java.util.Vector` that contains `String`, `Double`, or `DateTime` objects, depending on the type of the data within the item. Rich text is rendered into a `String` object in plain text. If the item has no value, an empty `Vector` is returned.

```
public double getItemValueDouble(String itemname) throws NotesException
```

The `getItemValueDouble` method returns the first value of the first item with the specified name. If the item is not numeric, the method returns `0.0`. If the item is multi-valued, only the first value is returned.

```
public int getItemValueInteger(String itemname) throws NotesException
```

The `getItemValueInteger` method returns the first value of the first item with the specified name. If the item is not numeric or if the item does not exist, the method returns `0`. For this reason, you should first call `hasItem` to determine whether the item exists, and if so, whether you need to distinguish the absence of a value from a value of `0`.

If the item is multi-valued, only the first value is returned. The `getItemValueInteger` method will round fractional values of 0.5 up and less than 0.5 down.

```
public String getItemValueString(String itemname) throws NotesException
```

The `getItemValueString` method returns the first value of the first item with the specified name. If the item has no value, is numeric, or is a date-time value, this method returns `null` (not an empty string). If multiple values exist, this method returns only the first value. If the item is a rich-text item, just the text is returned. Formatting characteristics and embedded objects are ignored.

```
public boolean hasItem(String itemname) throws NotesException
```

The `hasItem` method returns `true` if an item with the specified name exists within the document. It returns `false` otherwise.

```
public void makeResponse(Document parentDoc) throws NotesException
```

The makeResponse method makes the current document a response document of the specified document. This method will create or update a field called $Ref that contains the UNID of the specified parentDoc. Make sure you call the save method after calling makeResponse so that your changes are saved to the database.

```
public void putInFolder(String foldername) throws NotesException
```

```
public void putInFolder(String foldername, boolean createonfail) throws
NotesException
```

The putInFolder method puts the current document into the specified folder. If you specify createonfail to be false, an exception will be thrown if the folder does not exist. If you do not specify createonfail, the default value is true, so a folder will be created if it does not exist.

You can specify nested folders by using backslashes in the name, such as Basketball\\Lakers. You must use two slashes to represent a single slash in the name.

```
public boolean remove(boolean force) throws NotesException
```

The remove method removes the current document from the database. Special handling of the document occurs if it is modified by other users after the creation of the current Document object, but before the execution of remove. If the force parameter is false, the document is not deleted from the database if someone else modified the document. If force is true, the document is deleted regardless of what other users might have done to the same document.

```
public void removeFromFolder(String foldername) throws NotesException
```

The removeFromFolder method removes the document from the specified folder. Note that this method does not actually delete the document from the database; it just removes it from the folder.

You can specify nested folders by using backslashes in the name, such as Basketball\\Lakers. You must use two slashes to represent a single slash in the name.

```
public void removeItem(String itemname) throws NotesException
```

The removeItem method removes the specified item from the document. If more than one item has the specified name, all items with the name are removed. Make sure to call the save method to save your changes to the database.

```
public boolean renderToRTItem(RichTextItem rtitemname) throws NotesException
```

The renderToRTItem method renders the current document and its associated form as a graphic picture and stores it in the supplied rich-text item. The return value is true if the rendering was successful and false if it failed. It can fail if an input validation formula fails.

```
public Item replaceItemValue(String itemname, Object value) throws
NotesException
```

The replaceItemValue creates a new item with the specified name and stores the given value in the item. If one or more existing items are found with the same name in the document, they are deleted and replaced with the new item. If no previous item with the name is found, a new item is created. The return value is the newly created item.

You can use the replaceItemValue method to append additional items to a multi-valued item. First create a java.util.Vector that contains the existing values. Add the additional values to the Vector, and then call replaceItemValue to update the item.

```
public boolean save() throws NotesException
```

```
public boolean save(boolean force) throws NotesException
```

```
public boolean save(boolean force, boolean makeresponse) throws
NotesException
```

```
public boolean save(boolean force, boolean makeresponse, boolean markread)
throws NotesException
```

The save method saves the current document to the database. If you have made any modifications to the document object, you must call the save method to permanently save your changes. If the force parameter is true, any changes saved by another user while the current program is running are replaced. If the force parameter is false, the makeresponse parameter is used.

If the makeresponse parameter is true and a modification took place from another user, the current document becomes a response to the original document. If makeresponse is false or omitted, the save is canceled.

The markread parameter governs whether the document is marked as read. If true, it will be marked as read. If omitted or false, the document will not be marked as read.

```
public void send(String recipient) throws NotesException
```

```
public void send(java.util.Vector recipients) throws NotesException
```

```
public void send(boolean attachform, String recipient) throws NotesException
```

```
public void send(boolean attachform, java.util.Vector recipients) throws
NotesException
```

The send method sends the current document to the specified recipient or recipients. If the attachform parameter is true, the form is stored as an attachment to the message. The recipient string or recipients vector contains the names of the recipients. This parameter is used if no special field is within the document named SendTo. If a SendTo item is within the document, the parameter is ignored and the value in the field is used.

Several specially named items can be contained in a document to control the sending of email. Here are the special fields and their purposes:

Field Name	Values	Comments
BlindCopyTo	Names of people, groups, or mail-in databases	
Body	Email message content	
CopyTo	Names of people, groups, or mail-in databases	
DeliveryPriority	L, N, H	Low, Normal, or High priority.
DeliveryReport	0, 1	1 to return a report when the mail is delivered to the recipient.
Encrypt	0, 1	1 to encrypt mailed document. You can use the setEncryptOnSend property instead.
Form	Memo	Memo is usually the name of the form that is used for email.
MailFormat	M, T, E, B	Options to control rendering for cc:Mail recipients.
		M = Mail. The Body field of the document is rendered as text.
		T = Text. The contents of the document are rendered as text.
		E = Encapsulated. The document is encapsulated in a Notes database and attached.
		B = Both. Both text and encapsulated.
MailOptions	0, 1	1 to automatically mail the document when it is saved.
Principal	Names of people	This is the name of the person on whose behalf the mail is sent.
ReplyTo	Names of people, groups, or mail-in databases	This is useful if you use an agent to send mail but you want the responses to go to a person other than the agent's owner.
ReturnReceipt	0, 1	1 to send a receipt when the recipient opens the document.
SaveOptions	0, 1	1 to save a document that is mailed. You can use the saveMessageOnSend property instead.

PART

IV

CH

19

continues

continued

Field Name	Values	Comments
SendTo	Names of people, groups, or mail-in databases	Field is required within the form.
Sign	0, 1	1 to add an electronic signature to sign enabled fields. You can use the setSignOnSend property instead.
Subject	Subject line	

```java
import lotus.domino.*;
import java.util.*;

public class JavaAgent extends AgentBase {

   public void NotesMain() {

      try {
         Session session = getSession();
         AgentContext agentContext = session.getAgentContext();
         Database db = agentContext.getCurrentDatabase();
         // Create the email message
         Document email = db.createDocument();
         // Use the Email form
         email.appendItemValue("Form", "Memo");
         email.appendItemValue("Subject", "Do not send spam mail");
         Vector vTo = new Vector();
         vTo.addElement("Randy Tamura");
         vTo.addElement("John Smith");
         vTo.addElement("Fred Jones");
         // Domino will automatically save the message when sending it.
         email.setSaveMessageOnSend(true);
         // Send it. We don't need to save first.
         email.send(true, vTo);

      } catch(Exception e) {
         e.printStackTrace();
      }
   }
}
```

In the example, a document is created, the form is specified, and then the subject and recipients are given. The SaveMessageOnSend property is set to true to cause the message to be saved, and then the email is sent. You can also use an email message such as this to trigger an agent in a mail-in database. Create fields for communication to the mail-in database agent, fill them with values, and then send the message.

`public void sign() throws NotesException`

The sign method includes a digital security signature to the current document. A signature enables other people to verify the creator of the document. The signature is derived from the User ID and is based on the contents of the document. This method is not effective if the program is running on a server. Remember to call the save method for the document after signing it so that the changes will be saved to the database.

THE Outline CLASS

Class Definition

public class Outline extends Base

Properties

- getAlias/setAlias
- getComment/setComment

Methods

- addEntry (obsolete; use createEntry instead)
- createEntry
- getChild
- getFirst
- getLast
- getNext
- getNextSibling
- getParent
- getParentDatabase
- getPrev
- getPrevSibling
- moveEntry
- removeEntry
- save

The Outline class represents an outline within the Domino Designer. An outline is used to control navigation at the client level. An Outline object is a container for OutlineEntry objects. The primary function of the Outline class is to enable you to traverse and manipulate the OutlineEntry objects. If you manipulate the outline, be sure to call the save method to save your changes to the database.

In releases 5.0 and 5.0.1 it was possible to have free-standing OutlineEntry objects. As of release 5.0.2, Lotus has changed the interface so that OutlineEntry objects are always contained within an outline. As a result, the addEntry method is no longer necessary, and several other methods have been affected. Each routine that behaves differently beginning with 5.0.2 includes a description of the changes as of 5.0.2.

COMMON METHODS TO CREATE

```
Database.createOutline, Database.getOutline
```

PROPERTIES

```
public String getAlias() throws NotesException
```

```
public void setAlias(String alias) throws NotesException
```

The getAlias property returns the alias name for the current outline. The setAlias property routine can be used to set the alias to the specified string. Be sure to call the save method if you change the alias.

```
public String getComment() throws NotesException
```

```
public void setComment(String comment) throws NotesException
```

The getComment property returns the informational comment about the current outline. If you set the comment in the Domino designer, you can retrieve the value with getComment. The setComment property routine can be used to change the comment to the specified string. Be sure to call the save method if you change the comment.

METHODS

```
public void addEntry(OutlineEntry newEntry, OutlineEntry referenceEntry)
throws NotesException
```

```
public void addEntry(OutlineEntry newEntry, OutlineEntry referenceEntry,
boolean after) throws NotesException
```

```
public void addEntry(OutlineEntry newEntry, OutlineEntry referenceEntry,
boolean after, boolean asChild) throws NotesException
```

As of release 5.0.2 of Notes/Domino, the addEntry method is obsolete. You should use the createEntry method instead. The addEntry method is still available for backward compatibility. If you are using Release 5.0 or 5.0.1, here is a description of the function:

> The addEntry method adds the new OutlineEntry to the outline in relation to the reference entry. If the Boolean flag after is omitted or true, the new entry will be placed after the reference entry. If the Boolean flag asChild is true, the new entry will be created as a child of the reference entry. When asChild is true, the after flag must also be true. If you try to insert a child before the reference entry, an exception will be thrown.

> To add the very first entry to the outline, you can use null for the reference entry. Be sure to call the save method after modifying the outline.

```
public OutlineEntry createEntry(String newName) throws NotesException

public OutlineEntry createEntry(String newName, OutlineEntry referenceEntry)
throws NotesException

public OutlineEntry createEntry(String newName, OutlineEntry referenceEntry,
boolean after) throws NotesException

public OutlineEntry createEntry(String newName, OutlineEntry referenceEntry,
boolean after, boolean asChild) throws NotesException

public OutlineEntry createEntry(OutlineEntry fromEntry) throws NotesException

public OutlineEntry createEntry(OutlineEntry fromEntry, OutlineEntry
referenceEntry) throws NotesException

public OutlineEntry createEntry(OutlineEntry fromEntry, OutlineEntry
referenceEntry, boolean after) throws NotesException

public OutlineEntry createEntry(OutlineEntry fromEntry, OutlineEntry
referenceEntry, boolean after, boolean asChild) throws NotesException
```

In releases 5.0 and 5.0.1 of Domino, only the first syntax is available. In release 5.0.2 the other forms of createEntry are available and the last three forms replace the addEntry method.

The createEntry method creates a new OutlineEntry object. If you do not specify a referenceEntry, the new OutlineEntry is created at the end of the outline. If you specify a newName string, a new OutlineEntry is created with the specified name. If you specify a fromEntry, the new OutlineEntry is copied from fromEntry.

The createEntry method adds the new OutlineEntry to the outline in relation to the reference entry. If the Boolean flag after is omitted or true, the new entry will be placed after the reference entry. If the Boolean flag asChild is true, the new entry will be created as a child of the reference entry. When asChild is true, the after flag must also be true. If you try to insert a child before the reference entry, an exception will be thrown.

Be sure to call the save method after modifying the outline.

For example,

```
import lotus.domino.*;

public class JavaAgent extends AgentBase {
    public void NotesMain() {
        try {
            Session session = getSession();
            AgentContext agentContext = session.getAgentContext();
            Database db = agentContext.getCurrentDatabase();
            Outline ol = db.createOutline("MyOutline");
```

```
            OutlineEntry oe1 = ol.createEntry("Reference"); // Create free entry
            // Add the second entry prior to the Reference entry (after=false)
            OutlineEntry oe2 = ol.createEntry("Before Reference", oe1, false);
            // Add the third entry after the Reference entry (after=true)
            OutlineEntry oe3 = ol.createEntry("After Reference", oe1, true);
            // Add the next entry as a child of the reference entry.
            OutlineEntry oe4 = ol.createEntry("Below Reference as child",
                oe1, true, true);
            ol.save();
        } catch(Exception e) {
            e.printStackTrace();
        }
    }
}
```

The sample program will create three top-level outline entries and one second-level outline entry as a child of the reference entry.

`public OutlineEntry getChild(OutlineEntry entry) throws NotesException`

The getChild method returns the OutlineEntry of the first child of the specified OutlineEntry. It returns null if no child entry is found.

`public OutlineEntry getFirst() throws NotesException`

The getFirst method returns the first OutlineEntry object that is contained within the outline. It returns null if no entries exist.

`public OutlineEntry getLast() throws NotesException`

The getLast method returns the last OutlineEntry object that is contained within the outline. It returns null if no entries exist.

`public OutlineEntry getNext(OutlineEntry entry) throws NotesException`

The getNext method returns the OutlineEntry that follows the specified OutlineEntry. The nodes of the outline are visited in hierarchical order. That is, the first node is visited, then all its children, then its next sibling. It returns null if there is no next entry.

For example,

```
import lotus.domino.*;

public class JavaAgent extends AgentBase {
    public void NotesMain() {
        try {
            Session session = getSession();
            AgentContext agentContext = session.getAgentContext();
            Database db = agentContext.getCurrentDatabase();
            Outline ol = db.getOutline("MyOutline");
            // Get the first entry
            OutlineEntry oe = ol.getFirst();
            while (null != oe) {
                System.out.println(oe.getLabel());
                // Get the next entry
```

```
            oe = ol.getNext(oe);
        }
    } catch(Exception e) {
        e.printStackTrace();
    }
  }
}
```

The sample program gets an outline called MyOutline and then visits all the nodes of the outline in the order in which they are returned. Here is the output that is generated from the outline created from the example for the createEntry method:

```
Before Reference
Reference
Below Reference as child
After Reference
```

public OutlineEntry getNextSibling(OutlineEntry entry) throws NotesException

The getNextSibling method returns the next OutlineEntry at the same hierarchical level that follows the specified OutlineEntry. It returns null if no next entry is found. In the MyOutline example, if getNextSibling were used in place of getNext, the child node would be skipped and the following would be output:

```
Before Reference
Reference
After Reference
```

public OutlineEntry getParent(OutlineEntry entry) throws NotesException

The getParent method returns the OutlineEntry that is the parent of the specified OutlineEntry. It returns null if no parent is found, which means that the specified OutlineEntry is the top level.

public Database getParentDatabase() throws NotesException

The getParentDatabase method returns the database that contains the current outline.

public OutlineEntry getPrev(OutlineEntry entry) throws NotesException

The getPrev method returns the OutlineEntry that precedes the specified OutlineEntry. The nodes of the outline are visited in reverse hierarchical order. That is, all the children of a node are visited in reverse order followed by the node itself. It returns null if no previous entry exists.

public OutlineEntry getPrevSibling(OutlineEntry entry) throws NotesException

The getPrevSibling method returns the OutlineEntry at the same hierarchical level that precedes the specified OutlineEntry. It returns null if no preceding entry exists.

public void moveEntry(OutlineEntry theEntry, OutlineEntry referenceEntry) throws NotesException

```
public void moveEntry(OutlineEntry theEntry, OutlineEntry referenceEntry,
boolean after) throws NotesException
```

```
public void moveEntry(OutlineEntry theEntry, OutlineEntry referenceEntry,
boolean after, boolean asChild) throws NotesException
```

The moveEntry method moves an OutlineEntry from one spot in the outline to another. The entry is moved relative to the reference entry. If the Boolean flag after is omitted or true, the new entry will be placed after the reference entry. If the Boolean flag asChild is true, the new entry will be created as a child of the reference entry.

In releases 5.0 and 5.0.1, the asChild flag defaulted to true. As of release 5.0.2 and greater, the asChild flag default is false.

```
public void removeEntry(OutlineEntry entry) throws NotesException
```

The removeEntry method removes the specified OutlineEntry from the outline.

In releases 5.0 and 5.0.1, the removeEntry method would just remove the OutlineEntry from the outline. In release 5.0.2 and greater, the removeEntry method removes and destroys the specified OutlineEntry and all its children. An attempt to use the OutlineEntry or one of its children after it has been removed from the outline will throw an exception.

```
public int save() throws NotesException
```

The save method saves the current outline. You must call the save method or any changes you have made will be lost. A normal save will return zero.

THE OutlineEntry CLASS

Class Definition

```
public class OutlineEntry extends Base
```

Properties

- getAlias/setAlias
- getDatabase
- getDocument
- getEntryClass
- getFormula
- getFrameText/setFrameText
- getHideFormula/setHideFormula*
- getImagesText/setImagesText
- getKeepSelectionFocus/setKeepSelectionFocus*
- getLabel/setLabel

- getLevel
- getNamedElement
- getParent
- getType
- getURL
- getUseHideFormula/setUseHideFormula*
- getView
- hasChildren
- isHidden/setHidden
- isHiddenFromNotes/setHiddenFromNotes*
- isHiddenFromWeb/setHiddenFromWeb*
- isInThisDB
- isPrivate

Methods

- setAction
- setNamedElement
- setNoteLink
- setURL

The OutlineEntry class represents a single entry within an Outline object. An individual OutlineEntry can represent a named element, a link, or a variety of other possibilities. Essentially, an OutlineEntry will cause some sort of navigation by the user. Use the properties and methods to determine the type of OutlineEntry.

The properties marked with an asterisk (*) are new as of release 5.0.2 and might not appear in your documentation.

COMMON METHODS TO CREATE

Outline.createEntry

PROPERTIES

public String getAlias() throws NotesException

public void setAlias(String alias) throws NotesException

The getAlias property routine returns the alias name for the outline entry. You can use the setAlias property routine to change the alias name. The alias name is used for programmatic access to the OutlineEntry. For the name of the outline entry, use the getLabel/setLabel property methods.

```
public Database getDatabase() throws NotesException
```

The getDatabase property routine returns the database that is the resource link for an outline entry. This property is applicable only if the entry type is OUTLINE_TYPE_NOTELINK or OUTLINE_TYPE_NAMEDELEMENT and the entry class is OUTLINE_CLASS_DATABASE, OUTLINE_CLASS_DOCUMENT, or OUTLINE_CLASS_VIEW. In other cases, the getDatabase property will return null. You can query the OutlineEntry type using getType and the entry class using getEntryClass.

```
public Document getDocument() throws NotesException
```

The getDocument property routine returns the document that is the resource link for an outline entry. This property is applicable only if the entry type is OUTLINE_TYPE_NOTELINK and the entry class is OUTLINE_CLASS_DOCUMENT. In other cases, the getDocument property will return null.

```
public int getEntryClass() throws NotesException
```

The getEntryClass property returns an integer code that represents the class of the OutlineEntry. Here are the valid codes:

- OutlineEntry.OUTLINE_CLASS_DATABASE—(2194)
- OutlineEntry.OUTLINE_CLASS_DOCUMENT—(2190)
- OutlineEntry.OUTLINE_CLASS_FOLDER—(2197)
- OutlineEntry.OUTLINE_CLASS_FORM—(2192)
- OutlineEntry.OUTLINE_CLASS_FRAMESET—(2195)
- OutlineEntry.OUTLINE_CLASS_NAVIGATOR—(2193)
- OutlineEntry.OUTLINE_CLASS_PAGE—(2196)
- OutlineEntry.OUTLINE_CLASS_UNKNOWN—(2189)
- OutlineEntry.OUTLINE_CLASS_VIEW—(2191)

```
public String getFormula() throws NotesException
```

The getFormula property routine returns the formula for an action OutlineEntry. This property is applicable only if the entry type is OUTLINE_TYPE_ACTION. In other cases, the getFormula property will return an empty string. The setAction method is used to set the action formula.

```
public String getFrameText() throws NotesException
```

```
public void setFrameText(String framename) throws NotesException
```

The getFrameText property routine is used to get the name of the target frame for the entry's OnClick event. You can set the frame name with setFrameText.

```
public String getHideFormula() throws NotesException
```

```
public void setHideFormula(String formula) throws NotesException
```

The getHideFormula property returns a string that represents the hide-when formula. If there is no formula, it will return an empty string. Use the setHideFormula property routine to set the hide-when formula. This property is new with release 5.0.2.

```
public String getImagesText() throws NotesException
```

```
public void setImagesText(String imagename) throws NotesException
```

The getImagesText property is the name of the image resource (not a file) used to add an image next to the outline entry. Use setImagesText to set the name of the image resource.

```
public boolean getKeepSelectionFocus() throws NotesException
```

```
public void setKeepSelectionFocus(boolean keepFocus) throws NotesException
```

The getKeepSelectionFocus property returns true if the entry should keep the selection focus and false otherwise. This property is reset and set in the Domino designer with the check box Does Not Keep Selection Focus. Use setKeepSelectionFocus to set this property. This property is new with release 5.0.2.

```
public Outline getParent() throws NotesException
```

The getParent property returns the outline that contains the current OutlineEntry. This property is supported in release 5.0.2 and later.

```
public String getLabel() throws NotesException
```

```
public void setLabel(String label) throws NotesException
```

The getLabel property returns the text that is displayed for the OutlineEntry. Use the setLabel property routine to set the display text.

```
public int getLevel() throws NotesException
```

The getLevel property returns the indentation level of the OutlineEntry. Level 0 is the topmost level.

```
public String getNamedElement() throws NotesException
```

The getNamedElement returns the name of the Named element referenced by the outline entry. This property is applicable only if the entry type is OUTLINE_TYPE_NAMEDELEMENT. For any other entry type, the property will return an empty string.

```
public int getType() throws NotesException
```

The getType property returns an integer code that represents the type of the OutlineEntry. Here are the valid codes:

- OutlineEntry.OUTLINE_OTHER_FOLDERS_TYPE—(1589)
- OutlineEntry.OUTLINE_OTHER_UNKNOWN_TYPE—(1591)
- OutlineEntry.OUTLINE_OTHER_VIEWS_TYPE—(1588)
- OutlineEntry.OUTLINE_TYPE_ACTION—(2188)
- OutlineEntry.OUTLINE_TYPE_NAMEDELEMENT—(2187)
- OutlineEntry.OUTLINE_TYPE_NOTELINK—(2186)
- OutlineEntry.OUTLINE_TYPE_URL—(2185)

```
public String getURL() throws NotesException
```

The getURL property returns the URL associated with the OutlineEntry. This property is applicable only if the entry type is OUTLINE_TYPE_URL. For any other entry type, the property will return an empty string.

```
public boolean getUseHideFormula() throws NotesException
```

```
public void setUseHideFormula(boolean useformula) throws NotesException
```

The getUseHideFormula property returns true if the hide-when formula is active. If the hide-when formula is not used, the routine will return false. Use the setUseHideFormula property routine to set the property. This property is new with release 5.0.2.

```
public View getView() throws NotesException
```

The getView property returns the view associated with the OutlineEntry. This property is applicable only if the entry type is OUTLINE_TYPE_NOTELINK or OUTLINE_TYPE_NAMEDELEMENT and the entry class is OUTLINE_CLASS_VIEW. For any other entry type, the property will return null.

```
public boolean hasChildren() throws NotesException
```

The hasChildren property returns true if the OutlineEntry has child entries and false otherwise.

```
public boolean isHidden() throws NotesException
```

```
public void setHidden(boolean hidden) throws NotesException
```

The isHidden property returns true if the outline entry is hidden from you and false if it is visible. Use the setHidden property routine to set the hidden attribute.

```
public boolean isHiddenFromNotes() throws NotesException
```

```
public void setHiddenFromNotes(boolean hidden) throws NotesException
```

The isHiddenFromNotes property returns true if the OutlineEntry is hidden from Notes. It returns false if the OutlineEntry is visible from Notes. Use setHiddenFromNotes to set the property. This property is new with release 5.0.2.

```
public boolean isHiddenFromWeb() throws NotesException
```

```
public void setHiddenFromWeb(boolean hidden) throws NotesException
```

The isHiddenFromWeb property returns true if the OutlineEntry is hidden from Web browsers. It returns false if the OutlineEntry is visible from Web browsers. Use setHiddenFromWeb to set the property. This property is new with release 5.0.2.

```
public boolean isInThisDB() throws NotesException
```

The isInThisDB property returns true if the outline entry refers to an element in the current database and false otherwise.

```
public boolean isPrivate() throws NotesException
```

The isPrivate property returns true if the outline entry applies only to a specific user and false if it is public. As far as I can tell, as of release 5.0.2, no way to set the isPrivate attribute exists, either in the user interface or programmatically. Additionally, even if you could make the OutlineEntry private, no way to specify the user to whom it is private exists. So, this property routine will normally always return false. It might be implemented in a future release.

METHODS

```
public boolean setAction(String formula) throws NotesException
```

The setAction method sets the formula for an action outline entry. This method sets the outline entry type to OUTLINE_TYPE_ACTION. To retrieve the formula, use the getFormula property. If you pass a string that is not a valid formula, the stored formula will not be changed.

As of release 5.0.2, this method returns false if it completed successfully, and it returns true if the setAction failed. This is contrary to the documentation, so either the code or documentation might be changed in the future.

```
public boolean setNamedElement(Database db, String elementName, int
entryClass) throws NotesException
```

The setNamedElement method sets the OutlineEntry type to OUTLINE_TYPE_NAMEDELEMENT. You specify the database containing the named element, the element name, and the element class. The database argument cannot be `null`. See the `getEntryClass` property for a list of the classes.

As of release 5.0.2, this method returns `false` if it completed successfully, and it returns `true` if the `setNamedElement` failed. This is contrary to the documentation, so either the code or documentation might be changed in the future.

```
public boolean setNoteLink(Database db) throws NotesException
```

```
public boolean setNoteLink(Document doc) throws NotesException
```

```
public boolean setNoteLink(View view) throws NotesException
```

The `setNoteLink` method sets the `OutlineEntry` type to `OUTLINE_TYPE_NOTELINK`. It sets the resource link to the object that you supply. The method will set the entry class to one of the following: `OUTLINE_CLASS_DATABASE`, `OUTLINE_CLASS_DOCUMENT`, or `OUTLINE_CLASS_VIEW` depending on the type of the object you supply. The method returns `true` if it completed successfully.

As of release 5.0.2, this method returns `false` if it completed successfully, and it returns `true` if the `setNoteLink` failed. This is contrary to the documentation, so either the code or documentation might be changed in the future.

```
public boolean setURL(String url) throws NotesException
```

The `setURL` method sets the `OutlineEntry` type to `OUTLINE_TYPE_URL`. The entry class will be set to `OUTLINE_CLASS_UNKNOWN`. It sets the resource link to the URL that you supply. If you supply an empty string, the outline entry will not be changed from its previous setting.

As of release 5.0.2, this method returns `false` if it completed successfully, and it returns `true` if the `setURL` failed. This is contrary to the documentation, so either the code or documentation might be changed in the future.

THE Form CLASS

Class Definition

```
public class Form extends Base
```

Properties

- `getAliases`
- `getFields`
- `getFormUsers/setFormUsers`
- `getName`
- `getParent`
- `getReaders`
- `isProtectReaders/setProtectReaders`

- `isProtectUsers/setProtectUsers`
- `isSubForm`

Method

- `remove`

The `Form` class enables you to obtain and set information about a form in the database. You can find out the fields contained within the form, find out the name and aliases of the form, and control the form's users. You cannot, however, create a form with the `Form` class (or any other class). You must create the actual form in the Domino designer. You can obtain a form object from the `Database` class.

The fields of a form do not store values. Fields are named, and the Notes-rendering engine matches field names with a document's item names. When a document to be displayed has an item with the same name as a form's field, the item's contents are displayed in the form's field with the same name. For computed formulas, variable values are also retrieved from the underlying document's items with the same name.

COMMON METHODS TO CREATE

`Database.getForm, Database.getForms`

PROPERTIES

`public java.util.Vector getAliases() throws NotesException`

The `getAliases` property returns the alias names of the form. The routine returns a `Vector` of `String` objects, each representing an alias name. If there are no aliases, the `Vector` is empty. The list of names does not include the main name of the form. Use the `getName` property to obtain this name.

For example,

```
import lotus.domino.*;
import java.util.*;

public class JavaAgent extends AgentBase {
    public void NotesMain() {
        try {
            Session session = getSession();
            AgentContext agentContext = session.getAgentContext();
            Database db = agentContext.getCurrentDatabase();
            java.util.Vector forms = db.getForms();
            Form form = (Form) forms.elementAt(0);
            System.out.println("Form " + form.getName() + "; Aliases= "
                + form.getAliases());
        } catch(Exception e) {
            e.printStackTrace();
        }
    }
}
```

The example prints out the name and the aliases for the first form of the database.

`public java.util.Vector getFields() throws NotesException`

The `getFields` property returns a `Vector` of `String` objects. Each of the strings represents the name of one of the form's fields. If there are no fields, the `Vector` is empty.

`public java.util.Vector getFormUsers() throws NotesException`

`public void setFormUsers(java.util.Vector users) throws NotesException`

The `getFormUsers` property returns a `Vector` of `String` objects. Each string represents the name of a person or group that is allowed to create documents using the form. This list of users is stored within the form in the item named $FormUsers. If the $FormUsers field is empty or does not exist, the `Vector` is empty. Note that if the returned vector is empty, it means that the default ACL rules apply. It does not mean that no one is allowed to create documents using the form. You must access the ACL to find out the list of users.

You can modify the list of users within the Domino designer user interface on the Security tab of the Form properties box in the section titled Who Can Create Documents With This Form. You can also change the list of users with the `setFormUsers` property routine. The list of users cannot override the ACL settings for the database. It can only refine the list found in the ACL.

`public String getName() throws NotesException`

The `getName` property routine returns the name of the form. The name returned does not include any aliases. Use the `getAliases` property to obtain the names of the aliases.

`public Database getParent() throws NotesException`

The `getParent` property routine returns a `Database` object for the database that contains the form.

`public java.util.Vector getReaders() throws NotesException`

`public void setReaders(java.util.Vector users) throws NotesException`

The `getReaders` property returns a `Vector` of `String` objects. Each string represents the name of a person or group that is allowed to read documents using the form. This list of users is stored within the form in the item named $Readers. If the $Readers field is empty or does not exist, the `Vector` is empty. Note that if the returned `Vector` is empty, it means that the default ACL rules apply. It does not mean that no one is allowed to read documents using the form. You must access the ACL to find out the list of users.

You can modify the list of users within the Domino designer user interface on the Security tab of the Form properties box in the section titled Default Read Access for Documents

Created With This Form. You can also change the list of users with the `setReaders` property routine. The list of users cannot override the ACL settings for the database. It can only refine the list found in the ACL.

```
public boolean isProtectReaders() throws NotesException
```

```
public void setProtectReaders(boolean protect) throws NotesException
```

The `setProtectReaders` property routine can be used to protect the `$Readers` items from being overwritten by replication. If you call `setProtectReaders` with the value of `true`, the `$Readers` field will not be changed by replication. You can use the `isProtectReaders` property access routine to query the status of this flag.

```
public boolean isProtectUsers() throws NotesException
```

```
public void setProtectUsers(boolean protect) throws NotesException
```

The `setProtectUsers` property routine can be used to protect the `$FormUsers` items from being overwritten by replication. If you call `setProtectUsers` with the value of `true`, the `$FormUsers` field will not be changed by replication. You can use the `isProtectUsers` property access routine to query the status of this flag.

```
public boolean isSubForm() throws NotesException
```

The `isSubForm` property returns `true` if the form is a subform and `false` if it is a regular form.

METHODS

```
public void remove() throws NotesException
```

The `remove` method is used to permanently delete the form from the database.

CHAPTER REVIEW

1. What is a deletion stub? Explain its purpose. How can you tell whether a `Document` object is a deletion stub? Which method or property will create a deletion stub? What causes a deletion stub to be removed from a database?

2. What is the difference between the `setEncryptOnSend` property and the `encrypt` method? Suppose you are sending an email document and saving it in your mail database. Which one should you use? Can you use both? What is the effect of each?

3. Write a Java agent that will count the number of items in a document and print the answer.

4. What is the purpose of a digital signature on a document? Give two scenarios where this feature might be valuable in an application.

5. Write a Java agent that will traverse an outline visiting each OutlineEntry object. The program should visit all children of a node first before it visits the current node. Print out the name of each OutlineEntry as you visit it.

6. Write a Java agent that will inspect the ACL of a database, and then set the security attributes of a specific form so that only users with designer level access and above can create documents with the form.

7. A special field called $AssistMail is sometimes automatically added to a document. What is the purpose of this field and which property routine should you use to test for the field's existence?

8. Explain the difference between appendItemValue and replaceItemValue. Give a scenario where using appendItemValue is equivalent to replaceItemValue.

9. Write a Java agent that will go through one database and find all documents that were last accessed longer than 30 days ago. These documents should be copied to a separate, archive database. After they have been copied, they should be deleted from the original database. For this agent to function properly, what advanced Database property must be properly set?

10. Write a Java agent that will go through one database and find all documents that are larger than 10KB or that contain an attachment. These documents should be copied to a separate, archive database. After they have been copied, they should be deleted from the original database.

11. Three routines, getColumnValues, getFTSearchScore, and getParentView, are contained in the Document class. Consider what happens when a document appears in more than one view. What other classes in the Domino Objects model would be more appropriate to use to obtain these values? Why? (Hint: They might not appear in this chapter.)

12. What is the difference and relationship between a field on a form named TEST and an item in a document named TEST?

CHAPTER 20

WORKING WITH THE Item AND Formatting CLASSES

In this chapter

THE Item CLASS

Class Definition

public class Item extends Base

Properties

- getDateTimeValue/setDateTimeValue
- getLastModified
- getMIMEEntity
- getName
- getParent
- getText
- getType
- getValueDouble/setValueDouble
- getValueInteger/setValueInteger
- getValueLength
- getValues/setValues
- getValueString/setValueString
- isAuthors/setAuthors
- isEncrypted/setEncrypted
- isNames/setNames
- isProtected/setProtected
- isReaders/setReaders
- isSaveToDisk/setSaveToDisk
- isSigned/setSigned
- isSummary/setSummary

Methods

- abstractText
- appendToTextList
- containsValue
- copyItemToDocument
- parseXML
- remove
- transformXML

The Item class represents a data element within a Domino document. Each item has a name and either can have a single value or can contain multiple values. In addition, although it is not recommended, more than one item can have the same name in one document. Lotus uses this feature to implement rich-text items that can contain large amounts of data. The multiple items are internally linked to enable the storing of very large items.

Each item also has a type, which can be obtained using the getType property routine. The type indicates whether the value is a date/time, number, text item, or one of many other specialty items. Some examples of specialty items include rich-text, names, authors, and reader items. Rich-text items can contain text formatting as well as attachments and embedded objects. See the getType property description for more details.

COMMON METHODS TO CREATE

Document.appendItemValue, Document.copyItem, Document.getFirstItem, Document.replaceItemValue, Item.copyItemToDocument

PROPERTIES

public DateTime getDateTimeValue() throws NotesException

public void setDateTimeValue(DateTime dt) throws NotesException

The getDateTimeValue property access routine returns a DateTime object that represents the value of the item if it is a date/time item. If the item is some other type, the getDateTimeValue routine will return null. You can use the setDateTimeValue property routine to set the value of the item to a specified date/time value. The new date/time value will replace any previous values and will change the type of the item to Item.DATETIMES.

public DateTime getLastModified() throws NotesException

The getLastModified property routine returns the date and time that the current item was last modified.

public MIMEEntity getMIMEEntity() throws NotesException

The getMIMEEntity property routine returns the MIMEEntity object that this item represents. This is typically the Body item of a mailed Internet document. This property is available only with Domino 5.0.2 and later. See the MIMEEntity class for more information.

public String getName() throws NotesException

The getName property returns the item's name. An item's name is used to match with field names within forms. When a match occurs, the item's value is displayed in the corresponding field of the form. For example, suppose an item is named Address. When Domino displays a document with a form that contains a field named Address, the value of the document's Address item will be displayed on the form in the Address field. An item's name is also used in formula expressions, selection formulas, and other formula expressions within Domino.

public Document getParent() throws NotesException

The getParent property returns a Document object for the document that contains the current item.

public String getText() throws NotesException

public String getText(int maxlen) throws NotesException

The getText property routine returns the plain-text representation of the current item's value. Multiple values are separated with semicolons. Large values can be truncated, and non-text data such as bitmaps, file attachments, and embedded objects within a rich text field are ignored. Use the maxlen parameter to set the maximum number of characters to be returned.

public int getType() throws NotesException

The getType property returns an integer code that represents the data type of the item. Here are the valid codes:

- Item.ACTIONCD—(16)
- Item.ASSISTANTINFO—(17)
- Item.ATTACHMENT—(1084)
- Item.AUTHORS—(1076)
- Item.COLLATION—(2)
- Item.DATETIMES—(1024)
- Item.EMBEDDEDOBJECT—(1090)
- Item.ERRORITEM—(256)
- Item.FORMULA—(1536)
- Item.HTML—(21)
- Item.ICON—(6)
- Item.LSOBJECT—(20)
- Item.MIME_PART—(25)
- Item.NAMES—(1074)
- Item.NOTELINKS—(7)
- Item.NOTEREFS—(4)
- Item.NUMBERS—(768)
- Item.OTHEROBJECT—(1085)

- Item.QUERYCD—(15)
- Item.READERS—(1075)
- Item.RICHTEXT—(1)
- Item.SIGNATURE—(8)
- Item.TEXT—(1280)
- Item.UNAVAILABLE—(512)
- Item.UNKNOWN—(0)
- Item.USERDATA—(14)
- Item.USERID—(1792)
- Item.VIEWMAPDATA—(18)
- Item.VIEWMAPLAYOUT—(19)

`public double getValueDouble() throws NotesException`

`public void setValueDouble(double value) throws NotesException`

The getValueDouble returns the value of an item as a double-precision Java value. If the value is not numeric or empty, the property will return 0.0. If the item has multiple values, only the first value is returned. Be sure to check the data type before retrieving the value if you want to distinguish between a true zero value and a non-numeric or empty value.

The setValueDouble property routine will replace any existing value of the item with the value supplied and will change the type of the item to be Item.NUMBERS.

`public int getValueInteger() throws NotesException`

`public void setValueInteger(int value) throws NotesException`

The getValueInteger returns the value of an item as a Java integer value. If the value is not numeric or empty, the property will return 0. If the item has multiple values, only the first value is returned. This property will round a numeric value if it does not contain an integer. Be sure to check the data type before retrieving the value if you want to distinguish between a true zero value and a non-numeric or empty value.

The setValueInteger property routine will replace any existing value of the item with the value supplied and will change the type of the item to be Item.NUMBERS.

`public int getValueLength() throws NotesException`

The getValueLength property returns the length of the item, in bytes, including overhead. Because overhead is included in the length, you should not use the getValueLength property to check whether an item matches a given string's length.

```
public java.util.Vector getValues() throws NotesException
```

```
public void setValues(java.util.Vector values) throws NotesException
```

Use the getValues property routine to obtain all the values of an item. Although getValueDouble, getValueInteger, and getValueString return a convenient format, they only return the first value when an item has multiple values. The getValues property returns the same values as the Document.getItemValue method.

For a rich-text item, this property will return a Vector with a single element containing a plain-text rendering in a String. For text items, a Vector will be returned with String elements. For numbers, a Vector will be returned with Double elements. For date/time or date range values, a Vector of DateTime elements will be returned.

You can add, delete, or change values of a multi-valued item by retrieving the Vector of values within an item, updating the Vector, and then using the setValues property routine to change the item's values. The new item's type will be updated to match the type of the values supplied. For example, the type can be Item.NUMBERS, Item.DATETIMES, or Item.TEXT.

```
public String getValueString() throws NotesException
```

```
public void setValueString(String value) throws NotesException
```

The getValueString returns the value of an item as a Java String object. If the value is numeric or a date/time value, this routine will return an empty string. Rich-text items are rendered into plain text and there is no formatting. Embedded objects are not rendered. If the item has multiple values, only the first value is returned.

The setValueString property routine will replace any existing value of the item with the value supplied and will change the type of the item to be Item.TEXT.

```
public boolean isAuthors() throws NotesException
```

```
public void setAuthors(boolean authoritem) throws NotesException
```

The isAuthors property access routine returns true if the item is an Authors item, which contains a list of names. An Authors item only affects users who normally have Author-level ACL access. With Author-level ACL access, a user is normally restricted to editing documents that he or she has created. When an Authors item is created in a document, Author-level access is further restricted, and any such user can edit the document only if his or her name appears in the Authors item list. If a user has Author-level ACL access and the user's name (or an encompassing group name) does not appear in the list, he or she will have only Reader-level access to the document. When an Authors item appears in a document but it is empty, normal ACL rules apply.

An Authors item does not affect users with Editor-level ACL access or above, and it cannot be used to confer editing capabilities to users with a No Access, Depositor, or Reader ACL level.

```
public boolean isEncrypted() throws NotesException
```

```
public void setEncrypted(boolean encrypt) throws NotesException
```

The `isEncrypted` property returns `true` if the item is encrypted and `false` if it is not encrypted. Use the `setEncrypted` property routine to change the encryption status.

```
public boolean isNames() throws NotesException
```

```
public void setNames(boolean names) throws NotesException
```

The `isNames` property returns `true` if the item is a Names item and `false` if it is not. A Names item is a list of user, server, or group name strings. Names are stored in canonical format, for example, `CN=John Doe/OU=Engineering/O=Acme`.

Use the `setNames` property routine to indicate that the item represents a set of names.

```
public boolean isProtected() throws NotesException
```

```
public void setProtected(boolean names) throws NotesException
```

The `isProtected` property is `true` if the user needs at least Editor access to modify the item. Use the `setProtected` property routine to change the item's protected status. To change this property in the Domino Designer, highlight the field in the form designer and open the field's property box. In the Advanced tab, within the Security Options section, is a drop-down list. Enable the Must Have At Least Editor Access to Use option.

An example of this type of field can be found in the `Person` document of a Domino directory. Only an administrator can change a person's official name, but you can allow the person to change his or her own phone number.

```
public boolean isReaders() throws NotesException
```

```
public void setReaders(boolean readeritem) throws NotesException
```

The `isReaders` property access routine returns `true` if the item is a Readers item, which contains a list of names. When a Readers item is created in a document, access specified by the ACL is further restricted and a user can read the document only if his or her name (or an encompassing group name) appears in the Readers item list. Even with Editor access level or above, the user is restricted from reading the document if the user's name does not appear in the Readers item.

Appearance in the Readers item cannot override ACL access, and if the user's name has the No Access level, he or she still will not be able to read the document. If a Readers item appears in a document but is empty, normal ACL rules apply.

Use the `setReaders` property routine to change the item to or from a Readers item. Reader values are stored in canonical format, for example as `CN=Sam Smith/OU=Engineering/O=Acme`.

```
public boolean isSaveToDisk() throws NotesException
```

```
public void setSaveToDisk(boolean save) throws NotesException
```

The isSaveToDisk property routine returns true if the item will be saved to disk when the document is saved. It returns false if the item will not be saved. If you change the status of an item from saved to not saved, the item will be deleted when the document is saved.

Use the setSaveToDisk property routine to change the save status.

```
public boolean isSigned() throws NotesException
```

```
public void setSigned(boolean signed) throws NotesException
```

The isSigned property returns true if the item contains a signature, and false if not. The signature is derived from the User ID and serves as a verification of the creator of the data in the item as well as the item's contents.

For example:

```java
import lotus.domino.*;

public class JavaAgent extends AgentBase {
    public void NotesMain() {
        try {
            Session session = getSession();
            AgentContext agentContext = session.getAgentContext();
            Database db = agentContext.getCurrentDatabase();
            Document doc = db.createDocument();
            // Make sure we have a form for the document
            doc.appendItemValue("Form", "Memo");
            doc.appendItemValue("SendTo", "SignTester");
            doc.appendItemValue("Subject", "Sign Test");
            // Make the body a rich text item.
            RichTextItem body = doc.createRichTextItem("Body");
            body.setValueString("This is a signed rich text body");
            // Flag it to be signed
            body.setSigned(true);
            // Sign the field and save the document
            doc.save();
        } catch(Exception e) {
            e.printStackTrace();
        }
    }
}
```

The example will create a new document, fill in several fields, and sign the body field. The result will be a SEAL attribute on the body field.

The Document.sign method signs the entire document, whereas the Item.setSigned property signs only a single item.

```
public boolean isSummary() throws NotesException
```

```
public void setSummary(boolean summary) throws NotesException
```

The isSummary flag indicates whether an item can appear in a view or folder. If it is true, the item can appear in a view or folder, and if it is false, it cannot. Use the setSummary property routine to enable an item for viewing in a view or folder. Rich-text items cannot appear in a view or folder.

METHODS

```
public String abstractText(int maxlen, boolean dropvowels, boolean userdict)
throws NotesException
```

The abstractText method examines and abbreviates the text found in the current item. You specify the maximum length string, and it will return the abbreviated text. If you specify true for the dropvowels parameter, vowels will be dropped from the return string. If you specify true for the userdict parameter, Notes will use abbreviations found in the noteabbr.txt file.

The noteabbr.txt file should contain a list of abbreviations, one pair of words per line. Each line should contain first the word to be substituted followed by the abbreviation. For example:

```
telephone phone
maximum max
minimum min
onomatopoeia ono
abbreviation abbr
```

```
public void appendToTextList(String value) throws NotesException
```

```
public void appendToTextList(java.util.Vector values) throws NotesException
```

The appendToTextList method appends either a single String or a Vector of String objects to the end of the item. The existing item should be a text type item, but can contain either a single value or multiple values. You must invoke the Document.save method to save any changes you make to the item.

For example:

```
import lotus.domino.*;

public class JavaAgent extends AgentBase {
    public void NotesMain() {
        try {
            Session session = getSession();
            AgentContext agentContext = session.getAgentContext();
            Database db = agentContext.getCurrentDatabase();
            View view3 = db.getView("View3");
```

```
        // Retrieve a document
        Document doc = view3.getFirstDocument();
        // Get an item
        Item item = doc.getFirstItem("Field1");
        System.out.println("Field1 Initial Values:" + item.getValues());
        // Append an extra item to the field
        item.appendToTextList("Another");
        System.out.println("Field1 New Values:" + item.getValues());
        // Even though we appended to the item object, saving the
        // document will also save our changes to the item.
        doc.save();
      } catch(Exception e) {
        e.printStackTrace();
      }
    }
}
```

```
public boolean containsValue(Object value) throws NotesException
```

The containsValue method checks to see whether the supplied value matches one of an item's values. The method does not perform a text search for a word. It is intended to search a list of values within the item to see if one of the values matches the one supplied. The value parameter can be a String, Number, or DateTime value. If the value supplied is a distinguished name, it will match a common formatted name if the current item contains a list of Domino usernames.

Consider the following example. You are looking for the word *phone*. If an item contains the content *My phone is broken*, the containsValue method will return false. However, if an item contains a list of the values "radio" : "phone" : "television", the containsValue method will return true because one of the list's values is an exact match.

```
public Item copyItemToDocument(Document doc) throws NotesException
```

```
public Item copyItemToDocument(Document doc, String newname) throws
NotesException
```

The copyItemToDocument method copies the current item to the specified document. If newname is omitted or is the empty string, the item will keep its current name. If newname is specified, the newly copied item will have the given name. If an item already exists in the document with the specified name, the current item will replace, not append, the previous value.

If the current item is a RichTextItem object, all embedded objects, links, and attachments will not be copied to the destination document.

```
public org.w3c.dom.Document parseXML(boolean validated) throws
NotesException, java.io.IOException, org.xml.sax.SAXException
```

The parseXML method parses the XML content of the current item and creates a Document Object Model (DOM) Document tree from the XML. The validated parameter should be true if you want the XML validated and false if a non-validating parser should be used.

Non-validating parsers will check to make sure that the XML has valid syntax, but will not check that the XML conforms to a specific document type definition (DTD). The validating parser will check both the syntax and DTD conformance.

If the input contains relative or partial URLs, the parseXML method will resolve the partial URL as a page within the database that is the source of the InputStream. For example, if the URL books.dtd appears, parseXML will look for a page with the name books.dtd.

→ For an example of the parseXML method, **see** Chapter 25, "Processing XML with Domino." The section titled "A Simple DOM Example" illustrates the use of the Item.parseXML method as well as the Document.generateXML method.

```
public void remove() throws NotesException
```

The remove method deletes the current item from the document. After calling remove, you must call the Document.save method to save your changes to the database.

```
public void transformXML(Object style, XSLTResultTarget result) throws
NotesException, java.io.IOException, org.xml.sax.SAXException
```

The transformXML method transforms the current item using the specified XSL style object. The output is written to the resulting XSLTResultTarget object.

→ For a detailed example, **see** "Integrating XSL with Domino," in Chapter 23, page **719**. In that chapter, I show you how to use XSL as well as how you can use XSL with Domino.

THE DateTime CLASS

Class Definition

```
public class DateTime extends Base
```

Properties

- getDateOnly
- getGMTTime
- getLocalTime/setLocalTime
- getParent
- getTimeOnly
- getTimeZone
- getZoneTime
- isDST
- setLocalDate

Methods

- adjustDay
- adjustHour

- adjustMinute

- adjustMonth

- adjustSecond

- adjustYear

- convertToZone

- setAnyDate

- setAnyTime

- setNow

- timeDifference

- timeDifferenceDouble

- toJavaDate

The DateTime class is used in a variety of contexts within the Domino Objects classes. It is used to represent a universal date and time. That is, it stores time in Greenwich Mean Time and stores a time zone and daylight savings time flag for conversion to local time. For ease of input and display, you can use a two-digit year. If the year is less than 50, it represents a date of the format 20xx, whereas if the year is 50 or greater, it represents a date of the format 19xx. You can also use four-digit years to unambiguously represent a date for input or output.

COMMON METHODS TO CREATE

Session.createDateTime, Item.getDateTimeValue, Item.getLastModified,
DateRange.getEndDateTime, DateRange.getStartDateTime, Database.getCreated,
Document.getCreated, Document.getLastAccessed, Document.getLastModified,
View.getCreated, View.getLastModified, Database.getLastFTIndexed,
Database.getLastModified, Agent.getLastRun, AgentContext.getLastRun,
Replication.getCutoffDate, Registration.getExpiration

PROPERTIES

public String getDateOnly() throws NotesException

The getDateOnly property routine will return a String representation of the date part of the current DateTime. The date returned is the local date, not GMT time. The formatting is controlled by the operating system settings. In Windows, these are found in the control panel.

public String getGMTTime() throws NotesException

The getGMTTime property routine will return a String representation of the current DateTime converted to Greenwich Mean Time (time zone 0). The local time zone is determined from the operating system setting.

```
public String getLocalTime() throws NotesException
```

```
public void setLocalTime(String dt) throws NotesException
```

```
public void setLocalTime(java.util.Date dt) throws NotesException
```

```
public void setLocalTime(int hour, int minute, int second, int hundredth)
throws NotesException
```

The setLocalTime property enables you to get or set the DateTime object time with local time values. The local time will be converted to GMT time before saving in the DateTime object.

```
public Session getParent() throws NotesException
```

The getParent property returns the parent Session object that contains the DateTime object.

```
public String getTimeOnly() throws NotesException
```

The getTimeOnly property returns a string representation of just the time portion of the DateTime object. The time returned is local time, not GMT time. The formatting is controlled by the operating system settings. In Windows, these are found in the control panel.

```
public int getTimeZone() throws NotesException
```

The getTimeZone property routine returns an integer that represents the time zone of the current DateTime object. The integer is the value that must be added to the local time to get Greenwich Mean Time. Thus, the West Coast of the United States has a value of 8 and the East Coast has a value of 5. Values for locations east of GMT are negative. The range of values is from −12 to +12.

Note that the conventions for settings within Windows have an opposite sign. The Windows values are defined as the value that must be added to GMT to get local time. For example, the East Coast has a value of −5 and the West Coast has a value of −8.

The integer value returned is the time zone of the computer on which the program runs. This might be important if the client and server are running in different time zones. If the program is a CORBA/IIOP program, the time zone returned is for the Domino server.

PART

IV

CH

20

```
public String getZoneTime() throws NotesException
```

The getZoneTime property is useful for converting a given time to another time zone. You can think of this property as returning the time in a particular zone. Initially, the getZoneTime value is the same as the getLocalTime value. If you call the convertToZone method, the getZoneTime value as well as the getTimeZone and isDST values will all change. The value of getLocalTime will not change.

For example:

```
import lotus.domino.*;

public class JavaAgent extends AgentBase {
    public void NotesMain() {
        try {
            Session session = getSession();
            AgentContext agentContext = session.getAgentContext();
            DateTime dt = session.createDateTime("1/23/2000 11:00AM");
            System.out.println("Date Only: " + dt.getDateOnly());
            System.out.println("Time Only: " + dt.getTimeOnly());
            System.out.println("LocalTime: " + dt.getLocalTime());
            System.out.println("Time Zone: " + dt.getTimeZone());
            System.out.println("Is DST: " + dt.isDST());
            System.out.println("ZoneTime: " + dt.getZoneTime());
            System.out.println("Converting time.");
            dt.convertToZone(5, false);  // East Coast time zone
            System.out.println("LocalTime: " + dt.getLocalTime());
            System.out.println("Time Zone: " + dt.getTimeZone());
            System.out.println("Is DST: " + dt.isDST());
            System.out.println("ZoneTime: " + dt.getZoneTime());

        } catch(Exception e) {
            e.printStackTrace();
        }
    }
}
```

In the following sample output, notice that the value retrieved with getLocalTime does not change after converting the time zone. This enables you to retrieve both the local value and the time value of another time zone. Here is the sample output when generated from the West Coast of the United States:

```
Date Only: 01/23/2000
Time Only: 11:00:00 AM
LocalTime: 01/23/2000 11:00:00 AM PST
Time Zone: 8
Is DST: false
ZoneTime: 01/23/2000 11:00:00 AM PST
Converting time.
LocalTime: 01/23/2000 11:00:00 AM PST
Time Zone: 5
Is DST: false
ZoneTime: 01/23/2000 02:00:00 PM EST
```

```
public boolean isDST() throws NotesException
```

The isDST property returns true if daylight savings time is currently in effect and the computer is set to reflect daylight savings time. The property is false if daylight savings time is not in effect or if the computer is not set to observe daylight savings time. The property will also return false if no date component or no time component is within the DateTime object.

```
public void setLocalDate(int year, int month, int day) throws NotesException
```

```
public void setLocalDate(int year, int month, int day, boolean
preserveLocalTime) throws NotesException
```

The setLocalDate property sets the current DateTime object to the specified year, month, and day. The preserveLocalTime parameter is used to control adjustments that cross a daylight savings time boundary. If this parameter is true, a one-day (24-hour) adjustment will yield the same local time on the new day and the GMT time will be incremented or decremented by an hour to adjust. If the preserveLocalTime parameter is false, a one-day adjustment will cause the local time to gain or lose an hour when crossing a daylight savings time boundary.

METHODS

```
public void adjustDay(int nDays) throws NotesException
```

```
public void adjustDay(int nDays, boolean preserveLocalTime) throws
NotesException
```

The adjustDay method changes the current DateTime object by adding the specified number of days. The number of days to be added can be either positive or negative. The month and year values can also be affected by adjusting the day value. To obtain the next month, use adjustMonth instead of adding 30 days.

The preserveLocalTime parameter is used to control adjustments that cross a daylight savings time boundary. If this parameter is true, a one-day (24-hour) adjustment will yield the same local time on the new day, and the GMT time will be incremented or decremented by an hour to adjust. If the preserveLocalTime parameter is false, a one-day adjustment will cause the local time to gain or lose an hour when crossing a daylight savings time boundary.

```
public void adjustHour(int nHours) throws NotesException
```

```
public void adjustHour(int nHours, boolean preserveLocalTime) throws
NotesException
```

The adjustHour method changes the current DateTime object by adding the specified number of hours. The number of hours to be added can be either positive or negative. The adjustHour method can also affect the date if the adjustment crosses a midnight boundary.

The preserveLocalTime parameter is used to control adjustments that cross a daylight savings time boundary. If this parameter is true, a one-day (24-hour) adjustment will yield the same local time on the new day, and the GMT time will be incremented or decremented by an hour to adjust. If the preserveLocalTime parameter is false, a one-day adjustment will cause the local time to gain or lose an hour when crossing a daylight savings time boundary.

```
public void adjustMinute(int nMinutes) throws NotesException
```

```
public void adjustMinute(int nMinutes, boolean preserveLocalTime) throws
NotesException
```

The adjustMinute method changes the current DateTime object by adding the specified number of minutes. The number of minutes to be added can be either positive or negative. The adjustMinute method can also affect the hour and date if the corresponding boundary is crossed.

The preserveLocalTime parameter is used to control adjustments that cross a daylight savings time boundary. If this parameter is true, a one-day (24-hour) adjustment will yield the same local time on the new day, and the GMT time will be incremented or decremented by an hour to adjust. If the preserveLocalTime parameter is false, a one-day adjustment will cause the local time to gain or lose an hour when crossing a daylight savings time boundary.

```
public void adjustMonth(int nMonths) throws NotesException
```

```
public void adjustMonth(int nMonths, boolean preserveLocalTime) throws
NotesException
```

The adjustMonth method changes the current DateTime object by adding the specified number of months. The number of months to be added can be either positive or negative. The adjustMonth method can affect the year value if a year boundary is crossed.

The preserveLocalTime parameter is used to control adjustments that cross a daylight savings time boundary. If this parameter is true, a one-day (24-hour) adjustment will yield the same local time on the new day, and the GMT time will be incremented or decremented by an hour to adjust. If the preserveLocalTime parameter is false, a one-day adjustment will cause the local time to gain or lose an hour when crossing a daylight savings time boundary.

```
public void adjustSecond(int nSeconds) throws NotesException
```

```
public void adjustSecond(int nSeconds, boolean preserveLocalTime) throws
NotesException
```

The adjustSecond method changes the current DateTime object by adding the specified number of seconds. The number of seconds to be added can be either positive or negative. The adjustSecond method can affect the minute, hour, or date if the corresponding boundary is crossed.

The preserveLocalTime parameter is used to control adjustments that cross a daylight savings time boundary. If this parameter is true, a one-day (24-hour) adjustment will yield the same local time on the new day, and the GMT time will be incremented or decremented by an hour to adjust. If the preserveLocalTime parameter is false, a one-day adjustment will cause the local time to gain or lose an hour when crossing a daylight savings time boundary.

```
public void adjustYear(int nYears) throws NotesException
```

```
public void adjustYear(int nYears, boolean preserveLocalTime) throws
NotesException
```

The adjustYear method changes the current DateTime object by adding the specified number of years. The number of years to be added can be either positive or negative.

The preserveLocalTime parameter is used to control adjustments which cross a daylight savings time boundary. If this parameter is true, a one-day (24-hour) adjustment will yield the same local time on the new day, and the GMT time will be incremented or decremented by an hour to adjust. If the preserveLocalTime parameter is false, a one-day adjustment will cause the local time to gain or lose an hour when crossing a daylight savings time boundary.

```
public void convertToZone(int zone, boolean isDST) throws NotesException
```

The convertToZone method is used to convert the current DateTime value to another time zone. It does not actually change the GMT date-time value that is represented, only the time zone as displayed by the getTimeZone, isDST, and getZoneTime properties.

Note that the use of convertToZone does not cause the value retrieved with getLocalTime, getDateOnly, or getTimeOnly to change. This enables you to retrieve both the local value and the time value of another time zone.

The zone parameter can be a value from −12to +12 and represents the value that must be added to the local time zone number to obtain GMT. For example, the West Coast of the United States is 8 and the East Coast is 5. The isDST indicates whether daylight savings time is in effect.

See the example under the getZoneTime property.

```
public void setAnyDate() throws NotesException
```

Use the setAnyDate method to set the date component of the DateTime to a wildcard value. A wildcard value will match any date. The time component is not changed.

```
public void setAnyTime() throws NotesException
```

Use the setAnyTime method to set the time component of the DateTime to a wildcard value. A wildcard value will match any time. The date component is not changed.

```
public void setNow() throws NotesException
```

The setNow method sets the DateTime to the current date and time. The setNow method resets the isDST and TimeZone values to match the operating system's values.

```
public int timeDifference(DateTime dt) throws NotesException
```

```
public double timeDifferenceDouble(DateTime dt) throws NotesException
```

The timeDifference and timeDifferenceDouble methods compute the difference between the current DateTime and the one supplied as a parameter. The value returned is in seconds and represents the current DateTime object minus the DateTime parameter. You can use the timeDifferenceDouble to compute the difference between DateTime values that are larger than the capacity of an integer.

An integer can store values from –2,147,483,648 to +2,147,483,647, which is a little more than +/–68 years or +/–24,855 days. Use a Double if your date values might be more than these amounts.

```
public java.util.Date toJavaDate() throws NotesException
```

The toJavaDate method converts the current DateTime object to Java format. Java dates are stored in a different format from Domino's DateTime format. Java Date objects are stored as a long value and represent the number of milliseconds since January 1, 1970. Negative values represent times prior to 1970. In Java, you can also use the Calendar and GregorianCalendar classes to manipulate dates and times.

THE DateRange CLASS

Class Definition

public class DateRange extends Base

Properties

- getEndDateTime/setEndDateTime
- getParent
- getStartDateTime/setStartDateTime
- getText/setText

The DateRange class represents a range of dates and times. That is, it contains a starting DateTime and an ending DateTime. The range represents the interval between the starting and ending times. You can also associate a comment or text string with a DateRange object.

COMMON METHODS TO CREATE

Session.createDateRange

PROPERTIES

```
public DateTime getEndDateTime() throws NotesException
```

```
public void setEndDateTime(DateTime end) throws NotesException
```

You can use the setEndDateTime property routine to change the ending time for a DateRange object. Use the getEndDateTime to query the current ending date/time value.

```
public Session getParent() throws NotesException
```

The getParent property will return the Session object that contains the current DateRange object.

```
public DateTime getStartDateTime() throws NotesException
```

```
public void setStartDateTime(DateTime start) throws NotesException
```

You can use the setStartDateTime property routine to change the starting time for a DateRange object. Use the getStartDateTime to query the current starting date/time value.

```
public String getText() throws NotesException
```

```
public void setText(String text) throws NotesException
```

You can use the setText property routine to associate a text string or comment with a DateRange object. Use the getText to query the current text string.

THE RichTextItem CLASS

Class Definition

```
public class RichTextItem extends Item
```

Property

- getEmbeddedObjects

Methods

- addNewLine
- addPageBreak
- addTab
- appendDocLink
- appendParagraphStyle

- appendRTItem

- appendStyle

- appendText

- embedObject

- getEmbeddedObject

- getFormattedText

- parseXML

- transformXML

The RichTextItem class extends the Item class, which means that it inherits and you can use all the properties and methods of the Item class. RichTextItem objects enable you to include formatting such as fonts, colors, and styles. In addition, rich-text items can contain embedded objects and links to databases, views, or documents.

You can create a new RichTextItem object with the Document.createRichTextItem method. To obtain an existing rich-text item, you can use the getFirstItem method of the Document object, but you must explicitly cast the result to a RichTextItem.

Here is an example that shows how to append text, a rich-text style, and some document links:

```java
import lotus.domino.*;

public class JavaAgent extends AgentBase {
    public void NotesMain() {
        try {
            Session session = getSession();
            AgentContext agentContext = session.getAgentContext();
            Database db = agentContext.getCurrentDatabase();
            Document doc = db.createDocument();
            // Make sure to have a Form item in the document
            doc.appendItemValue("Form", "RTTest");
            // Now create the rich text item
            RichTextItem rti = doc.createRichTextItem("TextField");
            // The first text is normal
            rti.appendText("Hello, this is first.");
            // Create and append a Bold RichTextStyle
            RichTextStyle rts = session.createRichTextStyle();
            rts.setBold(RichTextStyle.YES);
            rti.appendStyle(rts);
            // Now append the text. It will be bold.
            rti.appendText("This is BOLD!");
            // Get ready to add a document link. First get a view
            View view1 = db.getView("View1");
            // Now get the first document of the view
            Document doclink = view1.getFirstDocument();
            // Append a doclink
            rti.appendDocLink(doclink, "This is my doclink comment",
                "Hotspot text");
```

```
        // Get the second document of the view
        doclink = view1.getNextDocument(doclink);
        // Append another doclink
        rti.appendDocLink(doclink);
        // Save all the changes
        doc.save();

    } catch(Exception e) {
        e.printStackTrace();
    }
  }
}
```

COMMON METHODS TO CREATE

Document.createRichTextItem, (RichTextItem) Document.getFirstItem, EmbeddedObject.getParent

PROPERTIES

public java.util.Vector getEmbeddedObjects() throws NotesException

The getEmbeddedObjects property returns a Vector that contains an EmbeddedObject for each of the embedded objects, links, or file attachments contained within the rich-text item. If you need to access rich-text items that are in the document, but not within a specific rich-text item, you must use the getEmbeddedObjects property routine of the Document object.

The getEmbeddedObjects method does not work on OS/2, UNIX, or the Macintosh.

METHODS

public void addNewLine() throws NotesException

public void addNewLine(int count) throws NotesException

public void addNewLine(int count, boolean newparagraph) throws NotesException

The addNewLine method adds one or more new lines to the current rich-text item. The count parameter specifies the number of new lines to add. If the newparagraph parameter is true (the default), the new line will be a paragraph separator. If it is false, the new line will not create a new paragraph. If the method is called without any parameters, a new line will be added that is not a paragraph.

public void addPageBreak() throws NotesException

public void addPageBreak(RichTextParagraphStyle style) throws NotesException

The addPageBreak method adds a page break to the end of the current rich-text item. If you specify a style, the new page will begin with the specified RichTextParagraphStyle.

```
public void addTab() throws NotesException
```

```
public void addTab(int count) throws NotesException
```

You can use the addTab method to add one or more tabs to the end of the current rich-text item. You can specify count, which indicates the number of tabs to add. If omitted, one tab will be added.

```
public void appendDocLink(Document doc) throws NotesException
```

```
public void appendDocLink(Database db) throws NotesException
```

```
public void appendDocLink(View view) throws NotesException
```

```
public void appendDocLink(Document doc, String comment) throws NotesException
```

```
public void appendDocLink(Database db, String comment) throws NotesException
```

```
public void appendDocLink(View view, String comment) throws NotesException
```

```
public void appendDocLink(Document doc, String comment, String hotspottext)
throws NotesException
```

```
public void appendDocLink(Database db, String comment, String hotspottext)
throws NotesException
```

```
public void appendDocLink(View view, String comment, String hotspottext)
throws NotesException
```

The appendDocLink method appends a doclink to the end of the current rich-text item. You can link to a document, a database, or a view (or folder) by specifying the appropriate object. You can optionally add a comment to be associated with the doclink. Finally, hotspottext is boxed text that appears instead of an icon. Note that hotspottext is ignored on the Web.

```
public void appendParagraphStyle(RichTextParagraphStyle style) throws
NotesException
```

The appendParagraphStyle is used to append a RichTextParagraphStyle object at the end of the current rich-text item. Any text following the style will be rendered using the attributes found within the style. The RichTextParagraphStyle controls attributes such as the text alignment, margins, and pagination. To control items such as font, color, bold, and italic, use the RichTextStyle class instead.

```
public void appendRTItem(RichTextItem item) throws NotesException
```

The appendRTItem method is used to append a rich-text item to the end of the current rich-text item. The specified item parameter is appended at the end of the current rich-text item.

`public void appendStyle(RichTextStyle item) throws NotesException`

The appendStyle method is used to append a RichTextStyle object at the end of the current rich-text item. Any text following the style will be rendered using the attributes found within the style. The RichTextStyle object controls attributes such as font, color, bold, and italic. To control items such as the paragraph's text alignment, margins, and pagination, use the RichTextParagraphStyle class instead.

`public void appendText(String text) throws NotesException`

The appendText method is used to append text to the end of the current rich-text item. If you want the text to appear with a particular style, you should append a RichTextStyle object before appending the text string.

`public EmbeddedObject embedObject(int type, String class, String source,`
`String name) throws NotesException`

The embedObject method appends a file, object, or object link to the current rich-text item. The valid values for type are

- EmbeddedObject.EMBED_ATTACHMENT—(1454)
- EmbeddedObject.EMBED_OBJECT—(1453)
- EmbeddedObject.EMBED_OBJECTLINK—(1452)

The class parameter is used to create an empty object from a particular application. The class parameter is used for the application name. This parameter is used with the EMBED_OBJECT type. The class parameter should be the empty string otherwise.

If you want to embed a file, specify null for the class parameter, use the EMBED_OBJECT or EMBED_ATTACHMENT type, and specify the filename for the source parameter. With EMBED_OBJECTLINK, the source parameter is the filename of the file to which you want to link.

The name parameter can be optionally used to specify a name for later retrieval of the object. It can be null.

Files can be attached on any Notes/Domino platform, but objects and object links are supported only on platforms that support OLE.

`public EmbeddedObject getEmbededObject(String name) throws NotesException`

The getEmbeddedObject method is used to retrieve a file attachment, object, or object link that is contained within the current rich-text item. To obtain a file attachment, use the filename (not its full path). For an object or object link, use the name that was supplied in the embedObject method call or the name that appears in the property box in the user interface.

```
public String getFormattedText(boolean striptabs, int linelength, int maxlen)
throws NotesException
```

The getFormattedText method formats and returns as plain text the text within the current rich-text item. If the striptabs parameter is true, tabs are stripped out of the result. The linelength parameter specifies the maximum number of characters per line. To use the default, use a 0 linelength. The maxlen parameter is the total maximum number of characters to return.

Non-textual data such as embedded objects and graphics are not returned from this method.

```
public org.w3c.dom.Document parseXML(boolean validated) throws
NotesException, java.io.IOException, org.xml.sax.SAXException
```

The parseXML method parses the XML content of the current rich-text item and creates a Document Object Model (DOM) Document tree from the XML. The validated parameter should be true if you want the XML validated and false if a non-validating parser should be used.

Non-validating parsers will check to make sure that the XML has valid syntax, but will not check that the XML conforms to a specific document type definition (DTD). The validating parser will check both the syntax and DTD conformance.

If the input contains relative or partial URLs, the parseXML method will resolve the partial URL as a page within the database that is the source of the InputStream. For example, if the URL books.dtd appears, parseXML will look for a page with the name books.dtd.

→ For an example of the parseXML method, **see** Chapter 25, "Processing XML with Domino." The section titled "A Simple DOM Example" illustrates the use of the Item.parseXML method as well as the Document.generateXML method.

```
public void transformXML(Object style, XSLTResultTarget result) throws
NotesException, java.io.IOException, org.xml.sax.SAXException
```

The transformXML method transforms the current rich-text item using the specified XSL style object. The output is written to the resulting XSLTResultTarget object.

→ For a detailed example, **see** Chapter 23, "Understanding the Extensible Stylesheet Language." In the section "Integrating XSL with Domino," I show you how to use XSL as well as how you can use XSL with Domino.

THE RichTextStyle CLASS

Class Definition

```
public class RichTextStyle extends Base
```

Properties

- getBold/setBold
- getColor/setColor

- getEffects/setEffects
- getFont/setFont
- getFontSize/setFontSize
- getItalic/setItalic
- getParent
- getPassThruHTML/setPassThruHTML
- getStrikeThrough/setStrikeThrough
- getUnderline/setUnderLine

The RichTextStyle class is used to add text styling characteristics to a rich-text item. By using the RichTextStyle class, you can change the font; the font size; color; and attributes such as italic, bold, and other effects. Different sections of text can have different style attributes. That is, the entire rich-text item does not have to have the same style. Several changes of style within one rich-text item are possible.

To use a RichTextStyle object, you first create the RichTextStyle object, change the attributes contained within it, and then append it to a rich-text item. You use the RichTextItem's appendStyle method to append the style, and then any text that you subsequently append to the rich-text item will have the attributes of the RichTextStyle.

If you will be using several styles within one paragraph, and especially if you will be reusing styles, it is a good idea to create several RichTextStyle objects, initialize each with its own attributes, and then append them as required within the rich-text item.

The default value for each RichTextStyle property is STYLE_NO_CHANGE. This enables you to modify some properties without affecting others.

To control margins and spacing for a rich-text paragraph, use the RichTextParagraphStyle class.

COMMON METHODS TO CREATE

```
Session.createRichTextStyle
```

PROPERTIES

```
public int getBold() throws NotesException
```

```
public void setBold(int bold) throws NotesException
```

The getBold and setBold property routines are used to obtain and set the bold attribute of the RichTextStyle. The valid values are

- RichTextStyle.YES—(1) turn on bold
- RichTextStyle.NO—(0) turn off bold

PART

IV

CH

20

- RichTextStyle.STYLE_NO_CHANGE—(255) maintain previous state
- RichTextStyle.MAYBE—(255) maintain previous state

```
public int getColor() throws NotesException
```

```
public void setColor(int color) throws NotesException
```

The getColor property access routine returns a code that represents the color for the text displayed within the RichTextStyle. The setColor property routine sets the color. The valid values are

- RichTextStyle.COLOR_BLACK—(0)
- RichTextStyle.COLOR_WHITE—(1)
- RichTextStyle.COLOR_RED—(2)
- RichTextStyle.COLOR_GREEN—(3)
- RichTextStyle.COLOR_BLUE—(4)
- RichTextStyle.COLOR_CYAN—(7)
- RichTextStyle.COLOR_YELLOW—(6)
- RichTextStyle.COLOR_MAGENTA—(5)
- RichTextStyle.COLOR_DARK_RED—(8)
- RichTextStyle.COLOR_DARK_GREEN—(9)
- RichTextStyle.COLOR_DARK_BLUE—(10)
- RichTextStyle.COLOR_DARK_CYAN—(13)
- RichTextStyle.COLOR_DARK_YELLOW—(12)
- RichTextStyle.COLOR_DARK_MAGENTA—(11)
- RichTextStyle.COLOR_GRAY—(14)
- RichTextStyle.COLOR_LIGHT_GRAY—(15)
- RichTextStyle.STYLE_NO_CHANGE—(255) maintain previous state

The color code values cannot be combined. Only a single value is returned.

```
public int getEffects() throws NotesException
```

```
public void setEffects(int effects) throws NotesException
```

The getEffects property routine returns a code that represents special effects styling. You can use setEffects to set the special effects. Here are the valid codes:

- RichTextStyle.EFFECTS_NONE—(0)
- RichTextStyle.EFFECTS_SUPERSCRIPT—(1)

- RichTextStyle.EFFECTS_SUBSCRIPT—(2)
- RichTextStyle.EFFECTS_SHADOW—(3)
- RichTextStyle.EFFECTS_EMBOSS—(4)
- RichTextStyle.EFFECTS_EXTRUDE—(5)
- RichTextStyle.STYLE_NO_CHANGE—(255) maintain previous state

public int getFont() throws NotesException

public void setFont(int font) throws NotesException

The getFont and setFont property routines are used to obtain and set the font attribute of the RichTextStyle. The valid values are

- RichTextStyle.FONT_ROMAN—(0)
- RichTextStyle.FONT_HELV—(1)
- RichTextStyle.FONT_COURIER—(4)
- RichTextStyle.STYLE_NO_CHANGE—(255) maintain previous state

public int getFontSize() throws NotesException

public void setFontSize(int size) throws NotesException

The getFontSize and setFontSize property routines are used to obtain and set the font size attribute of the RichTextStyle, in points. The valid values are an integer from 1–250, which represents the point size. There are 72 points to an inch. A value of RichTextStyle.STYLE_NO_CHANGE (255) is used to signify that the font size should not be changed.

public int getItalic() throws NotesException

public void setItalic(int italic) throws NotesException

The getItalic and setItalic property routines are used to obtain and set the italic attribute of the RichTextStyle. The valid values are

- RichTextStyle.YES—(1) turn on italic
- RichTextStyle.NO—(0) turn off italic
- RichTextStyle.STYLE_NO_CHANGE—(255) maintain previous state
- RichTextStyle.MAYBE—(255) maintain previous state

The STYLE_NO_CHANGE and MAYBE constants represent the same value.

PART

IV

CH

20

`public Session getParent() throws NotesException`

The getParent property returns the Session object that contains the current RichTextStyle object.

`public int getPassThruHTML() throws NotesException`

`public void setPassThruHTML(int passthru) throws NotesException`

The getPassThruHTML and setPassThruHTML property routines are used to obtain and set the PassThruHTML attribute of the RichTextStyle. The valid values are

- RichTextStyle.YES—(1) turn on pass-thru HTML
- RichTextStyle.NO—(0) turn off pass-thru HTML
- RichTextStyle.STYLE_NO_CHANGE—(255) maintain previous state
- RichTextStyle.MAYBE—(255) maintain previous state

The STYLE_NO_CHANGE and MAYBE constants represent the same value.

`public int getStrikeThrough() throws NotesException`

`public void setStrikeThrough(int strikethrough) throws NotesException`

The getStrikeThrough and setStrikeThrough property routines are used to obtain and set the strikethrough attribute of the RichTextStyle. The valid values are

- RichTextStyle.YES—(1) turn on strikethrough
- RichTextStyle.NO—(0) turn off strikethrough
- RichTextStyle.STYLE_NO_CHANGE—(255) maintain previous state
- RichTextStyle.MAYBE—(255) maintain previous state

The STYLE_NO_CHANGE and MAYBE constants represent the same value.

`public int getUnderline() throws NotesException`

`public void setUnderline (int underline) throws NotesException`

The getUnderline and setUnderline property routines are used to obtain and set the underline attribute of the RichTextStyle. The valid values are

- RichTextStyle.YES—(1) turn on underline
- RichTextStyle.NO—(0) turn off underline
- RichTextStyle.STYLE_NO_CHANGE—(255) maintain previous state
- RichTextStyle.MAYBE—(255) maintain previous state

The STYLE_NO_CHANGE and MAYBE constants represent the same value.

THE RichTextTab CLASS

Class Definition

public class RichTextTab extends Base

Properties

- getPosition
- getType

Method

- clear

The RichTextTab class represents a tab in a rich-text paragraph style. The attributes of the tab are effective in the scope of the rich-text paragraph style. Rich-text tabs can be aligned left, right, center, or decimal and appear in the ruler if it is displayed in the IDE.

COMMON METHODS TO CREATE

RichTextParagraphStyle.getTabs

PROPERTIES

public int getPosition() throws NotesException

The getPosition property routine returns the position of a tab within the rich-text paragraph style. The returned value is in a unit called *twips*. One centimeter is 567 twips and one inch is 1440 twips.

You can use two constants to convert twips to useful units. These are RichTextParagraphStyle.RULER_ONE_CENTIMETER and RichTextParagraphStyle.RULER_ONE_INCH. Here is an example of how you convert the result to useful units:

```
RichTextParagraphStyle rtps = session.createRichTextParagraphStyle();
rtps.setTab(1440, RichTextParagraphStyle.TAB_LEFT);
Vector tabs = rtps.getTabs();
RichTextTab tab = (RichTextTab) tabs.elementAt(0);
double pos = tab.getPosition();
System.out.println("First tab at: " +
    (pos/RichTextParagraphStyle.RULER_ONE_CENTIMETER) + " cm. ");
System.out.println("First tab at: " +
    (pos/RichTextParagraphStyle.RULER_ONE_INCH) + " in. ");
```

Here is the resulting output:

```
First tab at: 2.5396825396825395 cm.
First tab at: 1.0 in.
```

`public int getType() throws NotesException`

The getType property routine returns the type of tab that the current RichTextTab object represents. Here are the valid values:

- `RichTextParagraphStyle.TAB_LEFT`—(0)
- `RichTextParagraphStyle.TAB_RIGHT`—(1)
- `RichTextParagraphStyle.TAB_DECIMAL`—(2)
- `RichTextParagraphStyle.TAB_CENTER`—(3)

METHODS

`public void clear() throws NotesException`

The clear method clears a single tab definition from the ruler. This method does not remove a tab from a rich-text field.

THE RichTextParagraphStyle CLASS

Class Definition

`public class RichTextParagraphStyle extends Base`

Properties

- `getAlignment/setAlignment`
- `getFirstLineLeftMargin/setFirstLineLeftMargin`
- `getInterLineSpacing/setInterLineSpacing`
- `getLeftMargin/setLeftMargin`
- `getPagination/setPagination`
- `getRightMargin/setRightMargin`
- `getSpacingAbove/setSpacingAbove`
- `getSpacingBelow/setSpacingBelow`
- `getTabs`

Methods

- `clearAllTabs`
- `setTab`
- `setTabs`

The RichTextParagraphStyle class is used to control paragraph attributes such as margins and spacing and to control tab definitions. Attributes such as font, color, and so forth are found in the RichTextStyle class.

To use a RichTextParagraphStyle object, you first create the RichTextParagraphStyle object, change the attributes contained within it, and then append it to a rich-text item. Use the RichTextItem's appendParagraphStyle method to append the paragraph style, and then any text that you subsequently append to the rich-text item will have the attributes of the RichTextParagraphStyle.

COMMON METHODS TO CREATE

```
Session.createRichTextParagraphStyle
```

PROPERTIES

```
public int getAlignment() throws NotesException
```

```
public void setAlignment(int align) throws NotesException
```

The getAlignment property returns a code that represents the horizontal alignment type for the text within the paragraph. Here are the valid codes:

- RichTextParagraphStyle.ALIGN_LEFT—(0)
- RichTextParagraphStyle.ALIGN_RIGHT—(1)
- RichTextParagraphStyle.ALIGN_FULL—(2)
- RichTextParagraphStyle.ALIGN_CENTER—(3)
- RichTextParagraphStyle.ALIGN_NOWRAP—(4)

```
public int getFirstLineLeftMargin() throws NotesException
```

```
public void setFirstLineLeftMargin(int margin) throws NotesException
```

You use the getFirstLineLeftMargin to obtain the left margin of the first line of the paragraph. The returned value is in a unit called *twips*. One centimeter is 567 twips and one inch is 1440 twips.

The difference between setFirstLineLeftMargin and setLeftMargin is that setLeftMargin controls the margin for all lines and gives a block effect, whereas setFirstLineLeftMargin controls only the first line. By controlling the first line, you can create an indented effect for the first line or a hanging indent where all lines after the first are indented.

The two constants that you can use to convert twips to useful units are RichTextParagraphStyle.RULER_ONE_CENTIMETER and RichTextParagraphStyle.RULER_ONE_INCH. To convert a returned value to centimeters, divide the returned value by RULER_ONE_CENTIMETER.

You specify the first line left margin with the setFirstLineLeftMargin property routine call. The units are also twips. You can indicate a 1.5-inch left margin with the following call:

```
rtps.setFirstLineLeftMargin((int)(RichTextParagraphStyle.RULER_ONE_INCH*1.5));
➥// 1.5 inch left margin
```

```
public int getInterLineSpacing() throws NotesException
```

```
public void setInterLineSpacing(int spacing) throws NotesException
```

The getInterLineSpacing property routine returns a code that represents the vertical spacing between lines within the paragraph. Interline spacing can change within a given paragraph. Here are the valid codes:

- RichTextParagraphStyle.SPACING_SINGLE—(0)
- RichTextParagraphStyle.SPACING_ONE_POINT_50—(1)
- RichTextParagraphStyle.SPACING_DOUBLE—(2)

Use the setInterLineSpacing property routine to change the spacing. Use the spacing codes. The code SPACING_ONE_POINT_50 means one and one half line spacing.

```
public int getLeftMargin() throws NotesException
```

```
public void setLeftMargin(int margin) throws NotesException
```

The getLeftMargin property routine returns the left margin of all lines except the first line of each paragraph. The returned value is in a unit called *twips*. One centimeter is 567 twips and one inch is 1440 twips.

The difference between setFirstLineLeftMargin and setLeftMargin is that setLeftMargin controls the margin for all lines and gives a block effect, whereas setFirstLineLeftMargin controls only the first line. By controlling the first line, you can create an indented effect for the first line or a hanging indent where all lines after the first are indented.

The two constants that you can use to convert twips to useful units are RichTextParagraphStyle.RULER_ONE_CENTIMETER and RichTextParagraphStyle.RULER_ONE_INCH. To convert a returned value to centimeters, divide the returned value by RULER_ONE_CENTIMETER.

You specify the left margin with the setLeftMargin property routine call. The units are also twips. You can indicate a 0.65-inch left margin with the following call:

```
rtps.setLeftMargin((int)(RichTextParagraphStyle.RULER_ONE_INCH * 0.65));
➥// 0.65 inch left margin
```

```
public int getPagination() throws NotesException
```

```
public void setPagination(int pagination) throws NotesException
```

The getPagination property routine returns a code that indicates how page breaks will affect paragraphs. Here are the valid values for the code:

- RichTextParagraphStyle.PAGINATE_DEFAULT—(0)
- RichTextParagraphStyle.PAGINATE_BEFORE—(1)

- RichTextParagraphStyle.PAGINATE_KEEP_WITH_NEXT—(2)
- RichTextParagraphStyle.PAGINATE_KEEP_TOGETHER—(4)

Use the setPagination property call to change the pagination mode.

```
public int getRightMargin() throws NotesException
```

```
public void setRightMargin(int margin) throws NotesException
```

The getRightMargin property routine returns the right margin of each line of a paragraph. The returned value is in a unit called twips. One centimeter is 567 twips and one inch is 1440 twips.

The two constants that you can use to convert twips to useful units are RichTextParagraphStyle.RULER_ONE_CENTIMETER and RichTextParagraphStyle.RULER_ONE_INCH. To convert a returned value to centimeters, divide the returned value by RULER_ONE_CENTIMETER.

You specify the right margin with the setRightMargin property routine call. The units are also twips. You can indicate a 0.85-inch left margin with the following call:

```
rtps.setRightMargin((int)(RichTextParagraphStyle.RULER_ONE_INCH * 0.85));
➥// 0.85 inch right margin
```

```
public int getSpacingAbove() throws NotesException
```

```
public void setSpacingAbove(int spacing) throws NotesException
```

The getSpacingAbove property routine returns a code that represents the vertical spacing above each paragraph. Here are the valid codes:

- RichTextParagraphStyle.SPACING_SINGLE—(0)
- RichTextParagraphStyle.SPACING_ONE_POINT_50—(1)
- RichTextParagraphStyle.SPACING_DOUBLE—(2)

Use the setSpacingAbove with the same codes to set the spacing before the paragraph. The code SPACING_ONE_POINT_50 means one and one half line spacing.

```
public int getSpacingBelow() throws NotesException
```

```
public void setSpacingBelow(int spacing) throws NotesException
```

The getSpacingBelow property routine returns a code that represents the vertical spacing below each paragraph. Here are the valid codes:

- RichTextParagraphStyle.SPACING_SINGLE—(0)
- RichTextParagraphStyle.SPACING_ONE_POINT_50—(1)
- RichTextParagraphStyle.SPACING_DOUBLE—(2)

Use the setSpacingBelow with the same codes to set the spacing following the paragraph. The code SPACING_ONE_POINT_50 means one and one half line spacing.

```
public java.util.Vector getTabs() throws NotesException
```

The getTabs property returns a Vector of RichTextTab objects. Each element represents a tab within the RichTextParagraphStyle. See the RichTextTab class description for more information on the returned class.

METHODS

```
public void clearAllTabs() throws NotesException
```

The clearAllTabs method clears all tabs in the RichTextParagraphStyle object. This method clears all tabs defined in the ruler, but does not clear tabs in a rich-text field.

```
public void setTab(int position, int type) throws NotesException
```

The setTab method sets a single tab within the RichTextParagraphStyle. You must specify the tab position in a unit called twips. One centimeter is 567 twips and one inch is 1440 twips.

The two constants that you can use to convert useful units to twips are RichTextParagraphStyle.RULER_ONE_CENTIMETER and RichTextParagraphStyle.RULER_ONE_INCH. To convert centimeters to twips, multiply the number of centimeters by RULER_ONE_CENTIMETER. For example, 2.0*RULER_ONE_CENTIMETER is the number of twips in two centimeters.

There are four values you can use for the type of tab:

- RichTextParagraphStyle.TAB_LEFT—(0)
- RichTextParagraphStyle.TAB_RIGHT—(1)
- RichTextParagraphStyle.TAB_DECIMAL—(2)
- RichTextParagraphStyle.TAB_CENTER—(3)

For example:

```
RichTextParagraphStyle rtps = session.createRichTextParagraphStyle();
rtps.setTab(1440, RichTextParagraphStyle.TAB_LEFT);
Vector tabs = rtps.getTabs();
RichTextTab tab = (RichTextTab) tabs.elementAt(0);
double pos = tab.getPosition();
System.out.println("First tab at: " +
    (pos/RichTextParagraphStyle.RULER_ONE_CENTIMETER) + " cm. ");
System.out.println("First tab at: " +
    (pos/RichTextParagraphStyle.RULER_ONE_INCH) + " in. ");
```

Here is the resulting output:

```
First tab at: 2.5396825396825395 cm.
First tab at: 1.0 in.
```

```
public void setTabs(int count, int startposition, int interval) throws
NotesException
```

```
public void setTabs(int count, int startposition, int interval, int type)
throws NotesException
```

The setTabs method is used to set tabs at even intervals within the RichTextParagraphStyle. The count parameter specifies the number of tabs to be set. The startposition parameter and the interval are both specified in twips. The type code is the type of tab to be set. All tabs must have the same type.

One centimeter is 567 twips and one inch is 1440 twips.

The two constants that you can use to convert useful units to twips are RichTextParagraphStyle.RULER_ONE_CENTIMETER and RichTextParagraphStyle.RULER_ONE_INCH. To convert centimeters to twips, multiply the number of centimeters by RULER_ONE_CENTIMETER. For example, 2.0*RULER_ONE_CENTIMETER is the number of twips in two centimeters.

Here are the valid values for the type parameter:

- RichTextParagraphStyle.TAB_LEFT—(0)
- RichTextParagraphStyle.TAB_RIGHT—(1)
- RichTextParagraphStyle.TAB_DECIMAL—(2)
- RichTextParagraphStyle.TAB_CENTER—(3)

THE MIMEEntity CLASS

Class Definition

```
public class MIMEEntity extends Base
```

Properties

- getContentAsText
- getContentSubType
- getContentType
- getHeaders

PART

IV

CH

20

Methods

- getFirstChildEntity
- getNextSibling
- getParentEntity
- parseXML
- transformXML

The MIMEEntity class represents a Multipurpose Internet Mail Extensions (MIME) element. MIME entities can be nested, and for example, a multipart MIME message can have multiple parts and relations between the parts.

A typical mail message might have a text representation and an HTML representation of the same message. Each different representation would have a different MIME content type and subtype. In this example, the two parts would have MIME types text/plain and text/html.

There is a new Session property called isConvertMIME. When this is true (the default), MIME messages are automatically converted to rich text. If you set this property to false, you can obtain and process the individual MIME entities.

For example:

```java
import lotus.domino.*;

public class JavaAgent extends AgentBase {
    public void NotesMain() {
        try {
            Session session = getSession();
            AgentContext agentContext = session.getAgentContext();
            // Do the MIME thing, not rich text conversion
            session.setConvertMime(false);
            Database db = agentContext.getCurrentDatabase();
            View view3 = db.getView("View3");
            Document doc = view3.getFirstDocument();
            // Use Item, not RichTextItem for body
            Item item = doc.getFirstItem("Body");
            // Now get the primary mime entity
            MIMEEntity me = item.getMIMEEntity();
            // If there is no mime entity, throw up and get out
            if (null == me) throw new Exception("no me");
            // We have a MIMEEntity
            System.out.println("Mime Content Type: '" + me.getContentType()+ "'");
            System.out.println("Mime Content SubType: " + me.getContentSubType());
            System.out.println("Mime Headers: " + me.getHeaders());
            System.out.println("Mime Content as text: " + me.getContentAsText());
            MIMEEntity mec;
            // If this is multipart, then there will be children
            if (me.getContentType().equals("multipart") ) {
                // Get the first MIME child
                mec = me.getFirstChildEntity();
```

```
            while (null != mec) {
                System.out.println("****NEXT Mime child");
                System.out.println("Mime Content Type: " +
                        mec.getContentType());
                System.out.println("Mime Content SubType: " +
                        mec.getContentSubType());
                System.out.println("Mime Headers: " +
                        mec.getHeaders());
                System.out.println("Mime Content as text: " +
                        mec.getContentAsText());
                // Get the next MIME entity sibling
                mec = mec.getNextSibling();
            }
        }
    } catch(Exception e) {
        e.printStackTrace();
    }
    }
}
```

Here is the sample output:

```
Mime Content Type: 'multipart'
Mime Content SubType: alternative
Mime Headers: Content-Type: multipart/alternative;
➥boundary="=_alternative 0064D87385256870_="

Mime Content as text: This is a multipart message in MIME format.
****NEXT Mime child
Mime Content Type: text
Mime Content SubType: plain
Mime Headers: Content-Type: text/plain; charset="us-ascii"

Mime Content as text: text of message
****NEXT Mime child
Mime Content Type: text
Mime Content SubType: html
Mime Headers: Content-Transfer-Encoding: quoted-printable
Content-Type: text/html; charset="iso-8859-1"

Mime Content as text:
<br><font size=3D2 face=3D"sans-serif">text of message</font>
<br>
```

COMMON METHODS TO CREATE

`Item.getMIMEEntity`, `MIMEEntity.getFirstChildEntity`, `MIMEEntity.getNextSibling`, `MIMEEntity.getParentEntity`

PROPERTIES

`public String getContentAsText() throws NotesException`

The `getContentAsText` property returns the content of the `MIMEEntity` as a text string.

PART

IV

CH

20

> public String getContentSubType() throws NotesException

The getContentSubType returns the subtype as a string. If the ContentType header is text/plain, the getContentSubType returns plain.

> public String getContentType() throws NotesException

The getContentType returns the subtype as a string. If the ContentType header is multipart/alternative, the getContentType returns multipart.

> public String getHeaders() throws NotesException

The getHeaders property routine returns the RFC822 header fields as a single string. The header string contains new line characters to separate individual headers.

METHODS

> public MIMEEntity getFirstChildEntity() throws NotesException

The getFirstChildEntity method returns the first child MIMEEntity of the current MIMEEntity. If there is no child, the method will return null.

> public MIMEEntity getNextSibling() throws NotesException

The getNextSibling method returns the next sibling MIMEEntity of the current MIMEEntity. If there are no more siblings, the method will return null.

> public MIMEEntity getParentEntity() throws NotesException

The getParentEntity returns the parent MIMEEntity of the current MIMEEntity. If the current MIMEEntity has no parent, the method will return null.

> public org.w3c.dom.Document parseXML(boolean validated) throws
> NotesException, java.io.IOException, org.xml.sax.SAXException

The parseXML method parses the XML content of the current MIMEEntity and creates a Document Object Model (DOM) Document tree from the XML. The validated parameter should be true if you would like the XML validated and false if a non-validating parser should be used.

Non-validating parsers will check to make sure that the XML has valid syntax, but will not check that the XML conforms to a specific document type definition (DTD). The validating parser will check both the syntax and DTD conformance.

If the input contains relative or partial URLs, the parseXML method will resolve the partial URL as a page within the database that is the source of the InputStream. For example, if the URL books.dtd appears, parseXML will look for a page with the name books.dtd.

→ For an example of the parseXML method, **see** Chapter 25, "Processing XML with Domino." The section titled "A Simple DOM Example" illustrates the use of the Item.parseXML method as well as the Document.generateXML method.

```
public void transformXML(Object style, XSLTResultTarget result) throws
NotesException, java.io.IOException, org.xml.sax.SAXException
```

The `transformXML` method transforms the current `MIMEEntity` using the specified XSL style object. The output is written to the resulting `XSLTResultTarget` object.

→ For a detailed example, **see** Chapter 23, "Understanding the Extensible Stylesheet Language" in the section "Integrating XSL with Domino." In that chapter, I show you how to use XSL as well as how you can use XSL with Domino.

THE EmbeddedObject CLASS

Class Definition

```
public class EmbeddedObject extends Base
```

Properties

- getClassName
- getFileSize
- getName
- getObject
- getParent
- getSource
- getType
- getVerbs

Methods

- activate
- doVerb
- extractFile
- parseXML
- remove
- transformXML

The `EmbeddedObject` class is used to represent embedded or linked objects. It is also used for file attachments. You can activate the object, execute one of the object's verbs, or extract a file attachment.

COMMON METHODS TO CREATE

`Document.getAttachment`, `Document.getEmbeddedObjects`, `RichTextItem.embedObject`, `RichTextItem.getEmbeddedObject`, `RichTextItem.getEmbeddedObjects`

PART
IV
CH
20

PROPERTIES

`public String getClassName() throws NotesException`

The getClassName property returns the application name of the application that created the object.

`public int getFileSize() throws NotesException`

The getFileSize property returns the size of a file attachment, in bytes. This property returns 0 for embedded objects and links.

`public String getName() throws NotesException`

The getName property returns the name used to reference an object, link, or file attachment. If the object or object link does not have a name then this property returns null. If the object was created using the RichTextItem.embedObject method, this property returns the value that was specified in the name parameter.

`public int getObject() throws NotesException`

The getObject property returns the OLE handle, also sometimes known as the IUnknown or IDispatch handle. For object links, this property might or might not return a valid OLE handle, depending on the application used to create the object link. With the OLE handle, you can invoke methods or properties of the object if it supports OLE automation.

`public RichTextItem getParent() throws NotesException`

The getParent property returns the RichTextItem that contains the current EmbeddedObject, if applicable.

`public String getSource() throws NotesException`

The getSource property returns the internal name for the source document of an object or object link. For a file attachment, the source is the filename of the original file.

`public String getType() throws NotesException`

The getType property returns a code that represents the type of embedded object. Here are the valid codes:

- EmbeddedObject.EMBED_ATTACHMENT—(1454)
- EmbeddedObject.EMBED_OBJECT—(1453)
- EmbeddedObject.EMBED_OBJECTLINK—(1452)

```
public java.util.Vector getVerbs() throws NotesException
```

The getVerbs property returns a Vector of String elements. Each element represents one of the verbs or commands that the object supports. The EmbeddedObject must be an OLE/2 embedded object. Any other type of EmbeddedObject will throw an exception.

METHODS

```
public int activate(boolean show) throws NotesException
```

The activate method will cause OLE to load an embedded object or object link. If the show parameter is true, the OLE server application will display its user interface. The return value is an OLE handle to the object. It will return null if the embedded object or object link does not support OLE automation.

Domino agents running on a server must specify false for the show parameter. This method will throw an exception if invoked on a file attachment.

```
public void doVerb(String verb) throws NotesException
```

The doVerb method will invoke the specified verb in the EmbeddedObject.

```
public void extractFile(String path) throws NotesException
```

The extractFile method will extract the file attachment and write it to the disk at the specified path.

```
public org.w3c.dom.Document parseXML(boolean validated) throws
NotesException, java.io.IOException, org.xml.sax.SAXException
```

The parseXML method parses the XML content of the current EmbeddedObject and creates a Document Object Model (DOM) Document tree from the XML. The validated parameter should be true if you want the XML validated and false if a non-validating parser should be used.

Non-validating parsers will check to make sure that the XML has valid syntax, but will not check that the XML conforms to a specific document type definition (DTD). The validating parser will check both the syntax and DTD conformance.

If the input contains relative or partial URLs, the parseXML method will resolve the partial URL as a page within the database that is the source of the InputStream. For example, if the URL books.dtd appears, parseXML will look for a page with the name books.dtd.

→ For an example of the parseXML method, **see** Chapter 25, "Processing XML with Domino." The section titled "A Simple DOM Example" illustrates the use of the Item.parseXML method as well as the Document.generateXML method.

PART

IV

CH

20

```
public void remove() throws NotesException
```

The remove method removes the current EmbeddedObject. You must call the Document.save method to save your changes permanently in the database.

```
public void transformXML(Object style, XSLTResultTarget result) throws
NotesException, java.io.IOException, org.xml.sax.SAXException
```

The transformXML method transforms the current EmbeddedObject using the specified XSL style object. The output is written to the result XSLTResultTarget object.

→ For a detailed example, **see** "Integrating XSL with Domino," in Chapter 23, "Understanding the Extensible Stylesheet Language." In that chapter, I show you how to use XSL as well as how you can use XSL with Domino.

Chapter Review

1. What is the difference between the RichTextStyle class and the RichTextParagraphStyle class?

2. What is the special relationship between the RichTextItem class and the Item class? Can you encrypt a RichTextItem object? If yes, how? If no, why not?

3. What does the Summary flag indicate on an item? What is the impact of calling the setAuthors property with a value of true for an item?

4. The DateTime class has a method that you can use to convert a DateTime object to a Java Date (java.util.Date). Write a Java class that extends the DateTime class and adds a method that will take a Java Date as a parameter and convert it to a DateTime.

5. Write a Java agent that will extract data from an existing document. The document has three existing items: Author, Title, and ISBN. Your agent should read the existing Author, Title, and ISBN fields and format them into a new Body item. The Author should be bold, the Title should be bold and italic, and the ISBN should be in blue. Use three different font sizes for the three different items.

6. Write a Java application using CORBA and IIOP that is given a server name and database name. The application should go through the database and inspect each document in the database and find out which form it uses. The program should print a summary that displays all the form names and a count of how many times each form is used.

7. Write a Java agent that will go through all the forms of a specified database and create a master list of all the names of all the fields that appear on all the forms. Create an answer database. The answer database should have one document for each field found in the source database. The document should contain the field name and a count of how many forms contain that field name. The answer database should have a view containing field name and count. The view should be sorted by field name (you might need this view for lookup).

8. Write a Java agent that will examine each document of a database. The agent should find all documents that contain file attachments (but not other kinds of embedded objects). For each document that contains a file attachment, if the size is larger than 32KB, the agent should detach the file and save it in a special directory. It should then remove the file attachment from the document (and save the document).

9. Write a Java agent that is invoked with selected documents from a view. The agent should create one new document with a rich-text field in it. The rich-text field should contain one row of text plus a doclink for each row that was selected in the view. The text should be the contents from the first column of the view for each document.

CHAPTER 21

THE Registration, Newsletter, AND Log CLASSES

In this chapter

THE Registration CLASS

Class Definition

public class Registration extends Base

Properties

- getAltOrgUnit/setAltOrgUnit
- getAltOrgUnitLang/setAltOrgUnitLang
- getCertifierIDFile/setCertifierIDFile
- getCreateMailDb/setCreateMailDb
- getExpiration/setExpiration
- getIDType/setIDType
- getMinPasswordLength/setMinPasswordLength
- getOrgUnit/setOrgUnit
- getRegistrationLog/setRegistrationLog
- getRegistrationServer/setRegistrationServer
- getStoreIDInAddressBook/setStoreIDInAddressBook
- getUpdateAddressBook/setUpdateAddressBook
- isNorthAmerican/setNorthAmerican

Methods

- addCertifierToAddressBook
- addServerToAddressBook
- addUserProfile
- addUserToAddressBook
- crossCertify
- deleteIDOnServer
- getIDFromServer
- getUserInfo
- recertify
- registerNewCertifier
- registerNewServer
- registerNewUser
- switchToID

The Registration class is used to programmatically control user and server registration. You can obtain information about existing users as well as register new users. This class is not one you will use in your typical applications, but can be very useful in large organizations. You can, for example, use the Registration class in a linkage to HR or other applications to automate the registration of new users. Also, tool or utility companies can find this class useful.

You use the Registration class by following these general steps:

1. Create a new Registration object.
2. Set properties for the Registration object.
3. Invoke a method that performs the desired function.

For example, to register a new user you would do the following:

1. Create a Registration object.
2. Set values for at least the following properties: Certifier ID file, Org Unit(s), CreateMailDb, IDType, MinPasswordLength, Registration Log, Registration Server, UpdateAddressBook, Expiration, and North American.
3. Call registerNewUser for each user that has the same properties.

Other methods will require setting different properties, but the same general procedure applies to the various methods for the Registration class.

COMMON METHODS TO CREATE

Session.createRegistration

PROPERTIES

public java.util.Vector getAltOrgUnit() throws NotesException

public void setAltOrgUnit(java.util.Vector altorgunit) throws NotesException
Alternative names allow an extra name, usually in a language other than English, to be associated with a User ID. The getAltOrgUnit property routine returns a Vector of Strings that contain the alternative names for the organizational unit to use when creating User IDs. The setAltOrgUnit property routine can be used to set these names.

This property is new with Release 5.0.2 of Domino.

public java.util.Vector getAltOrgUnitLang() throws NotesException

public void setAltOrgUnitLang(java.util.Vector language) throws NotesException
Alternative names allow an extra name, usually in a language other than English, to be associated with a User ID. The getAltOrgUnitLang property routine returns the languages

associated with the alternative organizational unit names. Use the setAltOrgUnitLang property routine to set the languages.

This property is new with Release 5.0.2 of Domino.

```
public String getCertifierIDFile() throws NotesException

public void setCertifierIDFile(String filepath) throws NotesException
```

The getCertifierIDFile property routine returns the file path for the certifier ID that is used to create IDs. You can change the certifier ID by using the setCertifierIDFile property routine. You must specify the complete file path.

```
public boolean getCreateMailDb() throws NotesException

public void setCreateMailDb(boolean create) throws NotesException
```

The getCreateMailDb property routine indicates whether a mail database should be created when an ID file is created with the registerNewUser method. You can change the setting by calling the setCreateMailDb property routine with a value of true. The default is false.

```
public DateTime getExpiration() throws NotesException

public void setExpiration(DateTime date) throws NotesException
```

The getExpiration property routine returns the expiration date that is used when creating a new ID file. You can change the expiration date by calling the setExpiration routine.

```
public int getIDType() throws NotesException

public void setIDType(int type) throws NotesException
```

The getIDType property routine returns a code that indicates the type of ID file to create when calling registerNewUser, registerNewServer, or registerNewCertifier. You can change the ID type by calling the setIDType property routine with one of the valid codes. Here are the valid codes:

- Registration.ID_FLAT—(171)
- Registration.ID_HIERARCHICAL—(172)
- Registration.ID_CERTIFIER—(173)

```
public int getMinPasswordLength() throws NotesException

public void setMinPasswordLength(int len) throws NotesException
```

The minimum length of a password is stored in the ID file when it is certified. The user can later change the password, but it cannot be less than the specified length. Use getMinPasswordLength to query the current length setting and the setMinPasswordLength

routine to change the length. The length will apply to ID files registered with the
`registerNewUser`, `registerNewServer`, and `registerNewCertifier` methods.

`public String getOrgUnit() throws NotesException`

`public void setOrgUnit(String orgunit) throws NotesException`

The `getOrgUnit` and `setOrgUnit` property routines enable you to query and set the organizational unit that will be used when creating new IDs. If you want to specify a single organization unit, you can include the organization unit name within the string. However, if you want to include two or more levels of organization unit, you must use the fully distinguished syntax. For example, if a name to be registered is `John Doe/OrgA/OrgB/Acme`, you must specify the `setOrgUnit` string as `/OU2=OrgA/OU1=OrgB`. You must include the leading slash before the `OU2`.

`public String getRegistrationLog() throws NotesException`

`public void setRegistrationLog(String log) throws NotesException`

The `getRegistrationLog` and `setRegistrationLog` property routines are used to query and set the name of the Domino database that will be used to log the creation of new IDs. A typical name for this database might be `certlog.nsf`. There is no default logging database.

`public String getRegistrationServer() throws NotesException`

`public void setRegistrationServer(String server) throws NotesException`

The `getRegistrationServer` and `setRegistrationServer` property routines are used to obtain and set the name of the server that should be used to register new users and servers. The registration server name is used when creating a mail database and when the ID file is to be stored in the server's Domino Directory.

`public boolean getStoreIDInAddressBook() throws NotesException`

`public void setStoreIDInAddressBook(boolean flag) throws NotesException`

The `getStoreIDInAddressBook` property indicates whether a newly created ID file should be stored in the server's Domino Directory. If `true`, the ID file will be stored in the Domino Directory, and if `false`, it will not. Use the `setStoreIDInAddressBook` routine to change this property. The default is `false`.

`public boolean getUpdateAddressBook() throws NotesException`

`public void setUpdateAddressBook(boolean flag) throws NotesException`

The `setUpdateAddressBook` property routine controls whether a call to the `registerNewUser`, `registerNewServer`, or `registerNewCertifier` method will result in a new entry in the Domino Directory. If `true`, registering a new user will create the ID file and also create a new user, server, or certifier entry in the Domino Directory. If `false`, the ID file will be created, but an entry in the Domino Directory will not be created. You can use the `addCertifierToAddressBook`, `addServerToAddressBook`, or `addUserToAddressBook` method to add a user that was not added automatically at the time of registration.

If you set `setUpdateAddressBook` to `true`, you should not also use the `addxxxToAddressBook` methods because you will get two entries in the Domino Directory.

```
public boolean isNorthAmerican() throws NotesException
```

```
public void setNorthAmerican(boolean naflag) throws NotesException
```

The `isNorthAmerican` property routine returns `true` if the `registerNewUser`, `registerNewServer`, and `registerNewCertifier` methods will create a new North American ID file. The `setNorthAmerican` property routine enables you to change the type of ID file. If `true`, the ID will be a North American ID, and if `false`, it will be an international ID.

METHODS

```
public boolean addCertifierToAddressBook(String idfile) throws NotesException
```

```
public boolean addCertifierToAddressBook(String idfile, String password,
String location, String comment) throws NotesException
```

The `addCertifierToAddressBook` method is used to add a certifier ID file to the Domino Directory. The `idfile` parameter should be the full path to the ID file. The `password` parameter is the password for the ID file. You can also specify the `location` and `comment` fields of the Domino Directory record for the certifier.

The method will return `true` if the addition was successful and `false` if not.

```
public boolean addServerToAddressBook(String idfile, String server, String
domain) throws NotesException
```

```
public boolean addServerToAddressBook(String idfile, String server, String
domain, String password, String network, String adminname, String title,
String location, String comment) throws NotesException
```

The `addServerToAddressBook` method is used to create a new server record in the Domino Directory. The `idfile` should specify the full path to the server ID file. The `server` parameter is the server's name and the `domain` parameter is the domain of the server. The `password` parameter represents the password of the server's ID file. The `network` parameter is the Notes Named Network to which the server belongs. The `adminname` represents the administrator's name, and the `title` is the server's title. The `location` and `comment` fields are added to the corresponding fields of the Domino Directory.

The method will return `true` if the addition was successful and `false` if not.

```
public void addUserProfile(String username, String profile) throws
NotesException
```

The `addUserProfile` method will add the name of a set-up profile to the specified user's person record in the Domino Directory on the server. You must first call `setRegistrationServer` to specify the server to be used.

```
public boolean addUserToAddressBook(String idfile, String fullname, String
lastname) throws NotesException
```

```
public boolean addUserToAddressBook(String idfile, String fullname, String
lastname, String password, String firstname, String middleinit, String
mailserver, String mailfilepath, String fwdaddress, String location,
String comment) throws NotesException
```

The `addUserToAddressBook` method creates a person document in the Domino Directory that corresponds to the specified user. The `idfile` parameter must specify the full path name. The `fullname` represents the user's full name. The `lastname` parameter represents the user's last name. The `password` parameter is the user's password. The `firstname` and `middleinit` parameters contain the user's first name and middle initial. The `mailserver` parameter is the name of the Domino server that contains the user's mail database. The `mailfilepath` is the path to the mail database. The `fwdaddress` parameter contains the user's forwarding address. The `location` and `comment` fields are added to the corresponding fields of the Domino Directory.

The method will return `true` if the addition was successful and `false` if not.

```
public boolean crossCertify(String idfile) throws NotesException
```

```
public boolean crossCertify(String idfile, String certpassword, String
comment) throws NotesException
```

The `crossCertify` method is used to cross-certify a specific ID file. The `idfile` parameter specifies the full path to the ID file to be cross-certified. The `certpassword` parameter is the password for the certifier ID file, and the `comment` field represents a comment to be placed in the Domino Directory.

Although this method is a back-end class, it must be run within the Notes client. The password for the User ID file to be cross-certified will be requested in the process.

The method will return `true` if the cross-certification was successful and `false` if not.

For example:

```
import lotus.domino.*;

public class JavaAgent extends AgentBase {
    public void NotesMain() {
        try {
            Session session = getSession();
```

```
            AgentContext agentContext = session.getAgentContext();
            Registration reg = session.createRegistration();
            // First specify the certifier ID
            reg.setCertifierIDFile("c:\\notes50\\data\\IDs\\Cert.id");
            // and the registration server
            reg.setRegistrationServer("AdmServer/AcmeCorp");
            // Now cross-certify John Doe. Note John's password is required.
            // A user dialog box requesting John's password will appear.
            reg.crossCertify("c:\\notes50\\data\\IDs\\JohnDoe.id","certpw",
            ➥ "John is a good guy");

        } catch(Exception e) {
            e.printStackTrace();
        }
    }
}
```

public void deleteIDOnServer(String username, boolean isserverid) throws
NotesException

The deleteIDOnServer method is used to delete a User ID file that has been attached to the user document. This method does not remove the person document. You must specify the fully qualified username, including the organization. It can be abbreviated. For example, you can use Susan Smith/Acme, but Susan Smith will not work. The isserverid should be true for a server ID file and false for a user ID file.

public void getIDFromServer(String username, String filepath, boolean
isserverid) throws NotesException

The getIDFromServer method detaches a copy of the User ID file that has been attached to the specified username's person document in the Domino Directory. The ID file is written to the specified filepath. The isserverid should be true for a server ID file and false for a user ID file.

An exception will be thrown if the username is not found in the Domino Directory or if the person document does not have an ID file attached to it.

public void getUserInfo(String username, Stringbuffer mailserver,
StringBuffer mailfile, StringBuffer maildomain, StringBuffer mailsystem,
Vector profile) throws NotesException

The getUserInfo method returns information from the person document for the specified user. The mailserver parameter returns the name of the user's mail server. The mailfile parameter returns the mail file path information from the Domino Directory. The maildomain returns the user's mail domain. The mailsystem returns a string representation of the mail system type. Finally, the profile parameter returns a Vector of Strings, which represent the set-up profiles for this user.

| Note | As of Release 5.0.2B, a bug exists in this routine. The `mailsystem` values are returned in the `maildomain` parameter and the `mailsystem` parameter always returns an empty string. These anomalies could be fixed in any future maintenance release, so the main message here is to check the return values carefully. |

For example:

```
import lotus.domino.*;

public class JavaAgent extends AgentBase {
    public void NotesMain() {
        try {
            Session session = getSession();
            AgentContext agentContext = session.getAgentContext();
            Registration reg = session.createRegistration();
            reg.setRegistrationServer("AdmServer/Acme");
            StringBuffer mailserver = new StringBuffer(30);
            StringBuffer mailfile = new StringBuffer(30);
            StringBuffer maildomain = new StringBuffer(30);
            StringBuffer mailsystem = new StringBuffer(30);
            java.util.Vector vprof  = new java.util.Vector();
            reg.getUserInfo("Randy Tamura", mailserver, mailfile, maildomain,
            ➡ mailsystem, vprof);
            System.out.println("mailserver:" + mailserver);
            System.out.println("mailfile:" + mailfile);
            System.out.println("maildomain:" + maildomain);
            System.out.println("mailsystem:" + mailsystem);
            System.out.println("Vector profile:" + vprof);
        } catch(NotesException e) {
            System.out.println(e.id + ". " + e.text);
            e.printStackTrace();
        } catch(Exception e) {
            e.printStackTrace();
        }
    }
}
```

```
public boolean recertify(String idfile) throws NotesException
```

```
public boolean recertify(String idfile, String certpassword, String comment)
throws NotesException
```

The recertify method recertifies the specified ID file. The idfile parameter should specify the complete path to the ID file to be recertified. The certpassword parameter is the certifier password. A comment string can be specified and will be placed in the Domino Directory.

```
public boolean registerNewCertifier(String org, String idfile, String
userpassword) throws NotesException
```

```
public boolean registerNewCertifier(String org, String idfile, String
certpassword, String country) throws NotesException
```

The registerNewCertifier method creates and registers a new certifier ID file. The org parameter is used to specify the organization to which the new certifier belongs. The idfile is the full path to the location where the new certifier ID file will be created. The certpassword parameter is the password to be used in the certifier ID to be created.

You should set the setExpiration property, the setCertifierIDfile property, the setUpdateAddressBook, and optionally the setOrgUnit property before calling the registerNewCertifier method.

This method returns true if successful and false if not.

For example:

```
import lotus.domino.*;

public class JavaAgent extends AgentBase {
    public void NotesMain() {
        try {
            Session session = getSession();
            AgentContext agentContext = session.getAgentContext();
            Registration reg = session.createRegistration();
            // Set the ID that will certify the certifier ID
            reg.setCertifierIDFile("c:\\notes50\\data\\Cert.id");
            reg.setRegistrationServer("AdmServer/Acme");
            DateTime dt = session.createDateTime("1/1/2021");
            reg.setExpiration(dt);
            reg.setStoreIDInAddressBook(true);
            reg.setUpdateAddressBook(true);
            // Two additional levels of hierarchy
            reg.setOrgUnit("/OU2=OrgA/OU1=OrgB");
            // Dump out the current settings
            System.out.println("IDType: " + reg.getIDType());
            System.out.println("Create Mail Db: " + reg.getCreateMailDb());
            System.out.println("Expiration: " + reg.getExpiration());
            System.out.println("NA: " + reg.isNorthAmerican());
            System.out.println("Min PW: " + reg.getMinPasswordLength());
            System.out.println("OrgUnit: " + reg.getOrgUnit());
            System.out.println("Reg Log: " + reg.getRegistrationLog());
            System.out.println("Store ID in DD: " +reg.getStoreIDInAddressBook());
            System.out.println("Update AB: " + reg.getUpdateAddressBook());
            reg.registerNewCertifier("Acme","c:\\temp\\newcert.id", "secret", "");
        } catch(NotesException e) {
            System.out.println(e.id + ". " + e.text);
            e.printStackTrace();
        } catch(Exception e) {
            e.printStackTrace();
        }
    }
}
```

```
public boolean registerNewServer(String server, String idfile, String domain,
String password) throws NotesException
```

```
public boolean registerNewServer(String server, String idfile, String domain,
String serverpassword, String certpassword, String location, String comment,
String network, String adminname, String title) throws NotesException
```

The registerNewServer method is used to create a new server ID file and optionally register it in the Domino Directory. The server parameter is the server's name. The idfile should specify the full path to the server ID file, and the domain parameter is the domain of the server. The serverpassword parameter represents the password of the server's ID file, and the certpassword is the certifier password. The location and comment fields are added to the corresponding fields of the Domino Directory.

The network parameter is the Notes Named Network to which the server belongs. The adminname represents the administrator's name, and the title is the server's title.

You should set the setExpiration property, the setCertifierIDfile property, the setUpdateAddressBook, and optionally the setOrgUnit property before calling the registerNewServer method.

The method will return true if the method was successful and false if not.

```
public boolean registerNewUser(String lastname, String idfile, String server)
throws NotesException
```

```
public boolean registerNewUser(String lastname, String idfile, String server,
String firstname, String middleinit, String certpassword, String location,
String comment, String mailfilepath, String fwdaddress, String userpassword)
throws NotesException
```

```
public boolean registerNewUser(String lastname, String idfile, String server,
String firstname, String middleinit, String certpassword, String location,
String comment, String mailfilepath, String fwdaddress, String userpassword,
String altname, String altnamelang) throws NotesException
```

The registerNewUser method creates a new user ID file and optionally creates a person document in the Domino Directory that corresponds to the specified user. The lastname parameter is the user's last name. The idfile parameter must specify the full path name. The server parameter is the name of the Domino server that contains the Domino Directory. The firstname and middleinit parameters contain the user's first name and middle initial. The certpassword parameter is the certifier's password. The location and comment fields are added to the corresponding fields of the Domino Directory. The mailfilepath is the path to the mail database. The fwdaddress parameter contains the user's forwarding address. The userpassword parameter is the user's password.

The altname and altnamelang parameters are used to hold the alternative username and alternative username language. Alternative names allow an extra name, usually in a language other than English, to be associated with a User ID. The registerNewUser with alternative name support is available in release 5.0.2 of Domino and later.

You should set the setExpiration property, the setCertifierIDfile property, the setUpdateAddressBook, and optionally the setOrgUnit property before calling the registerNewServer method.

The method will return true if the addition was successful and false if not.

```
public String switchToID(String idfile, String userpassword) throws
NotesException
```

The switchToID method is used to switch to a different user ID file. The idfile parameter should contain the full path to the new ID file. The userpassword field contains the password of the new ID file.

The return String value is the username that corresponds to the new ID file that is in effect.

THE Newsletter CLASS

Class Definition

public class Newsletter extends Base

Properties

- getParent
- getSubjectItemName/setSubjectItemName
- isDoScore/setDoScore
- isDoSubject/setDoSubject

Methods

- formatDocument
- formatMsgWithDoclinks

The Newsletter class represents a collection of documents and can be used to create a single summary document that has links to the documents that are in the collection. After you create the summary document, it is common to send it as email or to use it like a table of contents within a database. In addition, the Newsletter class can be used to render a single document from the collection for use with email or for other purposes.

COMMON METHODS TO CREATE

Session.createNewsletter

PROPERTIES

`public Session getParent() throws NotesException`

The `getParent` property returns the `Session` object that contains the current `Newsletter` object.

`public String getSubjectItemName() throws NotesException`

`public void setSubjectItemName(String name) throws NotesException`

You use the `setSubjectItemName` property in conjunction with the `setDoSubject` property. If `setDoSubject` is `true`, a subject string will be formatted for each document by `formatMsgWithDoclinks`. The `formatMsgWithDoclinks` method will look at the `setSubjectItemName` property to find the name of the item that should be used for the subject string for each document. You must call `setSubjectItemName` before invoking `formatMsgWithDoclinks`.

You can query the current subject item name with `getSubjectItemName`.

`public boolean isDoScore() throws NotesException`

`public void setDoScore(boolean doit) throws NotesException`

The `isDoScore` and `setDoScore` property routines enable you to query and change whether a newsletter includes relevance scores. This property applies only to newsletter documents created with the `formatMsgWithDoclinks` method. For this property to take effect, you must change its value before calling `formatMsgWithDoclinks`. The document collection used to create the newsletter must be sorted. If it is not sorted, this property will have no effect. Sorted collections are the result of a call to the `FTSearch` method or agents that use search criteria. Unsorted collections result from references to `allDocuments` or `unprocessedDocuments` of various classes.

The property returns `true` if the newsletter should contain relevance scores and `false` if not.

`public boolean isDoSubject() throws NotesException`

`public void setDoSubject(boolean doit) throws NotesException`

The `isDoSubject` and `setDoSubject` property routines enable you to query and change whether a newsletter includes a subject string. This property applies only to newsletter documents created with the `formatMsgWithDoclinks` method. For this property to take effect, you must change its value before calling `formatMsgWithDoclinks`. The document collection used to create the newsletter must be sorted. If it is not sorted, this property will have no effect. You can use the `setSubjectItemName` property routine to specify the field that contains the subject in each document in the collection.

The property returns `true` if the newsletter should contain a subject string and `false` if not.

METHODS

```
public Document formatDocument(Database db, int docindex) throws
NotesException
```

The `formatDocument` method formats a single document of a newsletter collection. The `db` parameter specifies the database in which to create the resulting document. If you specify `null` for the database, the user's mail database is used. The `docindex` is used to specify the particular document within the collection that you want to render. Use 1 for the first document, 2 for the second document, and so forth.

The newly created document is not automatically saved or sent as email. You must call `Document.save` to save it in the database and `Document.send` to send it as email.

```
public Document formatMsgWithDoclinks(Database db) throws NotesException
```

The `formatMsgWithDoclinks` method is used to create a single document that contains a list of doclinks, one for each document in the newsletter collection. The `db` parameter is used as the database in which to create the document; however, the newly created document is not automatically saved unless you call the `Document.save` method.

The creation and formatting of the document will be controlled by the `isDoScore` and `isDoSubject` properties. If `isDoScore` is `true` (and the collection is sorted), the resulting document will contain a relevance score. If the `isDoSubject` property is `true` and the `getSubjectItemName` property contains a value, a subject (title) will be appended for each document.

For example:

```
import lotus.domino.*;

public class JavaAgent extends AgentBase {
    public void NotesMain() {
        try {
            Session session = getSession();
            AgentContext agentContext = session.getAgentContext();
            Database db = agentContext.getCurrentDatabase();
            DocumentCollection dc = agentContext.getUnprocessedDocuments();
            // Create the newsletter collection
            Newsletter nl = session.createNewsletter(dc);
            // Include the subject titles
            nl.setDoSubject(true);
            // Collect titles from each doc from the Subject field
            nl.setSubjectItemName("Subject");
            // Now create the Newsletter document
            Document doc = nl.formatMsgWithDoclinks(db);
            // Make sure it has a form for viewing
            doc.replaceItemValue("Form", "main");
```

```
        // Save it away in the database
        doc.save();

    } catch(Exception e) {
        e.printStackTrace();
    }
  }
}
```

THE Log CLASS

Class Definition

```
public class Log extends Base
```

Properties

- getNumActions
- getNumErrors
- getParent
- getProgramName/setProgramName
- isLogActions/setLogActions
- isLogErrors/setLogErrors
- isOverwriteFile/setOverwriteFile

Methods

- close
- logAction
- logError
- logEvent
- openAgentLog
- openFileLog
- openMailLog
- openNotesLog

The Log class can be used to log actions, events, or messages during program execution. This can be very valuable if you are trying to debug an intermittent problem. You can log information to a Domino database, log to a mail memo, log to a file, or log to an agent log.

A log can be very useful for scheduled agents because you can go back and find out information about the agent, for example, that was run during off-hours. You can inspect the log to make sure it ran properly.

PART
IV

CH

21

If you log to a mail memo, the mail will be sent when the log is closed. When you log to a Domino database, you must first create the database using the alog4.ntf template. You can manually create this database or you can create it in Java with the Database.createFromTemplate method. It is probably easier just to create it manually unless you will be creating many different logging databases and you want to automate the process. If you create the log manually, you must enable the Show Advanced Templates option in the New Database dialog box. Select the Agent Log template, which is alog4.ntf. Each log entry will contain the A$LOGTIME, A$LOGTYPE, A$PROGNAME, A$USER, and Form fields.

Note that the Session.createLog method creates a Log object, but it does not create a logging database.

COMMON METHODS TO CREATE

Session.createLog

PROPERTIES

`public int getNumActions() throws NotesException`

The getNumActions returns the number of actions logged since the creation of the Log object. The count initially starts at 0. If you close the log and reopen it, the count will reset to 0. It does not keep a persistent count of all actions logged to a database since the database was created.

`public int getNumErrors() throws NotesException`

The getNumErrors returns the number of errors logged since the creation of the Log object. The count initially starts at 0. If you close the log and reopen it, the count will reset to 0. It does not keep a persistent count of all errors logged to a database since the database was created.

For example:

```
import lotus.domino.*;

public class JavaAgent extends AgentBase {
    public void NotesMain() {
        try {
            Session session = getSession();
            AgentContext agentContext = session.getAgentContext();
            Log log = session.createLog("Test Log");
            log.openNotesLog("","AgentLog.nsf");
            log.logAction("Action number " + log.getNumActions()); // 0
            log.logAction("Action number " + log.getNumActions()); // 1
            log.logAction("Action number " + log.getNumActions()); // 2
            log.logError(5, "Error number " + log.getNumErrors()); // 0
            log.logError(6, "Error number " + log.getNumErrors()); // 1
            log.logError(7, "Error number " + log.getNumErrors()); // 2
            log.close();
```

```
      } catch(Exception e) {
         e.printStackTrace();
      }
   }
}
```

public Session getParent() throws NotesException

The getParent property returns the Session object that contains the current Log object.

public String getProgramName() throws NotesException

public void setProgramName(String name) throws NotesException

You can use the getProgramName property to return the name of the program that was specified in the createLog method. Use the setProgramName to change the name. The name is used to group messages in the agent log database. All messages from the same program are grouped together.

public boolean isLogActions() throws NotesException

public void setLogActions(boolean logit) throws NotesException

You can selectively enable or disable logging of actions with the setLogActions property. If true, actions will be logged with the logAction method. If false, a call to logAction will not actually log anything. The purpose of this call is to enable you to include logging calls throughout your program, but selectively turn off parts of the logging so that the log does not contain too many records to be useful.

public boolean isLogErrors() throws NotesException

public void setLogErrors(boolean logit) throws NotesException

You can selectively enable or disable logging of errors with the setLogErrors property. If true, errors will be logged with the logError method. If false, a call to logError will not actually log anything. The purpose of this call is to enable you to include logging calls throughout your program, but selectively turn off parts of the logging so that the log does not contain too many records to be useful.

public boolean isOverwriteFile() throws NotesException

public void setOverwriteFile(boolean overwrite) throws NotesException

If the isOverwriteFile property returns true, it indicates that for file logging the log should overwrite an existing log. If it returns false, file logging should append to an existing file. This property has no effect on database or mail logging. Use the setOverwriteFile property before calling the openFileLog to control the overwrite setting.

METHODS

`public void close() throws NotesException`

The close method closes the current log. If you are using a mail log, the method will mail the message to the recipients.

`public void logAction(String actionmsg) throws NotesException`

The logAction method is used to write a single log entry. The log can be either in a file, a Domino database, or an email memo. The actionmsg parameter is the text string to be logged.

If the action is logged to a Domino database, a document is created and an item with the name A$ACTION is created. This item contains the specified actionmsg.

For a mail memo, the message is appended to the Body item and if logging is to a file, a new line is appended.

`public void logError(int code, String errormsg) throws NotesException`

The logError method is used to write a single error log entry. The log can be either in a file, a Domino database, or an email memo. The errormsg parameter is the text string to be logged.

If the error is logged to a Domino database, a document is created and an item with the name A$ERRCODE is created to hold the error code. An additional item called A$ERRMSG is created in the same document to hold the specified errormsg.

For a mail memo, the message is appended to the Body item, and if logging is to a file, a new line is appended.

For example:

```
import lotus.domino.*;

public class JavaAgent extends AgentBase {
    public void NotesMain() {
        try {
            Session session = getSession();
            AgentContext agentContext = session.getAgentContext();
            Log log = session.createLog("Agent Error Log");
            log.openNotesLog("","AgentLog.nsf");
            try {
                log.logAction("Agent Started");

                // Place your logging code here

                } catch(NotesException e) {
                    log.logError(e.id, e.text); // Log the Notes error
                    System.out.println(e.id + ". " + e.text); // console output
                    e.printStackTrace();
                } catch(Exception e) {
```

```
                    e.printStackTrace();
                }
        log.logAction("Agent Finished");
        log.close();
        } catch(Exception e) {
            e.printStackTrace();
        }
    }
}
```

`public void logEvent(String msgtext, String queuename, int event, int severity) throws NotesException`

The `logEvent` method is used to send an event to a named queue. The `msgtext` parameter specifies the message to be sent. The `queuename` parameter is the name of the queue. If the `queuename` is an empty string, Domino will pick a queue. The `event` parameter is a code specifying the type of event, and the `severity` is a code for the severity of the event.

Use `logEvent` to log items to an operating system log or to get the attention of network monitors such as `openView` or `NetView`.

This method can only be used on a server and will not affect any other open database, file, or mail logs.

Here are the event codes:

- `Log.EV_ALARM`—(8)
- `Log.EV_COMM`—(1)
- `Log.EV_MAIL`—(3)
- `Log.EV_MISC`—(6)
- `Log.EV_REPLICA`—(4)
- `Log.EV_RESOURCE`—(5)
- `Log.EV_SECURITY`—(2)
- `Log.EV_SERVER`—(7)
- `Log.EV_UNKNOWN`—(0)
- `Log.EV_UPDATE`—(9)

Here are the severity codes:

- `Log.SEV_FAILURE`—(2)
- `Log.SEV_FATAL`—(1)
- `Log.SEV_NORMAL`—(5)
- `Log.SEV_WARNING1`—(3)
- `Log.SEV_WARNING2`—(4)
- `Log.SEV_UNKNOWN`—(0)

```
public void openAgentLog() throws NotesException
```

The openAgentLog method opens the agent log for the current agent. If the calling program is not an agent or is called from a CORBA/IIOP program, the method will fail.

The agent log is used to keep track of information about the last run for a particular agent. The agent log information is updated each time the agent is run, and each agent has its own separate agent log. You can examine the log in the Domino Designer interface. With the agent selected from the list of agents, select Agent, Log from the menus.

Note that writing to the agent log is different from writing to a Domino database from an agent. Use the openNotesLog method to open a Domino database for logging. You can see the agent log from the Domino Designer client by clicking on Agents in the design pane, and then choosing Agent, Log from the menus.

```
public void openFileLog(String filepath) throws NotesException
```

The openFileLog method opens the specified file for logging. If this method is called from the Notes client, the file will be opened on the user's local disk. If it is called from a server, for example in a scheduled agent, the agent owner (the last person to modify and save the agent) must be enabled to run unrestricted agents. Opening and using a file log is a restricted activity that restricted agents are not able to perform.

To run unrestricted agents, the user must be listed in the Run Unrestricted LotusScript/Java Agents field of the Agent Restrictions section of the Security tab of the server document.

Note

> Lotus documentation contains conflicting information about the openFileLog method. In some cases it indicates that the method cannot be invoked on a server and will return an error. In other places it indicates that the openFileLog is a restricted action and can be performed only by unrestricted agents. The actual checking might vary in different releases, so be sure to test your application to ensure compatibility.

To overwrite the file log, you should call the setOverwriteFile property routine with a value of true before opening the file log. Otherwise, new information will be appended to the existing file.

For example:

```
import lotus.domino.*;

public class JavaAgent extends AgentBase {
    public void NotesMain() {
        try {
            Session session = getSession();
            AgentContext agentContext = session.getAgentContext();
            Log log = session.createLog("Test Log");
            System.out.println("Restricted File log agent started");
            // If this agent is running on a server and the owner is not
            // authorized to run unrestricted agents, the following line
            // throws an error.
```

```
            log.openFileLog("c:\\temp\\test.txt"); // restricted operation
            log.logAction("I am authorized to run unrestricted agents!");
            log.close();
        } catch(NotesException e) {
            System.out.println(e.id + ". " + e.text);
            e.printStackTrace();
        } catch(Exception e) {
            e.printStackTrace();
        }
    }
}
```

public void openMailLog(java.util.Vector recipients, String subject) throws
NotesException

The openMailLog method is used to create a new mail memo that will be used for logging.
All logging statements will be placed in the email memo and it will be sent when the
Log.close method is called.

The recipients parameter is a Vector of String objects, each object representing the name
of a user. The subject parameter is the subject of the email.

This method is supported only for Domino agents.

public void openNotesLog(String server, String database) throws
NotesException

The openNotesLog method opens the specified database for logging on the specified server.
The database can be created from the StdR4AgentLog template, which has the name
alog4.ntf. The title of this database is Agent Log. You must enable the Show Advanced
Templates option in the New Database dialog box to see this template. Use of the template
is not required, but it is an easy way to create a log database and provides a form and view
for viewing the log entries.

If you specify an empty string for the server, the local machine is used for the server.

Each time you invoke either the logAction or logError a new document is created in the
database. Several items are automatically created in the document. Here are the items:

- Form—"Log Entry"
- A$PROGNAME—The program name
- A$LOGTIME—The date and time of log entry
- A$USER—The user at the time log entry is created
- A$LOGTYPE—"Action" or "Error"
- A$ACTION—The action message text (actions only)
- A$ERRCODE—The error code (errors only)
- A$ERRMSG—The error message text (errors only)

PART

IV

CH

21

THE Name CLASS

Class Definition

public class Name extends Base

Properties

- getAbbreviated
- getAddr821
- getAddr822Comment1
- getAddr822Comment2
- getAddr822Comment3
- getAddr822LocalPart
- getAddr822Phrase
- getADMD
- getCanonical
- getCommon
- getCountry
- getGeneration
- getGiven
- getInitials
- getKeyword
- getLanguage
- getOrganization
- getOrgUnit1
- getOrgUnit2
- getOrgUnit3
- getOrgUnit4
- getParent
- getPRMD
- getSurname
- isHierarchical

The Name class represents the name of a Notes user or Domino server. You can use the Name class to extract various components of a name. Although you can obtain the name in both abbreviated format and canonical format, it will not parse the name for some properties. For example, some naming standards enable you to specify a given name and surname in addition to the complete username. If the given name is supplied in the input (using G=), you can retrieve it using the `getGiven` property. However, if the given name is not supplied in the input as a separate component, Domino will not automatically parse it out from the complete name. The `getSurname` property works similarly and will not be automatically parsed out from the complete name. See the example under the `getCanonical` property routine.

COMMON METHODS TO CREATE

`Session.createName, Session.getUserNameList, Session.getUserNameObject, ACLEntry.getNameObject`

PROPERTIES

`public String getAbbreviated() throws NotesException`

The `getAbbreviated` property returns the current hierarchical name in abbreviated format. It returns `null` if the abbreviated form is not available.

For example:

```
import lotus.domino.*;

public class JavaAgent extends AgentBase {
   public void NotesMain() {
      try {
         Session session = getSession();
         AgentContext agentContext = session.getAgentContext();
         Name name = session.getUserNameObject();
         System.out.println("Canonical name: " + name.getCanonical());
         System.out.println("Abbreviated name: " + name.getAbbreviated());
         System.out.println("Common name: " + name.getCommon());
         System.out.println("Organization name: " + name.getOrganization());
         System.out.println("Given name: " + name.getGiven());
         System.out.println("Surname name: " + name.getSurname());
         System.out.println("Keyword name: " + name.getKeyword());

      } catch(Exception e) {
         e.printStackTrace();
      }
   }
}
```

Here is some sample output that is produced from the agent:

```
Canonical name: CN=Randy Tamura/O=GWCorp
Abbreviated name: Randy Tamura/GWCorp
Common name: Randy Tamura
Organization name: GWCorp
Given name:
Surname name:
Keyword name: GWCorp
```

Notice that the given name and surname are not specified in the name object, and so are not available in the output.

PART

IV

CH

21

```
public String getAddr821() throws NotesException
```

The getAddr821 property routine returns a string in the format specified by RFC 821 Address Format syntax. Simply put, this format is the one most of us are familiar with for Internet addresses. An example is RandyTamura@gwcorp.com. This format has a name followed by an @ sign followed by the Internet domain.

If the source input to the Name object did not contain an @ sign, this routine would return an empty string. If the string is input in RFC 822 format, the portion of the address corresponding to the name and domain will be parsed and returned.

```
public String getAddr822Comment1() throws NotesException

public String getAddr822Comment2() throws NotesException

public String getAddr822Comment3() throws NotesException

public String getAddr822LocalPart() throws NotesException

public String getAddr822Phrase() throws NotesException
```

The getAddr822Comment1, getAddr822Comment2, and getAddr822Comment3 properties will return the first three comments in an RFC 822 address format. Although there can be more than three comments, only the first three are available. A comment in RFC 822 consists of a string enclosed within parentheses that appear between the < and > in the address component. You can insert comments anywhere whitespace would be allowed. The returned string will not contain the enclosing parentheses. Here is the general format for an RFC 822 address:

```
"Phrase" <LocalPart @domain.com >
```

The getAddr822LocalPart and getAddr822Phrase will extract the local part and phrase from the address. Note that comments do not appear within the phrase part of the address.

For example:

```
import lotus.domino.*;

public class JavaAgent extends AgentBase {
    public void NotesMain() {
        try {
            Session session = getSession();
            AgentContext agentContext = session.getAgentContext();
            String sIName = "\"Randy Tamura (in phrase)\"
        ➥<(prior to name) RandyTamura(after name) @ (after at)gwcorp.com>";
            System.out.println("Source name string: " + sIName);
            Name iname = session.createName(sIName);
            System.out.println("Addr821: " + iname.getAddr821());
            System.out.println("Addr822 LocalPart: "+iname.getAddr822LocalPart());
            System.out.println("Addr822 Phrase: " + iname.getAddr822Phrase());
            System.out.println("Addr822 Comment1: " + iname.getAddr822Comment1());
```

```
              System.out.println("Addr822 Comment2: " + iname.getAddr822Comment2());
              System.out.println("Addr822 Comment3: " + iname.getAddr822Comment3());

        } catch(Exception e) {
             e.printStackTrace();
        }
    }
}
```

Here is the output for this example:

```
Source name string: "Randy Tamura (in phrase)"
➡<(prior to name) RandyTamura(after name) @ (after at)gwcorp.com>
Addr821: (prior to name) RandyTamura(after name) @ (after at)gwcorp.com
Addr822 LocalPart: (prior to name) RandyTamura(after name)
Addr822 Phrase: "Randy Tamura (in phrase)"
Addr822 Comment1: prior to name
Addr822 Comment2: after name
Addr822 Comment3: after at
```

public String getADMD() throws NotesException

The getADMD property routine will return the administration management domain name
(ADMD). The input must contain an ADMD component (A=). If no ADMD component
exists, the property will return the empty string (not null). See the example under the
getCanonical property.

public String getCanonical() throws NotesException

The getCanonical property routine will return a hierarchical name in canonical form.
Canonical form includes the component identifiers followed by an equal sign followed by
the value. Each component is separated from the next by a forward slash. If no canonical
value exists, the property will return the empty string.

For example:

```
import lotus.domino.*;

public class JavaAgent extends AgentBase {
    public void NotesMain() {
        try {
            Session session = getSession();
            AgentContext agentContext = session.getAgentContext();
            String sName = "CN=Randy Tamura/S=Specified/P=Arbitrary/OU1=X
            ➡/OU3=Y/OU2=Z/O=GWCorp";
            Name name = session.createName(sName);
            System.out.println("Input: " + sName);
            System.out.println("Canonical name: " + name.getCanonical());
            System.out.println("Abbreviated name: " + name.getAbbreviated());
            System.out.println("Common (CN=) name: " + name.getCommon());
            System.out.println("Country (C=) name: " + name.getCountry());
            if (null == name.getCountry()) System.out.println("Country Null");
            if (name.getCountry().equals(""))
                System.out.println("Country empty string");
```

PART

IV

CH

21

```
            System.out.println("Organization (O=) name: "+name.getOrganization());
            System.out.println("OrgUnit1 (OU1=) name: " + name.getOrgUnit1());
            System.out.println("OrgUnit2 (OU2=) name: " + name.getOrgUnit2());
            System.out.println("OrgUnit3 (OU3=) name: " + name.getOrgUnit3());
            System.out.println("OrgUnit4 (OU4=) name: " + name.getOrgUnit4());
            System.out.println("Given (G=) name: " + name.getGiven());
            System.out.println("Initials (I=) name: " + name.getInitials());
            System.out.println("Surname(S=) name: " + name.getSurname());
            System.out.println("Generation(Q=) name: " + name.getGeneration());
            System.out.println("ADMD (A=) name: " + name.getADMD());
            if (null == name.getADMD()) System.out.println("ADMD Null");
            if (name.getADMD().equals(""))
                System.out.println("ADMD empty string");
            System.out.println("PRMD (P=) name: " + name.getPRMD());
            System.out.println("Language name: " + name.getLanguage());
            System.out.println("Keyword name: " + name.getKeyword());
            System.out.println("Addr821: " + name.getAddr821());

        } catch(Exception e) {
            e.printStackTrace();
        }
    }
}
```

Note that in the input I have specified the organizational units out of order. In the output, the organizational unit numbers are omitted and implied. Here is the output from this program:

```
Input: CN=Randy Tamura/S=Specified/P=Arbitrary/OU1=X/OU3=Y/OU2=Z/O=GWCorp
Canonical name: S=Specified/CN=Randy Tamura/OU=Y/OU=Z/OU=X/O=GWCorp/P=Arbitrary
Abbreviated name: CN=Randy Tamura/S=Specified/P=Arbitrary/OU1=X
➥/OU3=Y/OU2=Z/O=GWCorp
Common (CN=) name: Randy Tamura
Country (C=) name:
Country empty string
Organization (O=) name: GWCorp
OrgUnit1 (OU1=) name: X
OrgUnit2 (OU2=) name: Z
OrgUnit3 (OU3=) name: Y
OrgUnit4 (OU4=) name:
Given (G=) name:
Initials (I=) name:
Surname(S=) name: Specified
Generation(Q=) name:
ADMD (A=) name:
ADMD empty string
PRMD (P=) name: Arbitrary
Language name:
Keyword name: GWCorp\X\Z\Y
Addr821:
```

```
public String getCommon() throws NotesException
```

The getCommon property routine returns the common name component (CN=) of the hierarchical name. If the name is a flat name from a previous release of Notes, getCommon will return the entire name. If no common name component is found, this property will return an empty string. See the example under the getCanonical property.

public String getCountry() throws NotesException

The getCountry property routine returns the country name component (C=) of the hierarchical name. If no country name component is found, this property will return an empty string. See the example under the getCanonical property.

public String getGeneration() throws NotesException

The getGeneration property routine returns the generation name (Q=) component of the hierarchical name (for example, Jr.). If no generation name component is found, this property will return an empty string. See the example under the getCanonical property.

public String getGiven() throws NotesException

The getGiven property routine returns the given name (G=) component of the hierarchical name. If no given name component is found, this property will return an empty string. Note that this property will not return a part of the common name; it will only return a value if the G= component is specified. Notes names define the common name (CN) rather than the Given, Initials, or Surname components. See the example under the getCanonical property.

public String getInitials() throws NotesException

The getInitials property routine returns the initials component (I=) of the hierarchical name. If no initials component is found, this property will return an empty string. Note that this property will not return a part of the common name, it will return a value only if the I= component is specified. Notes names define the common name (CN) rather than the Given, Initials, or Surname components. See the example under the getCanonical property.

public String getKeyword() throws NotesException

The getKeyword returns the country, organization, and organizational unit components of the name, separated by backslashes. The format is

Country\Organization\OrgUnit1\OrgUnit2\OrgUnit3\OrgUnit4

Any missing components are omitted, including the separator slash. This property is useful for extracting a string representation that can be used for organizing, sorting, or categorizing a group of names. The returned string is in hierarchical order and can therefore be used as a convenient sort key value.

public String getLanguage() throws NotesException

The getLanguage property returns the language tag associated with a name or the empty string if one is not defined. The language tags are two- or five-character abbreviations for a language and optionally a country. For example, here are a few of the more than 75 language codes:

```
en           English
en-au        English-Australia
en-gb        English-United Kingdom
en-us        English-United States
fr           French
fr-ca        French-Canada
ja           Japanese
zh-cn        Chinese-China
zh-hk        Chinese-Hong Kong
zh-tw        Chinese-Taiwan
```

See the Lotus documentation for the complete list of codes.

`public String getOrganization() throws NotesException`

The getOrganization property routine returns the organization component (O=) of the hierarchical name. If no organization component is found, this property will return an empty string. See the example under the getCanonical property.

`public String getOrgUnit1() throws NotesException`

`public String getOrgUnit2() throws NotesException`

`public String getOrgUnit3() throws NotesException`

`public String getOrgUnit4() throws NotesException`

The getOrgUnit*n* property routine returns an organization unit component (OU=) of the hierarchical name. Organization unit 1 is the highest level orgunit, just below the organizational level. Organization unit 2 is below orgunit 1. If no corresponding organization unit component exists, this property will return an empty string. See the example under the getCanonical property.

If only one organization unit exists, it is OU1, as in /OU1/O. For two names, the order is /OU2/OU1/O. If all organization units are present, it is OU4/OU3/OU2/OU1/O.

`public Session getParent() throws NotesException`

The getParent property routine returns the Session that contains the current Name object.

`public String getPRMD() throws NotesException`

The getPRMD property routine will return the private management domain name (PRMD). The input must contain a PRMD component (P=). If no PRMD component exists, the property will return the empty string (not null). See the example under the getCanonical property.

`public String getSurname() throws NotesException`

The `getSurname` property routine returns the surname name (S=) component of the hierarchical name. If no surname name component exists, this property will return an empty string. Note that this property will not return a part of the common name; it will return a value only if the S= component is specified. Notes names define the common name (CN) rather than the Given, Initials, or Surname components. See the example under the `getCanonical` property. Also note that the "N" in `getSurname` is not capitalized for this property routine.

`public boolean isHierarchical() throws NotesException`

The `isHierarchical` property routine returns `true` if the `Name` object has a hierarchical name and `false` if it is a flat name.

THE International CLASS

Class Definition

`public class International extends Base`

Properties

- getAMString
- getCurrencyDigits
- getCurrencySymbol
- getDateSep
- getDecimalSep
- getParent
- getPMString
- getThousandsSep
- getTimeSep
- getTimeZone
- getToday
- getTomorrow
- getYesterday
- isCurrencySpace
- isCurrencySuffix
- isCurrencyZero
- isDateDMY
- isDateMDY

- isDateYMD
- isDST
- isTime24Hour

The International class is used to hold properties that govern characteristics that vary from country to country. You can use the International class to inquire, for example, the currency symbol, the date and time separators, and the format used for displaying dates.

COMMON METHODS TO CREATE

Session.getInternational

PROPERTIES

public String getAMString() throws NotesException

The getAMString property returns the string that indicates a time between midnight and noon. For example, in English, this string is AM.

public int getCurrencyDigits() throws NotesException

The getCurrencyDigits returns the number of decimal digits for currency (number) formats.

public String getCurrencySymbol() throws NotesException

The getCurrencySymbol property returns the symbol used for currency. For example, it might be the dollar sign, yen sign, or pound symbol.

public String getDateSep() throws NotesException

The getDateSep property returns the symbol that is used to separate the month, day, and year of a date. For example, it might be a forward slash.

public String getDecimalSep() throws NotesException

The getDecimalSep property returns the character used to separate the whole number from the fractional part of a number. In some countries this character is a period (decimal point), and in other countries it might be a comma. Other separators can be used as well.

public Session getParent() throws NotesException

The getParent property returns the Session object that contains the current International object.

public String getPMString() throws NotesException

The getPMString property returns the string that indicates a time between noon and midnight. For example, in English, this string is PM.

`public String getThousandsSep() throws NotesException`

The `getThousandsSep` property returns the character that is used to separate numbers over one thousand. This character is used between groups of three digits. This character is commonly a comma, but in Europe, it is sometimes a period.

`public String getTimeSep() throws NotesException`

The `getTimeSep` character is used to separate hours, minutes, and seconds. This character is frequently a colon.

`public int getTimeZone() throws NotesException`

The `getTimeZone` property returns an integer representing the time zone. This value can be positive or negative and normally is the number of hours that must be added to the local time zone to obtain Greenwich Mean Time. For example, Los Angeles has a value of 8. The East Coast of the United States has a value of 5.

`public String getToday() throws NotesException`

The `getToday` property returns the string that means today in a time-date specification. In English, the string is `Today`.

`public String getTomorrow() throws NotesException`

The `getTomorrow` property returns the string that means tomorrow in a time-date specification. In English, the string is `Tomorrow`.

`public String getYesterday() throws NotesException`

The `getYesterday` property returns the string that means yesterday in a time-date specification. In English, the string is `Yesterday`.

`public boolean isCurrencySpace() throws NotesException`

The `isCurrencySpace` property returns `true` if the currency format should have a space between the currency symbol and the number. It returns `false` if not.

`public boolean isCurrencySuffix() throws NotesException`

The `isCurrencySuffix` property returns `true` if the currency symbol should be after the number. It returns `false` if the currency symbol should be before the number. For dollars, the symbol is before the number.

`public boolean isCurrencyZero() throws NotesException`

The `isCurrencyZero` property returns `true` if fractional currency values should have a zero before the decimal point (actually the `DecimalSep` character). If `false`, fractional currency values do not need to have a zero. This property is not applicable to UNIX platforms.

```
public boolean isDateDMY() throws NotesException
```
The isDateDMY property returns true if the date format is day, then month, and then year.

```
public boolean isDateMDY() throws NotesException
```
The isDateMDY property returns true if the date format is month, then day, and then year.

```
public boolean isDateYMD() throws NotesException
```
The isDateYMD property ;returns true if the date format is year, then month, and then day.

```
public boolean isDST() throws NotesException
```
The isDST property returns true if time formatting includes daylight savings time.

```
public boolean isTime24Hour() throws NotesException
```
The isTime24Hour property returns true if the time formatting uses 24-hour notation. It returns false if 12-hour notation is used.

CHAPTER REVIEW

1. Write a Domino agent that can be invoked when a new document arrives (for example, a mail-in database). The document that arrives should have user information such as last name, first name, server, and so forth. From this information, register the new user on the specified server. You can include whatever information you feel is appropriate in the incoming document.

2. Explain the difference between addUserToAddressBook and registerNewUser.

3. What is a registration log? Why might it be a good idea to create and use a registration log?

4. What is the difference between an organizational unit and an organization?

5. Write an agent that will run periodically (for example, once a day) that will be contained in a discussion database. The agent should do a full text search and create a newsletter document that contains links to all new documents that contain the keyword XML. The agent should mail the newsletter document to you. Note that each day's newsletter should contain references to documents that you have not previously seen. If no new documents contain XML, it should not send the email.

6. Enhance the agent created in Exercise 5 so that it checks the number of new documents. If three or fewer documents exist, render the actual documents in the email message rather than sending links. If more than three new documents exist, just send the doclinks in the newsletter.

7. Enhance the agent created in Exercise 5 (or 6) to add logging to a Notes database. Add an action in the log database when the agent starts and when the agent is finished. Log the number of documents that are found. Log any errors that are detected during processing and any other actions you feel appropriate.

8. Write an agent that will run in an agent log database. It should run daily and delete any log entries that are more than 14 days old.

9. Explain the difference between RFC 821 and RFC 822 formatted Internet names. Which format can contain comments?

10. Sarah obtained a Name object through the Session.getUserNameObject method. She then tried to get the last name of the user by using the Name.getSurname property. It returned the empty string. Why?

11. Why is it a good idea to use values from the International class when developing applications that might be used by people from several countries?

PART V

ENTERPRISE INTEGRATION USING XML, JAVA, AND DOMINO

CHAPTER **22**

INTRODUCTION TO EXTENSIBLE MARKUP LANGUAGE (XML)

In this chapter

WHAT IS XML?

If you have been watching the industry press for the last year or two, I'm sure you have noticed that the number of articles about the Extensible Markup Language (XML) has been growing. Microsoft has made XML an important initiative and has even mentioned it in a television commercial. Lotus is placing heavy emphasis on XML and is devoting major development resources to this technology. Other companies including IBM, Oracle, and Sun are likewise placing special emphasis on XML.

Why is there so much interest in XML? Is this just industry hype or is something more substantial here? And just what is XML, anyway? In this chapter, I'll answer these questions and provide you with an overview of XML.

THE IMPORTANCE OF XML

Let me jump to my conclusion first, and in this chapter and the next few, I'll try to convince you that my conclusion is true. XML truly is an important technology, and these vendors are on to something besides their own self interest. XML will be good for not only the computing industry, but also potentially every industry that uses the Internet. Are you aware of many industries that are not now or will not in the future be using the Internet?

XML is fundamentally important because it provides a standardized structural framework—a syntax for exchanging data. This is an important first step in improving data exchange between and among computer programs. In many ways, XML is as important for data as Java is for programming. Let me give you an analogy so you can understand the significance (and limitations) of XML.

In written and spoken languages there is both a syntax and a semantic content to information. Syntax in English, for example, governs the use and placement of nouns, verbs, commas, semicolons, and periods. A common English sentence format is a subject followed by a verb followed by a direct object. Declarative sentences end with a period.

Syntax rules for French, Italian, or Spanish, of course, are different from the rules for English. However, many of the rules are similar or are the same. The rules for Japanese are completely different and use a completely different set of symbols as well.

What if we could come up with a common syntax for all these languages? In other words, all languages would require sentences to be in a particular format. The words in the sentences could be in the Spanish, French, or Japanese vocabularies, but the syntax would be the same in all languages. This would not enable a Spanish speaker to understand English, but we could standardize sentence structure and whether question marks are right side up or upside down.

Would this be a significant accomplishment? I think so. However, for written and spoken languages, I'm not sure that it would be worthwhile to even try to standardize human language syntax for a huge variety of reasons. For computers, though, it is a much more modest goal with potentially great benefits.

XML provides a common syntax for computer programs to communicate. Syntax for computer programs is much more important than it is for people. In written and spoken languages a person can typically make himself or herself understood by using a few words, even in the incorrect order. For programs, the order and choice of words is very important.

The power of XML lies in the fact that it standardizes the format for information to flow from one program to another. Although this is a very important first step, it will not automatically allow all programs to communicate. Even if two programs understand the XML syntax, if one program is using one vocabulary and the second is using a different vocabulary, the two programs will not be able to hold a conversation. In fact, now that the syntax is standardized with XML, our next big challenge is to standardize XML vocabularies.

Over the next several years, I expect that many standardized XML vocabularies will begin to emerge. In addition, with the advent of a standardized syntax, common tools are possible. Tools for generating, parsing, and processing XML are possible because the syntax has been standardized. Tools for editing XML and for converting XML to and from other formats are possible. Microsoft Internet Explorer already supports XML, and other Web browsers will soon add support for XML. Because Microsoft believes in the importance of XML, you can be sure that it will provide many XML tools, and other vendors are joining the XML party as well. Vendors such as Lotus, IBM, Sun, Netscape, and Oracle are all providing XML support in their products.

XML, HTML, AND WORD MEANINGS

Now that you have an introduction to the importance of XML, let's take a look at a simple XML example. XML files are simple text files. Here is our first XML example:

```
<?xml version="1.0"?>
<message>
Hello, World!
</message>
```

This is our Hello, World! example again. You'll notice right away that the format is similar to HTML. Despite its similarity to HTML, you should understand that XML is neither a superset nor subset of HTML. The purpose of HTML is to format information for display and presentation in Web browsers. The primary purpose of XML is to express information for computer-to-computer transactions. Because people frequently create HTML, most Web browsers are very forgiving of syntax errors and will process incorrect HTML files. XML, on the other hand, will typically be created by programs and read by programs and is much more strict and rigid with regard to syntax.

A new specification called XHTML was released as a W3C recommendation (essentially a standard) in January 2000. This is a reformulation of HTML 4 using XML syntax. It is clear from this recommendation that HTML is moving toward XML now and for the future. You can find the XHTML recommendation at http://www.w3.org/TR/xhtml1/.

XML files must begin with an XML declaration. As of this writing, the only version is 1.0, but the declaration must specify the version number so that documents using future versions can be distinguished from version 1.0. Here is an example of the XML declaration:

```
<?xml version="1.0"?>
```

Following the version number, our sample XML document has only a single element, the `<message>` element. This element is made up of a starting tag, the content, and its ending tag. Ending tags, as in HTML, begin with a slash. Within an XML file, you can have nested elements, and element starting tags can contain attributes.

Note that there is no final tag such as `<?/xml>` or `</xml>`. The declaration line does not have a matching end tag.

The next question you might have is: "How is the `<message>` tag defined and what does it mean?" That is actually two questions, but I'll answer both of them for you. The answer is best summed up by Humpty Dumpty speaking to Alice in Lewis Carroll's *Through the Looking Glass*:

> "When *I* use a word," Humpty Dumpty said in rather a scornful tone, "it means just what I choose it to mean—neither more nor less."
>
> "The question is," said Alice, "whether you *can* make words mean so many different things."
>
> "The question is," said Humpty Dumpty, "which is to be master—that's all."

With XML, you are the master. You can choose the vocabulary for your application, and you don't have to worry about the syntax because the rules are predefined. In the previous example, I made up the element name message. It seemed like a nice element name, so I just used it. If you are writing your own application, you can use your own element names and provide your own structure to your documents. All these aspects of your XML documents are defined in a Document Type Definition (DTD) that I describe in the section titled "Document Type Definitions (DTDs)."

XML-Based Languages

As you might imagine, defining your own XML-based language can be fun and interesting. However, unless you can get the rest of the world to adopt your language, it will not be useful for communicating with other people or programs. The key to making a widely accepted XML-based language is to define an application domain and to standardize the XML language for that domain by bringing together interested parties.

Many XML-based languages already exist: Synchronized Multimedia Integration Language (SMIL), Mathematical Expressions (MathML), metadata (Resource Description Framework—RDF), and Wireless Markup Language (WML), to name just a few. In addition to this list, industrial groups such as financial institutions and manufacturing companies are developing XML-based standards for transactions within their industries.

The beauty of XML is that it can be used for in-company proprietary applications as well as inter-company standardized communications. By standardizing the XML syntax, a variety of tools and applications can be developed that will greatly ease the processing of XML-based information.

XML Syntax

Here is a more complicated example of an XML file:

```
<?xml version="1.0" encoding="UTF-8" ?>
<!-- Lotus-Domino (Release 5.0.2b - December 16, 1999
➥on Windows NT/Intel)  -->
<viewentries toplevelentries="3">
 <viewentry position="1" unid="4AD9B08B6BE05A0F88256756007E2B64"
➥noteid="8F6" siblings="3">
  <entrydata columnnumber="0" name="Form">
   <text>CtlSection</text>
  </entrydata>
 </viewentry>
 <viewentry position="2" unid="140F6C949D3993C38825687E0014DB23"
➥noteid="92E" siblings="3">
  <entrydata columnnumber="0" name="Form">
   <text>Listbox</text>
  </entrydata>
 </viewentry>
 <viewentry position="3" unid="246A24BC5CFDEECD8825687E00150BBF"
➥noteid="932" siblings="3">
  <entrydata columnnumber="0" name="Form">
   <text>Listbox</text>
  </entrydata>
 </viewentry>
</viewentries>
```

This example, as you can probably tell, was generated by Domino. The first line is the XML declaration and the second line is a comment that lets you know that Domino generated the file. Here is the Domino comment, which gives you the version and the date of the release (not the current date) along with platform information:

```
<!-- Lotus-Domino (Release 5.0.2b - December 16, 1999
➥on Windows NT/Intel)  -->
```

This XML file was generated as the result of a ?ReadViewEntries URL command, which is supported in Domino release 5.0.2 and above. Here is an example of the syntax for the ?ReadViewEntries URL command:

```
http://Host/Database/ViewName?ReadViewEntries
```

More details about this command can be found in Chapter 7, "Using Hypertext Markup Language (HTML) for Page Design."

The XML file shown here is for a view that displays three documents and has one column. The column name is Form and in this case displays the form used for the Domino document.

I won't delve into a complete description of this example, but a couple of points are worth noting. First, all XML documents have a single main element. In this example, the main element is <viewentries> and can be found just below the Domino comment line. Second, elements can be nested, and within the <viewentries> element there are three <viewentry>

elements. In turn, within each <viewentry> element there is an <entrydata> element, and within the <entrydata> element you find a <text> element.

This hierarchical containment within an XML document is typical. Also notice that on some element start tags you find attributes. For example, the <viewentries> tag has one attribute called toplevelentries. The <entrydata> tag has two attributes, columnnumber and name.

In XML, all attributes must always be enclosed in either single or double quotes. HTML is more forgiving, and you can find HTML files with attributes not enclosed in quotes. Notice in the ReadViewEntries example that even numeric values are enclosed in quotes.

Unlike HTML, XML is case sensitive. All the Domino-generated elements are lowercase. If you define your own XML, be sure to have a convention for your element names. Using all lowercase is a simple and useful convention.

In HTML, some elements such as <HR> do not have an end tag. XML does not allow a start tag without an end tag. XML does allow a shorthand notation for elements that do not contain content. The following are synonymous:

```
<mytag></mytag>
```

and

```
<mytag />
```

The second notation is simply a shorthand form for the first version. You can also include attributes, as in

```
<mynote priority="Important" timeframe="Immediate" />
```

PROCESSING XML

There are two aspects to processing XML. One aspect is the generation of XML from a data source. The original data can be from a Domino database, a relational database, text file, spreadsheet, or any other type of object. The resulting XML file can contain as much or as little data as you like and depends on your application. If you don't include all the original information in your XML file, of course, you will not be able to perform a round trip export and import. Chapter 24, "Serving XML from Domino," focuses on the generation and serving of XML documents.

The second aspect of processing an XML file involves reading an XML file and then doing something with it. You can, for example, read an XML file and create documents in a Domino database or a relational database. You can read an XML file and create transactions in a financial accounting system. You can read an XML file and display a multimedia presentation. Of course this list is endless. Chapter 25, "Processing XML with Domino," focuses on reading and interpreting XML files.

WHAT IS THE EXTENSIBLE STYLESHEET LANGUAGE (XSL)?

The Extensible Stylesheet Language is a language that uses XML syntax. It provides a powerful mechanism to process XML files. There are two primary purposes for XSL. The first is similar to the purpose for stylesheets in HTML. That is, to format documents for display to users by specifying font faces, font sizes, styles, and so forth. The second purpose of XSL, and the one I will primarily discuss in this book, is for the transformation of an XML document.

When you transform an XML document with XSL, you can convert it to another XML document, to HTML, or to another format you specify. This transformation aspect of XML and XSL is very powerful because it enables you to separate the content of the data from its presentation. For example, using the same source XML data document, you can combine it with different XSL stylesheets and display the data with different formatting and filtering. I discuss XSL in Chapter 23, "Understanding the Extensible Stylesheet Language (XSL)."

The concept of separating content from format has been a part of Notes and Domino since the very beginning but has now attracted industry interest. In Notes and Domino, you have long been able to combine Domino documents, which store data, with Domino forms, which specify formatting. XML provides these capabilities with XML documents for data and XSL stylesheets for formatting.

WELL-FORMED AND VALID DOCUMENTS

You now know that XML is used to describe information and that an XML file must conform to rigidly defined rules. What are these rules and how are they defined? There are two sets of rules. The first set of rules applies to all XML files and governs XML syntax in general.

For example, XML files must begin with a `<?xml version="1.0"?>` declaration. In addition, XML start and end tags must be properly nested. The following will properly display in most Web browsers but is not properly nested because the italic tag (`<I>`) should be terminated before the bold tag (`<B>`). XML would signal this as an error because tags must be nested and cannot overlap.

```
<B><I>Bold-Italic Text</B></I>
```

These types of rules apply to all XML files, regardless of the particular vocabulary being used. If an XML file conforms to these general XML rules it is called *well formed*. There are many more rules for XML. The actual specification is "Extensible Markup Language (XML) 1.0" and is W3C Recommendation REC-xml-19980210, dated February 10, 1998. A copy of this specification is in Appendix A, and you can also find it on the Web at `http://www.w3.org/TR/REC-xml`.

The second set of rules goes beyond the concept of a well-formed document and controls the application-specific elements used for a specific document type. Thus, the rules for SMIL are different from the rules for MathML, and these are different from the rules for WML. Each separate language, called a document type, has a separate set of rules.

The specification that controls each document type is called a Document Type Definition (DTD). An XML document that is well formed and also complies with its DTD is called a *valid* XML document. An XML parser is a program that analyzes the syntax of an XML document. Most parsers will check to make sure that an XML document is well formed. Parsers that check that a document is valid in addition to being well formed are called validating XML parsers.

DOCUMENT TYPE DEFINITIONS (DTDs)

Document Type Definition (DTD) files provide the XML parser with information about the structure of your document. DTDs specify, for example, the name of the root node of your document tree, which is the name of your document type. In HTML, the document type is HTML and the <HTML> element is the root node of the tree and encompasses all other elements of the document.

In addition to the root node or document type, DTDs also describe the other elements of the document and their attributes. To illustrate the syntax of DTDs, I'll show you the DTD for the ?ReadViewEntries URL command for Domino. This URL command enables you to obtain the information from a view in XML format. You can then manipulate the view information and present it in a Web browser in your own custom format.

Before I show you the DTD, let's look at an example using the built-in Domino URL command called ?ReadViewEntries. This command will return the data for a view in XML format. Here is the logical XML structure of the view as returned by ?ReadViewEntries:

```
<viewentries toplevelentries="n">
   <!-- Each viewentry is one row -->
   <viewentry ViewEntryAttributes>
      <!-- Each entrydata is one column -->
      <entrydata columnnumber="n" indent="n" name="str" category="bool">
         <!-- data goes here -->
      </entrydata>
      <!-- More entrydata items here -->
   </viewentry>
</viewentries>
```

The data for a particular view is returned using this logical structure. To make the example concrete, let's look at some specific data for a view. Here is an example of a view with three rows. The text that follows is returned to the browser when the ?ReadViewEntries URL command is sent to Domino.

```
<?xml version="1.0" encoding="UTF-8"?>
<!-- Lotus-Domino (Release 5.0.2b - December 16, 1999 on Windows NT/Intel) -->
<viewentries toplevelentries="3">
  <viewentry position="1" unid="3B2AE4A1A73B94A0882568800068BE2A"
➥noteid="936" siblings="3">
    <entrydata columnnumber="0" name="TxtField">
      <text>MyText</text></entrydata>
    <entrydata columnnumber="1" name="NumField">
      <number>3.17</number></entrydata>
    <entrydata columnnumber="2" name="DateField">
```

```
        <datetime>20000229T144700,00-08</datetime></entrydata>
      <entrydata columnnumber="3" name="NameField">
        <text>CN=John Doe/O=GWCorp</text></entrydata>
  </viewentry>
  <viewentry position="2" unid="D4C32FE24E65ABB1882568800068CEE3"
  ➡noteid="93A" siblings="3">
    <entrydata columnnumber="0" name="TxtField">
      <text>Second Doc</text></entrydata>
    <entrydata columnnumber="1" name="NumField">
      <number>2</number></entrydata>
    <entrydata columnnumber="2" name="DateField">
      <datetime>19840516</datetime></entrydata>
    <entrydata columnnumber="3" name="NameField">
      <text>CN=Eric Tamura/O=GWCorp</text></entrydata>
  </viewentry>
  <viewentry position="3" unid="CC3A6588F4265C4E8825688000693560"
  ➡noteid="93E" siblings="3">
    <entrydata columnnumber="0" name="TxtField">
      <text>ZZ - Last Doc</text></entrydata>
    <entrydata columnnumber="1" name="NumField">
      <number>-27.46</number></entrydata>
    <entrydata columnnumber="2" name="DateField">
      <datetime>T152200,00</datetime></entrydata>
    <entrydata columnnumber="3" name="NameField">
      <text></text></entrydata>
  </viewentry>
</viewentries>
```

In this example, notice that each row of the view is represented by one <viewentry> element. Within each <viewentry>, each column is represented by one <entrydata> element. Within each <entrydata> element, the simple type (such as text or number) is specified along with the column content. As mentioned previously, all attributes are enclosed with double quotes, even numeric values. For example, the attribute siblings is specified as siblings="3", not siblings=3.

The following attributes can be returned for the <viewentry> element as of version 5.0.3 for Domino:

- position—A character string of numbers, separated by periods representing the entry's position in the hierarchy.

- unid—The document's universal ID. It is a hexadecimal string of 32 characters. If the entry is not a document, the attribute is omitted.

- noteid—The document's note ID. It is a hexadecimal string of up to eight characters. If the entry is not a document, the attribute is omitted.

- children—The number of entries that are children of the current entry within the view hierarchy.

- siblings—The number of entries that are siblings at the current level in the hierarchy, including the current element.

- descendants—The number of entries that are descendants of the current entry (including itself).

- collapsed—This Boolean value is true if the current entry is collapsed.

- response—This Boolean value is true if the current entry is a response document.

- conflict—This Boolean value is true if the current entry is a save or replication conflict document.

- categorytotal—This Boolean value is true if the current entry is a category total entry.

- markedfordel—This Boolean value is true if the current entry is marked for deletion.

- unread—This Boolean value is true if the current entry is unread (new with 5.0.3).

- unreadchildren—This Boolean value is true if any children of the current entry are unread (new with 5.0.3).

- relevance—This integer is the relevance score for the current entry, if applicable (new with 5.0.3).

Consider the following line from the example:

```
<viewentry position="3" unid="CC3A6588F4265C4E8825688000693560"
➥noteid="93E" siblings="3">
```

In this line, the position, unid, noteid, and siblings attributes have been specified. Although this line has been taken out of context, you can tell that it is in position 3 within the view because of the position attribute. The other attributes provide additional information.

THE ?ReadViewEntries DTD

To understand DTDs, it is usually easier to see an example than to read a specification. I'm going to show you the DTD for the ?ReadViewEntries URL command and explain its parts. In this way you'll see a specific, useful example of a DTD while I explain the purpose of its statements. Because I'll explain DTDs with examples, I will not cover every option in a DTD, only the major options. This will be enough to get you started. If you're curious, DTDs are covered in full detail in the XML recommendation (specification) in Appendix A.

The DTD is a bit lengthy, but this is partly because of the embedded comments. Don't be intimidated by its length. As we go through it, you'll see that it really isn't that complicated.

```
<!--
ViewEntries.dtd
    These types represent the information required to support
    the ?ReadViewEntries URL command that generates XML.
-->
<!--********************************************************-->
<!-- * Basic Types                                        * -->
<!--********************************************************-->

<!ENTITY % boolean "( true | false )">
<!ENTITY % hex "CDATA">
<!ENTITY % integer "CDATA">
<!-- NOTEIDs are 4-8 hex chars -->
<!ENTITY % noteid "CDATA">
```

```
<!-- UNIDs are 32 hex chars -->
<!ENTITY % unid "CDATA">

<!--
Domino TIMEDATEs are represented in ISO8601 basic format,
for example:
    19990713T060306,52+05
TIMEDATEs can have just a time, or just a date.
These use only the part of the ISO8601 representation
that are appropriate:
    T060306,52
    19990713
-->

<!ELEMENT datetime ( #PCDATA )>

<!-- Attributes for <datetime>:
    dst:            was daylight savings in effect
                    when this time was recorded?
-->
<!ATTLIST datetime
    dst             %boolean;        "false"
    >

<!--
This entity describes the attributes that can appear
on any of the potential root elements in the DTD.
-->

<!ENTITY % root.attrs "
    version         CDATA           #IMPLIED
    ">

<!--***************************************************-->
<!-- * Items                                         * -->
<!--***************************************************-->

<!ENTITY % simple.types "
    text |
    number |
    datetime |
    textlist |
    numberlist |
    datetimelist
    ">

<!ELEMENT text ( #PCDATA )>
<!ELEMENT number ( #PCDATA )>
<!ELEMENT textlist ( text* )>
<!ELEMENT numberlist ( number* )>
<!ELEMENT datetimelist ( datetime*, datetimepair* )>
<!ELEMENT datetimepair ( datetime, datetime )>

<!--
This is the output of the ?ReadViewEntries URL.
All of the requested entries are output as a list
of <viewentry> elements in a <viewentries> element.
```

```
    The nesting implied by categories and response hierarchies
    is flattened out.
    -->

    <!ELEMENT viewentries ( viewentry* )>

    <!-- Attributes for <viewentries>:
        toplevelentries:    The number of top-level entries
                            in the entire view.
    -->
    <!ATTLIST viewentries
        %root.attrs;
        toplevelentries %integer;       #IMPLIED
        >


    <!-- Each line in the view becomes an <viewentry> element. -->

    <!ELEMENT viewentry ( entrydata* )>
    <!ATTLIST viewentry
        position        CDATA           #IMPLIED
        unid            %unid;          #IMPLIED
        noteid          %noteid;        #IMPLIED
        children        %integer;       #IMPLIED
        siblings        %integer;       #IMPLIED
        descendants     %integer;       #IMPLIED
        collapsed       %boolean;       #IMPLIED
        response        %boolean;       #IMPLIED
        conflict        %boolean;       #IMPLIED
        categorytotal   %boolean;       #IMPLIED
        markedfordel    %boolean;       #IMPLIED
        unread          %boolean;       #IMPLIED
        unreadchildren  %boolean;       #IMPLIED
        relevance       %integer;       #IMPLIED
        >


    <!ELEMENT entrydata ( %simple.types; )>

    <!-- Attributes for <entrydata>:
        category:       Is this entry data the name of a category?
    -->
    <!ATTLIST entrydata
        columnnumber    %integer;       #IMPLIED
        indent          %integer;       #IMPLIED
        name            %string;        #IMPLIED
        category        %boolean;       #IMPLIED
        >


<!-- end of ViewEntries.dtd -->
```

The first point to notice in the DTD is that despite its length, it has only four types of statements. The first type is just a comment. Comments are formatted like this:

```
<!--    Any comment text      -->
```

The text within the comment can span multiple lines, as you see in the example.

The other three types of statements are <!ENTITY>, <!ELEMENT>, and <!ATTLIST>. Entities are used for symbolic substitution. That is, you can define a symbol and a replacement string.

The replacement string will be used in place of the symbol in the appropriate context. Elements are the fundamental unit of XML; examples are `<viewentries>`, `<entrydata>`, and `<viewentry>`. The `<!ATTLIST>` specification is used to specify the list of attributes that can be associated with a particular element.

So, at a high level, it is relatively easy to understand the purpose of the various components of a DTD. I'll now explain each of these statement types in more detail.

THE `<!ENTITY>` DECLARATION

You define entities with the `<!ENTITY>` declaration. The two types of entities are general entities and parameter entities. There are two types because their use depends on where and when the substitution of the entity occurs.

General entities are defined in the DTD and can be used in the XML file. To declare a general entity, you use the following syntax:

```
<!ENTITY entname "entvalue">
```

In the syntax description, *entname* refers to the entity name and *entvalue* refers to the entity's value. Here are some general entity declaration examples:

```
<!ENTITY copw "Copyright (c) 2000">
<!ENTITY allr "All rights reserved.">
<!ENTITY frm "the super-ultra framis contraption">
```

When you refer to a general entity, you use an ampersand (&) before the entity name and a semicolon (;) following the name. When the XML file is parsed, the general entity will be replaced with its specified value. One common use for general entities is to enable you to specify special characters that are otherwise part of the XML syntax. Here is an example:

```
<math>
  &copw; &allr;
  A &lt; B is true if A is less than B.
  A &gt; B is true if A is greater than B.
</math>
```

In this example, the `copw` general entity previously defined will be replaced with the copyright statement, and the `allr` general entity will be replaced with the `All rights reserved` phrase. The `lt` entity is built in and will be replaced with a less than (<) character.

Parameter entities defined in the DTD are used for substitution within the DTD only. Parameter entities enable you to use shorthand notation within the DTD. To reference a parameter entity, you use a percent sign (%) before the entity name and a semicolon (;) following the name. You cannot use parameter entities in the XML file itself.

Armed with this knowledge, let's look back at the first few lines of the `ViewEntries` DTD:

```
<!ENTITY % boolean "( true | false )">
<!ENTITY % hex "CDATA">
<!ENTITY % integer "CDATA">
```

As you can see, all three of these entities include a percent sign. This indicates that the entities are parameter entities. General entities do not use the percent sign. Parameter entity references are similar to general entity references, except that parameter entities use a percent sign (%) instead of an ampersand (&) at the beginning and a semicolon at the end of the reference. As you browse through the rest of the DTD, you can see several references of both the `boolean` and `integer` entities. Notice that they are referenced as in the following:

```
descendants    %integer;      #IMPLIED
collapsed      %boolean;      #IMPLIED
```

The parameter entity references begin with a percent (%) and end with a semicolon (;). I explain the purpose of the `#IMPLIED` keyword later in the section describing `<!ATTLIST>`. The `integer` reference will be replaced by the string `CDATA`, which stands for character data. The `boolean` reference will be replaced by the string (`true` | `false`). Note that the beginning and ending quotes will not be included in the substitution string. Boolean values must be specified by one of the following strings: `true` or `false`. The vertical bar means that in the XML file, any one of the choices is acceptable. You see the vertical bar again in the definition of the parameter entity called `simple.types`. Here is the definition for `simple.types`:

```
<!ENTITY % simple.types "
    text |
    number |
    datetime |
    textlist |
    numberlist |
    datetimelist
    ">
```

Notice that the entity definition can extend beyond one line. In this case the definition spans multiple lines to make reading the definition easier.

As mentioned previously, the main reason for defining entities is so that we can use meaningful names in the definitions. For example, the definition showing that the `descendants` attribute is an `integer` using the entity

```
descendants    %integer;      #IMPLIED
```

is much clearer than its equivalent without using the entity

```
descendants  CDATA   #IMPLIED
```

Note that the XML specification also distinguishes between *parsed* and *unparsed* entities. Parsed entities are those that are to be sent to the XML processor. Unparsed entities are not processed by the XML processor and can contain binary data, such as images or any other information useful to the application but not parsed by the XML processor.

You can also use external entities, which are references to files or other Web resources. Here is an example of a reference to a file:

```
<!ENTITY decls SYSTEM "sysdecls.xml">
```

THE <!ELEMENT> TYPE DECLARATION

An element in XML is comprised of a start tag, the element's content, and the element's end tag. For example, consider the following:

```
<message>
Hello, World!
</message>
```

This is an example of a single element with a start tag of `<message>`, an end tag of `</message>`, and content of `Hello, World!` In general, remember that an element encompasses all the content from the start tag through the end tag. A tag can be just a part of an element.

The `<!ELEMENT>` type declaration is used to specify the name of the element and its valid content. Here is the syntax:

```
<!ELEMENT Name contentspec>
```

The element `Name` is case sensitive. The `contentspec` can be one of the two keywords `EMPTY` or `ANY` or a list of character data and/or children. Here are some examples from the `ViewEntries` DTD:

```
<!ELEMENT text ( #PCDATA )>
<!ELEMENT number ( #PCDATA )>
<!ELEMENT textlist ( text* )>
<!ELEMENT numberlist ( number* )>
```

The first two element types, `text` and `number`, consist of parsed character data (`#PCDATA`). Here are some examples you could see in an XML file:

```
<text>This is my text</text>
<number>3.17</number>
<number>Alpha characters?</number>
```

The `<text>` element and the first `<number>` element are self-explanatory. The second `<number>` example requires a little more explanation. You can tell from the DTD definition of `text` and `number` that they are defined identically with (`#PCDATA`). For this reason, it should not be a surprise that the second number example in XML is allowed to contain alphabetic characters. However, something doesn't seem right about this. How do we check and enforce the fact that a `<number>` should contain only valid numbers?

There are two aspects to the answer. The first deals with the generation of the XML and the second with the parsing of the XML if it was generated from another source. When Domino generates the XML for a `?ReadViewEntries` request, it will look at the item data type and generate the appropriate element types. Although there might be ways to fool Domino, under normal circumstances this will always result in the appropriate type being generated.

When you are parsing data that was generated from another source, you will need to check the data type yourself as you parse the input. Although the element name is `<number>`, nothing in the DTD forces the content to be numeric. Therefore, the XML parser itself will not enforce the content to be numeric. If this is important to your application (it might not be), you will handle it as part of your application. I explain more about parsing XML in Chapter 25.

Continuing with our examples, look at the following few lines from the DTD:

```
<!ELEMENT textlist ( text* )>
<!ELEMENT numberlist ( number* )>
<!ELEMENT datetimelist ( datetime*, datetimepair* )>
<!ELEMENT datetimepair ( datetime, datetime )>
```

Notice that the `<textlist>` element is specified as a text element followed by an asterisk (*). This syntax means that a `<textlist>` element can contain zero or more instances of `<text>` elements. Here are some examples:

```
<textlist>
  <text>This is text</text>
  <text>Another text item</text>
</textlist>

<textlist/>

<textlist><text>Text item</text></textlist>
```

The first `<textlist>` has two `<text>` children, the second example has none, and the third has one. A `<numberlist>` is similar to a `<textlist>` but contains `<number>` elements instead of `<text>` elements.

When the contents of an element contain more than one name, separated by commas, each name represents a child element. The specified child elements must all be included, in order. A `<datetimelist>` is zero or more `<datetime>` elements followed by zero or more `<datetimepair>` elements. A `<datetimepair>` element is one `<datetime>` element followed immediately by another `<datetime>` element. Neither of the `<datetime>` elements in a `<datetimepair>` is optional.

Here are the special characters that can be used following an element name:

- *—Asterisk: Zero or more occurrences of an element.
- +—Plus sign: One or more occurrences of an element.
- ?—Question mark: Zero or one occurrence of an element.

Using these special characters in addition to the alternative choice character (vertical bar |), and the sequential character (comma ,) you can make very complex patterns describing an element's content.

Here are some examples:

```
<!ELEMENT part ( head, (para | body)*, foot )>
<!ELEMENT section ( front, body, back? )>
<!ELEMENT datelist ( dateitem+ )>
```

```
<!ELEMENT generalitem ( text | number | datetime )>
```

You can also use parameter entities as shorthand for the element's content:

```
<!ELEMENT entrydata ( %simple.types; )>
```

Using the previous definition of the simple.types entity, this would be equivalent to the following specification:

```
<!ELEMENT entrydata (
    text |
    number |
    datetime |
    textlist |
    numberlist |
    datetimelist
    ) >
```

By using the simple.types entity, the entrydata specification can easily be changed if new types are added at a later time.

THE <!ATTLIST> DECLARATION

The <!ATTLIST> declaration is used to specify an element's attribute list. Let's take a simple example to begin our study of attribute lists:

```
<!ENTITY % root.attrs "
    version         CDATA           #IMPLIED
    ">

<!ATTLIST viewentries
    %root.attrs;
    toplevelentries %integer;       #IMPLIED
    >
```

The first token after the keyword ATTLIST is the name of the element associated with the attribute list. This is the specification for the <viewentries> element's attributes. In this case notice that root.attrs is a parameter entity, which means that it will be substituted when the DTD is parsed. This entity is used so that any XML element that is a root element can contain a set of common attributes. In our sample DTD, we have only one root element (<viewentries>) and only one root attribute (version).

Looking back at the definition of the integer parameter entity, we see that it is defined as CDATA. Thus, after substitution, the attribute declaration is equivalent to the following:

```
<!ATTLIST viewentries
    version         CDATA           #IMPLIED
    toplevelentries CDATA           #IMPLIED
    >
```

The CDATA keyword, as I've mentioned before, stands for character data and means that each of these two attributes can contain character data. Besides the CDATA type, which is also known as the string type, an attribute value can be either a tokenized type or an enumerated type. Tokenized types enable you to refer from one element to another element. Tokenized types are not used in the ViewEntries DTD and are beyond the scope of our discussion. We have seen an example of the enumerated type with Boolean attributes. Here is an example:

```
<!ENTITY % boolean "( true | false )">

<!ATTLIST viewentry
    response        %boolean;      #IMPLIED
>
```

In this example, the boolean parameter entry will expand to the enumerated type (true | false). Following the enumerated type definition, you can include a default value, as in the following:

```
<!ATTLIST example
    response        %boolean;      "false"
>
```

This indicates that false is the default value.

Finally, a keyword indicates whether the attribute is optional or required. The #IMPLIED keyword means that the attribute is optional. The #REQUIRED keyword indicates that the attribute is required. The keyword #FIXED means that the attribute must match a fixed value. Here are some examples:

```
<!ATTLIST example
    name         CDATA          #REQUIRED
    response     %boolean;       #IMPLIED
    style        CDATA          #FIXED "standard"
>
```

Here is some text from an XML file that would comply with this attribute definition:

```
<example name="first" style="standard">
<example name="second" response="true" style="standard">
```

CONDITIONAL SECTIONS

Sometimes during the development of a DTD you might want to conditionally include or exclude parts of the definition. You can do this with the INCLUDE or IGNORE keywords. Here is how you use them:

```
<![INCLUDE[
    . . . included contents. . .
]]>
<![IGNORE[
    . . . ignored contents. . .
]]>
```

You can also use parameter entities instead of the keywords. For example:

```
<!ENTITY % mainversion "INCLUDE">
<!ENTITY % newversion  "IGNORE">
<![%mainversion;[
    . . . included contents. . .
```

```
]]>
<![%newversion;[
    . . . ignored contents. . .
]]>
```

You can use this feature for a very simple version control or for debugging. You can also use this feature to test some new DTD definitions without disturbing definitions already in place.

THE <!DOCTYPE> DECLARATION

The <!DOCTYPE> declaration describes the XML document type. The <!DOCTYPE> declaration defines the root element, which is the parent element of all the other elements of the document. You can have at most one <!DOCTYPE> declaration within an XML file and therefore at most one root element. The declaration specified can be either inline or it can be in an external file (or both).

Here is an XML file with a self-contained <!DOCTYPE> declaration:

```
<?xml version="1.0">
<!DOCTYPE message [
<!ELEMENT message (#PCDATA)>
]>
<message>Hello, World!</message>
```

In this example, I have defined the document type inline and have specified that the root element (and in this case the only element) is the message element. I could use an external reference for my DTD as follows:

```
<!DOCTYPE viewentries SYSTEM "ViewEntries.dtd">
```

This example specifies that the viewentries element is the root element and the DTD to use is contained in the ViewEntries.dtd file. Here is a sample with an external DTD reference:

```
<?xml version="1.0">
<!DOCTYPE viewentries SYSTEM "ViewEntries.dtd">
<viewentries toplevelentries="1">
  <viewentry position="1" unid="3B2AE4A1A73B94A0882568800068BE2A"
  ➥noteid="936" siblings="1">
    <entrydata columnnumber="0" name="TxtField">
      <text>MyText</text></entrydata>
    <entrydata columnnumber="1" name="NumField">
      <number>3.17</number></entrydata>
    <entrydata columnnumber="2" name="DateField">
      <datetime>20000229T144700,00-08</datetime></entrydata>
    <entrydata columnnumber="3" name="NameField">
      <text>CN=John Doe/O=GWCorp</text></entrydata>
  </viewentry>
</viewentries>
```

VALIDATION

You might have noticed that in the XML that is generated automatically by Domino, a `<!DOCTYPE>` declaration is not included. A `<!DOCTYPE>` declaration is optional and is required only if you want the XML processor to validate the document. As you might recall, an XML document is well formed if it conforms to all the rules of XML. It is valid if there is a `<!DOCTYPE>` declaration associated with the XML document and the document conforms to the declaration.

All the DTD declarations are required only if you want to validate your XML document. What are the advantages or disadvantages of validating a document? If you are obtaining a document from an unknown source, you might want to validate the document. Validating the document will enable the XML processor to check the types of elements, their attributes, and the element nesting to ensure that they conform to a DTD.

If you are processing an XML document from a known source, for example the `?ReadViewEntries` URL, you might want to skip the validation. Validation takes time within the process receiving the XML (such as a Web browser) and you might want to assume that the XML generated by Domino is in the correct format. In fact, because the `?ReadViewEntries` URL does not include a `<!DOCTYPE>` declaration, there is no way to validate the XML document, even if you wanted to. The only way to validate the document would be to provide your own DTD, similar to the one that I showed you earlier in this chapter, and add the `<!DOCTYPE>` declaration to the Domino-generated XML before processing the file.

SUMMARY

XML is a powerful technology and will become more important in time. It is important because it provides a standardized format, a syntax for data exchange and communication. Because the Internet is connecting more and more computers, the need for exchanging data continues to grow.

By providing a common syntax for the specification of documents, XML allows the creation of entire libraries of tools such as parsers, translators, and XML generators. As these tools become more plentiful, and as XML data becomes more plentiful, the value of the tools will increase because they can be used in so many different contexts.

As of releases 5.0.2 and 5.0.3, Domino provides a set of tools for creating (`?ReadViewEntries`), parsing, and translating XML files. Domino has its own dialect of XML (called DXL) for representing the data contained in a Domino database. The `?ReadViewEntries` URL command exposes a part of this language.

In the next few chapters, I'll give you more information on translating, serving, and parsing XML files with Domino and Java.

CHAPTER REVIEW

1. Create a sample hierarchical XML file that describes your office or a room in your home. The elements of your office can be the furniture and its subcomponents. Do the same for your car.

2. Describe some of the similarities and differences between XML and HTML.

3. What is the difference between a well-formed XML document and a valid XML document?

4. What is the difference between a general entity and a parameter entity?

5. Using the Domino Designer (at release 5.0.2 or later), design a form with three fields and a view with three columns. Each field should appear in one column of the view. Enter a few documents, and using Microsoft Internet Explorer version 5.0 (or later), display the view with the ?ReadViewEntries URL. Create additional fields or vary the field types in the form and repeat your experiment. How does the generated XML vary?

6. Enhance the database created in question 5 by adding some response forms and making a hierarchical view. Can you generate XML files with some of the additional viewentry attributes? Do these attributes contain the content you expect? Why or why not?

7. Create a DTD for the XML files you made in question 1.

8. Consider one of your business applications. It could be an inventory, financial, sales, or any other application. Assuming you could handle security issues, is there some subset of the information in this application that might be useful to your customers? Is there some subset of this information that you are now transmitting to vendors, suppliers, or customers on paper that could save you money if automated? Take a small piece of the application and create a sample XML file containing information you would like to transfer. Create a DTD for the file when you are finished. Could you easily use XML for this purpose? Why or why not?

UNDERSTANDING THE EXTENSIBLE STYLESHEET LANGUAGE (XSL)

In this chapter

WHAT IS XSL?

The Extensible Stylesheet Language (XSL) is an XML-based language that can be used to transform and format XML documents. The transformation of XML documents means that XSL can be used to describe the transformation of one XML document into another XML document, an HTML document, or some other type of document. When you use XSL formatting, you use the XSL syntax to describe characteristics such as pages, paragraphs, borders, and other kinds of document formatting characteristics. The standards for XSL formatting are not as mature as for transformations; as of this writing they are still at the Working Draft level and have not yet reached the Recommendation level. Therefore, XSL formatting will not be covered in this book.

This chapter describes the November 16, 1999 version of the XSL Transformations (XSLT) 1.0 document. As of that date, XSLT 1.0 is a World Wide Web Consortium (W3C) Recommendation and as a result, it is relatively stable and suitable for implementation.

WHAT CAN YOU DO WITH XSLT?

As mentioned, XSLT is a language for describing transformations of XML documents. The most typical transformations are from XML to XML, XML to HTML, and XML to text files. XSLT can be used for all these purposes. In addition, XSLT can be used on either the client or the server.

Note

Converting one XML document to another XML document occurs when you have data stored in one dialect of XML and you want to convert it to another dialect. This can occur, for example, when you want to transmit data from one application to another or from your system to a business partner.

On the server, it would be typical to transform an XML document using XSLT to HTML. Then any Web server, including Domino, could be used to serve the resulting HTML to the Web browser. The browser doesn't really even need to be aware that XML was involved in the generation of the HTML.

When used on the client, an XML- and XSLT-enabled browser must be used. Microsoft Internet Explorer 5 is the only browser at the time of this writing that provides this XML and XSLT support. When used at the client, an XML document and an XSLT transform document are both served to the browser. The browser then performs the transformation at the client and displays the transformed document. Microsoft implemented IE5 before the standardization of XSLT, so its version of XSLT is slightly different from the November 16, 1999 Recommendation. You should carefully test your implementation if you will be using client-side XSL.

XALAN, XERCES, AND THE APACHE XML PROJECT

The Apache Software Foundation is a non-profit group that provides organizational, legal, and financial support for open-source projects. It originated from the Apache Web server open-source group. It has now expanded and has several other projects, including the Apache XML project.

The Apache XML project has several subprojects, including two that are important to readers of this book. The Xalan project consists of open-source versions of XSLT processors in both Java and C++. The Java version is based on the LotusXSL processor developed by Lotus, which has contributed the source code to the Apache XML project. The LotusXSL processor (and, therefore, the Xalan processor) is a transformation engine based on the W3C specifications. It will accept as input an XML document and an XSLT document that specifies the transformation, and will produce as output an XML or HTML document.

Because the source code came from Lotus, it has been fairly easy for Lotus to integrate the Xalan package into Notes and Domino. Starting with release 5.0.3, the `transformXML` method has been included on the `EmbeddedObject`, `Item`, and `MIMEEntity` Java classes. Note that the `transformXML` method is available only in Java, not LotusScript. The `transformXML` method calls Xalan. In the implementation, you can sometimes see references to Xalan and other times to LotusXSL, but they refer to the same code.

Xerces is the Apache XML project for XML parsers. IBM donated the XML4J source code to the Apache Xerces project. The C++ version originated from IBM's XML4C code. Again, because the original source code came from IBM, Lotus has integrated the code directly into Domino. The `parseXML` method calls Xerces. In addition, the Xalan package also uses the Xerces code to read and parse the XML before and during transformation.

Note	You might be wondering about the names Xalan and Xerces. I suppose the first criterion for the names was that they begin with X. This quickly narrows the choices. Xalan is the name of a rare musical instrument and Xerces was named after the Xerces blue butterfly.

XSL TRANSFORMATIONS

The main purpose of XSLT is the transformation of XML documents, so let's now take a look at how the transformation takes place. As I've mentioned, transformations take a source XML document and use an XSL document to control the transformation. As a simple example, consider the following XML document:

```
<?xml version="1.0" ?>
<doc title="Hello World Example">
Hello there, World
</doc>
```

This XML document has only a single element, the <doc> element. Here is an XSL stylesheet that we can apply to the XML source document:

```
<?xml version="1.0"?>
<xsl:stylesheet xmlns:xsl="http://www.w3.org/1999/XSL/Transform" version="1.0">
  <xsl:output method="html" indent="yes"/>

  <xsl:template match="/">
    <xsl:apply-templates/>
  </xsl:template>

  <xsl:template match="doc">
    <html>
      <head><title><xsl:value-of select="@title"/></title></head>
      <body bgcolor="#ffffff" text="#000000">
        <h2 align="center"><xsl:value-of select="@title"/></h2>
        <xsl:apply-templates/>
      </body>
    </html>
  </xsl:template>

</xsl:stylesheet>
```

XSL has a reputation, probably somewhat justly deserved, that it is complicated. As you can tell, the XSL document is four times as long as the document that it is transforming. After you break down the XSL file into component pieces, however, it is relatively straightforward.

The XSL stylesheet begins with the XML declaration, just like any XML file. Following the header is the first XSL element, <xsl:stylesheet>. Notice that a colon follows a prefix of xsl. This convention is called a namespace, and XSL uses a separate namespace so that its commands can be separated from any output that might be generated. Namespaces are described in detail on the Web at http://www.w3.org/TR/REC-xml-names/.

The xmlns:xsl attribute is used to specify the version of the XSL transform specification that should be used. In this case, we are using version 1.0.

The <xsl:output> element is used to indicate that the output will be HTML. Note that as of this writing, Microsoft Internet Explorer 5 does not support this element. This is not a problem, however, because Internet Explorer can still convert XML to HTML without the element.

The definitions for two template rules are next defined in the XSL file. Template rules are a key to the transformation of XML documents because they specify how the transformation should take place.

TEMPLATE RULES

Several template rules can exist within a stylesheet, as we have seen. Each template rule normally contains a match attribute. The match attribute is used to define the context in which the template rule applies. That is, template rules apply only in certain contexts, and the match attribute informs the XSL process when the particular template rule is appropriate.

Conceptually, when processing an XML document, it is first read and parsed into memory. The resulting parsed document is specified as a tree. The XSL stylesheet instructions are then processed, with the XML tree as input. The result of processing the XML input and the XSL instructions is another tree, which can then be output in a variety of formats. Because you control the output format, in addition to XML or HTML, you can write the output in any format you desire.

The `match` attribute of a template rule specifies which nodes of the input XML tree apply to the template rule. If the template rule applies to a particular node, the instructions within the template rule are used to construct the output.

The parsed XML tree contains both a root node and a root element. The root node is considered the top of the tree. The only content of the root node is a single child, which is the root element of the XML tree. The root element contains all the other elements in the tree. In our XML example, the `<doc>` element is the root element. Thus, the parent of the `<doc>` element is the tree's root node.

Let's consider the first template in the XSL stylesheet:

```
<xsl:template match="/">
  <xsl:apply-templates/>
</xsl:template>
```

The `match` attribute with a single slash matches the root node (not root element) of the XML tree. Because it matches this root node, the XSL processor automatically processes it. It is analogous to the `main` program in Java.

At any point in the processing, one node of the input tree is considered to be the current node. When processing starts, the current node is the root node. The template that best matches the current node is selected and processed. Processing typically involves recursively matching and processing subsidiary nodes of the current node.

Let's return to our example. Because the single slash matches the root node, the template is selected and processed. The `<xsl:apply-templates/>` element is then processed. This instruction tells the XSL processor to recursively process any of the children of the current node.

The root node has just one child, which in this example is the `<doc>` element node. The XSL processor will look for any templates that match the `<doc>` element. Amazingly, there is one:

```
<xsl:template match="doc">
  <html>
    <head><title><xsl:value-of select="@title"/></title></head>
    <body bgcolor="#ffffff" text="#000000">
      <h2 align="center"><xsl:value-of select="@title"/></h2>
      <xsl:apply-templates/>
    </body>
  </html>
</xsl:template>
```

In this template, you can see that the `match` attribute indicates that the template rule applies when the node is a `<doc>` element. Following the beginning tag, you can see a set of HTML tags. These tags are sent directly to the output without modification.

Within the `<title>` tags, you see the expression

```
<xsl:value-of select="@title"/>
```

The `<xsl:value-of>` element is used to obtain the value of the expression specified in the `select` attribute. An `@` symbol is used to indicate that the name refers to an attribute name, not a tag name. In this case, because the current node is the `<doc>` node, the `@title` refers to the `title` attribute of the `<doc>` tag. Here is the corresponding line in the source XML file:

```
<doc title="Hello World Example">
```

Combining this source with the XSL line

```
<head><title><xsl:value-of select="@title"/></title></head>
```

produces the following output line:

```
<head><title>Hello World Example</title></head>
```

The `<h2>` tag is handled similarly. Following the `<h2>` tag, you see that we are to recursively handle all children of the `<doc>` element because an `<xsl:apply-templates/>` element exists. As mentioned, this element means that we should form a list of all children of the current node and recursively process each element of the list. In this particular example, no other tags exist, but some static text is within the `<doc>` tags. This text will be sent to the output stream.

Here is the HTML that results from processing the input XML file with the XSL file:

```
<html>
<head>
<title>Hello World Example</title>
</head>
<body text="#000000" bgcolor="#ffffff">
<h2 align="center">Hello World Example</h2>
Hello there, World
</body>
</html>
```

Note that because of the parsing of the original input and the processing of trees, the output nodes and line breaks can appear differently from the input. For example, notice that a line break is after the `<head>` tag. Also notice that the `text` and `bgcolor` attributes are reversed. These minor changes do not alter the meaning of the HTML output, however.

PATTERN MATCHING

Patterns are very important to transformations because patterns are used to search for a particular context. They are used in `select` attributes and `match` attributes. We have seen the use of the `/` pattern, which matches the root node (not the root element). I have also shown you the pattern `@title`, which matches the `title` attribute on the current node.

You can specify a constant such as doc within the match attribute, as in

```
<xsl:template match="doc">
```

This pattern will match a doc element in the source tree. A node with a specific parent can be specified, as in noteinfo/created. This string means to look for a created element that is found within a noteinfo element. If you want to specify that noteinfo can be any ancestor, you use the syntax noteinfo//created.

Here is an example:

```
<xsl:template match="noteinfo/created">
     <tr><td>Document created</td><td><xsl:value-of select="." /></td></tr>
</xsl:template>
```

This code fragment will match the following fragment:

```
<noteinfo>
   <created> 991105 </created>
</noteinfo>
```

The value of the `<xsl:value-of>` element will be the date that is found within the `<created>` element.

If you append square brackets onto a pattern, it adds a condition. For example, item[@name="form"] matches an item element with a name attribute of form. For example, the pattern would match the following:

```
<item name='form'><text>Memo</text></item>
```

If you use a numeric value within the brackets, it specifies a child number, starting from 1. For example, item[2] means the second item element.

The asterisk * is used to indicate all elements. So you can specify textlist/* to match all immediate children of a textlist element. The pattern textlist//* would indicate all descendents of the textlist element.

The period is used to indicate the current node. Review the following expression:

```
<xsl:value-of select="."/>
```

This expression is used to obtain the value of the current node.

Several built-in functions are useful in patterns:

- position()—Returns the current node's position relative to its parent. For example, if a node is the first child of its parent, position() will return 1.
- text()—Matches any text node.
- processing-instruction()—Matches any processing instruction.
- last()—Returns the position of the last node of a group.

This list of expressions is actually part of the XPath language, which is designed to address parts of an XML document. The language is very rich and includes the capability to manipulate strings, use numbers and Booleans, and refer to sets of nodes. The XPath language version 1.0 is a W3C Recommendation as of November 16, 1999. Refer to `http://www.w3.org/TR/xpath` for the XPath specification.

DOMINO EXTENSIBLE LANGUAGE (DXL)

New with release 5.0.3 of Domino is the capability to generate DXL, which is an XML-based language defined by Lotus for describing elements of a Domino database. The implementation as of 5.0.3 is a subset of the capabilities of Domino, but the language will be extended over time. In 5.0.2, the `?ReadViewEntries` URL command was introduced. This was the first exposure of DXL. In 5.0.3, documents and items can be obtained in XML format.

The data types supported in 5.0.3 DXL are text, datetime values, and numbers as well as lists of each of these types. You can obtain the XML for a document by using the `generateXML` method of the `Document` class. Note that the `generateXML` method is available only in Java, not LotusScript. Assuming that `doc` is a `Document` object, you can easily generate the DXL for the document:

```
String sDXL = doc.generateXML();
```

The generated XML will be stored in the string variable. Here is some sample output from this method:

```
<document form='local'>
<noteinfo noteid='8F6' unid='9D13E3F0DCD373D485256282000CD1BF'>
 <created><datetime>19951127T212001,27-05</datetime></created>
 <modified><datetime dst='true'>19990623T133106,15-07</datetime></modified>
</noteinfo>
<item name='PriorityFlag'><text>0</text></item>
<item name='country'><text/></item>
<item name='RLANTag'><text/></item>
<item name='Cost'><number>5</number></item>
<item name='PortName'><text>TCPIP</text></item>
<item name='PhoneNumber'><text>home.notes.net</text></item>
<item name='$UpdatedBy' names='true'>
 <textlist><text>CN=Rob Slapikoff/O=Iris</text></textlist>
</item>
<item name='$Revisions'>
 <datetimelist><datetime>19951127T212121,38-05</datetime></datetimelist>
</item>
</document>
```

A DXL `<document>` element contains a `<noteinfo>` element and a series of `<item>` elements, one for each item stored in the document. The `noteid` and the universal ID (`unid`) are attributes of the `<noteinfo>` element.

The <document> element can have four optional attributes. The attributes for the <document> element are

- parent—The unid of the parent document if the current document is a response or conflict document.
- response—True if the current document is a response document. The default is false.
- form—The name of the form for the document.
- conflict—True if the current document is a save conflict or a replication conflict document. The default is false.

The <noteinfo> element contains information about the creation datetime as well as the datetime of the last modification to the document.

Items within the document are defined by <item> elements. Rich text items are not supported as of release 5.0.3. In addition to the name attribute, three additional attributes exist. Each of these attributes defaults to false. The attributes are as follows:

- authors—This is true if the item is an Authors item.
- names—This is true if the item is a Names item.
- readers—This is true if the item is a Readers item.

See the $UpdatedBy item in the sample DXL output for an example of a names item.

DISPLAYING DOCUMENT ITEMS

As an exercise in using XSL, I'll show you an example that takes Domino DXL and formats it into displayable HTML. The XSL file that does the transformation converts the DXL into an HTML table of two columns. The left column is the item name and the right column is the value. The first three rows represent document information and the rest of the table contains the items. The items within the table are sorted in ascending order based on the item name. Listing 23.1 is the Items.xsl document that is used for the transformation.

LISTING 23.1 THE Items.xsl DOCUMENT

```
<?xml version="1.0"?>
<xsl:stylesheet xmlns:xsl="http://www.w3.org/1999/XSL/Transform" version="1.0">
  <xsl:output method="html" indent="yes"/>

  <xsl:template match="/">
    <xsl:apply-templates/>
  </xsl:template>

  <xsl:template match="document">
    <html>
      <head><title>UNID:<xsl:value-of select="noteinfo/@unid"/></title></head>
```

continues

LISTING 23.1 CONTINUED

```
        <body bgcolor="#ffffff" text="#000000">
        <center><h2>Document Items</h2></center>
        <table bgcolor="#c0c0c0">                  <!-- Begin HTML table -->
          <xsl:apply-templates select="noteinfo"/>
          <!-- select all item elements -->
          <xsl:apply-templates select="item" >
              <xsl:sort select="@name" /> <!-- sort based on name attribute -->
          </xsl:apply-templates>                    <!-- end of sorted grouping -->
        </table>                                     <!-- End HTML table -->
        </body>
    </html>
  </xsl:template>

  <!-- Information at the document level -->
  <xsl:template match="noteinfo">
    <tr><td>UNID</td><td><xsl:value-of select="@unid"/></td></tr>
    <xsl:apply-templates/>    <!-- noteinfo/created and noteinfo/modified -->
  </xsl:template>

  <xsl:template match="noteinfo/created">
     <tr><td>Document created</td><td><xsl:value-of select="." /></td></tr>
  </xsl:template>

  <xsl:template match="noteinfo/modified">
     <tr><td>Last Modified</td><td><xsl:value-of select="." /></td></tr>
  </xsl:template>

 <!-- Information for each item -->
 <xsl:template match="item">
    <tr><td><xsl:value-of select="@name"/></td>   <!-- The item's name  -->
        <td><xsl:apply-templates/></td>           <!-- the item's value -->
    </tr>
  </xsl:template>

</xsl:stylesheet>
```

Don't be intimidated by the relative complexity of this XSL document; I'll explain all its parts. However, before I explain how this XSL document works, let me first show you some sample output that was produced by this stylesheet. See Figure 23.1 for an example. The XML input data for this document is from my personal address book and is similar to the sample XML data found in the section "Domino Extensible Language (DXL)," earlier in this chapter. The XML data represents a record for the home.notes.net connection from my personal address book.

In Figure 23.1 you can see the table on the left as formatted by the browser as well as the actual HTML code on the right. This HTML code was generated on the Domino server using the release 5.0.3 transformXML method of the Item class. This method takes an XML document and an XSL document, transforms the XML document, and produces a result. Here are the first few lines of the XML input file:

```
<document form='local'>
<noteinfo noteid='8F6' unid='9D13E3F0DCD373D485256282000CD1BF'>
```

```
<created><datetime>19951127T212001,27-05</datetime></created>
<modified><datetime dst='true'>19990623T133106,15-07</datetime></modified>
</noteinfo>
```

Figure 23.1
XSL was used to convert a DXL document to HTML.

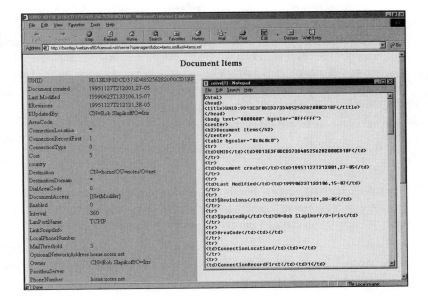

As in our first XSL example, the first template rule matches the root node because it contains a forward slash. This template causes the <document> element template rule to be invoked using the <xsl:apply-templates/> element. A pattern match will then be found for the <document> element and the second template rule processes a document element.

In the XSL file you can see that the second template rule begins processing with the <html> tag. The <xsl:value-of> tag found in the title has an interesting select attribute. The attribute is specified as noteinfo/@unid. The line in the XSL file is as follows:

```
<head><title>UNID:<xsl:value-of select="noteinfo/@unid"/></title></head>
```

At the point this element is processed, the current node is the <document> element. Thus, the select clause refers to children of the <document> element. In this case, the noteinfo child element is selected, and then its unid attribute's value is used. The attribute is indicated because of the @. If you look carefully at Figure 23.1, you can see that the title line contains the string UNID and a long hexadecimal string. The HTML output produced is the following:

```
<head><title>UNID:9D13E3F0DCD373D485256282000CD1BF</title></head>
```

The next few lines are regular HTML, and they begin the body of the document, define an h2 header, and begin the table of document items. The following line means that the XSL processor should select all noteinfo elements and apply the associated templates:

```
<xsl:apply-templates select="noteinfo"/>
```

When this occurs, the following template rule is invoked:

```
<xsl:template match="noteinfo">
  <tr><td>UNID</td><td><xsl:value-of select="@unid"/></td></tr>
  <xsl:apply-templates/>    <!-- noteinfo/created and noteinfo/modified -->
</xsl:template>
```

This rule will output some HTML table tags and then select the unid attribute of the current node. In the context of this template, the current node is the noteinfo node. Notice that because this template's current node is the noteinfo node, the select clause is different from that found in the document node even though both expressions refer to the same attribute. The following is the expression from the document node:

```
<xsl:value-of select="noteinfo/@unid"/>
```

The following is the expression as found in the noteinfo node:

```
<xsl:value-of select="@unid"/>
```

The difference between the two is the context of the template rule. When the context is the document node, you must specify both the child node and its attribute, but within the noteinfo node, you can just specify the attribute's name.

Following the unid row, an `<xsl:apply-templates/>` instruction is encountered. This will cause a search for any templates that match children of the noteinfo element.

Here is the XML that is currently being scanned:

```
<noteinfo noteid='8F6' unid='9D13E3F0DCD373D485256282000CD1BF'>
  <created><datetime>19951127T212001,27-05</datetime></created>
  <modified><datetime dst='true'>19990623T133106,15-07</datetime></modified>
</noteinfo>
```

Note that two children are in the noteinfo element. They are the `<created>` element and the `<modified>` element. The `<created>` element will match the following template rule:

```
<xsl:template match="noteinfo/created">
  <tr><td>Document created</td><td><xsl:value-of select="." /></td></tr>
</xsl:template>
```

This template rule will output another row of the table with some static text as well as the value of the datetime value representing the document's creation. Refer to Figure 23.1 to see the second row for an example of this output.

After the `<created>` element is processed, the `<modified>` element is processed. This element will match the following template rule:

```
<xsl:template match="noteinfo/modified">
  <tr><td>Last Modified</td><td><xsl:value-of select="." /></td></tr>
</xsl:template>
```

This rule operates in the same manner as the `<created>` template. The output from this rule can be seen in the third line of the table in Figure 23.1.

At this point the `noteinfo` element has been completely processed. Control returns to the `<document>` template rule. The next few statements in this rule are

```
<!-- select all item elements -->
<xsl:apply-templates select="item" >
    <xsl:sort select="@name" /> <!-- sort based on name attribute -->
</xsl:apply-templates>                 <!-- end of sorted grouping -->
```

These three statements will handle all the `item` elements in the XML file. The instructions cause the selection of all `item` elements, sorting them by the attribute called `name`, and individually applying any template rules that correspond to the `item` element. If you refer to Figure 23.1, you'll see that after the first three lines (that are generated by the `noteinfo` processing) all the items are sorted by item name.

This brings us to the processing of each individual item. Items are handled by the following template rule:

```
<!-- Information for each item -->
<xsl:template match="item">
    <tr><td><xsl:value-of select="@name"/></td>  <!-- The item's name  -->
        <td><xsl:apply-templates/></td>          <!-- the item's value -->
    </tr>
</xsl:template>
```

For each item, we select the item's `name` attribute to place in the first column. The item's value is handled by the `<xsl:apply-templates/>` instruction. The default for any element that does not match a template rule is to just pass its text data to the output. In this case, the values will be displayed in the second column of the table.

That's it. We've made it through the XSL file. As you have seen in this example, template rules are the heart of the transformation. Each template rule matches a small section of the source tree. The processing starts at the top of the XML tree, finds matching patterns, sequentially and recursively processes template rules, and builds the resulting output tree.

OTHER XSL ELEMENTS

In addition to the XSL elements that I've already described, you can use several other important XSL elements to control the transformation of the source to the desired output. You can create dynamic elements and attributes with the `<xsl:element>` and `<xsl:attribute>` elements.

CREATING DYNAMIC ELEMENTS

The `<xsl:element>` element is used to create dynamic elements. As a simple example, consider the following XSL code:

```
<xsl:element name="qqq">
value
</xsl:element>
```

This code produces the following output:

```
<qqq>
value
</qqq>
```

Of course, this is not particularly interesting because you could have generated this manually. For a more interesting example, suppose you have the following XML file:

```
<?xml version='1.0'?>
<doc tag="test">
doc content
</doc>
```

Associated with the XML file is the following XSL file fragment:

```
<xsl:template match="doc">
 <xsl:element name="{@tag}">
  <xsl:value-of select="." />
 </xsl:element>
</xsl:template>
```

The resulting output of these statements is the following:

```
<test>
doc content
</test>
```

This example is much more interesting because the actual element called <test> is dynamically generated from the tag attribute of the <doc> element in the original source XML file.

The new concept here is that we are using braces (curly brackets) around the @tag attribute to indicate that the tag attribute's value should be used rather than the literal string within the quotes.

CREATING DYNAMIC ATTRIBUTES

In addition to creating dynamic elements, you can assign dynamic attributes to element tags with the <xsl:attribute> element. Here is a simple example. Suppose you have the following XSL stylesheet fragment:

```
<xsl:template match="doc">
<A>
<xsl:attribute name="HREF">http://www.lotus.com</xsl:attribute>
Go to Lotusland
</A>
</xsl:template>
```

Here is the resulting output:

```
<A HREF="http://www.lotus.com">
Go to Lotusland
</A>
```

The `<xsl:attribute>` element creates an attribute on the most recent start tag element. It will work only if no output has been generated for the tag yet. For example, suppose the input was the following:

```
<xsl:template match="doc">
<A>
Go to Lotusland
<xsl:attribute name="HREF">http://www.lotus.com</xsl:attribute>
</A>
</xsl:template>
```

In this case the output would be

```
<A>
Go to Lotusland
</A>
```

The attribute is not applied because text has already been generated for the element. Let's now look at a more interesting dynamic example. Consider the following XML input file:

```
<?xml version='1.0'?>
<doc>
<link html="A">
<url>http://www.lotus.com</url>
<text>Go to Lotus</text>
</link>
</doc>
```

Here is the associated XSL stylesheet fragment:

```
<xsl:template match="link">
<xsl:element name="{@html}">
 <xsl:attribute name="HREF">
   <xsl:value-of select="url"/>
 </xsl:attribute>
 <xsl:value-of select="text" />
</xsl:element>
</xsl:template>
```

Finally, here is the resulting output:

```
<A HREF="http://www.lotus.com">Go to Lotus</A>
```

In this example, the element name `<A>` is generated as the content of the HTML attribute of the `<link>` tag. The HREF attribute is generated with a fixed name. The content of the HREF attribute is specified by the `<url>` element of the XML input. The `<text>` element of the input is used to generate the contents within the `<A>` element.

CREATING COMMENTS

You can create comments with the `<xsl:comment>` element. Here is a simple example:

```
<xsl:template match="/">
<xsl:comment>This is a test version. Be careful!</xsl:comment>
</xsl:template>
```

This template generates the following output:

```
<!--This is a test version. Be careful!-->
```

REPETITION

You can use the `<xsl:for-each>` element to repeatedly process a group of nodes. You use the `select` attribute of the element to specify the group of nodes to be processed. Here is an example:

```
<xsl:template match="document">
  <table>
  <xsl:for-each select="item">
  <tr><td><xsl:value-of select="@name"/></td>
     <td><xsl:apply-templates/></td>
  </tr>
  </xsl:for-each>
  </table>
</xsl:template>
```

This example will create a row for each item within a table. Each row has two columns; the first contains the name and the second column contains the value.

CONDITIONAL PROCESSING

The `<xsl:if>` element is used to conditionally process the content of the element. You use the `test` attribute to supply the conditional expression. Here is an example that inserts colons between the members of a `textlist`:

```
<xsl:template match="textlist">
 <xsl:for-each select="text">
    <xsl:apply-templates/>
    <xsl:if test="not(position()=last())">: </xsl:if>
 </xsl:for-each>
</xsl:template>
```

In addition to the `<xsl:if>` element, a `<xsl:choose>` element exists, which is similar to a Java `switch` statement. Three related elements also exist: `<xsl:choose>`, `<xsl:when>`, and `<xsl:otherwise>`. Here is the syntax for these statements:

```
<xsl:choose>

  <xsl:when test="expression1">
    <!-- First case -->
  </xsl:when>
  <xsl:when test="expression2">
    <!-- Second case -->
  </xsl:when>
  <xsl:when test="expression3">
    <!-- Third case -->
  </xsl:when>
  <xsl:otherwise>
    <!-- Otherwise case -->
  </xsl:otherwise>

</xsl:choose>
```

XSL ELEMENT SUMMARY

Additional elements are contained in the XSLT language. I have tried to describe the important elements and give you examples so you can get started with XSL. The definitive reference for the XSLT language can be found on the Web at http://www.w3.org/TR/xslt.

Now I'll explain how we can use Domino's transformXML method to convert the XML to HTML using XSLT and send it to Web browsers.

INTEGRATING XSL WITH DOMINO

Release 5.0.3 provides an important new method called transformXML. This method is available on the EmbeddedObject, Item, and MIMEEntity Java classes. These methods are not available in LotusScript. It is also available on the RichTextItem class because it inherits the method from the Item class.

To illustrate the use of the transformXML method, I'm going to create a Domino database called TransXSL.nsf. In this database I'll create a form for entering XML, XSL, and HTML code as well as a view and an agent. In Figure 23.2 you can see the XMLSource form.

PART

V

CH

23

Figure 23.2
The XMLSource form can be used for XML, XSL, or HTML.

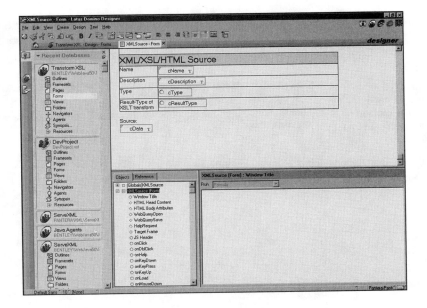

The cName field is used to hold the name of the document, and cDescription can be used for a description. The cType and cResultType fields hold a code of X for XML, S for XSL, or H for HTML. Finally, the cData field is used to hold the source for the document. Figure 23.3 shows you the Items.xsl document that was shown previously in Listing 23.1.

Figure 23.3
The Items.xsl document is used to format DXL items.

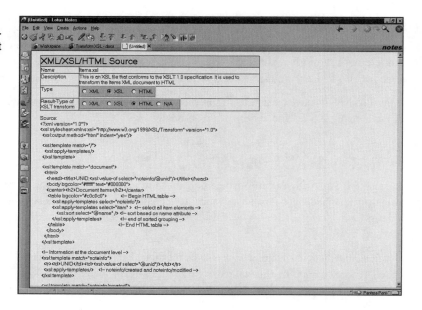

The database also contains a view called the docs view. This view shows the name and description for each XMLSource document of the database. This view is sorted by name so that it can be used for lookups in the Java agent. You can see the view in Figure 23.4.

Figure 23.4
The docs view is sorted by name so that it can be used for lookups.

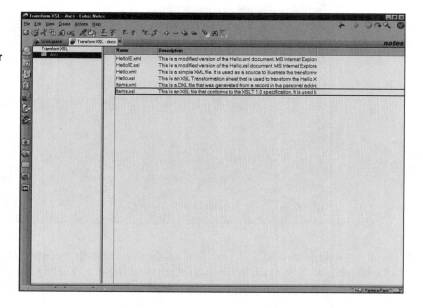

Now that you have seen the form and view used for this database, I'll show you the Java agent that is used to serve XML, XSL, and HTML documents. The reason a Java agent is required is that when serving XML documents, the proper MIME type must be used. Domino automatically uses the MIME type of `text/html`. This is an appropriate default for HTML pages, but it will not work for XML pages. To set the MIME type, we use a Java agent, store the documents in a Domino database, and indicate the appropriate MIME type to use by using fields in the document. Listing 23.2 contains the `Serve.java` agent that is used to serve the documents from the database.

LISTING 23.2   THE `Serve.java` AGENT

```java
import lotus.domino.*;
import java.io.*;

public class JavaAgent extends AgentBase {

  public void NotesMain() {

    try {
      Session session = getSession();
      AgentContext agentContext = session.getAgentContext();
      Database db = agentContext.getCurrentDatabase();
      View view=db.getView("docs");    // Get the view object

      // Parse the URL arguments
      AgentParameters pt = new AgentParameters();
      pt.parseParameters(session);
      PrintWriter out = getAgentOutput();          // web server output

      // Obtain the doc and xsl URL parameters
      String docName = pt.getString("doc");    // Looking for doc=name
      String docXslName = pt.getString("xsl");  // Looking for xsl=name
      Document doc = null;
      Document docXsl = null;

      // See if we got a doc parameter.
      if (null == docName || docName.equals("")) {
        // Document name not specified, get first document of view
        doc = view.getFirstDocument();
        docName = doc.getItemValueString("cName"); // Get this doc's name
      }
      else {
        doc = view.getDocumentByKey(docName);
      }

      // Assume we will convert the XML
      boolean bDoConvert = true;
      if (null == docXslName || docXslName.equals("")) {
        // output XML for transformation at client.
        bDoConvert = false;
      }
      else {
```

continues

LISTING 23.2 CONTINUED

```
                    // We have an XSL document
                    docXsl = view.getDocumentByKey(docXslName);
                }

            String sType = null;
            if (bDoConvert )  {
                // We're converting the source document
                Item iXml = doc.getFirstItem("cData");
                Item iXsl = docXsl.getFirstItem("cData");
                sType = docXsl.getItemValueString("cResultType");
                // Output the MIME type
                out.println(getMimeType(sType));
                out.println("");   // blank line to terminate header

                XSLTResultTarget outxsl = new XSLTResultTarget();

                outxsl.setCharacterStream(out);
                iXml.transformXML(iXsl, outxsl); // Transform the XML
            }
            else {
                sType = doc.getItemValueString("cType");
                // Just output the data natively
                out.println(getMimeType(sType));
                out.println("");   // blank line to terminate header
                out.println(doc.getItemValueString("cData"));
            }


        } catch(Exception e) {
            e.printStackTrace();
        }
    }

    // Convert the cType field to a Content type header
    public String getMimeType(String sType) {
        if (sType.equals("X")) {
            return("Content-Type: text/xml");
        }
        else {
            if (sType.equals("S")) {
                return("Content-Type: text/xsl");
            }
            else {
                if (sType.equals("H")) {
                    return("Content-Type: text/html");
                }
                // default if unknown
                return("Content-Type: text/xml");
            }
        }
    }
}
```

This agent uses the AgentParameters class that was described in Chapter 13, "Creating Java Agents with the Domino Designer IDE." The AgentParameters class parses parameters in the URL and makes them available using simple methods.

After initializing, obtaining the docs view object, and parsing the parameters, the agent obtains the PrintWriter object that will be used to send information back to the browser.

The URL can have two parameters, the doc parameter and the xsl parameter. The doc parameter specifies the main document to be served. The xsl parameter, if present, means that the document should be processed with the transformXML method before being returned to the browser. Here is a sample URL that contains both the doc and xsl parameters:

```
http://<server>/TransXsl.nsf/Serve?OpenAgent&doc=Items.xml&xsl=Items.xsl
```

If the doc parameter is specified, the document is obtained from the view. The program does not handle the case when the document is not found in the view. This is left as an exercise for the reader.

If an xsl parameter is found, the bDoConvert flag is set and used to determine whether transformation processing should be done. The MIME type is determined from the cResultType field. The getMimeType method will convert the single character to a string that can be used as an HTTP header. For most conversions, the XML will be converted to HTML and the resulting MIME type will be HTML.

The following three lines actually do the transform:

```
XSLTResultTarget outxsl = new XSLTResultTarget();
outxsl.setCharacterStream(out);
iXml.transformXML(iXsl, outxsl); // Transform the XML
```

The Item object iXml contains the XML source document. The Item object iXsl contains the XSL transformation document, and the outxsl object contains the output specification. The outxsl object is of the class org.apache.xalan.xslt.XSLTResultTarget. Because an implicit import exists for this package, it is abbreviated XSLTResultTarget. In this example, I have specified that the output for the XSL transformation should be sent directly to the output stream that will go back to the browser. Other alternatives exist for handling the output as I describe in the next section.

XSLTResultTarget

The XSLTResultTarget class is contained in the org.apache.xalan.xslt package. This class is used to specify the output of the XSLT transformation. The output can be directed to a java.io.Writer, as shown in the previous example, or it can be sent to three other types of output destinations. The output destinations can be

- java.io.OutputStream—This is a stream of bytes.
- java.io.Writer—This is a stream of characters. Characters in Java are Unicode, so this is not equivalent to a stream of bytes.
- org.w3c.dom.Node—This is a node of a DOM tree.
- java.lang.String—This is the name of an output file in the file system.

You either can set the type of output in the constructor of the XSLTResultTarget or you can instantiate the object and change the output type with a method call.

Here are the constructors for the XSLTResultTarget class:

- XSLTResultTarget()—The default constructor
- XSLTResultTarget(java.io.OutputStream byteStream)
- XSLTResultTarget(java.io.Writer charStream)
- XSLTResultTarget(org.w3c.dom.Node node)
- XSLTResultTarget(java.lang.String filename)

The property routines of the XSLTResultTarget class appear in the following section.

```
public java.io.OutputStream getByteStream()
```

```
public void setByteStream(java.io.OutputStream byteStream)
```
The getByteStream property routine returns the byte stream that was used in the constructor or the setByteStream routine. The getByteStream routine will return null if the output was not set to a byte stream. The setByteStream property routine sets the output to a byte stream.

```
public java.io.Writer getCharacterStream()
```

```
public void setCharacterStream(java.io.Writer characterStream)
```
The getCharacterStream property routine returns the character stream that was used in the constructor or the setCharacterStream routine. The getCharacterStream routine will return null if the output was not set to a character stream. The setCharacterStream property routine sets the output to a character stream.

```
public String getFileName()
```

```
public void setFileName(String filename)
```
The getFileName property routine returns the filename that was used in the constructor or the setFileName routine. The getFileName routine will return null if the output was not set

to a filename. The `setFileName` property routine sets the output to a file with the specified filename.

```
public org.w3c.dom.Node getNode()
```

```
public void setNode(org.w3c.dom.Node node)
```

The `getNode` property routine returns the node that was used in the constructor or the `setNode` routine. The `getNode` routine will return `null` if the output was not set to a node. The `setNode` property routine sets the output to a tree with the specified node as the root.

The following is an example of how you would output the transformed information to a file instead of an output stream:

```
XSLTResultTarget outxsl = new XSLTResultTarget();
outxsl.setFileName("c:\\temp\\myfile.html");
iXml.transformXML(iXsl, outxsl); // Transform the XML
```

USING XSL WITH INTERNET EXPLORER 5

Because Microsoft Internet Explorer 5 was released before the November 16, 1999 Recommendation for XSLT and XPath, its implementation varies slightly from the Recommendation. Microsoft has pledged to follow the standard, so by the time you read this, they might have a new browser that conforms to the Recommendation.

A few important differences exist between Microsoft's implementation of XSL and the Domino (LotusXSL and Xalan) implementation. This list is not meant to be exhaustive, so you might run into additional differences.

First, Internet Explorer uses a different version on its `<xsl:stylesheet>` element. Here is what you should use with Internet Explorer:

```
<xsl:stylesheet xmlns:xsl="http://www.w3.org/TR/WD-xsl"
                xmlns="http://www.w3.org/TR/REC-html40" version="1.0">
```

Note that the `WD-xsl` means Working Draft for xsl.

The Internet Explorer version of XSL does not handle built-in template rules. Two important built-in rules as follows:

```
<!-- Built-in Template Rules -->
  <xsl:template match="text()">
    <xsl:value-of select="."/>
  </xsl:template>

  <xsl:template match="*">
    <xsl:apply-templates/>
  </xsl:template>
<!-- End Built-in Template Rules -->
```

If you place these template rules at the beginning of your own XSL document, you can make Internet Explorer behave closer to the standard operation. Note that template rules at the end of an XSL document override template rules toward the beginning. For this reason, you want to place these rules at the very beginning so they act as default rules. Any of your own rules that follow will take precedence over these defaults.

Finally, you can place the following processing instruction in your XML file:

```
<?xml-stylesheet type="text/xsl" href="yourfile.xsl"?>
```

When you add this processing instruction to your XML file, it informs Internet Explorer of the location of your XSL file and tells it to process the XML file before display. As of this writing, I have been unable to get Internet Explorer to work with a Domino agent specification in the href field. This might be because of the requirement for question marks and ampersands in the URL. Also it might be caused by security concerns. Internet Explorer might be restricting the XSL file to be on the same server and within the same relative directory as the original XML file.

In any case, Internet Explorer does seem to process the XML and XSL files when both are stored locally on your disk. You can test this by creating some small XML and XSL files locally and using Internet Explorer to display them.

CHAPTER REVIEW

1. What is the difference between the root node and the root element of an XML tree? Which is the "real" root of the tree?

2. What exactly is the purpose of an XSL template rule? What causes a template rule to be invoked? What pattern matches the root node?

3. Write an expression to extract the value of the noteid attribute of the current node.

4. Why does XSLT use a namespace? For extra credit, explore and read about namespaces on the Web and write about what you find.

5. What is the XPath language? For extra credit, explore and read about XPath on the Web and write about what you find.

6. Does the order of the template rules make a difference? If so, which rules take precedence?

7. In Listing 23.2, the Serve.java agent does not handle the case when a document or XSL document is specified incorrectly. Add error-handling code to check for this case and prepare a message for the user. Use a Java Exception to implement this feature.

8. Create an XML file and an XSL stylesheet. Use the XSL file to transform the XML to HTML and display the result with Microsoft Internet Explorer. You can use the local file system and any text editor.

9. Write a Java program that will read your Domino Directory (the public name and address book), create a list of users in XML, and then process the list with an XSL document. Use XSL to sort the names in order by last name. Display the result in HTML to a browser.

CHAPTER 24

SERVING XML FROM DOMINO

In this chapter

USING PAGES, FORMS, AND VIEWS TO SERVE XML

Probably one of the easiest ways to get started serving XML from Domino is to use its built-in capabilities of pages, forms, and views. By enabling the Treat Content as HTML Option for pages, forms, and views, you can serve XML from Domino. The HTML option essentially tells Domino not to add its standard HTML element tags around the content. Even though you are generating XML instead of HTML, the option still works fine. By using this option, you can generate your own XML in forms, pages, and views. Let's look at some examples to see how this is done.

USING PAGES FOR XML

If you would like to follow along, you can create a new Domino database or use an existing database. For my example, I created a database called ServeXML.nsf. If you want to follow along, you can create a database with this same name.

In Figure 24.1, I have created a page in the Domino designer that represents an employee record. You can see this page in the background. In the foreground you can see the Microsoft Internet Explorer browser and its display of this XML.

> **Note**
>
> Your version of Internet Explorer might not display the XML properly because Domino serves this page with an HTTP header MIME type of text/html rather than text/xml. Some older versions of Internet Explorer version 5 do not check the contents of the data, only the MIME type. Newer versions check the first line to see if it begins with <?xml. If so, it displays the page using XML formatting rather than HTML formatting. In the section "Using Domino Agents to Serve XML," I show you how you can set the MIME type to overcome this problem.
>
> In addition, versions of the Domino server up to and including R5.0.2c will report error messages if you attempt to export XML text in this way. You must upgrade the Domino Server to R5.0.3 to obtain this functionality.

On the left side of the page, you can see the Page properties box. In the Web Access section, you enable the Treat Page Contents as HTML property. This enables the page contents to flow through to the browser without additional HTML tags added by Domino. In Internet Explorer 5, the XML tags are displayed using different colors for different parts of the XML file. The default XSL Stylesheet in Internet Explorer 5 determines the appearance of the XML served by Domino.

Although this page illustrates how XML can be used on a page, it is not very practical because the information is hard coded on the page. For a more practical application, you can use Domino forms and documents to generate your XML.

USING FORMS FOR XML

To use a form with XML, you can create a field on a form in each location where you would like to substitute data values. See Figure 24.2 for an example of how you can convert a hard-coded page into a form that can be used with XML. I created a form called Employee to input and display fields with XML.

Figure 24.1
You can use Domino pages to serve static XML.

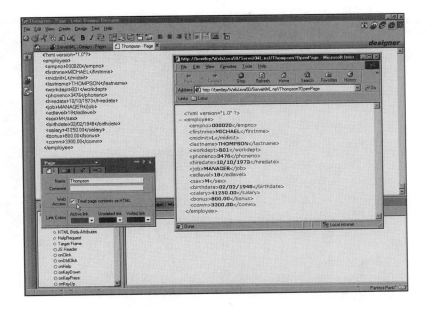

PART

V

CH

24

Figure 24.2
You can use Domino forms with documents to serve XML.

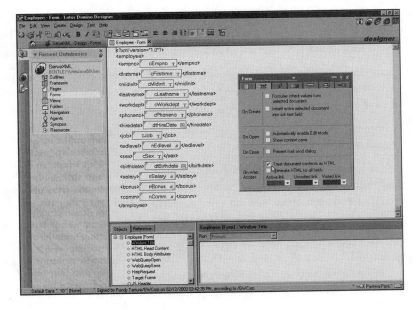

In Figure 24.2 also notice that I have enabled the form property Treat Document Contents as HTML in the On Web Access section of the Form properties box. This option is located on the Defaults tab (the second tab) in the Form properties box.

Figure 24.3 shows a view that I created called `Employees`. I added three documents to the database; two of the documents are displayed in Internet Explorer in separate windows.

Figure 24.3
By using a form, Domino documents can be displayed as XML.

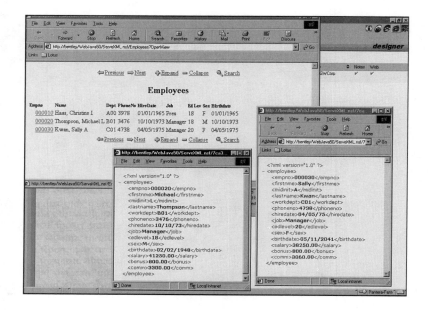

You can see that, by using a form, creating documents that display XML is easy. The main drawback of the approach shown so far is that for an end user, the input form is pretty ugly. A user should not have to deal with angle brackets.

Fortunately, we can solve the user interface situation and still take advantage of everything we've done so far. The method is to use two forms for the same document. One form will be used for user input and the second form will be used for our XML formatting.

In Figure 24.4 you can see the additional form, called `EmployeeInput`. The original `Employee` form can still be used for output of XML to the browser.

Notice also in Figure 24.4 that I have included a controlled access section to hold some of the information for the employee. Controlled access sections will not completely prevent unauthorized users from viewing the information. You should use encryption keys to completely prevent unauthorized viewing of information.

On the Web, however, you can more easily control the information a user can see by controlling which forms are used for display. If you have multiple forms for a document, you can use a view's form formula to specify which form will be used to display the document. In this case, set the `Employees` view's form formula to `Employee`. Then, even though the document is created with the `EmployeeInput` form, it will be displayed with the `Employee` form in its XML format.

Figure 24.4
One form can be used for input and another can be used to display the document as XML.

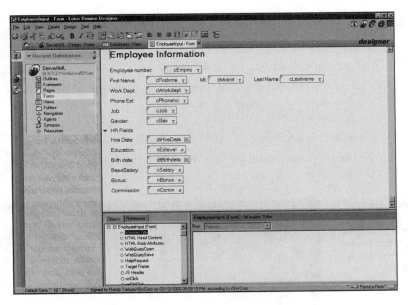

You set the form formula for a view by opening the view in the Domino designer and then highlighting the words Form Formula in the left side of the programmer's pane. On the right side you enter the formula `"Employee"` (including the quotes).

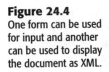

Note

You would probably not directly display the XML to the user, either. You will typically use XSL transformations to convert the XML to a formatted HTML document. I cover XSL formatting in Chapter 23, "Understanding the Extensible Stylesheet Language (XSL)." I'm directly displaying the XML output using the default XSL Stylesheet in Internet Explorer in this chapter so you can see the XML that is generated before transformation using XSL within Domino.

USING VIEWS FOR XML

In addition to using forms to serve XML, you can also use views. Views are very useful because, when you use views, you can send an XML file that contains aggregated data. That is, you can send information for a collection of documents rather than just a single document.

To use views, it is usually most convenient to embed the view within a page. When you embed the view within a page, you can add information in front of the view data as well as after the view data. Here is an example:

1. Create a view called `EmployeesXML`. Make sure that you enable the Treat View Contents as HTML option in the View properties box. Also be sure to disable the Show Column Headings option within the Style tab of the View properties box.

2. The first column of the view should contain the following formula: `"<employee>"` + `"<empno>"` + cEmpno + `"</empno>"`. See Figure 24.5 for an example of the first column in the programmer's pane. The <employee> and <empno> tags have been created as separate strings to highlight the XML structure.

3. Each of the remaining columns (except the last column) should have a formula such as the following: `"<fieldtag>"` + *fieldname* + `"</fieldtag>"`, for example, `"<lastname>"` + cLastName + `"</lastname>"`.

4. If the field is a numeric or date field, you must surround the field name with @Text().

5. The last column should contain the field definition followed by a closing `"</employee>"`.

Figure 24.5
Each column should contain start and end tags. The first and last columns also contain a group tag.

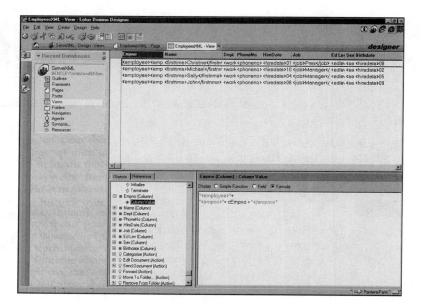

After you have created a view with fields for your documents, you can create your page. The page will contain the beginning and ending tags and the embedded view.

1. Create a new page in the Domino designer. Call the new page EmployeesXML. At the top of the page include the line `<?xml version="1.0"?>`. Below this line, add the line `<employees>`. Be sure to enable the Treat Page Contents as HTML property.

2. Embed the EmployeesXML view. Make sure the option Display Using HTML is enabled in the Web Access section of the Embedded View properties box (see Figure 24.6). This option will prevent the view from being displayed with the Domino View Java applet.

3. Following the embedded view, add a line that has `</employees>`.

Figure 24.6
Use a page with an embedded view to add beginning and ending tags around the view data.

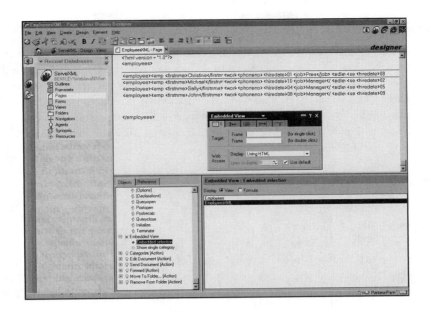

After you have created your page, you can display it in Microsoft Internet Explorer. Figure 24.7 shows the output from the page with an embedded view.

Figure 24.7
The XML for a view contains information from multiple documents.

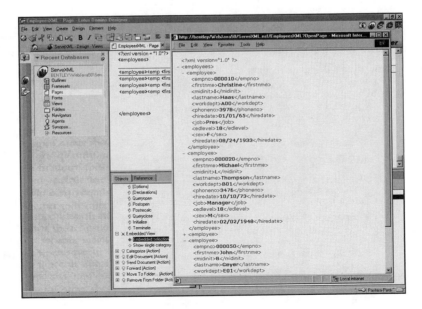

Notice that each document in the Domino database becomes one row of the view. Each row of the view becomes a hierarchical section of the resulting XML. Each hierarchical section is contained within the `<employee>` XML element.

Using Domino Agents to Serve XML

Although using pages, forms, and views to display Domino data is very easy and straight-forward, you will sometimes need to include logic in the generation of the XML. For example, you might want to generate XML only for employees within a certain department, who make a certain salary, or who work for a particular manager. In Domino, you can implement these kinds of queries using views. However, someone must predefine these views in advance. You cannot use views for ad hoc queries. To generate dynamic XML, one method is to use Domino agents.

You can use an agent to generate XML in the same way as you generate HTML. In Chapter 13, "Creating Java Agents with the Domino Designer IDE," I showed you how to use an agent to serve HTML and XML.

Recall from Chapter 13 that you can invoke a Java agent on the Domino server by using a URL. When the agent is invoked, it can obtain a `PrintWriter` object through the `getAgentOutput` method of the `AgentBase` class. Because your agent extends the `AgentBase` class, this method is effectively in your agent's class. After you have the `PrintWriter` object, you can use it to send a stream of characters back to the Web browser. This stream of characters can be HTML or XML.

Here is the agent I showed you in Chapter 13. This agent uses the `AgentParameters` class that is included in the Java script library for the database. The `AgentParameters` class parses the parameters passed in the agent's URL string.

```java
import lotus.domino.*;
import java.io.*;
import java.util.*;

public class JavaAgent extends AgentBase {

    public void NotesMain() {
        PrintWriter out = getAgentOutput();
        try {

            Session session = getSession();
            AgentContext agentContext = session.getAgentContext();

            AgentParameters pt = new AgentParameters();
            pt.parseParameters(session);

            String filepath = pt.getString("filepath");//Get the requested db name
            if (null == filepath) {
                // If none supplied, use this database
                filepath = agentContext.getCurrentDatabase().getFilePath();
            }
            // dbname should now have a valid value

            String server = session.getServerName();

            DbDirectory  dbd = session.getDbDirectory(server);
```

```
        if (null == dbd) {
           out.println("Error - Unable to get DbDirectory");
           throw new Exception();
        }

        Database db = dbd.openDatabase(filepath);
        printDBXML(db, out, pt);        // Output the xml

   } catch(NotesException e) {
      out.println(e.id + " " + e.text);
      e.printStackTrace(out);
   } catch(Exception e) {
      e.printStackTrace(out);
   }
   finally {
      out.flush();
      out.close();
   }
}

void printDBXML(Database db, PrintWriter out, AgentParameters pt) {
   try {
      out.println("Content-Type: text/xml");
      out.println("<?xml version='1.0'?>");
      out.println("<database filename='" + db.getFileName() +
                        "' filepath='" + db.getFilePath() +

                        "' server='" + db.getServer() + "'>");
      out.println("<title>" + db.getTitle() + "</title>");
      out.println("<created>" + db.getCreated().toString() + "</created>");
      out.println("<lastmodified>" + db.getLastModified().toString() +
                  "</lastmodified>");
      if (db.isFTIndexed()) {
         out.println("<ftindexed>" + db.getLastFTIndexed().toString() +
                     "</ftindexed>");
      }
      if (null != pt.getString("managers")) {
         out.println("<managers>");
         Vector vMgr = db.getManagers();
         for (int iMgr=0; iMgr < vMgr.size(); iMgr++) {
            out.println("<manager>" + vMgr.elementAt(iMgr).toString() +
                        "</manager>");
         }
         out.println("</managers>");
      }
      out.println("</database>");
   } catch(NotesException e) {
      out.println(e.id + " " + e.text);
      e.printStackTrace(out);
   } catch(Exception e) {
      e.printStackTrace(out);
   }

   }
}
```

PART

V

CH

24

Figure 24.8 shows the resulting output from the execution of this sample program. The URL used is

```
http://Server/Directory/ServeXML.nsf/dbxml
```

The *server* and *directory* items must match your server and directory names. ServeXML.nsf is the database name, and dbxml is the agent name. Notice that case is not important for the agent name. The name in the database is DbXML, but an all-lowercase name was specified in the URL. Note that the ?OpenAgent command in the URL has been omitted. This is permitted if the name dbxml is not ambiguous. If multiple design elements with the same name are in your database, you should use the ?OpenAgent command.

Figure 24.8
A Domino agent can create a dynamic XML document.

To specify the filepath or managers parameter to the agent, you must use the following syntax:

```
http://Server/Directory/ServeXML.nsf/dbxml?openagent[&filepath=dbpath]
➡[&managers]
```

If you supply a parameter, you must also use the openagent keyword for Domino. The *dbpath* value is used as the name of the database to use.

Let's examine the printDBXML method in more detail. If you review the Java code, you'll notice that the first statement specifies the MIME type. The code for the Java output routine will examine the output lines and, if they conform to the syntax for an HTTP header, they will be used as a header instead of as content. A *header* has the format of a token followed by a colon followed by a space and then a value. The first output line fits the description and is used as an HTTP header:

```
Content-Type: text/xml
```

The second output line does not fit the format for an HTTP header and is used as the first line of the actual output stream. In this case, it is our XML declaration line:

```
<?xml version='1.0'?>
```

Notice that I used single quotes around the version number because the entire string was enclosed in double quotes. You can use either type of quotes. If you look carefully at Figure 24.8, you'll notice that Internet Explorer is actually displaying double quotes around the version number. This is because IE has parsed the input and is displaying the parsed input reformatted for output.

In the main body of the routine, the agent accesses some of the database properties and formats them in XML syntax. In this case, the database filename, file path, creation date, and some other attributes are formatted for display.

One optional parameter is the keyword `managers`. If this keyword is appended to the URL, the list of database managers is displayed along with the other attributes. In Figure 24.9 you can see the output from a URL that requests the `names.nsf` database and its managers.

Figure 24.9
An agent can treat URL parameters as query parameters to create dynamic XML.

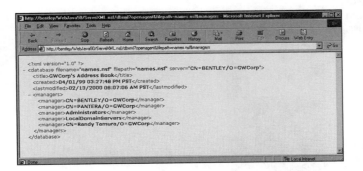

CASE STUDY USING WIRELESS MARKUP LANGUAGE

Now that I've shown you how to use pages, forms, views, and agents to serve XML, I'd like to give you a more detailed case study example. This example is based on the Wireless Markup Language (WML). In only a few pages I won't explain all the options of WML, but I'll show you the basics.

If you are interested in this application of XML, you can find out more details on the Web at the following address: `http://updev.phone.com`. At this site you can download the developer's kit for WML. For this case study, I'm using the beta version 4.0 of the toolkit. By the time you read this, version 4.0 might be final and some changes might be in the WML language or syntax from the example I'm showing you here.

If you want to follow along with this case study, you will need to obtain a copy of the developer's kit for WML. Without it, you should be able to read and understand the text, but you will not be able to actually try the database.

WHAT ARE WML AND WAP?

WML is a language based on XML that is used for wireless devices. *WAP* stands for *Wireless Access Protocol* and is the communications protocol used to deliver WML documents. Information on WAP can be found at `http://www.wapforum.org/`. Most of the time the hardware devices are wireless phones; however, the development kit comes with a simulator that you can use with a standard HTTP server. WML is like a very simplified version of HTML that uses XML syntax. It is simplified because the amount of data to be transmitted to the device must be very small. The device typically handles about 1000–1500 bytes at a time. This is very small compared to the typical Web page.

The basic display unit of information in WML is called a *card*. Typically, a WAP device will download a *deck*, which consists of one or more cards. A card is analogous to a Web page but, as mentioned, typically contains much less data. Within a card, you can display lists of information, use hyperlinks to other cards, and even display small icon-like graphics. Figure 24.10 shows you a picture of the simulator for Windows that comes with the development kit.

Figure 24.10
The phone simulator showing a WML card served from Domino.

Figure 24.10 shows the output of a WML card in the display window. Domino WML Demo appears in the top line. This simulator does not represent a specific cellular phone, but rather a functional equivalent. The functions on the simulator can be used to test and debug a WML application.

The architectural model for WML includes two programmable function keys that are located just under the display window of the simulator. The left programmable key is called the *accept* key, and the right programmable key is called the *options* key. You can add labels to these keys. In Figure 24.10 the accept key has the default label of OK. The right key has been programmed with the label About. If the user presses the About key, another card will be displayed with information about the demo.

Here is a very simple WML card deck. A deck is a WML document that contains one or more cards accessible with a single URL:

```
<?xml version="1.0"?>
<!DOCTYPE wml PUBLIC "-//PHONE.COM//DTD WML 1.1//EN"
"http://www.phone.com/dtd/wml11.dtd" >
<wml>
<card>

<p>News<br/>
Now hear this! Domino serves WML!
</p>

</card>
</wml>
```

Figure 24.11 shows you the output on the simulator for the first WML card deck.

Figure 24.11
The phone simulator showing a simple WML card served from Domino.

If you examine both the XML file and the figure, understanding the components should be fairly straightforward. A WML card deck is identified by the `<wml>` element. Individual cards are identified by the `<card>` element. In this example I have used only a single card, but I could have multiple `<card>` elements within one `<wml>` card deck.

Within a `<card>`, the `<p>` element identifies text that should be displayed in the window. Like HTML, blanks and other whitespace are converted to a single blank. The text is automatically wrapped to multiple lines if necessary. As in all XML files, you must properly terminate all elements with a closing tag.

If an element consists of only a singleton tag, you can close it with a slash before the ending angle bracket. For example, `<br/>` is a singleton element that is opened and closed with the same tag. The `<br/>` syntax is interchangeable with `<br></br>` in that it represents an empty XML element. As you might have guessed, the XML `<br/>` tag does the same as the HTML `<br>` tag, for example, creates a new line. Because every start tag must have an end tag in XML, using this syntax makes it easier and is just a shorthand notation for the string `<br></br>`.

SERVING WML WITH DOMINO

Now that you've seen an example of a WML card deck, you can move on to the decision of how to implement this application with Domino. Several choices are possible:

1. Implement each separate WML card deck as a page within Domino. Each page would be addressed as a separate, named URL.

2. Use a single form with multiple documents. Each document would represent one WML card deck. You need a view with this approach to selectively retrieve the desired document.

3. Use Domino agents to programmatically generate WML to send to the device.

4. Use Java servlets similar to Domino agents to generate WML to send to the device.

5. Use a combination of the previous methods.

For this case study, I have used option number 5. That is, I used several techniques because of a variety of considerations. Although this makes the demonstration a little bit more complicated, it makes it more interesting and enables me to illustrate more points as I describe the implementation.

My first thought on implementing the WML case study was to use a form, documents, and a view. This approach allows as many different card decks as needed for an application. Each card deck is represented by a single Domino document. When I first implemented this, I discovered that the WML simulator (and probably the real WAP/WML devices) requires the use of a specialized MIME type. The MIME type is used in the WAP or HTTP header section of the transmission. The header for HTML has the following format:

```
Content-Type: text/html
```

For WAP/WML, the corresponding header must be

```
Content-Type: text/vnd.wap.wml
```

Unfortunately, if you are just using forms and documents, you cannot specify the MIME type. You can specify the MIME type only if you use a server-based program such as an agent or servlet. Thus, because of the MIME type restriction, I decided to use a Java agent to deliver the document.

> **Note**
>
> Do not confuse the HTML <HEAD> element with the HTTP header. The HTML <HEAD> element contains HTML markup such as the <TITLE> tag. The Domino Designer contains a form event called HTML Head Content (previous versions called this event HTML Header) that can be used to specify the <HEAD> element content.
>
> The HTTP header is where the MIME type is specified along with many other header variables. The HTTP header is discussed in great detail in Chapter 11, "JavaScript Techniques with Domino." It is not part of the HTML document but is transmitted by the HTTP protocol.

CREATING THE WMLCard FORM

Even though I decided to use Java to deliver the final documents to the device, I could still use forms, documents, and views to prepare the data for sending. By using forms and documents, I could make the authoring of WML files relatively easy. In Figure 24.12 you can see the WMLCard form that I created.

In Figure 24.12 you can see that, in addition to the name and description of the card deck, I have three fields that are used to store WML information: cCard, cCardHeader, and cCardTrailer. The cCardHeader and cCardTrailer fields are computed fields that contain constants that must be included for each WML card deck. You can see the formula for the cCardHeader field in the figure. By standardizing the header and trailer fields, each card deck will have uniform wrapper information, making it easier to change in the future.

Figure 24.12
The WMLCard form is used to create simple WML card decks.

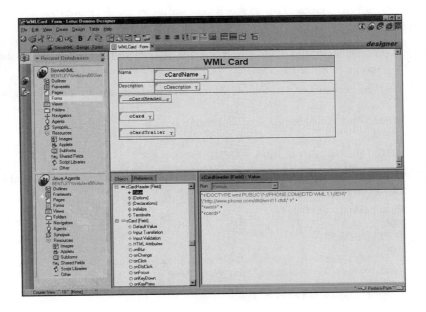

The cCard field is the field that contains the actual WML for the card deck itself. Figure 24.13 illustrates the WML file for the main menu that I showed you in Figure 24.10. At this point you don't need to understand the syntax of this WML file, but you should be able to see some correlation between the input and the display on the phone. I'll explain the WML syntax shortly.

Figure 24.13
The WML card deck for the main menu.

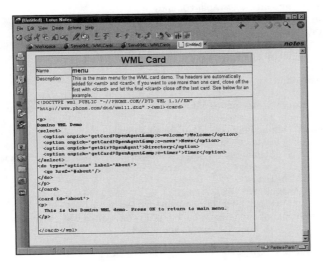

CREATING THE WMLCards VIEW

After you have created the form, you will also need a view that you can use to look up the various WML cards. This view is a very simple view. To create it, follow these steps:

1. Create a new view called WMLCards.

2. The view should contain only a single column called the CardName column. The column should be sorted ascending.

3. The contents of the column should be the cCardName field of the WMLCard form.

When you have finished, close and save the view.

CREATING THE getCard JAVA AGENT

After you create the form, documents, and view you can create a Java agent that will display the documents to the device.

```java
import lotus.domino.*;
import java.io.*;
import java.util.*;

// Initial Implementation of getCard.java routine.
public class JavaAgent extends AgentBase {

    public void NotesMain() {

        try {
            Session session = getSession();
            AgentContext agentContext = session.getAgentContext();

            // Parse the URL arguments
            AgentParameters pt = new AgentParameters();
              pt.parseParameters(session);

            PrintWriter out = getAgentOutput();
            out.println("Content-Type: text/vnd.wap.wml");
            out.println("");       // Header ends with blank line
            out.println("<?xml version='1.0'?>");  // Write the XML header.
            Database db = agentContext.getCurrentDatabase();
            View v;
            Document doc;

            String cardName = pt.getString("c"); // Looking for c=CardName
            // if there is a card name,
            if (null != cardName && !cardName.equals("")) {
                v = db.getView("WMLCards");        // Get the cards view
                doc = v.getDocumentByKey(cardName); // Get the card name
                if (null == doc) {    // Card not found
                    out.println(
                        "<!DOCTYPE wml PUBLIC \"-//PHONE.COM//DTD WML 1.1//EN\"
                        \"http://www.phone.com/dtd/wml11.dtd\" >");
                    out.println("<wml><card><p>Error, card "+ cardName +
                        " not found.</p></card></wml>");
                }
                else {
```

```
                    // Get Header
                    String cCardHeader = doc.getItemValueString("cCardHeader");
                    // Get the WML Card
                    String cCard = doc.getItemValueString("cCard");
                    // Get Trailer
                    String cCardTrailer = doc.getItemValueString("cCardTrailer");
                    out.println(cCardHeader);  // Output the data
                    out.println(cCard);  // Output the data
                    out.println(cCardTrailer); // Output the data
                }
            }
            else {
                out.println(
                "<!DOCTYPE wml PUBLIC \"-//PHONE.COM//DTD WML 1.1//EN\"
                 \"http://www.phone.com/dtd/wml11.dtd\" >");
                out.println(
                "<wml><card><p>No card specified in URL.</p></card></wml>");
            }
        } catch(Exception e) {
          e.printStackTrace();
        }
    }
}
```

Here are some points to notice in the Java program:

1. The `Content-Type` is specified as `text/vnd.wap.wml`.

2. Look for a parameter of the format `c=CardName`. This card name is the key you will look up in the view.

3. If you are unsuccessful in obtaining the requested card, you send an error message to the device.

4. If you are successful in obtaining the document, you send the three fields `cCardHeader`, `cCard`, and `cCardTrailer`.

Let's recap what you have accomplished so far. You have created a form, a view, and a Java agent. The `WMLCard` form will be used to create your WML documents. The `WMLCards` view is used by the `getCard` Java agent to retrieve the card decks. Each card document has a name, which is also the key into the `WMLCards` view. You inform the Java agent which card you want to display by using a keyword parameter in the URL. Here is a sample URL:

`http://<server>/<database>.nsf/getCard?OpenAgent&c=news`

The c parameter identifies the card name we want to display. The agent will send the appropriate MIME `Content-Type` followed by the data in the three fields of the appropriate document. It will find the document by using the key to look up the document in the view.

UNDERSTANDING BASIC WML SYNTAX

Now that we have the basic infrastructure to display a card, let's turn our attention to the actual WML syntax. Here is the WML source code for the main menu card deck. It does not contain either the header or trailer information, which will be added by the agent automatically.

```
<wml>
<card>
<p>
Domino WML Demo
<select>
  <option onpick="getCard?OpenAgent&amp;c=welcome">Welcome</option>
  <option onpick="getCard?OpenAgent&amp;c=news">News</option>
  <option onpick="getDir?OpenAgent">Directory</option>
  <option onpick="getCard?OpenAgent&amp;c=timer">Timer</option>
</select>
<do type="options" label="About">
  <go href="#about"/>
</do>
</p>
</card>

<card id="about">
<p>
  This is the Domino WML demo. Press OK to return to main menu.
</p>
</card>
</wml>
```

This card deck contains two cards within the <wml> element. The first card is the main menu. The <p> tag indicates that the text that follows is ordinary text and should just be displayed in the window.

The <select> element indicates the browser should display a list of selections. <option> elements are contained within the <select> element. Each <option> element represents a single choice on the screen and will act as a link to a new card.

Notice that the URLs that are included in the onpick attribute are relative URLs. They will be constructed within the current database. The &amp entity will be replaced with an ampersand (&). The complete URL for the Welcome card is

```
http://<server>/<database>.nsf/getCard?OpenAgent&c=welcome
```

The <do> element enables you to associate an action with one of the programmable buttons. In this case, the options button, which is on the right side of the phone simulator, is specified. The label for this button is About. The <go> element indicates that the browser should transfer to the URL #about. This name refers to a card that is contained in the same card deck. The remaining tags close out the associated elements.

The second card has the ID about that was referenced in the first card. When the options button is pressed, this second card will be displayed. The accept button displays the word OK by default, and the default action is to return to the previously displayed card. The default operation is similar to the Back button of a Web browser.

ADDING A DIRECTORY

At the beginning of this chapter I showed you an example of an employee directory stored in XML. Wouldn't it be nice if we could use this directory to access the phone numbers of the employees? In particular, suppose we could tap into that employee directory, present a menu of the employees, allow the user to select an employee, and then call the employee's extension.

Wow! Because the phone directory is stored on the server and served out to the phone using WML, it is always up-to-date. No address book is stored in the phone itself. No speed dial numbers are in the phone to update. Just update the Domino database storing the phone numbers and, when the server phone numbers are updated, the phone accesses the latest numbers. A user can select a person by name, and then press the Call button. Let's see how this is done.

Our first step in enhancing the WML application is to update the view. We want to create a WML card for each employee to be displayed. Because this is a simplified example, I haven't taken care of the case when more names than will fit on the screen exist. Remember that each card deck should be in the range of 1000–1500 characters. If you are interested, you can tackle this job on your own.

In the `WMLCards` view, I have changed the `CardName` column formula to be the following:

```
@If(@Contains(Form; "Employee");"e*"+cEmpno;cCardName)
```

This formula works as follows: If the form used to create the document contains the word `Employee`, append e* to the employee number and use this as the key. This enables the use of either the `Employee` or `EmployeeInput` form for original input of the employee information. If it was not an employee form, then assume it was the `WMLCard` form and use the `cCardName` field as the key for the document.

The `WMLCards` view will be used to serve either the cards as before or the employee records. As you can see in Figure 24.14, you can easily distinguish the employee records because they begin with e* (for example, e*00020).

PART
V

CH

24

Figure 24.14
The `WMLCards` view contains employee numbers and card names.

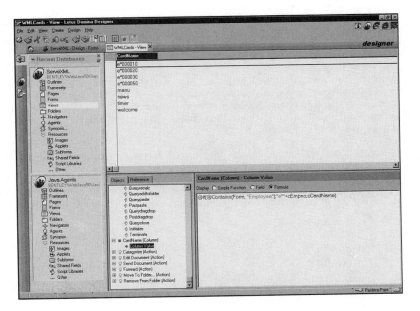

ADDING THE EmployeesWML VIEW

If you look back at the syntax for making a `<select>`/`<option>` list, you see that this list can easily be constructed by creating a view with the Treat View Contents as HTML option. I'll create the EmployeesWML view for this purpose.

To create the EmployeesWML view, follow these steps:

1. Create a new view called EmployeesWML with a single column called Name.
2. In the view style attributes, turn off the Show Column Headings attribute.
3. In the advanced view properties, enable the Treat View Contents as HTML property.
4. For the contents of the Name column, use the following formula:

```
"<option onpick=\"getCard?OpenAgent&amp;e=e*" + cEmpno +"\">" +
cLastname + ", " + cFirstnme + "</option>"
```

Here is an example of how one row would appear in the view:

```
<option onpick="getcard?OpenAgent&amp;e=e*000020">
Thompson, Michael</option>
```

Normally, it would be ideal to embed the EmployeesWML view in a page. You could then add header and trailer information and the WML would be complete. Unfortunately, if you do this, you cannot change the HTTP/WAP MIME Content-Type. This is the same problem we saw previously. As before, we can circumvent this problem by creating an agent to display the information. In this case, we will create a new agent called the getDir agent.

ADDING THE getDir JAVA AGENT

The getDir agent will generate the card containing the `<select>` and `<option>` WML statements for selecting the employees from a list. Here is an example of the WML output we want from this agent:

```
<?xml version='1.0'?>
<!DOCTYPE wml PUBLIC "-//PHONE.COM//DTD WML 1.1//EN"
"http://www.phone.com/dtd/wml11.dtd" >
<wml><card><p><select>
<option onpick="getCard?OpenAgent&amp;e=e*000010">Haas, Christine</option>
<option onpick="getCard?OpenAgent&amp;e=e*000020">Thompson, Michael</option>
<option onpick="getCard?OpenAgent&amp;e=e*000030">Kwan, Sally</option>
<option onpick="getCard?OpenAgent&amp;e=e*000050">Geyer, John</option>
</select></p></card></wml>
```

To create this WML output, the agent will use the EmployeesWML view that we made in the previous section. Note that all the `<option>` lines are generated from the view. This allows a variable number of lines but would need to be modified somewhat to handle the small number of screen lines of the phone. Here is the code for the Java getDir Java agent:

```
import lotus.domino.*;
import java.util.*;
import java.io.*;

public class JavaAgent extends AgentBase {
```

```
public void NotesMain() {

    try {
        Session session = getSession();
        AgentContext agentContext = session.getAgentContext();
        PrintWriter out = getAgentOutput();

        out.println("Content-Type: text/vnd.wap.wml");
        out.println("");        // Header ends with blank line
        out.println("<?xml version='1.0'?>");  // Write the XML header.
        out.println("<!DOCTYPE wml PUBLIC \"-//PHONE.COM//DTD WML 1.1//EN\"
                    \"http://www.phone.com/dtd/wml11.dtd\" >");
        out.println("<wml><card><p><select>");

        Database db = agentContext.getCurrentDatabase();
        View view = db.getView("EmployeesWML");
        ViewEntryCollection vec = view.getAllEntries();
        Vector columns;
        ViewEntry ve;
        String optValue;
        ve = vec.getFirstEntry();

        // For each view entry
        while (null != ve) {
            // Get the value of the columns, we only need first
            columns = ve.getColumnValues();
            // Get first column value
            optValue = (String) columns.elementAt(0);
            out.println(optValue);
            ve = vec.getNextEntry();

        }
        out.println("</select></p></card></wml>");

    } catch(Exception e) {
        e.printStackTrace();
    }
  }
}
```

Figure 24.15 shows the output of the agent in the phone simulator.

ENHANCING THE getCard JAVA AGENT

Our final task for the WML application is to enhance the getCard agent so that it can display not only the defined WML cards but also information from the employee directory. Here is a sample URL that we will use to obtain employee information:

```
http://<server>/<database>.nsf/getCard?OpenAgent&e=e*000010
```

With this URL, we would like the getCard agent to obtain employee information. Notice that the key for employee information is e, not c. The c parameter was used for cards, the e parameter is used for employee information. The difference between these two cases is similar to the difference between a statically generated HTML page and a dynamic page generated by a Domino agent. The c parameter serves mainly static cards, and the e parameter is used to dynamically generate employee information and to enable the user to actually call the employee on the phone.

Figure 24.15
Domino serves the most current employee directory information.

Here is the updated getCard Java agent:

```java
import lotus.domino.*;
import java.io.*;
import java.util.*;

public class JavaAgent extends AgentBase {

    public void NotesMain() {

        try {
            Session session = getSession();
            AgentContext agentContext = session.getAgentContext();

            // Parse the URL arguments
            AgentParameters pt = new AgentParameters();
              pt.parseParameters(session);

            PrintWriter out = getAgentOutput();
            out.println("Content-Type: text/vnd.wap.wml");
            out.println("");      // Header ends with blank line
            out.println("<?xml version='1.0'?>");  // Write the XML header.
            Database db = agentContext.getCurrentDatabase();
            View v;
            Document doc;

            String cardName = pt.getString("c"); // Looking for c=CardName
            // if there is a card name,
            if (null != cardName && !cardName.equals( "" )) {
                v = db.getView("WMLCards");        // Get the cards view
                doc = v.getDocumentByKey(cardName); // Get the card name
                if (null == doc) {    // Card not found
                    out.println(
                        "<!DOCTYPE wml PUBLIC \"-//PHONE.COM//DTD WML 1.1//EN\"" +
                        \"http://www.phone.com/dtd/wml11.dtd\" >");
                    out.println("<wml><card><p>Error, card "+cardName +
                        " not found.</p></card></wml>");
```

```
        }
        else {
            // Get Header
            String cCardHeader = doc.getItemValueString("cCardHeader");
            // Get the WML Card
            String cCard = doc.getItemValueString("cCard");
            // Get Trailer
            String cCardTrailer = doc.getItemValueString("cCardTrailer");
            out.println(cCardHeader);  // Output the data
            out.println(cCard);  // Output the data
            out.println(cCardTrailer); // Output the data
        }
    }
    else {
        String empNo = pt.getString("e");   // Looking for e=Empno
        if (null != empNo && !empNo.equals( "")) {
            v = db.getView("WMLCards");        // Get the cards view
            doc = v.getDocumentByKey(empNo); // Get the employee number
            if (null == doc) {   // Employee not found
                out.println(
                    "<!DOCTYPE wml PUBLIC \"-//PHONE.COM//DTD WML 1.1//EN\"
                        \"http://www.phone.com/dtd/wml11.dtd\" >");
                out.println("<wml><card><p>Error, employee "+empNo +
                    " not found.</p></card></wml>");
            }
            else {
                // Employee was found
                out.println(
                    "<!DOCTYPE wml PUBLIC \"-//PHONE.COM//DTD WML 1.1//EN\"
                        \"http://www.phone.com/dtd/wml11.dtd\" >");
                out.println("<wml><card>");
                out.println("<do type=\"options\" label=\"Call\">");
                out.println("<go href=\"wtai://wp/mc;" +
                        doc.getItemValueString("cPhoneno") + "\"/>");
                out.println("</do><p>");
                out.println(doc.getItemValueString("cFirstnme") + " " +
                        doc.getItemValueString("cMidInit") + ". " +
                        doc.getItemValueString("cLastname") + "<br/>");
                out.println("Extension: " +
                        doc.getItemValueString("cPhoneno") + "<br/>");
                out.println("Department: " +
                        doc.getItemValueString("cWorkdept") + "<br/>");
                out.println("</p></card></wml>");
            }
        }
        else {
            // No "c" and no "e"
            out.println(
                    "<!DOCTYPE wml PUBLIC \"-//PHONE.COM//DTD WML 1.1//EN\"
                        \"http://www.phone.com/dtd/wml11.dtd\" >");
            out.println(
                "<wml><card><p>No card specified in URL.</p></card></wml>");
        }
    }
} catch(Exception e) {
    e.printStackTrace();
}
```

```
    }
}
```

Figure 24.16 shows the image of the phone when you click the entry for Christine Haas.

Figure 24.16
You can click the Call button to call the employee.

The WML card information generated by the agent for a single employee is as follows:

```
<?xml version='1.0'?>
<!DOCTYPE wml PUBLIC "-//PHONE.COM//DTD WML 1.1//EN"
➥"http://www.phone.com/dtd/wml11.dtd" >
<wml><card>
<do type="options" label="Call">
<go href="wtai://wp/mc;3978"/>
</do><p>
Christine I. Haas<br/>
Extension: 3978<br/>
Department: A00<br/>
</p></card></wml>
```

Notice in this WML the options button has the label Call. When it is clicked, the href uses the URL with the wtai protocol. This is the *Wireless Telephony Application Interface*. The wtai protocol is used to actually dial the phone. In this case, only the telephone extension number is present, but it can obviously and easily be extended to external phone numbers, long distance, or international phone numbers.

The rest of the card's information is relatively self-explanatory.

SUMMARY

In this chapter I've shown you several methods for generating and sending XML data to a client device. You can use pages, forms, and views. In addition to the built-in mechanisms for generating XML, you can use Java agents to generate XML as well.

I showed you a case study using WML, which is an XML-based language for wireless applications. The application used Domino forms, documents, views, and Java agents to display WML information. By using the power of Domino, you can supply mobile users with a server-based phone book. The advantage of a server-based phone book is that, when the server copy of the information is updated, the mobile phones will have immediate access to the new information. If a phone number is updated, the next time a user looks up the name, it will be updated in the phone and can be used for dialing purposes.

The real purpose of the case study was not to provide you with an industrial-strength WAP/WML phone application. Instead, it was to illustrate the power of XML and how you can use Domino today to generate XML using a variety of techniques. Your application for XML might be completely different, but you should be able to use the techniques presented in this chapter.

CHAPTER REVIEW

1. Give four different methods for generating and serving XML to a client device. Explain the pros and cons of each method.

2. Suppose you need to set the MIME header for your document to a particular type. For example, suppose the client device wanted to use the Synchronized Multimedia Integration Language (SMIL) and the MIME header Content-Type: text/smil. What implementation technique would you use and why?

3. Suppose the MIME header was not a problem and you could serve your document with the standard Domino text/html MIME header. Suppose each document in your Domino database represented one widget. You want to send XML to the client with information about each widget within an element, such as <widget>. Which implementation technique would you favor? Why?

4. In the WML case study, I created and used a Java agent called getDir. This agent used a view called EmployeesWML. What was the advantage of using this view? What effort did I save within the Java agent by using the view rather than logic within the agent itself?

5. What is the advantage of using two forms with a single document—one for data input and one for XML formatting?

6. What is the purpose of the form formula? Is it attached to a form or a view?

7. Write a Java agent that will accept a parameter n=lastname, which will find the name in the Domino directory (Name and Address book) and serve data to a WML client. The data to be served should include the name, phone number, and email address of the user.

8. Think about Domino single-category views. Develop a scenario where you could use single-category views to traverse a hierarchical menu tree with WML. How could you use single-category views to implement the traversal? Test your ideas by implementing a small test application.

PROCESSING XML WITH DOMINO

THE W3C DOCUMENT OBJECT MODEL

In this book, I've described several object models. In Part IV, "The Domino Objects for Java," I told you about the Domino Objects, an object model that describes Domino databases and their contents. I also described the JavaScript Document Object Model in Chapter 8, "The JavaScript Language and the Document Object Model," in Chapter 9, "The JavaScript Window and Document Objects," and in Chapter 10, "The JavaScript Form and Form Elements."

Now I'd like to describe another object model, also called a Document Object Model (DOM). This DOM, as you might expect, is similar to the previous document object models I've described, but different. Although it originated from the JavaScript DOM, its purpose has been expanded. The purpose of the W3C Document Object Model is to describe an application programming interface object model for processing XML and HTML documents. It describes the logical structure of documents. It is a platform-neutral and programming language-neutral definition.

Two levels of this specification exist. Level 1 was approved as a W3C Recommendation on October 1, 1998. Domino supports Level 1 of the DOM. Level 2 is currently being developed and, as of May, 2000 is a Candidate Recommendation, but has not yet reached Recommendation status. Level 2 contains all of Level 1 and includes extra features such as namespaces, style sheets, and event handling. Because Domino supports only Level 1 of the specification, the rest of this chapter will describe Level 1. If you are interested in Level 2, you can find it at `http://www.w3c.org/TR/DOM-Level-2`. The Level 1 specification can be found at `http://www.w3c.org/TR/REC-DOM-Level-1`.

The Level 1 specification contains two modules, a Core module and an HTML module. The *Core* module enables you to traverse a DOM hierarchical tree structure and extract data found within the structure. You can also create new nodes of the tree. The *HTML* module adds additional interfaces for handling HTML-specific elements such as the <BODY>, <FORM>, and other elements of HTML. In this chapter, I discuss only the Core module, which is supported by Domino.

THE DOCUMENT OBJECT MODEL LEVEL 1 CORE

The textual syntax for XML is relatively easy to read and understand. The angle brackets enclose element tags, and the attributes are denoted by a name, an equal sign, and a value that must be contained within either single or double quotation marks. This syntax is easy to create and understand both by computer programs and people. This textual syntax, however, is not really convenient for processing by programs.

A more useful format for processing by computer programs is a *hierarchical tree structure*. In this tree structure, the highest level of the tree represents the outermost element of the XML document. This element is also called the *root* element. Layers of the tree represent containment. Lower levels of the hierarchy represent elements that are enclosed or contained within higher-level elements.

A tree structure is useful because algorithms for traversing trees are well known. Most tree traversal algorithms are recursive, but they can also be iterative. *Traversing* a tree involves starting at the root and processing each node in a well-defined order. Because DOM trees are organized by containment, traversal can be sideways among siblings or by depth, which will "drill down" into the details of a specific element.

The DOM Level 1 Core Java binding consists of 17 Java interfaces and 1 Java class. The Domino implementation of the XML parser is based on the IBM XML4J processor. This processor has been donated to the Apache XML project and in that context is also known as the Xerces Java parser.

Figure 25.1 shows the DOM Core Level 1 class and interface hierarchy. The lines indicate inheritance, so, for example, the Document interface inherits from or extends the Node interface. The Text interface extends the CharacterData interface, which in turn extends the Node interface.

Figure 25.1
The W3C Document Object Model Core Level 1 inheritance diagram.

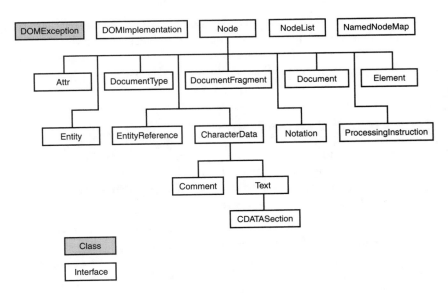

As you can see from Figure 25.1, only one class is defined in the W3C DOM, which is the DOMException class. This class extends the java.lang.RuntimeException class. The DOMException class defines the various exception codes that can occur while executing the DOM routines.

Each of the various interfaces represents an object within the DOM tree or is used in the processing of the tree. As you can tell, most of the interfaces extend the Node interface. The Node interface and each derived class represent a node of the tree. The NodeList interface is used to hold a list of nodes, much like a Java Vector. The list can be accessed by index values that begin at 0. The NamedNodeMap allows access to nodes by name rather than an index value. The DOMImplementation class can be used to determine which features are available in the specific DOM implementation.

PART
V

CH
25

The APIs are defined with interfaces instead of classes because this decouples the implementation from its interface. In other words, an implementation can define its own classes as long as it exposes methods that are defined within the interface. An implementation could, for example, use a single Java class to implement two or more DOM interfaces.

In this chapter, I will take a few liberties with the terminology to make the text easier to read. When interfaces are used, say the Document interface, technically the class used to implement the Document interface might be any kind of class, and an object corresponding to the class might be any kind of object as long as it implements the Document interface. Thus, technically I should speak of objects that implement the Document interface. However, this adds more complexity than clarity to the text. It is much easier to speak of a Document object rather than an object that implements the Document interface. With that caveat, I'll try to be technically precise, but occasionally I'll speak of Document objects, Element objects, or Nodes. In practice, most DOM implementations will map a single interface to a single class, so my descriptions are really not too incorrect in practice.

Because interfaces are used, factory methods within the Document interface are used to create additional nodes in the tree. For example, the Document interface includes the methods createComment, createElement, createEntityReference, and so on. This structure is similar to the idea in Domino Objects, which uses a Session object or a Database object to create elements within the given context.

THE DOM STRUCTURE

Each node within a DOM tree is represented by a Node. The Node interface provides a rich set of traversal and access methods, and you can traverse a DOM tree and access its data solely by using the Node interface. For some applications, this can be desirable based on either the programmer's background or the characteristics of the application.

In addition to the single Node processing model, the DOM provides a class (interface) inheritance model that I showed you in Figure 25.1. If you are more accustomed to object-oriented programming and want to use a more object-based programming model, you can use these interfaces instead of the generic Node interface. For example, you can use an Element object with the method getTagName instead of the more generic getNodeName of the Node interface. Each of these methods will return the same result for an Element node, but the getTagName is more descriptive and specific to the context of an Element node.

Table 25.1 shows the various types of nodes that can appear in a DOM tree and the types of children that each node allows.

TABLE 25.1   TABLE OF NODE TYPES

Node Type	Description	Children
Document	Only a single Document node is in the tree. This node represents the entire document.	Element (max of one), ProcessingInstruction, Comment, DocumentType

Node Type	Description	Children
DocumentFragment	This lightweight type can be used to store parts of one or more trees during construction.	Element, ProcessingInstruction, Comment, Text, CDATASection, EntityReference
DocumentType	In DOM Level 1, this node stores only a list of available entities and notations in the document. This object is read-only.	None allowed
EntityReference	Entity references can appear in the DOM model when an entity reference is in the source document. These are optional, however, because the XML processor can expand and replace any entity references.	Element, ProcessingInstruction, Comment, Text, CDATASection, EntityReference
Element	An element node represents an XML (or HTML) element in the source document.	Element, ProcessingInstruction, Comment, Text, CDATASection, EntityReference
Attr	An attribute object refers to a single attribute of an Element.	Text, EntityReference
Processing Instruction	A processing instruction contains information from the XML processing instruction in the source document.	None allowed
Comment	A comment. This is the text within the <!-- and -->.	None allowed
Text	This is text found between the start and end tags of an element or as a child of an Attr object.	None allowed

PART

V

CH

25

continues

TABLE 25.1   CONTINUED

Node Type	Description	Children
CDATASection	A CDATASection is used to escape character sequences that might otherwise be considered markup.	None allowed
Entity	The Entity interface is used to represent an XML entity. Parsers can expand entity definitions, so they are optional.	Element, ProcessingInstruction, Comment, Text, CDATASection, EntityReference
Notation	The Notation interface is used to represent an XML notation declared in the DTD. These are used for processing instruction targets.	None allowed

A SIMPLE DOM EXAMPLE

It is often easier to understand new conceptual ideas when you see an example. The following example illustrates the new Domino parseXML method (added in release 5.0.3) of the Item class. Here is the first method of a Java agent. It is designed to generate XML from the personal address book and then parse it with parseXML.

```
public void NotesMain() {

    try {
        Session session = getSession();
        AgentContext agentContext = session.getAgentContext();
        DbDirectory dbdir = session.getDbDirectory("");
        Database db = dbdir.openDatabase("Names.nsf");
        DocumentCollection dc = db.getAllDocuments();
        // Just pick up the first document of the database
        Document doc = dc.getFirstDocument();
        // Generate some XML from the personal address book.
        String sXml = doc.generateXML();
        System.out.println(sXml);  // Display the XML source
        // We create a new temp item to contain the XML, but we do not
        // save it back to the database
        Item iXml = doc.replaceItemValue("iXml", sXml);

        // Now parse the XML that was generated
        org.w3c.dom.Document domdoc = iXml.parseXML(false);
        System.out.println("Parsed OK");
        // Get the root element
        org.w3c.dom.Element docelem = domdoc.getDocumentElement();
        System.out.println("docelem: " + docelem.getTagName());
```

```
        // Print the tree, starting at the root
        printTree(docelem);

    } catch(Exception e) {
        e.printStackTrace();
    }
}
```

In the `NotesMain` method, I get the personal address book and then obtain the first document in the database. From this document, I generate XML and place it in the string variable `sXml`. I create a Domino `Item` using the generated XML. This temporary `Item` is not saved back to the database.

After the XML is stored in the `Item`, you can use the `parseXML` method. This method will create a DOM tree and return the `Document` object. In the program, you can see that I have defined the variable to be of the class `org.w3c.dom.Document`. I have used the fully qualified name to distinguish it from a Domino `Document` object. After the `Document` object has been obtained, I can get the main document `Element` with the `getDocumentElement` method.

A difference exists between the `Document` object and the document `Element`. The `Document` object is the parent of the document `Element`, and a single node represents each. The `Document` object provides a context for the tree, is used to create other objects, and provides information about the document as a whole. The document `Element` is the topmost (or outermost) XML element. As such, it is also sometimes called the root element.

After obtaining the document `Element`, I call the `printTree` routine to print out the contents of the tree. The `printTree` routine will recursively traverse the tree, printing the nodes as it traverses the nodes.

Here is the code for the `printTree` method:

```
public void printTree(org.w3c.dom.Node node) {

    boolean isElem = printNode(node);  // Visit the node
    org.w3c.dom.NodeList nl = node.getChildNodes(); // get all children
    if (null != nl) { // Check that the NodeList is not empty
        org.w3c.dom.Node cNode = nl.item(0);
        while (null != cNode) {
            printTree(cNode);      // Recurse
            cNode = cNode.getNextSibling();
        }
    }
    // If the node was an Element node, then print the closing tag
    if (isElem) {
        // finish off this node.
        System.out.println("</" + node.getNodeName() + ">");
    }
}
```

The `printTree` method will print a tree by first printing out the root node and then printing out each child in order. After they have been printed, if the top of the tree is an `Element` node, an end tag must also be printed.

The first statement of the method will print the current node, which represents the top of this tree structure. The getChildNodes method of the Node interface returns a NodeList. A NodeList is conceptually very similar to a java.util.Vector. You can iterate through the NodeList by using the item method with an index. The indices for the NodeList begin at 0. If the getChildNodes method returns null, the current node does not have any children.

The while loop will cycle through each node in the NodeList, beginning with the first item. The getNextSibling routine of the Node interface enables you to get the next node. As you get each node, you call the printTree method on that node. This will recursively visit each node.

The only remaining method to investigate is the printNode method. Here is the code for printNode:

```java
public boolean printNode(org.w3c.dom.Node node) {
    // If the node is an element node, print the opening tag
    if (node.ELEMENT_NODE == node.getNodeType()) {
        System.out.print("<" + node.getNodeName() );

        // Get ready to append all the attributes
        org.w3c.dom.NamedNodeMap nmap = node.getAttributes();
        if (null != nmap) {
            for (int i=0; i < nmap.getLength(); i++) {
                System.out.print(" " + nmap.item(i).getNodeName() +
                    "=\"" + nmap.item(i).getNodeValue() + "\"" );
            }
        }

        System.out.print(">");
        return (true); // This is an element
    }
    else {
        // If the node is a text node, just print the data
        if (node.TEXT_NODE == node.getNodeType()) {
            System.out.print( ((org.w3c.dom.Text) node).getData() );
        }
        else {
            // Otherwise, we don't handle it. Just print a message.
            System.out.println("Node: " + node.getNodeName() +
                ", type=" + node.getNodeType() );
        }
    }
    // Anything else is not an Element type node
    return (false);
}
```

The printNode routine examines the current node's type with the getNodeType method. Table 25.2 is a list of the available node types and the associated Java constants.

Table 25.2   Java Constant Names for Node Types

Node Type	Java Constant	Value
Document	DOCUMENT_NODE	9
DocumentFragment	DOCUMENT_FRAGMENT_NODE	11
DocumentType	DOCUMENT_TYPE_NODE	10
EntityReference	ENTITY_REFERENCE_NODE	5
Element	ELEMENT_NODE	1
Attr	ATTRIBUTE_NODE	2
ProcessingInstruction	PROCESSING_INSTRUCTION_NODE	7
Comment	COMMENT_NODE	8
Text	TEXT_NODE	3
CDATASection	CDATA_SECTION_NODE	4
Entity	ENTITY_NODE	6
Notation	NOTATION_NODE	12

PART

V

CH

25

If the current node is an Element node, the program will obtain the element's name with the getNodeName method. After printing the element's name, it obtains the attributes with the getAttribute method. This method returns a NamedNodeMap object. A NamedNodeMap enables you to access nodes by name rather than by index. The NodeList provides an indexed method of access to the attributes.

If any attributes are found, the program will loop through each attribute, printing the attribute name and value with an equal sign between them and quotation marks to enclose the value of the attribute. Finally, the program will print a closing angle bracket to indicate the end of the tag. For an element, the routine will return a true value, indicating that the node represents an Element.

If the node is a Text node, the program will print out the value of the node. Otherwise, if it is not a Text node, the program just prints the node's name and type.

For the following input

```
<item name='PriorityFlag'><text>0</text></item>
<item name='country'><text/></item>
```

the program will produce the following output:

```
<item name="PriorityFlag"><text>0</text>
</item>
<item name="country"><text></text>
</item>
```

You can see that the output is not formatted identically with the input. However, the logical meaning of both the input and output trees are the same. Make sure you understand why the output is formatted differently from the input. I'll leave it as an exercise for the reader to modify the programs to produce output that is formatted similarly to the input format of this example.

THE DOM APPLICATION PROGRAMMING INTERFACE

This section describes each DOM interface as well as the DOMException class. Because the API is specified mainly as a set of interfaces, the implementation is free to provide a different class structure.

The classes and interfaces of the DOM are all contained in the org.w3c.dom package. In the class and interface definitions, the package name is omitted. However, when you incorporate the use of this API with the Domino Objects API, you might need to qualify the interfaces. For example, the Domino Objects API has a class called Document and the DOM API also has an interface called Document. To clarify which name is referenced, you can use a fully qualified name such as org.w3c.dom.Document.

THE DOMException CLASS

```
public abstract class DOMException extends RuntimeException {
    public DOMException(short code, String message) {
        super(message);
        this.code = code;
    }
    public short    code;
    // ExceptionCode
    public static final short    INDEX_SIZE_ERR            = 1;
    public static final short    DOMSTRING_SIZE_ERR        = 2;
    public static final short    HIERARCHY_REQUEST_ERR = 3;
    public static final short    WRONG_DOCUMENT_ERR    = 4;
    public static final short    INVALID_CHARACTER_ERR = 5;
    public static final short    NO_DATA_ALLOWED_ERR   = 6;
    public static final short    NO_MODIFICATION_ALLOWED_ERR = 7;
    public static final short    NOT_FOUND_ERR            = 8;
    public static final short    NOT_SUPPORTED_ERR        = 9;
    public static final short    INUSE_ATTRIBUTE_ERR      = 10;
}
```

The DOMException class is specified as an abstract class. Each implementation of the DOM specification must provide an implementation of this class. Exceptions can be thrown by the underlying DOM routines. This class defines the errors that can occur.

THE Document INTERFACE

```
public interface Document extends Node {
    public DocumentType      getDoctype();
```

```
public DOMImplementation  getImplementation();
public Element            getDocumentElement();
public Element            createElement(String tagName) throws DOMException;
public DocumentFragment   createDocumentFragment();
public Text               createTextNode(String data);
public Comment            createComment(String data);
public CDATASection       createCDATASection(String data)
                                  throws DOMException;
public ProcessingInstruction createProcessingInstruction(String target,
                                  String data) throws DOMException;
public Attr               createAttribute(String name)  throws DOMException;
public EntityReference    createEntityReference(String name)
                                  throws DOMException;
public NodeList           getElementsByTagName(String tagname);
}
```

The Document interface represents the outermost container for the XML (or HTML) document. As you saw in the previous example, you can use the getDocumentElement to obtain the root element of the document. The other methods enable you to create and obtain information in the DOM tree.

PROPERTIES

```
public DocumentType getDocType();
```

The getDocType property routine returns a DocumentType object. The document type of the DOM is meant to provide information from the DTD. In Level 1, the DocumentType interface essentially just provides access to the entities and does not provide full access to all the DTD information.

```
public DOMImplementation getImplementation();
```

The getImplementation property returns a DOMImplementation object. This object is meant to encapsulate properties and methods that are not dependent on a specific instance of the Document Object Model. See the DOMImplementation description in this chapter for more information.

```
public Element getDocumentElement();
```

The root element of the DOM tree is called the *document* element. You can retrieve this element from the Document object through the getDocumentElement property routine. Suppose iXml is a Domino Item object. The following will parse the contained XML, return the DOM document, and then retrieve the document element:

```
org.w3c.dom.Document domdoc = iXml.parseXML(false);
  // Get the root element
  org.w3c.dom.Element docelem = domdoc.getDocumentElement();
```

METHODS

```
public Element createElement(String tagName) throws DOMException;
```

The createElement method will create a new object that implements the Element interface. An Element extends a node, so all the Node properties and methods are also available. The tagName parameter specifies the name (not the type) of the Element to create.

```
public DocumentFragment createDocumentFragment();
```

A DocumentFragment is a lightweight component that can be used instead of a complete Document object. A DocumentFragment might be useful in the construction or parsing of an XML document, similar to the use of a temporary variable. The createDocumentFragment method is used to create a DocumentFragment object.

```
public Text createTextNode(String data);
```

A Text object is used to store the text of an Element or Attr object within the DOM tree. The createTextNode method is used to create a Text object.

```
public Comment createComment(String data);
```

The createComment method creates and returns a Comment node. The Comment object can be used to obtain the text of the comment.

```
public CDATASection createCDATASection(String data) throws DOMException;
```

A CDATA section is used to escape sections of text that might otherwise appear to be markup. The CDATASection object is used to handle this type of object in the DOM tree. CDATA sections cannot be nested, and the only delimiter recognized for this type of section is]]>. All other markup is included within the data.

Here is an example:

```
<![CDATA[
This appears <asif>it is markup</asif>
even though it is not.
]]>
```

Note that the <asif> element within the CDATA section will be treated as text, even though it appears as if it is markup.

The CDATASection interface extends the Text interface but provides no additional properties or methods.

```
public ProcessingInstruction createProcessingInstruction(String target,
String data) throws DOMException;
```

The createProcessingInstruction method creates and returns a ProcessingInstruction node. Processing instructions are a way to store processor-specific instructions within a document.

```
public Attr createAttribute(String name) throws DOMException;
```

The createAttribute method creates an Attr (attribute) node with the specified name. This method will create the Attr node as a free-standing node. To be useful, it should be attached to an Element node with the setAttributeNode method of Element. You can also create an attribute directly on an Element node with the setAttribute method of the Element.

```
public EntityReference createEntityReference(String name) throws
DOMException;
```

The createEntityReference method creates an EntityReference node with the specified name. If entities and references to them are in the original source document, the processor might not expand the references. This method can be used to explicitly create a reference to an entity.

```
public NodeList getElementsByTagName(String tagName) throws DOMException;
```

The getElementsByTagName method returns a NodeList that contains a list of all the Elements that have the specified tagName. They are returned in the order that would be obtained by a preorder traversal of the DOM tree. The special value of "*" for tagName matches all tags in the tree.

THE DocumentFragment INTERFACE

```
public interface DocumentFragment extends Node {
}
```

Document fragments are designed to provide a lightweight alternative to a Document object. The DocumentFragment interface extends the Node interface. As you can tell, no additional properties or methods are available in Level 1 beyond those available in a Node, so this interface clearly passes the test of being lightweight. This interface might be expanded in future releases of the DOM specification.

THE Node INTERFACE

```
public interface Node {
  // NodeType
  public static final short   ELEMENT_NODE             = 1;
  public static final short   ATTRIBUTE_NODE           = 2;
  public static final short   TEXT_NODE                = 3;
  public static final short   CDATA_SECTION_NODE       = 4;
  public static final short   ENTITY_REFERENCE_NODE    = 5;
  public static final short   ENTITY_NODE              = 6;
  public static final short   PROCESSING_INSTRUCTION_NODE = 7;
  public static final short   COMMENT_NODE             = 8;
  public static final short   DOCUMENT_NODE            = 9;
  public static final short   DOCUMENT_TYPE_NODE       = 10;
  public static final short   DOCUMENT_FRAGMENT_NODE   = 11;
  public static final short   NOTATION_NODE            = 12;
```

```
    public String          getNodeName();
    public String          getNodeValue() throws DOMException;
    public void            setNodeValue(String nodeValue) throws DOMException;
    public short           getNodeType();
    public Node            getParentNode();
    public NodeList        getChildNodes();
    public Node            getFirstChild();
    public Node            getLastChild();
    public Node            getPreviousSibling();
    public Node            getNextSibling();
    public NamedNodeMap    getAttributes();
    public Document        getOwnerDocument();
    public Node            insertBefore(Node newChild, Node refChild)
                               throws DOMException;
    public Node            replaceChild(Node newChild, Node oldChild)
                               throws DOMException;
    public Node            removeChild(Node oldChild) throws DOMException;
    public Node            appendChild(Node newChild) throws DOMException;
    public boolean         hasChildNodes();
    public Node            cloneNode(boolean deep);
}
```

The Node interface is probably the most important interface in the DOM API. All elements of the DOM tree are Nodes, and you can traverse the DOM tree by using the Node methods. Other interfaces, such as the Element interface, extend the Node interface to provide a higher-level conceptual model for the Node in the tree and merely serve as a programming convenience. Although the interface defines the capability to create child nodes, children might not be allowed for certain types of nodes such as Text nodes. If an attempt is made to add a child node, a DOMException will be raised.

You can determine the type of the current node by using the getNodeType property routine.

PROPERTIES

```
public short getNodeType();

public String getNodeName();

public String getNodeValue() throws DOMException;

public void setNodeValue(String nodeValue) throws DOMException;
```

The value of the Node name and value depend on the type of node. Table 25.3 lists the correspondence between the DOM objects and the Node properties.

TABLE 25.3   DOM OBJECT Node PROPERTIES

DOM Object	Node Type	Node Name	Node Value
Element	ELEMENT_NODE	tagName	null
Attr	ATTRIBUTE_NODE	Name of attribute	Value of attribute

DOM Object	Node Type	Node Name	Node Value
Text	TEXT_NODE	#text	Content of text node
CDATASection	CDATA_SECTION_NODE	#cdata-section	Content of the CDATA-Section
EntityReference	ENTITY_REFERENCE_NODE	Name of entity referenced	null
Entity	ENTITY_NODE	Entity name	null
ProcessingInstruction	PROCESSING_INSTRUCTION_NODE	target	Entire content excluding the target
Comment	COMMENT_NODE	#comment	Content of the comment
Document	DOCUMENT_NODE	#document	null
DocumentType	DOCUMENT_TYPE_NODE	document type name	null
DocumentFragment	DOCUMENT_FRAGMENT_NODE	#document-fragment	null
Notation	NOTATION_NODE	notation name	null

The value in the Node Type column is the name of the Java integer constant that will be returned for the getNodeType method. The getNodeName routine will return a text string with the content of the column called Node Name. The getNodeValue routine will return the contents indicated in the Node Value column. The setNodeValue routine accepts a string value. If a particular type of node does not allow the setting of a value, a DOMException with the value NO_MODIFICATION_ALLOWED_ERR will be raised.

```
public Node getParentNode();
```
The getParentNode property routine will return the parent of the current node. If a Node has not been added to the tree, the parent node will be null. Document, DocumentFragment, and Attr nodes will always return null for the parent node.

```
public NodeList getChildNodes();
```
The getChildNodes property returns a NodeList of all the children of the current node. If no children exist, the NodeList will be empty. The child nodes contained in the NodeList will actively reflect any changes made to them subsequent to the creation of the NodeList. They are not static snapshots of the nodes.

```
public Node getFirstChild();
```

```
public Node getLastChild();
```

The getFirstChild and getLastChild property routines will return the first or last child of the current node, respectively. If no children exist, the property routine will return null.

```
public Node getPreviousSibling();
```

```
public Node getNextSibling();
```

The getPreviousSibling and getNextSibling property routines respectively will return the previous or next node at the same level as the current node. If no corresponding node exists, the property routine will return null.

```
public NamedNodeMap getAttributes();
```

The getAttributes property routine will return a NamedNodeMap of the attributes for the current Element node. If the current node is not an Element, the property will return null.

```
public Document getOwnerDocument();
```

The getOwnerDocument returns the Document that is associated with the current node. This Document object can be used to create new nodes. If the current node is a Document, the property will return null.

METHODS

```
public Node insertBefore(Node newChild, Node refChild) throws DOMException;
```

The insertBefore method will insert the newChild node prior to the refChild node in the list of children for the current node. If refChild is null, the new node will be appended to the end of the tree. If refChild is not a child of the current node, or if the current node is read-only, a DOMException will be raised. If the newChild node was created from a different document or would cause a circular reference in the tree, a DOMException will be raised. If the newChild is already in the tree, it will first be removed before being reinserted. If the newChild is a DocumentFragment, all the children are inserted in the same order into the DOM tree.

```
public Node replaceChild(Node newChild, Node oldChild) throws DOMException;
```

The replaceChild method will replace the oldChild node with the newChild node in the list of children for the current node. If oldChild is not a child of the current node, or if the current node is read-only, a DOMException will be raised. If the newChild node was created from a different Document or would cause a circular reference in the tree, a DOMException will be raised. If the newChild is already in the tree, it will first be removed before being reinserted.

```
public Node removeChild(Node oldChild) throws DOMException;
```

The removeChild method will remove the oldChild node with the newChild node in the list of children for the current node. If oldChild is not a child of the current node, or if the current node is read-only, a DOMException will be raised.

```
public Node appendChild(Node newChild) throws DOMException;
```

The appendChild method will append the newChild node to the end of the list of children for the current node. If the current node is read-only, a DOMException will be raised. If the newChild node was created from a different document or would cause a circular reference in the tree, a DOMException will be raised. If the newChild is already in the tree, it will first be removed before being reinserted.

```
public boolean hasChildNodes();
```

The hasChildNodes method returns true if the current node has child nodes and false otherwise.

```
public Node cloneNode(boolean deep);
```

The cloneNode makes a copy of the current node. The new node does not have a parent. If the deep parameter is false, only the current node and attributes (if the node is an Element) are copied. If the deep parameter is true, the clone will contain a copy of the entire subtree of the current node. You should specify the deep parameter to be true if you want to copy the text of an Element because the textual information is contained in the Text children of the Element node.

THE NodeList INTERFACE

```
public interface NodeList {
    public Node       item(int index);
    public int        getLength();
}
```

The NodeList interface represents a list of nodes. It is similar to a Java Vector. You can access each node in the list by using the item method and by supplying an index. The getLength method will return the number of nodes in the list.

```
public Node item(int index);
```

The item method returns the node at the specified index. If no such index is found, the method will return null. This method will not raise any exceptions.

```
public int getLength();
```

The getLength method returns the number of elements in the NodeList.

THE NamedNodeMap INTERFACE

```
public interface NamedNodeMap {
    public Node    getNamedItem(String name);
    public Node    setNamedItem(Node arg)         throws DOMException;
    public Node    removeNamedItem(String name)   throws DOMException;
    public Node    item(int index);
    public int     getLength();
}
```

The NamedNodeMap interface is used to implement a list of items that can be accessed by either name or index. The items within the list are all nodes. You can add and remove nodes from the list.

```
public Node getNamedItem(String name);
```

The getNamedItem method returns the node with the specified name. If no item with the given name is found, the method will return null. This method will not raise any exceptions.

```
public Node setNamedItem(Node arg) throws DOMException;
```

The setNamedItem method sets the node with the specified name. A NamedNodeMap cannot contain nodes with duplicate names. If you call setNamedItem with a node that duplicates the name of a node already in the NamedNodeMap, the node is replaced. The returned node represents the old node that was replaced. If no replacement was made, null is returned.

```
public Node removeNamedItem(String name) throws DOMException;
```

The removeNamedItem method removes the node with the specified name. The returned node is the node that was removed. If the name is not found, a DOMException is raised.

```
public Node item(int index);
```

The item method returns the node at the specified index. If no such index is found, the method will return null. This method will not raise any exceptions.

```
public int getLength();
```

The getLength method returns the number of elements in the NamedNodeMap.

THE Element INTERFACE

```
public interface Element extends Node {
    public String    getTagName();
    public String    getAttribute(String name);
    public void      setAttribute(String name, String value) throws DOMException;
    public void      removeAttribute(String name) throws DOMException;
    public Attr      getAttributeNode(String name);
    public Attr      setAttributeNode(Attr newAttr) throws DOMException;
    public Attr      removeAttributeNode(Attr oldAttr) throws DOMException;
```

```
    public NodeList  getElementsByTagName(String name);
    public void      normalize();
}
```

The `Element` interface is used to handle element tags. An element tag can contain attributes. However, attributes are not considered children of the `Element`. You can retrieve or set an attribute as a string or as a node. If you use the `String` methods, entities are not expanded, and any text that appears like an entity is treated as literal text. To process entity references, use the `Node` routines, such as `getAttributeNode`.

Consider the following XML fragment:

```
<doc name="Holiday" place="Southwest">
  <item type="Western"/>
  <item type="Movies"/>
</doc>
```

In this example, the `<doc>` element has two child `<item>` elements, but the `name` and `place` attributes are retrieved from the `Element` node through the `getAttribute` method or the `getAttributes` method inherited from the `Node` interface.

PROPERTIES

```
public String getTagName();
```

The `getTagName` property routine returns the tag name of the current `Element`. This property is read-only.

METHODS

```
public String getAttribute(String name);
```

The `getAttribute` property routine returns the string value of the named attribute. It will return the empty string if no such attribute is found.

```
public void setAttribute(String name, String value) throws DOMException;
```

The `setAttribute` method sets the named attribute with the specified value.

```
public void removeAttribute(String name) throws DOMException;
```

The `removeAttribute` method removes the named attribute from the element. If the attribute has a default value, the default value will be reinstated.

```
public Attr getAttributeNode(String name);
```

The `getAttributeNode` property routine returns the value of the named attribute as an `Attr` node. The method will return `null` if no such attribute exists.

```
public Attr setAttributeNode(Attr newAttr) throws DOMException;
```

The setAttributeNode method sets the named attribute with the specified Attr node. If the attribute is replacing another attribute with the same name, the old attribute is returned; otherwise, null is returned.

```
public Attr removeAttributeNode(Attr oldAttr) throws DOMException;
```

The removeAttributeNode method removes the named attribute. The removed attribute is returned. If the attribute is not found, an exception is raised.

```
public NodeList getElementsByTagName(String name);
```

The getElementsByTagName method returns a NodeList of all the elements that match the specified tag name. If you use "*" as the name, it matches all elements. The nodes are returned in the order they would be visited in a preorder traversal (visit a node first, and then its children).

```
public void normalize();
```

The normalize method normalizes the element tree by combining adjacent Text nodes into a single Text node. Text nodes are then only separated by markup. This method enables you to construct a tree without regard to preceding or following nodes. After a tree or subtree has been constructed, you can normalize it to combine adjacent Text nodes.

THE Attr INTERFACE

```
public interface Attr extends Node {
  public String              getName();
  public boolean             getSpecified();
  public String              getValue();
  public void                setValue(String value);
}
```

The Attr interface is used to store attribute values attached to an Element. Attr nodes are not explicitly kept within an Element tree. They can be accessed only through the Element to which they are attached.

PROPERTIES

```
public String getName();
```

The getName property routine returns the name of the attribute.

```
public boolean getSpecified();
```

The getSpecified property routine returns true if the attribute has been specified in the original document or through the setValue method and false if not. After the value is set to true, the only way to reset it to its original state is to delete the attribute.

```
public String getValue();
```

```
public void setValue(String value);
```

The getValue property routine gets the value of the attribute, and the setValue property routine sets the value of the attribute.

THE CharacterData INTERFACE

```
public interface CharacterData extends Node {
  public String   getData()throws DOMException;
  public void     setData(String data) throws DOMException;
  public int      getLength();
  public String   substringData(int offset, int count) throws DOMException;
  public void     appendData(String arg) throws DOMException;
  public void     insertData(int offset, String arg) throws DOMException;
  public void     deleteData(int offset, int count) throws DOMException;
  public void     replaceData(int offset, int count, String arg)
  ➥throws DOMException;
}
```

The CharacterData interface is used by both the Text interface and the Comment interface to represent character data within the tree. You can get and set the string data and insert, delete, replace, and append additional data to the string. No DOM objects correspond directly to a CharacterData node. All offsets in the various routines begin at 0.

PROPERTIES

```
public String getData() throws DOMException;
```

```
public void setData(String data) throws DOMException;
```

The getData property routine returns the character data as a string. The setData routine sets the current value of the character data.

```
public int getLength();
```

The getLength property routine returns the length of the character data.

METHODS

```
public String substringData(int offset, int count) throws DOMException;
```

The substringData method extracts a substring from the character data beginning at the specified offset for the given count. If the count is negative or greater than the length of the string, an exception is raised.

```
public void appendData(String arg) throws DOMException;
```

The appendData method appends the new string to the end of the existing character's string.

```
public void insertData(int offset, String arg) throws DOMException;
```

The insertData method inserts the new arg string at the specified offset in the existing character's string.

```
public void deleteData(int offset, int count) throws DOMException;
```

The deleteData method deletes characters from the character data beginning at the specified offset for the given count. If the count is negative or greater than the length of the string, an exception is raised.

```
public void replaceData(int offset, int count, String arg) throws
DOMException;
```

The replaceData method replaces characters from the character data beginning at the specified offset for the given count with the new arg string. If the count is negative or greater than the length of the string, an exception is raised.

THE Comment INTERFACE

```
public interface Comment extends CharacterData {
}
```

The Comment interface is used to identify a node as a comment. This interface extends the CharacterData interface but does not add any unique properties or methods.

THE Text INTERFACE

```
public interface Text extends CharacterData {
  public Text  splitText(int offset) throws DOMException;
}
```

The Text interface extends the CharacterData interface and includes all its properties and methods. The only unique method provided by the Text interface is the splitText method.

METHODS

```
public Text splitText(int offset) throws DOMException;
```

The splitText method splits the current Text node by creating a new Text node sibling. The current Text node will contain text up to the offset (starting at 0). After the call, the length of the current node will be equal to the offset. A new Text node will be created immediately following the current Text node and will contain the remainder of the characters.

THE CDATASection INTERFACE

```
public interface CDATASection extends Text {
}
```

CDATA sections are used to escape characters that would otherwise be treated as markup. The CDATASection interface extends the Text interface but does not add any unique properties or methods.

THE DocumentType INTERFACE

```
public interface DocumentType extends Node {
    public String          getName();
    public NamedNodeMap     getEntities();
    public NamedNodeMap     getNotations();
}
```

The DocumentType interface is used to retrieve the name and other information from the Document Type Definition (DTD). In Level 1, only the entities and notations are available.

PROPERTIES

```
public String getName();
```

The getName property routine obtains the name of the DTD. This is the name that immediately follows the DOCTYPE keyword.

```
public NamedNodeMap getEntities();
```

The getEntities property routine returns a NamedNodeMap that contains the general entities defined in the DTD. Parameter entities, which are used only within the DTD itself, are not returned.

```
public NamedNodeMap getNotations();
```

The getNotations property routine returns a NamedNodeMap that contains the notations defined in the DTD. Notations are used for external references.

THE Entity INTERFACE

```
public interface Entity extends Node {
    public String     getPublicId();
    public String     getSystemId();
    public String     getNotationName();
}
```

The Entity interface is used to model the entity value. You can obtain the name and value using the base Node class. The properties that extend the node interface are used for external entities. Note that the processor can expand entities before they are placed in the tree, so entity definitions might not be available.

PROPERTIES

```
public String getPublicID();
```

The getPublicID property routine returns the public ID defined for the entity in the DTD.

```
public String getSystemID();
```

The getSystemID property routine returns the system ID defined for the entity in the DTD.

```
public String getNotationName();
```

The getNotationName property routine returns the name for a declared notation. This is the name that follows the NDATA keyword in the DTD.

THE EntityReference INTERFACE

```
public interface EntityReference extends Node {
}
```

The EntityReference interface is used for references to entities. Note that the processor can expand entities so that an entity reference in the original source document might not appear in the DOM tree.

THE Notation INTERFACE

```
public interface Notation extends Node {
   public String      getPublicId();
   public String      getSystemId();
}
```

The Notation interface represents a notation declared in the DTD. It is used either by a processing instruction or by an unparsed entity.

PROPERTIES

```
public String getPublicID();
```

The getPublicID property routine returns the public ID defined for the notation in the DTD.

```
public String getSystemID();
```

The getSystemID property routine returns the system ID defined for the notation in the DTD.

THE ProcessingInstruction INTERFACE

```
public interface ProcessingInstruction extends Node {
    public String    getTarget();
    public String    getData();
    public void       setData(String data) throws DOMException;
}
```

The ProcessingInstruction interface is used to store an XML processing instruction within the document. Processing instructions contain information that can be used by the processor to control the processing of the document.

PROPERTIES

```
public String getTarget();
```

The getTarget property routine returns the target of the processing instruction. The target is the first token found after the markup that begins the processing instruction.

```
public String getData();
```

The getData property routine returns the data portion of the processing instruction. The data portion is the content staring at the first non-white space text after the target and until the character immediately preceding the ?> that ends the processing instruction.

THE DOMImplementation INTERFACE

```
public interface DOMImplementation {
    public boolean    hasFeature(String feature, String version);
}
```

The purpose of the DOMImplementation interface is to hold any information that is not dependent on a specific implementation of DOM. You can obtain the DOMImplementation object through the getImplementation property of the Document object.

METHODS

```
public boolean hasFeature(String feature, String version);
```

The hasFeature method returns true if the DOM supports the specified feature and version. The only supported strings for the feature of DOM Level 1 are xml and html. For DOM Level 1, the version string should be 1.0.

The Domino implementation as of release 5.0.3 supports only the XML feature, not the HTML feature. The feature string is not case sensitive.

The following code will print true for the hasFeature method:

```
org.w3c.dom.Document domdoc = iXml.parseXML(false);
org.w3c.dom.DOMImplementation di = domdoc.getImplementation();
System.out.println("Has feature xml 1.0: " + di.hasFeature("xml", "1.0"));
```

YET ANOTHER DOM TREE PRINTING PROGRAM

Earlier in this chapter I gave you an example of a program that would print out a simplified DOM tree. Here is another program that covers other Node types and is more complete:

```java
import org.w3c.dom.*;
import java.io.*;

// Print XML DOM Tree
class PrintDOMTree {
  // Constructor
  public PrintDOMTree() {};

  // Prints the specified Dom tree node, recursively. */
  public void printTree(Node node, PrintWriter out)  {
    int type = node.getNodeType();
    switch (type)  {
        // Print the main document node (root element)
        case Node.DOCUMENT_NODE: {
          out.println("Content-type: text/xml");  // Print the MIME type
          out.println("");                         // Close out header
          out.println("<?xml version=\"1.0\" ?>");
          printTree(((org.w3c.dom.Document)node).getDocumentElement(), out);
          break;
        }

        // Print an Element and its attributes plus child nodes (if they exist)
        case Node.ELEMENT_NODE: {
          out.print("<" + node.getNodeName());
          NamedNodeMap attrs = node.getAttributes();
          for (int i = 0; i < attrs.getLength(); i++) {
            Node attr = attrs.item(i);
            out.print(" " + attr.getNodeName() +
                      "=\"" + attr.getNodeValue() + "\"");
          }
          out.println(">");

          NodeList cNodes = node.getChildNodes();
          if (null != cNodes) {
            int len = cNodes.getLength();
            for (int i = 0; i < len; i++)
             printTree(cNodes.item(i),out);
          }

          out.println("");
          out.println("</" + node.getNodeName() + ">");

          break;
        }

        // Print Text nodes
        case Node.TEXT_NODE: {
          out.print(node.getNodeValue());
          break;
        }

        // Print CDATA sections
```

```
        case Node.CDATA_SECTION_NODE: {
            out.print("<![CDATA[" + node.getNodeValue() + "]]>");
            break;
        }

        // Print Entity reference nodes
        case Node.ENTITY_REFERENCE_NODE: {
            out.print("&" + node.getNodeName() + ";");
            break;
        }

        // Print processing instruction
        case Node.PROCESSING_INSTRUCTION_NODE: {
            out.print("<?");
            out.print(node.getNodeName()); // target
            String cPI = node.getNodeValue(); // The processing instruction
            out.print(" " + cPI + "?>");
            break;
        }
    }

  }
}
```

This program operates in roughly the same manner as the previous program, but in this one I use a `switch` statement instead of a set of nested `if` statements. Now that you have seen the complete DOM API, how the printing program works should be clearer.

As you know, only a single `Document` node is in the tree. When this is encountered, the XML header is output. The `Element` node handles the `Element` tags and their attributes. The other nodes don't really do too much work.

CREATING A DOM TREE FROM SCRATCH

In addition to using the DOM API for parsing and processing an XML document, you can use the DOM API to create a tree from scratch. Here is a Domino agent that can run as a Web agent and return XML to a browser. The XML is generated dynamically by calling the DOM API. After the tree has been built, it uses the `printTree` routine from the previous section to print and send the XML to the browser.

```
import lotus.domino.*;
import java.io.*;
import org.w3c.dom.*;

public class JavaAgent extends AgentBase {

  public void NotesMain() {
     try {
        Session session = getSession();
        AgentContext agentContext = session.getAgentContext();
        Database db;              // Domino Database

        PrintWriter out = this.getAgentOutput();
```

```java
org.w3c.dom.Document doc = (org.w3c.dom.Document)Class.
            forName("com.ibm.xml.dom.DocumentImpl").newInstance();

Element root = doc.createElement("Session");

Attr attrIsOnServer = doc.createAttribute("IsOnServer");
attrIsOnServer.setValue(session.isOnServer()?"true":"false");
root.setAttributeNode(attrIsOnServer);

Attr attrNotesVersion = doc.createAttribute("NotesVersion");
attrNotesVersion.setValue(session.getNotesVersion() );
root.setAttributeNode(attrNotesVersion);

Attr attrPlatform = doc.createAttribute("Platform");
attrPlatform.setValue(session.getPlatform() );
root.setAttributeNode(attrPlatform);

Attr attrServerName = doc.createAttribute("ServerName");
attrServerName.setValue(session.getServerName() );
root.setAttributeNode(attrServerName);

Element username = doc.createElement("UserName");
username.appendChild(doc.createTextNode(session.getUserName()));
root.appendChild(username);

Element commonusername = doc.createElement("CommonUserName");
commonusername.appendChild(doc.createTextNode(
                          session.getCommonUserName() ));
root.appendChild(commonusername);

Element url = doc.createElement("URL");
url.appendChild(doc.createTextNode(session.getURL()));
root.appendChild(url);

Element urldatabase = doc.createElement("URLDatabase");
db = session.getURLDatabase();
urldatabase.appendChild(doc.createTextNode(db.getFilePath()));
root.appendChild(urldatabase);

Element addressbooks = doc.createElement("AddressBooks");
java.util.Vector ab = session.getAddressBooks();
Element addressbk;
for(int i=0; i < ab.size();++i) {
  db = (Database) ab.elementAt(i);
  addressbk = doc.createElement("AddressBook");
    addressbk.appendChild(doc.createTextNode(db.getFilePath()));
    addressbooks.appendChild(addressbk);
}
root.appendChild(addressbooks);

Element agentctx = doc.createElement("AgentContext");

Element currentdb = doc.createElement("CurrentDatabase");
db = agentContext.getCurrentDatabase();
currentdb.appendChild(doc.createTextNode(db.getFilePath()));
agentctx.appendChild(currentdb);
```

```
        Element effectiveusername = doc.createElement("EffectiveUserName");
        effectiveusername.appendChild(doc.createTextNode(
                            agentContext.getEffectiveUserName()  ));
        agentctx.appendChild(effectiveusername);
        root.appendChild(agentctx);

        doc.appendChild(root);
        PrintDOMTree pt = new PrintDOMTree();

        pt.printTree(doc, out);
      }
    catch (Exception e) {
      System.err.println(e);
      }
    }
}
```

The beginning few lines of the agent represent the familiar code that obtains a session, agent context, and agent's output `PrintWriter`. The next statement is as follows:

```
org.w3c.dom.Document doc = (org.w3c.dom.Document)Class.
                forName("com.ibm.xml.dom.DocumentImpl").newInstance();
```

This statement requires some explanation. Recall that a `Document` node represents the root node of a DOM tree. `Document` is a Java interface, not a class. As you might know, you cannot create an object with a type that has been defined as an interface. In other words, you cannot directly create a new `Document` object. The following statement will not work:

```
org.w3c.dom.Document doc = new org.w3c.dom.Document(); // DOES NOT WORK
```

You can instantiate only an object of a class, not an interface. It turns out that the `xml4j.jar` file does contain a class you can use to instantiate a document: It is the `com.ibm.xml.dom.DocumentImpl` class. This class is the one that actually implements the `Document` interface. I've used the `forName` and `newInstance` methodology to create the object because you might want to use another class that implements the `Document` interface. For example, if you were using the Xerces implementation from the Apache organization, the full class name would be `org.apache.xerces.dom.DocumentImpl`. You would substitute this name for the IBM name.

After the document has been created, you can create an `Element`. In this case, the root (first) `Element` will represent a Domino session. After the root `Element` has been created, I create four attributes of the `Session` node. These are for the `IsOnServer`, `NotesVersion`, `Platform`, and `ServerName` attributes. After each attribute has been created, I attach it to the root element with the `setAttributeNode` method.

The remainder of the program queries attributes of the Domino `Session` class and formats them as XML. Here is some sample output from the agent:

```
<?xml version="1.0" ?>
<Session IsOnServer="true" NotesVersion="Build V503_02152000 |
➥February 15, 2000       " Platform="Windows/32"
➥ServerName="CN=BENTLEY/O=GWCorp">
<UserName>
CN=BENTLEY/O=GWCorp
```

```
</UserName>
<CommonUserName>
BENTLEY
</CommonUserName>
<URL>
</URL>
<URLDatabase>
web.nsf
</URLDatabase>
<AddressBooks>
<AddressBook>
names.nsf
</AddressBook>
</AddressBooks>
<AgentContext>
<CurrentDatabase>
Testing\TestXML.nsf
</CurrentDatabase>
<EffectiveUserName>
CN=Randy Tamura/O=GWCorp
</EffectiveUserName>
</AgentContext>
</Session>
```

Of course, your output will contain different information. The formatting of the tree was accomplished by the printTree routine of the PrintDOMTree class.

CHAPTER REVIEW

1. Explain why the DOM nodes are defined as interfaces rather than classes in Java. What is the difference between an interface and a class?

2. What is the difference between an Element and a Node?

3. In the section titled "A Simple DOM Example," I created an agent that would traverse a DOM tree and print formatted XML as the output. The formatting in the example is not the same as that provided by Domino's generateXML method. Update the example to format the output so that the line breaks occur at the same locations as in the input. Also, your output should contain tags such as <text/> instead of <text></text>.

4. Suppose you have an employee database. Documents in the database contain employee name, ID number, address, and other information. Write a Java agent that will be called with a parameter to identify the employee. The agent should look up the employee in a view, obtain the corresponding document, and then create an XML DOM tree from the document contents. It should then format the tree and send it back to the browser in XML format.

5. What is a NamedNodeMap, and how is it used? What are the differences and similarities between a NamedNodeMap and a NodeList?

6. Write a Java agent that can take an XML file as input and then call the parseXML method to create a DOM tree. The program should then traverse the DOM tree and create a Domino document for the data found in the tree. For example, suppose the

root element is <order> and represents a customer order. Subsidiary elements might include customer number or customer name as well as the identifiers for the items to be ordered. After parsing the XML, the program should process the order by creating a Domino document from the information.

7. Write a Java program that can read an email document (for example, Memo form). From the Domino document, it should create an XML file that contains the usual fields: SendTo, CopyTo, and so on. Write a corresponding reader program to read and parse the XML and convert it to an email message.

8. Create an XML data format to represent Access Control Lists (ACLs). After you have done that, write a Domino agent that can read the ACL in XML format and apply it to a real database to update the ACL. Hint: Try your program on a test database. If a bug is in your program, you can get locked out of the database without a way to fix the ACL.

9. Create an XML data format for representing new users. Use the Domino Registration class to write a routine to register new users based on the XML data input.

CHAPTER 26

INTEGRATING DOMINO WITH RELATIONAL DATABASES USING JDBC

In this chapter

WHY INTEGRATE WITH RELATIONAL DATABASES?

When you read books about Lotus Notes and Domino technology it might seem as if Domino can solve all your database needs. It is, after all, a database system. When and why would it make sense to integrate Domino with a relational database system (RDB) such as IBM's DB2, Oracle, Microsoft's SQL Server, or some other system?

A variety of reasons explain why it would make good sense to integrate a relational database system with Domino. First, you might already have an application that uses a relational database system. In this case, it can be much simpler to integrate Domino rather than try to convert or port the application. Second, certain kinds of applications are better suited to a relational database system rather than Domino.

Although Domino is a database system, its strength is as a document database. That is, Domino excels where the information is unstructured—email, workflow, Web pages, knowledge management, discussion databases, and any application where a significant communication component as well as a database component exists.

Relational databases (RDBs) excel where the data is structured, for example, where you potentially might have a huge amount of data but most of it is in the same format. Applications where you are counting things such as inventory, accounting, or record keeping are good candidates for relational databases. Applications where you need real-time access to a central repository of data are another class of application for RDBs.

Try to use the proper tool for the job. Thus, when implementing your inventory management system, you should use an RDB, but when implementing email, use Domino. It should be clear, then, that good reasons exist to have both Domino and a relational database system implemented within the same company. In fact, it is almost hard to imagine any company that might have Domino that would *not* have a relational database system for some other application.

So, given the fact that your company probably has both Domino and an RDB, are there times when you would want to integrate the two? Again, it almost seems obvious that you would want to be able to tie them together. For example, your linked systems could provide an email to an ordering clerk when inventories run low. Your Web site, powered by Domino, could contain the latest pricing information from your RDB. You might want to keep customer purchasing information in an RDB but make it accessible for knowledge mining. Of course, this type of list can be easily extended or applied to your business. I'm sure you can come up with several ideas immediately.

INTRODUCTION TO IBM's DB2

For illustration in this chapter, I'm going to use IBM's DB2. Because Lotus is an IBM subsidiary, synergies exist between Domino and DB2. In particular, Lotus has developed a special DB2 Lotus Software Extension (LSX). You can access DB2 using JDBC, which is the Java standard for relational database access. The Domino Enterprise Connection Services

(DECS) interface also enables Domino to access DB2 data using a simple form user interface.

After you have installed DB2, you can use the Control Center to add and modify tables, users, and many other data control elements such as triggers and indexes. Figure 26.1 shows the DB2 Control Center.

Figure 26.1
The DB2 Control Center enables you to modify system information about your databases.

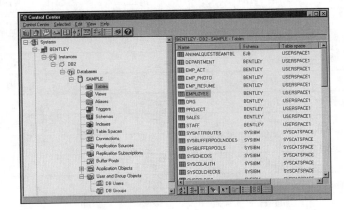

Notice that you can control multiple systems, multiple instances of DB2, and then different databases within DB2. I have highlighted the EMPLOYEE table from the SAMPLE database. The SAMPLE database is included with the standard DB2 installation, so if you have DB2, you can follow along. If you don't have DB2, you can create a table in your own database system. The examples I will show will not require complex features of your database system. My intention is to show you how to integrate Domino and your database system using Java, not to explain in depth how to use DB2 or any other database system.

REVIEWING AND UPDATING COLUMNS

Figure 26.2 shows a dialog box that enables you to alter column definitions in the EMPLOYEE table.

Figure 26.2
You can view and alter columns within the DB2 Control Center.

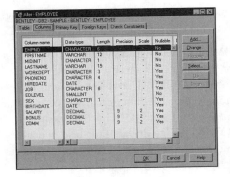

PART
V

CH
26

Similar capabilities exist in all RDB systems. You can control the name, data type, and length of each field within a table. In this example, the EMPLOYEE table has the characteristics shown in Table 26.1.

TABLE 26.1 DATA CHARACTERISTICS FOR THE EMPLOYEE TABLE

Column Name	Data Type	Length	Precision	Scale	Nullable
EMPNO	Character	6			No
FIRSTNME	Varchar	12			No
MIDINIT	Character	1			No
LASTNAME	Varchar	15			No
WORKDEPT	Character	3			Yes
PHONENO	Character	4			Yes
HIREDATE	Date				Yes
JOB	Character	8			Yes
EDLEVEL	SmallInt				No
SEX	Character	1			Yes
BIRTHDATE	Date				Yes
SALARY	Decimal		9	2	Yes
BONUS	Decimal		9	2	Yes
COMM	Decimal		9	2	Yes

The primary key for the EMPLOYEE table is the EMPNO column.

USING JAVA DATABASE CONNECTIVITY

Java Database Connectivity (JDBC) is the Java standard for accessing relational databases. A Java program that uses JDBC consists of several components. In addition to the Java application program, a JDBC manager provides the JDBC API (application programming interface). The JDBC manager is a database-independent layer providing general JDBC services. The JDBC manager relies on a set of JDBC drivers to provide the actual database access.

The database vendors, such as IBM or Oracle, typically write JDBC drivers. By providing a JDBC driver, the database vendor provides access to the database for Java programmers. Because each vendor typically provides the JDBC driver, the functionality of the drivers can vary from vendor to vendor. Although the basic functionality is common, advanced features are typically database-specific. In addition to the JDBC database-specific drivers, Sun Microsystems provides a JDBC-ODBC bridge driver. This bridge enables Java JDBC programs to access any database that already has an ODBC driver. ODBC stands for *Open Database Connectivity* and is a Microsoft database API standard.

You can find the JDBC API routines in the `java.sql` package. So, at the beginning of any program that accesses JDBC, you should import the `java.sql` package with a statement such as

```
import java.sql.*;
```

LOADING A DATABASE DRIVER

The first step in using JDBC to access a relational database is to load the database driver. As mentioned, these drivers are usually shipped with the database system itself. For example, IBM's DB2 ships with a Java JDBC driver. It is typically located in the `db2java.zip` file in the `sqllib\java` directory. The JDBC-ODBC database driver is located in the `classes.zip` file that is shipped with the Java Development Kit (JDK) or with various compilers and IDEs.

Make sure that you list the driver's Zip or jar file in the `CLASSPATH` variable or its IDE equivalent. Here are the actual names of the driver classes for DB2 and ODBC:

```
DB2       COM.ibm.db2.jdbc.app.DB2Driver (for applications)
DB2       COM.ibm.db2.jdbc.net.DB2Driver (for applets)
ODBC      sun.jdbc.odbc.JdbcOdbcDriver
```

Note that the capitalization of the names is critical. In particular, the `COM` of the IBM driver is specified in all capital letters. Using capital letters was the original Java recommendation, although most package names now (including Sun's) do not follow this convention.

After you know the name of the class that represents the driver, you load it using the `Class` `newInstance` method. Here are some examples:

```
Class.forName("COM.ibm.db2.jdbc.app.DB2Driver").newInstance();
Class.forName("sun.jdbc.odbc.JdbcOdbcDriver").newInstance();

String driver="COM.ibm.db2.jdbc.app.DB2Driver";
Class.forName(driver).newInstance();
```

You usually use the `newInstance` method to instantiate the driver because this enables you to use various drivers and choose the appropriate driver at runtime rather than when the Java program is compiled. As a developer, you might not know the specific database or driver that might be required at runtime.

If you will be using JDBC in Domino agents, see the section titled "The Java Security Context, Agents, and JDBC" for additional information on loading the driver within an agent.

MAKING A DATABASE CONNECTION

After the database driver has been loaded, you can use it to connect to a database. To locate a database with JDBC, specify the database name in URL syntax. Here is the naming syntax:

```
jdbc:<subprotocol>:<db identification>
```

Here are two examples:

```
jdbc:db2:sample
```

```
jdbc:odbc:sample
```

To connect to the database, use the URL with a `java.sql.Connection` object. You obtain the `Connection` object from the `DriverManager`. Here is an example:

```
String url = "jdbc:db2:sample";
Connection con;
con = DriverManager.getConnection(url,"<user name>", "<password>");
```

If you will be using JDBC in Domino agents, see the section titled "The Java Security Context, Agents, and JDBC," later in this chapter, for additional information on making a connection within an agent. In particular, you must use an alternative method to obtain a connection within an agent.

EXECUTING A QUERY

After you have connected to the database, you can execute a query by creating a `Statement` object. A `ResultSet` object contains the result of the query. Here is how you create a statement and execute a query:

```
Statement st = con.createStatement();
String query = "Select * from EMPLOYEE where EMPNO < '000100'";

ResultSet rs = st.executeQuery(query);
```

The `ResultSet` contains the records retrieved by the query. One record is considered the current record. You can retrieve fields from the current record by various `getXXX` methods (such as `getString`, `getDouble`, `getDate`, and so on). You can loop through the results by calling the `next` method of the `ResultSet`. Although a valid current record exists, `next` returns `true`. When you have reached the end of the `ResultSet` and no more records exist, `next` returns `false`.

You can call `getString` to return a field from the current record as a `String` object. If you call `getDate`, the field is returned as a `java.sql.Date`, and if you call `getDouble`, you can retrieve a numeric field as a double precision floating-point value. Each routine has an integer parameter that specifies which field of the current record to return. The fields of the `ResultSet` are numbered starting from 1 (not 0).

PUTTING IT ALL TOGETHER

Here is a sample program that shows all the components of a simple JDBC program:

```
import java.sql.*;

class JdbcDb2 {
    public static void main(String args[]) {
        String driver = "COM.ibm.db2.jdbc.app.DB2Driver";
        String url = "jdbc:db2:sample";
        //String driver = "sun.jdbc.odbc.JdbcOdbcDriver";
        //String url = "jdbc:odbc:sample";
```

```
try {
    System.out.println("Starting");
    // Load the Datatbase driver
    Class.forName(driver).newInstance();
    // Enable the Logging String
    DriverManager.setLogStream(java.lang.System.out);
    // Connect to the database
    Connection con;
    con = DriverManager.getConnection(url,"<user name>", "<password>");
    System.out.println("Using driver "+driver+", on database "+url);

    // Create a statement
    Statement st = con.createStatement();
    String query = "Select EMPNO, LASTNAME, FIRSTNME, HIREDATE,
    ➥SALARY from EMPLOYEE where EMPNO < '000100'";

    // Execute the SQL statement
    ResultSet rs = st.executeQuery(query);
    // Loop through each record of the result set
    while (rs.next()) {
        System.out.print("EMPNO: " + rs.getString(1));
        System.out.print(": " + rs.getString(2)+", "+rs.getString(3));
        System.out.print(", hired: " + rs.getDate(4));
        System.out.println(", salary: " + rs.getDouble(5));
    }
    System.out.println("Done");
    // Close the statement and the connection
    st.close();
    con.close();
}
catch (Exception e) {
    e.printStackTrace();
}
}
}
```

The program begins by assigning two variables, the driver name and the database URL specification. After printing a message, the program loads the DB2 driver.

The `DriverManager.setLogStream` method is used to enable logging messages from the driver. The messages are not standardized, and some drivers can print out more or different information from others.

After setting the logging stream, the program connects to the database by using the `getConnection` method of the `DriverManager`. The `createStatement` method creates a `Statement` object, and the `executeQuery` method executes the SQL query and produces a `ResultSet`. The `while` loop prints out each record of the `ResultSet`.

The `Statement` and `Connection` objects are both closed at the end of the program.

Here is the output produced by the sample program:

```
Starting
DriverManager.getConnection("jdbc:db2:sample")
    trying driver[className=COM.ibm.db2.jdbc.app.DB2Driver,
    ➥context=null,COM.ibm.db2.jdbc.app.DB2Driver@1d3376]
```

PART

V

CH

26

```
getConnection returning driver[className=COM.ibm.db2.jdbc.app.DB2Driver,
➥context=null,COM.ibm.db2.jdbc.app.DB2Driver@1d3376]
Using driver COM.ibm.db2.jdbc.app.DB2Driver, on database jdbc:db2:sample
EMPNO: 000010: HAAS      , CHRISTINE, hired: 1965-01-01, salary: 52750.0
EMPNO: 000020: THOMPSON  , MICHAEL  , hired: 1973-10-10, salary: 41250.0
EMPNO: 000030: KWAN      , SALLY    , hired: 1975-04-05, salary: 38250.0
EMPNO: 000050: GEYER     , JOHN     , hired: 1949-08-17, salary: 40175.0
EMPNO: 000060: STERN     , IRVING   , hired: 1973-09-14, salary: 32250.0
EMPNO: 000070: PULASKI   , EVA      , hired: 1980-09-30, salary: 36170.0
EMPNO: 000090: HENDERSON , EILEEN   , hired: 1970-08-15, salary: 29750.0
Done
```

USING DIFFERENT DRIVERS

Because of the architecture of JDBC, it is possible to use essentially the same program with different drivers. Two comments at the beginning of the sample program specify the use of the JDBC ODBC driver instead of the native DB2 driver.

```
String driver = "sun.jdbc.odbc.JdbcOdbcDriver";
String url = "jdbc:odbc:sample";
```

If these two statements are used to specify the driver and database, here are the first few lines of the resulting output:

```
Starting
DriverManager.getConnection("jdbc:odbc:sample")
    trying driver[className=sun.jdbc.odbc.JdbcOdbcDriver,
    ➥context=null,sun.jdbc.odbc.JdbcOdbcDriver@1d336c]
*Driver.connect (jdbc:odbc:sample)
JDBC to ODBC Bridge: Checking security
No SecurityManager present, assuming trusted application/applet
JDBC to ODBC Bridge 1.1001
Current Date/Time: Fri Feb 18 23:12:56 PST 2000
Loading JdbcOdbc library
Allocating Environment handle (SQLAllocEnv)
hEnv=57867356
Allocating Connection handle (SQLAllocConnect)
hDbc=57867516
Connecting (SQLDriverConnect), hDbc=57867516, szConnStrIn=DSN=sample;
➥UID=<server>;PWD=<password>
*Connection.getMetaData
*DatabaseMetaData.getDriverName
Get connection info string (SQLGetInfo), hDbc=57867516, fInfoType=6, len=300
DB2CLI.DLL
Driver name:    JDBC-ODBC Bridge (DB2CLI.DLL)
*DatabaseMetaData.getDriverVersion
Get connection info string (SQLGetInfo), hDbc=57867516, fInfoType=7, len=300
05.02.0000
Driver version: 1.1001 (05.02.0000)
Caching SQL type information
*Connection.getMetaData
*DatabaseMetaData.getTypeInfo
Allocating Statement Handle (SQLAllocStmt), hDbc=57867516
hStmt=56822624
Get type info (SQLGetTypeInfo), hStmt=56822624, fSqlType=0
Number of result columns (SQLNumResultCols), hStmt=56822624
value=19
```

```
Get connection info string (SQLGetInfo), hDbc=57867516, fInfoType=10, len=300
03.51.0000
Fetching (SQLFetch), hStmt=56822624
Column attributes (SQLColAttributes), hStmt=56822624, icol=1, type=2
value (int)=12
Column attributes (SQLColAttributes), hStmt=56822624, icol=1, type=3
value (int)=128
Get string data (SQLGetData), hStmt=56822624, column=1, maxLen=129
BLOB
Get integer data (SQLGetData), hStmt=56822624, column=2
value=-98
Get integer data (SQLGetData), hStmt=56822624, column=3
value=2147483647
```

This is only about one tenth of the trace output. As you can tell, the JDBC ODBC driver produces much more verbose output for debugging purposes than does the DB2 driver. Running the program again but without the tracing enabled produces the following result:

```
Starting
Using driver sun.jdbc.odbc.JdbcOdbcDriver, on database jdbc:odbc:sample
EMPNO: 000010: HAAS, CHRISTINE, hired: 1965-01-01, salary: 52750.0
EMPNO: 000020: THOMPSON, MICHAEL, hired: 1973-10-10, salary: 41250.0
EMPNO: 000030: KWAN, SALLY, hired: 1975-04-05, salary: 38250.0
EMPNO: 000050: GEYER, JOHN, hired: 1949-08-17, salary: 40175.0
EMPNO: 000060: STERN, IRVING, hired: 1973-09-14, salary: 32250.0
EMPNO: 000070: PULASKI, EVA, hired: 1980-09-30, salary: 36170.0
EMPNO: 000090: HENDERSON, EILEEN, hired: 1970-08-15, salary: 29750.0
Done
```

The most interesting point to notice is that the same database produces slightly different results depending on the driver used to access the database. The ODBC driver strips off the trailing blanks from the name fields, while the DB2 native driver retains trailing blanks. Because these are VARCHAR fields and trailing blanks might not actually be stored in the fields, determining which of the two drivers is correct is difficult. One could probably argue that either return value is correct.

When you are developing JDBC applications, be sure to test your program with various drivers that might be used at runtime, and make sure you get the results you expect. Minor differences, such as the inclusion of trailing blanks (or not), can affect comparison or other operators in Java. In addition, different drivers will have different performance characteristics. Some drivers can definitely have performance advantages over others. Finally, because of differences in data types, transferring data from an RDB to a Domino database can result in improper rounding or conversions. Be careful to check data as it is converted.

THE LOTUS DOMINO DRIVER FOR JDBC

The chapter thus far has been about using standard Java and JDBC to access relational databases, and nothing has required the use of Notes or Domino. I now want to cover the Lotus Domino Driver for JDBC (LDDJ). Contrary to what you might think, this driver is not for accessing relational databases from Domino. Instead, this is a JDBC driver (as we saw with DB2) for using Java and JDBC to access Domino databases as if they were relational.

PART

V

CH

26

In other words, we can create and use a JDBC program with Java and access documents in a Domino database as if they were records of a relational database. Here is what you must do to use LDDJ:

1. Install the Lotus Domino Driver for JDBC software. You can download this software from the Lotus Web site at http://www.lotus.com/home.nsf/welcome/techzone.

2. Update your execution classpath to include the JdbcDomino.jar file, which contains the driver. Also ensure that the executable DLLs from LDDJ are available.

3. If required by your IDE, update the IDE classpath or the environment variable for your computer.

4. Update the JDBC driver name to lotus.jdbc.Domino.DominoDriver.

5. Update the URL to the name jdbc:Domino:/<dbpath.nsf>/<server>. If the database path contains more than one level, you must use backslashes (\). Because the backslash is an escape character, you must use two consecutive backslashes to indicate a single backslash.

Here is an example of two lines that specify the driver and a sample database:

```
String driver = "lotus.jdbc.domino.DominoDriver";
String url = "jdbc:domino:/WebJava50\\DomJDBC.nsf/BENTLEY";
```

As always, the driver name is case sensitive, so be sure to use the proper case for the name. The URL string shows how to specify a database that is one level down. The WebJava50 directory is below the data directory. The DomJDBC.nsf database is on the BENTLEY server. You must use backslashes because the string following the forward slash is the name of the server.

Here is a query line used to specify the query:

```
String query = "Select cEmpno, cLastname, cFirstnme, dtHireDate,
➡nSalary from Employee where cEmpno < '000100' order by cEmpno";
```

When obtaining data from a Domino database, you can use either forms or views as if they were relational tables. If you use forms, Domino will search each document to see if it has a form item with the specified form name. This can take a substantial amount of time if the database is very large. If you use a view, documents in the view will be retrieved.

Normally in Domino, field names are not case sensitive. However, when you use LDDJ, field, form, and view names are all case sensitive. You must make sure that when you specify a name, the case is properly specified or the name will not be found.

If you use views and also specify an ORDER BY clause in the SELECT statement, make sure the ordering is the same as that found in the view. If it is different, Domino must create a temporary table and re-sort the documents in the correct order. This can be a substantial performance penalty, and the user must have read/write access to the database to create the temporary index.

In addition to using forms and views as if they were tables, LDDJ has a concept called the *universal relation*. You can think of this relation as a list of all the documents of the database. You access this virtual table by using the name of the database in place of a table name. The user must have read/write access to the database to use the universal relation, even for SELECT statements. Here is an example:

```
String query = "Select cEmpno, cLastname, cFirstnme, dtHireDate,
➥nSalary from ServeXML where cEmpno < '000100' order by cEmpno";
```

Even though this select statement has an ORDER BY clause, sorting is ignored for the universal relation. This type of query is useful if you want to retrieve documents that were not all created from the same form or that do not appear in the same view.

Here is the previous example JDBC program that has been modified to work with LDDJ:

```
import java.sql.*;

class JdbcDomino {
    public static void main(String args[]) {
        //String driver = "COM.ibm.db2.jdbc.app.DB2Driver";
        //String url = "jdbc:db2:sample";
        //String driver = "sun.jdbc.odbc.JdbcOdbcDriver";
        //String url = "jdbc:odbc:sample";
        String driver = "lotus.jdbc.domino.DominoDriver";
        String url = "jdbc:domino:/WebJava50\\DomJDBC.nsf/BENTLEY";
        try {
            System.out.println("Starting");
            // Load the Datatbase driver
            Class.forName(driver).newInstance();
            // Enable the Logging String
            //DriverManager.setLogStream(java.lang.System.out);
            // Connect to the database
            Connection con;
            con = DriverManager.getConnection(url);
            System.out.println("Using driver " + driver + ", on database " + url);

            // Create a statement
            Statement st = con.createStatement();
            String query = "Select cEmpno, cLastname, cFirstnme, dtHireDate,
➥nSalary from Employee where cEmpno < '000100' order by cEmpno";

            // Execute the SQL statement
            ResultSet rs = st.executeQuery(query);
            // Loop through each record of the result set
            while (rs.next()) {
                System.out.print("EMPNO: " + rs.getString(1));
                System.out.print(": " + rs.getString(2) + ", " + rs.getString(3));
                System.out.print(", hired: " + rs.getDate(4));
                System.out.println(", salary: " + rs.getDouble(5));
            }
            System.out.println("Done");
            // Close the statement and the connection
            st.close();
            con.close();
        }
```

```
         catch (Exception e) {
            e.printStackTrace();
         }
      }
   }
```

Here is the output produced by this Java JDBC program:

```
Starting
Using driver lotus.jdbc.domino.DominoDriver, on database
➥jdbc:domino:/WebJava50\ServeXML.nsf/BENTLEY
EMPNO: 000010: Haas, Christine, hired: 1965-01-01, salary: 52750.0
EMPNO: 000020: Thompson, Michael, hired: 1973-10-10, salary: 41250.0
EMPNO: 000030: Kwan, Sally, hired: 1975-04-05, salary: 38250.0
Done
```

Note that this Domino database does not have all the information that was contained in the DB2 database, so only three records are displayed in the output. You can see that the format produced by this program is the same as the DB2-based program. I included the ORDER BY clause in the SELECT statement because I retrieved the information using a Domino form, not a view. Without the ORDER BY clause, the resulting data is not sorted.

ACCESSING RELATIONAL DATABASES FROM DOMINO AGENTS

In this chapter I've shown you how to access relational databases using JDBC from an ordinary Java program. Let's now look at how you can do the same thing from a Java agent. Because a Java agent is just a Java program, if we have our environment set up properly, we should be able to access relational databases and incorporate the data with Domino.

For this example, I'm going to be using an Employee XML form. This form can be used to display XML data from Domino documents. I will use JDBC to access a DB2 database to populate the documents.

This agent relies on the DB2 JDBC driver. Because Domino's class loader will load the agent, and the DB2 driver uses the Java Native Interface (JNI), you must specify the DB2 driver in the class path variable for Domino's loader. The JNI enables a Java program to call external modules such as DLL files for Windows. The Domino class path is specified in the Notes.ini file with the parameter name JavaUserClasses. You will need a line in your Notes.ini file to specify the db2java.zip file. Here is an example:

```
JavaUserClasses=D:\sqllib\java\db2java.zip;<other jar/zip files>
```

If you run this agent from the Notes client, you must modify the Notes.ini file for the Notes client. If the agent will run on the server, you must modify Domino's Notes.ini file.

Here is the Java agent that reads the DB2 database and populates the Domino documents:

```
import lotus.domino.*;
import java.sql.*;
import java.util.Properties;
import java.util.Enumeration;
```

```java
public class JavaAgent extends AgentBase {
    static final int icEmpno    = 1;    // Field 1
    static final int icFirstnme = 2;    // Field 2
    static final int icMidinit  = 3;    // Field 3
    static final int icLastname = 4;    // Field 4
    static final int icWorkdept = 5;    // Field 5
    static final int icPhoneno  = 6;    // Field 6
    static final int icHiredate = 7;    // Field 7
    static final int icJob      = 8;    // Field 8
    static final int icEdlevel  = 9;    // Field 9
    static final int icSex      = 10;   // Field 10
    static final int icBirthdate = 11;  // Field 11
    static final int icSalary   = 12;   // Field 12
    static final int icBonus    = 13;   // Field 13
    static final int icComm     = 14;   // Field 14

    public void NotesMain() {

        // Declare driver here so we can use it in both the
        // try and finally blocks.
        Driver drv = null;

        try {
            Session session = getSession();
            AgentContext agentContext = session.getAgentContext();
            Database db = agentContext.getCurrentDatabase();
            View empview = db.getView("Employees"); // Get the employees view

            String dbuser = "<user>";
            String dbpassword = "<password>";

            String driver = "COM.ibm.db2.jdbc.app.DB2Driver";
            String url = "jdbc:db2:sample";
            //String driver = "sun.jdbc.odbc.JdbcOdbcDriver";
            //String url = "jdbc:odbc:sample";
            System.out.println("Starting");
            // Load the Datatbase driver, explicitly into Object
            drv = (Driver) Class.forName(driver).newInstance();
            // Enable the Logging String
            DriverManager.setLogStream(java.lang.System.out);
            // Connect to the database
            Connection con;
            // The following line will not work with Agent security contexts
            // con = DriverManager.getConnection(url, dbuser, dbpassword);
            Properties p = new Properties();
            p.put("user", dbuser);
            p.put("password", dbpassword);
            con = drv.connect(url, p);    // Connect directly using DB driver
            System.out.println("Using driver " + driver + ", on database "+ url);

            // Create a statement
            Statement st = con.createStatement();
            String query ="Select EMPNO, FIRSTNME, MIDINIT, LASTNAME, WORKDEPT,"+
                    "PHONENO, HIREDATE, JOB, EDLEVEL, SEX, BIRTHDATE, SALARY," +
                    "BONUS, COMM from EMPLOYEE";

            // Execute the SQL statement
            ResultSet rs = st.executeQuery(query);
```

```java
        Document doc;
        // Loop through each record of the result set
        while (rs.next()) {
            // Get the data from the database
            String cEmpno = rs.getString(icEmpno);
            String cFirstnme = rs.getString(icFirstnme);
            String cMidinit  = rs.getString(icMidinit);
            String cLastname = rs.getString(icLastname);
            String cWorkdept = rs.getString(icWorkdept);
            String cPhoneno  = rs.getString(icPhoneno);
            java.sql.Date dtHiredate = rs.getDate(icHiredate);
            String cJob     = rs.getString(icJob);
            int iEdlevel    = rs.getInt(icEdlevel);
            String cSex     = rs.getString(icSex);
            java.sql.Date dtBirthdate = rs.getDate(icBirthdate);
            double dSalary = rs.getDouble(icSalary);
            double dBonus  = rs.getDouble(icBonus);
            double dComm   = rs.getDouble(icComm);

            // Look up the document in the view
            doc = empview.getDocumentByKey(cEmpno); // get the document
            if (null == doc) {
                // Document does not exist, create it.
                doc = db.createDocument();
                doc.replaceItemValue("Form", "Employee");
                System.out.println("Empno "+cEmpno+" does not exist, created.");
            }
            // Document exists. Now replace all values
            doc.replaceItemValue("cEmpno", cEmpno);
            doc.replaceItemValue("cFirstnme", cFirstnme);
            doc.replaceItemValue("cMidinit", cMidinit);
            doc.replaceItemValue("cLastname", cLastname);
            doc.replaceItemValue("cWorkdept", cWorkdept);
            doc.replaceItemValue("cPhoneno", cPhoneno);
            doc.replaceItemValue("dtHireDate", dtHiredate.toString());
            doc.replaceItemValue("cJob", cJob);
            doc.replaceItemValue("nEdlevel", new Integer(iEdlevel));
            doc.replaceItemValue("cSex", cSex);
            doc.replaceItemValue("dtBirthdate", dtBirthdate.toString());
            doc.replaceItemValue("nSalary", new Double(dSalary));
            doc.replaceItemValue("nBonus", new Double(dBonus));
            doc.replaceItemValue("nComm", new Double(dComm));

            // Save document.
            doc.save(true, true);
            System.out.println("Empno " + cEmpno + " saved.");
        }
        System.out.println("Done");
        // Close the statement and the connection
        st.close();
        con.close();

    } catch(NotesException e) {
        System.out.println("Error " + e.id + ". " + e.text);
        e.printStackTrace();
    } catch(Exception e) {
        e.printStackTrace();
```

```
        } finally {
           try {
              // Deregister any associated drivers
              Enumeration eDrivers = DriverManager.getDrivers();
              for ( ; eDrivers.hasMoreElements(); ) {
                 System.out.println("Drivers not empty.");
                 DriverManager.deregisterDriver((Driver) eDrivers.nextElement());
              }
           } catch(Exception e) {
              e.printStackTrace();
           }
        }
     }
}
```

If you want to use this agent, substitute your server name and the password at the appropriate places in the program. In this program, note that I have defined static constants to represent the field numbers. The program first connects to the DB2 database, accesses the records, and creates a result set.

After the result set is created, the program loops through one record at a time and updates the documents in the Domino database. Note that database record deletions are not handled. If a record exists in the DB2 database but not in Domino, a corresponding document will be created. Each value is stored in the Domino document, and then the document is saved. The program continues through the result set until all the documents have been processed.

THE JAVA SECURITY CONTEXT, AGENTS, AND JDBC

If you noticed, the code to get the Database driver for the agent is a little different from the code I showed you before that used `DriverManager.getConnection`. Although the `getConnection` method will work fine in a regular Java application, it might have problems when running in a Domino agent. The reason is that for Domino agents, each agent is given its own Java security context. This has implications for the JDBC DB drivers because the `DriverManager` attempts to share the database drivers.

If you use the `getConnection` method, the first agent to run will load the database driver using the `Class.forName` method, and everything will work fine. At the time it is loaded, however, the database driver is associated with the security context of this first agent. When the second agent loads and issues the `Class.forName`, Java will notice that the class is already loaded and will not load it again, even though it is in a different security context. When the second agent then issues a call to `getConnection`, the `DriverManager` will go through its list of available drivers, including their security contexts, and will not be able to find a match because this second agent has a separate security context. The driver manager will then throw a `SQLException` indicating "No Suitable Driver."

To avoid these problems, explicitly create a database driver object and call the `connect` method directly. In this way, the `DriverManager` does not need to find the driver first before

PART
V
CH
26

making a connection. This technique also has the added benefit that it is slightly more efficient. Here is the connection code:

```
Properties p = new Properties();
p.put("user", dbuser);
p.put("password", dbpassword);
con = drv.connect(url, p);      // Connect directly using DB driver
```

Because you manage the database driver, you must be sure to deregister it at the end of the program after you have finished. For this reason, I have included the deregistration in a finally block for the agent. By including it in a finally block, even if exceptions are detected during execution, the driver will be deregistered. If you do not deregister the database driver, each time the agent is run an additional driver will be registered, you will have a memory leak, and eventually you will run out of memory. Here is the code to deregister the driver:

```
try {
   // Deregister any associated drivers
   Enumeration eDrivers = DriverManager.getDrivers();
   for ( ; eDrivers.hasMoreElements(); ) {
      System.out.println("Drivers not empty.");
      DriverManager.deregisterDriver((Driver) eDrivers.nextElement());
   }
} catch(Exception e) {
   e.printStackTrace();
}
```

USING DOMINO AGENTS TO SERVE XML FROM RELATIONAL DATABASES

You have seen how to use Domino agents to access both relational databases and Domino documents. Let's now examine how you can use Domino's programmability features to serve XML from a relational database.

Suppose you want to use the Employee database in DB2 to produce a phone directory. In this case you don't want to duplicate the data in a Domino database; you just want to access DB2 and return an XML file containing the phone list. Here is a example agent:

```
import lotus.domino.*;
import java.sql.*;
import java.io.*;
import java.util.Properties;
import java.util.Enumeration;

public class JavaAgent extends AgentBase {
      static final int icEmpno    = 1;    // Field 1
      static final int icFirstnme = 2;    // Field 2
      static final int icMidinit  = 3;    // Field 3
      static final int icLastname = 4;    // Field 4
      static final int icWorkdept = 5;    // Field 5
      static final int icPhoneno  = 6;    // Field 6
```

```java
public void NotesMain() {

    Driver drv = null;
    try {
        Session session = getSession();
        AgentContext agentContext = session.getAgentContext();
        PrintWriter out = getAgentOutput();

        // Parse the URL arguments
        AgentParameters pt = new AgentParameters();
        pt.parseParameters(session);

        String dbuser = "<user>";
        String dbpassword = "<password>";

        String driver = "COM.ibm.db2.jdbc.app.DB2Driver";
        String url = "jdbc:db2:sample";
        // String driver = "sun.jdbc.odbc.JdbcOdbcDriver";
        // String url = "jdbc:odbc:sample";
        System.out.println("Starting");
        // Load the Datatbase driver
        drv = (Driver) Class.forName(driver).newInstance();
        // Enable the Logging String
        DriverManager.setLogStream(java.lang.System.out);
        // Connect to the database
        Connection con;
        Properties p = new Properties();
        p.put("user", dbuser);
        p.put("password", dbpassword);
        con = drv.connect(url, p);
        System.out.println("Using driver " + driver + ", on database " + url);

        // Create a statement
        Statement st = con.createStatement();
        String query ="Select EMPNO, FIRSTNME, MIDINIT, LASTNAME, WORKDEPT,"+
                        "PHONENO from EMPLOYEE order by LASTNAME";

        // Execute the SQL statement
        ResultSet rs = st.executeQuery(query);
        Document doc;
        out.println("Content-Type: text/xml");
        out.println("");

        out.println("<?xml version='1.0'?>");  // Write the XML header.
        out.println("<phonelist>");
        // Loop through each record of the result set
        while (rs.next()) {
            // Get the data from the database
            String cEmpno    = rs.getString(icEmpno);
            String cFirstnme = rs.getString(icFirstnme);
            String cMidinit  = rs.getString(icMidinit);
            String cLastname = rs.getString(icLastname);
            String cWorkdept = rs.getString(icWorkdept);
            String cPhoneno  = rs.getString(icPhoneno);

            out.println("<employee empno=\""+ cEmpno + "\">");
            out.println("<firstname>" + cFirstnme + "</firstname>");
```

```
                    out.println("<midinit>" + cMidinit + "</midinit>");
                    out.println("<lastname>" + cLastname + "</lastname>");
                    out.println("<dept>" + cWorkdept + "</dept>");
                    out.println("<phone>" + cPhoneno + "</phone>");
                    out.println("</employee>");
                }
                out.println("</phonelist>");

                System.out.println("Done");
                // Close the statement and the connection
                st.close();
                con.close();

            } catch(NotesException e) {
                System.out.println("Error " + e.id + ". " + e.text);
                e.printStackTrace();
            } catch(Exception e) {
                e.printStackTrace();
            } finally {
                try {
                    Enumeration eDrivers = DriverManager.getDrivers();
                    for ( ; eDrivers.hasMoreElements(); ) {
                        System.out.println("Drivers not empty.");
                        DriverManager.deregisterDriver((Driver) eDrivers.nextElement());
                    }
                } catch(Exception e) {
                    e.printStackTrace();
                }
            }
        }
    }
}
```

This agent is designed to be used with a URL. Suppose the name of this agent is PhoneList. You would invoke the agent with a URL such as

```
http://<server>/<database.nsf>/PhoneList?OpenAgent
```

This will invoke the agent and return an XML data stream. If you are using a browser that is capable of recognizing XML, it will be displayed appropriately. Notice that the SQL SELECT statement sorts the list by ascending last name.

By using URL parameters, you can have the agent produce a phone number for a specific department, sort by other fields, select a subset of records, or even search for a particular person by name or employee number.

You could alternatively produce HTML instead of XML. This would enable you to access the information from a regular browser without the need for additional translating, parsing, or formatting.

Another interesting modification is to keep statistics on the queries received. You can keep these statistics directly in the Domino database. By keeping statistics about the queries, you can gain valuable management information. You can then provide built-in queries or add other features based on the information your clients are requesting.

COMBINING WORKFLOW WITH RELATIONAL DATABASES

Workflow commonly uses email to track transactions through an enterprise. By using email, you can automate messages and tasks that users would otherwise have to perform manually. For example, suppose you are working in a human resources department and certain tasks must be performed when an employee's work anniversary or birthday occurs. This type of system could easily be accomplished by using Domino alone. However, perhaps you already have personnel information stored in your DB2 database and you would prefer not to duplicate the information. By using an agent that is triggered monthly, you could receive an email message about all the birthdays within the month.

Here is an agent that accesses a DB2 database to find birthdays. It sends an email message to a specified recipient for all the birthdays occurring in the current month.

```java
import lotus.domino.*;
import java.sql.*;
import java.util.*;

public class JavaAgent extends AgentBase {
    static final int icEmpno     = 1;   // Field 1
    static final int icFirstnme  = 2;   // Field 2
    static final int icMidinit   = 3;   // Field 3
    static final int icLastname  = 4;   // Field 4
    static final int icWorkdept  = 5;   // Field 5
    static final int icPhoneno   = 6;   // Field 6
    static final int icHiredate  = 7;   // Field 7
    static final int icJob       = 8;   // Field 8
    static final int icEdlevel   = 9;   // Field 9
    static final int icSex       = 10;  // Field 10
    static final int icBirthdate = 11;  // Field 11
    static final int icSalary    = 12;  // Field 12
    static final int icBonus     = 13;  // Field 13
    static final int icComm      = 14;  // Field 14

    public void NotesMain() {

        // Declare driver here so we can use it in both the
        // try and finally blocks.
        Driver drv = null;

        try {
            Session session = getSession();
            AgentContext agentContext = session.getAgentContext();
            Database db = agentContext.getCurrentDatabase();
            View empview = db.getView("Employees"); // Get the employees view

            String dbuser = "<user>";
            String dbpassword = "<password>";
            String mailrecipient = "<mail recipient>";

            String driver = "COM.ibm.db2.jdbc.app.DB2Driver";
            String url = "jdbc:db2:sample";
            //String driver = "sun.jdbc.odbc.JdbcOdbcDriver";
            //String url = "jdbc:odbc:sample";
            System.out.println("Starting");
```

```java
// Load the Datatbase driver, explicitly into Object
drv = (Driver) Class.forName(driver).newInstance();
// Enable the Logging String
DriverManager.setLogStream(java.lang.System.out);
// Connect to the database
Connection con;
// The following line will not work with Agent security contexts
// con = DriverManager.getConnection(url, dbuser, dbpassword);
Properties p = new Properties();
p.put("user", dbuser);
p.put("password", dbpassword);
con = drv.connect(url, p);      // Connect directly using DB driver
System.out.println("Using driver " + driver + ", on database "+ url);

// Create a statement
Statement st = con.createStatement();
String query ="Select EMPNO, FIRSTNME, MIDINIT, LASTNAME, WORKDEPT,"+
        "PHONENO, HIREDATE, JOB, EDLEVEL, SEX, BIRTHDATE, SALARY," +
        "BONUS, COMM from EMPLOYEE";

// Execute the SQL statement
ResultSet rs = st.executeQuery(query);
Document doc;
// Loop through each record of the result set
while (rs.next()) {
    // Get the data from the database
    String cEmpno = rs.getString(icEmpno);
    String cFirstnme = rs.getString(icFirstnme);
    String cMidinit  = rs.getString(icMidinit);
    String cLastname = rs.getString(icLastname);
    String cWorkdept = rs.getString(icWorkdept);
    String cPhoneno  = rs.getString(icPhoneno);
    java.sql.Date dtHiredate = rs.getDate(icHiredate);
    String cJob     = rs.getString(icJob);
    int iEdlevel    = rs.getInt(icEdlevel);
    String cSex     = rs.getString(icSex);
    java.sql.Date dtBirthdate = rs.getDate(icBirthdate);
    double dSalary = rs.getDouble(icSalary);
    double dBonus  = rs.getDouble(icBonus);
    double dComm   = rs.getDouble(icComm);

    java.util.Date dtToday = new java.util.Date();      // Today
    if (dtToday.getMonth() == dtBirthdate.getMonth()) {
        // Anyone who's birthday is this month
        doc = db.createDocument();
        doc.replaceItemValue("Form", "Memo");
        doc.replaceItemValue("Subject", "Birthday this month: "
            + cLastname);
        doc.replaceItemValue("Body", "Hello. " + cFirstnme + " "
            + cLastname + " has a birthday this month." +
            "The birthdate is " + dtBirthdate.toString());
        doc.send(mailrecipient);
        System.out.println("Empno " + cEmpno + " sent.");
    }
}
System.out.println("Done");
// Close the statement and the connection
st.close();
```

```
        con.close();

    } catch(NotesException e) {
      System.out.println("Error " + e.id + ". " + e.text);
      e.printStackTrace();
    } catch(Exception e) {
      e.printStackTrace();
    } finally {
      try {
         // Deregister any associated drivers
         Enumeration eDrivers = DriverManager.getDrivers();
         for ( ; eDrivers.hasMoreElements(); ) {
            System.out.println("Drivers not empty.");
            DriverManager.deregisterDriver((Driver) eDrivers.nextElement());
         }
      } catch(Exception e) {
         e.printStackTrace();
      }
    }
  }
}
```

This example is similar to the previous examples, but you can see how you can combine the strengths of Domino with email simply by using the Document.send method.

CHAPTER REVIEW

1. Give three sample scenarios where it would make sense to combine Domino with a relational database system. Your examples should combine the strengths of Domino with the strengths of the relational database system.

2. Write a standalone Java program to access the EMPLOYEE table. It should print out a list of employees who have more than 20 years of service. The list should be sorted starting with the person with the longest service record.

3. What is a JDBC database driver? What is the advantage of using a database retrieval architecture that includes drivers?

4. What is a JDBC database connection? Give two different methods for obtaining a database connection.

5. Why should you be careful to unload a database driver that you have loaded?

6. If you will be using a database driver or any program that uses Java Native Interface (JNI) to access external DLL modules, what must you do to enable the Domino class loader to find the classes?

7. Suppose you have written an agent that accesses a relational database with JDBC. It works the first time, but every subsequent time it fails with the error message "No Suitable Driver." What is wrong, and how can you correct it?

8. Update the PhoneList agent to produce HTML. Use HTML <table> tags to format the phone list.

9. Update the PhoneList agent to take a URL parameter that specifies sorting. Provide sorts for last name, first name, department, and employee number.

PART

V

CH

26

Using IBM WebSphere for Java Servlets and Java Server Pages (JSP)

In this chapter

What Is a Servlet?

Servlets are server-based Java programs that can be added to a Web server to provide additional functions to a Web site. Servlets are invoked by a special URL specification. When the Web server sees a special servlet URL, it turns over the request to a servlet manager. The servlet manager then loads and executes the servlet.

In many ways, servlets are similar to Domino agents for the Web. They provide a way to produce customizable output to Web users. When static Web pages are used, all users have the same experience. When a program such as a servlet or agent produces the HTML or XML for the user, logic can be used to create a unique user experience. You typically customize the output for the user based on knowledge of the user, which usually requires a login, based on parameters of the URL, or based on other factors unique to the Web site.

For content customization, the servlet can examine the parameters of the URL or cookie values. These are both important methods for servlets to receive parameterized information to control their execution. The output of the servlet is sent to an output stream that is sent back to the client. Typically the clients are Web browsers, and servlets communicate using the HTTP protocol, but this is not a requirement for servlets. For form-based input, servlets can obtain parameter information from input fields on the form.

The servlet manager is responsible for controlling the lifetime of the servlet. That is, it controls when the servlet is loaded and when it is discarded from memory. After servlets are loaded, they are generally kept memory-resident unless a severe memory constraint exists. Thus, servlets have an advantage over similar, older technologies such as CGI (Common Gateway Interface).

Comparison of Servlets to Other Server-Based Technologies

In addition to servlets, several other server-based technologies work with Web servers. One of the oldest of these add-in technologies is CGI. CGI provides the capability to enable server programmability through the use of executable modules. Each time a request is made, the server must load the executable module (a process). It will then execute, and it will be deleted from memory. The overhead of repeatedly loading, executing, and deleting modules can be very expensive in server resources. For rarely used functions this might not be a problem, but it does not provide scalability for high-volume Web applications.

In addition to the older CGI technology, many newer programmability options exist. For example, Microsoft provides Active Server Pages (ASP); Domino provides agents; Java Server Pages (JSPs) exist; and middleware servers such as Allaire's ColdFusion, BEA's Weblogic, and IBM's WebSphere exist. Each of these technologies offers various strong and weak points in providing server-based capabilities.

It would be impossible to cover all these technologies in this chapter, so I'm going to focus on the products and technologies that are the most relevant for Lotus Domino, XML, and Java users. In this chapter I discuss servlets in general, Java Server Pages, and how Domino integrates with WebSphere and DB2. I end this chapter with an example that shows how you can serve XML documents using the combined technologies of Domino, WebSphere, and DB2.

THE JAVA SERVLET DEVELOPMENT KIT (JSDK)

The Java Servlet Development Kit is a set of Java classes and information that can be used to develop servlets. The `jsdk.jar` file containing the JSDK classes ships with Domino, so you can use servlets with Domino.

If you have not read Chapter 11, "JavaScript Techniques with Domino," I suggest that you read at least the section titled "Client/Server Communication with HTTP." In that chapter I describe the HTTP protocol, requests, responses, headers, and cookies. It is important to understand the basics of the HTTP protocol because the coding and operation of servlets correspond to many HTTP concepts.

Before continuing, make sure you understand the difference between the GET and POST methods. The HTTP GET method passes parameters through the URL, while POST sends data through the body of the HTTP request. Although many other HTTP request methods exist, the GET and POST methods are by far the most important.

HELLO WORLD SERVLET

It is usually easiest to explain new concepts with an example. Two levels of abstractions exist for servlets. The highest level of abstraction is the generic servlet, which is not dependent on HTTP—it can be used with a variety of protocols. The second level of abstraction takes the generic servlet class and extends it to handle HTTP specifically.

For all servlets, the model includes a request, which comes from a client; a service, which is implemented by the servlet; and a response, which is sent back to the client. The `javax.servlet.GenericServlet` class implements a generic servlet.

The `javax.servlet.HttpServlet` class extends the `GenericServlet` class with methods that are unique to the HTTP protocol. Here is an example of a servlet:

```java
import java.io.*;

import javax.servlet.*;
import javax.servlet.http.*;

public class HelloServlet extends HttpServlet {

    public void doGet (HttpServletRequest req, HttpServletResponse res)
         throws ServletException, IOException {
      PrintWriter    out;

      res.setContentType("text/html");
      out = res.getWriter();

      out.println("<html>");
      out.println("<head><title>Hello World Servlet</title></head>");
```

```
        out.println("<body>");
        out.println("<h1>Hello World Servlet!</h1>");
        out.println("</body>");
        out.println("</html>");
    }
}
```

In this example, you see only a single method, the doGet method. This method is part of the HttpServlet class and, by default, returns an error message. We override the default in the HelloServlet class to return the HTML page.

The method takes two parameters, the request and the response. The request is encapsulated in the HttpServletRequest object, and the response is in the HttpServletResponse object. The doGet method also has a throws clause in the method declaration. This indicates that the two specified exceptions ServletException and IOException are not handled within the method and might be thrown to the caller of this method.

The first executable line sets the content type for the result. The content type will be sent in the HTTP header for the response. In this case, the content type is set to text/html. The next statement obtains the PrintWriter object that can be used for output back to the client. This call is analogous to the getAgentOutput method for Domino agents. After you have obtained the PrintWriter, you can send HTML output to this writer. In Figure 27.1 you can see the output produced by this servlet as well as the HTML source that was sent to the browser.

Figure 27.1
A servlet sends HTML output to the Web browser.

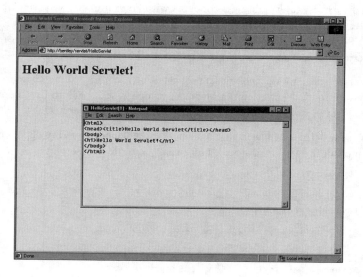

The URL that was used to generate the output is

```
http://<server>/servlet/HelloServlet
```

Note that the name of the servlet is case sensitive. Be sure to use the proper case when invoking a servlet.

SERVING XML FROM A SERVLET

By making just two small changes to our HTML servlet, we can turn it into a servlet that will serve XML instead of HTML. Here is the same servlet, but used to serve XML instead of HTML:

```java
import java.io.*;

import javax.servlet.*;
import javax.servlet.http.*;

public class HelloXMLServlet extends HttpServlet {

    public void doGet (HttpServletRequest req, HttpServletResponse res)
        throws ServletException, IOException {
      PrintWriter    out;

      res.setContentType("text/xml");
      out = res.getWriter();

      out.println("<?xml version='1.0' ?>");
      out.println("<html>");
      out.println("<head><title>Hello World Servlet</title></head>");
      out.println("<body>");
      out.println("<h1>Hello World Servlet!</h1>");
      out.println("</body>");
      out.println("</html>");
    }
}
```

In addition to changing the name, I've changed only the content type to text/xml, and I've inserted an XML declaration line. In Figure 27.2 notice that the browser now displays formatted XML instead of HTML.

Figure 27.2
Servlets can be used for XML as well as HTML.

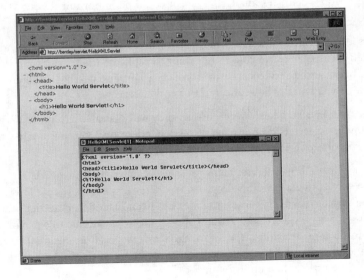

SERVLETS VERSUS DOMINO AGENTS

Servlets are similar to Domino agents in many ways. Both servlets and agents enable you to provide programmable output to an HTTP request. Some differences exist between servlets and agents, however. In this section I'll describe these differences to allow you to choose the appropriate tool for your job.

Domino agents are stored in a Domino database. This allows them to use Domino security mechanisms such as ACLs. Domino agents are run by default with the security level of the agent's owner (the last person to modify and save the agent). Alternatively, you can run the agent with the security level of the Web user if you check the Run Agent as Web User flag of the For Web Access section on the Design tab of the Agent properties box. See Figure 27.3 for an example.

Figure 27.3
Agents can run with the Web user's security level.

Because agents are stored in a Domino database, they can be replicated from one server to another. This enables you to distribute an agent to multiple Web database sites. However, note that, by default, replicated agents are set to run on only one specified server.

Agents are loaded and executed each time a URL request is made for execution. Although this overhead is relatively small, this aspect could be important if your Web site is getting millions of hits.

Servlets are stored in the server's file system. In some cases this can provide you with enhanced security because you do not want to replicate the servlet functionality to other servers. Because the servlets are not stored in a Domino database, there is no chance for the function to accidentally be replicated to another server.

Servlets are a Java standard, which means they will operate with most Web servers and environments. Servlets do not need to be dependent on Domino in any way. In some cases, implementation of a Java standard is preferable for portability.

Servlets are loaded by a servlet manager when they are first invoked. They stay in memory until the servlet manager shuts down or an operator removes them. This policy for the lifetime of a servlet means that after a servlet has been loaded, it does not incur the overhead of loading for each subsequent request. For some applications, this performance benefit can be very important. In addition, because the servlet is memory resident, it can cache some results and use other performance-enhancing features, such as connecting to databases ahead of time rather than upon request.

To summarize simply, with agents you can use Domino security features that can improve your security. With servlets you can typically optimize performance for large-scale applications.

THE HttpServlet CLASS

Let's return now to the HttpServlet class, which will serve as the base class for any HTTP servlet that you write. The Servlet interface, which an HttpServlet implements, includes three important methods: the init, destroy, and service methods. The init method is called when the servlet is loaded into memory. The init method can also be called at the request of the operator to reinitialize the servlet. The init method is guaranteed to be called before the first invocation of the service method.

The destroy method is called before the unloading of the servlet. During the destroy method, the servlet should clean up any memory or other resources acquired, and it can write out configuration information or close files.

The service method is provided as part of the Servlet interface. In the GenericServlet class, you can use this method to provide arbitrary services upon request. Within the HttpServlet class, the base class implements this method, parses the HTTP request string, and calls one of several HTTP-specific methods. This approach makes writing an HTTP servlet much easier than writing a generic servlet to handle HTTP. You must implement only those requests that are applicable to your application. Here are the HTTP methods you can implement:

- doDelete—Handles the HTTP DELETE method
- doGet—Handles the HTTP GET method
- doHead—Handles the HTTP HEAD method
- doOptions—Handles the HTTP OPTIONS method
- doPost—Handles the HTTP POST method
- doPut—Handles the HTTP PUT method
- doTrace—Handles the HTTP TRACE method

Each of these methods has the same parameters:

```
void doMethod(HttpServletRequest req, HttpServletResponse resp)
```

You have seen previously that by implementing the doGet method, you can return HTML or XML to the Web browser. Typically, you should also implement at least the doPost method. Fortunately, you can implement the code once and forward on the request. Here is an example:

```
public void doPost (HttpServletRequest req, HttpServletResponse res)
        throws ServletException, IOException {
    doGet(req, res);
}
```

PART

V

CH

27

In this case, the doPost method invokes the doGet method. Of course, you can implement the doPost method and invoke it from doGet. You can also have completely different implementations for the two routines. The default behavior if you do not implement a method is for the servlet engine to return an error code to the browser.

In addition to the HTTP method routines, you should also consider implementing the getLastModified servlet method. When the browser is requesting a page, it can issue a request for a page only if it has been modified since a particular time and date. For static files, the Web server can determine this information by itself. However, for servlets, the Web server and servlet engine have no way to know the last modified information because it can change dynamically.

When the servlet engine is returning a response to the browser, it will call the getLastModified routine to obtain a date/time to return to the browser. In addition, before retrieving a page, it will call the routine before issuing a doGet. If the time/date is the same as the previous time/date, the doGet will be skipped and the server can return a code to the browser indicating that it is safe to use the cached version of the page content. Here is the signature for the getLastModified method:

```
protected long getLastModified(HttpServletRequest req)
```

Notice that the getLastModified method returns a long value. This is the format for a Java Date value. It is expressed as the integer number of milliseconds since January 1, 1970, GMT. The value you return should be rounded or truncated to the nearest second. You can accomplish this by the following:

```
long timeValue = <calculated value>;
timeValue = timeValue / 1000 * 1000; // Truncate to nearest second
return timeValue;
```

It does not matter whether you round or truncate, but you must be consistent in your use of the value you return.

THE ServletRequest INTERFACE

The ServletRequest interface defines information that a servlet can obtain about the specific request. The information obtained from the ServletRequest interface does not depend specifically on the HTTP protocol. Some methods, such as getParameter, are useful in both a GenericServlet and an HttpServlet.

```
public Object getAttribute(String name)
```

```
public void setAttribute(String name, Object object)
```

The getAttribute method returns the specified named attribute. Attributes are named following the same convention as package names. The purpose of attributes is to obtain information that is not otherwise handled by the interface.

The `setAttribute` method sets the value of the attribute with the given name. It can be used to pass information to nested servlets.

public Enumeration getAttributeNames()

The `getAttributeNames` method returns an `Enumeration` containing the names of all attributes associated with the request.

public String getCharacterEncoding()

The `getCharacterEncoding` method returns the character set encoding for the input or `null` if no character encoding is specified.

public int getContentLength()

The `getContentLength` method returns the MIME-specified content length or `-1` if the length is not known.

public String getContentType()

The `getContentType` method returns the MIME content type of the request or `null` if the type is not known.

public ServletInputStream getInputStream() throws IOException

The `getInputStream` method returns an input stream that can be used to read binary data from the request. You cannot use both this method and the `getReader` method. If you call `getInputStream` after calling `getReader`, an exception will be thrown.

public String getParameter(String name)

The `getParameter` method returns the `String` value of the specified parameter name. In an `HttpServlet`, the value can be specified in the URL or it can be specified in fields posted from a form. If multiple values exist for the specified parameter, only the first is returned. You can use the `getParameterValues` method to obtain all the values for a specified name. If the specified parameter does not exist, `null` is returned.

public Enumeration getParameterNames()

The `getParameterNames` method returns an `Enumeration` of `String` objects containing the parameters for this request. If no parameters exist, the `Enumeration` will be empty.

public String[] getParameterValues()

The `getParameterValues` method returns an array of `String` objects containing the values of all the parameters for this request. If no parameters exist, the return value will be `null`.

```
public String getProtocol()
```
The getProtocol method returns a string representing the protocol. It is in the format *protocol/major.minor*. For example, if the request is for HTTP 1.1, the resulting string will be HTTP/1.1.

```
public BufferedReader getReader() throws IOException
```
The getReader method returns a buffered reader for reading text from the request. You cannot use both this method and the getInputStream method. If you call getReader after calling getInputStream, an exception will be thrown.

```
public String getRemoteAddr()
```
The getRemoteAddr method returns a string representing the IP address of the client that sent the request.

```
public String getRemoteHost()
```
The getRemoteHost method returns a string representing the fully qualified hostname of the client that sent the request. It can potentially return the dotted-string form of the IP address.

```
public String getScheme()
```
The getScheme method returns a string representing the scheme of the URL of the request. For example, an HTTP request would return http.

```
public String getServerName()
```
The getServerName method returns a string representing the server that has received the request.

```
public int getServerPort()
```
The getServerPort method returns an integer of the port number that received the request.

EXAMPLE OF getParameter

The getParameter routine is an important method because it enables you to get the URL parameters that are passed to the servlet. Here is a simple servlet that obtains a parameter and displays it. If no parameter is found, it substitutes a constant.

```
import java.io.*;

import javax.servlet.*;
import javax.servlet.http.*;
```

```
public
class ParamServlet extends HttpServlet {

    public void doGet (HttpServletRequest req, HttpServletResponse res)
      throws ServletException, IOException  {
       PrintWriter    out;

      try {
          res.setContentType("text/html");
          out = res.getWriter();
          out.println("<html>");
          out.println("<head><title>Parameter Example</title></head>");
          out.println("<body>");
          // Get from URL: ?myname=Name
          String name = req.getParameter("myname");
          if (null == name) {
             name = "Stranger";
          }
          out.println("<h1>Hello, " + name + "<h1>");
          out.println("</body></html>");
      }
       catch (Exception e) {
           e.printStackTrace();
      }
    }
}
```

In Figure 27.4 you can see the result of invoking the servlet several times. Each time, the servlet is passed a different parameter. This parameter is used to generate the name shown in the Web browser.

Figure 27.4
A servlet can access URL parameters to customize the output.

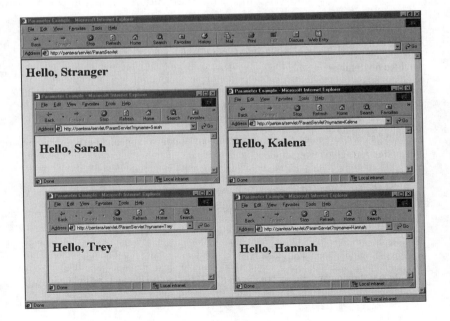

THE HttpServletRequest INTERFACE

The HttpServletRequest interface extends the ServletRequest interface and defines request-specific information for the servlet. The majority of methods of the HttpServlet class use an HttpServletRequest object to pass incoming parameters about the request. When you extend the HttpServlet class and implement one of these methods, you will be passed an HttpServletRequest object. For example, the doGet, doPost, doHead, and the other doXXX methods of HttpServlet all use an HttpServletRequest object as the first parameter. Because this interface extends ServletRequest, you can call methods of either interface in your servlet.

Here are the methods of the HttpServletRequest interface.

```
public String getAuthType()
```
The getAuthType method returns the authentication type for the request.

```
public Cookie[] getCookies()
```
The getCookies method returns an array of cookie objects containing all the cookies of this request.

```
public long getDateHeader(String name)
```
The getDateHeader method returns the value of the named header converted to a long value. The value represents the number of milliseconds since January 1, 1970, GMT. If the header cannot be converted to a date, an exception will be thrown. The name is not case sensitive.

```
public String getHeader(String name)
```
The getHeader method returns the value of the named header. The name is not case sensitive.

```
public Enumeration getHeaderNames()
```
The getHeaderNames method returns an Enumeration of String objects that represent all the header names of the request.

```
public int getIntHeader(String name)
```
The getIntHeader method returns the value of the named header converted to an integer. The name is not case sensitive.

```
public String getMethod()
```
The getMethod method returns the HTTP method (GET, POST, HEAD, and so on) expressed as a string.

`public String getPathInfo()`

The getPathInfo method returns any extra path information following the servlet path. It does not include the query string.

`public String getPathTranslated()`

The getPathTranslated method returns any extra path information following the servlet path after it has been translated to a real path. It does not include the query string.

`public String getQueryString()`

The getQueryString method returns the string that follows a question mark (?) in the URL. If no query string exists, the method returns null.

`public String getRemoteUser()`

The getRemoteUser method returns the name of the user making the request. The information can be supplied by HTTP authentication. If no associated user exists, the method returns null.

`public String getRequestedSessionId()`

The getRequestedSessionId method returns the session ID requested by the client. This can be different from the current session ID if the requested session ID was invalid.

`public String getRequestURI()`

The getRequestURI method returns the URI string from the first line of the HTTP request. It does not include the query string. This string includes both the servlet path and the path info.

`public String getServletPath()`

The getServletPath method returns the part of the URL that corresponds to the servlet that is being invoked.

`public HttpSession getSession()`

`public HttpSession getSession(boolean create)`

The getSession method returns an HttpSession object that is associated with the current request. If called without a parameter, a session will be created if one does not exist. If called with a parameter of false, the session will not be created if it does not already exist and the method will return null. This method must be called before any output is sent to the response.

`public boolean isRequestedSessionIdValid()`

The isRequestedSessionIdValid method returns true if a valid associated session exists.

PART

V

CH

27

```
public boolean isRequestedSessionIdFromCookie()
```

The isRequestedSessionIdFromCookie method returns true if the session ID was obtained from the client in a cookie and false if not.

```
public boolean isRequestedSessionIdFromURL()
```

The isRequestedSessionIdFromURL method returns true if the session ID was obtained from the client as part of a URL and false if not.

THE ServletResponse INTERFACE

The ServletResponse interface defines an object that is generated by the servlet engine and is passed to the servlet. This object contains information that allows the servlet to communicate back to the client. It is also the base interface for the HttpServletResponse interface, which is generally used with the HTTP protocol.

```
public String getCharacterEncoding()
```

The getCharacterEncoding method returns the character set encoding used for the MIME body of the response. In HTTP, this information is passed from the client through the Accept-Charset HTTP header.

```
public ServletOutputStream getOutputStream() throws IOException
```

The getOutputStream method returns an output stream that can be used to send binary data to the client. You cannot use both this method and the getWriter method. If you call this method after calling getWriter, an exception will be thrown.

```
public PrintWriter getWriter() throws IOException
```

The getWriter method returns a print writer for returning text data to the client. You cannot use both this method and the getOutputStream method. If you call this method after calling getOutputStream, an exception will be thrown. You should call setContentType before calling getWriter.

```
public void setContentLength(int length)
```

The setContentLength method sets the content length for the response. It will override any previous length specification. If called, this method must be called before sending any output to the underlying output stream.

```
public void setContentType(String type)
```

The setContentType method sets the content type for the response. It will override any previous type specification. If called, this method must be called before sending any output to the underlying output stream.

THE HttpServletResponse INTERFACE

The HttpServletResponse interface extends the ServletResponse interface. It adds methods that are specific to the HTTP protocol. Objects representing HttpServletResponse are passed to the doXXX methods of the HttpServlet class.

public void addCookie(Cookie cookie)

The addCookie method adds the specified cookie to the response. You can call this routine multiple times to add more than one cookie, but the calls must occur before the response is committed to the output stream because cookies are passed in the HTTP header.

public boolean containsHeader(String name)

The containsHeader method returns true if the specified name has already been set in the response header and false otherwise.

public String encodeRedirectURL(String url)

The encodeRedirectURL method encodes a URL for use with the sendRedirect method. The URL must be an absolute URL. You must call this method before calling sendRedirect so that session tracking is properly handled. This method is distinct from encodeURL because redirection URLs can require different encoding from other URLs.

public String encodeURL(String url)

The encodeURL method encodes a URL by adding a session ID in it. Any URL that is returned by the servlet should use this method so that session tracking is properly handled for all browsers.

public void sendError(int code) throws IOException

public void sendError(int code, String message) throws IOException

The sendError method sends an error response with the specified code to the client. If the message is provided, it will be sent as the response body. This method immediately sends the response, so no further output to the response should be made after calling this method.

public void sendRedirect(String url) throws IOException

The sendRedirect method sends a temporary redirect (code 302) using the specified URL. The URL should be an absolute URL; a relative URL will cause an exception to be thrown. This method immediately sends the response, so no further output to the response should be made after calling this method.

PART

V

CH

27

```
public void setDateHeader(String name, long date)
```

The setDateHeader method is used to set a header field with the specified name in date format. The date supplied should be a long value that represents the number of milliseconds since January 1, 1970, GMT. This method will overwrite any previous header with the same name and should be called before any output is committed to the underlying output stream.

```
public void setHeader(String name, String value)
```

The setHeader method is used to set a header field with the specified name. This method will overwrite any previous header with the same name and should be called before any output is committed to the underlying output stream.

```
public void setIntHeader(String name, int value)
```

The setIntHeader method is used to set a header field with an integer value with the specified name. This method will overwrite any previous header with the same name and should be called before any output is committed to the underlying output stream.

```
public void setStatus(int code)
```

```
public void setStatus(int code, String message)
```

The setStatus method is used to set the status code of the response. This method will overwrite any previous status code and should be called before any output is committed to the underlying output stream. If the message is provided, it will be sent as the response body.

USING COOKIES IN A SERVLET

The HTTP protocol is a stateless protocol; that is, each request and response is processed separately. No information is kept from one transaction to the next. Although this is suitable for some applications, others require at least some persistence of information from one HTTP request to another. For example, an electronic shopping cart application must keep track of the items that are in the cart. Of course, many other examples exist.

Through the use of cookies, client and server can exchange persistent information. The information is passed through HTTP headers. In Chapter 11, in the section titled "Cookies," I explain how cookies work from a client perspective. In this section, I describe the Cookie class, which is used within servlets to implement the server side of cookie baking.

The following is the Cookie constructor.

```
public Cookie(String name, String value)
```

A cookie object is created with an initial name/value pair. The name must be valid as an HTTP/1.1 token value and must not begin with a $. If the name is not valid, an exception will be thrown. After the cookie has been created, the value and other properties can be changed, but the name cannot be changed.

The following are the `Cookie` property methods.

```
public String getComment()
```

```
public void setComment(String purpose)
```

The `getComment` and `setComment` methods are used to get and set the comment that describes the purpose of the cookie. If the comment has not been defined, the `getComment` property routine will return a `null`.

```
public String getDomain()
```

```
public void setDomain(String pattern)
```

The `getDomain` and `setDomain` methods are used to get and set the domain pattern string for the cookie. The domain pattern begins with a dot (`.lotus.com`). Hosts within the DNS zone (`www.lotus.com` but not `www.java.lotus.com`) can see the cookie.

```
public int getMaxAge()
```

```
public void setMaxAge(int maxage)
```

The `getMaxAge` and `setMaxAge` methods are used to get and set the maximum age for the cookie, in seconds. Negative values mean that the cookie should not persist on the client, and a zero value will cause the cookie to be deleted from the client.

```
public String getName()
```

The `getName` method is used to return the name of the cookie. The name is set with the cookie constructor and cannot be subsequently changed.

```
public String getPath()
```

```
public void setPath(String uri)
```

The `getPath` and `setPath` methods are used to get and set the path attribute for the cookie. The `getPath` routine returns the prefix of all the URL paths for which the cookie is valid. It returns `null` if the path is not defined.

```
public boolean getSecure()
```

```
public void setSecure(boolean secure)
```

The `getSecure` and `setSecure` methods are used to get and set a flag that indicates whether the cookie should only be sent through a secure channel, such as HTTPS.

```
public String getValue()

public void setValue(String value)
```

The getValue and setValue methods are used to get and set the current value of the cookie. Version 0 cookies should avoid the use of whitespace and special characters.

```
public int getVersion()

public void setVersion(int version)
```

The getVersion and setVersion methods are used to get and set the version number of the cookie. Version 0 corresponds to the original Netscape cookie specification and is used by default. Version 1 complies with RFC 2109.

COOKIE EXAMPLE

The following example shows you how to set a cookie and retrieve it. The first time it is run, you will see the output "You sent no cookies." After the initial execution, it will display a table showing CChip as the name and with the value Tasty.

```
import java.io.*;

import javax.servlet.*;
import javax.servlet.http.*;

public
class CookieServlet extends HttpServlet {

    public void doGet (HttpServletRequest req, HttpServletResponse res)
       throws ServletException, IOException {
        PrintWriter     out;

        res.setContentType("text/html");
        out = res.getWriter();
        Cookie cookie = new Cookie("CChip", "Tasty");
        res.addCookie(cookie);

        try {
           out.println("<html>");
           out.println("<head><title>Cookie Example</title></head>");
           out.println("<body>");
           // Retrieve the cookies
           Cookie[] cookies = req.getCookies();
           if (null != cookies) {
              // There are some cookies. Format them.
              out.println("<table border='3'>");
              out.println("<tr><td>COOKIE</td><td>VALUE</td></tr>");
              for (int i=0; i < cookies.length; i++) {
                 out.print("<tr><td>" + cookies[i].getName() + "</td>");
                 out.println("<td>" + cookies[i].getValue()+ "</td></tr>");
              }
              out.println("</table>");
           }
```

```
        else {
            out.println("You sent no cookies.");
        }
        out.println("</body></html>");

    }
    catch (Exception e) {
        e.printStackTrace();
    }

} // doGet

}
```

When this program is run for the first time, a new cookie with the name CChip and the value Tasty is created. It is sent to the browser along with the displayed information "You sent no cookies." At this point the browser does have the cookie value and will store it. If the user subsequently executes the same program, the browser will automatically send the cookie back to the server. The server will then find a cookie in the array returned from the getCookies method. It will then format the array as a table and return it to the browser.

Note

Depending on your browser version, the browser might automatically send a cookie for sessionid. If so, the first time you run the program, it might display the sessionid rather than the message.

ACCESSING DOMINO OBJECTS FROM A SERVLET

Now that I have shown you how you can create an HTTP servlet that is completely independent of Domino, let's take a look at how you can integrate the Domino objects with a servlet.

You can integrate Domino with a servlet by initializing the Domino environment, creating a session, and then terminating the environment. Here is a program that just starts the Domino environment and prints information from Domino:

```
import java.io.*;

import javax.servlet.*;
import javax.servlet.http.*;
import lotus.domino.*;

public
class DominoServlet extends HttpServlet {

    public void doGet (HttpServletRequest req, HttpServletResponse res)
        throws ServletException, IOException  {
        PrintWriter     out;
```

```
        res.setContentType("text/html");
        out = res.getWriter();

        try {
           // Initialize Domino on this thread
           NotesThread.sinitThread();
           // Create a session
           Session session = NotesFactory.createSession();
           // Get the Notes/Domino version
           String version = session.getNotesVersion();

           out.println("<html>");
           out.println("<head><title>Domino Example</title></head>");
           out.println("<body>");
           out.println("<h1>Running Domino " + version + "</h1>");

           out.println("<h2>on platform: " + session.getPlatform() + "</h2>");
           out.println("<h2>User is: " + session.getUserName() + "</h2>");
           out.println("</body></html>");

        }
        catch (NotesException e) {
           System.out.println(e.id + ". " + e.text);
           e.printStackTrace();
        }
        catch (Exception e) {
           e.printStackTrace();
        }
        finally {
           // Make sure to terminate the environment
           NotesThread.stermThread();
        }

   } // doGet

}
```

In this example, I have imported the lotus.domino package. After setting the content type, I initialize Domino on the current thread. The NotesFactory.createSession method will create a session using the server's ID. After I have obtained the session, I can access various informational methods. I combine this information with HTML to produce the output. Figure 27.5 shows the output produced by the program.

Figure 27.5
A servlet can access Domino objects.

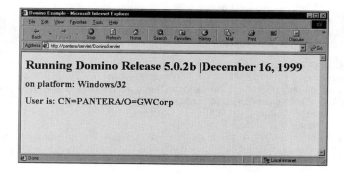

After you are able to initialize Notes and create a session, you can access databases and the rest of the Domino objects hierarchy. Use the techniques and classes described throughout this book to implement your application.

If you are using WebSphere as your servlet manager, you must make sure that the Domino objects jar file (Notes.jar) is in the WebSphere class path.

USING JDBC TO ACCESS DB2 FROM A SERVLET

We have seen servlets used with and without Domino. Let's now examine how we can use servlets with JDBC and a DB2 database. Here is a version of a JDBC program that runs within a servlet:

```
import java.io.*;

import javax.servlet.*;
import javax.servlet.http.*;
import java.sql.*;

public
class DB2Servlet extends HttpServlet {

    public void doGet (HttpServletRequest req, HttpServletResponse res)
      throws ServletException, IOException  {
      PrintWriter    out;

     res.setContentType("text/html");
     out = res.getWriter();

      String driver = "COM.ibm.db2.jdbc.app.DB2Driver";
      String url = "jdbc:db2:sample";
      //String driver = "sun.jdbc.odbc.JdbcOdbcDriver";
      //String url = "jdbc:odbc:sample";
      try {
         System.out.println("Starting");
         // Load the Datatbase driver
         Class.forName(driver).newInstance();
         // Enable the Logging String
         DriverManager.setLogStream(java.lang.System.out);
         // Connect to the database
         Connection con;
         con = DriverManager.getConnection(url,"<user>", "<password>");
         System.out.println("Using driver " + driver +", on database "+url);

         // Create a statement
         Statement st = con.createStatement();
         String query = "Select EMPNO, LASTNAME, FIRSTNME, HIREDATE, SALARY
         ➥from EMPLOYEE where EMPNO < '000100'";

         out.println("<html>");
         out.println("<head><title>DB2 Example</title></head>");
         out.println("<body>");

         out.println("<table border='3'>");
         out.println("<tr><td>EMPNO</td><td>NAME</td><td>HIRED</td>
```

```
➥<td>SALARY</td></tr>");
    // Execute the SQL statement
    ResultSet rs = st.executeQuery(query);
    // Loop through each record of the result set
    while (rs.next()) {
        out.print("<tr><td>" + rs.getString(1) + "</td>");
        out.print("<td>" +rs.getString(2)+", "+rs.getString(3)+"</td>");
        out.print("<td>" + rs.getDate(4) + "</td>");
        out.println("<td>" + rs.getDouble(5)+ "</td></tr>");
    }
    out.println("</table>");
    out.println("</body></html>");
    // Close the statement and the connection
    st.close();
    con.close();
}
catch (Exception e) {
    e.printStackTrace();
}
    }
}
```

In this sample servlet, I connect to a DB2 database using the DB2 driver. After the connection is made, I execute a SQL query on the database. After the query has completed, I loop through the result set, formatting each of the results obtained into an HTML table. See Figure 27.6 for the resulting output as presented in a Web browser.

Figure 27.6
A table of values generated from a relational database.

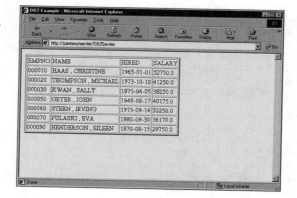

THE DOMINO SERVLET MANAGER

A servlet manager, sometimes called a servlet engine, is used to load and unload servlets. It is also used to provide a context for servlets so they can obtain the request and response objects. Domino provides a built-in servlet engine for this purpose.

By default, servlet support is not enabled. To enable servlet support, you must update the server document within the Domino Directory (public name and address book). In the server document, click the Internet Protocols tab and then select the Domino Web Engine tab. You will find a section titled Java Servlets. Within this section, change the value in the Java Servlet Support field from None to Domino Servlet Manager. You use the Third Party Servlet Support option when you want to use WebSphere as your servlet manager.

You can leave the default values for Servlet URL Path (/servlet) and Class Path (domino/servlet). The Servlet URL field indicates the trigger that will cause Domino to look for a servlet as opposed to a database. For example, a URL of the format

```
http://<server>/servlet/<servletname>
```

is recognized as a servlet because of the keyword servlet in the URL path.

The Class Path field is the location relative to the Domino data directory where the servlet class files are located. For example, if the Domino data directory is D:/Domino/Data, the servlet directory is D:/Domino/Data/domino/servlet.

After the Domino servlet manager is enabled, you must copy the Java class files to the servlet directory, and they can be invoked from URLs. Note that you must also load the HTTP task within Domino, which is the Web server task.

USING THE WEBSPHERE SERVLET MANAGER WITH DOMINO

In addition to using the Domino Servlet Manager, you can use IBM's WebSphere Application Server as your servlet manager. WebSphere provides additional functionality that is not provided by Domino's servlet engine. The two most important features provided by WebSphere are Java Server Pages and Enterprise Java Beans (EJBs). The current version of WebSphere is 3.0, but I describe version 2.0 in this book because at this time, version 2.0 is the one that is shipping with Domino. All the features described in this chapter should apply equally to version 3.0 of WebSphere as well.

Java Server Pages allow you to intermix HTML with Java program snippits. This enables you to use HTML for the majority of your Web pages and to provide some programmability using Java. I'll give you more details about JSPs in the next section.

EJBs provide a component-based model for combining Web technology with Java and with relational databases. The purpose of EJBs is to enable a separation of functions so database experts can provide high-level, object-oriented access to databases. Application experts can use these access components to quickly write enterprise applications.

EJB support requires the Advanced Edition of the WebSphere Application server. I will not be discussing EJBs in detail in this book.

When you use the WebSphere servlet manager, you must move your servlet class files to the WebSphere\AppServer\servlets directory. Note that this is different from the default location if you use the Domino servlet manager.

CONFIGURING SERVLETS WITH WEBSPHERE

After you have installed WebSphere, you can use a browser to configure and administer it. Four major areas of control are in the WebSphere administration application. They are Setup, Servlets, Security, and Server Execution Analysis.

In the Setup section you can control the administrator password, database connection management, directory services, Java Engine settings, Session management, user profiles, and virtual hosts.

The Java Engine settings enable you to set parameters for the Java Virtual Machine. One of the most important fields in this section is one that allows you to set the Application Server Classpath. When you develop your servlet, you might need to reference external JAR or Zip files. Either you must specify these files within the system classpath and tell WebSphere to use the system classpath or you must specify these files explicitly in the WebSphere classpath. See Figure 27.7 for the Application Server Classpath field.

Figure 27.7
WebSphere uses the Application Server Classpath field to find JAR and Zip files.

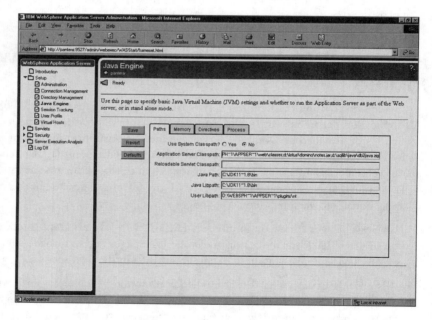

If you receive a ClassNotFound error, check the WebSphere classpath within the Java Engine section. You can also specify a reloadable servlet classpath. This classpath is useful if you are doing development. If any class has changed that was loaded from the reloadable servlet classpath, all servlets, classes, and sessions are invalidated and reloaded when the change is detected. Any classes used by Java objects that must be serialized cannot be placed in the reloadable path.

In the Security section you can add and remove users and groups that are authorized for WebSphere. In the Server Execution Analysis section you can control JVM debugging, logging, and monitoring.

Figure 27.8 shows the Servlet Configuration page, which enables you to review and update a servlet's settings. You can control whether the servlet is loaded at startup and whether the servlet is currently loaded.

Figure 27.8
The Servlet Configuration page enables you to see and modify a servlet's settings.

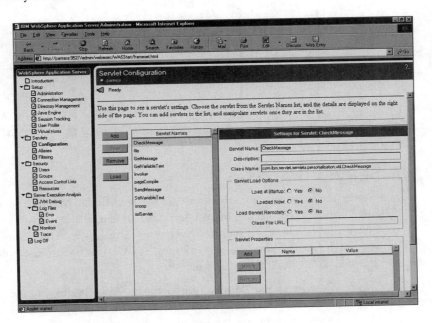

In addition to the servlet configuration, you can control servlet *aliases*. An alias allows WebSphere to automatically invoke a servlet when a specific file extension is used in a URL or when a particular directory is specified (see Figure 27.9).

You can see from Figure 27.9 that when the /servlet directory is found in the URL path, the invoker servlet is invoked. This servlet actually invokes the servlet specified in the URL. Any filename with the format *.jsp (or *.jhtml or *.shtml) will cause the page to be compiled and treated as a Java Server Page (JSP). Java Server Pages are described in the next section.

PART
V

CH

27

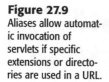

Figure 27.9
Aliases allow automatic invocation of servlets if specific extensions or directories are used in a URL.

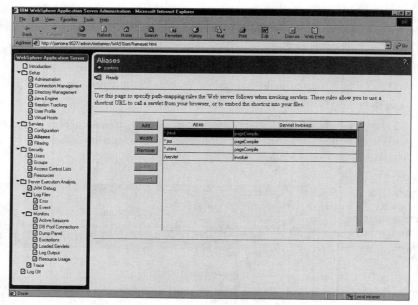

JAVA SERVER PAGES

Java Server Pages provide a method for combining static HTML with Java to produce dynamic output. The objective of Java Server Pages is to allow a separation of formatting code from program logic. In standard servlets, even the static HTML must be specified in the Java servlet itself. With Java Server Pages, HTML can be expressed directly as HTML and the Java code is highlighted as separate.

The Domino servlet engine does not support JSPs. To use them, you must use WebSphere. JSP support is enabled by default, so no special configuration is required. When using the Domino Web server, you place the JSP files in the Domino\html directory along with any other HTML pages, even though you are using the WebSphere server. If you are using another Web server, such as IIS, the location of your JSP files is dependent on your Web server.

If you use both Domino and WebSphere, you should install Domino first, and then install WebSphere, because WebSphere can configure itself to work with the Domino HTTP server. In addition, you must modify the Domino directory Java Servlets section in the Domino Web Engine tab of the Internet Protocols tab of the Server document. The Java Servlet Support field should indicate that a third-party servlet engine will be used. For more information, review the release notes for both Domino and WebSphere for the versions you are using.

Here is an example of a Java Server Page that uses the Domino objects:

```
<html>
<head><title>Domino Example</title></head>
<body>
<%
  try   {
      // Initialize Domino on this thread
      lotus.domino.NotesThread.sinitThread();
      // Create a session
      lotus.domino.Session session = lotus.domino.NotesFactory.createSession();
      // Get the Notes/Domino version
      String version = session.getNotesVersion();
      out.println("<h1>Running Domino  " +   version + "</h1>");
      out.println("<h2>on  platform: " + session.getPlatform() + "</h2>");
      out.println("<h2>User is: "   + session.getUserName() + "</h2>");
  }
  catch (lotus.domino.NotesException e) {
      System.out.println(e.id +  ". "  + e.text);
      e.printStackTrace();
  }
  catch (Exception e)  {
      e.printStackTrace();
  }
  finally  {
   //   Make sure to terminate the environment
      lotus.domino.NotesThread.stermThread();
  }
%>
</body>
</html>
```

The filename for this program is `Domino.jsp`. The JSP extension indicates that this is a Java Server Page. The output from this JSP is identical to Figure 27.5; refer to that figure and the associated servlet to see how the JSP compares.

COMBINED EXAMPLE SHOWING DOMINO, WEBSPHERE, XML, JDBC, AND DB2 IN A JSP

The title of this section is probably the most acronym-filled title in this book. It's a good thing we're near the end of the book. By now, you've mastered these acronyms and you know what they mean. In this section, I'll create a JSP that is served by the Domino Web server and WebSphere. WebSphere will convert the JSP into a servlet, compile it, and execute it. The servlet will use JDBC to access a DB2 database and format the data into XML. The XML is then handed to Domino, which will send the result to the browser.

Here is the JSP:

```
<% response.setContentType("text/xml"); %>

<?xml version="1.0" ?>
<html>
```

```
<head><title>XML Display of Directory</title></head>
<body>
<table border='3'>
<tr><td>EMPNO</td><td>NAME</td><td>HIRED</td><td>SALARY</td></tr>
<%
        String driver = "COM.ibm.db2.jdbc.app.DB2Driver";
        String url = "jdbc:db2:sample";
        //String driver = "sun.jdbc.odbc.JdbcOdbcDriver";
        //String url = "jdbc:odbc:sample";
        try {
           // Load the Datatbase driver
           Class.forName(driver).newInstance();
           // Enable the Logging String
           java.sql.DriverManager.setLogStream(java.lang.System.out);
           // Connect to the database
           java.sql.Connection con;
           con = java.sql.DriverManager.getConnection
           ➥(url,"<user>","<password>");
           System.out.println("Using driver "+driver+", on database " + url);

           // Create a statement
           java.sql.Statement st = con.createStatement();
           String query = "Select EMPNO, LASTNAME, FIRSTNME, HIREDATE,
           ➥SALARY from EMPLOYEE where EMPNO < '000100'";
           // Execute the SQL statement
           java.sql.ResultSet rs = st.executeQuery(query);
           // Loop through each record of the result set
           while (rs.next()) {
              out.print("<tr><td>" + rs.getString(1) + "</td>");
              out.print("<td>" + rs.getString(2) + ", " +
              ➥rs.getString(3) + "</td>");
              out.print("<td>" + rs.getDate(4) + "</td>");
              out.println("<td>" + rs.getDouble(5)+ "</td></tr>");
           }
           out.println("</table>");
           // Close the statement and the connection
           st.close();
           con.close();
        }
        catch (Exception e) {
           e.printStackTrace();
        }

%>
</body>
</html>
```

The result of executing the JSP can be seen in Figure 27.10. The result is XML by virtue of the fact that the MIME type is set to text/xml and the first line of output contains the XML version number. The rest of the file is actually HTML, so by changing these two features, the JSP could easily be converted to return HTML instead of XML.

Of course, you could also process the resulting XML with XSL to format it into HTML. Note that, because JSPs do not allow you to import Java class libraries, you must use the fully qualified package and class names. For example, you must use the name java.sql.Connection rather than the abbreviated name Connection.

Figure 27.10
Java Server Pages can return XML as well as HTML.

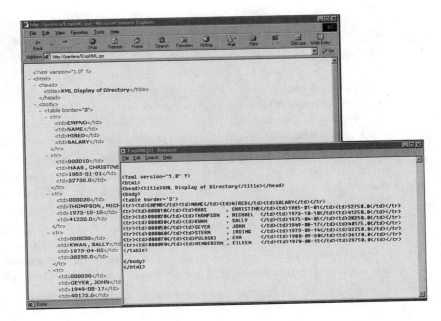

Details of the use of JDBC can be found in Chapter 26, "Integrating Domino with Relational Databases Using JDBC."

Within the Java portion of a JSP, you can refer to the following names:

- out—Refers to a PrintWriter that can be used for output
- request—Refers to the request object and corresponds to the HttpServletRequest interface
- response—Refers to the response object and corresponds to the HttpServletResponse interface

CHAPTER REVIEW

1. Describe the relative merits of using servlets instead of Domino agents. When would you use one type of program as opposed to the other?

2. In Chapter 24, I describe serving WML (Wireless Markup Language), which is an XML-based language. Create a Java servlet that can be used to serve WML. The WML files can be stored within the file system, a Domino database, or as a relational database. Try to make your program flexible enough to easily support all three types of data sources.

3. What is the purpose of the doGet method of the HttpServlet class? What is the difference between the doGet and doPost methods? What is the difference between the HTTP GET and POST methods? (Hint: Some information about HTTP appears in Chapter 11, "JavaScript Techniques with Domino.")

4. In the examples for accessing Domino, I used the `NotesThread.sinitThread` method. Why? Could alternative methods be used to initialize the Domino environment? If so, update one of the examples using an alternative initialization technique.

5. Write a servlet that can be used to save a user's name and password. You should use cookies to implement the servlet. Because cookies are stored on the user's local disk, you should encrypt the password. You can use any technique to encrypt the password. The first time a user visits the servlet's URL, it should request a username and password. Subsequent calls should recognize that the user has previously logged in.

6. In the last section of this chapter, I showed you a sample servlet that accessed a relational database and produced XML. Update the example to change the tags to more meaningful element names such as `<empno>`, `<name>`, and so on. Also add an XSL translation to format the output to HTML from your newly created XML.

7. Create a servlet that will read your Domino directory (public name and address book) and format information based on a query parameter. You should have several possible query parameters. For example, you should be able to look up someone by first name, last name, or Internet username. Look up the user and format the result.

8. Create a Java Server Page that performs the same function as that in exercise 7.

Extensible Markup Language (XML) 1.0

The XML Recommendation

This appendix contains the full text of the XML 1.0 recommendation of February 10, 1998. A W3C recommendation is an industry standard recommendation. This specification is actually very short, and if you are going to be doing any XML work, I recommend that you read the entire specification.

The specification also can be obtained on the Internet at the following address: `http://www.w3.org/TR/REC-xml`.

XML 1.0 W3C Recommendation of 10-February-1998

Extensible Markup Language (XML) 1.0 REC-xml-19980210

Extensible Markup Language (XML) 1.0

W3C Recommendation 10-February-1998

This version

```
http://www.w3.org/TR/1998/REC-xml-19980210
http://www.w3.org/TR/1998/REC-xml-19980210.xml
http://www.w3.org/TR/1998/REC-xml-19980210.html
http://www.w3.org/TR/1998/REC-xml-19980210.pdf
http://www.w3.org/TR/1998/REC-xml-19980210.ps
```

Latest version

```
http://www.w3.org/TR/REC-xml
```

Previous version

```
http://www.w3.org/TR/PR-xml-971208
```

Editors

Tim Bray, Textuality and Netscape (tbray@textuality.com)

Jean Paoli, Microsoft (jeanpa@microsoft.com)

C. M. Sperberg-McQueen, University of Illinois at Chicago (cmsmcq@uic.edu)

Abstract

The Extensible Markup Language (XML) is a subset of SGML that is completely described in this document. Its goal is to enable generic SGML to be served, received, and processed on the Web in the way that is now possible with HTML. XML has been designed for ease of implementation and for interoperability with both SGML and HTML.

Status of this document

This document has been reviewed by W3C Members and other interested parties and has been endorsed by the Director as a W3C Recommendation. It is a stable document and may be used as reference material or cited as a normative reference from another document. W3C's role in making the Recommendation is to draw attention to the specification and to promote its widespread deployment. This enhances the functionality and interoperability of the Web.

This document specifies a syntax created by subsetting an existing, widely used international text processing standard (Standard Generalized Markup Language, ISO 8879:1986(E) as amended and corrected) for use on the World Wide Web. It is a product of the W3C XML Activity, details of which can be found at http://www.w3.org/XML. A list of current W3C Recommendations and other technical documents can be found at http://www.w3.org/TR.

This specification uses the term URI, which is defined by [Berners-Lee et al.], a work in progress expected to update [IETF RFC1738] and [IETF RFC1808]. The list of known errors in this specification is available at http://www.w3.org/XML/xml-19980210-errata.

Please report errors in this document to xml-editor@w3.org.

EXTENSIBLE MARKUP LANGUAGE (XML) 1.0

TABLE OF CONTENTS

Appendices

A. References

A.1 Normative References

A.2 Other References

B. Character Classes

C. XML and SGML (Non-Normative)

D. Expansion of Entity and Character References (Non-Normative)

E. Deterministic Content Models (Non-Normative)

F. Autodetection of Character Encodings (Non-Normative)

G. W3C XML Working Group (Non-Normative)

1. INTRODUCTION

Extensible Markup Language, abbreviated XML, describes a class of data objects called XML documents and partially describes the behavior of computer programs which process them. XML is an application profile or restricted form of SGML, the Standard Generalized Markup Language [ISO 8879]. By construction, XML documents are conforming SGML documents.

XML documents are made up of storage units called entities, which contain either parsed or unparsed data. Parsed data is made up of characters, some of which form character data, and some of which form markup. Markup encodes a description of the document's storage layout and logical structure. XML provides a mechanism to impose constraints on the storage layout and logical structure.

A software module called an XML processor is used to read XML documents and provide access to their content and structure. It is assumed that an XML processor is doing its work on behalf of another module, called the application. This specification describes the required behavior of an XML processor in terms of how it must read XML data and the information it must provide to the application.

1.1 ORIGIN AND GOALS

XML was developed by an XML Working Group (originally known as the SGML Editorial Review Board) formed under the auspices of the World Wide Web Consortium (W3C) in 1996. It was chaired by Jon Bosak of Sun Microsystems with the active participation of an XML Special Interest Group (previously known as the SGML Working Group) also organized by the W3C. The membership of the XML Working Group is given in an appendix. Dan Connolly served as the WG's contact with the W3C.

The design goals for XML are

1. XML shall be straightforwardly usable over the Internet.
2. XML shall support a wide variety of applications.
3. XML shall be compatible with SGML.
4. It shall be easy to write programs which process XML documents.
5. The number of optional features in XML is to be kept to the absolute minimum, ideally zero.
6. XML documents should be human-legible and reasonably clear.
7. The XML design should be prepared quickly.
8. The design of XML shall be formal and concise.
9. XML documents shall be easy to create.
10. Terseness in XML markup is of minimal importance.

This specification, together with associated standards (Unicode and ISO/IEC 10646 for characters, Internet RFC 1766 for language identification tags, ISO 639 for language name codes, and ISO 3166 for country name codes), provides all the information necessary to understand XML Version 1.0 and construct computer programs to process it.

This version of the XML specification may be distributed freely, as long as all text and legal notices remain intact.

1.2 TERMINOLOGY

The terminology used to describe XML documents is defined in the body of this specification. The terms defined in the following list are used in building those definitions and in describing the actions of an XML processor:

may

Conforming documents and XML processors are permitted to but need not behave as described.

must

Conforming documents and XML processors are required to behave as described; otherwise they are in error.

error

A violation of the rules of this specification; results are undefined. Conforming software may detect and report an error and may recover from it.

fatal error

An error which a conforming XML processor must detect and report to the application. After encountering a fatal error, the processor may continue processing the data to search for further errors and may report such errors to the application. In order to support correction of errors, the processor may make unprocessed data from the document (with intermingled character data and markup) available to the application. Once a fatal error is detected, however, the processor must not continue normal processing (i.e., it must not continue to pass character data and information about the document's logical structure to the application in the normal way).

at user option

Conforming software may or must (depending on the modal verb in the sentence) behave as described; if it does, it must provide users a means to enable or disable the behavior described.

validity constraint

A rule which applies to all valid XML documents. Violations of validity constraints are errors; they must, at user option, be reported by validating XML processors.

App

A

well-formedness constraint

A rule which applies to all well-formed XML documents. Violations of well-formedness constraints are fatal errors.

match

(Of strings or names:) Two strings or names being compared must be identical. Characters with multiple possible representations in ISO/IEC 10646 (e.g. characters with both precomposed and base+diacritic forms) match only if they have the same representation in both strings. At user option, processors may normalize such characters to some canonical form. No case folding is performed. (Of strings and rules in the grammar:) A string matches a grammatical production if it belongs to the language generated by that production. (Of content and content models:) An element matches its declaration when it conforms in the fashion described in the constraint **Section 3: Element Valid**.

for compatibility

A feature of XML included solely to ensure that XML remains compatible with SGML.

for interoperability

A non-binding recommendation included to increase the chances that XML documents can be processed by the existing installed base of SGML processors which pre-date the WebSGML Adaptations Annex to ISO 8879.

2. DOCUMENTS

A data object is an *XML document* if it is well-formed, as defined in this specification. A well-formed XML document may in addition be valid if it meets certain further constraints.

Each XML document has both a logical and a physical structure. Physically, the document is composed of units called entities. An entity may refer to other entities to cause their inclusion in the document. A document begins in a "root" or document entity. Logically, the document is composed of declarations, elements, comments, character references, and processing instructions, all of which are indicated in the document by explicit markup. The logical and physical structures must nest properly, as described in **Section 4.3.2 Well-Formed Parsed Entities**.

2.1 WELL-FORMED XML DOCUMENTS

A textual object is a well-formed XML document if:

1. Taken as a whole, it matches the production labeled document.
2. It meets all the well-formedness constraints given in this specification.
3. Each of the parsed entities which is referenced directly or indirectly within the document is *well-formed*.

Document

```
[1] document    ::= prolog element Misc*
```

Matching the *document* production implies that:

1. It contains one or more elements.
2. There is exactly one element, called the root, or document element, no part of which appears in the content of any other element. For all other elements, if the start-tag is in the content of another element, the end-tag is in the content of the same element. More simply stated, the elements, delimited by start- and end-tags, nest properly within each other.

As a consequence of this, for each non-root element C in the document, there is one other element P in the document such that C is in the content of P, but is not in the content of any other element that is in the content of P. P is referred to as the *parent* of C, and C as a *child* of P.

2.2 CHARACTERS

A parsed entity contains *text*, a sequence of characters, which may represent markup or character data. A *character* is an atomic unit of text as specified by ISO/IEC 10646 [ISO/IEC 10646]. Legal characters are tab, carriage return, line feed, and the legal graphic characters of Unicode and ISO/IEC 10646. The use of "compatibility characters," as defined in section 6.8 of [Unicode], is discouraged.

Character Range

```
[2] Char    ::= #x9 | #xA | #xD | [#x20-#xD7FF]    /* any Unicode character,
              | [#xE000-#xFFFD] | [#x10000-          excluding the surrogate
              #x10FFFF]                              blocks, FFFE, and FFFF. */
```

The mechanism for encoding character code points into bit patterns may vary from entity to entity. All XML processors must accept the UTF-8 and UTF-16 encodings of 10646; the mechanisms for signaling which of the two is in use, or for bringing other encodings into play, are discussed later, in **Section 4.3.3 Character Encoding in Entities**.

2.3 COMMON SYNTACTIC CONSTRUCTS

This section defines some symbols used widely in the grammar.

S (white space) consists of one or more space (#x20) characters, carriage returns, line feeds, or tabs.

White Space

```
[3] S       ::= (#x20 | #x9 | #xD | #xA)+
```

Characters are classified for convenience as letters, digits, or other characters. Letters consist of an alphabetic or syllabic base character possibly followed by one or more combining characters, or of an ideographic character. Full definitions of the specific characters in each class are given in **Appendix B: Character Classes**.

A Name is a token beginning with a letter or one of a few punctuation characters, and continuing with letters, digits, hyphens, underscores, colons, or full stops, together known as name characters. Names beginning with the string "xml", or any string which would match ((('X'|'x') ('M'|'m') ('L'|'l'))), are reserved for standardization in this or future versions of this specification.

Note

> The colon character within XML names is reserved for experimentation with name spaces. Its meaning is expected to be standardized at some future point, at which point those documents using the colon for experimental purposes may need to be updated. (There is no guarantee that any name-space mechanism adopted for XML will in fact use the colon as a name-space delimiter.) In practice, this means that authors should not use the colon in XML names except as part of name-space experiments, but that XML processors should accept the colon as a name character.

An Nmtoken (name token) is any mixture of name characters.

Names and Tokens

```
[4] NameChar    ::= Letter | Digit | '.' | '-' | '_' | ':' | CombiningChar |
                    Extender
[5] Name        ::= (Letter | '_' | ':') (NameChar)*
[6] Names       ::= Name (S Name)*
[7] Nmtoken     ::= (NameChar)+
[8] Nmtokens    ::= Nmtoken (S Nmtoken)*
```

Literal data is any quoted string not containing the quotation mark used as a delimiter for that string. Literals are used for specifying the content of internal entities (EntityValue), the values of attributes (AttValue), and external identifiers (SystemLiteral). Note that a SystemLiteral can be parsed without scanning for markup.

Literals

```
[9]  EntityValue   ::= '"' ([^%&"] | PEReference | Reference)* '"'
                     | "'" ([^%&'] | PEReference | Reference)* "'"
[10] AttValue       ::= '"' ([^<&"] | Reference)* '"'
                     | "'" ([^<&'] | Reference)* "'"
[11] SystemLiteral  ::= ('"' [^"]* '"') | ("'" [^']* "'")
[12] PubidLiteral   ::= '"' PubidChar* '"' | "'" (PubidChar - "'")* "'"
[13] PubidChar      ::= #x20 | #xD | #xA | [a-zA-Z0-9] | [-'()+,./:=?;!*#@$_%]
```

2.4 CHARACTER DATA AND MARKUP

Text consists of intermingled character data and markup. *Markup* takes the form of start-tags, end-tags, empty-element tags, entity references, character references, comments, CDATA section delimiters, document type declarations, and processing instructions.

All text that is not markup constitutes the *character data* of the document.

The ampersand character (&) and the left angle bracket (<) may appear in their literal form only when used as markup delimiters, or within a comment, a processing instruction, or a

CDATA section. They are also legal within the literal entity value of an internal entity declaration; see **Section 4.3.2: Well-Formed Parsed Entities**. If they are needed elsewhere, they must be escaped using either numeric character references or the strings "`&amp;`" and "`&lt;`", respectively. The right angle bracket (>) may be represented using the string "`&gt;`", and must, for compatibility, be escaped using "`&gt;`" or a character reference when it appears in the string "`]]>`" in content, when that string is not marking the end of a CDATA section.

In the content of elements, character data is any string of characters which does not contain the start-delimiter of any markup. In a CDATA section, character data is any string of characters not including the CDATA-section-close delimiter, "`]]>`".

To allow attribute values to contain both single and double quotes, the apostrophe or single-quote character (') may be represented as "`&apos;`", and the double-quote character (") as "`&quot;`".

Character Data

```
[14] CharData        ::= [^<&]* - ([^<&]* ']]>' [^<&]*)
```

2.5 COMMENTS

Comments may appear anywhere in a document outside other markup; in addition, they may appear within the document type declaration at places allowed by the grammar. They are not part of the document's character data; an XML processor may, but need not, make it possible for an application to retrieve the text of comments. For compatibility, the string "`--`" (double-hyphen) must not occur within comments.

Comments

```
[15] Comment         ::= '<!--' ((Char - '-') | ('-' (Char - '-')))* '-->'
```

An example of a comment:

```
<!-- declarations for <head> & <body> -->
```

2.6 PROCESSING INSTRUCTIONS

Processing instructions (PIs) allow documents to contain instructions for applications.

Processing Instructions

```
[16] PI              ::= '<?' PITarget (S (Char* - (Char* '?>' Char*)))? '?>'
[17] PITarget        ::= Name - (('X' | 'x') ('M' | 'm') ('L' | 'l'))
```

PIs are not part of the document's character data, but must be passed through to the application. The PI begins with a target (`PITarget`) used to identify the application to which the instruction is directed. The target names "`XML`", "`xml`", and so on are reserved for standardization in this or future versions of this specification. The XML Notation mechanism may be used for formal declaration of PI targets.

2.7 CDATA SECTIONS

CDATA sections may occur anywhere character data may occur; they are used to escape blocks of text containing characters which would otherwise be recognized as markup. CDATA sections begin with the string "`<![CDATA[`" and end with the string "`]]>`":

CDATA Sections

```
[18]  CDSect        ::= CDStart CData CDEnd
[19]  CDStart       ::= '<![CDATA['
[20]  CData         ::= (Char* - (Char* ']]>' Char*))
[21]  CDEnd         ::= ']]>'
```

Within a CDATA section, only the CDEnd string is recognized as markup, so that left angle brackets and ampersands may occur in their literal form; they need not (and cannot) be escaped using "`&lt;`" and "`&amp;`". CDATA sections cannot nest.

An example of a CDATA section, in which `<greeting>` and `</greeting>` are recognized as character data, not markup:

```
<![CDATA[<greeting>Hello, world!</greeting>]]>
```

2.8 PROLOG AND DOCUMENT TYPE DECLARATION

XML documents may, and should, begin with an *XML declaration* which specifies the version of XML being used. For example, the following is a complete XML document, well-formed but not valid:

```
<?xml version="1.0"?>
<greeting>Hello, world!</greeting>
```

and so is this:

```
<greeting>Hello, world!</greeting>
```

The version number "`1.0`" should be used to indicate conformance to this version of this specification; it is an error for a document to use the value "`1.0`" if it does not conform to this version of this specification. It is the intent of the XML working group to give later versions of this specification numbers other than "`1.0`", but this intent does not indicate a commitment to produce any future versions of XML, nor if any are produced, to use any particular numbering scheme. Since future versions are not ruled out, this construct is provided as a means to allow the possibility of automatic version recognition, should it become necessary. Processors may signal an error if they receive documents labeled with versions they do not support.

The function of the markup in an XML document is to describe its storage and logical structure and to associate attribute-value pairs with its logical structures. XML provides a mechanism, the document type declaration, to define constraints on the logical structure and to support the use of predefined storage units. An XML document is *valid* if it has an associated document type declaration and if the document complies with the constraints expressed in it. The document type declaration must appear before the first element in the document.

Prolog

```
[22] prolog          ::= XMLDecl? Misc* (doctypedecl Misc*)?
[23] XMLDecl         ::= '<?xml' VersionInfo EncodingDecl? SDDecl? S? '?>'
[24] VersionInfo     ::= S 'version' Eq (' VersionNum ' | " VersionNum ")
[25] Eq              ::= S? '=' S?
[26] VersionNum      ::= ([a-zA-Z0-9_.:] | '-')+
[27] Misc            ::= Comment | PI | S
```

The XML *document type declaration* contains or points to markup declarations that provide a grammar for a class of documents. This grammar is known as a document type definition, or *DTD*. The document type declaration can point to an external subset (a special kind of external entity) containing markup declarations, or can contain the markup declarations directly in an internal subset, or can do both. The DTD for a document consists of both subsets taken together.

A *markup declaration* is an element type declaration, an attribute-list declaration, an entity declaration, or a notation declaration. These declarations may be contained in whole or in part within parameter entities, as described in the well-formedness and validity constraints below. For fuller information, see **Section 4: Physical Structures**.

Document Type Definition

```
[28] doctypedecl  ::= '<!DOCTYPE' S Name (S ExternalID)? S? [   VC: Root Element
                      ('[' (markupdecl | PEReference | S)*      Type ]
                      ']' S?)? '>'
[29] markupdecl   ::= elementdecl | AttlistDecl | EntityDecl [  VC: Proper
                      | NotationDecl | PI | Comment              Declaration/PE
                                                                 Nesting ]
                                                              [  WFC: PEs in
                                                                 Internal Subset]
```

The markup declarations may be made up in whole or in part of the replacement text of parameter entities. The productions later in this specification for individual nonterminals (`elementdecl`, `AttlistDecl`, and so on) describe the declarations *after* all the parameter entities have been included.

> **VALIDITY CONSTRAINT: Root Element Type.** The Name in the document type declaration must match the element type of the root element.

> **VALIDITY CONSTRAINT: Proper Declaration/PE Nesting.** Parameter-entity replacement text must be properly nested with markup declarations. That is to say, if either the first character or the last character of a markup declaration (`markupdecl` above) is contained in the replacement text for a parameter-entity reference, both must be contained in the same replacement text.

> **WELL-FORMEDNESS CONSTRAINT: PEs in Internal Subset.** In the internal DTD subset, parameter-entity references can occur only where markup declarations can occur, not within markup declarations. (This does not apply to references that occur in external parameter entities or to the external subset.)

Like the internal subset, the external subset and any external parameter entities referred to in the DTD must consist of a series of complete markup declarations of the types allowed by the non-terminal symbol `markupdecl`, interspersed with white space or parameter-entity references. However, portions of the contents of the external subset or of external parameter entities may conditionally be ignored by using the conditional section construct; this is not allowed in the internal subset.

External Subset

```
[30] extSubset      ::= TextDecl? extSubsetDecl
[31] extSubsetDecl  ::= ( markupdecl | conditionalSect | PEReference | S )*
```

The external subset and external parameter entities also differ from the internal subset in that in them, parameter-entity references are permitted *within* markup declarations, not only *between* markup declarations.

An example of an XML document with a document type declaration:

```
<?xml version="1.0"?>
<!DOCTYPE greeting SYSTEM "hello.dtd">
<greeting>Hello, world!</greeting>
```

The system identifier `"hello.dtd"` gives the URI of a DTD for the document.

The declarations can also be given locally, as in this example:

```
<?xml version="1.0" encoding="UTF-8" ?>
<!DOCTYPE greeting [
<!ELEMENT greeting (#PCDATA)>
]>
<greeting>Hello, world!</greeting>
```

If both the external and internal subsets are used, the internal subset is considered to occur before the external subset. This has the effect that entity and attribute-list declarations in the internal subset take precedence over those in the external subset.

2.9 STANDALONE DOCUMENT DECLARATION

Markup declarations can affect the content of the document, as passed from an XML processor to an application; examples are attribute defaults and entity declarations. The standalone document declaration, which may appear as a component of the XML declaration, signals whether or not there are such declarations which appear external to the document entity.

Standalone Document Declaration

```
[32] SDDecl    ::= S 'standalone' Eq ((" '" ('yes' | 'no') "'")    [ VC: Standalone
                 | ('"' ('yes' | 'no') '"'))                          Document
                                                                      Declaration ]
```

In a standalone document declaration, the value `"yes"` indicates that there are no markup declarations external to the document entity (either in the DTD external subset, or in an external parameter entity referenced from the internal subset) which affect the information passed from the XML processor to the application. The value `"no"` indicates that there are or may be such external markup declarations. Note that the standalone document declaration only denotes the presence of external *declarations*; the presence, in a document, of references to external *entities*, when those entities are internally declared, does not change its standalone status.

If there are no external markup declarations, the standalone document declaration has no meaning. If there are external markup declarations but there is no standalone document declaration, the value "no" is assumed.

Any XML document for which standalone="no" holds can be converted algorithmically to a standalone document, which may be desirable for some network delivery applications.

> **VALIDITY CONSTRAINT: Standalone Document Declaration.** The standalone document declaration must have the value "no" if any external markup declarations contain declarations of:
> - attributes with default values, if elements to which these attributes apply appear in the document without specifications of values for these attributes, or
> - entities (other than amp, lt, gt, apos, quot), if references to those entities appear in the document, or
> - attributes with values subject to *normalization*, where the attribute appears in the document with a value which will change as a result of normalization, or
> - element types with element content, if white space occurs directly within any instance of those types.

An example XML declaration with a standalone document declaration:

```
<?xml version="1.0" standalone='yes'?>
```

2.10 WHITE SPACE HANDLING

In editing XML documents, it is often convenient to use "white space" (spaces, tabs, and blank lines, denoted by the nonterminal S in this specification) to set apart the markup for greater readability. Such white space is typically not intended for inclusion in the delivered version of the document. On the other hand, "significant" white space that should be preserved in the delivered version is common, for example in poetry and source code.

An XML processor must always pass all characters in a document that are not markup through to the application. A validating XML processor must also inform the application which of these characters constitute white space appearing in element content.

A special attribute named xml:space may be attached to an element to signal an intention that in that element, white space should be preserved by applications. In valid documents, this attribute, like any other, must be declared if it is used. When declared, it must be given as an enumerated type whose only possible values are "default" and "preserve". For example:

```
<!ATTLIST poem   xml:space (default|preserve) 'preserve'>
```

The value "default" signals that applications' default white-space processing modes are acceptable for this element; the value "preserve" indicates the intent that applications preserve all the white space. This declared intent is considered to apply to all elements within the content of the element where it is specified, unless overriden with another instance of the xml:space attribute.

The root element of any document is considered to have signaled no intentions as regards application space handling, unless it provides a value for this attribute or the attribute is declared with a default value.

2.11 END-OF-LINE HANDLING

XML parsed entities are often stored in computer files which, for editing convenience, are organized into lines. These lines are typically separated by some combination of the characters carriage-return (#xD) and line-feed (#xA). To simplify the tasks of applications, wherever an external parsed entity or the literal entity value of an internal parsed entity contains either the literal two-character sequence "#xD#xA" or a standalone literal #xD, an XML processor must pass to the application the single character #xA. (This behavior can conveniently be produced by normalizing all line breaks to #xA on input, before parsing.)

2.12 LANGUAGE IDENTIFICATION

In document processing, it is often useful to identify the natural or formal language in which the content is written. A special attribute named xml:lang may be inserted in documents to specify the language used in the contents and attribute values of any element in an XML document. In valid documents, this attribute, like any other, must be declared if it is used. The values of the attribute are language identifiers as defined by [IETF RFC 1766], "Tags for the Identification of Languages":

Language Identification

```
[33] LanguageID   ::= Langcode ('-' Subcode)*
[34] Langcode     ::= ISO639Code | IanaCode | UserCode
[35] ISO639Code   ::= ([a-z] | [A-Z]) ([a-z] | [A-Z])
[36] IanaCode     ::= ('i' | 'I') '-' ([a-z] | [A-Z])+
[37] UserCode     ::= ('x' | 'X') '-' ([a-z] | [A-Z])+
[38] Subcode      ::= ([a-z] | [A-Z])+
```

The Langcode may be any of the following:

- a two-letter language code as defined by [ISO 639], "Codes for the representation of names of languages"

- a language identifier registered with the Internet Assigned Numbers Authority [IANA]; these begin with the prefix "i-" (or "I-")

- a language identifier assigned by the user, or agreed on between parties in private use; these must begin with the prefix "x-" or "X-" in order to ensure that they do not conflict with names later standardized or registered with IANA

There may be any number of Subcode segments; if the first subcode segment exists and the Subcode consists of two letters, then it must be a country code from [ISO 3166], "Codes for the representation of names of countries." If the first subcode consists of more than two letters, it must be a subcode for the language in question registered with IANA, unless the `Langcode` begins with the prefix `"x-"` or `"X-"`.

It is customary to give the language code in lower case, and the country code (if any) in upper case. Note that these values, unlike other names in XML documents, are case insensitive.

For example:

```
<p xml:lang="en">The quick brown fox jumps over the lazy dog.</p>
<p xml:lang="en-GB">What colour is it?</p>
<p xml:lang="en-US">What color is it?</p>
<sp who="Faust" desc='leise' xml:lang="de">
  <l>Habe nun, ach! Philosophie,</l>
  <l>Juristerei, und Medizin</l>
  <l>und leider auch Theologie</l>
  <l>durchaus studiert mit heißem Bemüh'n.</l>
</sp>
```

The intent declared with `xml:lang` is considered to apply to all attributes and content of the element where it is specified, unless overridden with an instance of `xml:lang` on another element within that content.

A simple declaration for `xml:lang` might take the form

```
xml:lang  NMTOKEN  #IMPLIED
```

but specific default values may also be given, if appropriate. In a collection of French poems for English students, with glosses and notes in English, the `xml:lang` attribute might be declared this way:

```
<!ATTLIST poem   xml:lang NMTOKEN 'fr'>
<!ATTLIST gloss  xml:lang NMTOKEN 'en'>
<!ATTLIST note   xml:lang NMTOKEN 'en'>
```

3. LOGICAL STRUCTURES

Each XML document contains one or more *elements*, the boundaries of which are either delimited by start-tags and end-tags, or, for empty elements, by an empty-element tag. Each element has a type, identified by name, sometimes called its "generic identifier" (GI), and may have a set of attribute specifications. Each attribute specification has a name and a value.

Element

```
[39] element    ::= EmptyElemTag
                  | STag content ETag    [ WFC: Element Type Match ]
                                         [ VC: Element Valid ]
```

This specification does not constrain the semantics, use, or (beyond syntax) names of the element types and attributes, except that names beginning with a match to `(('X'|'x')('M'|'m')('L'|'l'))` are reserved for standardization in this or future versions of this specification.

WELL-FORMEDNESS CONSTRAINT: Element Type Match. The *Name* in an element's end-tag must match the element type in the start-tag.

VALIDITY CONSTRAINT: Element Valid. An element is valid if there is a declaration matching `elementdecl` where the *Name* matches the element type, and one of the following holds:

1. The declaration matches `EMPTY` and the element has no content.
2. The declaration matches `children` and the sequence of child elements belongs to the language generated by the regular expression in the content model, with optional white space (characters matching the nonterminal `S`) between each pair of child elements.
3. The declaration matches `Mixed` and the content consists of character data and child elements whose types match names in the content model.
4. The declaration matches `ANY`, and the types of any child elements have been declared.

3.1 START-TAGS, END-TAGS, AND EMPTY-ELEMENT TAGS

The beginning of every non-empty XML element is marked by a *start-tag*.

Start-tag

```
[40] STag        ::= '<' Name (S Attribute)* S? '>'   [ WFC: Unique Att Spec ]
[41] Attribute   ::= Name Eq AttValue                 [ VC: Attribute Value Type ]
                                         [ WFC: No External Entity References ]
                                            [ WFC: No < in Attribute Values ]
```

The `Name` in the start- and end-tags gives the element's type. The `Name`-`AttValue` pairs are referred to as the attribute specifications of the element, with the `Name` in each pair referred to as the *attribute name* and the content of the `AttValue` (the text between the ' or " delimiters) as the *attribute value*.

WELL-FORMEDNESS CONSTRAINT: Unique Att Spec. No attribute name may appear more than once in the same start-tag or empty-element tag.

VALIDITY CONSTRAINT: Attribute Value Type. The attribute must have been declared; the value must be of the type declared for it. (For attribute types, see **Section 3.3 Attribute-List Declarations**.)

WELL-FORMEDNESS CONSTRAINT: No External Entity References. Attribute values cannot contain direct or indirect entity references to external entities.

WELL-FORMEDNESS CONSTRAINT: No < in Attribute Values. The replacement text of any entity referred to directly or indirectly in an attribute value (other than "<") must not contain a <.

An example of a start-tag:

```
<termdef id="dt-dog" term="dog">
```

The end of every element that begins with a start-tag must be marked by an *end-tag* containing a name that echoes the element's type as given in the start-tag:

End-tag

```
[42] ETag          ::= '</' Name S? '>'
```

An example of an end-tag:

```
    </termdef>
```

The text between the start-tag and end-tag is called the element's *content*:

Content of Elements

```
[43] content    ::= (element | CharData | Reference | CDSect | PI | Comment)*
```

If an element is *empty*, it must be represented either by a start-tag immediately followed by an end-tag or by an empty-element tag. An *empty-element tag* takes a special form:

Tags for Empty Elements

```
[44] EmptyElemTag ::= '<' Name (S Attribute)* S? '/>'  [ WFC: Unique Att Spec ]
```

Empty-element tags may be used for any element which has no content, whether or not it is declared using the keyword EMPTY. For interoperability, the empty-element tag must be used, and can only be used, for elements which are declared EMPTY.

Examples of empty elements:

```
    <IMG align="left"
     src="http://www.w3.org/Icons/WWW/w3c_home" />
    <br></br>
    <br/>
```

3.2 ELEMENT TYPE DECLARATIONS

The element structure of an XML document may, for validation purposes, be constrained using element type and attribute-list declarations. An element type declaration constrains the element's content.

Element type declarations often constrain which element types can appear as children of the element. At user option, an XML processor may issue a warning when a declaration mentions an element type for which no declaration is provided, but this is not an error.

An *element type declaration* takes the form:

Element Type Declaration

```
[45] elementdecl   ::= '<!ELEMENT' S Name S '       [ VC: Unique Element
                       contentspec S? '>'              Type Declaration ]
[46] contentspec   ::= 'EMPTY' | 'ANY' | Mixed | children
```

where the Name gives the element type being declared.

> **VALIDITY CONSTRAINT: Unique Element Type Declaration.** No element type may be declared more than once.

Examples of element type declarations:

```
<!ELEMENT br EMPTY>
<!ELEMENT p (#PCDATA|emph)* >
<!ELEMENT %name.para; %content.para; >
<!ELEMENT container ANY>
```

3.2.1 ELEMENT CONTENT

An element type has *element content* when elements of that type must contain only child elements (no character data), optionally separated by white space (characters matching the nonterminal S). In this case, the constraint includes a content model, a simple grammar governing the allowed types of the child elements and the order in which they are allowed to appear. The grammar is built on content particles (*cps*), which consist of names, choice lists of content particles, or sequence lists of content particles:

Element-content Models

```
[47] children   ::= (choice | seq) ('?' | '*' | '+')?
[48] cp         ::= (Name | choice | seq) ('?' | '*' | '+')?
[49] choice     ::= '(' S? cp ( S? '|' S? cp )* S? ')'   [ VC: Proper
                                                           Group/PE Nesting ]
[50] seq        ::= '(' S? cp ( S? ',' S? cp )* S? ')'   [ VC: Proper Group/PE
                                                           Nesting ]
```

where each Name is the type of an element which may appear as a child. Any content particle in a choice list may appear in the element content at the location where the choice list appears in the grammar; content particles occurring in a sequence list must each appear in the element content in the order given in the list. The optional character following a name or list governs whether the element or the content particles in the list may occur one or more (+), zero or more (*), or zero or one times (?). The absence of such an operator means that the element or content particle must appear exactly once. This syntax and meaning are identical to those used in the productions in this specification.

The content of an element matches a content model if and only if it is possible to trace out a path through the content model, obeying the sequence, choice, and repetition operators and matching each element in the content against an element type in the content model. For compatibility, it is an error if an element in the document can match more than one occurrence of an element type in the content model. For more information, see **Appendix E: Deterministic Content Models**.

VALIDITY CONSTRAINT: Proper Group/PE Nesting. Parameter-entity replacement text must be properly nested with parenthetized groups. That is to say, if either of the opening or closing parentheses in a choice, seq, or Mixed construct is contained in the replacement text for a parameter entity, both must be contained in the same replacement text.

For interoperability, if a parameter-entity reference appears in a choice, seq, or Mixed construct, its replacement text should not be empty, and neither the first nor last non-blank character of the replacement text should be a connector (| or ,).

Examples of element-content models:

```
<!ELEMENT spec (front, body, back?)>
<!ELEMENT div1 (head, (p | list | note)*, div2*)>
<!ELEMENT dictionary-body (%div.mix; | %dict.mix;)*>
```

3.2.2 MIXED CONTENT

An element type has *mixed content* when elements of that type may contain character data, optionally interspersed with child elements. In this case, the types of the child elements may be constrained, but not their order or their number of occurrences:

Mixed-content Declaration

```
[51] Mixed        ::= '(' S? '#PCDATA' (S? '|' S? Name)* S? ')*'
                  | '(' S? '#PCDATA' S? ')'       [ VC: Proper Group/PE
                                                    Nesting ]
                                                  [ VC: No Duplicate Types ]
```

where the Names give the types of elements that may appear as children.

> **VALIDITY CONSTRAINT: No Duplicate Types.** The same name must not appear more than once in a single mixed-content declaration.

Examples of mixed content declarations:

```
<!ELEMENT p (#PCDATA|a|ul|b|i|em)*>
<!ELEMENT p (#PCDATA | %font; | %phrase; | %special; | %form;)* >
<!ELEMENT b (#PCDATA)>
```

3.3 ATTRIBUTE-LIST DECLARATIONS

Attributes are used to associate name-value pairs with elements. Attribute specifications may appear only within start-tags and empty-element tags; thus, the productions used to recognize them appear in **Section 3.1: Start-Tags, End-Tags, and Empty-Element Tags**. Attribute-list declarations may be used

- To define the set of attributes pertaining to a given element type.
- To establish type constraints for these attributes.
- To provide default values for attributes.

Attribute-list declarations specify the name, data type, and default value (if any) of each attribute associated with a given element type:

Attribute-list Declaration

```
[52] AttlistDecl     ::= '<!ATTLIST' S Name AttDef* S? '>'
[53] AttDef          ::= S Name S AttType S DefaultDecl
```

The Name in the AttlistDecl rule is the type of an element. At user option, an XML processor may issue a warning if attributes are declared for an element type not itself declared, but this is not an error. The Name in the AttDef rule is the name of the attribute.

When more than one `AttlistDecl` is provided for a given element type, the contents of all those provided are merged. When more than one definition is provided for the same attribute of a given element type, the first declaration is binding and later declarations are ignored. For interoperability, writers of DTDs may choose to provide at most one attribute-list declaration for a given element type, at most one attribute definition for a given attribute name, and at least one attribute definition in each attribute-list declaration. For interoperability, an XML processor may at user option issue a warning when more than one attribute-list declaration is provided for a given element type, or more than one attribute definition is provided for a given attribute, but this is not an error.

3.3.1 ATTRIBUTE TYPES

XML attribute types are of three kinds: a string type, a set of tokenized types, and enumerated types. The string type may take any literal string as a value; the tokenized types have varying lexical and semantic constraints, as noted:

Attribute Types

```
[54] AttType        ::= StringType | TokenizedType | EnumeratedType
[55] StringType     ::= 'CDATA'
[56] TokenizedType  ::= 'ID'                    [ VC: ID ]
                                                [ VC: One ID per Element Type ]
                                                [ VC: ID Attribute Default ]
                      | 'IDREF'                 [ VC: IDREF ]
                      | 'IDREFS'                [ VC: IDREF ]
                      | 'ENTITY'                [ VC: Entity Name ]
                      | 'ENTITIES'              [ VC: Entity Name ]
                      | 'NMTOKEN'               [ VC: Name Token ]
                      | 'NMTOKENS'              [ VC: Name Token ]
```

VALIDITY CONSTRAINT: ID. Values of type ID must match the Name production. A name must not appear more than once in an XML document as a value of this type; i.e., ID values must uniquely identify the elements which bear them.

VALIDITY CONSTRAINT: One ID per Element Type. No element type may have more than one ID attribute specified.

VALIDITY CONSTRAINT: ID Attribute Default. An ID attribute must have a declared default of #IMPLIED or #REQUIRED.

VALIDITY CONSTRAINT: IDREF. Values of type IDREF must match the Name production, and values of type IDREFS must match Names; each Name must match the value of an ID attribute on some element in the XML document; i.e. IDREF values must match the value of some ID attribute.

VALIDITY CONSTRAINT: Entity Name. Values of type ENTITY must match the Name production, values of type ENTITIES must match Names; each Name must match the name of an unparsed entity declared in the DTD.

VALIDITY CONSTRAINT: Name Token. Values of type NMTOKEN must match the Nmtoken production; values of type NMTOKENS must match Nmtokens.

Enumerated attributes can take one of a list of values provided in the declaration. There are two kinds of enumerated types:

Enumerated Attribute Types

```
[57] EnumeratedType  ::= NotationType | Enumeration
[58] NotationType    ::= 'NOTATION' S '(' S? Name (S? '|' S? Name)* S?
                         ')' [ VC: Notation Attributes ]
[59] Enumeration     ::= '(' S? Nmtoken (S? '|' S? Nmtoken)* [ VC:
                         S? ')'                              Enumeration ]
```

A NOTATION attribute identifies a notation, declared in the DTD with associated system and/or public identifiers, to be used in interpreting the element to which the attribute is attached.

> **VALIDITY CONSTRAINT: Notation Attributes.** Values of this type must match one of the notation names included in the declaration; all notation names in the declaration must be declared.

> **VALIDITY CONSTRAINT: Enumeration.** Values of this type must match one of the Nmtoken tokens in the declaration.

For interoperability, the same Nmtoken should not occur more than once in the enumerated attribute types of a single element type.

3.3.2 ATTRIBUTE DEFAULTS

An attribute declaration provides information on whether the attribute's presence is required, and if not, how an XML processor should react if a declared attribute is absent in a document.

Attribute Defaults

```
[60] DefaultDecl  ::= '#REQUIRED' | '#IMPLIED'
                    | (('#FIXED' S)? AttValue)[ VC: Required Attribute ]
                                             [ VC: Attribute Default Legal ]
                                             [ WFC: No < in Attribute
                                              Values ]
                                             [ VC: Fixed Attribute Default ]
```

In an attribute declaration, #REQUIRED means that the attribute must always be provided, #IMPLIED that no default value is provided. If the declaration is neither #REQUIRED nor #IMPLIED, then the AttValue value contains the declared default value; the #FIXED keyword states that the attribute must always have the default value. If a default value is declared, when an XML processor encounters an omitted attribute, it is to behave as though the attribute were present with the declared default value.

> **VALIDITY CONSTRAINT: Required Attribute.** If the default declaration is the keyword #REQUIRED, then the attribute must be specified for all elements of the type in the attribute-list declaration.

> **VALIDITY CONSTRAINT: Attribute Default Legal.** The declared default value must meet the lexical constraints of the declared attribute type.

VALIDITY CONSTRAINT: Fixed Attribute Default. If an attribute has a default value declared with the #FIXED keyword, instances of that attribute must match the default value.

Examples of attribute-list declarations:

```
<!ATTLIST termdef
          id      ID      #REQUIRED
          name    CDATA   #IMPLIED>
<!ATTLIST list
          type    (bullets|ordered|glossary)  "ordered">
<!ATTLIST form
          method  CDATA   #FIXED "POST">
```

3.3.3 ATTRIBUTE-VALUE NORMALIZATION

Before the value of an attribute is passed to the application or checked for validity, the XML processor must normalize it as follows:

- a character reference is processed by appending the referenced character to the attribute value
- an entity reference is processed by recursively processing the replacement text of the entity
- a whitespace character (#x20, #xD, #xA, #x9) is processed by appending #x20 to the normalized value, except that only a single #x20 is appended for a "#xD#xA" sequence that is part of an external parsed entity or the literal entity value of an internal parsed entity
- other characters are processed by appending them to the normalized value

If the declared value is not CDATA, then the XML processor must further process the normalized attribute value by discarding any leading and trailing space (#x20) characters, and by replacing sequences of space (#x20) characters by a single space (#x20) character.

All attributes for which no declaration has been read should be treated by a non-validating parser as if declared CDATA.

3.4 CONDITIONAL SECTIONS

Conditional sections are portions of the document type declaration external subset which are included in, or excluded from, the logical structure of the DTD based on the keyword which governs them.

Conditional Section

```
[61] conditionalSect      ::= includeSect | ignoreSect
[62] includeSect          ::= '<![' S? 'INCLUDE' S? '[' extSubsetDecl ']]>'
[63] ignoreSect           ::= '<![' S? 'IGNORE' S? '[' ignoreSectContents*
                              ']]>'
[64] ignoreSectContents   ::= Ignore ('<![' ignoreSectContents ']]>'
                              Ignore)*
[65] Ignore               ::= Char* - (Char* ('<![' | ']]>') Char*)
```

Like the internal and external DTD subsets, a conditional section may contain one or more complete declarations, comments, processing instructions, or nested conditional sections, intermingled with white space.

If the keyword of the conditional section is INCLUDE, then the contents of the conditional section are part of the DTD. If the keyword of the conditional section is IGNORE, then the contents of the conditional section are not logically part of the DTD. Note that for reliable parsing, the contents of even ignored conditional sections must be read in order to detect nested conditional sections and ensure that the end of the outermost (ignored) conditional section is properly detected. If a conditional section with a keyword of INCLUDE occurs within a larger conditional section with a keyword of IGNORE, both the outer and the inner conditional sections are ignored.

If the keyword of the conditional section is a parameter-entity reference, the parameter entity must be replaced by its content before the processor decides whether to include or ignore the conditional section.

An example:

```
<!ENTITY % draft 'INCLUDE' >
<!ENTITY % final 'IGNORE' >

<![%draft;[
<!ELEMENT book (comments*, title, body, supplements?)>
]]>
<![%final;[
<!ELEMENT book (title, body, supplements?)>
]]>
```

4. PHYSICAL STRUCTURES

An XML document may consist of one or many storage units. These are called *entities*; they all have *content* and are all (except for the document entity, see below, and the external DTD subset) identified by *name*. Each XML document has one entity called the document entity, which serves as the starting point for the XML processor and may contain the whole document.

Entities may be either parsed or unparsed. A *parsed entity's* contents are referred to as its replacement text; this text is considered an integral part of the document.

An *unparsed entity* is a resource whose contents may or may not be text, and if text, may not be XML. Each unparsed entity has an associated notation, identified by name. Beyond a requirement that an XML processor make the identifiers for the entity and notation available to the application, XML places no constraints on the contents of unparsed entities.

Parsed entities are invoked by name using entity references; unparsed entities by name, given in the value of ENTITY or ENTITIES attributes.

General entities are entities for use within the document content. In this specification, general entities are sometimes referred to with the unqualified term *entity* when this leads to no ambiguity. Parameter entities are parsed entities for use within the DTD. These two types of entities use different forms of reference and are recognized in different contexts. Furthermore, they occupy different namespaces; a parameter entity and a general entity with the same name are two distinct entities.

4.1 Character and Entity References

A *character reference* refers to a specific character in the ISO/IEC 10646 character set, for example one not directly accessible from available input devices.

Character Reference

```
[66] CharRef      ::= '&#' [0-9]+ ';'
                    | '&#x' [0-9a-fA-F]+ ';'        [ WFC: Legal Character ]
```

> **WELL-FORMEDNESS CONSTRAINT: Legal Character.** Characters referred to using character references must match the production for Char.

If the character reference begins with "&#x", the digits and letters up to the terminating ; provide a hexadecimal representation of the character's code point in ISO/IEC 10646. If it begins just with "&#", the digits up to the terminating ; provide a decimal representation of the character's code point.

An *entity reference* refers to the content of a named entity. References to parsed general entities use ampersand (&) and semicolon (;) as delimiters. *Parameter-entity references* use percent sign (%) and semicolon (;) as delimiters.

Entity Reference

```
[67] Reference    ::= EntityRef | CharRef
[68] EntityRef    ::= '&' Name ';'      [ WFC: Entity Declared ]
                                        [ VC: Entity Declared ]
                                        [ WFC: Parsed Entity ]
                                        [ WFC: No Recursion ]
[69] PEReference  ::= '%' Name ';'      [ VC: Entity Declared ]
                                        [ WFC: No Recursion ]
                                        [ WFC: In DTD ]
```

> **WELL-FORMEDNESS CONSTRAINT: Entity Declared.** In a document without any DTD, a document with only an internal DTD subset which contains no parameter entity references, or a document with "standalone='yes'", the Name given in the entity reference must match that in an entity declaration, except that well-formed documents need not declare any of the following entities: amp, lt, gt, apos, quot. The declaration of a parameter entity must precede any reference to it. Similarly, the declaration of a general entity must precede any reference to it which appears in a default value in an attribute-list declaration. Note that if entities are declared in the external subset or in external parameter entities, a non-validating processor is not obligated to read and process their declarations; for such documents, the rule that an entity must be declared is a well-formedness constraint only if standalone='yes'.

> **VALIDITY CONSTRAINT: Entity Declared.** In a document with an external subset or external parameter entities with "standalone='no'", the Name given in the

entity reference must match that in an entity declaration. For interoperability, valid documents should declare the entities amp, lt, gt, apos, quot, in the form specified in **Section 4.6: Predefined Entities**. The declaration of a parameter entity must precede any reference to it. Similarly, the declaration of a general entity must precede any reference to it which appears in a default value in an attribute-list declaration.

WELL-FORMEDNESS CONSTRAINT: Parsed Entity. An entity reference must not contain the name of an unparsed entity. Unparsed entities may be referred to only in attribute values declared to be of type ENTITY or ENTITIES.

WELL-FORMEDNESS CONSTRAINT: No Recursion. A parsed entity must not contain a recursive reference to itself, either directly or indirectly.

WELL-FORMEDNESS CONSTRAINT: In DTD. Parameter-entity references may only appear in the DTD.

Examples of character and entity references:

```
Type <key>less-than</key> (&#x3C;) to save options.
This document was prepared on &docdate; and
is classified &security-level;.
```

Example of a parameter-entity reference:

```
<!-- declare the parameter entity "ISOLat2"... -->
<!ENTITY % ISOLat2
        SYSTEM "http://www.xml.com/iso/isolat2-xml.entities" >
<!-- ... now reference it. -->
%ISOLat2;
```

4.2 ENTITY DECLARATIONS

Entities are declared thus:

Entity Declaration

[70]	EntityDecl	::= GEDecl | PEDecl
[71]	GEDecl	::= '<!ENTITY' S Name S EntityDef S? '>'
[72]	PEDecl	::= '<!ENTITY' S '%' S Name S PEDef S? '>'
[73]	EntityDef	::= EntityValue | (ExternalID NDataDecl?)
[74]	PEDef	::= EntityValue | ExternalID

The Name identifies the entity in an entity reference or, in the case of an unparsed entity, in the value of an ENTITY or ENTITIES attribute. If the same entity is declared more than once, the first declaration encountered is binding; at user option, an XML processor may issue a warning if entities are declared multiple times.

4.2.1 INTERNAL ENTITIES

If the entity definition is an EntityValue, the defined entity is called an *internal entity*. There is no separate physical storage object, and the content of the entity is given in the declaration. Note that some processing of entity and character references in the literal entity value may be required to produce the correct replacement text: see **Section 4.5: Construction of Internal Entity Replacement Text**.

APP

A

An internal entity is a parsed entity.

Example of an internal entity declaration:

```
<!ENTITY Pub-Status "This is a pre-release of the
specification.">
```

4.2.2 EXTERNAL ENTITIES

If the entity is not internal, it is an *external entity*, declared as follows:

External Entity Declaration

```
[75] ExternalID    ::= 'SYSTEM' S SystemLiteral
                     | 'PUBLIC' S PubidLiteral S SystemLiteral
[76] NDataDecl     ::= S 'NDATA' S Name               [ VC: Notation Declared ]
```

If the NDataDecl is present, this is a general unparsed entity; otherwise it is a parsed entity.

> **Validity Constraint: Notation Declared.** The Name must match the declared name of a notation.

The SystemLiteral is called the entity's *system identifier*. It is a URI, which may be used to retrieve the entity. Note that the hash mark (#) and fragment identifier frequently used with URIs are not, formally, part of the URI itself; an XML processor may signal an error if a fragment identifier is given as part of a system identifier. Unless otherwise provided by information outside the scope of this specification (e.g. a special XML element type defined by a particular DTD, or a processing instruction defined by a particular application specification), relative URIs are relative to the location of the resource within which the entity declaration occurs. A URI might thus be relative to the document entity, to the entity containing the external DTD subset, or to some other external parameter entity.

An XML processor should handle a non-ASCII character in a URI by representing the character in UTF-8 as one or more bytes, and then escaping these bytes with the URI escaping mechanism (i.e., by converting each byte to %HH, where HH is the hexadecimal notation of the byte value).

In addition to a system identifier, an external identifier may include a *public identifier*. An XML processor attempting to retrieve the entity's content may use the public identifier to try to generate an alternative URI. If the processor is unable to do so, it must use the URI specified in the system literal. Before a match is attempted, all strings of white space in the public identifier must be normalized to single space characters (#x20), and leading and trailing white space must be removed.

Examples of external entity declarations:

```
<!ENTITY open-hatch
        SYSTEM "http://www.textuality.com/boilerplate/OpenHatch.xml">
<!ENTITY open-hatch
        PUBLIC "-//Textuality//TEXT Standard open-hatch boilerplate//EN"
        "http://www.textuality.com/boilerplate/OpenHatch.xml">
<!ENTITY hatch-pic
        SYSTEM "../grafix/OpenHatch.gif"
        NDATA gif >
```

4.3 PARSED ENTITIES

4.3.1 THE TEXT DECLARATION

External parsed entities may each begin with a *text declaration*.

Text Declaration

```
[77] TextDecl          ::= '<?xml' VersionInfo? EncodingDecl S? '?>'
```

The text declaration must be provided literally, not by reference to a parsed entity. No text declaration may appear at any position other than the beginning of an external parsed entity.

4.3.2 WELL-FORMED PARSED ENTITIES

The document entity is well-formed if it matches the production labeled document. An external general parsed entity is well-formed if it matches the production labeled extParsedEnt. An external parameter entity is well-formed if it matches the production labeled extPE.

Well-Formed External Parsed Entity

```
[78] extParsedEnt      ::= TextDecl? content
[79] extPE             ::= TextDecl? extSubsetDecl
```

An internal general parsed entity is well-formed if its replacement text matches the production labeled content. All internal parameter entities are well-formed by definition.

A consequence of well-formedness in entities is that the logical and physical structures in an XML document are properly nested; no start-tag, end-tag, empty-element tag, element, comment, processing instruction, character reference, or entity reference can begin in one entity and end in another.

4.3.3 CHARACTER ENCODING IN ENTITIES

Each external parsed entity in an XML document may use a different encoding for its characters. All XML processors must be able to read entities in either UTF-8 or UTF-16.

Entities encoded in UTF-16 must begin with the Byte Order Mark described by ISO/IEC 10646 Annex E and Unicode Appendix B (the ZERO WIDTH NO-BREAK SPACE character, #xFEFF). This is an encoding signature, not part of either the markup or the character data of the XML document. XML processors must be able to use this character to differentiate between UTF-8 and UTF-16 encoded documents. Although an XML processor is required to read only entities in the UTF-8 and UTF-16 encodings, it is recognized that other encodings are used around the world, and it may be desired for XML processors to read entities that use them. Parsed entities which are stored in an encoding other than UTF-8 or UTF-16 must begin with a text declaration containing an encoding declaration:

Encoding Declaration

```
[80] EncodingDecl      ::= S 'encoding' Eq ('"' EncName '"' |  "'" EncName
                           "'" )
```

```
[81] EncName        ::= [A-Za-z] ([A-Za-z0-9._] | '-    /* Encoding name
                    ')*                                     contains only
                                                           Latin characters */
```

In the document entity, the encoding declaration is part of the XML declaration. The EncName is the name of the encoding used.

In an encoding declaration, the values "UTF-8", "UTF-16", "ISO-10646-UCS-2", and "ISO-10646-UCS-4" should be used for the various encodings and transformations of Unicode/ISO/IEC 10646, the values "ISO-8859-1", "ISO-8859-2", ... "ISO-8859-9" should be used for the parts of ISO 8859, and the values "ISO-2022-JP", "Shift_JIS", and "EUC-JP" should be used for the various encoded forms of JIS X-0208-1997. XML processors may recognize other encodings; it is recommended that character encodings registered (as *charsets*) with the Internet Assigned Numbers Authority [IANA], other than those just listed, should be referred to using their registered names. Note that these registered names are defined to be case-insensitive, so processors wishing to match against them should do so in a case-insensitive way.

In the absence of information provided by an external transport protocol (e.g. HTTP or MIME), it is an error for an entity including an encoding declaration to be presented to the XML processor in an encoding other than that named in the declaration, for an encoding declaration to occur other than at the beginning of an external entity, or for an entity which begins with neither a Byte Order Mark nor an encoding declaration to use an encoding other than UTF-8. Note that since ASCII is a subset of UTF-8, ordinary ASCII entities do not strictly need an encoding declaration.

It is a fatal error when an XML processor encounters an entity with an encoding that it is unable to process.

Examples of encoding declarations:

```
<?xml encoding='UTF-8'?>
<?xml encoding='EUC-JP'?>
```

4.4 XML PROCESSOR TREATMENT OF ENTITIES AND REFERENCES

The table below summarizes the contexts in which character references, entity references, and invocations of unparsed entities might appear and the required behavior of an XML processor in each case. The labels in the leftmost column describe the recognition context:

Reference in Content

as a reference anywhere after the start-tag and before the end-tag of an element; corresponds to the nonterminal content.

Reference in Attribute Value

as a reference within either the value of an attribute in a start-tag, or a default value in an attribute declaration; corresponds to the nonterminal AttValue.

Occurs as Attribute Value

as a Name, not a reference, appearing either as the value of an attribute which has been declared as type ENTITY, or as one of the space-separated tokens in the value of an attribute which has been declared as type ENTITIES.

Reference in Entity Value

as a reference within a parameter or internal entity's literal entity value in the entity's declaration; corresponds to the nonterminal EntityValue.

Reference in DTD

as a reference within either the internal or external subsets of the DTD, but outside of an EntityValue or AttValue.

	Entity Type				Character
	Parameter	Internal General General	External Parsed	Unparsed	
Reference in Content	Not recognized	Included	Included if validating	Included	Forbidden
Reference in Attribute Value	Not recognized	Included in literal	Forbidden	Forbidden	Included
Occurs as Attribute Value	Not recognized	Forbidden	Forbidden	Notify	Not recognized
Reference in Entity Value	Included in literal	Bypassed	Bypassed	Forbidden	Included
Reference in DTD	Included as PE	Forbidden	Forbidden	Forbidden	Forbidden

4.4.1 NOT RECOGNIZED

Outside the DTD, the % character has no special significance; thus, what would be parameter entity references in the DTD are not recognized as markup in content. Similarly, the names of unparsed entities are not recognized except when they appear in the value of an appropriately declared attribute.

4.4.2 INCLUDED

An entity is *included* when its replacement text is retrieved and processed, in place of the reference itself, as though it were part of the document at the location the reference was recognized. The replacement text may contain both character data and (except for parameter entities) markup, which must be recognized in the usual way, except that the replacement text of entities used to escape markup delimiters (the entities amp, lt, gt, apos, quot) is always treated as data. (The string "AT&T;" expands to "AT&T;" and the remaining ampersand is not recognized as an entity-reference delimiter.) A character reference is *included* when the indicated character is processed in place of the reference itself.

4.4.3 INCLUDED IF VALIDATING

When an XML processor recognizes a reference to a parsed entity, in order to validate the document, the processor must include its replacement text. If the entity is external, and the processor is not attempting to validate the XML document, the processor may, but need not, include the entity's replacement text. If a non-validating parser does not include the replacement text, it must inform the application that it recognized, but did not read, the entity.

This rule is based on the recognition that the automatic inclusion provided by the SGML and XML entity mechanism, primarily designed to support modularity in authoring, is not necessarily appropriate for other applications, in particular document browsing. Browsers, for example, when encountering an external parsed entity reference, might choose to provide a visual indication of the entity's presence and retrieve it for display only on demand.

4.4.4 FORBIDDEN

The following are forbidden, and constitute fatal errors:

- the appearance of a reference to an unparsed entity.
- the appearance of any character or general-entity reference in the DTD except within an EntityValue or AttValue.
- a reference to an external entity in an attribute value.

4.4.5 INCLUDED IN LITERAL

When an entity reference appears in an attribute value, or a parameter entity reference appears in a literal entity value, its replacement text is processed in place of the reference itself as though it were part of the document at the location the reference was recognized, except that a single or double quote character in the replacement text is always treated as a normal data character and will not terminate the literal. For example, this is well-formed:

```
<!ENTITY % YN '"Yes"' >
<!ENTITY WhatHeSaid "He said &YN;" >
```

while this is not:

```
<!ENTITY EndAttr "27'" >
<element attribute='a-&EndAttr;'>
```

4.4.6 NOTIFY

When the name of an unparsed entity appears as a token in the value of an attribute of declared type ENTITY or ENTITIES, a validating processor must inform the application of the system and public (if any) identifiers for both the entity and its associated notation.

4.4.7 BYPASSED

When a general entity reference appears in the EntityValue in an entity declaration, it is bypassed and left as is.

4.4.8 INCLUDED AS PE

Just as with external parsed entities, parameter entities need only be included if validating. When a parameter-entity reference is recognized in the DTD and included, its replacement text is enlarged by the attachment of one leading and one following space (#x20) character; the intent is to constrain the replacement text of parameter entities to contain an integral number of grammatical tokens in the DTD.

4.5 CONSTRUCTION OF INTERNAL ENTITY REPLACEMENT TEXT

In discussing the treatment of internal entities, it is useful to distinguish two forms of the entity's value. The *literal entity value* is the quoted string actually present in the entity declaration, corresponding to the non-terminal EntityValue. The *replacement text* is the content of the entity, after replacement of character references and parameter-entity references.

The literal entity value as given in an internal entity declaration (EntityValue) may contain character, parameter-entity, and general-entity references. Such references must be contained entirely within the literal entity value. The actual replacement text that is included as described above must contain the *replacement text* of any parameter entities referred to, and must contain the character referred to, in place of any character references in the literal entity value; however, general-entity references must be left as-is, unexpanded. For example, given the following declarations:

```
<!ENTITY % pub    "&#xc9;ditions Gallimard" >
<!ENTITY   rights "All rights reserved" >
<!ENTITY   book   "La Peste: Albert Camus,
&#xA9; 1947 %pub;. &rights;" >
```

then the replacement text for the entity "book" is:

```
La Peste: Albert Camus,
© 1947 Éditions Gallimard. &rights;
```

The general-entity reference "&rights;" would be expanded should the reference "&book;" appear in the document's content or an attribute value.

These simple rules may have complex interactions; for a detailed discussion of a difficult example, see **Section D: Expansion of Entity and Character References**.

4.6 PREDEFINED ENTITIES

Entity and character references can both be used to *escape* the left angle bracket, ampersand, and other delimiters. A set of general entities (amp, lt, gt, apos, quot) is specified for this purpose. Numeric character references may also be used; they are expanded immediately when recognized and must be treated as character data, so the numeric character references "<" and "&" may be used to escape < and & when they occur in character data.

All XML processors must recognize these entities whether they are declared or not. For interoperability, valid XML documents should declare these entities, like any others, before using them. If the entities in question are declared, they must be declared as internal entities whose replacement text is the single character being escaped or a character reference to that character, as shown below.

```
<!ENTITY lt      "&#38;#60;">
<!ENTITY gt      "&#62;">
<!ENTITY amp     "&#38;#38;">
<!ENTITY apos    "&#39;">
<!ENTITY quot    "&#34;">
```

Note that the < and & characters in the declarations of "lt" and "amp" are doubly escaped to meet the requirement that entity replacement be well-formed.

4.7 NOTATION DECLARATIONS

Notations identify by name the format of unparsed entities, the format of elements which bear a notation attribute, or the application to which a processing instruction is addressed.

Notation declarations provide a name for the notation, for use in entity and attribute-list declarations and in attribute specifications, and an external identifier for the notation which may allow an XML processor or its client application to locate a helper application capable of processing data in the given notation.

Notation Declarations

```
[82] NotationDecl    ::= '<!NOTATION' S Name S (ExternalID | PublicID)
                         S? '>'
[83] PublicID        ::= 'PUBLIC' S PubidLiteral
```

XML processors must provide applications with the name and external identifier(s) of any notation declared and referred to in an attribute value, attribute definition, or entity declaration. They may additionally resolve the external identifier into the system identifier, file name, or other information needed to allow the application to call a processor for data in the notation described. (It is not an error, however, for XML documents to declare and refer to notations for which notation-specific applications are not available on the system where the XML processor or application is running.)

4.8 DOCUMENT ENTITY

The *document entity* serves as the root of the entity tree and a starting-point for an XML processor. This specification does not specify how the document entity is to be located by an

XML processor; unlike other entities, the document entity has no name and might well appear on a processor input stream without any identification at all.

5. CONFORMANCE

5.1 VALIDATING AND NON-VALIDATING PROCESSORS

Conforming XML processors fall into two classes: validating and non-validating. Validating and non-validating processors alike must report violations of this specification's well-formedness constraints in the content of the document entity and any other parsed entities that they read.

Validating processors must report violations of the constraints expressed by the declarations in the DTD, and failures to fulfill the validity constraints given in this specification. To accomplish this, validating XML processors must read and process the entire DTD and all external parsed entities referenced in the document.

Non-validating processors are required to check only the document entity, including the entire internal DTD subset, for well-formedness. While they are not required to check the document for validity, they are required to *process* all the declarations they read in the internal DTD subset and in any parameter entity that they read, up to the first reference to a parameter entity that they do *not* read; that is to say, they must use the information in those declarations to *normalize* attribute values, *include* the replacement text of internal entities, and supply *default attribute values*. They must not process entity declarations or attribute-list declarations encountered after a reference to a parameter entity that is not read, since the entity may have contained overriding declarations.

5.2 USING XML PROCESSORS

The behavior of a validating XML processor is highly predictable; it must read every piece of a document and report all well-formedness and validity violations. Less is required of a non-validating processor; it need not read any part of the document other than the document entity. This has two effects that may be important to users of XML processors:

- Certain well-formedness errors, specifically those that require reading external entities, may not be detected by a non-validating processor. Examples include the constraints entitled *Entity Declared*, *Parsed Entity*, and *No Recursion*, as well as some of the cases described as *forbidden* in **Section 4.4: XML Processor Treatment of Entities and References**.
- The information passed from the processor to the application may vary, depending on whether the processor reads parameter and external entities. For example, a non-validating processor may not *normalize* attribute values, *include* the replacement text of internal entities, or supply *default attribute values*, where doing so depends on having read declarations in external or parameter entities.

For maximum reliability in interoperating between different XML processors, applications which use non-validating processors should not rely on any behaviors not required of such processors. Applications which require facilities such as the use of default attributes or internal entities which are declared in external entities should use validating XML processors.

6. Notation

The formal grammar of XML is given in this specification using a simple Extended Backus-Naur Form (EBNF) notation. Each rule in the grammar defines one symbol, in the form

```
symbol     ::= expression
```

Symbols are written with an initial capital letter if they are defined by a regular expression, or with an initial lower case letter otherwise. Literal strings are quoted.

Within the expression on the right-hand side of a rule, the following expressions are used to match strings of one or more characters:

#xN

> where N is a hexadecimal integer, the expression matches the character in ISO/IEC 10646 whose canonical (UCS-4) code value, when interpreted as an unsigned binary number, has the value indicated. The number of leading zeros in the #xN form is insignificant; the number of leading zeros in the corresponding code value is governed by the character encoding in use and is not significant for XML.

[a-zA-Z], [#xN-#xN]

> matches any character with a value in the range(s) indicated (inclusive).

[^a-z], [^#xN-#xN]

> matches any character with a value *outside* the range indicated.

[^abc], [^#xN#xN#xN]

> matches any character with a value not among the characters given.

"string"

> matches a literal string matching that given inside the double quotes.

'string'

> matches a literal string matching that given inside the single quotes.

These symbols may be combined to match more complex patterns as follows, where A and B represent simple expressions:

(*expression*)

> expression is treated as a unit and may be combined as described in this list.

A?

> matches A or nothing; optional A.

A B

> matches A followed by B.

A | B

> matches A or B but not both.

A - B

> matches any string that matches A but does not match B.

A+

> matches one or more occurrences of A.

A*

> matches zero or more occurrences of A.

Other notations used in the productions are:

/* ... */

> comment.

[wfc: ...]

> well-formedness constraint; this identifies by name a constraint on well-formed documents associated with a production.

[vc: ...]

> validity constraint; this identifies by name a constraint on valid documents associated with a production.

APPENDICES

A. REFERENCES

A.1 NORMATIVE REFERENCES

IANA

(Internet Assigned Numbers Authority) *Official Names for Character Sets*, ed. Keld Simonsen et al. See `ftp://ftp.isi.edu/in-notes/iana/assignments/character-sets`.

IETF RFC 1766

IETF (Internet Engineering Task Force). *RFC 1766: Tags for the Identification of Languages*, ed. H. Alvestrand. 1995.

ISO 639

(International Organization for Standardization). *ISO 639:1988 (E). Code for the representation of names of languages*. [Geneva]: International Organization for Standardization, 1988.

ISO 3166

(International Organization for Standardization). ISO 3166-1:1997 (E). *Codes for the representation of names of countries and their subdivisions—Part 1: Country codes* [Geneva]: International Organization for Standardization, 1997.

ISO/IEC 10646

ISO (International Organization for Standardization). ISO/IEC 10646-1993 (E). Information technology—Universal Multiple-Octet Coded Character Set (UCS)—Part 1: Architecture and Basic Multilingual Plane. [Geneva]: International Organization for Standardization, 1993 (plus amendments AM 1 through AM 7).

Unicode

The Unicode Consortium. *The Unicode Standard, Version 2.0*. Reading, Mass.: Addison-Wesley Developers Press, 1996.

A.2 OTHER REFERENCES

Aho/Ullman

Aho, Alfred V., Ravi Sethi, and Jeffrey D. Ullman. *Compilers: Principles, Techniques, and Tools*. Reading: Addison-Wesley, 1986, rpt. corr. 1988.

Berners-Lee et al.

Berners-Lee, T., R. Fielding, and L. Masinter. *Uniform Resource Identifiers (URI): Generic Syntax and Semantics*. 1997. (Work in progress; see updates to RFC1738.)

Brüggemann-Klein

> Brüggemann-Klein, Anne. *Regular Expressions into Finite Automata*. Extended abstract in I. Simon, Hrsg., LATIN 1992, S. 97-98. Springer-Verlag, Berlin 1992. Full Version in Theoretical Computer Science 120: 197-213, 1993.

Brüggemann-Klein and Wood

> Brüggemann-Klein, Anne, and Derick Wood. *Deterministic Regular Languages*. Universität Freiburg, Institut für Informatik, Bericht 38, Oktober 1991.

Clark

> James Clark. Comparison of SGML and XML. See `http://www.w3.org/TR/NOTE-sgml-xml-971215`.

IETF RFC1738

> IETF (Internet Engineering Task Force). *RFC 1738: Uniform Resource Locators (URL)*, ed. T. Berners-Lee, L. Masinter, M. McCahill. 1994.

IETF RFC1808

> IETF (Internet Engineering Task Force). *RFC 1808: Relative Uniform Resource Locators*, ed. R. Fielding. 1995.

IETF RFC2141

> IETF (Internet Engineering Task Force). *RFC 2141: URN Syntax*, ed. R. Moats. 1997.

ISO 8879

> ISO (International Organization for Standardization). ISO 8879:1986(E). *Information processing—Text and Office Systems—Standard Generalized Markup Language (SGML)*. First edition—1986-10-15. [Geneva]: International Organization for Standardization, 1986.

ISO/IEC 10744

> ISO (International Organization for Standardization). ISO/IEC 10744-1992 (E). *Information technology—Hypermedia/Time-based Structuring Language (HyTime)*. [Geneva]: International Organization for Standardization, 1992. *Extended Facilities Annexe*. [Geneva]: International Organization for Standardization, 1996.

B. Character Classes

Following the characteristics defined in the Unicode standard, characters are classed as base characters (among others, these contain the alphabetic characters of the Latin alphabet, without diacritics), ideographic characters, and combining characters (among others, this class contains most diacritics); these classes combine to form the class of letters. Digits and extenders are also distinguished.

Characters

```
[84] Letter      ::= BaseChar | Ideographic
[85] BaseChar    ::= [#x0041-#x005A] | [#x0061-#x007A] | [#x00C0-#x00D6]
                   | [#x00D8-#x00F6] | [#x00F8-#x00FF] | [#x0100-#x0131]
                   | [#x0134-#x013E] | [#x0141-#x0148] | [#x014A-#x017E]
                   | [#x0180-#x01C3] | [#x01CD-#x01F0] | [#x01F4-#x01F5]
                   | [#x01FA-#x0217] | [#x0250-#x02A8] | [#x02BB-#x02C1]
                   | #x0386 | [#x0388-#x038A] | #x038C | [#x038E-#x03A1]
                   | [#x03A3-#x03CE] | [#x03D0-#x03D6] | #x03DA | #x03DC
                   | #x03DE | #x03E0 | [#x03E2-#x03F3] | [#x0401-#x040C]
                   | [#x040E-#x044F] | [#x0451-#x045C] | [#x045E-#x0481]
                   | [#x0490-#x04C4] | [#x04C7-#x04C8] | [#x04CB-#x04CC]
                   | [#x04D0-#x04EB] | [#x04EE-#x04F5] | [#x04F8-#x04F9]
                   | [#x0531-#x0556] | #x0559 | [#x0561-#x0586]
                   | [#x05D0-#x05EA] | [#x05F0-#x05F2] | [#x0621-#x063A]
                   | [#x0641-#x064A] | [#x0671-#x06B7] | [#x06BA-#x06BE]
                   | [#x06C0-#x06CE] | [#x06D0-#x06D3] | #x06D5
                   | [#x06E5-#x06E6] | [#x0905-#x0939] | #x093D
                   | [#x0958-#x0961] | [#x0985-#x098C] | [#x098F-#x0990]
                   | [#x0993-#x09A8] | [#x09AA-#x09B0] | #x09B2
                   | [#x09B6-#x09B9] | [#x09DC-#x09DD] | [#x09DF-#x09E1]
                   | [#x09F0-#x09F1] | [#x0A05-#x0A0A] | [#x0A0F-#x0A10]
                   | [#x0A13-#x0A28] | [#x0A2A-#x0A30] | [#x0A32-#x0A33]
                   | [#x0A35-#x0A36] | [#x0A38-#x0A39] | [#x0A59-#x0A5C]
                   | #x0A5E | [#x0A72-#x0A74] | [#x0A85-#x0A8B] | #x0A8D
                   | [#x0A8F-#x0A91] | [#x0A93-#x0AA8] | [#x0AAA-#x0AB0]
                   | [#x0AB2-#x0AB3] | [#x0AB5-#x0AB9] | #x0ABD | #x0AE0
                   | [#x0B05-#x0B0C] | [#x0B0F-#x0B10] | [#x0B13-#x0B28]
                   | [#x0B2A-#x0B30] | [#x0B32-#x0B33] | [#x0B36-#x0B39]
                   | #x0B3D | [#x0B5C-#x0B5D] | [#x0B5F-#x0B61]
                   | [#x0B85-#x0B8A] | [#x0B8E-#x0B90] | [#x0B92-#x0B95]
                   | [#x0B99-#x0B9A] | #x0B9C | [#x0B9E-#x0B9F]
                   | [#x0BA3-#x0BA4] | [#x0BA8-#x0BAA] | [#x0BAE-#x0BB5]
                   | [#x0BB7-#x0BB9] | [#x0C05-#x0C0C] | [#x0C0E-#x0C10]
                   | [#x0C12-#x0C28] | [#x0C2A-#x0C33] | [#x0C35-#x0C39]
                   | [#x0C60-#x0C61] | [#x0C85-#x0C8C] | [#x0C8E-#x0C90]
                   | [#x0C92-#x0CA8] | [#x0CAA-#x0CB3] | [#x0CB5-#x0CB9]
                   | #x0CDE | [#x0CE0-#x0CE1] | [#x0D05-#x0D0C]
                   | [#x0D0E-#x0D10] | [#x0D12-#x0D28] | [#x0D2A-#x0D39]
                   | [#x0D60-#x0D61] | [#x0E01-#x0E2E] | #x0E30
                   | [#x0E32-#x0E33] | [#x0E40-#x0E45] | [#x0E81-#x0E82]
                   | #x0E84 | [#x0E87-#x0E88] | #x0E8A | #x0E8D
                   | [#x0E94-#x0E97] | [#x0E99-#x0E9F] | [#x0EA1-#x0EA3]
                   | #x0EA5 | #x0EA7 | [#x0EAA-#x0EAB] | [#x0EAD-#x0EAE]
                   | #x0EB0 | [#x0EB2-#x0EB3] | #x0EBD | [#x0EC0-#x0EC4]
                   | [#x0F40-#x0F47] | [#x0F49-#x0F69] | [#x10A0-#x10C5]
                   | [#x10D0-#x10F6] | #x1100 | [#x1102-#x1103]
                   | [#x1105-#x1107] | #x1109 | [#x110B-#x110C]
                   | [#x110E-#x1112] | #x113C | #x113E | #x1140 | #x114C
                   | #x114E | #x1150 | [#x1154-#x1155] | #x1159
                   | [#x115F-#x1161] | #x1163 | #x1165 | #x1167 | #x1169
                   | [#x116D-#x116E] | [#x1172-#x1173] | #x1175 | #x119E
                   | #x11A8 | #x11AB | [#x11AE-#x11AF] | [#x11B7-#x11B8]
                   | #x11BA | [#x11BC-#x11C2] | #x11EB | #x11F0 | #x11F9
                   | [#x1E00-#x1E9B] | [#x1EA0-#x1EF9] | [#x1F00-#x1F15]
                   | [#x1F18-#x1F1D] | [#x1F20-#x1F45] | [#x1F48-#x1F4D]
```

```
                         | [#x1F50-#x1F57] | #x1F59 | #x1F5B | #x1F5D
                         | [#x1F5F-#x1F7D] | [#x1F80-#x1FB4] | [#x1FB6-#x1FBC]
                         | #x1FBE | [#x1FC2-#x1FC4] | [#x1FC6-#x1FCC]
                         | [#x1FD0-#x1FD3] | [#x1FD6-#x1FDB] [#x1FE0-#x1FEC]
                         | [#x1FF2-#x1FF4] | [#x1FF6-#x1FFC] | #x2126
                         | [#x212A-#x212B] | #x212E | [#x2180-#x2182]
                         | [#x3041-#x3094] | [#x30A1-#x30FA] | [#x3105-#x312C]
                         | [#xAC00-#xD7A3]
[86] Ideographic    ::= [#x4E00-#x9FA5] | #x3007 | [#x3021-#x3029]
[87] CombiningChar  ::= [#x0300-#x0345] | [#x0360-#x0361] | [#x0483-#x0486]
                         | [#x0591-#x05A1] | [#x05A3-#x05B9] | [#x05BB-#x05BD]
                         | #x05BF | [#x05C1-#x05C2] | #x05C4 | [#x064B-#x0652]
                         | #x0670 | [#x06D6-#x06DC] | [#x06DD-#x06DF]
                         | [#x06E0-#x06E4] | [#x06E7-#x06E8] | [#x06EA-#x06ED]
                         | [#x0901-#x0903] | #x093C | [#x093E-#x094C] | #x094D
                         | [#x0951-#x0954] | [#x0962-#x0963] | [#x0981-#x0983]
                         | #x09BC | #x09BE | #x09BF | [#x09C0-#x09C4]
                         | [#x09C7-#x09C8] | [#x09CB-#x09CD] | #x09D7
                         | [#x09E2-#x09E3] | #x0A02 | #x0A3C | #x0A3E | #x0A3F
                         | [#x0A40-#x0A42] | [#x0A47-#x0A48] | [#x0A4B-#x0A4D]
                         | [#x0A70-#x0A71] | [#x0A81-#x0A83] | #x0ABC
                         | [#x0ABE-#x0AC5] | [#x0AC7-#x0AC9] | [#x0ACB-#x0ACD]
                         | [#x0B01-#x0B03] | #x0B3C | [#x0B3E-#x0B43]
                         | [#x0B47-#x0B48] | [#x0B4B-#x0B4D] | [#x0B56-#x0B57]
                         | [#x0B82-#x0B83] | [#x0BBE-#x0BC2] | [#x0BC6-#x0BC8]
                         | [#x0BCA-#x0BCD] | #x0BD7 | [#x0C01-#x0C03]
                         | [#x0C3E-#x0C44] | [#x0C46-#x0C48] | [#x0C4A-#x0C4D]
                         | [#x0C55-#x0C56] | [#x0C82-#x0C83] | [#x0CBE-#x0CC4]
                         | [#x0CC6-#x0CC8] | [#x0CCA-#x0CCD] | [#x0CD5-#x0CD6]
                         | [#x0D02-#x0D03] | [#x0D3E-#x0D43] | [#x0D46-#x0D48]
                         | [#x0D4A-#x0D4D] | #x0D57 | #x0E31 | [#x0E34-#x0E3A]
                         | [#x0E47-#x0E4E] | #x0EB1 | [#x0EB4-#x0EB9]
                         | [#x0EBB-#x0EBC] | [#x0EC8-#x0ECD] | [#x0F18-#x0F19]
                         | #x0F35 | #x0F37 | #x0F39 | #x0F3E | #x0F3F
                         | [#x0F71-#x0F84] | [#x0F86-#x0F8B] | [#x0F90-#x0F95]
                         | #x0F97 | [#x0F99-#x0FAD] | [#x0FB1-#x0FB7] | #x0FB9
                         | [#x20D0-#x20DC] | #x20E1 | [#x302A-#x302F] | #x3099
                         | #x309A
[88] Digit          ::= [#x0030-#x0039] | [#x0660-#x0669] | [#x06F0-#x06F9]
                         | [#x0966-#x096F] | [#x09E6-#x09EF] | [#x0A66-#x0A6F]
                         | [#x0AE6-#x0AEF] | [#x0B66-#x0B6F] | [#x0BE7-#x0BEF]
                         | [#x0C66-#x0C6F] | [#x0CE6-#x0CEF] | [#x0D66-#x0D6F]
                         | [#x0E50-#x0E59] | [#x0ED0-#x0ED9] | [#x0F20-#x0F29]
[89] Extender       ::= #x00B7 | #x02D0 | #x02D1 | #x0387 | #x0640 | #x0E46
                         | #x0EC6 | #x3005 | [#x3031-#x3035] | [#x309D-#x309E]
                         | [#x30FC-#x30FE]
```

The character classes defined here can be derived from the Unicode character database as follows:

- Name start characters must have one of the categories Ll, Lu, Lo, Lt, Nl.

- Name characters other than Name-start characters must have one of the categories Mc, Me, Mn, Lm, or Nd.

- Characters in the compatibility area (i.e. with character code greater than #xF900 and less than #xFFFE) are not allowed in XML names.

- Characters which have a font or compatibility decomposition (i.e. those with a "compatibility formatting tag" in field 5 of the database—marked by field 5 beginning with a <) are not allowed.

- The following characters are treated as name-start characters rather than name characters, because the property file classifies them as Alphabetic: [#x02BB-#x02C1], #x0559, #x06E5, #x06E6.

- Characters #x20DD-#x20E0 are excluded (in accordance with Unicode, section 5.14).

- Character #x00B7 is classified as an extender, because the property list so identifies it.

- Character #x0387 is added as a name character, because #x00B7 is its canonical equivalent.

- Characters ':' and '_' are allowed as name-start characters.

- Characters '-' and '.' are allowed as name characters.

C. XML AND SGML (NON-NORMATIVE)

XML is designed to be a subset of SGML, in that every valid XML document should also be a conformant SGML document. For a detailed comparison of the additional restrictions that XML places on documents beyond those of SGML, see [Clark].

D. EXPANSION OF ENTITY AND CHARACTER REFERENCES (NON-NORMATIVE)

This appendix contains some examples illustrating the sequence of entity- and character-reference recognition and expansion, as specified in **Section 4.4 XML Processor Treatment of Entities and References**.

If the DTD contains the declaration

```
<!ENTITY example "<p>An ampersand (&#38;#38;) may be escaped
numerically (&#38;#38;#38;) or with a general entity
(&amp;amp;).</p>" >
```

then the XML processor will recognize the character references when it parses the entity declaration, and resolve them before storing the following string as the value of the entity "example":

```
<p>An ampersand (&#38;) may be escaped
numerically (&#38;#38;) or with a general entity
(&amp;amp;).</p>
```

A reference in the document to "&example;" will cause the text to be reparsed, at which time the start- and end-tags of the "p" element will be recognized and the three references will be recognized and expanded, resulting in a "p" element with the following content (all data, no delimiters or markup):

```
An ampersand (&) may be escaped
numerically (&#38;) or with a general entity
(&amp;).
```

A more complex example will illustrate the rules and their effects fully. In the following example, the line numbers are solely for reference.

```
1 <?xml version='1.0'?>
2 <!DOCTYPE test [
3 <!ELEMENT test (#PCDATA) >
4 <!ENTITY % xx '&#37;zz;'>
5 <!ENTITY % zz '&#60;!ENTITY tricky "error-prone" >' >
6 %xx;
7 ]>
8 <test>This sample shows a &tricky; method.</test>
```

This produces the following:

- in line 4, the reference to character 37 is expanded immediately, and the parameter entity "xx" is stored in the symbol table with the value "%zz;". Since the replacement text is not rescanned, the reference to parameter entity "zz" is not recognized. (And it would be an error if it were, since "zz" is not yet declared.)

- in line 5, the character reference "<" is expanded immediately and the parameter entity "zz" is stored with the replacement text "<!ENTITY tricky "error-prone" >", which is a well-formed entity declaration.

- in line 6, the reference to "xx" is recognized, and the replacement text of "xx" (namely "%zz;") is parsed. The reference to "zz" is recognized in its turn, and its replacement text ("<!ENTITY tricky "error-prone" >") is parsed. The general entity "tricky" has now been declared, with the replacement text "error-prone".

- in line 8, the reference to the general entity "tricky" is recognized, and it is expanded, so the full content of the "test" element is the self-describing (and ungrammatical) string. *This sample shows a error-prone method.*

E. DETERMINISTIC CONTENT MODELS (NON-NORMATIVE)

For compatibility, it is required that content models in element type declarations be deterministic.

SGML requires deterministic content models (it calls them "unambiguous"); XML processors built using SGML systems may flag non-deterministic content models as errors.

For example, the content model ((b, c) | (b, d)) is non-deterministic, because given an initial b the parser cannot know which b in the model is being matched without looking ahead to see which element follows the b. In this case, the two references to b can be collapsed into a single reference, making the model read (b, (c | d)). An initial b now clearly matches only a single name in the content model. The parser doesn't need to look ahead to see what follows; either c or d would be accepted.

More formally: a finite state automaton may be constructed from the content model using the standard algorithms, e.g. algorithm 3.5 in section 3.9 of Aho, Sethi, and Ullman [Aho/Ullman]. In many such algorithms, a follow set is constructed for each position in the regular expression (i.e., each leaf node in the syntax tree for the regular expression); if any position has a follow set in which more than one following position is labeled with the same element type name, then the content model is in error and may be reported as an error.

Algorithms exist which allow many but not all non-deterministic content models to be reduced automatically to equivalent deterministic models; see Brüggemann-Klein 1991 [Brüggemann-Klein].

F. Autodetection of Character Encodings (Non-Normative)

The XML encoding declaration functions as an internal label on each entity, indicating which character encoding is in use. Before an XML processor can read the internal label, however, it apparently has to know what character encoding is in use—which is what the internal label is trying to indicate. In the general case, this is a hopeless situation. It is not entirely hopeless in XML, however, because XML limits the general case in two ways: each implementation is assumed to support only a finite set of character encodings, and the XML encoding declaration is restricted in position and content in order to make it feasible to autodetect the character encoding in use in each entity in normal cases. Also, in many cases other sources of information are available in addition to the XML data stream itself. Two cases may be distinguished, depending on whether the XML entity is presented to the processor without, or with, any accompanying (external) information. We consider the first case first.

Because each XML entity not in UTF-8 or UTF-16 format *must* begin with an XML encoding declaration, in which the first characters must be '<?xml', any conforming processor can detect, after two to four octets of input, which of the following cases apply. In reading this list, it may help to know that in UCS-4, '<' is "#x0000003C" and '?' is "#x0000003F", and the Byte Order Mark required of UTF-16 data streams is "#xFEFF".

- 00 00 00 3C: UCS-4, big-endian machine (1234 order)
- 3C 00 00 00: UCS-4, little-endian machine (4321 order)
- 00 00 3C 00: UCS-4, unusual octet order (2143)
- 00 3C 00 00: UCS-4, unusual octet order (3412)
- FE FF: UTF-16, big-endian
- FF FE: UTF-16, little-endian
- 00 3C 00 3F: UTF-16, big-endian, no Byte Order Mark (and thus, strictly speaking, in error)
- 3C 00 3F 00: UTF-16, little-endian, no Byte Order Mark (and thus, strictly speaking, in error)

- **3C 3F 78 6D:** UTF-8, ISO 646, ASCII, some part of ISO 8859, Shift-JIS, EUC, or any other 7-bit, 8-bit, or mixed-width encoding which ensures that the characters of ASCII have their normal positions, width, and values; the actual encoding declaration must be read to detect which of these applies, but since all of these encodings use the same bit patterns for the ASCII characters, the encoding declaration itself may be read reliably

- **4C 6F A7 94:** EBCDIC (in some flavor; the full encoding declaration must be read to tell which code page is in use)

- other: UTF-8 without an encoding declaration, or else the data stream is corrupt, fragmentary, or enclosed in a wrapper of some kind

This level of autodetection is enough to read the XML encoding declaration and parse the character-encoding identifier, which is still necessary to distinguish the individual members of each family of encodings (e.g. to tell UTF-8 from 8859, and the parts of 8859 from each other, or to distinguish the specific EBCDIC code page in use, and so on).

Because the contents of the encoding declaration are restricted to ASCII characters, a processor can reliably read the entire encoding declaration as soon as it has detected which family of encodings is in use. Since in practice, all widely used character encodings fall into one of the categories above, the XML encoding declaration allows reasonably reliable in-band labeling of character encodings, even when external sources of information at the operating-system or transport-protocol level are unreliable.

Once the processor has detected the character encoding in use, it can act appropriately, whether by invoking a separate input routine for each case, or by calling the proper conversion function on each character of input.

Like any self-labeling system, the XML encoding declaration will not work if any software changes the entity's character set or encoding without updating the encoding declaration. Implementors of character-encoding routines should be careful to ensure the accuracy of the internal and external information used to label the entity.

The second possible case occurs when the XML entity is accompanied by encoding information, as in some file systems and some network protocols. When multiple sources of information are available, their relative priority and the preferred method of handling conflict should be specified as part of the higher-level protocol used to deliver XML. Rules for the relative priority of the internal label and the MIME-type label in an external header, for example, should be part of the RFC document defining the text/xml and application/xml MIME types. In the interests of interoperability, however, the following rules are recommended.

- If an XML entity is in a file, the Byte-Order Mark and encoding-declaration PI are used (if present) to determine the character encoding. All other heuristics and sources of information are solely for error recovery.

- If an XML entity is delivered with a MIME type of text/xml, then the charset parameter on the MIME type determines the character encoding method; all other heuristics and sources of information are solely for error recovery.

- If an XML entity is delivered with a MIME type of application/xml, then the Byte-Order Mark and encoding-declaration PI are used (if present) to determine the character encoding. All other heuristics and sources of information are solely for error recovery.

These rules apply only in the absence of protocol-level documentation; in particular, when the MIME types text/xml and application/xml are defined, the recommendations of the relevant RFC will supersede these rules.

G. W3C XML Working Group (Non-Normative)

This specification was prepared and approved for publication by the W3C XML Working Group (WG). WG approval of this specification does not necessarily imply that all WG members voted for its approval. The current and former members of the XML WG are:

Jon Bosak, Sun *(Chair)*

James Clark *(Technical Lead)*

Tim Bray, Textuality and Netscape *(XML Co-editor)*

Jean Paoli, Microsoft *(XML Co-editor)*

C. M. Sperberg-McQueen, U. of Ill. *(XML Co-editor)*

Dan Connolly, W3C *(W3C Liaison)*

Paula Angerstein, Texcel

Steve DeRose, INSO

Dave Hollander, HP

Eliot Kimber, ISOGEN

Eve Maler, ArborText

Tom Magliery, NCSA

Murray Maloney, Muzmo and Grif

Makoto Murata, Fuji Xerox Information Systems

Joel Nava, Adobe

Conleth O'Connell, Vignette

Peter Sharpe, SoftQuad

John Tigue, DataChannel

W3C Document Notice

The name and trademarks of copyright holders may NOT be used in advertising or publicity pertaining to this document or its contents without specific, written prior permission. Title to copyright in this document will at all times remain with copyright holders.

This formulation of W3C's notice and license became active on April 05 1999 so as to account for the treatment of DTDs, schema's and bindings. See the older formulation for the policy prior to this date. Please see our Copyright FAQ for common questions about using materials from our site, including specific terms and conditions for packages like libwww, Amaya, and Jigsaw. Other questions about this notice can be directed to site-policy@w3.org.

webmaster
(last updated by reagle on 1999/04/99.)

INDEX

Q–R

The IT site
you asked for...

InformIT is a complete online library delivering
information, technology, reference, training, news,
and opinion to IT professionals, students,
and corporate users.

Find IT Solutions Here!

www.informit.com